Landscaping with Herbs

Acknowledgments

Very simply, this book would not have been written without the support of my wife, Jeanne. Not only was she a fine editor that saw to it I sent off polished work, but she was also an invaluable listener. She is a very remarkable and wonderful person.

There are many people who have assisted me over the past two years, too many to list them all and their contributions of thoughts and design suggestions. It has been a privilege to work with three special people who helped me from the beginning—and even before that: Mary Medalia, Betty McSorley and Judy Zugish. Mary is known fondly as the Herb Lady at Seattle's Pike Place Market, where she has been selling the finest herbs in the Northwest for some 30 years. No finer herbs can be found anywhere, and no finer lady either. Betty McSorley, like Mary, was an unwavering source of enthusiasm. It seemed both had the answers every time I came knocking. I can't thank Betty enough for her moral support and all-consuming interest in the secrets of herbs that rubbed off on me the very first time we met. You may find her at the *GARDEN GATE* in Rochester, WA. Judy is someone you just have to meet. She's like an effervescent herb tea, an exciting package of herbal mysteries you simply can't tire of. She is owner of the *BOUQUET BANQUE* in Marysville, WA. Many invaluable thoughts and ideas about the herbs in this text were offered by Mary, Betty and Judy.

A group of people that deserve specific mention are the many library staff employees that ran their tails off searching for obscure and little used books. They like that sort of thing I understand. My special thanks to Rivka and Darlene and Kitty and Jim and Ardith and Eddie at the Chehalis Library. Many thanks to Heidi Mercado, Librarian of the Chemistry Library at the University of Washington, and I can't begin to thank enough Anna Zeigler for her assistance from the depths of the University's Herbarium. Joy Mastroguiseppe of the Marion Ownbey Herbarium of Washington State University identified nearly 120 weird worts, so that correct natural histories could be compiled about the herbs in this text. Between Joy and Steve Gibbs, also from the Washington State Cooperative Extension Services, I was able to gather a remarkable amount of inside data about herbs.

Growers, sellers and nomenclature buffs as I am can be grateful for Dr. A. O. Tucker's input on the accepted scientific nomenclature of the herbs. Dr. Tucker, Co-Curator of the Delaware State College Herbarium, has done extensive research in nomenclature of herbs, particularly those stubborn families like Oregano, Mint, Lavender and Rosemary. We should all be indebted to him for this exhaustive research. (See, "Nomenclature of the Culinary Herbs and Potherbs," Chap. 3 in *Herbs, Spices & Medicinal Plants*, Vol I, Cracker & Simon, 85.)

Other valuable people include the Zimmerman's of the Fall City Herb Farm, Michele Nash, Gail Schilling, Angelo Pellegrini, Irving Scherer, John Eccles and many more who shared their gardens with us. I am grateful to Kelly Powell for his interest, time and equipment which most certainly helped me provide better pictures than I would otherwise have composed. And if it were not for Leone Seidel, on her typewriter and computer, who made writing fun, I'd have lost my patience and courage long ago.

Table 1
Key to Plant Symbols

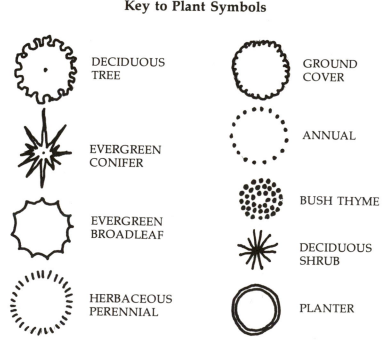

DECIDUOUS TREE

EVERGREEN CONIFER

EVERGREEN BROADLEAF

HERBACEOUS PERENNIAL

GROUND COVER

ANNUAL

BUSH THYME

DECIDUOUS SHRUB

PLANTER

How to Use This Book

Because I am so involved in the lives of herbs, people expect me to know what an herb is. I can only answer, "any plant that you find useful". The definition of an herb has changed through the centuries, replaced in some cases by more specific terminology: vegetable, grain, fruit, etc. and recently, "ornamental". Many plants with an historical use, and once considered herbs, are now merely ornamental plants to many gardeners. You would be surprised at the number of medicinal gems in your gardens, a pharmacy by medieval standards: Quince, Christmas Rose, Honeysuckle, Hollyhock, Pussywillow, Trillium, Oregon Grape, Alder, Oak, Larkspur, Lily of the Valley, Juniper berries. You name it, someone classified it as a medicinal. This indiscriminate labelling has not simplified the herbalist's task of sorting through the real from the imaginary medicinal plants. But they remain with us in our gardens because someone once found them useful.

They are pretty. That is sufficient for me. We may grow some herbs because they scent our environment. Is that stretching the term a bit? Not at all. Jasmine and Mock Orange have been used this way for centuries. My point is that plants are herbs if you use them—even to surround your home as screens, or use them for shade, fragrance or food for the birds—no matter what end use is in store, they are being applied to your daily life.

What then is this book doing describing only a selection of herbs, predominantly culinary, out of the multitude? Two reasons: 1) I am interested in those herbs that are less thought of as ornamentals than they should be, plants that are left out of most landscaping texts and designs for lack of data about their qualities, other than culinary; and 2) I am restricting myself to herbs with which I have had experience. There are literally thousands of true medicinal herbs that could be included. Some you know, such as Foxglove. But many you possibly don't recognize as herbs, but still cultivate for their beauty, such as Peonies, St. John's Wort and the Passion Flower. After reading this book I hope you will be more venturesome. Just because someone says it's an herb shouldn't ruin the fun of growing a new plant you have found. Instead, look up its history. Like Yarrow it might have saved an empire, like Hyssop bathed the wounds of our Lord Jesus Christ, like Monarda blushed m'lady's cheeks, or like Dyers Camomile supplied the khaki color for camouflaged uniforms. Herbs are special, or they wouldn't be herbs.

Each chapter of this book is divided into three sections. The first section describes a form of landscaping. This is a general overview, the purpose of which is to introduce you to the theme of such a landscape so you can choose ornamental herbs more wisely. Certain restrictions on plant uses are described and must be examined before designing or redesigning the gardens of a homesite. Use Table 1, Key to Plant Symbols, when examining the architectural designs in this book.

The second section closely examines a selection of herbs. This selection is by no means exclusive. They are chosen to some extent to emphasize the chapter's theme. In this way the basic landscape covered by each chapter is better understood. Other ornamental plants that are chosen as companions to herbs in feature gardens are only mentioned throughout in order to simplify the comparisons that are made between the habits and ornamental characteristics of herbs. They are more easily visualized when only a small number of comparisons are used. Forgive me if I did not use your favorite ornamental. Remember this book is intended to spur you to experiment and adventure.

In order to get the most from this book first decide objectively what landscape you have or are interested in looking at. If you are undecided then read all of the first sections of each chapter for insight and certainly follow this with readings from some of the many books listed in the bibliography. Then read again the first section of the chapter that most closely defines what you seek. Can you see your homesite in that context? The more easily definable your landscape is the easier it will be to choose ornamental herbs that fit.

Now make an inventory of the valuable ornamental plants in your landscape or those that you want to have as neighbors to herbs. Study the tables in the appendices and select six to a dozen herbs that exhibit similar characteristics or sound intriguing. Locate them via the index and read about their needs and desires. Examples are given that compare or contrast other plants so you can get a grasp of the herb's nature. Consider their value to you as well. You may prefer a culinary herb to a pretty one.

Once you have your list, read the last section of the chapter that corresponds to your landscape. This will give you an idea of how some herbs have been used in actual settings. Some landscapes can accommodate many herbs, others are able to adequately present no more than a dozen. Purchase those that remain on your list and let them loose in your landscape to entertain you and your guests.

Remember, an ornamental herb doesn't require use. Certainly I recommend that you experiment with using it, for to make it valuable you must know what it is capable of doing for you. Once you have shared that knowledge with other gardeners you will then know why herbs are exciting ornamentals. Be a bridge between the past and the future, experiment with herbs.

I have limited the use of uncommon terminology or scientific terms to those in the following glossary:

CHEMOTYPE/CHEMOVAR—a chemically distinct variety or cultivar that is identical to the species but distinguished only by its fragrance or chemical make-up.

CULTIVAR—horticulturally derived variation of a species.

CUTTING—portion of plant (severed by a sharp knife) for purposes of propagation.

DRIFT—a grouping of identical plants arranged in a variety of shapes combined with other drifts of plants in such a way to encourage the sense of motion in a planting.

ESPALIER—woody herbs (including trees) wired to a trellis or wall, sometimes in decorative patterns.

"FORMAL"—a garden designed geometrically but included in another landscape form as a separate, and often isolated, garden.

FILTERED SHADE—Partial shade found in forests where patches of sun brighten the scene only momentarily.

INFLORESCENCE—the flowering or reproductive part of a plant.

INFORMAL BORDER—plants natural, not pruned to decorative or geometric shapes.

LIVING SCREEN—barrier over 3' of plants (may include espaliered).

MEAD—region where low grasses, wildflowers and herbs compose the lawn.

PARTIAL SHADE—sun for part of the day.

POTPOURRI—fragrant mixture of herbs in a container that is stoppered and used as an air freshener.

QUAD—garden arrangement of four square beds surrounded by a hedge or fence.

ROOT DIVISION/CROWN DIVISION—severing of reproductive roots or a plant's crown into pieces for purposes of propagation.

POLYMORPHIC—variable in habit and foliage characteristics (occurs within a species).

RUGOSE—wrinkled and pitted (usually refers to a leaf texture).

SIMPLES—simple herbal remedy for a simple ailment.

START—rooted cutting.

SPORT—branch or foliage with atypical characteristics.

SACHET—cloth bag containing fragrant herbs, usually used as is to scent articles of clothing or fabric.

STREWING HERBS—fragrant herbs thrown to the floor and crushed underfoot to scent rugs and freshen the air.

STANDARD—a form of topiary that makes a woody perennial herb represent a tree, with a ball of foliage atop a bare trunk.

TISANE—mixture of fragrant and flavorful herbs in a cloth bag (tea bag) to be used to make an infusion for medicinal purposes (a medicinal tea).

TOPIARY—pruning and training evergreen woody herbs to take on recognizable shapes or characteristics.

VARIETY—variation of the species with stable characteristics.

VOLATILES—chemicals that escape from a plant under normal conditions that we perceive as scent.

Virtually every plant mentioned in this book has been used in some fashion to let it qualify as an herb. I dwell only on the significant ones. But where in the botanical world do all of these herbs and plants fit? Without man they are unlabeled but still have a history to tell, one of the most fascinating histories imaginable, evolution. The plant kingdom is at least one billion years old, and many scientists say as old as four billion years if unicellular plants (Algae, etc.) are added. They came from nothing and created an Eden.

Let's take a quick look at how plants fit together; who their relatives are. Table 2 is a family tree of the herbs. A few plants other than those in this book are added to give a better picture of their family life. When these herbs evolved in history is another story and a long and controversial one. Suffice it to say the wind pollinated plants were some of the oldest plants, Sweet Bay, Witch Hazel, Birch, Magnolias, etc. The daisied flowers so plentiful today were relatively late in coming, relying as they do on the pollinators such as insects and birds. You may want to refer to this table as you are reading to see how an herb evolved, who its cousins are and which ornamentals could be joined in a feature garden that's all in the family.

Table 2
Key to Botanical Classification of Herbs
Family Tree of Herbs

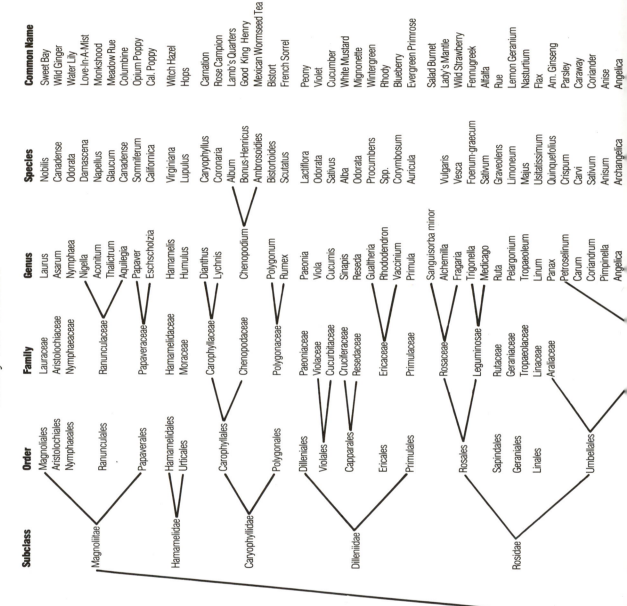

Class	Subclass	Order	Family	Genus	Species	Common Name
		Magnoliales	Lauraceae	Laurus	Nobilis	Sweet Bay
		Aristolochiales	Aristolochiaceae	Asarum	Canadense	Wild Ginger
		Nymphaeales	Nymphaeaceae	Nymphaea	Odorata	Water Lily
		Ranunculales	Ranunculaceae	Nigella	Damascena	Love-In-A-Mist
				Aconitum	Napellus	Monkshood
				Thalictrum	Glaucum	Meadow Rue
				Aquilegia	Canadense	Columbine
		Papaverales	Papaveraceae	Papaver	Somniferum	Opium Poppy
				Eschscholzia	Californica	Cal. Poppy
		Hamamelidales	Hamamelidaceae	Hamamelis	Virginiana	Witch Hazel
		Urticales	Moraceae	Humulus	Lupulus	Hops
		Carophyllales	Carophyllaceae	Dianthus	Caryophyllus	Carnation
				Lychnis	Coronaria	Rose Campion
			Chenopodaceae	Chenopodium	Album	Lamb's Quarters
					Bonus-Henricus	Good King Henry
					Ambrosoidies	Mexican Wormseed Tea
		Polygonales	Polygonaceae	Polygonum	Bistortoides	Bistort
				Rumex	Scutatus	French Sorrel
		Dilleniales	Paeoniaceae	Paeonia	Lactiflora	Peony
		Violales	Violaceae	Viola	Odorata	Violet
			Cucurbitaceae	Cucumis	Sativus	Cucumber
		Capparales	Cruciferaceae	Sinapis	Alba	White Mustard
			Resedaceae	Reseda	Odorata	Mignonette
		Ericales	Ericaceae	Gualtheria	Procumbens	Wintergreen
				Rhododendron	Spp.	Rhody
				Vaccinium	Corymbosum	Blueberry
		Primulales	Primulaceae	Primula	Auricula	Evergreen Primrose
		Rosales	Rosaceae	Sanguisorba minor		Salad Burnet
				Alchemilla	Vulgaris	Lady's Mantle
				Fragaria	Vesca	Wild Strawberry
			Leguminosae	Trigonella	Foenum-graecum	Fennugreek
				Medicago	Sativum	Alfalfa
		Sapindales	Rutaceae	Ruta	Graveolens	Rue
		Geraniales	Geraniaceae	Pelargonium	Limoneum	Lemon Geranium
			Tropaeolaceae	Tropaeoleum	Majus	Nasturtium
		Linales	Linaceae	Linum	Usitatissimum	Flax
			Araliaceae	Panax	Quinquefolius	Am. Ginseng
		Umbellales		Petroselinum	Crispum	Parsley
				Carum	Carvi	Caraway
				Coriandrum	Sativum	Coriander
				Pimpinella	Anisum	Anise
				Angelica	Archangelica	Angelica

Magnoliitae

Hamamelidae

Caryophyllidae

Dilleniidae

Rosidae

Magnoliatae

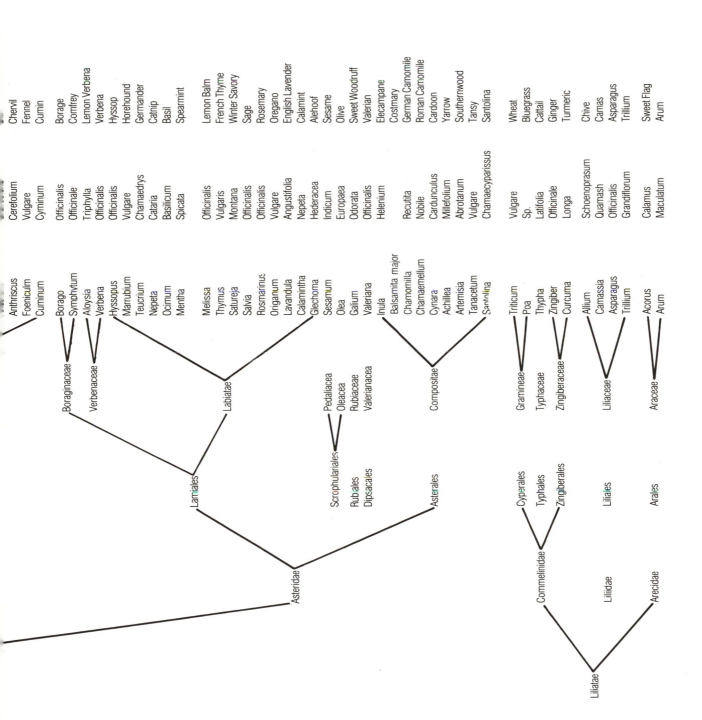

Chapter 1 / INTRODUCTION

All gardeners including herbs in their gardens do so for the same reason: they are more than pretty plants. Even if you haven't raised one, the word "herb" still conjures images of ancient mages and contemporary apothecaries apportioning plant parts for innumerable and frequently unfathomable reasons.

Quickly off the tip of the tongue come recollections of many commonly encountered herbs: annuals such as Summer Savory, Chervil and Dill; herbaceous perennials such as Lovage, Roman Camomile and Fennel; woody perennials like Sage, Thyme and Rue; vines like Hops and Jasmine; bulbs of Chives and Saffron; and the winter-blooming shrub Witch Hazel.

Included in herbal gardens could be Snakeroot, Felon Herb, Hindheal, Herb-of-Grace, Rattlesnake, Mosquito plant, Five Fingers, Lion's Mouth, King's Cure-All, Starwort, Alecoast and Bugloss—names not easy to remember but coined by centuries of use.

Mankind has always put great value on herbs and flowers. In past times they were valued ornamentally as well as for more practical reasons. Only recently, due to the declining use of herbs in medicines and the wide selection of rugged ornamentals gathered from all over the world, have the lackluster herbs fallen by the wayside to become, in many cases, unappreciated weeds.

Before the evolution of a settled society, man's chief interest in plants was for nourishment, with other uses arising quickly as men established homesites. In the Paleolithic Period of the Stone Age (30,000–11,000 B.C.) men were nomadic, following grazing herds of large mammals. With them, either accidentally or by choice, went the seeds of plants they used most often. Ruins from the Mesolithic Period (11,000–5,000 B.C.) have revealed much about the developing dependence upon plants. For example, evidence found at archeological sites showed that Mesolithic fishermen in southeastern Asia began propagating roots and cuttings of specific plants in order to supply themselves with plant dyes, extracts for fish poisons, fibers for nets and bark for textiles.

Food, shelter and religious rituals were the first uses of herbs, followed quickly by clothing and eventually cure-alls. When it was discovered that some plants could combat diseases, our ancestors began to investigate the world around them in more detail in hopes of finding the "bread of life" that would sustain them forever. Since the search began, less than a few hundred out of hundreds of thousands of plant species have proved valuable as either a medicine or a producer of quality seeds, fruits, bark, roots or leaves. Improvements from selective breeding techniques, that is, planting the seed of only the finest of each year's stock (e.g. the hardiest, a heavy producer or one that shows special new traits) have evolved many new forms and adapted herbs to fit every environment in the world.

One of the first uses of herbs was as an element in sacrificial rites performed on altars.

For primitive man a beautiful flower was a powerful talisman, the bearer of magical abilities, a ward fending off devils and demons in the dark of night. Though many of the powers associated with herbs are certainly fantasy, deep within this convoluted world of herb lore are true powers. Even today 40% of the medicines prescribed by doctors are derived from plants.

Undoubtedly the most significant role herbs have played throughout man's history is in medicine. Every culture, past and present, has relied on the widely varied philosophies of its shamen and physicians to keep the human body free from disease and discomfort. The Greek scholar, Theophrastus, a pupil of Aristotle in the fourth century B.C., first classified over three hundred simples (herbal remedies for simple ailments). Dioscorides, a Greek physician in the first century after Christ, compiled an herbal that for 15 centuries was a standard tome for those practicing the art of medicine.

Other scholars such as Hippocrates, Aristotle, Galen, Dodens, and master gardeners Charlemagne, Gerarde, Parkinson, and learned writers Jon Gardener, Dr. William Turner, Culpepper and Sir Francis Bacon were all involved with the evolution of the art of healing into the science of medicine.

Because diet has always been a controlling factor in man's pursuit of a more healthful life, herbs have played a significant role in reaching that goal. Many positive effects of herbal remedies once attributed to magic can be explained by the presence of vitamins and minerals. The diets of our forebears chronically lacked many vital nutrients. The results from consuming herbs containing these nutrients were often dramatic. The mystery of Scurvy Grass, *Cochlearia officinalis,* its ability to heal the bleeding gums formerly developing in late winter, lies in its high concentration of Vitamin C and its early appearance in spring just when needed. Such positive effects helped bolster the notion that herbs were indeed magic. The vast, worldwide health food industry thrives today, in part, because of this notion.

We need not believe all the tales we hear about miracle or magical herbal remedies but we should respect the herbs for the history they represent. Although mysticism has been replaced by the demands of a consumer society, still with us after untold centuries are herbal products such as cosmetics, perfumes, candies, liqueurs, vitamins, foods, medicines, gums, teas, tobaccos, dyes, soaps, oils, incense, disinfectants, toiletries, decorative gifts, fermented beverages and fragrances for stationery and fabrics.

There are also unlimited culinary uses of herbs to consider. Herbs such as Lovage and Parsley flavor soups while Salad Burnet adds zest to a salad. Saffron and Chives flavor cheese, Dill and Basil perk up a butter. Rosemary and Savory go well with all meats, but Fennel and fish are a match to remember. Borage finds a place in cake decorating while Poppy and Caraway seeds make delicious candy. Hosts of Mints create hundreds of hearty summer ices.

Herbs have innumerable cosmetic uses: wash waters and ointments for skin and hair care and fragrances for perfumes are by far the most popular. As decorations the various plant parts such as seeds, seed pods, leaves and flowers provide interesting dried materials for floral arrangements that range in design from simple swags hung over doors and flower petal designs on greeting cards to concerted works of art.

Herbs have an ageless quality that is still appreciated. Because they are a vast kingdom of riches which can readily be exploited there is magic in herbs even to this day. It is this magic that lures poets and playwrights to praise and glorify herbs. Religions deify them. Mages and scientists philosophise on them. Herbalists and cosmeticians swear by them. Gourmets relish them. Artists portray them. Cosmologists predict by them. Gardeners adore and pamper them.

For at least 12,000 years man has been a farmer, a gardener and a landscaper. Like native trees and shrubs, herbs were used in landscaping around primitive dwellings. Herbs were chosen for their utility in medicines, religion, cooking and food preparation; whereas trees and shrubs were usually chosen for protection from enemies and weather. The earliest landscapers attempting to confine and recreate natural settings quickly learned that gardens were more manageable when only one small niche in nature was captured and defined within the boundaries of a given plot of land. Even the most minute garden became a milestone for mankind. Each one embraced nature and defined life over and over and over again through good times and bad, reminding people how much they are a part of the world, how much they need it. Through those centuries the occupants of castles, cabins and condominiums have conspired to copy this ancient rite.

As people, politics, and plant lore changed so did the design of gardens. Gardens became sanctuaries not only around individual homesites but for community parks, commons, church yards, and governmental precincts as well. As communities grew the need for protective cover gave way to enticing gardens, signatures of influential people. The huge herb gardens of Charlemagne tended by hundreds of gardeners in the early 9th century are an example.

Natural terrain in many new lands engendered new ideas. Rocky Mediterranean coastlands and mideastern deserts, the Asian Steppes and European mountains, African tropics and the misty British Isles all yielded to the touch of gardeners and joined the ranks of landscape forms. Landscaping today reflects the amalgamated history of hundreds of nations and countless people and customs.

Plants have been such an intimate part of human evolution that whether we are the student or the teacher of herb lore, we can all be comfortable collecting and arranging them according to our tastes. The tastes of some may run to rigid geometric designs based on perfect symmetry, as in the *formal* landscape. Others, however, are enamored of imitating nature's randomness and so fashion an *informal* landscape.

Gently winding paths, intersecting in great hyperbolic arcs with patios and plantings, are the stuff of the practitioners of *contemporary* landscaping. A smattering of this and a bit of that neatly yet naturally snuggled into beds of bark and crushed rock suits them fine.

Like a flood ravaged valley, the *rock garden* landscape is strewn with boulders large and small. Randomly scattered tuffets of bold color add a sense of brightness to the scene. Nearby in a secluded meadow, flowers, as though sown midst the frenzy of a gypsy dance, create chaotic drifts of color characteristic of the *wild garden* landscape.

Those who prefer to square dance, tame this natural chaos into a checkerboard of raised beds, then summarily surround and subdue it all with a low fence or hedge. Contrast in this *dooryard* landscape is seen in textures and heights and greens and golds. It is a garden where beneficial herbs are favored over ornamentals.

As our megalopolises grow and engulf us, landscapes diminish in size, yet even the smallest space can be enhanced by walk enveloped *ponds*. Here a tiny spring and a few aquatic herbs suffice as a soliloquy on life. The last watering place a refreshing landscape reflecting serenity and constancy, emphasizes for us again the depth of the bond between man and nature.

When the decision to landscape is made, we necessarily design before planting. It is important to read about and study the various landscape forms—to venture out on weekends to see what the neighbors have done or what types of plants we prefer, visit nurseries and garden centers to determine what is actually available and at what price. This planning stage can take months to years.

Once the desired form of landscape is decided upon we are a giant step closer but a significant amount of planning, not to mention work, remains ahead. The first task takes us to the library, or the bookstore, again, where ideas for garden and landscape designs may be found. From there, with notes on preferences and availabilities determined in earlier explorations we can begin to sketch in our minds and on paper what we want to create. In the final stages the development of a sustainable budget is required.

It is now necessary to obtain the herbs that have been chosen for a design. To be frank this task can become troublesome. Herbs have an overabundance of names which at their best are confusing when the time comes to order a particular plant. Oswego Tea, Beebalm, Mountain Mint and Mountain Balm are all common names for the popular North American flower *Monarda didyma,* used by the Oswego Indians long before the Americas were discovered by Europeans. Other species of this genus are *M. punctata,* sold as Horsemint, and *M. fistulosa,* sold as Wild Bergamot. Cultivars include 'Prairie Night', 'Salmon Queen', etc. Though they add to the list of names, cultivar names often solve some of the "which is which" problems that arise with closely related varieties.

Further confusion of genus and species assignments by botanists have shifted in a game of botanical musical chairs with the new names not yet widely known or even accepted. A good example is Marjoram, or we should say Oregano. Not affecting the plant in the least, but confusing us is the switching of the *Majorana* genus to *Origanum.* Therefore, *M. hortensis,* known as Sweet Marjoram, is now *O. majorana* and *M. onites,* Pot Marjoram, is *O. onites.* Other Oreganos with a confusing assortment of botanical and common names are *O. vulgare,* Wild Marjoram; and *O. dictamnus,* Hop Marjoram. All are often sold simply as Oregano.

In order to purchase by mail it is often best to first know well the exact genus and species of each plant desired. Plant identification will be important when your search for seeds yields packets labeled only by genus: Lavender, Thyme, Oregano, Calendula, Savory. Often more than one species or variety of plant can be grown from a packet of seed labeled in such a roughshod way. Results are generally more exciting than a nuisance.

Preferable for landscaping are potted starts of exactly the species we want. Only a few nurseries and fewer garden centers stock more than a dozen herb starts suitable as ornamentals. Gardeners living in large metropolitan areas have more, but still inadequate opportunities. However, thanks to garden catalogs and especially herb and native plant sales sponsored by enthusiasts, desired materials can be found.

With the selected plants in hand you can begin propagating. Propagation is required for two reasons. First, because several of the same species will usually be required, you must propagate for quantity. Secondly, different sizes, shapes and types of conditioning may be needed to fit a particular herb to a design and they will not generally be available the way you would like them.

Many herbs also have more bad growing habits than do "plastic" ornamental plants purchased from nurseries. So even if you can find the species you want it may need taming, or perhaps a little understanding, before it is transferrable to the landscape. Let us not forget that a considerable amount of effort goes into taming all ornamental plants by the growers before they are put on sale for landscape use.

Propagation is an important step because it helps us fully understand the plants we will be dealing with and enjoying. Learning to recognize the seasonal changes an herb goes through as well as the variances throughout its life cycle will be very useful. Cultural problems can more easily be distinguished from disease and unexpected insect damage. Constant vigilance will allow you to catch the creation of a "sport", or new variety. Many sports can only be propagated by cuttings. Just as valuable is the benefit from being able to identify seeds and seedlings. Later when the garden is flourishing, weeding will repay you for all the toil expended in creating your landscape through sales of these "exotic" herbs at plant sales.

Whether a garden's design is functional, such as a play yard, patio, entrance way or service yard, or fictional, with a pond, rockfield, or miniature meadow enveloped by a small forest, one of the basic landscape forms must be adhered to as a framework. An integrated landscape plan is the background in which one or more garden designs are woven. The whole bears the creative signature of its owner.

The landscaped garden is the evidence by which neighbors and visitors judge gardeners. The more expressive a design, the more viewers will be impressed, whether or not they themselves are gardeners, for it will be obvious to them that this ground has been shaped by a skilled hand. Choosing ornamental herbs for special plantings in a landscape will multiply the homeowner's pleasures because of the many and more favorable comments from fascinated visitors.

The landscaped homesite is a piece of art, a creative work with form and beauty and benefit. It is possible to dwell here on a dozen different methods to describe how landscaping is brought into focus and metamorphosed from thoughts and things into an artistic design. Hundreds of books are available on just that subject. However, whatever words are chosen to describe beauty and artistry, and whatever method is taken to achieve them, neither is important unless we really enjoy landscaping, reading about techniques and designs and above all, enjoy what gardeners have done throughout history, *experimenting.*

The concepts for using herbs in landscaping must be dug spadeful by spadeful out of bygone tomes on lore and sifted carefully for meaningful ideas that can be reoriented to the needs of today's gardeners and their homesites. Tables and charts of ornamental plants rarely include even a few herbs and too much reading can lead to disinterest. Experimenting is an exciting and more rewarding solution.

Experimenting begins when the herbs are finally introduced to the landscape. Now we must take a trip back in time as we become involved in integrating ancient herbs with a 20th century landscape. By definition they are beneficial as well as beautiful. They are a delightful, ofttimes eccentric "old family" of plants, containing annuals, biennials, herbaceous perennials, woody and evergreen perennials, vines, bulbs and shrubs.

Herbs can be used to influence or enhance garden designs in many ways. In our landscape we may either recall ancient moments with carefully chosen and arranged herbs or merely make use of their gifts for ourselves and enable us to share with others the rich knowledge we have garnered. We may wish to recreate historical periods and places using garden designs of those times as well as the precise species of plants grown by the people of the century represented. Many of the culinary and medicinal herbs are no longer used and may be difficult to find, but well worth the search if only to preserve a portion of history as a living plant. Though many medicinal herbs are no longer recognized as possessing therapeutic value, they are a glorious flora that can be displayed ornamentally in physick gardens. Herbs can also be planted to individual themes according to their use as fragrant, culinary, cosmetic or decorative material sources.

If we choose to accent the use of herbs, then plantings such as salad greens like Salad Burnet, Caraway, Chervil and Chives would be good choices. Or perhaps our favorite teas of Mint, Anise, Lemon Balm and Camomile. Other groups may contain heady spices like Sage, Savory, Basil and Oregano.

We may want to combine herbs useful in floral arrangements using seeds of Dill, Calendula and Borage, or seed pods of Violets, Coriander and Rue, or the bamboo-like stalks of Lovage which, when cut, become cylinders and circles. Flowers from silvery Wormwood form tall backgrounds for sunny buttons of Santolina and spikes of Wooly Betony and mauve-stained Sage.

Some may design a garden that will tell a story using herbs that help recreate historical periods, such as the formal gardens of the Governor's Palace in Colonial Williamsburg, VA, reminiscent of 18th century gardens in Europe and America. Others recreate gardens of historical places such as a reconstructed village: Plymouth Plantation,

Plymouth, MA landscaped in the style of 17th century American dooryard and kitchen gardens, or the Hancock Shaker Village, Pittsfield, MA with replicas of Shaker gardens. Physick gardens contain only medicinal plants. They are abundant today as historical gardens or active centers of research at universities around the world. The University of Washington, Seattle, WA displays hundreds of medicinal herbs in its four acres of formal gardens. Designed in 18th century style is the Pennsylvania Hospital physick garden, Philadelphia, PA, the first American hospital. Often these gardens are used as living laboratories and reference libraries for studies ranging from history and anthropology to biochemistry and pharmacognosy (the study of drugs obtained from nature).

Observing another world from our doorstep is a common desire and choosing ornamental herbs can help achieve that goal. Landscapes using herbs give us gardens embedded in history. We can enter into fantasy among the herbs in our garden. We can enjoy a refreshing patch of grey nestled in light green and see peasants stooping to pick delicate yellow and blue flowers for fragrant herbal potpourris destined for noble courts in Rome and Athens. These herbs are Camomile and Lavender. The market for their flowers remains unchanged since ancient times. In the distance, rolling drifts of purple foliage break against a wall of tall green giants with beaded hair. Brown-skinned workers harvest these crops so they may be consecrated by priests and entombed with pharaohs. These workers are Egyptian slaves harvesting 'Krishna' Basil and Coriander seed.

Some gardeners may simply wish to include a few herbs here and there that they use on occasion, very likely for cooking, such as Thyme, Marjoram, Rosemary, Basil and Sage; simple herbs easily raised and endlessly enjoyed season after season.

There are a few who will choose to design the essence of a dreamworld with fabulously foliaged plants exuding rich and exotic scents, a garden designed to ensorcell, a garden that provokes you to wonder at the beauty of those lifeforms we call herbs. Wandering in this Eden your senses are forever on the verge, but just out of reach, of being satiated by the myriad of miracle plants you can see, touch and smell. Thoughts that at one time kept you from believing in the mystical power of herbs are winnowed from your wonderment by a crafty guide. You leave knowing your hands could also create this dreamworld and all the elixirs of the ancient herbalists. You feel kindred to them.

Fragrance is an important ornamental characteristic. Perfumes, cosmetics, mouth washes and body soaps all conspire to invoke sensual reminiscences by copying the herbal scents of Jasmine, Lavender, Lemon Balm, Lemon Verbena, and Patchouli. Gardens devoted to fragrant foliages and flowers are the most delightful of any that can be designed. Thick and rich herbal odors, sweet and spicy scents seem to resurrect for us our youthful, carefree days and tender memories of moments our hearts had carefully hidden.

You may ask what all that has to do with the ornamental aspects of herbs. *It is the other half to a whole.* You can always buy an ornamental plant but you do not have an herb unless you know its heritage. There are a few fortunate herbs, though planted with no eye to utility, which have qualities that have let them get by as ornamentals; Wormwood, Rue, Germander and Santolina. However, without a use or a history, an herb is usually not an ornamental but a weed.

Landscaping is one of man's proudest pursuits. Its ancient roots are so deep in our history that it has become an integral part of our lives. From time to time changing customs devalue certain plants or artistic forms but the varieties of designs and materials always increase with each new generation of gardeners. Because the garden is a necessary part of our lives we expend a vast amount of effort in making it into something in which we can find our place in nature, appreciate and utilize. Today in our landscapes it is possible to combine the world's most beautiful flowers with the most honorable of all plants, the herbs. A landscape that includes herbs is a constant reminder of how much the kingdom of plants has become a part of our lives.

Next time you are strolling past a neighbor's think about what you are really seeing. In truth it is another world, small and separate from the real world, a wellspring of comfort and passion and security in troubled and unsettled times—a companion. When this other world includes herbs it is a sign that someone has sought beyond the beauty of nature and chosen to interweave a little of the history of man into his living space.

Herbs are more than plants. They simultaneously spice the food we eat and provide our bodies with nutrients vital for healthful living. They scent every minute of our day. They can cure melancholy as well as cancer. They are friends that are growing among the plants in our garden making life more enjoyable and more livable.

Chapter 2 / SECTION 1

The Fragrant Garden

The distinguishing quality of many herbs is their fragrance. Because of their characteristic odors, even after a single encounter, fragrant herbs are never forgotten. Enchanting, arousing, sensational, sublime, erotic, and heavenly are usual descriptions by visitors to fragrant gardens who have for the first time experienced the odors of many common herbs that they can grow in their home garden.

Fragrant plants and herbs enable the home gardener to enjoy a multitude of scents. Lemon scents can be found in Lemon Balm, *Melissa officinalis*; Lemon Verbena, *Aloysia triphylla*; Lemon Grass, *Cymbopogon citratus*; Lemon Thyme, *Thymus* × *citriodorus*; Lemon Geraniums, *Pelargonium limoneum*; *Eucalyptus maculata* var. *citriodora*; and Mock Orange, *Philadelphus* × *lemoinei*. Pineapple can be had by growing Pineapple Mint, *Mentha suaveolens*; Pineapple Weed, *Chamomilla suaveolens*; Pineapple Sage, *Salvia elegans*; and Mock Orange, *Philadelphus* 'Enchantment'. Minty scents can be enjoyed as shrubs such as Mintbush, *Prosanthera*; American Pennyroyal, *Hedeoma pulegioides*; Bible Leaf *Balsamita major*; Korean Mint, *Agastache rugosa*; and Calamint, *Calamintha nepeta*. The fragrance of Caraway seed can be enjoyed as a garden herb in Caraway Thyme, *Thymus herba-barona*. A clump of Basil provides a sweet cinnamon, ginger or clove scent. Anise scents are produced by Fennel, *Foeniculum vulgare*; Anise Hyssop, *Agastache foeniculum*; Sweet Cicely, *Myrrhis odorata*; and Goldenrod, *Solidago odorata*. These herbs have been a source of the spice of life for untold millions of housewives, peasants and industrious lords and ladies in every century past. What treasures they are, to be able to please so many people for so long. Let them please you too.

Most people become interested in growing fragrant herbs simply because they are traditional herbal scents; Spearmint, Peppermint, Lemon Verbena, Rose, Wintergreen, Lemon Balm, Camomile, Lavender, Rosemary and Ginger. Sometimes a small gift of a potpourri or bouquet carried home from a friend's garden is enough to entice another gardener into growing herbs, if only for their scent. Secreted away in sachets or potpourri jars, collections of dried herbs can enliven and purify the air indoors with just the shake of a hand. It is certainly possible to do the same from a pressurized can filled with an herbal fragrance but not with the same satisfying effect, nor the same sense of self achievement. Because we have grown the herbs ourselves, the room smells of our success as a gardener and herbalist, in the same way that a bright bouquet of dazzling flowers rewards our gardening talents.

More precious than potpourris are the essences of herbs. These are the herb's fragrant oils. They have been extracted and captured in tiny, dram vials. The essences of Rosemary, Pennyroyal, Rose, Clove and Jasmine are but a few. These and many more are used to scent potpourris and sachets, herb pillows, linen, and clothing. For elegant dining, essences can be used to scent tablecloths, napkins, artificial or dried flowers in a bouquet, fingerbowl water and candles. Furniture, drapes and carpets can be scented for special effects. Essences can also be used to scent stationery and writing inks, party costumes, talcum powder and soap, dried arrangements, decorative ornaments, macrame and embroidered fabrics. Commercial products containing herbal scents and flavors include toothpaste, candy, gum, mouthwash, room spray, shampoos, bath powders and cosmetics.

The sweet herbs: Mint, Lavender, Lemon Balm, Sweet Cicely, Rosemary, Costmary, Southernwood, Camomile, Sweet Flag, Santolina and Thyme have been in household use for millenia, primarily in wash waters and for strewing. Strewing herbs were thrown to the floor and trod or sat upon in order to enjoy their fragrance. For wash waters they were enclosed in a cloth bag and steeped in boiling water for a few minutes. The scented water was then used as a rinse water for dustcloths and floor mops. There is no reason to avoid strewing herbs today. Prior to vacuuming, strew your favorite fragrant herb near doorways or in halls, or in bedrooms and baths. Crush the herb underfoot then sweep or vacuum. The scent will cling to carpets and refresh the air for hours, masking the unwanted dusty odor that accompanies vacuuming. Three herbs are recommended: Pennyroyal, Lemon Geranium and Basil. All three are also repellants and may deter fleas from traveling through carpets.

A few herbs are grown for their use in food preparation, added to give a special dish a delicious taste and odor; Basil, Sage, Thyme and Oregano for example. These herbs are easily grown in any garden soil and may be used either fresh or dried. The drying process invariably reduces a significant proportion of the fragrant component of an herb's essence. Fresh herbs should be preserved by freezing them whole in either water or oil or ground into a paste. In the same way an oil will extract a flower's fragrance for perfume, that same desirable chemical fraction will be held in an oil for use in cooking. Freezing will extend the storage life of an oil herb paste indefinitely.

A fragrant herb garden becomes a large perfume vat where scents are mixed by breezes, wafted on the wind to our noses, forever varying. Formulas are being created spontaneously. For the gardener, our whole life's work is not unlike that of a professional perfumer. Careful combinations of several herbal fragrances can create floral perfumes and pockets of single scents that can please and entertain anyone. In a fragrant garden, we can see all the components of our perfume vat. We can amble along and touch them, call them into life as they are needed.

There are a few steadfast guidelines to follow and this chapter will present them for you to consider next time you have a new plant in hand and wonder where to place it in the landscape. First, the highly fragrant herbs should be used as magnets, to draw attention to less spectacular herbs. To design a garden that projects an aroma that is self-generating and inviting we need to use those few herbs that provide remarkable results: Lavender, Sage, Mint, Rosemary, Camomile, Basil, Coriander, Wormwood, Southernwood and Savory. Thyme is indeed fragrant but not without crushing the leaves. So too are Catnip, Monarda, Anise, Costmary and most of the common herbs.

One approach to planning a fragrant magnet is mixing herbs of similar fragrance for a combined effect that is more intense that any individual herb by itself. In this case, anise-scented herbs such as Fennel, Sweet Cicely and Chervil may be grouped to join forces, producing a penetrating fragrance noticeable at some distance. Another approach uses an intensely fragrant herb in a grouping of many others, such as a border of daisy-like flowers of *Celmisia*, *Anthemis* and *Senecio* alternated with clumps of German Camomile.

Plant fragrant herbs as the focal point of a garden feature. (Fig. 1) Once visitors have discovered the whereabouts of the inviting scent, the handling begins, and sometimes never stops. Making sampling worthwhile is important for it encourages further handling. This, of course, multiplies the aroma, making the stop worthwhile. It is here that other aromatic plants and herbs are planted, ones with equally surprising fragrances but a bit more secre-

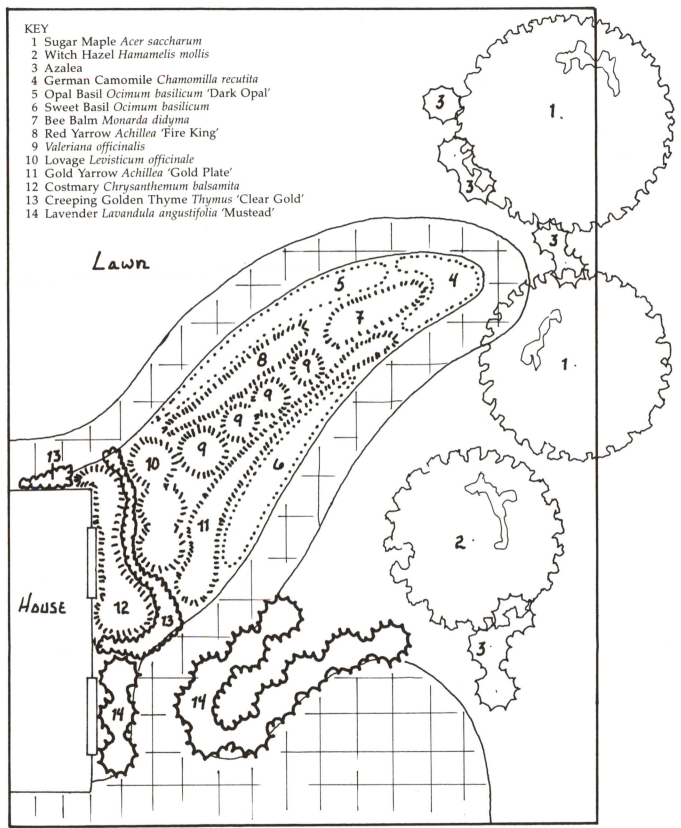

KEY
1 Sugar Maple *Acer saccharum*
2 Witch Hazel *Hamamelis mollis*
3 Azalea
4 German Camomile *Chamomilla recutita*
5 Opal Basil *Ocimum basilicum* 'Dark Opal'
6 Sweet Basil *Ocimum basilicum*
7 Bee Balm *Monarda didyma*
8 Red Yarrow *Achillea* 'Fire King'
9 *Valeriana officinalis*
10 Lovage *Levisticum officinale*
11 Gold Yarrow *Achillea* 'Gold Plate'
12 Costmary *Chrysanthemum balsamita*
13 Creeping Golden Thyme *Thymus* 'Clear Gold'
14 Lavender *Lavandula angustifolia* 'Mustead'

Lawn

House

Fig. 1. A fragrant garden using the most fragrant herbs for a self generating scent. A short cut is provided by a ground hugging mat of Creeping Thyme (13) that clambers over and around stepping stones.

tive about showing them.

Walking close to a fence along which Fennel is grown as a screen, the fragrance of anise is apparent. If Fennel is mixed with Camomile, Catnip and annual pinks in the sun, or Violets, Primroses and Mint in partial shade, the scent is divine. Surround small gardens with a border of fragrant herbs by using a frame of Lavender, Basil, German Camomile or Santolina. A circular frame of Chives, with purple globes cavorting about in the air, is a dramatic strategy for a simple arrangement of fragrant plants in a small yard.

Second, for the best results fragrant herbs must be located in strategic spots and planted where they can be touched. Pockets of fragrant herbs should be located close to leisure areas such as paths, barbeque pits, patios, home entrances, entrances from the street or driveway, around gates, swings, home foundations or in pass-throughs of fences and hedges within the landscape. These are places where a visitor may chance to brush the foliage of nearby herbs or stop to take a deeper breath of a scent on the wind. Plants we can brush past and caress fondly with our hands or feet, filling the air with their freshness, is what a fragrant garden is all about.

The highly fragrant herbs should be the primary elements of an entrance design. (Fig. 2) Patios, porches and doorways provide many alternatives for the lover of fragrant herbs. These are areas where people stop to admire your gardens, move about leisurely and rest for a moment, enjoying the scents that come their way.

For the simple open and uncluttered porch, low, mounded perennial and annual herbs are best. They should be placed at the junctions of the incoming walks. Contrasting foliage may be added according to the demands of the landscape design. But the overall design should take into account that the most fragrant herbs should be placed adjacent to the walks and porch edges where they will be brushed and handled. Steps leading up to the porch are candidates for those herbs that can be planted in the cracks or to the side that creep in and out and are trod upon, releasing an inviting aroma. Along the porch, low bushes that do not obstruct the view of the garden but still provide some cover for those sitting on the porch are needed: Lavender, Southernwood, Santolina, Rosemary, Sage and Wormwood are examples.

If a walk leads to the street or sidewalk, a procession of these fragrant herbs should flow with it, extending part way down the walk for an enjoyable entrance theme. At the sidewalk, Wormwood or Winter Savory, both neatly trimmed and contrasted with low growing junipers, and a ground cover of bark or gravel, provide a fragrant welcome for those approaching from the street. A popular, living ground cover is the blue-flowered *Nepeta mussinii*, a dwarf species of Catnip. Moderately low herbs should be planted near the driveway, punctuating the entrance that will be used by guests arriving by car. The evergreen herbs Southernwood, Wormwood, Santolina, and Bush or Creeping Thymes are appropriate.

Fragrant herbs can also make a rewarding gatestop. (Fig. 3) Whether planted around the gate post, in the path of the swinging gate door, or in a direct line of foot traffic, they will release cheery notes of fragrance to anyone entering. Guests will go out of their way to use such a splendid entrance precisely because of the regaling greeting. Useful herbs for this gate stop task are Lavender, Hyssop, Santolina, Sage and Winter Savory. They all form dense clumps of woody parts that can handle rough useage quite well but can be pruned at any time to keep a neat and trim appearance. For heavy gates it is wise to drive a stake close to the center of the clump where the gate is required to stop. A few non-woody herbs for this use are the Mints, Lemon Balm, Costmary and Roman Camomile. A Rosemary standard in a heavy pot can also be used. Fragrant vines of Jasmine and Honeysuckle, *Lonicera*, growing along the gate door or over it in an arch add heavy floral scents to the gate stopper's contribution each time the gate is used.

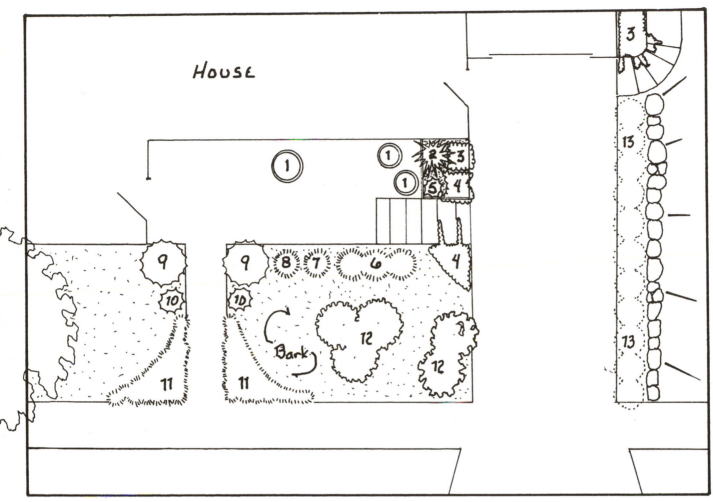

Fig. 2. Entrance ways cloaked in fragrant herbs and a patio surrounded by highly scented plants for an enjoyable rest stop.

KEY
1 potted herbs
2 *Thuya orientalis*
3 Oregano Thyme *Thymus pulegioides* 'Oregano-scented'
4 Cr. Red Thyme *Thymus pulegioides* 'Kermesinus'
5 Southernwood *Artemisia abrotanum*
6 Lemon Balm *Melissa officinalis*
7 Peppermint Geranium *Pelargonium tomentosum*
8 Variegated Lemon Balm
9 Lavender *Lavandula angustifolia* 'Hidcote'
10 Dwarf Lavender *Lavandula angustifolia* 'Nana'
11 Dwarf Catnip *Nepeta mussinii*
12 Grey Birch *Betula populifolia*
13 German Camomile/bulbs/Calendula

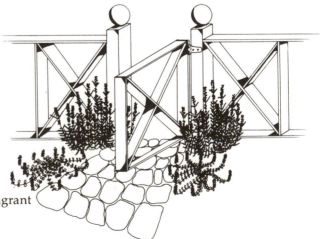

Fig. 3. Gate entrance that entertains the visitor with fragrant herbs Lavender and Thyme as the door is opened.

Back doors, kitchen doors and patios have a need of a special group of fragrant herbs: the Mints, Artemisias, Fennel, Lovage, Lemon Balm, Lavender, Camomile and Chives. Since most herbs are grown to be used as samples and simples, all of these provide household potions and necessities. The Mints and Camomiles for teas and cool drinks, icings and candies. Fennel, Lovage and Chives find their way into virtually every meal whether a salad, a soup, main course or dessert. Lavender, Lemon Balm and the *Artemisias* such as Wormwood, Southernwood and White Mugwort become indispensable scents for room deodorizers, baths and washwaters.

Along frequently used paths, fragrant herbs may be featured as borders or mass plantings. (Fig. 4) Mass plantings should be located on curves or junctions of paths where a pause in the stroll is customary. Borders should feature a mixture of the most colorful and fragrant herbs. In general both sides of a path should have an identical fragrant planting for the fullest effect. In a small garden, this may be impractical as well as limiting the number of fragrant herbs that can be employed. Matched borders of mixed species at either side of a path are attractive and an ideal solution to limited space problems. Along curving walks from the public sidewalk to the main entrance of a home, a line on both sides with mixed fragrant herbs adds an inviting aromatic note in any landscape. The changing foliage, colors, and the coming and going of flowers ensures an entertaining arrangement the year around.

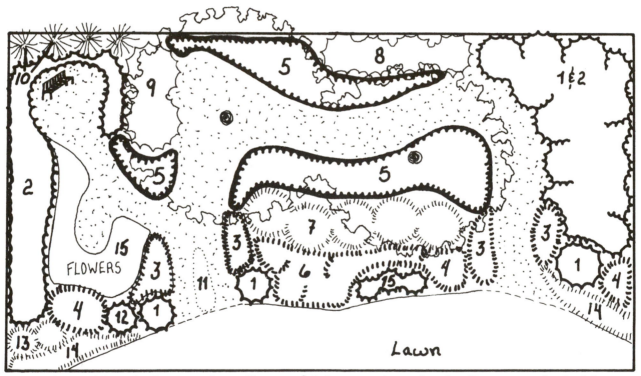

Fig. 4. Massed plantings for self-generated fragrant airs and a dazzling array of colorful flowers for an enchanting garden.

KEY

1 Lavender *Lavendula angustifolia* 'Hidcote'
2 *Santolina chamaecyparissus*
3 Bible Leaf *Balsamita major*
4 *Valeriana officinalis*
5 Florists' Violet *Viola odorata*
6 herbaceous perennials
7 Sweet Cicely *Myrrhis odorata*
8 Rhododendron
9 Rhododendron
10 Mock Orange *Philadelphus* sp.
11 German Camomile *Chamomilla recutita*
12 Southernwood *Artemisia abrotanum*
13 *Astilbe* spp.
14 Scented Geraniums *Pelargomium* spp.
15 Fragrant annuals

The third guideline for planting highly fragrant herbs in the landscape is to use containers. (Figures 8, 28 and 51) For over 8 centuries Venetian housewives have nurtured thriving gardens in simple clay pots on slender balconies overlooking the canals. Then, as today, fragrant herbs were used to purify and mask unwanted odors in the air that entered the house. Containers are practical because they can be carried wherever a certain scent is desired. Windows should be graced with fragrant plants, either in a garden or in a container such as a window box. Window boxes were most popular during the 17th and 18th centuries. Flowers and fragrant herbs such as Mignonette, Violets, Gilliflowers (the Carnations and Pinks), Basil, Camomile, Scented Geraniums, Dwarf Lavender and Mints were grown.

Containers have always been used in landscaping to accent a particular plant. Fragrant turf seat covers of Roman Camomile were a medieval treat. Other mat-forming herbs such as Thyme and Corsican Mint were also used. One container is asking a lot of any scented plant, so to be effective it must not only be highly fragrant but also easy to grow and hardy. The Mock Orange and Lime are classic examples of a single plant used to scent a small courtyard or secluded patio. Whether the container used to emphasize a fragrant plant is a fashionable urn, window box, turfed seat or hanging planter, several herbs are quite suitable: Roman or German Camomile, Lavender, Rosemary, Basil, several Mints, Pennyroyal, Calamint and the Jasmines. (Figures 12 and 50)

A fourth guideline for planting a fragrant garden is to use fragrant herbs as prominent borders, hedges, ground covers or screens. A border is a general term implying a demarcation in the landscape using plant materials. Borders are used on edges of open areas such as lawns and patios. They are used as a frame around gardens or as a line of foliage paralleling paths and fences. The term "hedge" refers to the use of woody perennials. Hedges are commonly used for major divisions between garden patterns within the landscape.

Often a tall dense border will achieve the same screening effect as a fence. A living screen, which implies a background border plant that is over 3 ft. high and used to hide something from view, provides a natural barrier in the landscape. Maintenance of an herbaceous screen, one that is gone in winter months, is far less demanding than hedges of evergreen or espaliered plants. During the growing season, little or no pruning is needed to keep the screen looking neat and natural. Herbs that make useful fragrant screens are the herbaceous perennials: Tansy, Giant Alliums, White Mugwort, Fennel, Meadowsweet, *Filipendula ulmaria,* and Valerian.

Ground covers are one of the most popular uses of fragrant herbs. New varieties are steadily being developed labeled "mat-forming" or "procumbent". They can immediately be put to use as ground covers. A thin crack between bricks or stones in a path will accommodate many. Under or amidst larger plants and in open expanses, these low-growing forms will spread into one another to create dense covers, from knee-deep to thinner than the sole of a shoe. Consider a fragrant ground cover effective when an acceptable scent comes naturally to passersby. Increase the number of plants or the area involved as necessary. For most fragrant herbs, 25 sq. ft., a patch 5 × 5 ft., is a minimum and many patches should approach 100 sq. ft. if a dominating scent is desired in the landscape.

A fifth guideline in landscaping with fragrant plants is to assist them in their task of releasing an identifiable scent by taking advantage of air currents. (Figures 5A, 5B and 5C) Before any landscaping is begun, the prevailing wind directions should be determined. Wind breaks and shade plants are designed into the landscape from this data. Slowing or stopping winter winds, but not sunlight, keeps a home warmer with less energy. Directing summer breezes to where we want them will cool outdoor leisure areas as well as funnel fragrant air from special beds. If possible, they must be directed to perform in a reliable manner, such as generating a wind through a breezeway or trapping warm air with an

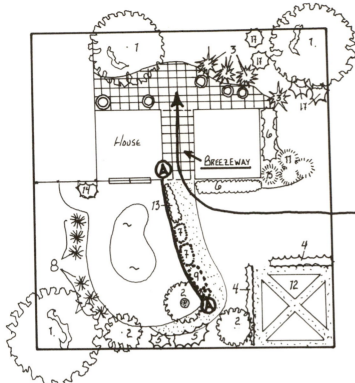

Fig. 5A. Direct breezes along a screen AA and through a breezeway to front patio. A paved patio warmed by the sun assists in drawing a parcel of air toward it through the breezeway.

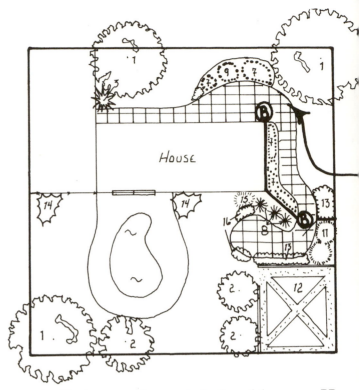

Fig. 5B. A gate at the upwind edge of the screen BB forces wind down the beds to where it is wanted. Wind currents breeching the screen become turbulent passing over and pick up more scents from foliage while delayed over the warmed patio.

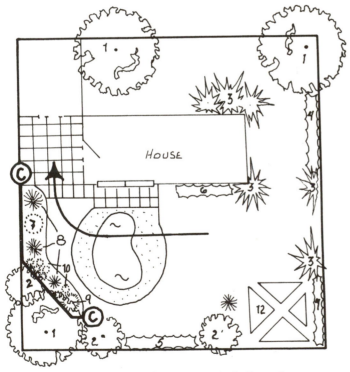

Fig. 5C. Shrubbery and trees upwind direct breezes toward the house and courtyard. A hot driveway beyond is effective in drawing a breeze through the courtyard.

KEY
1 Fl Cherry *Prunus* sp.
2 Dwarf Apple *Malus* spp.
3 *Juniperus horizontalis*
4 Holly *Ilex aquifolia*
5 Barberry *Berberis darwinii*
6 Yew *Taxus*
7 Fragrant annuals
8 Roses
9 Carnation *Dianthus*
10 Basils *Ocimum basilicum*
11 *Valeriana officinalis*
12 KITCHEN GARDEN
13 Roman Camomile *Chamaemellum nobile* var. *florepleno*
14 Southernwood *Artemisia abrotanum*
15 Lemon Balm *Melissa officinalis*
16 Oregano Thyme *Thymus pulegioides* 'Oregano-scented'
17 Azaleas

enclosed patio. The task is not simple and often not possible due to existing vegetation or predicted interference from plants growing in neighboring yards. It is best to design for the prevailing winds of the summer months, the time of year that most fragrant plants abound. Wind direction may change throughout the seasons so be thoughtful about where a screen might be best put to use.

In the landscape, wind screens of living hedges create turbulence, divert breezes and stir foliage gently, helping it release its scent. Upon encountering a barrier, the flow of air will rise creating turbulence on either side. On the leeward side of a fence, a parcel of air is trapped, warmed slightly, and given a chance to pick up more of a fragrance and hold it longer. If the fence sits at a slight angle to the wind's direction of travel, the breeze turns and follows the fence, picking up any odors from foliage planted along it. Obstacles upwind can be added to stop the wind from moving in that direction also, such as a slight cant to the tip of the fence or shrubbery.

At the downwind side, we must give the wind a chance to move freely away or if possible, to draw it along. A breezeway may be designed into the home through which fragrant air will be vented. In the front garden a large entrance patio of stone will act as a hot spot to help draw air through the breezeway. Foliage planted along the perimeter of the patio will slow incoming winds from other directions. During the summer months, delicious scents winnow through the breezeway and across the patio, providing enjoyment as well as entertainment. Large areas of concrete, patios of brick, sand or gravel, driveways, or expanses of lawn unshaded by trees, create warm surfaces that help drive a breeze. Hot air rising from these areas must be replaced by nearby air currents and it is those we have diverted to move in this direction. Sunny spots also give the warmer air an opportunity to extract more odor-producing substances from any herbs within its bounds.

To better enjoy fragrant plants let's look at some of the volatiles that we perceive as odors released by both flowers and foliage. Although the term fragrance is easily defined it is extremely difficult to identify the chemicals we are smelling. It is even more difficult to categorize herbs or flowers by their odor. Many produce several fragrant compounds. The Mint family is a good example of a multitude of odors, from subtle apple to spicy lime, yet all are only overtones to the predominant mint scent. As an example, in the essence of Peppermint, *Mentha* × *piperita*, are the spicy, mint-scented chemicals menthol and menthone as well as pinene and eucalyptol, which have a camphoraceous scent.

The herbs discussed in this book will be given an odor classification according to Table 3. This is intended for those who have never had an opportunity to sniff a particular herb and may be curious. The herbs were chosen to be representative of the odor of the fragrance chemicals listed. Chemicals are mentioned in the text for each herb if they are known so that a better understanding of the fragrance of an herb is possible. A table certainly does not substitute for the real adventure, but it may spark curiosity.

A fragrance is merely one component in a plant's arsenal of chemicals that protect and defend it. An herb releases a fragrance as a measure to ensure its reproductive success. Like petal colors, flower odors attract pollinators—moths, flies, butterflies, wasps and many birds. On the other hand, fragrant foliages act as cautionary signs to animals indicating that this plant is not to be nibbled. Quite often these foliages have a disagreeable taste reinforcing the signal to browsers and grazers.

Two such chemicals that have ulterior motives are camphor, produced by some of the Artemisias, and methylepijasmonate, the major scent-producing chemical in the flowers of Jasmine. Camphor is allelopathic. It is an herbicide that when washed to the ground, effectively kills germinating seeds around the plant, thus eliminating herbaceous competition. Methylepijasmonate is one of the most highly regarded fragrant chemicals. It is a scent particularly attractive to many flying insects. Although man does not resemble a bug in any

Table 3
Odor Classification and Chemicals Responsible for Some Herbal Fragrances

Odor Class	Fragrance Chemicals	Herb
SPICY	Asarole	Ginger
	Anethol	Anise
	Carvone	Caraway
	Cinnamonaldehyde	Cinnamon
	Citral, Citronellal	Lemon Balm
	Cuminal	Cumin
	Eugenol	Clove
	Fenchone, Chavicol	Fennel
	Farnesol	Lime
	Limonene	Pineapple Mint
	Menthol, Menthone, Piperitone	Pepper Mint
	Methylsalicylate	Wintergreen
	Myrcene	Hop
	Pulegone	Pennyroyal
	Cymene, Terpinene, Linalool*	
CAMPHORACEOUS	Pinene	Hyssop
	Camphor, Borneol	Rosemary
	Thujone, Eucalyptol	Sage
	Thymol	Thyme
	Farnescene, Cedral, Bisabolol*	
FLORAL	Azulene, Chamazulene	Camomile
	Geraniol	Rose
	Irone	Violet
	Methylepijasmonate	Jasmine
	Phenylethylalcohol, Benzyl acetate*	
HERBACEOUS	Carvacrol	Oregano
	Coumarin	Woodruff, Hay
	Phenylacetic acid	Honey
	Umbeliferone, Phellandrene, Ionone*	
ALLIACEOUS	Allyldisulfide, allicin	Garlic

*Not found in sufficient quantity to impart its odor to a specific herb.

way, human chemistry also utilizes this attractant scent. We do not understand it, but the fragrance apparently evolved over many millions of years to lure and is so successful that even man finds these scents enticing, and uncommonly attractive often to the point of being sensually arousing.

There are also many herbs that contain fragrant and tasty chemicals for us to enjoy when we eat. When we use an herb in cooking some of its fragrance is lost immediately. We can smell it. Yet some is retained in the fat and oil of the concoction before us. What is most important is to retain the true fragrance and flavor of the herb by harvesting, preserving and storing it in the best way possible. We know this is not always possible. In many cases we are accustomed to the odor and taste of the herb only in its preserved state. Odor chemicals are odoriferous simply because they are volatile, that is they are easily released to the air from the plant material. To enjoy these special aromas, evident only at harvest, careful procedures

Plate 1

Harvest of gold. Ornamental herbs from the garden for decoration. Flowers of Lavender Cotton, Feverfew, Calendula and Green Santolina.

ELECAMPANE

" Excellent herbs had our fathers of old—
Excellent herbs to ease our pain—
Alexander and Marigold,
Eyebright, Orris and Elecampane,
Basil, Rocket, Valerian, Rue,
(Almost singing themselves they run),
Vervain, Dittany, Call-me-to-you—
Cowslip, Melilot, Rose of the Sun.
Anything green that grew out of the mould
Was an excellent herb to our fathers of old.
RUDYARD KIPLING.

In no haven other than an herb garden can reading be pursued with more enjoyment especially when true scents can be called forth to supplement fine poetry.

Fragrant magnet of Valerian in the center square in a formal garden, Medicinal Herb Garden, Univ. of Washington, Seattle, WA.

Fragrant magnet in dooryard design using 'Cinnamon Basil (lower right) at waist level where it is accessible to hands and Roman Camomile (center) that signals its presence from a turf seat that doubles as the raised bed's frame.

Luring the visitor to closer inspection in a fragrant garden is Southernwood. Here where a path encounters a perennial bed the garden also displays Ginger Mint and Oregano (in bloom behind).

Plate 2

Fragrant frame of spicy 'Dark Opal' Basil around a bed of fragrant Roses at the home of Irving Scherer, Chehalis, WA.

Fragrant herbs jutting into a rocky pathway where they will be brushed by passersby. Blue and pink Hyssop, Creeping Savory, Roman Camomile and Thyme are visible.

German Camomile lounging on a walk where it will be stepped on, releasing its apple scent to the entire yard.

Wooly Thyme plunging over a precipice just behind a sitting chair at the home of Michele Nash, Mercer Island, WA.

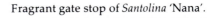

Fragrant gate stop of *Santolina* 'Nana'.

Entrance theme from driveway. Evergreens, Southernwood, Lemon Balm, Creeping Thyme, Dwarf Catnip and Violets decorate this compact feature.

must be followed to retain more volatile chemicals as well as preventing others from degenerating during storage.

There are countless ways to preserve herbs: candy, cheese, vinegar, butter and, of course, drying are most common. Which is best? Let's find out. First, it must be remembered that the volatile, odoriferous chemicals are for the most part not water soluble. Dropping them into hot stew will be quite rewarding but only briefly. Preserving the herb in oil and cooking at a low heat for a short period ensures the trapping of aromatic chemicals.

Second, most herbal aromas are not single chemicals but conglomerations of several or more. During preservation some are lost and others, that are more stable, become prominent. Take, for example, the ripening of Coriander seed. When picked slightly green, it is spicy but muted by a heavy waxy odor. When fully ripe its scent is sharp, spicy and sweet. The task before every gardener of herbs is to experiment with different methods of preservation to determine how you like your herbs stored in order to yield the aroma you enjoy the most.

Third, pick no herb before its time. That is very easy for me to say but I am the first to violate this principle by slipping out of my kitchen any day of the year to snip off a piece of fresh herb. Nothing can compare. Not even the best stored product. But to be sure that the material being stored is at its very best, know when to harvest it. Taste it. Smell it. Dry a little and see if it's bitter or musty. When it smells the way you want it to, harvest it. To give you a little help there are three rules of thumb. 1) Never harvest when water or dew are on the plant. They must be air dry. You may have to compromise with the weather on this one. 2) Harvest before the heat of the day. Transpiration reduces the levels of an undetermined number of the herb's constituents during the late afternoon. Never harvest (for storage) in the evening. 3) Harvest just prior to blooming.

Some of the chemicals stored are attractants for pollinators, they are pleasing to us as well as bugs, and they are present in their highest concentration prior to and during blooming. However, once an herb blooms other chemical changes occur that often decrease the quality of its fragrance and interfere with its storage ability. Let's take Basil as an example. The fresh herb is highly fragrant, but exceedingly so just prior to blooming. More than 15 chemicals are responsible for the aroma of Basil as you smell it out in the garden. Basil produces some chemicals that attract pollinators; they are concentrated on the flowering tops, on bracts and calyxes. Chemicals that repel flying insects are found on leaves and stems, while other repellant chemicals on leaves taste badly, inhibiting chewing insects. Many other fragrant chemicals that are part of the herb's machinery for life are exuded along with water during periods of rapid transpiration in late afternoon. This process can be rapid enough to cause wilting on hot sunny afternoons.

Basil is best harvested at midday and in mid-to late summer when its flowers have just opened. Flower tops are included because of their contribution of floral and sweetly spiced scents. But to fully preserve all of these chemicals there is little to do but freeze the harvested material. This is a costly option. Second to that is pesto. Although, if you do not choose to entertain recipes that call for pesto, because of the cheese (milk-free diets) or salt (low-sodium diets), the best preservation method is an oil paste.

Let's discuss some of the ways to preserve herbs. Table 4 shows the four basic types of preservation. In decreasing order of energy requirement they are freezing, solvents, absorbents and drying. Each is accompanied by specific methods.

Freezing requires considerable energy. Freeze dried herbs are essentially a commercial product only. Storing whole herbs in air-tight containers in the home freezer is the most satisfactory way of preserving the true nature of an herb. However, it is costly and worth the expense for only two herbs, French Tarragon and Lemon Verbena. Loss of volatiles still occurs but at a reduced rate. Storage is limited to 6–8 months. Freezer storage is valuable

Table 4
Methods of Preserving Herbs

High Energy ————————————————————————→ *Low Energy*

FREEZING	: Freeze Dried		Freezer Storage
SOLVENT	: Alcohol, Vegetable oil, Vinegar, Cheese, Butter, Syrup		
ABSORBENT	: Sugar		Salt
DRYING	: Oven	Microwave	Air

Low Energy

only to those who enjoy a refreshing cup of herb tea. Make your herb blends for teas before freezing. Go so far as to put the materials in tea bags (which provide extra protection). Herbs that must be preserved this way to yield a true off-the-plant flavor and fragrance are German Camomile, Catnip, Fennel, Sweet Cicely, Anise, Lemon Verbena, Mint, Anise Hyssop, Calamint, Chervil, Lemon Balm and Pineapple Sage.

The Solvent method offers the widest variety of options. Alcohol preservation is least common because of the cost and limited culinary use. It is an excellent method to extract fragrant oils and volatiles from herbs however. Most, if not all, alcohol products are in fact already herbally flavored. Rosemary, Mint, Thyme and the green seeds of Sweet Cicely, Lovage, Anise and Fennel are preserved nicely in whiskey or Vermouth for use in marinades, candies, mixed drinks and punch.

Vinegar is used for certain salad and marinade herbs such as Basil, Tarragon, Savory, Rosemary, Sweet Marjoram and Garlic Chives. Use only distilled white vinegar and do not use wet material or too much. A vinegar extraction is strengthened by repeated changes for fresh material. It may be necessary to filter the vinegar to keep it clear.

Cheese is a solvent of sorts. It contains many fats, sugars and oils that can retain a significant proportion of an herb's chemical signature. Of course, the cheese itself has a major influence on the product. Cream cheese, Brie, Mozarella and other soft mild cheeses are best to blend with fresh herbs. Allow some period of aging, 1 week to 10 days, before using. The shelf life is usually less than 1–2 months. Herbs are either folded into the cheese or blended at low speed.

An herb butter can effectively preserve an herb for several months. Fresh herbs are chopped, or better yet, blended into butter (margarine for milk-free diets) in a ratio of 1 Tbsp. herb to 2 Tbsp. butter. Heat the mixture to boiling and simmer for 8–10 minutes. Pour into a mold and refrigerate. The mixture will separate, yielding a colored top layer that retains the herb's fragrant signature. This layer is good for spreads and pastries. The herb-rich bottom layer is good for stews, soups and basting broths. Powdered herbs can also be used. Mix them 1:4.

Preserving herbs in vegetable oil is another choice method for retaining natural freshness. For dishes such as salad dressings, oriental stir-fries, gravy and sauces or marinades, the oil method proves this point. The bite of Basil, mellow richness of Tarragon and sweet perfection of Sweet Marjoram remains intact. Mix fresh herbs 4:1 and puree in a blender. Use soybean, sesame, peanut or safflower oils. A little sugar and salt can be added to extend shelf life, preserve color and to some extent, extract fragrant oils. Ascorbic acid (Vitamin C) can also be added to extend shelf life and preserve color. Use ½ teaspoon of each to 1 pint of puree. This product should be refrigerated, and has a shelf life of 3–4 months (without additives) or up to 6 months (with salt and/or ascorbic acid).

When using solvent methods to preserve do not overlook the advantage of herb blends. Not only can remarkable products emerge but some extra shelf life will result when herbs such as Basil, Sage, Savory, Rosemary and Thyme are added. These herbs all confer some antimicrobial activity to herb mixtures. Favorite recipes can be made more quickly by having the herb mixture at hand in oil or butter form, such as for soups and stews.

Herb syrups are in essence the same as fruit syrups. Sugar becomes the preserving material. Herbs are prepared by using either an infusion (steeping herbs in boiled water for 5–10 minutes) or a decoction (bringing herbs and water to a boil and simmering for 5–10 minutes). A little sugar (1 tsp. per cup) may be added to facilitate extraction of aromatic oils. The strained liquid is then converted to a syrup by adding 2 c. of sugar per cup of liquid and boiling to desired consistency. Mint Syrup is most famous but Basil, Ginger and Violet Syrup are just as easily prepared.

Sugar and salt are absorbent materials that trap volatile chemicals. Layer herbs and either absorbent in pint jars and seal tightly. Salt preserves for a longer period of time but is not as useful for those on salt restricted diets. Sugar, flavored by Lemon Verbena, Lemon Balm, Rosemary, Mint, Scented Geraniums, Lemon or 'Krishna' Basil and Chervil is excellent for cookies, pastries, oriental cuisine and teas.

Drying is the most popular method of preserving herbs. Air drying removes about 80% of a plant's moisture and is used for large volumes of material. Oven drying can remove up to 90% although its main advantage is to dry a small amount of herbs quickly. A microwave oven can be used to dry a minute amount of herb extremely quickly.

Air drying should be done in the shade. Herbs producing seeds are bound and covered by paper bags which are then hung under eves or on a covered porch. Check them periodically for dryness. Oven drying is accomplished with either a wire screen to hold plucked leaves or a rack of slim dowling for whole plants. The latter yields a coarse product that may require cleaning to remove stems before use. Three temperature levels are used in this book to indicate how warm an oven should be to adequately dry a specific herb: Low 80–90°F, Medium 90–110°F, and High 110–140°F. It is not practical to offer an average drying time for all herbs but expect oven drying to require from 4 to 12 hours. A convection oven will usually halve the drying time.

The microwave oven is useful for drying very small amounts (1 teaspoon to a few tablespoons) of an herb for either immediate use or simply because no more can be harvested. A gardener cultivating only one French Thyme does not need to spend 2–4 hours drying a handful when 10 minutes in a microwave will suffice. In addition, some recipes, particularly something quick, call for powdered herbs as opposed to whole fresh herbs. When no dried herb is available the microwave comes to the rescue with dried material that is easily powdered in no time at all.

When using a microwave to dry herbs be sure to place them on a paper towel. Do not cover them. Give branches room to wilt so that they do not cross. Set the microwave on *Defrost*. Do not use a normal setting unless the oven is designed to handle dehydration. Most fresh herbs require from 8–15 minutes on defrost to dry fully. Resetting for successive 3–5 minute periods is recommended so neither the herb nor the oven is overheated. Microwave dried Chives, Lemon Balm, Calamint, Savory, Rosemary and French Thyme are superior to the radiant-oven dried product.

Let's take a look at some of the world's most fragrant herbs; evergreen herbs such as Creeping Thyme, Roman Camomile, Creeping Rosemary and Lavender; semievergreen shrubs such as Wormwood, Creeping Savory and Southernwood; herbaceous perennials Valerian, Mint and Fennel; vines of Jasmine; and annuals German Camomile, Coriander and Basil.

Chapter 2 / SECTION 2

Herbs for a Fragrant Garden

Many of the most popular fragrant ground covers come from the Thyme family. Creeping Thyme comes in many forms to suit all tastes and fit all designs. They all tend to grow more densely if heavily pruned in early spring and a sunny, warm niche is necessary for a full fragrance. Although their flowering periods vary it is their most fragrant period and must not be discouraged. Masses of Thyme flower spikes, however, create a traffic jam of bees and butterflies so beware of planting them in leisure areas if you are not a fan of bees, or they of you.

Some Creeping Thymes produce an abundance of fertile seed that may be sown along sidewalks or between steps or paving stones. An easy tool for simplifying the transfer of seedlings to the garden walk is a seed tray composed of a dozen parallel troughs, ⅜ in. wide and ¾ in. deep. Slender rows of well rooted, healthy plants, one seedling to the inch, may be transplanted directly into the cracks between paving stones or steps using this technique.

A mixture of more than two species is best, as it provides more color and foliage contrast as well as a margin of safety in any one spot. Combinations always appear to be wrestling in a confusion of intermingling colors in joyful pursuit of one another. If kept trimmed in early spring with a lawn mower set high, cultivars of *T. praecox* and *T. pulegioides* form dense mats valuable for the fragrant mead. Do not forget to plant a significant quantity of spring and fall bulbs along with Creeping Thyme covers to produce a year round show of color and fragrance.

The genus *Thymus* is easily the most confusing of all the culinary herbs. Over 150 species, varieties, and cultivars exist world-wide and taxonomic data is difficult to find or interpret. The classification used for Thyme in this text is based on the fabulous work of Harriet Flannery, *A Study of the Taxa of Thymus Cultivated in the United States.*

The Creeping Thymes covered in this discussion are: Moroccan Thyme, *T. brousonetti;* Tuffeted Thyme, *T. caespititius;* Caraway Thyme, *T. herba-barona;* Peter Davis Thyme, *T. leucotrichus;* Mother-of-Thyme, *T. pulegioides;* and Wild Thyme, *T. praecox* ssp. *arcticus.* Several Thymes have only cultivar designations. Those discussed here are 'Clear Gold', 'Doone Valley', 'Linear Leaf Lilac' and 'Long Leaf Gray'. There are an unlimited number of discrepancies in popular nomenclature. For example, the legendary *T. serpyllum* is rarely cultivated and is unknowingly represented (or substituted for) by *T. pulegioides* or *T. praecox. T. nummularius* is invariably *T. pulegioides.* Of those Thymes that have no species designation, 'Long Leaf Gray' is sold as *T. glabrous loevyanus, T. lanicaulis* and *T. thracicus,* while 'Linear Leaf Lilac' is sold as either *T. panonnicus* or *T. marshallianus* (Marshall Thyme).

In order to assist you in choosing a Creeping Thyme to experiment with, those discussed here will be separated by approximate height into two categories: prostrate (less than 3 in. and rooting along branches at nodes) and mounding (forming either procumbent or decumbent spreading mounds over 3 in. high). Procumbent (branches lying flat on the ground) and decumbent (branch tips ascending) habits do not always root at every node, but at the branch ends.

Several handsome prostrate Creeping Thymes are widely available from herb growers. In general, these are less then 3 in. high, including flowering stems: *T. caespititius* and its cultivar 'Tuffet', and *T. praecox ssp. arcticus* and its cultivars 'Mayfair', 'White Moss', 'Pink Chintz', 'Coccineus', 'Languinosus', and 'Halls Wooly'.

The prostrate Creeping Thymes are characterized by tiny leaves, compact habit, and dense mats that are scarcely higher than the pebbles they may find themselves growing among. The most popular are *T. praecox* ssp. *articus* 'White Moss', with shiny, green leaves, and 'Languinosus', or Wooly Thyme, with exceedingly hairy leaves and stems. They grow no higher than the thickness of stem and leaves as they creep along in hot, sunny sites. They are tough herbs that can take considerable traffic and as such, are perfect for dampening footfalls on stony ground. Such a heavenly soft walk is also fragrant as these two Thymes release their aromas when crushed. 'Languinosus', with its fuzzy, grey-green leaves, is not hardy in damp soils during winter months so should be grown in a well drained, sandy soil in full sun or partial shade. In the latter it tends to thicken into a fluffy 2 in. carpet but loses its resilience to foot traffic. 'Halls Wooly' is quite similar to 'Languinosus', growing as a somewhat thicker blanket but it is highly regarded for its prolific flower production.

Two other highly ornamental and pancake-thin ornamental Creeping Thymes of this subspecies are 'Pink Chintz' and 'Coccineus'. They display prominent pink and magenta flowers on shiny, dark green mats of exceptional beauty. These two herbs look their best slithering among fissures in rocks or paving, their flowers crowding the cracks so colorfully at bloomtime it is as if someone had spilled cherry frosting in the garden. Add to this their delicious Thyme aroma and it's an experience you will want to share with everyone.

T. Praecox ssp. *articus* 'Mayfair' also has an admirable, dark green foliage but it has butter-yellow spots on some leaves, in no regular pattern, that often engulf entire leaves yet avoid others completely. In some cases, a whole branch is dressed in gold with nary a spot of green. 'Mayfair' has a splendid, thick garment of rose in midsummer.

As its name implies, *T. caespititius* is caespitose. Rather than quickly spreading it stops to form small tuffets or mounds; the cultivar 'Tuffet' decidedly so. This striking habit and its light green, needle-like leaves make it an uncommonly beautiful Creeping Thyme for open rocky areas, dry bed streams, as a border in knots and parterres or part of a contemporary feature. Not only does this Thyme look better emerging from a sandy bed, it grows and spreads faster. In average garden soil, use ½–1 in. layer of sand where it is to grow.

'Doone Valley' is best described as a harlequin Thyme because of its uncertain origin, fleeting lemon scent, splashy colors (glossy, dark green leaves with some branch tips dipped in gold), its summer cloak of rose-purple so thick the plant is barely visible, and the shedding of its golden variegation in the summer. This prostrate mat is temperamental about soils, particularly damp ones, so during winter a layer of sand will help see it through. 'Mayfair' closely resembles 'Doone Valley' but has more widespread variegation that does not vanish in summer. Both are sold as Golden or Creeping Golden Thyme.

The Creeping Thymes, forming spreading mounds that are generally over 3 in. high, and as much as 8–10 in., are divided into two categories: 1) a compact spreading mat, and 2) a mound. The first contains *T. leucotrichus* and *T. pulegioides* and its cultivars 'Fosterflower', 'White Magic', 'Oregano-scented', and 'Kermesinus'. Those of the second category that form slow-spreading mounds are *T. brousonetti*, *T.* 'Clear Gold', *T. pulegioides* 'Gold Dust', *T. herba-barona*, *T.* 'Nutmeg', *T.* 'Linear Leaf Lilac', and *T.* 'Long Leaf Gray'. These categories are not clearly defined because many Thymes are polymorphic, that is, quite variable in habit. A significant factor interfering with their habit is sexual variability; some plants bear only female flowers. This proclivity results in a slightly different appearance of the herb from its male/female counterpart.

A spreading mat may be either procumbent or decumbent and forms a loose, rapidly spreading ground cover. Most representative of this habit is *T. pulegioides* and its cultivars. All are incorrectly sold as *T. serpyllum.* Mother-of-Thyme is the correct common name, however. The spreading mats of Mother-of-Thyme include the beautiful cultivars 'Fosterflower', named after Gertrude Foster, and 'White Magic', both white-flowering, and the lavender or purple-flowering 'Oregano-scented'.

Both white-flowering cultivars are very hardy Creeping Thymes with a good Thyme fragrance. 'White Magic' is somewhat lemon-scented. These 3–6 in. mats are two of the finest mead herbs because of their hardiness and resilience to foot traffic. They will both do well in partial shade with a well drained soil of average fertility.

'Oregano-scented' is also sold as Oregano Thyme, *T. serpyllum* or *T. nummularius.* The name 'Oregano-scented' is a bit presumptuous, but it does have a pleasant Thyme scent with a rich, woodsy note. It has fairly large, dark green leaves and produces a moderate supply of lavender flowers. 'Kermesinus' resembles 'Oregano-scented' except for a heavier flower spike of rose-purple and a somewhat less dense habit.

A less commonly cultivated spreading Thyme is Peter Davis, *T. leucotrichus.* It forms a grey-green, open mat 3–4 in. high. It blooms very early with colorful flower spikes of showy pink flowers marked by especial beauty. Its biting, spicy scent and flavor is a result of thymol mixed with borneol, camphor, and limonene. This Creeping Thyme and *T. brousonetti* create a dazzling pink carpet when in bloom about mid-May and are best as ground covers along paths, in sunny meads, rock gardens, and design motifs in parterres.

The slow spreading, mounding Thymes are often simply rangy sub-shrubs only 6–10 in. high, but they tend to root at branch tips and carry on as though not satisfied to stay in place like bush Thymes.

The Thyme just mentioned, *T. brousonetti,* or Moroccan Thyme, bears the most glorious flowers of any Thyme, shooting out in ½ in. trumpets clustered into a pastel pink pompom. Its foliage is green with a medicinal or resinous odor composed of cymene, myrcene, and carvacrol. This Creeping Thyme is hardy to Zone 8 with protection and should be given a sandy soil and a thick sandy layer beneath to protect it in winter.

Two Creeping Thymes, *T.* 'Clear Gold' and *T. pulegioides* 'Gold Dust', are both sold as Golden or Creeping Golden Thyme. They have mottled leaves of yellow-green and lavender flowers. The basic difference between them is the more compact habit of 'Gold Dust'. Both form a 4–8 in., slowly spreading ground cover of a decumbent habit. They are best used in a mixed planting ground cover where only modest color contrast is desired. Their lavender-pink flowers do not become them; the combination of pink and yellow-green is not complimentary.

Caraway Thyme, *T. herba-barona* and *T.* 'Nutmeg', are two fairly compact mounding herbs that from one whiff you would think could only be harvested in a dreamland. They are strongly fragrant and quick to spread into an 18 in. wide prostrate mat from 2–6 in. high. They contribute a heavenly odor to the garden air as they flow beneath our feet, spreading from cracks between paving stones on a sunny walk. The chemistry of both is similar, a pure caraway fragrance from carvone and a spicy note of limonene. Either of these Thymes are exciting culinary spices for spaghetti sauces, chili, and pot roast or other stewed meats and vegetables.

Two Thymes that spread slowly in diffuse, thinly foliaged mounds, are *T.* 'Linear Leaf Lilac' and *T.* 'Long Leaf Gray'. These two unique Thymes have hairy or ciliated grey-green leaves that are long, slender, and on the former, somewhat curved. Their purple or lilac flowers are a prominent feature in early summer and both combine well in a widespaced mixed border with Dwarf Catnip, *N. mussinni,* to provide a silver lining along a driveway or sunny walk in winter as well as summer. Their sparsely foliaged branches do not form a simple rosette (spider web), resembling instead the writhing tentacles of a sea monster groping about indiscriminately. They give character to any rock garden or austere contemporary garden feature and should be grown to contrast with other slow spreading herbs and plants such as *T. caespititius* and *T. leucotrichus* in an informal border. For contemporary designs they can be paired with Dwarf Germander; Incana Santolina; and Speedwell, *Veronica prostrata,* for a spectacular foliage and flower show as well as a neat and attractive blend of textures in winter.

Once a highly revered medicinal of Egyptian physicians, Camomile has never strayed more than a doorstep away from man's needs. In more than one language the name given this herb implies apple-scented. From castle lawns, bench seats, and window sills via medieval Venice to 16th century London then in wooden buckets strapped to the sides of Conestoga wagons that crossed America, Camomile is one of the most desirable of all herbs.

Many forms of Camomile exist, from sweet-flowered cultivars for teas and tisanes to the flowerless turfs that adorned castle keeps. More than one genus is involved and there is still much confusion on botanical placement. For simplicity it is important to remember that the annual Camomile comes from the *Chamomilla* genus, *C. recutita [Matricaria recutita, M. chamomilla]* and is commonly called Roumainian or German Camomile. The perennial Camomile comes from the genus *Chamaemelum. Chamaemelum nobile* is the popular creeping species called Roman Camomile. Other Camomiles include Pineapple Weed, *Chamomilla suaveolens,* smelling of tart pineapples; fruity scented *Matricaria suffruticosa,* from S. Africa; *Anthemis cotula,* a medicinal weed called Stinking Camomile, Mayweed or Dog Fennel; *A. cupaniana,* an aromatic grey-foliaged herb resembling Roman Camomile; and two other *Anthemis* species, *A. sancti-johannes* and *A. tinctoria,* the Marguerite, that are not scented but common ornamentals in the perennial garden.

Chamaemelum nobile, Roman Camomile, is a mat-forming perennial that has the sweetest, most deliciously scented foliage of any plant. There are rayless, single and double-flowered cultivars. A cultivar, Lawn Camomile, *C. n.* 'Trenague' is a non-flowering turf variety that can be mown to form a lawn of spongy carpet smelling of apples right out of an oven. This cultivar forms attractive tight rosettes of foliage like verdant spiny starfish. Roman Camomile was popular in medieval days as a covering on benches.

Flowers may be discouraged on Roman Camomile, except the double flowered forms, which are the most pleasantly scented, to improve the fragrance of the foliage. It must not be allowed to become rangy as it cannot spread effectively unless firmly pressed into the soil. Planted in loose moist soils and kept mown to no more than 2 in., Camomile will develop into a dense mat suitable for sitting. Either full sun or partial shade are acceptable to Camomile.

As a fragrant perennial ground cover, Roman Camomile should, and can be, a part of every landscape. Its phenomenal fragrance is a special feature to which few plants can lay claim. Use it as a path covering in a wilderness, dry bed ravine in wild and informal settings, an aromatic entrance theme around the paving stones leading through a contemporary homesite to the door, a floor covering in an open forest glade, a mead herb, or a turf bench or lawn manicured to furry softness in a formal garden.

During medieval days a bench was usually a flat-topped pile of earth pushed against the side of a castle wall or into a mound elsewhere. On top was Roman Camomile, essentially a fragrant plant grown as a seat cover. 'Trenague' developed as a turf variety and was most popular because of its dense habit and lack of flowers. As a cover it must be cut back regularly and grown in full sun in cool climates, or partial shade in hot.

Because it can be mown and trimmed, Roman Camomile is a valuable counterpart to turf grass even in the most formal, feature garden. In fact, its aromatic gift makes it so superior to grass in formal design that grass just cannot compare.

Spilling uncontrolled across a rocky barren slope, Roman Camomile creates a bold dendritic pattern like the many fingers of a river reaching out into the sea. In an intermittent stream-bed it will keep to the moist areas and thicken beautifully in wet depressions in full sun. Rock walls or escarpments, provided with planting pockets full of rich soils, clothed all in Roman Camomile, are thrilling sights and a splendid treat for the nose.

The annual German Camomile is a highly aromatic, flower-bearing herb used to scent wash waters for hair rinses and medicinal baths, in medicinal ointments or teas and candies. Camomile tea has been a favorite nightcap for thousands of years. It is a weedy, profusely blooming annual that will self-sow in any soil, exposure or climate. It is frost hardy and in cooler climes will grow surrounded by snow, provided the ground does not freeze. It excells in full sun, developing small 12 in. diameter bushes that become encased under hundreds of ½ in. daisies. Its talent for self-sowing is unsurpassed by any herb, and possibly most weeds. If it were not for its unequalled fragrance it would certainly rank with Chickweed. For unmixed borders or mass plantings give each plant 12 in. from center. Overcrowding simply ruins its handsome bushy nature so avoid it. Be sensible—be ruthless when thinning.

A limed clayey soil produces the most fragrant flower, which is the result desired. The apple-scent comes from the flower, not the foliage, and is strongest when planted in groups of several or more plants. No agitation is required for German Camomile to scent an entire yard day and night. Its apple-scent, created by a combination of camphoraceous, herbaceous and spicy scents that include the chemicals azulene and anethol, is best in mid-afternoon, which is the time of day the flowers should be picked. For the finest aroma in a tea, flowers should not be allowed to age more than a few days after first opening. To protect successive crops of German Camomile from losing their fine fragrance, be sure no Mayweed, *Anthemis cotula*, grows in any abundance near your garden. German Camomile readily crosses with Mayweed, to its disadvantage.

German Camomile lends itself well to hard, dry areas where little else will grow without extensive soil renovation. Rocky banks, ravines, rock walls, brick walks, and along driveways and sidewalks where afternoon sun may produce intense heat are favorite spots of this delightful weed. Its seed may be sown where it is to grow and in poor soils this is recommended. It transplants well, even when in full bloom, if plenty of soil is taken up and water applied after planting. Sown in spring it will bloom by midsummer and continue for two months or more. Left on the plants, the flowers retain their scent through most of the season.

German Camomile is a versatile herb for a medium to low border or ground cover use in wild and informal designs on hot, dry sites. Given free reign, its light tolerance and frost hardiness both improve with time from self-sown individuals. Be careful. Its shade tolerance will allow it to germinate under other plants, grow through them rapidly, and emerge into the light to flourish, eventually bestowing its host with what appears to be a cloak of daisies but also robbing it of water and nutrients. Take care in the wild garden where it is allowed to sow and grow freely as it will overtake other slower germinating and maturing plants. Thin a stand early to improve the chances of other self-sowing, wild herbs. In rich soils it may grow tall and slender instead of bushy, so be sure to thin into clumps, not singles, so they will support themselves without staking or toppling over in heavy rain.

German Camomile has been used in exceedingly long or intricate borders in formal parterres where its self-sowing attribute, a time and labor saving boon, provide a profusion of highly fragrant daisies all summer giving it a stature no other single annual herb enjoys. It is an easily established ground cover in meadows and sunny glades or as an area of color balance in the contemporary garden that features other annuals or biennials, such as the vegetable garden. In the informal perennial bed it is an excellent transition planting.

In any vegetable garden German Camomile is a valuable bee plant that attracts many winged creatures, thus improving yield. In the dooryard garden it is grown along paths where it can be easily harvested and its seeds will drop harmlessly to the path where trodden underfoot, they are unlikely to propagate uncontrollably or at the expense of a pampered neighbor.

German Camomile can be seeded directly into containers for displays around doors, porches, and patios. It can be sown repeatedly all year for a continual show of bloom from early spring, if plants are begun in cold frames, through late fall. The pleasant ah-inspiring, apple-scent of German Camomile in full bloom is an event that must be experienced. Rich soils beget slender plants and should be avoided. Do not overfertilize. Do not cut plants back but allow long cascading branches to form.

The flowers of German Camomile are the source of Camomile tea and yield the best flavor of all the Camomiles. What a treat it is to be able to step out onto the patio and pluck a few flowers from a hanging planter of Camomile for a quick cup of one of history's most famous teas.

On the other side of that Conestoga wagon going west, in another part of the castle near a pond, or powdered and sealed in a pharaoh's tomb for spiritual defense, Mint, in any of its hundreds of guises, never left its master's side. The *Mentha* are among the finest aromatic plants in the world. They come packaged as hardy perennials that can literally be chopped into pieces and easily regrown spreading indefinitely in all directions. They must be allowed to fall onto walks and pavement, which they will do with nary a second thought, so foot traffic will trample and crush their succulent leaves, releasing their scent—pulegone, menthol, piperitone and carvone. If left alone, they will sprout tall thin stalks with fuzzy spires of honey-and mint-scented flowers in midsummer. To determine how good a stand of Mint is, count the bees; if you lose count, it's good.

Mint adds sparkle to any niche, doing best in filtered shade where the soil remains moist, humusy and slightly acidic. Variegated foliages and a multitude of fragrance highlights are possible: fuzzy, light green, apple-scented leaves of Applemint; cream-splashed leaves smelling of pineapples in Pineapple Mint; leaves with emerald and gold stains and a spicy hint of ginger in Ginger Mint; round, purplish leaves with a fragrance of oranges in Orange Mint; the aroma of limes, lemons, melons, Creme-de-Menthe, and many more are possible. Of the Mints available, Silver Mint is the least useful, being unornamental and marginally fragrant.

Many Mints may be sown where they are to grow, although cuttings are required for most cultivars. They multiply rapidly in any case but need uprooting and replanting every 4 years, or when the foliage becomes spindly or diseased. In warm, moist climates where wilt, caused by the disease organism Verticillium, is possible, a cultivar series of the Peppermint species called 'Mitcham' is a valuable resistant form. Two commonly available are 'Todd's Mitcham' and 'Murray Mitcham'. 'Black Mitcham' *M.* × *piperita* var. *piperita,* is a commercial cultivar. They are all powerfully menthol-scented and superior to Spearmint and Peppermint. Crossing occurs in gardens with many species or cultivars so strangers will suddenly appear in older stands. Literally hundreds of species and cultivars of Mint are known. Some of the finest ornamentals were discovered in mixed Mint plantings.

Cultivating Mints can be quite distressing, or remarkably easy, to propagate depending on your point view. In any case, to succeed the first time and prevent Mint from achieving the status of Bermuda Grass or Morning Glory in your garden, plant it in a container that is embedded at least 6 in. into the soil. The boundary should be unbroken, in other words, bricks are not sufficient, and must extend 2 in. or more above the soil surface.

Very few of the Mints are not hardy, and in general all will thrive for many years if well mulched. A top dressing of manure each spring and fall is beneficial. Many are marginally scented for a fragrant garden unless crushed and passed under the nose. Those with the finest fragrance are English Pennyroyal, *Mentha pulegium;* Pineapple Mint, *M. suaveolens;* Water Mint, *M. aquatica;* Spearmint, *M. spicata;* 'Orange', 'Lime' and 'Lemon' Mints, *M.* × *piperita* var. *citrata;* Corsican Mint, *M. requienii;* and Black Mint, *M.* × *piperita* var. *vulgaris.*

Orange, Black, Lime, Ginger and Pineapple Mints are the most valuable members of this genus for both landscaping and culinary uses. Orange, Lime and Lemon are all cultivars of the same species *M.* × *piperita* var. *citrata* and vary only in the citrousy pique. Orange is by far the most pleasant. They are tolerant of full shade, emerge early and form robust masses in short order. Lime has a larger leaf and darker color, which is a rich purple-green. They have rose-colored flowers that smell divine.

Black Mint is a rapidly spreading, dark purple Mint cultivated for menthol, which can constitute 90% of its oil. This Mint can literally numb the tongue. Confine it, for it is a vigorous and adventuresome herb that develops beastly stolons (a trailing shoot) that can easily breech a 4", above-ground guard and burrow 10–12 in. to escape. Fortunately it is far superior to most other culinary Mints and is an exciting cultivar of Peppermint to grow.

The golden hue of Ginger Mint, *M.* × *gracilis* var. *variegata,* changes in intensity with the seasons and the amount of sunlight it receives. At its peak in late summer it is a superb, low-growing, quickly spreading ground cover in a sunny or semi-shady spot in gardens with both light and dark ornamentals. Its leaf is attractively serrated and its "ginger" scent is indeed spicy and delicious.

Pineapple Mint, *M. suaveolens,* is apparently the rich cousin of Apple Mint, *M. villosa* var. *alopecuroides.* The latter is a pleasant herb, but Pineapple Mint is racy. It likes full sun and an ultra-rich, moist soil. It is much slower growing than its cousin, and its light green leaf with creamy or white markings makes it an excellent feature or a ground cover in high visibility areas. Pair it with dark green companions, avoiding the yellows. Entirely white sports are commonplace. Replant it periodically for finest fragrance. Pineapple Mint's fragrance will diminish as a planting crowds so choose fragrant cuttings wisely to propagate only the best.

Corsican or Creme-de-Menthe Mint, *Mentha requienii,* has a cool, minty aroma that causes considerable searching by visitors for it is hard to find once its penetrating mint scent has been detected. A small patch will give a false impression of huge expanses of Mint nearby. These bright green mats often resemble a clump of *Sedum* from a distance. Growing at times to one or more inches, though normally less, the dense tight mats are smooth enough for marbles to roll across with ease. Damp, rich soils in full sun are recommended and light foot traffic will not set it back too much. In midsummer a film of miniscule blue flowers appears suddenly, lasting a month or more.

A perennial in warmer climates, Corsican Mint will die back in late fall after a hard frost but reseeds itself and reappears by early summer from the tiniest amount of material, to grow again next season. It spreads rapidly during early summer. A small handsized clump may spread 12 in. outward by the end of summer in ideal locations and travel in tiny, bright green rivulets along cracks to spread into an open area between paving stones. Clumps may be lifted with ease and replanted by pressing them into loose soil.

Corsican Mint is a valuable ground cover among plantings of dwarf materials. Fascinating miniature effects can be created using this Mint as a "grass". Dwarf plants appear to be of real proportions from a distance. It lends itself well to soil contouring for dwarf displays imitating grassy mounds, or meadows with a meandering stream of colored stones, or miniature parterre designs using Corsican Mint and inert materials in convoluted designs with heavenly scents.

Corsican Mint is also a candidate for turfed seats. Simply consider the bench as a large container and treat the Mint as a potted herb. It must be grown as a tightly packed ground cover no higher than half the depth of a finger nail. Do not use a rich soil. This Mint should be watered daily and to compensate for frequent watering, mineral supplements, particularly iron, should be added to keep the foliage a verdant green. It may be grown in the same pot with other plants provided there is not competition for nutrients. Large containers with fair-sized shrubs and trees, such as Sweet Bay and Lemon Verbena, are best.

English Pennyroyal, *M. pulegium*, is evergreen to Zone 6. Like most mints it spreads slowly during warm spells in winter months. Its dense habit makes it valuable as a fragrant winter herb for walks and patios where it should be encouraged to spread between cracks directly in the line of foot traffic. Although mouth wateringly fragrant, a tea of English Pennyroyal is relatively toxic because of the chemical pulegone. It is, however, an effective insect repellant when rubbed on the hands and face and is the most valuable herb for strewing or in wash waters for home use.

A variety of English Pennyroyal, Hoary Pennyroyal, *M. pulegium* var. *gibraltarica*, is sold as Gibraltar Mint. It has fuzzy narrow leaves and bears much of the Pennyroyal fragrance. This herb is of somewhat more erect habit and can grow in full sun in moist spots. This herb is sometimes incorrectly sold as Silver Mint.

Two less commonly cultivated herbs, also with delicious minty aromas worth investigating, are Lesser Calamint, *Calamintha nepeta*, and American Pennyroyal, *Hedeoma pulegioides*. Calamint resembles Pennyroyal, *Mentha pulegium*, in habit including its leaves, which are somewhat fuzzy and serrated. It has a strong, sweet flavor and minty odor, not at all camphoraceous. As such, it is well suited as a culinary spice on fish and pork, in sauces, gravies, potato salad and fresh in a green salad accompanying pickled condiments. It is much more fragrant during bloom and thick clumps should be cultivated, spreading onto walks and patios, over low retaining walls or into any damp, sunny or partly shaded area that is well traveled. Two species, *C. nepeta* and *C. sylvatica*, and four subspecies exist. *C. nepeta* subsp. *nepeta* is the most commonly cultivated Lesser Calamint. *C. nepeta* subsp. *glandulosa* has a more delicate flavor and is sometimes referred to as Nepetella.

American Pennyroyal, *Hedeoma* spp., are perennials and annuals native to North and South America and a number of species are often substituted for one another. Although Hedeoma means "sweet odor," only one species, *H. pulegioides*, resembles the strong, pleasant Pennyroyal aroma from *Mentha pulegium*. Its wiry, Summer Savory-like habit makes it difficult to place in the ornamental garden but in a good soil and full sun it yields a fine mint scent for strewing or wash waters. It prefers a dry, sandy soil, flowers profusely, and reseeds itself, growing rapidly in a single season to full size. It is a perennial but does not often survive cold winters, as will English Pennyroyal. Several species of *Hedeoma* are used as oregano in the tropical Americas. *Hedeoma floribundum*, is one example, and called Mexican Oregano because of its prominent scent.

Another deliciously fragrant herb is Winter Savory, *Satureja montana*. A subspecies, Creeping Savory, *Satureja m.* ssp. *pilosa*, stands about 4 in. high spreading to a 24 in. wide clump. In late summer, tiny flowers, giving the impression of a light snowcover, give a boost to its camphoraceous fragrance with a honey-sweet note. The latter has much less foliage than the bush form and is, therefore, better suited as a fragrant herb. It excels in a poor, dry, sandy soil and may best be used falling from walls and over rocky ledges where its dangling branches are tousled by the wind and are all the more fragrant.

The larger form of the species, *S. montana*, is a dense mound resembling a hedgehog.

It has a mellow camphoraceous aroma. Its neat appearance and slick shiny leaves are bright and attractive. It is a variable species so plants from 6 to 14 in. will emerge from the same package of seed. The most entertaining form is Pygmy Savory, *S. montana* ssp. *pygmaea*. It forms a dense, very dark green bush 8–10 in. in diameter. Its shiny savory leaves are more sharply pointed than the species and not a fraction of an inch on any branch is leafless. Varieties and subspecies occur frequently in purchased seed. Cuttings are easily rooted however, so if a choice specimen is cultivated, cuttings, not seed, should be used for propagation. Plenty of deep water and a rocky, well drained, limed soil will produce the most fragrant plants.

Although the culinary value of Winter Savory is not as fine as that of the annual Summer Savory, it is evergreen, can be harvested year round, and is significantly more ornamental. It grows several inches per year up to its full size. For a healthy, dense bush prune heavily in early spring and again lightly after blooming.

Winter Savory is best planted among evergreen borders that run in and out of the sun. It savors the drip line on the sunny side of trees and hotspots in rock fields in northern exposures that receive little afternoon sun. It is a long-lived, hardy herb with glossy, dark green foliage used to create accents in ornamental gardens with conifers and other broadleaf evergreens. It often shares the limelight with other small-leaved herbs such as Bush Thyme, Hyssop, and Germander, and ornamentals such as Box, Bayberry, and Miniature Roses. It has long been a formal garden herb for natural form borders of mounded bushes or neatly trimmed hedges and topiary.

The small stature of Winter Savory makes it a valuable rock garden herb, where it appears to be most at home. Whether perched on a stone escarpment, among boulders its size or greater, or scattered over rocky expanses, it needs to be seen and smelled so keep it close enough for curious hands to caress it as visitors wander past. Its branches are slow to heal so plants should be pruned and not jut out onto paths.

Prostrate or Creeping Rosemary, *Rosmarinus officinalis* var. *prostratus,* looks for all the world like Creeping Savory but for its larger, more spicily scented leaves that have a downy backside. It is perfect for the entrance gate that must swing through a patch, releasing its pungent aroma as a gay greeting. It is not generally tolerant of foot traffic so it is best grown on ledges and along open, sunny banks that have a path close enough for groping hands to find a fragrant purchase with every grasp. In most climates Prostrate Rosemary must be grown in containers to be brought indoors for the winter. The plant must be trimmed of unsightly or damaged branches and potted in late summer. They may be left outdoors only in Zones 8–10. Numerous varieties are available. 'Lockwood de Forest' has a lighter green foliage than others and keeps its dark blue flowers longer. Other cultivars include 'Golden Prostrate' and 'Kenneth Prostrate.'

All of the Prostrate Rosemarys should be seen cascading down wide-stepped entrances and grouped so that their warm, camphoraceous fragrance dominates the site. Use them at the feet of patio benches, flowing from containers, planted between paving stones, in rock gardens or among dwarf materials in contemporary features. Around the kitchen doors or barbeque grills it is easily plucked and savored in grilled foods, salads, and meat stews. Sausage and meat can be smoked to a tangy flavor using a cup of leaves thrown onto the hot coals when cooking outdoors. Rosemary has been used as an incense for more than 5000 years. Until early in this century, Rosemary Oil was burned to prevent the spread of disease by insects. Rosemary's "intoxicating fragrance" (which is its name in Chinese) is from an exhilarating combination of camphoraceous and spicy chemicals—borneol, eucalyptol, camphene, camphor and pinene.

ROSEMARY CHIPS

10 fried tortillas (broken into "chips")
2 Tbsp. butter or margarine
1 tsp. powdered Chives
½ tsp. Paprika
½ tsp. powdered Rosemary

Mix ingredients in pan. Bring to boil and pour over chips to coat them. Spread chips on baking sheet and bake in oven at 425° several minutes or until crisp. Serve alone or with fresh Chive Dip.

For a low maintenance border in either formal or informal settings, Lavender, *Lavandula* spp., is choice. One of the best known herbs due to its penetrating, yet perfume-quality fragrance, Lavender is available in many cultivars and species for use in the landscape. The differences are not major, limited to leaf size and shape, flower color and flower stalk length.

The hardy perennial Lavenders include English Lavender, *Lavandula angustifolia*, Spike Lavender, *L. latifolia* and Lavandin, *L. × intermedia,* a hybrid of the former two. A selection of cultivars of English lavender include: those with dark violet flowers, 'Munstead', which is lower growing and more compact, 'Hidcote', 'Mitcham Gray', a form quick to reach a full height of 18 in., 'Lodden Blue' and 'Nana Atropurpurea'; those with lavender blue flowers include 'Compacta', 'Gray Lady', 'Irene Doyle' and 'Twickle Purple'; a pink-flowered cultivar 'Rosea'; and white-flowered 'Alba' and 'Nana Alba'. Lavandin cultivars Dr. A. O. Tucker considers choice for landscaping include 'Dutch', 'Grappenhall', 'Grosso' and 'Hidcote Giant'.

Many Lavenders are tender perennials and restricted to the southern landscape unless they are potted and brought indoors in winter. In general, these species are not hardy below 10°F, regrowing poorly from damaged wood and most certainly dying if their roots are frozen. The most decorative and hardiest is *L. stoechas*, Stoechade or Spanish Lavender. It was once known as Stickadove. It is a sweet scented lavender, with short, narrow leaves and flowers that form a compact inflorescence about ½ in. thick and from 1–2 in. long with pink or lavender colored bracts and purple flowers. Of the six subspecies, *L.s.* ssp. *penduculata* has flower spikes shooting out on 6–8 in. stalks that bob around in the wind like tiny purple balloons, and *L.s.* ssp. *stoechas* 'Alba' has white flowers.

French Lavender, *L. dentata*, has fuzzy leaves serrated their entire length, giving the plant a soft appearance. Its lax growth habit gives it an unkempt look so prune early each spring and again in the fall. New growth improves its fragrance as it is not as strongly scented as other Lavenders. French Lavender is a winter-blooming species and in cooler climates (Zone 8 and colder) must be potted so its beauty can be enjoyed indoors. It is sometimes sold as Fringed Lavender.

Other species, less commonly available but fascinating ornamentals, include Wooly Lavender, *L. lanata,* with soft, downy-white leaves; the strangely scented Fringed Lavender, *L. multifida*, with light green, fern-like foliage and tufts of blue flowers; and *L. pinatta* which resembles the latter (including the common name) except for a pine-like scent. Neither is hardy below 20°F.

Lavender most commonly cohabits in an ornamental garden with other grey foliaged herbs and plants. Its tall, slender, purple flower spikes seem to be the perfect contrast for the thick, silvery, blue and pink-spotted spikes of Veronica Incana and Wooly Betony. Silver Thyme and Dittany often share a site with Dwarf or 'Mitcham Gray' Lavender in rockeries, knots, and narrow informal borders. Its neat, low maintenance style is indispensable and particularly noteworthy for its "ever-grey" winter use in a deciduous planting.

Lavender's optimum use is in matching borders along entrance paths, the perimeter of patios and along sunny walks and fragrant stops by benches in the secluded sections of a garden. Along paths they must fall onto the paving. Planting Lavender near hot dry surfaces extends their life and assists them in growing more densely and compactly. Like Thyme, Lavender must be protected from dampness by a layer of sand beneath its foliage. At least 2 in. is recommended. Part of this depth may be provided by porous paving materials such as brick, gravel, and stone. A sandy, well limed soil helps Lavender project a dependable fragrance and prolong its blooming season. 'Irene Doyle' Lavender can be cut immediately upon flowering and will develop a second crop of flowers lasting late into fall.

As a contemporary landscape herb, Lavender is becoming more popular. Try it in a sand feature for the front garden. Use a compact cultivar, 'Hidcote' or 'Twickle Purple' and gather around it a small collection of Clove Pinks with a bevy of Birdsfoot Violets scattered hither and thither across the dune-like expanse. Beach Wormwood, or Cinquefoil, with yellow or red flowers, can be used as well for more color and variety if desired.

Lavender has been used in formal arrangements as a perimeter border hedge on banks that surround knots and parterres to restrict entrance and encourage the visitor to enjoy the garden within. As such, it is a fragrant and colorful boundary.

In the wild or informal garden, Lavender should be a back border, providing a light background for dark foliaged herbs and ornamentals or clumped in several groups of 2, 3, and 5 for bright patches of blue and grey, looking like whales basking in the sun at the surface of an ocean of flowers.

The chemicals chiefly responsible for that legendary Lavender scent are linalool, borneol, eucalyptol, and fenchone. Citrousy notes in English Lavender are from limonene and pinene and its spicy notes from geraniol and ocimene. Stoechade Lavender and Spike Lavender, *L. latifolia,* contain camphors and terpenes yielding a strong medicinal odor. The sweet floral scent of French Lavender, *L. dentata,* is due to fenchone and geraniol.

In late summer, tall blue and purple flower spikes add immensely to the power of Lavender's clear, invigorating scent. They remind us of bath salts and perfume, fine stationery and room deodorizers. Not all Lavenders smell alike, though none is unpleasant. They all deserve to be experimented with for first-hand experience by the gardener they are intended to please. Lavender was once called the herb of war, a strange title considering its fragrance, but was once used as an antiseptic. Its oil was used on surgical incisions or mixed with the oil of Rosemary and burned as incense to purify the air in surgeries. Valuable as potpourri material today, Lavender flowers retain their fragrance for many years after drying.

Wormwood, *Artemisia absinthum,* is a hardy, semi-evergreen perennial with a fragrance that is bitter and pine-like. It is a scent that can be overpowering and is often described as medicinal. Thujone and terpenes are the primary camphoraceous chemicals in Wormwood, yet from a distance the scent is fruity and similar to the fragrance of Roman Camomile. When in bloom, the flower spikes form a yellow haze of tiny, button flowers that add a pure camphor highlight to the Wormwood scent. Wormwood plumes dry easily and are fine arranging material, doubling as an air deodorizer. Beware, however, of its proclivity to cause an allergenic response both in the respiratory system and the skin. Indoors the scent of Wormwood is less pungent and suggests a medicinal cleanliness pleasant in kitchens, bathrooms, and moldy basements. Wormwood's strange scent should not cause it to be banished from the fragrant garden. It is an invaluable accent to many evergreens in simple arrangements, its fragrance mingling with theirs to yield an overall richness. The odor of Wormwood is often more appealing when it can mingle with the heavier scents of Roses, Carnations, and Camomile. Wormwood contributes a tingling surprise hard to create otherwise.

Although a single Wormwood bush is dense, its feathery appearance may grow ragged unless trimmed back each spring and again after blooming. Wormwood may be kept cut to any desired height during the growing season if pruning is not severe. Planted about 18–24 in. apart, and regularly pruned, Wormwood forms a dense, medium height border from 24–30 in. Although it can grow to 48 in. during flowering and be a bit messy, the flowers heavy with pollen give a sunny contrast to dark spires of other fragrant flowers in a mixed border. Roman Wormwood, *A. pontica,* resembles Wormwood but for its extremely delicate foliage. It is less hardy, requires full sun and is not evergreen. Roman Wormwood is at its formal best as a small potted herb or in a grey garden.

Wormwood adds a silver lining in any ornamental garden. Its satiny, grey-green foliage stands out on glum, overcast days, providing relief from the many monotonous dark green evergreens of winter gardens. Due to its feathery foliage, Wormwood resembles some conifers and thus fits well in ornamental designs that use weeping or pendulous elements in evergreen features. Its natural, untrimmed habit is the one most easily managed and the best way to feature it. When trimmed into a neat hedge, it is becoming only in a formal garden as a border and requires constant attention, although there it will be in close company with other plants in need of constant attention. In the informal or wild garden, Wormwood should be grown as a back border snug with the forest front. It is most appealing intermingling with a woodland of spruce and fir. Use it as a patchy, traversable ground cover between widely spaced trees. Let it spill abruptly from the forest's edge onto a lawn without benefit of a perennial bed. This recalls the pattern of sparsely vegetated conifer forests in the mountainous regions of the western U.S.

For a wild effect, intersperse into the latter example a smattering of tall and slender wildflowers and herbs such as Foxglove, Monkshood, Lupine, Clary or Silver Sage and Kniphofia. In wide expanses of wilderness combine Wormwood and other larger, grey-foliaged, gaily-flowered shrubs such as Garden Sage and a mixture of its ornamental cousins of the genus *Salvia;* Lavender; Russian Sage, *Perovskia;* Carnations; Incana Santolina; and Pearly Everlasting, *Helichrysum lanatum.*

Wormwood is grown in the dooryard garden for its double value as a repellant. It can be a chemical repellant or a companion plant in the vegetable garden. An infusion of 1 c. Wormwood, 1 tsp. vegetable oil, and 1 c. water diluted and sprayed onto foliage acts as a short term insect repellent and will also prevent dampoff. It is important to keep the strength of such a solution quite weak (diluted until the Wormwood odor is just apparent) or it is toxic to seedlings as well as the fungus it is intended to control. The use of Wormwood medicinally as a vermifuge for either animals or man is not advised because of its toxicity.

'Silver Mound' Artemisia is a desirable ground cover for the fragrant garden. A number of ornamental Artemisias can be substituted; all are attractive and aromatic particularly along paths in sunny, hot recesses and rockeries. *A. frigida* 'Silver Mound'; *A. lanata; A. genipi;* and *A. schmidtiana* 'Nana' are all sold as Silver Mound and form handsome mounds that appear to be silvery furballs growing from 6–18 in. Another handsome ground cover, Beach Wormwood or Old Woman, *Artemisia stellerana,* has wooly white leaves shaped like the leaf of White Oak. It grows from 6–12 in. in full sun or part shade but needs a sandy or well-drained soil. It is deciduous and bears modest yellow flowers in summer.

Fennel, *Foeniculum vulgare,* spontaneously comes to mind as a screening herb. It is tall, approaching 5–6 ft. in good soils, and will grow in thick clumps without diminishing its fragrance. Fennel foliage exudes the most marked anise scent of all *Umbelliferae,* including Anise. (Though perhaps if Anise, at a diminutive 1 ft., could grow to 6 ft., it too might contribute more of its essence to the garden's atmosphere.) Its genus name, *Foeniculum,* means fragrant hay. Fennel contains some of the chemicals that give Anise its fragrance: anethol, fenchone, and pinene. Fennel Oil also carries camphene, myrcene, limonene and ocimene.

Sweet and Bitter Fennel differ in fragrance. Wild or Bitter Fennel, *Foeniculum vulgare* ssp. *vulgare,* contains more fenchone and limonene and less anethol than Sweet Fennel.

Fennel is a rapid grower in rich, damp soils. Foliage color varies with soil conditions, being yellow-green in poor, sandy soils and dark blue-green in rich clays. Soils little change its fragrance, however. A spring application of manure should not be forgotten. A single plant may self-sow into a sizable patch in 1–2 years, although close planting in the beginning will achieve the same results. Plants may be set 6 in. apart for a very dense screen. It is often treated as an annual because of its rapid growth from seed sown in early spring to full-sized plants in one season but yields significantly more seed in following years. Fennel is far more fragrant during flowering, from late summer throughout autumn. Its umbels grow very large with bright yellow flowers and fruits tasting of anise seed.

Fennel is an excellent fragrant herb for screening or along the back border. Its habit is somewhat unkempt when grown as a single plant in a perennial border but becomes quite elegant when packed into a dense back border drift with an entourage of Fernleaf Tansy, White Mugwort, Valerian, Astilbe, Foxglove, *Digitalis* spp., and Meadow Rue, *Thalictum aquilegiifolium* 'Purple Cloud'. This combination provides a dark green back border 3–4 ft. high and a flower display from spring through fall. For a thicker screen, Fennel can be cut back in early summer to as low as 18 in.

In a contemporary fragrant garden or a kitchen garden, Finocchio, *F. v.* ssp. *vulgare* var. *azoricum,* or Sweet Fennel, *F. v.* ssp. *vulgare* var. *dulce,* can be surrounded with Southernwood and Blue Sage with a low accenting border of either *Santolina neapolitana* or an assortment of ornamental and edible Alliums including Chives, *A. schoenoprasum;* yellow *A. moly* and *A. flavum; A. pulchellum;* the delightful *A. karataviense;* and the white Garlic Chive, *A. tuberosum.*

A red variety of Fennel can be substituted for a change of color using Red or Bronze Fennel. *F. v.* ssp. *v.* 'Rubrum'. Red Fennel has a purple or reddish-brown hue and readily replaces the species in any design. It is especially useful for bold and colorful vertical balance in an informal or contemporary landscape. It is as hardy as the species but does not take to partial shade and should be grown in rich, moist soil in full sun for the best color development. The dried herb is indistinguishable from the species. Sweet Fennel is a commercial variety with larger fruits having a higher essential oil content. This variety can grow to 7 ft.

At the base of the stalk of Finocchio just at ground level, the stem is swollen into a 3–6 in. "bulb" that is served as a steamed or baked vegetable. It imparts a sweet, delicate Anise flavor to combination vegetable dishes, soups, and stuffings or may be eaten alone as a side dish. It may be purchased at grocery stores under the names Finocchio or Anise Root. To encourage bulb formation wait till midsummer to plant out.

FINOCCHIO SIDE DISH

Surround a beef roast in last hour of cooking with:

> 2 c. Finnocchio (large wedges)
> 3 c. Mushrooms
> 2 Green Peppers (sliced into rings)
> 1 Red Pepper (sliced into rings)

Remove from juices and serve separately.

Plate 3

Path junction planted on both sides with identical low growing Lavender for a fragrant greeting at the Medicinal Herb Garden, Univ. of Washington, Seattle, WA.

Mass planting of Garden Sage to create an extravagant atmosphere behind a bench in the Medicinal Herb Garden, Univ. of Washington, Seattle, WA.

Decorative containers of herbs at the entrance to the home of Michele Nash, Mercer Island, WA.

Containers on an out building at the Bouquet Banque, Marysville, WA.

Fragrant turf seat composed of Creeping Golden Thyme backed by Orange Mint, Peppermint and a potted Lemon Verbena.

Fragrant screen of Sweet Fennel in kitchen garden of John Eccles, Winlock, WA.

Plate 4

'White Moss' Thyme creeping around rocks on a step.

Young plant of Crimson Thyme trying hard to show off in early summer.

Looking down on a patch of 'Mayfair' Thyme.

Patch of 'Pink Chintz' Thyme working its way down a rock wall.

A bright fragrant border of 'Clear Gold' Thyme creeps beneath a turf seat. The rose flowers belong to a clump of Wild Thyme which is part of the turf seat.

Plate 5

'Oregano-scented' Thyme cultivated in the kitchen garden at ome of Judith Zugish.

'White Moss' Thyme in bloom. It is neighbor to 'Long Leaf Gray' Thyme with French Thyme behind in the garden of Michele Nash, Mercer Island, WA.

A bed of Orange Mint in bloom.

A carpet of Creme-de-Menthe Mint creates a flower-studded meadow beneath a 6 in. tall Dwarf Sage and a globe of *Santolina* 'Nana'.

ineapple Mint frequently produces all white sports among its reme-on-lime variegated foliage that truly smells of pineapples.

A barrel of English Pennyroyal in bloom reaches out to passersby.

Plate 6

Calamint in early spring before a growth of tiny pink flowers on pendulous stalks, Medicinal Herb Garden, Univ. of Washington, Seattle, WA.

Pygmy Savory in a border of containers that provides support for a raised bed in a dooryard garden. Its neighbors include Chive, Dwarf Snapdragons and Dwarf Lavender.

Spanish or Stoechade Lavender in regal splendor at its post by a gate.

Silver Mound, *Artemisia lanata* forms a cheerful flowing mound for steps and terraces.

Wormwood and Chives form a fragrant frame around Comfrey in this contemporary feature.

CHICKEN SOUP

1 c. Noodles	1 Tbsp. Fennel
Boullion	1 Tbsp. Calendula
1 c. Water	½ tsp. Chives
1 c. Tomato quarters	½ tsp. Oregano
1 c. Green Pepper	1 tsp. Lovage
1 c. diced precooked Chicken	

Fennel foliage is dried easily at a medium temperature (90–110°F.). If 1 tsp. of Fennel is needed, dry ½ c. (packed) of fresh foliage in a microwave oven on *defrost* for 5–10 minutes. Then it can be more finely ground and evenly and esthetically applied to many recipes. Fresh Fennel is used on baked fish, lamb, or pork cuts by covering the meat in a relatively thick layer of 2–3 fronds. In other recipes Fennel is used dried to spread it evenly and avoid tangled, seaweed-like clumps of soggy Fennel.

Fresh Fennel can be eaten as a pot herb. Boiled in the gravy from the meat main course it yields a sweetened gravy and a tasty vegetable dish. Fresh Fennel can be used to make a butter by blending 1 c. of foliage in ½ c. butter, but the dried product powdered and boiled for 3 minutes is superior. A sweet butter can be made by plucking ½ c. of Fennel flowers and boiling for 3 min. in butter and straining. Fennel butter will keep for 3–4 months in a refrigerator.

Fennel seed can be used as well, providing a strong Anise flavor, but they require long cooking to soften. Green seeds, however, are easily crushed and used in recipes for rice, steamed vegetables and pudding to add sweetness. Green Fennel seeds make one of the finest herb teas that can come from a garden. Use 1 tsp. of crushed green seeds per cup or 1 Tbsp. of Fennel flowers.

CHICKEN HEARTS

1½ lbs. Chicken hearts
4 Tbsp. Fennel butter
Boullion
½ tsp. Fennel
½ tsp. Basil
½ tsp. Sweet Marjoram
½ tsp. Chives

Use no water, but add ¼ c. sherry after hearts are fully cooked in butter. Then add herbs, etc.

BAKED CHICKEN

Baste 1 chicken in 4 Tbsp. Fennel butter combined with 4 Tbsp. honey, ½ tsp. boullion, and ½ tsp. Fennel.

Place chicken in covered baking dish with ¼ c. sherry.
Add 4–6 cloves garlic.
Continue to baste while baking at 275 F. for 1½–2 hours.
Add 1 tsp. Lovage and ¼ tsp. Rosemary to juices to make gravy.

Many canned foods can be enlivened with a liberal dose of Fennel when cooking: soups, stews, noodles, and rice or potato entrees. Breads and biscuits benefit from an addition of crushed green seeds and apple, peach, or rhubarb pies sprinkled with the same become a new treat.

GUACAMOLE

> 2 Avocados
> 1 Tomato
> ¼ c. Chives (fresh chopped)
> ¼ tsp. salt
> 1 Tbsp. lemon juice
> 1 Tbsp. Fennel
> ½ tsp. Sweet Marjoram

Mix ingredients on slow speed to chunky consistency. Let stand at least 3 hours (in refrigerator) before serving.

CHIP DIP

> 6 oz. non-dairy dressing or sour cream
> 1 tsp. Honey
> 1 Tbsp. Fennel
> ½ tsp. Rosemary
> 1 Tbsp. Chives (fresh chopped)
> 1 Tbsp. Red Bell Pepper (finely chopped)

Refrigerate 24 hours before serving.

Coming with the highest recommendation as an annual border for a fragrant garden is Basil, *Ocimum spp.*—one of the world's most fragrant herbs. Although not always highly revered for its flavor, Basil has been in cultivation for thousands of years. Before the Egyptians farmed it along the Nile in 2500 B.C., Holy or Sacred Basil, *O. sanctum,* had been a sacred herb of India many centuries, perhaps millenia, earlier. Grown for food, spice, incense, and perfume, Basil is renowned for its ginger, clove, or licorice fragrance, three of the most widely traded spices in man's history. Basil is not a substitute for them but an herb with a fragrance all its own, at once strong and delicious.

The fragrant garden is imperfect without a border of Basil bolting to flower in the hot, summer sun. The peak of Basil's power comes just as flowers begin to open in mid-summer and the hotter the climate the more fragrant Basil will be. An enclosed patio will be saturated with its aroma using only 20 plants, penetrating the air regardless of wind or rain. Indoors, a half dozen or more plants hanging to dry send their spicy scent to every corner of the home. Basil, planted with Coriander, Camomile, and Summer Savory, recreates in any landscape the aroma of the spice markets of ancient times.

Basil requires a dry, well-drained soil. The source of water should be infrequent on the surface but available at depth. In the border, Basil plants should be underlain by bark or gravel to keep the surface dry—sawdust and mulch keep the soil too cool so are unsuitable. It is important to remember that poor soils will give the sweet Basils a pungent clove-like accent while rich soils and excess moisture impart a sweeter, licorice odor.

Most of the cultivars of Basil can be assigned a scent based on their chemical makeup. Although there will be some variation from soil to soil and climatic factors, the chemotypes of Basil are relatively stable.

The cultivated Basils include Lemon Basil, *Ocimum americanum;* Spice Basil, *O.* 'Spice'; Hoary Basil, *O. canum;* Sweet Basil, *O. basilicum;* Sacred Basil, *O. sanctum;* and Camphor Basil, *O. kilimandscharicum.*

There are two cultivars of the *O. sanctum* group: the green, ginger-scented 'Sri' Tulsi and the purple, clove-scented 'Krishna' Tulsi. They are both holy herbs in the Hindu religion. The purple foliaged Tulsi also has beautiful purple flowers and 'Sri' Tulsi, yellow-green.

The cultivars of *O. basilicum* are organized by Helen Darah in her manuscript *THE CULTIVATED BASILS,* into four categories: 1) tall, 3 ft., and slender; 2) large-leaved, to 2½ ft.; 3) dwarf, small leaves; and 4) compact, thyrsiflora.

The most commonly cultivated Basils fall into the two middle categories. The second includes 'Lettuce Leaf', 'Italian', and 'Crispum', the widely recognized culinary Sweet Basils with large glabrous green leaves, which may be "much puckered and crumpled" as Parkinson wrote of them centuries ago. The only pure purple cultivar is in this category, *O. b.* 'Dark Opal'. *O. b.* var. *minimum,* Bush Basil, is a cultivar of the dwarf category. It has small leaves, ½–1 in., and a handsomely dense habit.

An exquisite new Basil with a silver lining comes to us from Fox Hill Farm, Parma, MI. 'Silver Fox' is a variegated cultivar of the fine leaf Basil variety *O.b.* var. *minimum.* 'Silver Fox' has a touch of white on the margin of its pea-green leaves and is well endowed with a rich gingery scent. Give it a decorative container and feature it on a hot, sunny patio or in a fragrant garden for the summer, but invite it in for the winter to charm your guests with its abundance.

The fourth category is represented by a Sweet Basil whose flower spike grows into a crowded arrangement of lavender flowers that tend to form a spiral called a thyrsus. The 'Thyrsiflora' Basil, *O. b.* cv., is exceptionally beautiful, growing from 12–18 in. as a sturdy bush. It is an exceptionally useful culinary cultivar with an anise flavor and fragrance formed by two delicious chemicals, methylchavicol and linalool.

O. canum, Hoary Basil, and its cultivars are identified by chemotype only (fragrance chemicals). They do not appear to be different otherwise, distinguished by lemony (citral), camphor (camphor) and spicy (methyl cinnamate) scents. 'Lemon', 'Camphor' and 'Licorice' are common names for these cultivars. They are all identical, characterized by elliptic-lanceolate leaves pointed at both ends, hairy and pale green. Flowers are cream colored.

Lemon Basil, either *O. basilicum* 'Citriodorum' or *O. americanum,* which are identical, grow to 18 in. with a less bushy habit than Sweet Basil. Their leaves are narrow, light green, and inflorescences are lax and unattractive. Its pleasant lemon taste and fragrance has a gingery note.

'Spice' Basil has a complicated history of hybridization, so much so that no botanical name has been assigned to this diverse group, recognized by green, serrated leaves that are delicately scented and often mottled with purple. Its flowers are pink, quite large and showy. The aroma of the plant is delightfully spicy in a way no other Basil can compare.

A woody perennial Basil sold as Tree Basil may be any of 3 species *O. gratissimum,* a large shrub; hoary Basil, *O. canum,* a clove-scented cultivar; and 'Sri' Tulsi, *O. sanctum.* The first species is generally regarded as Tree Basil. None are spectacular as ornamentals.

Although the cultivated Basils are grown as annuals throughout the northerly latitudes, a large number of them are short-lived perennials that can be potted, wintered indoors, and replanted again the following spring, and the next, etc. The gardener needs only to give each specimen a try as a houseplant. It will need good illumination and a cool, dry soil that is not overly fertilized to keep them robust and slow growing. Begin their internment with a heavy pruning, before they are transplanted from the garden in mid-summer. Bring them in while the weather is still warm.

Not all of the Basils are suitable as ornamentals. The most popular cultivars used in landscape design are the Sweet Basils including 'Crispum', 'Bush' and 'Dark Opal', the purple 'Krishna' Tulsi, 'Spice' Basils, and 'Thyrsiflora'. Basils listed by their fragrance such as 'Cinnamon', 'Lemon', 'Camphor', or 'Licorice' can be any species, although they most commonly are cultivars of *O. canum* or hybrids of *O. canum* and *O. basilicum*. The seeds a gardener receives virtually always contain at least a few plants not identical with the majority. To the Basil grower this can be an enjoyable discovery, to the landscape gardener, a nuisance. Two frequent substitutions are 'Camphor' Basil, *O. canum* for Camphor Basil, *O. kilimandscharicum*, and 'Sri Tulsi' Basil, *O. sanctum* for Tree Basil, which most commonly refers to *O. gratissimum*.

The kitchen garden in any landscape is the proper environment for the Basils of leggy, obese, or sloppy habits, such as 'Lemon', Cinnamon', 'Licorice', 'Camphor', 'Lettuce Leaf' or the black sheep that is not representative of the package label. The latter should be set aside if they are remarkable, protected from cross pollination and either propagated from cuttings or seed.

The ornamental Basils are fabulous border herbs. Their powerful fragrance readily percolates into the garden air come rain or shine. Dense, solid color borders are as easy as planting seeds where they are to grow. Formal gardens and courtyards, as ancient as Egypt, relied on Basil to cleanse and refresh the air. Knots and parterres benefit from Basils since a number of contesting cultivars may be played one against the other. Opal is frequently used in formal or contemporary landscaping with 'Bush' and 'Spice' Basils.

Borders of Basil from giant swaths 2–3 ft. wide along palatial entranceways, to simple frames around beds of fragrant ornamentals circumscribed by a patio are possible. Plants should be spaced 8–12 in. for the Sweet Basils, 6–8 in. for 'Bush', 'Lemon', and 'Dark Opal' to give a dense, unbroken border. Planted closely, Basil becomes somewhat leggy so keep the spacing wider in less sunny sites to encourage sturdier growth. Double wide rows, set 12 in. apart on center, strengthens the bold color of Sweet Basils and magnifies their rich and spicy aroma.

The chemovars and hybrids of *O. canum* are suitable for dooryard and wild gardens. Some have glossy leaves with purple markings or purple stems and pink flowers. They require fair-sized clumps of 6–8 plants to provide a good garden fragrance. These are the cultivars known by their fragrance; i.e., 'Cinnamon' Basil, etc. They are tall, to 3 ft. or more, and really need constant pruning to give them shape. Place them where they will be brushed by visitors. Plant at their feet a ground cover that is exceptionally low and fragrant, such as Creeping Thyme, Corsican Mint, or Lawn Camomile.

In the contemporary setting, 'Dark Opal', 'Spice' Basil, 'Thyrsiflora', and 'Krishna' Basil are suitable for feature gardens. With ingenuity others can certainly be tried but these four are more easily worked into designs because of their purple hues and pink flowers. Combine them with grey-foliaged herbs and plants such as *Santolina* 'Nana' pruned to smooth globes, Dwarf Sage, Clove Pinks, Dittany, or *Origanum microphyllum,* or as a free style feature with ground covers of Beach Wormwood, Veronica Incana, Wooly Betony or *Cerastium tomentosum.* Gold or yellow-green foliages also go well with the purple Basils: herbs such as Golden Sage, Golden Oregano, Gold Lemon Thyme, Dwarf Feverfew, and *Santolina viridis.*

'Dark Opal', 'Krishna', 'Bush', 'Spice', and 'Crispum' should be planted in thick drifts in informal borders. Use at least 2 cultivars and keep them adjacent to one another for better appreciation of flowers and fragrance.

The black sheep of the fragrant herbs is Coriander, *Coriandrum sativum*. Its unfortunate name, meaning bug-like, referring to its odor, is a misnomer. The Coriander scent is indeed a fragrance and not goat-like or foul as some have described it. Of course, as odors go, not everyone agrees. Linnaeus, in his pioneering work on fragrance, categorized Coriander in 'hircine' company and added aside, *"aliis grati aliis ingrati"*, that is, "pleasant to some, unpleasant to others".

Coriander leaves and the seeds when unripe are a bit off, but the odor is best described as a heavy, waxy scent that is only unpleasant when stuffed under the nose. It is a rich, warm, old wax aroma when used in a planting with other fragrant herbs and flowers and should be included, for it supplies an important fraction to the overall fragrance just as do civet and musk in perfumes. The odor of Coriander is a combination of scents from spicy terpinene (common to Caraway and Cumin), citrus and camphoraceous notes from pinene and other terpenes, and spicy overtones due to linalool (which can comprise as much as 80–90% of the oil). Coriander should not compete with musk or onion-scented herbs and flowers. Choose floral and spicy scents and keep the population of Coriander to less than half that of any of the other herbs in a mixed planting. You will be surprised at its performance.

The best Coriander comes from the central part of Russia and China where unknown natural factors are present that give us the sweet and spicy Coriander seed used in fine culinary recipes for pizza and pasta sauce. They are a rare sweet treat just off the plant before fully dry, becoming a dried spice that has been desired by cooks for as long as the spice trade has been in existence. Hot summers are an important prerequisite so time the planting of this annual so that seeds ripen during the heat of summer. It is generally recommended that ripe Coriander be harvested in early morning with the dew clinging to the seeds preventing them from bursting open explosively during handling. Plants should be pulled and bound then covered with paper bags and stored in a dry location. The foliage of Coriander (Cilantro) can be used fresh or dried at medium or high heat.

Thickly-sown drifts in wild gardens and wild retreats in kitchen gardens are the finest ways to enjoy the many talents of Coriander. Until it flowers and sets seed it is a weedy fellow with a funny odor. Its continuously emerging flocks of small pinkish flowers slowly metamorphose in the summer heat into glistening green globes that are crispy and sweet. By late summer, thousands of decorative tan beads bob about on rapidly thinning plants. Eventually the entire plant browns, remaining erect and proud, awaiting the gardener to pluck it from the ground at harvest time.

This sequence is quite ornamental when the proper design criterion are taken into consideration. First, light green backgrounds or contrasting materials are needed to accent the green or dark green foliage of Coriander as well as inhance its tan, beaded skeleton in late summer. Second, Coriander requires full sun and plenty of room. Close spacing makes for spindly plants susceptible to wind and rain damage. In any garden, give Coriander plants 12–18 in. of growing room. Third, locate a bee plant, an herb well endowed with nectar-rich flowers, close by to attract pollinators. Flies and wasps adore Coriander. Bees do not avoid it, but do not go out of their way to patronize it either. Monarda, Basil, German Camomile, and Borage are 4 bee herbs, any one of which can accompany Coriander in an arrangement.

In the kitchen garden, Coriander can be grown as a border. A double border, rows 12 in. apart, should be planted on the south side of a back border of Crinkled or 'Lettuce Leaf' Basil, or as a screen behind a front border of 'Dark Opal' or 'Krishna' Basil. Or it can be used to encircle a central patch of pole beans with an outside border of ornamental Kale or a red-leaf Lettuce. In a wild patch in the kitchen garden, combine Coriander, German Camomile, *Nigella*, Dill, Summer Savory, and Lemon Basil for a highly fragrant and beneficial garden of tasty seeds and foliage.

The perimeter bed in a dooryard garden is a safe site for Coriander. Let it share a mixed border with medium height, red and pink Yarrows, tucked in a narrow bed behind Miniature Roses, Feverfew and German Camomile. Here it can also be grown with 'Cinnamon' and 'Licorice' Basils and German Camomile, with a background of Garden Sage. These gardens exude perfumes that are easily described as enticing.

The most fragrant of the herbs recommended for growing in containers are the Jasmines. Their ability to arouse the emotions is legendary. One of the greatest treasures of history's mightiest monarchs was the essence of Jasmine. It has been used to scent everything from the lace cuffs on King Herod's royal robes to the sails of Cleopatra's ships. In centuries past, fields of Jasmine were grown only for the wealthy and powerful. Today they belong to every gardener.

Most Jasmines are not hardy in northern climates. Gardeners in these latitudes shrug their shoulders and sigh at their misfortune. Yet all the Jasmine species may be successfully grown in containers, from the minute *J. polyanthus*, whose evergreen foliage drapes daintily over pots with hundreds of fragrant white flowers, to the large twining bush *J. odoratissimum* and the heavy vines of *J. officinalis*.

J. officinalis, hardy to Zone 6, is a rapidly growing vine easily woven or wired onto a trellis anchored in a container. It blooms from early summer through fall and needs no trimming until through flowering in late fall. Flowers form predominantly on new wood. Therefore, last year's wood must be pruned off each fall, leaving young branchlets on one or more permanent trunks that may reach a total length of 15 ft.

J. grandiflorum is the most valued by perfumers, having the highest concentration of those chemicals that give Jasmine its beguiling power, methylanthranilate and benzyl esters. It blooms from July to October. Flowers should be picked during August for the most satisfying results in potpourris and sachets. This species can also be grown on a trellis.

J. sambac, Arabian Jasmine, is an evergreen that will bloom for most of the year. Move the container indoors during colder months and enjoy its perfume throughout its long blooming season. *J. sambac* is one of the Jasmines used for blending with Chinese tea. (There may be, perhaps, some use for such a blend since the flowers offer some antimicrobial activity to the mixture.) Another delicious, homemade, after-dinner tea is made with equal proportions of fresh *J. sambac* flowers and Camomile with a dash of roasted Chicory.

Containers should be located near windows and doors frequently open, in sunny breezeways, courtyards, or partially enclosed patios. A featured area in the garden consisting of a bench in a cul-de-sac surrounded by dense foliage, so as to seclude the site, is ideal for several pots of flowering Jasmines secreted away to create a bewitching atmosphere.

One of the most easily cared for and reliably fragrant herbs is Valerian, *Valeriana officinalis*. The flower plume of Valerian is referred to as having "heliotrope-like breath", an intoxicating fragrance, variously described, but most certainly floral and fruity. The legendary perfume Spikenard contained Valerian predominantly from the species *V. celtica*. Over one hundred species are known and though some are valuable for their fragrant flowers, other produce a spicy, luxuriantly aromatic root cherished by perfumers. Still others, such as *V. officinalis*, are grown commercially for their medicinal value as a powerful, non-addicting sedative.

Generally called Valerian today, instead of Fu, a handle from Greek times alluding to its malodorous airs during the drying process, this herb is still valuable today as a sedative. A few species commonly cultivated include Speick or Celtic Nard, *V. celtica*, which harks from the Alps and provides the ingredients for perfumes; Indian Valerian, *V. wallichii*; and Japanese Valerian or Kesso, *V. officinalis* var. *latifolia*. *V. sitchensis* from the steppes of Russia is considered the most important species for medicinal preparations, a reputation shared with *V. mexicana* from the New World. Some novel species include a 12 in. dwarf form, *V. arizonica*;

Elder-leaved Valerian, *V. sambucifolia;* and a low growing Marsh Valerian, *V. dioica* from Great Britian. These are mentioned because the many suppliers of Valerian do not always identify the species of the roots they sell for horticultural purposes.

The root oils contain pinene, camphene and limonene as well as a number of aromatic bornyl esters that are created during drying. The fragrance, which can be imitated by valerianic ether, is prized in India and the Mid-East. Strangely enough, it is the unpleasant smelling valerianic acid in the oil that is used as an intermediary in perfume manufacturing. It is one of those scents that is necessary to the final product's wide spectrum of odors, appealing to our sense of smell because it is more pleasing to encounter a mixture of fragrances than any single one. This is undoubtedly why a fragrant garden is so hypnotic—perhaps more so with Valerian about because of its sedative properties. Research indicates the active principles in Valerian root are truly central nervous depressants, but they are also highly unstable. The shelf life of the root is little more than a few months and any preparation that involves more than a simple infusion will destroy these active chemicals, rendering the medicine useless (except for the placebo effect which has also been studied and found to be a significant factor in successful treatments with Valerian).

Valerian's place in the fragrant garden is as a background herb. Its flowers are white or pink, highly fragrant, easily dried and everlasting. It blooms in early summer and lasts for several weeks. Do not get too close or the odor becomes heavy and can be regarded as putrid. From a distance the disgusting odors are diluted and the legendary heoliotrope fragrance dominates. To work an enchantment in your garden use at least 6 clumps. Arrange them along a pathway where they will be sheltered from winds or unite them at a central spot. Provide each clump at least 24 in. spacing and several years of maintenance-free flowering will be forthcoming. It is a hardy, herbaceous perennial that for the most part appreciates a heavy moist soil. *V. mexicana* and *V. sitchensis* can handle drier soils. It tolerates partial shade but is more fragrant in full sun. Depending upon the species, Valerian should be replanted every 4–6 years to thin the root system. It will grow from 3–6 ft. and makes a thin screen or border.

As a fragrant herb Valerian gives a special touch to compact features in formal or contemporary landscapes. Every garden needs a fragrant drift of Valerian and it is especially suited to wild and informal designs fitting into an arrangement with Meadow Rue, *Thallictrum glaucum,* Fennel and Astilbe. Valerian is a natural component along the forest front. In an informal landscape it should be tucked into a thicket of shrubbery or low trees.

A dapper herb for the fragrant and/or formal garden is the Curry Plant, *Helichrysum italicum* ssp. *siitalicum,* which entertains us with its near spherical shape, 12–18 in., and long-fingered, blue-silver foliage. One or two, wintered over in a cold frame (it is hardy to about 28°F) or greenhouse, are useful for turning a dull feature of conifers into an eye-catching arrangement. Its spicy scent is unquestionably that of Curry spice. Though most popular as a fragrant, silvered decorative material for wreaths and swags it can be used to spice an omelette or in breading fried chicken.

It prefers full sun and a sandy or a rocky, alkaline soil that remains dry. Its wispy, carefree habit adds a little informality in a formal arrangement with the Santolinas and Bush Thymes neatly trimmed into manageable mounds of comfortable size. Let *Origanum microphyllum* and Bush Basil share the scene for an immensely useful, fragrant and attractive feature garden.

Chapter 2 / SECTION 3

A Walk Through a Fragrant Garden

Visiting a fine garden is always an adventure. Examining the prize possessions of another gardener and enjoying the fruits of someone else's labor is a joy for anyone whether a gardener or not. Let's take a stroll through a small fragrant garden now. (Fig. 6) Descending the stairs from a deck to the garden in the early evening we feel the punch of a warm and spicy breeze wafting back over us. Our last step is cushioned by deep sand. The sand, as a source of the heat, draws air into the narrow garden keeping the air in motion even on calm days. It is an enclosed garden with a bowling green inside an oval path. Raised beds around the perimeter are stuffed with everchanging herbs and flowers, many of which are highly fragrant, scenting the entire yard during their reign, while others offer up their aromas to gentle carressing. "They are like shy people", Louise Beebe Wilder wrote, in *The Fragrant Garden,* "who find it difficult to open their hearts save at the magic of a sympathetic touch." If we delved no further in this garden than the drawing of deep breaths we would still go away enlightened. Being gardeners however, we've been this route before. We know that abstinence is impossible. Fragrance is nature's most powerful come-on, a lure no creature can foreswear.

Greeting us at the bottom of the steps is a pungent, spicy scent mixed with camphor. Ahead and to the left against a simmering block wall are 2 yellow-flowered herbs: Wormwood, an ancient vermifuge and narcotic, and Dwarf Feverfew, *Chrysanthemum parthenium* 'Selaginoides', a medicinal of reputable value in fever control. The grey-green, feathery foliage of Wormwood is a stark contrast to the vivid, lime-green oak leaf foliage of its neighbor. Their scents are not unpleasant but a brief encounter is encouraged.

A spicy sweetness in the air seems to come from everywhere and beckons us forward. A tall feathery Tansy with yellow buttons sprinkled all over its top bows to us as we pass and the heat from the sand draws us up a whiff of something waxy, an invigorating odor on a hot summer day. The shorter member of this duo by the stairsteps entertains us with a marbled foliage of creamy white and emerald-green. Our host gently prods it into action with a sandaled foot. A moment later Hawaiian drums throb in our ears and plantations of pineapples ripening in the hot South Pacific sun appear in our mind. Pineapple Mint is true to its namesake.

Moving on, we brush aside a groping branch of Variegated Hops that clings tenaciously to the stair railing. Though not scented, its 12 in. maple-like leaves are smeared with white in fascinating patterns imitating the little pot of Pineapple Mint at our feet.

We stroll past a sentinel Juniper standing guard at the corner of the stairs. At our feet a

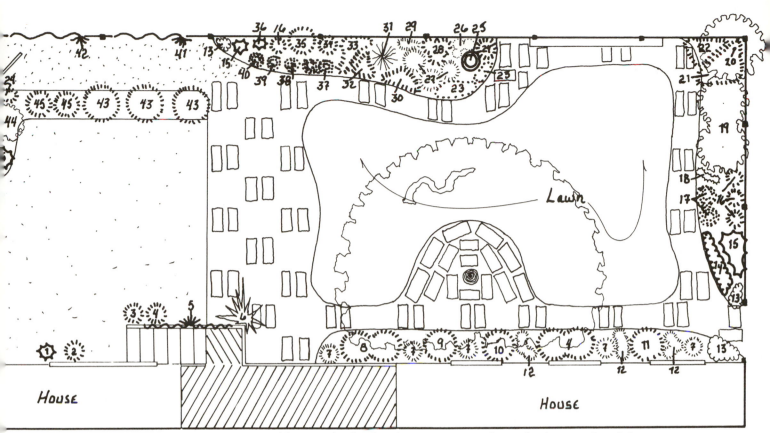

Fig. 6. A Fragrant garden. Dozens of fragrant herbs dangle or creep into the path of passersby giving up their scents for our enjoyment.

KEY

1 Wormwood *Artemisia absinthum*
2 Feverfew *Chrysanthemum parthenium*
3 Tansy *Tanacetum vulgare*
4 Pineapple Mint *Mentha suaveolens*
5 Variegated Hop *Humulus japonicus*
6 *Juniperus communis*
7 Columbine *Aquilegia* sp.
8 Orange Mint *Mentha* × *piperita* var. *citrata*
9 Lime Mint *Mentha* × *piperita* var. *citrata*
10 Black Mint *Mentha* × *piperita* var. *vulgaris*
11 Golden Mint *Mentha* × *gracilis* var. *variegata*
12 Rocambole *Allium sativa* var. *ophioscorodon*
13 Silver Mound *Artemisia lanata*
14 Cr. Red Thyme *Thumus praecox* 'Coccineus'
15 Southernwood *Artemisia abrotanum*
16 White Mugwort *Artemisia lactiflora*
17 Golden Lemon Thyme *Thymus* × *citriodorus* 'Aureus'
18 Dwarf Carnation *Dianthus caryophyllus*
19 Lilac *Syringa vulgaris*
20 Sweet Spire *Itea virginica*
21 Sweet Cicely *Myrrhis odorata*
22 Curly Mint *Mentha aquatica* var. *crispa*
23 Opal Basil *Ocimum basilicum* 'Dark Opal'
24 Lemon Balm *Melissa officinalis*
25 Sweet Bay *Laurus nobilis*
26 Lemon Geranium *Pelargonium melissinum*
27 Peony *Paeonia* spp.
28 *Valeriana officinalis*
29 Foxglove *Digitalis*
30 Lady's Mantle *Alchemilla vulgaris*
31 Blueberry *Vaccinium macrocarpon*
32 Grapefruit Mint *Mentha suaveolens* var.
33 Dwarf Monarda *Monarda didyma* 'Granite Pink'
34 Fernleaf Tansy *Tanacetum vulgare* 'Crispum'
35 Sweet Fennel *Foeniculum vulgare*
36 Roman Wormwood *Artemisia pontica*
37 Wedgewood Thyme *Thymus* 'Wedgewood English'
38 Tuffeted Thyme *Thymus caespititius*
39 Cr. Golden Thyme *Thymus* 'Clear Gold'
40 'Pink Chintz' Thyme *Thymus praecox* ssp. *articus*
41 Arabian Jasmine *Jasminum officinalis*
42 *Jasminum nudiflorum*
43 Lovage *Levisticum officinale*
44 Mock Orange *Philadelphus* sp.
45 Comfrey, Red flr. *Symphytum officinale* 'Coccineum'

cool red brick patio quickly pulls the heat from our soles as we enter the patchy shade of an old man apple. Crossing to the far corner we pass another Juniper sentinel softening the sharp line of a block wall. An arm of the patio extends ahead as a path following the wall leads ever deeper into the shade of the apple tree.

A slender raised bed at our feet is overflowing quite prodigiously with multihued herbs. Our host tells us that many mints reside here mixed incomprehensibly at times. His foot glides through the yellow and green speckled foliage of Ginger Mint and a spicy but still minty aroma evolves in the cool shade. Lacy, light green stems with bobbing daisies poke out here and there, among the mints sometimes as a dense bush, and others as single, thread-thin waifs with a solitary apple-scented flower. The faint apple aroma that comes and goes with the breeze is not from the apples now swelling on the branches above us but from this weedy annual, German Camomile. Little or no movement is needed for Camomile to raise its scent to all the world.

That South Seas aroma reaches us again and nearby is a great green mat of Pineapple Mint, speckled with white as if someone had spilled paint. Quite remarkably several branches of this mint are entirely white. A neighboring, dark green mint is melded subtly with red hues producing a purplish cast from a distance. A swipe of the foot and a delectable minty aroma surrounds us. It is the pure menthol scent Black Mint produces, rarely bitter, spicy or camphoraceous as Spearmint or Peppermint can be, and is highly fragrant even in the shade.

Other mints growing here are Apple Mint, a tall fuzzy leafed mint with fruity overtones. Curly Mint is an ornamental mint with tattered and gnarled leaves that make a colorful bright spot in a partially shaded garden. Horse Mint resembles a wooly, light green spearmint. Spearmint and Peppermint, the most common mints grown, are rather weedy but provide a good mint scent and flavor for little effort.

Appearing as little pools of green molasses, the irresistible Corsican Mint grows here and there self-sown between cracks in the path's bricks. It is a pleasant minty weed that needs no help to spread. We sidestep onto the grass a moment as 3 toddlers on tricycles roar past. The path along the perimeter of the lawn provides an excellent runway for children. The walk was designed with them in mind and adds versatility to a small backyard which serves as an elegant garden, an entertaining arena and a playground. The flowing lines of the warm, rusty red brick hide its utility well.

The last few feet of this mint garden are graced by the most fragrant of all the Mints, English Pennyroyal. Its perky perfume we are told is rarely absent from this end of the garden. Low growing and resilient to traffic, Pennyroyal is allowed to venture onto the walk where it is constantly crushed underfoot, scenting the entire yard on windy days. American Pennyroyal, *Hedeoma pulegioides,* is equally fragrant our host tells us although more upright and bushy in habit. Several plants of it reside across the path. Both are nicknamed Mosquito Plant for their uncanny ability to repel those vicious predators. On hot summer nights a centerpiece for outdoor use must include Pennyroyal to create an effective repellent.

The brick walk divides here, rising gently and entering the kitchen garden ahead, and to the left appearing to descend into a thicket. The thicket is composed of two venerable Lilacs surrounded by other bushes. A fuzzy, green herald immediately ahead on the leading edge of this thicket garden draws our attention. It is a cool, green carpet of Silver Mound, a miniature *Artemisia.* Neat, rounded humps spill casually over the rock ledge taking its shape and scenting the air ever so faintly with a sweet, absinthe scent.

Upon examining it closely we notice another Artemisia close by, Old Man, or Southernwood. In spring the crisp, pine scent of Old Man mingles perfectly with the rich Lilacs and Camomiles. Old Man has been a favorite nosegay for centuries. It is easily cared for and added to every indoor bouquet at our host's dinners.

Another *Artemisia* appearing tall and thin beside its relatives is White Mugwort. Its sweet smelling, yellow-white plume in late summer through autumn is a perfect harbinger of fall for a fragrant garden. Gentle autumn rains by no means spoil its fragrance, often carrying it on misty breezes to where it can be widely appreciated.

A small flowering willow ahead resides in a bed of Sweet Cicely and 'Lime' Mint. 'Lime' Mint has a tart, crisp, citrus note that makes an iced lemonade a special treat.

An inviting bench located at the halfway point around the small garden gives us a moment to rest and enjoy the garden from a sunny perspective. Twining at our backs is Hall's Honeysuckle, *Lonicera japonica,* sporting fragrant pink blooms that last from spring until fall. From below the bench creeps some of the Lime Mint while gobs of apple-scented blossoms of German Camomile peek out in search of sunlight adding to the informal charm.

The color-splashed beds further on attract our attention and we leave the bench to continue our journey. The thought of more new sights and smells piques our interest. Before we reach the raised garden we encounter a tub of Sweet Bay nobly perched in the center of a wide spot in the path. Grown for culinary use this bay is given a spot to bask in the sun.

Approaching the garden a tingling citrus scent greets us. In a large pot is Lemon Verbena emitting a barely perceptible fragrance of grated lemon peel. When touched it literally explodes as if we were squeezing lemons. Nearby, contributing to the lemon-scented air, is a Lemon Balm and a stand of Lemon-Scented Geranium, *Pelargonium limoneum,* with large maple-like leaves. Working together these 3 fragrant herbs yield a pleasant lemon odor recognizable from a distance. Flowing in front of the lemon-scented herbs are *Santolina neapolitana* and Opal Basil for a mellow, silver-blue and purple front border smelling of ginger cakes.

Tucked up against the fence is a low screen of Fragrant Goldenrod, *Solidago odorata.* Though we often speak unkindly of this genus, our host tells us that botanists have found that the Goldenrods do not contribute to the pollen problem. We should be grateful for this because the sweet-scented Goldenrod combines beauty and fragrance in a slender perennial package that never fails to please. From this species an anise essence is obtained, which is also the odor it imparts to the garden here. Others of the genus were once considered as a source of latex rubber. Goldenrod, available in many varieties and cultivars, remains a favorite border and screen plant with showy panicles of lemon-yellow, orange and bronze flowers.

An assortment of Peonies, *Paeonia* sp., join together in providing a crowd of blooms for color and entertainment. Some Peonies are scented: 'Elsa Sags', 'Pink Parfait', 'Vivid Rose', 'Joseph Christie' and 'Kelway's Glorious' for example. Don't think that growing Peonies is out of line in an herb garden. The Peony is one of the oldest herbs. Once used as a medicine, it received its name from the Greek physician to the gods, Paeonia. Even before the Greeks and Romans, who reputedly cultivated hundreds of varieties, they were revered centuries earlier by the Chinese, who grew them in temple gardens. Their attractive foliage provides a medium height background for a selection of Creeping Thymes along the front border. From behind the Peonies spills a dwarf Bee Balm, 'Granite Pink', with pink spidery flowers, and round-leaved or Grapefruit Mint, with large, purplish, fragrant leaves. The wind's invisible hands, as if in possession of a secret formula, are at work gently shaking the proper mixtures of essence from these herbs, rewarding us with a whiff of one of her price-less perfumes.

Rising like a feathery screen at the back of the garden are Garden Heliotrope and Fennel. The former is no longer in full bloom and scenting the entire garden, but the honey and vanilla odor is still unmistakable when we crush a flower. Although the root is a powerful sedative, it is the flowering portion of Garden Heliotrope that is valuable today as a highly fragrant everlasting plume for gardens and dried arrangements. The Fennel is in bloom and we are told that this is its most fragrant period. The anise scent encountered while observing Goldenrod close up is strong enough here to be sensed from a distance. Known as the "candy plant" by our host's children it is kept to the back for its own protection. Its sugar-sweet, anise-flavored leaves and flowers are a delicious breath freshener, a perky treat while gardening or a sweet spice for many delicately flavored dishes. We are told that rice was not a favorite food at our host's table until he began adding several green herbs and the flower umbels of Fennel for sweetness. Leftover rice is a thing of the past.

Fennel's other neighbors are Fernleaf Tansy and a graceful wand of blue-green Meadow Rue, *Thallictrum glaucum,* bearing clusters of musk-scented, yellow flowers that shed their fragrance best during late evening hours. Used here as screens, both make a pleasant contrast to their feathery neighbor.

Primarily for show is a narrow rivulet of red-flowering Yarrow, streaming into a pool of white and pink yarrow. Deep green foliage raises this ruddy sea aloft to ripple in the breeze.

Bent wearily and solemn over its charges before it is a small screen of White Mugwort just behind the Yarrow. Its heavy flower heads are beginning to form their fragrant plumes for fall, drooping over the Yarrow and a compact gold-leaved bush at its feet. This bright patch of yellow and light green is Golden Sage, more compact than Garden Sage and equally provocative in cooking. Beside it is an exquisite Tangerine Southernwood with an orange or lemon twist. A modest, blue-grey puff of *Artemisia lanata* brings this small garden to a neat finish.

Our guide gestures us on. There is more. Immediately ahead is a living screen that separates the sandbox from a pathway. It's a strangely herbed border garden. Among the screen of herbs is one that is quite unique and dominant. The herb is Lovage, a tall, tropical-looking plant with the unmistakable odor of Celery. The jungle-thick Lovage screen, looking like a queue of giant Celery plants, forms a dense barrier to sounds as well as sights.

On our right is a screen of espaliered vines whose flowers are so fragrant we must stop to catch our breath. That scent is familiar. "Jasmine, nature's most fragrant flower. Almost sacred, isn't it?" our guide whispers, referring to the intense feeling this flower's odor arouses. It has also been judged "sensual". If we look closer we can find more than one species joining forces here. Espaliered on the fence are vines of Poet's Jasmine and Winter Jasmine, whose flowers bloom before foliage appears in early spring, and an Arabian Jasmine, the flowers of which are prized for blends with tea, is trained on a trellis from a container.

The afternoon sun baking the damp, wood chip walk has created a hot and steamy air in this fragrant corridor. With the gate closed ahead a mixture of odors cling tenaciously to the air about us. Faintly hidden on the air is a hint of lemons, apples, anise, and a heavy note of Jasmine and gingered Celery. It is a mixture that seems to have been blended together like a recipe for a rare and precious perfume or a great epicurean banquet.

Self-sowing with gay abandon along the path is German Camomile again, its scent commingling and reminding us of spicy apple-butter. Scattered also by their own will and fortune are Coriander, Lemon Balm, and Borage. The scent of Coriander introduces a strange mongrel note in this collection of oversweet fragrances, a note not at all unpleasant. A Mock Orange, *Philadelphus* × *lemoinei,* introduces a lemon fragrance to the garden in very early spring. Our host explains that the Lemon Balm, strategically situated at the base of the gate in the path of the door, almost equals the scent of the Mock Orange whenever the gate is opened.

Staring through the gate dreamily, we can see that our host's garden does not end but becomes a dark, fern-dominated world under a huge walnut where other exciting herbs are surely hidden. This, however, is the end of our stroll through a fragrant garden. We turn and shortcut through the Lovage screen back across the sandbox to the house for the sun is setting and dinner, highlighted by herbs from this very garden, awaits us.

Chapter 3 / SECTION 1

Formal Gardens for Beauty

Formal garden design is never seen anywhere in nature. It is distinct from other landscape forms which take at least some of their cue from the natural world around us. True formal landscapes are a massive undertaking. These are the grand gardens we visit on holidays or associated with a museum, public edifice, or historical monument. These gardens, like that shown in Figure 7, are pieces of art.

The formal landscape is designed to be shared. It is open and inviting, creative, not secretive, and overflowing with little details that beg to be seen, lauded, and loved. Formal designs incorporate round, square, or rectangular beds and may be dotted with ponds or cut by waterways. Intricate topiary, trimmed hedges, vine-smothered arbors, outbuildings for leisure, great urns, exotic herbs, breathtaking beds of a single flower species, elegant lawn furniture, statuary, ponds, palatial staircases, and a liberal application of expansive walks are all a part of formal design. The non-natural aspect is an attractive feature. The ability of a gardener to soften the geometric rigidity with herbs and flowers in all their glory is the crucial path to success.

To venture ahead let us examine the general principles used in any formal design. The first, and most important, is that a pattern must be balanced, whether it is a small decorative plot or an entire landscape. A balanced formal garden does not require geometric symmetry, but such has been the most common method. Asymmetric gardens are becoming popular today, but require considerable knowledge of landscape art.

Second, walkways in the vicinity of "formals" must be wide. Spacious paths give the impression of larger-than-life gardens and are a feature of the landscape to provoke a sense of motion and to open the vista. A path may widen around, pass between, or simply end at one or more formal gardens. However, the garden must be highly visible from the central point, and wide, well directed paths promote this image. (Fig. 8)

Path materials are also important. Solid colors and textures such as concrete, gravel, cobblestone, sawdust, bark or turf do not themselves distract from the panorama of gardens and other features in the landscape. They encourage the eye to keep moving. Brick or stone slab paving set in an unpatterned fashion will be less distracting than in patterns such as herringbone. The latter are intrinsically entertaining and may be used elsewhere, such as an enticing lead-in to a special feature, but never adjacent to a feature. A break in the pattern, such as a 90° rotation, deliberate off-set, different pattern, or a change in paving materials such as from brick to a graveled section bordered by curbs, is used to herald a change in the landscape. It provides a meaningful stopping point for the eye, thereby assisting in discovering a new display—another formal garden—and directing all emphasis there.

Third, water in ponds, streams, or canals are important elements in formal gardens. Shallow ponds striking canal-like into a landscape and bordered by beds of brilliant flowers

Fig. 7. A collection of formal gardens including variations on the maze designed by DeVries in the 16th century for royalty.

and herbs is a Dutch feature, while slender channels of water flowing perpendicularly to a central walk and bordered by elaborate containers of fragrant herbs are a Persian theme. In shallow reflecting ponds water promotes relaxation in any landscape. Unlike inert objects, water, as well as garden plants, appeals to all of our senses, thereby drawing our minds away from the mundane and tedious. Ponds or fountains (Fig. 8) are included as the center of a design or a shallow trough may be featured nearby, in imitation of a medieval dipping well. (Fig. 9) In many regions a pond is a necessity to alter the level of humidity in its vicinity. In dry climates, the humidity allows the gardener to employ otherwise difficult species. A shallow, wide pond is far more effective than a small deep one and should be located in the sun or in the immediate area where it is to furnish humidity.

Fourth, statuary, topiary, and containerized herbs are an integral part of a formal garden. Statues bring emotions in to play with displays of humorous personages, animals in predicaments, frightening beasts whose attacks have been frozen into terrifying poses, or cheerful frolicking creatures from myth or legend. Containers of splendid flowers and strange foliage momentarily draw the viewer's attention from the strict geometry of formal landscapes.

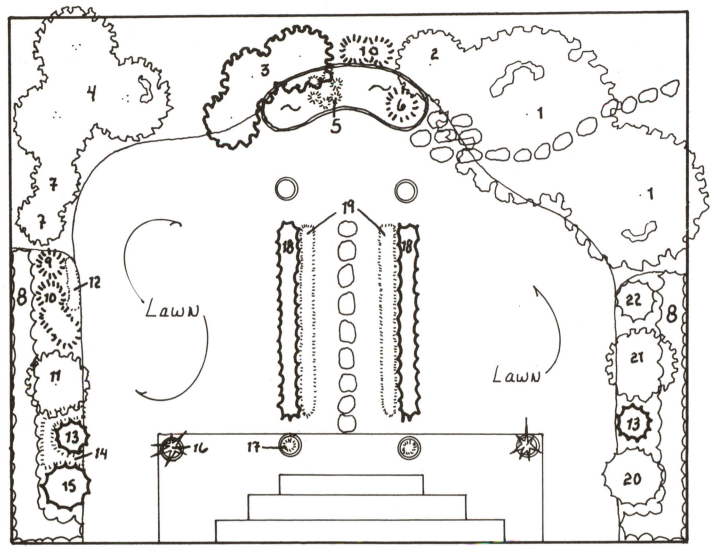

Fig. 8. A formal landscape on a grand scale.

KEY

1 Elm *Ulmus glabra* 'Pendula'
2 Sweet spire *Itea virginica*
3 Witch Hazel *Hamamelis mollis*
4 Birch *Betula pendula*
5 Cattail *Thyphus latifolia*
6 Sweet flag *Acorus calamus*
7 Lilac *Syringa vulgaris*
8 Holly *Ilex aquifolium*
9 Lovage *Levisticum officinale*
10 *Valeriana officinalis*
11 Tamarisk *Tamarix tetranda*
12 'Skeleton-leaf Lemon' Geranium *Pelargonium graveolens*
13 *Santolina neapolitana*
14 Lady's Mantle *Alchemilla* spp.
15 Lavender *Lavandula angustifolia*
16 potted Rosemary (pair) *Rosmarinus* 'Tuscan Blue'
17 potted Jasmine (pair) *Jasminum sambac*
18 Southernwood *Artemisia abrotanum*
19 Saffron/bulbs/Basil
20 *Eleagnus pungens*
21 Japanese apricot *Prunus mume*
22 Oregon Grape *Mahonia aquifolium*

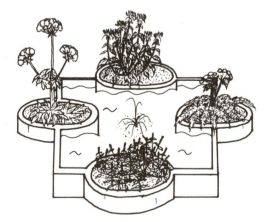

Fig. 9. 16th century formal courtyard pond for residences in hot, dry zones to assist in the cultivation of water loving herbs such as Angelica, Monarda, Sweet Cicely and Mint.

Fascinating works of topiary, including bonsai, espalier and the estrade, are forms of art which stir emotions. Estrade, Figure 10, are standards, a lollipop structure—frivolous entities to amuse visitors. They may also be admired for the craft employed in their making for they require considerable skill to create. They are trained to one or more tiers, each the same or a different shape—spheres, cones, or discs.

Fig. 10A.
Wreath Standard in Holly.　　**Fig. 10B.** Dome Standard.　　**Fig. 10C.**
　　　　　　　　　　　　　　　　　　　　　　　　　　　　Globe Standard.

Espalier involves the training of shrubs or trees to a shape upon a vertical surface such as trellis or wall. It is the least difficult kind of topiary to exploit. Spirals, sunbursts and candelabra are common espalier designs used. It is often used to train apple and pear trees or to add charm to an otherwise drab fence or garage wall by using a flowering plant in a pleasant design that may repeat an existing pattern in a patio, lawn furniture or the architectural cutwork of the home.

An espaliered fruit plant is healthier and yields considerably more than the natural form. Fewer branches are providing fruit and all are given maximum exposure to sunlight. The design is inherently more open and therefore less prone to the spread of disease. Flowering stone fruits benefit from this technique in wet climates, particularly where an overhang protects them from rainfall.

Bonsai is the most demanding of topiary works and is essentially an art form requiring a great deal of time, effort and creative skill. Bonsai are exhibited alone or in groupings in virtually any setting, whether formal or informal, with the added dimension to a landscape that no other topiary work has—inspiration. Bonsai can be shaped to evoke deep feelings of joy or sadness and can accent other landscape features to bring out hidden forms.

A popular and special form of formal garden is to be found in metropolitan neighborhoods. It is the rooftop garden, composed entirely of container grown plants. Narrow containers 18–24 in. deep, typically of pre-formed concrete or wood planking with plastic liners, may be arranged to accommodate a long walk in the open air high above the bustling world below.

The rooftop container garden is inherently formal because of the rectangular contours of both the building and the containers employed. It is therefore a simple matter to construct a formal garden. Roof gardens are a great asset not only because they create beauty in an otherwise barren environment but also because they yield fresh herbs and vegetables from otherwise wasted space. Metropolitan rooftop gardens place unique demands on the garden concept, the foremost of which is size. Many rooftops provide fewer than 1,000 sq. ft. of space, or an area 33 ft. or less on each side, roughly half the average American front garden

Plate 7

Specimen of 'Camphor' Basil, *O. canum,* in a dooryard garden.

The lustrous rich appearance of a 'Cinnamon' Basil goes well in any perennial contemporary feature.

hining white ground cover of Beach Wormwood in partial ade encircling a clump of Chervil.

Single specimen of 'Spice' Basil.

ettuce Leaf' Basil and Bush Basil—a comparison of the largest nd smallest leaved Basils.

A fragrant border in a kitchen garden of 'Dark Opal', Lemon and 'Lettuce Leaf' Basils.

Plate 8

Fragrant herbs awaiting passersby. Several herbs combine here to give an all year display of fragrance and color. From left, Winter Savory, Lady's Mantle and 'Dark Opal' Basil. Peonys, Archangel and *Santolina neapolitana* are background herbs.

A partially closed knot of Sweet Basil, 'Dark Opal' Basil, Chives and Dwarf Feverfew with a frame of carrots as a part of a 17th century kitchen garden replica.

Curly Mint with cheerful dark green ruffles is a choice feature garden Mint, from garden of John Eccles, Winlock, WA.

Stream channel in formal setting with Marsh Marigold, *Caltha palustris,* Sweet Flag and Water Mint in the Cascara Circle of the Medicinal Herb Garden, University of Washington, Seattle, WA.

Pond with Sweet Flag and Water Lily in Garden of Judith Zugish, Marysville, Washington.

A fragrant path between the forested perimeters of a checkerboard garden lined with a fragrant white flowering Rosemary, Medicinal Herb Garden, University of Washington, Seattle, WA.

Plate 9

Golden Lemon Thyme in a perimeter bed with Shasta Daisy, Hyssop and Lemon Balm.

…ecimen of Miniature Thyme.

The compact busy nature of Silver Thyme (center) and Lavender Cotton (right) make them invaluable herbs for formal or informal applications.

…mound of 'Broadleaf English' Thyme joins Chives, Sage and …ooly Betony on this raised bed feature. Blue spires of Dwarf …tnip rise in the background.

'Narrow Leaf French' Thyme shares this dry desert site with Spanish Lavender.

Plate 10

Lavender and *Santolina chamaecyparissus* blooming with blue and gold colors in a mixed border on a sloping perimeter of a formal garden at the Medicinal Herb Garden, University of Washington, Seattle, WA.

The marked contrast of a feathery species of Lavender Cotton, *Santolina neapolitana,* and a broad-leaved Lion's Paw or Lady's Mantle, *Alchemilla* sp. makes a splendid feature in this contemporary scene in the gardens of Judith Zugish, Marysville WA.

A blue green puff of Garden Rue, with a collar of Corsican Mint, joins Creeping Golden Thyme and French Thyme in this evergreen perennial bed.

An ancient mound of Corsican Rue in a square at the Medicinal Herb Garden, University of Washington, Seattle, WA.

Germander blooming in perennial border in garden of Judith Zugish, Marysville, WA.

in suburbia. Other problems to be dealt with include: water cost/supply, wind and air pollution.

One landscaping principle that is difficult to incorporate into rooftop gardens is the tying together of the immediate landscape with features in the distance so that they enhance one another. Architecture is a formal element in such environments. Formality in landscaping, which was once quite commonly related to architecture, may again be the inspiration for a gardener to design a formal garden around the skyline. The raised beds could frame a scene in the distance such as mountains or near or distant skyline. Perhaps a pattern in the fashion of the cutwork parterre could adopt the architecture of an adjacent and dominating building to the garden.

One design that is best expressed is the maze. Figure 11 is such an example. This garden design makes use of far-off vistas of mountains as well as neighboring architecture and yet it captures the true spirit of a maze because it can be seen throughout the year and

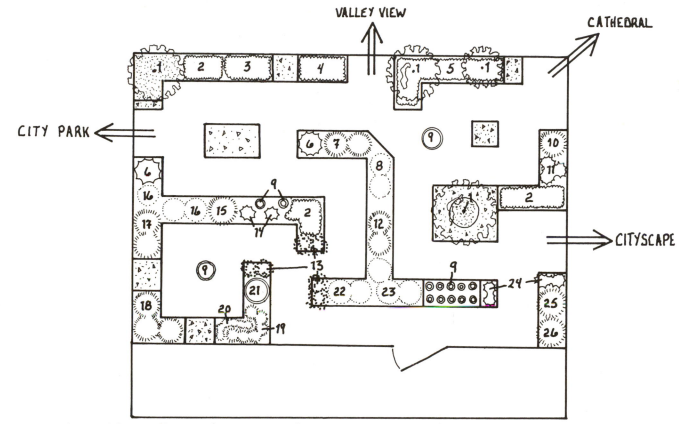

Fig. 11. Metropolitan rooftop maze garden.
KEY
1 Dwarf fruit trees *Malus* sp.
2 Turf Camomile *Chamaemellum nobile* 'Trenague'
3 Caraway Thyme *Thymus herba-barona*
4 Red flowering Thyme *Thymus praecox* 'Coccineus'
5 Sweet Woodruff/Violets
6 Southernwood *Artemisia abrotanum*
7 Peony *Paeonia* spp.
8 Mums
9 potted herbs
10 *Allium karataviense*
11 Winter Savory *Satureja montana*
12 Shasta Daisy *Chrysanthemum maximum*
13 French and Silver Thyme *Thymus* 'Argenteus', *T. vulgaris* 'Narrow Leaf French'
14 Dwarf Sage *Salvia officinalis* 'Nana'
15 Golden Mint *Mentha* × *gracilis* var. *variegata*
16 *Calendula officinalis*
17 Pineapple Mint *Mentha suaveolens*
18 Orange Mint *Mentha* × *piperita* var. *citrata*
19 Chive *Allium schoenoprassum*
20 Dwarf Feverfew *Chrysanthemum parthenium* 'Selaginoides'
21 potted Sweet Bay *Laurus nobilis*
22 Opal Basil *Ocimum basilicum* 'Dark Opal'
23 Sweet Basil *Ocimum basilicum*
24 Azalea
25 'Moonshine' Yarrow *Achillea clypeolata*
26 Painted Daisy *Chrysanthemum coccineum*

incorporates many evergreen plants for winter beauty. Lounge areas for both sun-and-shade-lovers are provided and there is an accent on the more fragrant herbs to counteract the unpleasant, polluted air of the city.

The fifth principle for constructing any formal design is that the formal garden must be isolated within the landscape. It must be surrounded by a barrier which sharply delineates it from its surroundings and restricts entry. It may be either framed so it is visible from without or enclosed for complete privacy. The frame might be wattle, picket, ranch or rail fencing, a low to medium height hedge, or a stone wall that doubles as a sitting bench. It might be enclosed by a board fence, brick wall or a tall trellis clothed in a thicket of vines and espaliered herbs, depending upon the site and the intentions of the gardener.

The enclosed formal garden is refered to as the *Hortus Conclusus*, literally, a contained garden (see Chapter 7). Those of the 12th century are little different from the enclosed patio of today, provided there are herbs and potted plants within (Fig. 12). The smaller formal pleasure gardens originated as extended rooms located within the inner bailey of a castle, the grounds adjacent to the door of a castle keep's bedchamber or hall. The herber and an orchard would surround the keep, but still be within the castle walls, tucked into a part of the outer bailey. Smaller castles with little room for gardens or those situated on unsuitable soils placed the garden a short walk from the main gate and, if possible, visible from a tower window for entertainment, or from the barbicans for protection. These gardens were fenced within wattle, stone, wooden palisades (thick boards nailed side-by-side), or impenetrable shrubbery such as that about which King James I wrote as he gazed from his jail cell window overlooking the garden outside the castle wall:

And Hawthorn hedges knit
That no one, though he were walking by
Might there within scarce anyone espy.

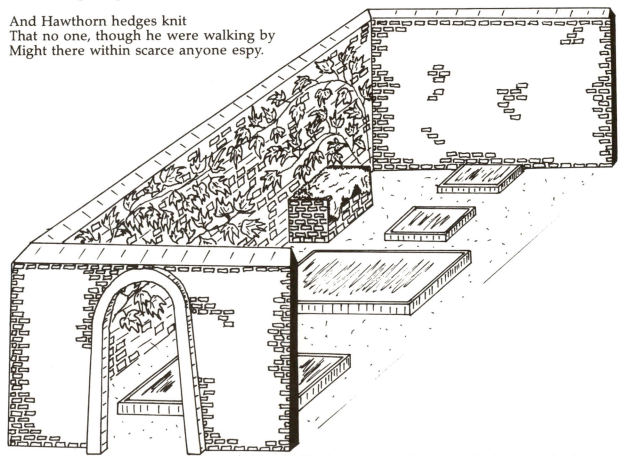

Fig. 12. Hortus Conclusus, looking into the walled herber shown in Fig. 50. An herb garden for the small metropolitan yard.

Near the end of the 19th century, formalism was replaced by the informal and natural look. Small "formals" were relegated to a patch off to the side of the estate, so that lavish and elegant gardens were not forgotten but appreciated on a more modest scale. Three kinds of "formals" were designed for their beauty and incorporated into the landscape. These gardens were the *knot*, the *parterre* and the *maze.* Let's examine each one in more detail.

The *knot* was one of the earliest pleasure gardens. Within a square or rectangular bed, a design was created with herbs and colored earth that resembled a piece of knotted rope. Some examples are shown in Figures 13 through 20. Figure 13 shows one of the most popular designs, originating in the 16th century. It is composed of three separate borders. The garden design in Figure 14 comprised only two interweaving borders. Figure 15 is essentially a single border but quite complicated. The designs in Figures 16 and 17 were popular knots in the American colonies during the late 16th and early 17th centuries. These were the domain of many low-growing beneficial herbs, not necessarily in trimmed borders but rather linear and triangular beds of many varied species. Figures 18 and 19 are examples of modern knots.

Fig. 13. Popular 16th century knot design composed of three borders.

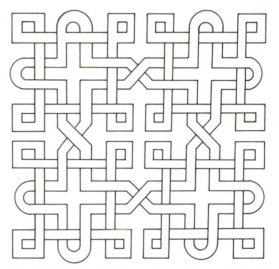

Fig. 14. A simplified version of a multibordered knot from 16th century.

Fig. 15. A single border closed knot design. Interstices are occupied by colored earth for a low border or by flowers if a taller border is used.

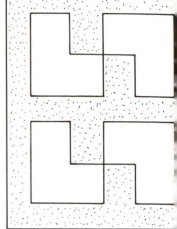

Fig. 16. Simple knot from colonial American period.

Fig. 17. Simple knot from colonial American period.

Fig. 18. Contemporary knot for today's gardener. This design can be merged with a sidewalk or patio.

Fig. 19. Contemporary knot

During the 16th century the knot reached its peak as a popular pleasure garden. Within the raised bed framework a knot could assume an unlimited number of designs. Knots were just as likely to be animal caricatures, the heraldry of a castle's lord (Fig. 20), as religious, mystic or astrological symbols. Whether enjoyed from afar, as an ornamental garden near benches or sitting lawns, or criss-crossed by footpaths, the knot contained both ornamental and beneficial herbs. The "open" knot allows more space for maintaining and harvesting beneficial herbs while the interstices of a "closed" knot were filled with flowers. Virtually any low-growing herb could be worked into the interstices of a knot.

Fig. 20. Heraldry in a knot.

Though there are many ways to approach the design of a knot, several principles are universally observed. First, and most important, the herbs selected should be of markedly different foliage colors to create a strong sense of contrast. Second, all the plants should be about the same height at maturity. Spreading herbs can be corralled but if one herb requires pruning, the others should also be trimmed to maintain a uniform height and appearance. Annuals or perennials can be used, alone or in combination. Tall herbs are generally unsuitable for a knot garden because they will hide a portion of the garden from view or unbalance the design. The knot is intended to be a centerpiece, a feature garden to be strolled about and admired from nearby. Choose herbs that grow less than 24 in. and with a relatively dense habit. Ground covers below 6 in. are best for the interstices or borders surrounding a knot. If a smaller garden is planned, it is important to note that foliage colors produce more appealing and distinct patterns than do flowering plants. Flowers might well be used, however, to fill the interstices of the knot.

Of the perennial herbs, a few should be tried first. Bushy, evergreen candidates, easy to work with and propagate, include Wormwood, Southernwood, Santolina, Germander, Hyssop, Rue, Winter Savory, Thyme and Lavender. The only drawback to evergreen or woody perennials is the difficulty of maintaining a continuous border of 2 dozen or more plants. These herbs might be better grown as closely spaced mounds for easy maintainence and to make replacement of dying plants less tedious.

On the other hand, the best herbaceous perennials include Oregano, the Mints, Chives and Dwarf Feverfew. If an herbaceous perennial garden is desired, two Oreganos will quickly fill the bill. Wild Marjoram, *Origanum vulgare,* with a dark green foliage and Golden Oregano, *O. vulgare* 'Aureum' which has yellow green leaves. Either Apple Mint for a soft green or Orange Mint for a deep purple-green could be used for contrast. The Mints make excellent knot herbs, filling their boxes snugly and providing a tremendous experience for the nose. The variegated Mints are choice for contrast, but solid green colors are necessary for a proper knot.

Starting with annuals is the best way to become familiar with the knot design. Both the plants and the garden are short-lived, allowing for other ideas and designs to follow them. A few of the best herbs for this use are Curly Parsley, Caraway, Sweet Marjoram, German Camomile, Calendula and Basil. They can be accompanied by annual flowering plants, such as Marigolds and Alyssums, or even vegetables such as Carrots, Lettuce, flowering Kale, etc. The Basils are the choice herb with which to experiment. Foliage colors range from dark green in 'Cinnamon' Basil, a range of greens with Sweet Basil and Bush Basil, the light green of Lemon Basil, and the dark purples of Opal' and 'Krishna' Basil.

The dimensions of a knot depend upon the plant materials used in it. The more compact herbs and lower-growing ground covers are used in knots as small as 30 sq. ft. Slim, well-trimmed hedges of *Santolina,* Germander, Hyssop or Thyme may be only 6–8 inches in cross-section, or large hedges of Rosemary, Compact Lavender, Bay and Southernwood may be at least 12 in. As a rule of thumb a border should be no wider than one-tenth the shortest dimension of the garden. An 8 in. Thyme hedge will look its best in a small garden of only 30–50 sq. ft., where its leaves and flowers can play an important role. A border of English Lavender, trimmed to 12–24 in., will require a garden that is at least 20–30 ft. on a side.

The interstices of a knot may not only be filled with flowers and ground covers but inert earths or organic materials. It was for the knot and parterre that colored earths were formulated. Intense color is vital to accent the design or balance the color of foliage. Table 5 lists the choices of fill materials that may be used and Table 6, Coloring Agents. Materials such as crushed coal (black), lime (white), or the two combined (blue) provide striking accents for grey foliages, a popular choice for 3 centuries. Crushed brick or tiles (red/yellow), crushed green sand or slate (green/grey or blue/green) all lend character to a design. Organic materials such as sawdust (yellow/red/brown), wood chips (brown), manures (dark brown/black) and even turf (green) are used in gardens with changing designs, thus improving the soil as well as decorating it. Many sizes and colors of crushed rock are available to us today, including cinders (red), lava rock (red/browns/black), gravel (grey), granite (pink or white), quartzite (pink/white) and fabricated concrete mixes of all colors. Pebbles, cobbles, brick, tile, sea shells, boards and even bones have been used as fill.

Table 5
Fill For Knots and Parterres

INORGANIC	*ORGANIC*
Crushed Rock, gravel	Mulch
Sand	Sawdust
Oyster shell	Woodchips
	Bagged manure

Table 6
Coloring Agents

Black	Crushed coal[1] or charcoal, steer manure[2]
Brown	Wood chips, chicken manure[2]
White	Lime, oyster shell, Dolomite chips, Quartzite, sand
Blue	Lime and charcoal, colored sand
Green	Greensand, grass[3]
Yellow	Crushed brick, sawdust
Red	Crushed brick, sawdust (cedar or redwood)

1. Coal will leave a toxic residue of metals if used regularly
2. Commercially prepared, bagged and pasteurized
3. Use low growing Bentgrass, Fescue, etc.

You will find the knot an immensely gratifying garden. The garden shown in Figure 13 is easy to lay out and simple to plant. It is a basic knot that was popular because of its versatility. In only ten steps, a knot garden like that in Figure 13 can become the center of attraction in your landscape. Table 7 describes the step-by-step construction of this design.

Table 7
Ten Steps To a Knot Garden

STEP 1— Measure off the outside dimensions of garden. All four sides must be equal.

STEP 2— Find center of square (C) and center of each side (#1–4).

STEP 3— Drive stake at each point, 1 through 4, and with stake or trowel tied on the end of string sketch a half circle beginning at each point. Start at a distance (equal to the width of the border desired) from C, the center point.

These lines sketched will be the centerline of one border. Border width should be about 1/10 of the width of the square.

STEP 4— From center point C sketch a circle. The outermost edge (point 5) should equal the distance from the lobe of the first design to the edge of the square.

STEP 5— Measure off border width and sketch inner circle.

STEP 6— Where points 1–4 on edges intercept inner edge of circle will be the four outside corners of the square. Sketch straight lines between intercept points.

STEP 7— Sketch inner border of square according to intended border width.

STEP 8— Identify crossovers.

STEP 9— When planting annual borders, plant seeds in order of germination, longest first, to properly time emergence. Bloom times should also be planned for.

STEP 10— Fill interstices by either coloring the soil surface using one of the recommended soil conditioners, a ground cover or flowers (e.g., Alyssums).

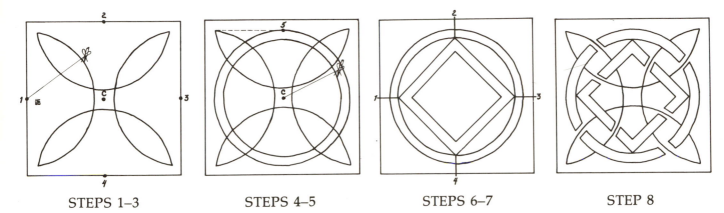

STEPS 1–3   STEPS 4–5   STEPS 6–7   STEP 8

The best method for transferring a complicated design from paper to the ground is probably one you have already encountered while doing cross-word puzzles and scrambled picture games. The picture to be copied is overlaid with a grid of squares. (Fig. 21) The garden plot that will receive the design is also gridded. It is important to remember that the number of squares used on both must be equal though the dimensions will differ. The transfer process is performed by walking from square to square on the garden plot and sketching onto the soil that portion of the design on the picture for the same square. Even the most complicated patterns may be copied with this method.

Fig. 21. Parterre garden design rendered into grid for transfer to garden site. The garden site is gridded in the same fashion and the design traced onto the soil using lime or a trowel.

The flamboyant *parterre* is the most fanciful and intricate garden pattern ever designed. It was evolved to fulfill the wildest dreams of the lovers of formal gardens. Early parterres relied predominantly on colored earths and less on herbs, effectively allowing an increase in the scale of the design with less gardening effort. The parterre, as the name implies, was literally level with the ground and not composed of raised beds, again requiring less gardening effort yet appearing orderly and distinct.

Figures 22 and 23 are examples of a parterre. With the ground already tilled either could be laid out on a weekend. Two alternate designs have been reproduced here to show the versatility. Figure 22 will be set directly into an existing lawn, the paths at 3 ft. wide, easily accommodate a lawnmower. The beds will be filled with numerous flowering and evergreen herbs which may include the ornamental dwarf Catnip, miniature Roses, Feverfew, Camomile, Anise Hyssop, Golden Oregano, Santolina, Rue, English Lavender, 'Rosea' Lavender, Wooly Betony, Monarda and Golden and Dwarf Sage. This is a garden with a blend of colors that are bright and cheerful. It is essentially a garden which does not hug the property line but holds a classical pose in the very center of the lawn.

Fig. 22. Background parterre set directly into the lawn. Paths remain grass.

KEY
  1 Golden Sage *Salvia officinalis* 'Icterina'
  2 Dwarf Feverfew *Chrysan. parthenium*
  3 Lemon Balm *Melissa off.* var. *variegata*
  4 Cr. Thyme *Thymus pulegioides*
  5 Roses
  6 Miniature Roses
  7 *Santolina viridis*
  8 *Santolina chamaecyparrissus*
  9 Lavender *Lavandula angustifolia* 'Hidcote'
 10 Bee Balm *Monarda didyma*
 11 *Santolina neapolitana*

Fig. 23. Metropolitan courtyard parterre.

KEY
  1 *Juniperus communis*
  2 Mignonette *Reseda odorata*
  3 Opal Basil *Ocimum basilicum* 'Dark Opal'
  4 Golden Sage *Salvia officinalis* 'Aurea'
  5 Dwarf Sage *Salvia officinalis* 'Nana'
  6 Cr. Red Thyme *Thymus praecox* ssp. *articus* 'Coccineus'
  7 Dwarf Lavender *Lavandula angustifolia* 'Nana'
  8 Variegated Lemon Balm *Melissa officinalis* var. *variegata*
  9 White Cr. Thyme 'Foster flower' *Thymus pulegioides*
 10 Silver/Golden Lemon Thyme
 11 Golden Oregano *Origanum vulgare* 'Aureum'

Figure 23 may be used in a crowded metropolitan neighborhood, where it can become the entire back garden. The scale of the garden is less, 30 x 30 ft. with a surrounding 5 ft. strip of lawn. The beds are 18 in. wide. A rusty red brick has been chosen to match that of the building. The plants chosen are beneficial herbs, including Basil, Oregano, Thyme, Sage and Rosemary, and here and there are patches of ground cover, to allow foot traffic. The central looping border is composed primarily of evergreens for winter beauty. The interconnecting beds are herbaceous perennials and annuals. Four columnar junipers in ornate pots reside in the corners. It is a garden of considerable beauty and benefit for the enlightened metropolitan gardener.

The completed parterre says much about a home owner. It is quite obvious that an appreciation of art is paramount and on a grand scale. But the art must also instruct: that is, teach the viewer about the beauty of two unrelated, but united subjects, geometry and nature. Although the parterre is the medium in which the two so perfectly come together, combining the two is not easy. It is an art.

The parterre was intended to be fairly large, certainly no less than 300–400 sq. ft. The reason was simple—in too small an area a loss of clarity in the design would result. The prime reason for using colored earths was to help refine the image and also decrease the need for maintenance when the garden was boosted to stupendous proportions. Palatial parterres in the 17th and 18th centuries ranged from ¼ acre to several, and quite often, several parterres were interconnected to create one garden feature of immense size.(Fig. 7)

Figure 24 shows a parterre composed of only one plant species, a box hedge, circa 17th century. The English parterre, Figure 25 substituted lawn for earths and the beds were gorged with elegant flowers. Compartmented parterres used geometric subunits that were reversed and connected back-to-back (Fig. 26). Like the links in a chain, these subunits would be used to form intricate patterns from the simple quad to many dozens of units interconnected into an even larger pattern. For the ultrastylish, it became fashionable to own a parterre patterned after embroidery designs or after the architectural scrollwork (cutwork) of their mansions, such as in Figures 25 and 26.

Fig. 24. Single border parterre.

Before choosing herbs for a parterre it is important to determine the background material. Color is applied in the garden just as a painter applies pigments to a canvas to create a painting. The color of the fill is chosen to either contrast or harmonize with the surrounding landscape. As the large size of a parterre is imposing in any landscape, choose the background wisely.

Dark backgrounds will suit light green or grey foliage plants. Black, blue, or chocolate colored earths suggest both an emptiness and vastness that needs to be filled by bright colors such as the yellows of Golden Oregano, Dwarf Feverfew, Golden Creeping and

Fig. 25. English parterre: central oval may be either a bowling green or reflecting pool, paths are grass or Roman Camomile and beds of colorful flowers dazzle the eyes from all around as statuary or topiary grace the circled areas.

Fig. 26. Compartmented and/or Cutwork parterre.

Golden Lemon Thyme, variegated Melissa, and Ginger Mint or the silver-lining herbs, Silver Horehound, Silver Germander, Wooly Lavender, Wooly Betony, Silver or Clary Sage and Silver Thyme.

Brick-red materials add a warmth and depth to a landscape and require the verdant greens of *Santolina viridis,* Myrtle, Germander, Roman Camomile, Curly Parsley, Lemon Verbena, Basil, miniature Roses, Pennyroyal, Holly, and virtually all of the golden variegated varieties and cultivars.

Cooler colors, blue, yellow and white, convey a joyful cordial feeling and are best combined with the fragrant and richly robed herbs such as the scented Geraniums with their fabulous foliage patterns, *Santolina neapolitana,* German Camomile, Silver Germander, Basil, Rue, Dittany, Creeping Red and Wooly Thyme, the dark glossy green Mother-of-Thyme,

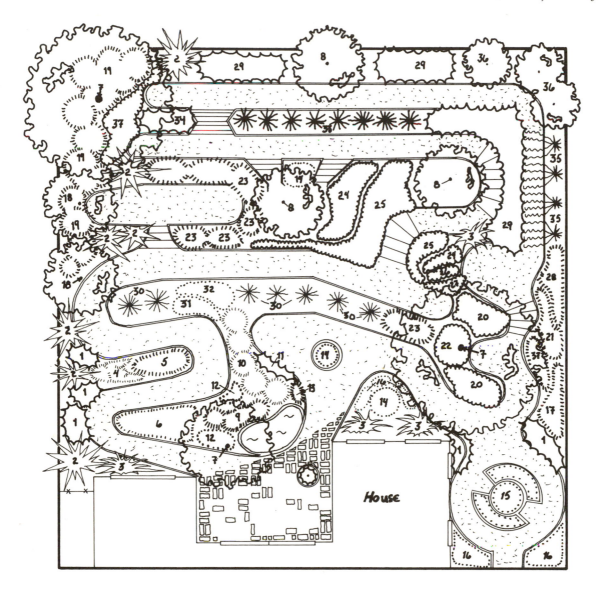

Fig. 27. Maze in informal design on sloping terrain.

KEY

1 Southernwood *Artemisia abrotanum*
2 Mugo Pine *Pinus* spp.
3 Creeping Juniper *Juniperus horizontalis*
4 *Dahlia* selection
5 Valerian *Valeriana officinalis*
6 *Iris* spp.
7 English Walnut *Juglans regia*
8 Apple *Malus* sp.
9 Angelica *Angelica atropurpurea*
10 Peony (selection)
11 Golden Sage *Salvia officinalis* 'Icterina'
12 *Monarda didyma* Bee Balm
13 Golden Oregano *Origanum vulgare* 'Aureum'
14 Calendula *Calendula officinalis*
15 KITCHEN GARDEN
16 annual flowers
17 Meadow Rue *Thalictrum glaucum*
18 Hazelnut *Corylus*
19 Sword Fern *Polystichum* sp.
20 Violets *Viola* spp.

21 Primroses *Primula* spp.
22 Wild Ginger *Asarum hartwegii*
23 Lovage *Levisticum officinale*
24 'White Magic' Thyme *Thumus praecox* ssp. *articus*
25 Cr. Red Thyme *Thymus pulegioides* 'Kermesinus'
26 Golden Thyme *Thymus* 'Clear Gold'
27 Oregano Thyme *Thymus pulegioides* 'Oregano-scented'
28 Fern Leaf Tansy *Tanacetum vulgare* 'Crispum'
29 Lavender *Lavandula angustifolia* 'Hidcote'
30 Roses *Rosa* sp.
31 'Bush' Basil *Ocimum basilicum*
32 Opal Basil *Ocimum basilicum* 'Dark Opal'
33 Blueberry *Vaccinium angustifolium*
34 Azalea *Rhododendron obtusum* 'Coccineum'
35 Grape *Vitus vinifera*
36 Italian Prune *Prunus*
37 Sweet Woodruff *Gallium odorata*

'Pink Chintz' and Caraway Thymes.

The parterre is best planted with hardy evergreen perennials: Lavender, Thyme, Germander, Box, Hyssop, Holly, Yew, Myrtle, Bay, Santolina, Rue and Rosemary. However, in today's bustling world, gardeners do not always stay in one location long enough to enjoy such a laborious design. It is also more satisfying to reap a harvest, if possible, from any garden, be it even the most classical. A parterre using herbaceous perennials and annuals is not at all illogical and may well have been more common than medieval writers would like us to believe. The only rule this is breaking, which must be weighed carefully in designing the garden, is the loss of clarity of the design.

It is vital for the parterre to provide a continual display of flowers or colorful foliages. The beds are generally planted with a homogeneous mixture of evergreen and flowering plants having staggered bloom times. It was popular among the better medieval landscapers to interpose more than one pattern, using each blooming species to create another design. The flowers were arranged in the beds so that they yielded a clearly defined design by themselves alone—a design within a design. The parterre was also used to incorporate into the home site a wooded section of the estate. That is, trees were assembled onto the design in an orderly way. Fruit and nut-bearing trees were used primarily but botanical gardens included every tree possible for the purposes of instruction. With a little planning ingenuity, a home owner can design a parterre around existing trees and shrubs, using them to an advantage.

The *maze,* such as in Figure 7, has enjoyed sporadic popularity throughout the last 3,000 years. This queer, but delightful design was originally developed as a game in commemoration of the fall of Troy (the maze reproduced the convoluted walls of the great fortress). The game was introduced into Europe and Great Britain by the Romans and used as a training arena for mounted knights to hone their riding skills. In medieval times, shepherds and mercenary men-at-arms were fond of maze games and scratched them onto bare soil anywhere.

The maze endured as a feature for entertainment and was a popular festival activity. Rules of the game required a participant to "thread" or "tread the maze" for accuracy and speed. The maze was generally cut from turf with little or no embellishment. Inner borders took on any form, from stone walls to hedges. They were often built without plant materials. Many famous and legendary mazes were constructed of stones or excavated onto flat terrain. Such patterns were equally pleasant to observe in winter and existed as landscape features long after they grew old and useless. Some mazes have existed for centuries.

The maze or labyrinth is described as a convoluted path that utilizes diversions such as cul-de-sacs and circuitous dead ends to tantalize and entertain. A maze may also be a single continuous, albeit tortuous, pathway, inescapable without completing the course, incorporating switchbacks and spirals. Where the former is a challenge, the latter is suspenseful and landscaped more cleverly with containers, statuary and benches.

Although still formal by definition, a maze need not use hundreds of closely clipped hedges and borders, but beds of flowers and herbs paralleling the paths. If the symmetry requirement of a formal maze design is relaxed, as if taking it out of a square frame and letting the pathways fall back again to refill an entire landscape, the path may now be viewed as a meandering wild garden walk, as in Figure 27. The fact that it is a maze will not be revealed immediately, thus adding to the enchantment. Homeowners on steep slopes or forested grounds may consider this scheme. A single path need not hinder the gardener from normal chores. Some stepping stones hidden here and there aid in traversing the yard without having to "thread the maze".

Now let us turn to some of history's most famous formal garden herbs; evergreens such as Germander, Rue, Hyssop, Santolina, Rosemary and Thyme; pond dwellers Angelica and Sweet Flag; and winter-blooming herbs Witch Hazel and Saffron.

Chapter 3 / SECTION 2

Herbs for Formal Gardens

The bush Thymes are veterans of detail design in the formal landscape. They are characterized as small evergreen bushes with spade- or needle-like leaves and cylindrical or pom-pom-shaped flower heads. They grow from 4 to over 16 in. in an erect, mounded habit. The upright growth is an obvious difference from the spreading mat-forming habit of the Creeping Thymes you may also cultivate. They may be trimmed into hedges, grown as solitary mounds, or carefully pruned into shapes or topiary. There are many species and cultivars which are easily confused. It is quite common to receive a cultivar different than what was ordered, particularly if using a common name.

Most of the Thymes conform to an approximate height classification. As an example, 'Narrow Leaf French' Thyme rarely exceeds 16 in. and if healthy, keeps a well mounded shape for 3–5 years. The Bush Thymes in this section are organized by height so that they may be selected for a particular landscape use more easily. Remember, categorizing Thyme by height is not exact because of the polymorphic nature of individual species. The first category includes the dwarf, or low-growing and sprawling Bush Thymes, *T. camphoratus, T. carnosus, T.* 'Argenteus', *T.* 'Wedgewood English', and *T. vulgaris* 'Miniature', which keep a profile of less than 10 in. In the mid-range, between 8–12 in. high, are *T. capitatus, T. × citriodorus,* and *T. hyemalis.* Those Bush Thymes that grow to over 10 in. in the prime of life are *T. mastichina, T.* 'Broadleaf English' and *T. vulgaris.*

The tiniest of all the Bush Thymes is *T. vulgaris* 'Miniature'. It is a delightful cultivar that exactly resembles the species except for its diminutive size. It forms a dense, upright, fastigiate (all branches rise suddenly upward—e.g., the Lombardy Poplar) bush of tiny, dark grey-green leaves harboring the same delicate aroma of common French Thymes. If you do not use much Thyme in the kitchen this is the cultivar to grow.

'Miniature' Thyme is very hardy and holds its shape longer than the larger *T. vulgaris* cultivars. Trim it lightly in the fall to remove any flowers that may have graced the little plant (it generally does not flower). It grows slowly to about 6 in., forming a nice symmetrical bush that requires virtually no maintenance. Specimens of 'Miniature' Thyme are a common substitute for *T. richardii* ssp. *nitidus* and *T. carnosus.*

The rock garden, a dwarf feature in a dooryard or contemporary garden and the formal parterre are the choice sites for 'Miniature' Thyme. Other dwarf or miniature herbs that can accompany it include Dwarf Germander, *Santolina* 'Nana', *Origanum microphyllum*, Curly Parsley, Pygmy Savory, Miniature Roses, Dwarf Sage, Corsican Mint, and two tiny Creeping Thymes 'Languinosus' or 'White Moss'.

Camphor Thyme, *T. camphoratus*, is also a small 4–6 in. bush, with thick, dark green leaves that have a thin, fleecy-white underside. It has not been reported to flower in cultivation. It has a biting, Rosemary-like scent. The oil of Camphor Thyme contains pinene, terpinyl acetate, borneol, and camphene. It is not hardy below 10°F. and must be potted and brought indoors during extended cold spells.

Camphor Thyme resembles *T. zygis* and they are commonly substituted for one another although the latter is much less available. *T. zygis* is a larger, less compact bush with lavender flowers and a stronger thymol scent. It is presently a commercial source of Thyme Oil. Both have a strong fragrance and bitter flavor that is not as appealing as that of French Thyme. Use clippings for strewing and in fragrant bouquets or as an aromatic ornamental in the garden in the same niche as 'Miniature' Thyme.

Another diminutive Thyme often substituted for *T. camphoratus* is *T. carnosus*. 'Miniature' Thyme is also substituted as well. *T. carnosus* is a small 4–6 in. compact bush with dark green leaves that have a thick felty coat on their undersides. It also generally blooms—the flowers are white—unlike either of its substitutes that do not flower. It has a distinct resinous odor and is bitter.

Among the mid-range Bush Thymes is one of the most famous ornamental Thymes, Silver Thyme, *T.* 'Argenteus'. It forms a small dense mound instead of a symmetrical bush. Strong, woody, decumbent branches determine the shape of these mounds and wise pruning can help to shape Silver Thyme into a work of art. Although a single plant will not grow more than 6–8 inches from center, after some time its branches will take root near the tip and the crown will die. It is possible, but infrequent, that healthier clumps will spread 2–3 ft. before the crown dies, leaving many smaller Silver Thymes in a 'fairy ring'. A rocky ground cover will forestall this event.

The leaves of Silver Thyme are olive-green with a cream or yellow-white margin. Their odor is similar to French Thyme but less spicy and often citrus-like. Plants sold as Silver Lemon Thyme are not a distinct cultivar and do tend to lose their lemon scent. Careful propagation is necessary to maintain this emerging cultivar (chemotype). In fall, leaves predominantly at branch tips have a margin of pink or red.

Silver Thyme provides the gardener with a sparkling flat-topped mound that is a charmer in any landscape design. Arrangements with conifers or broadleaf evergreens can be given a boost in character with the glittering accent of Silver Thyme to draw attention. Always use dark ground covers such as fly ash, cinders and crushed lava rock, or basalt chips to bring out the detail in this entertaining herb.

The rock garden is the place to feature it alone or in sparse company with Dittany and *Origanum microphyllum.* But in the perennial bed it is an attractive herb that brightens even the sunniest spots. Although it can grow in partial shade its overall shape and hardiness are superior in full sun.

Since full sun improves its informal habit, use it in informal and wild borders, displaying an irregularly advancing front where the herb will receive no more than a trimming-off of flower stalks at year's end. Silver Thyme is a very beautiful ground cover in contemporary settings that do not cover large areas and has been used as such in formal settings around statues, urns, and sundials, at the center of knots or to fill in large portions of a design ensemble in parterres (i.e. heraldry, non-geometric artwork, etc.). Solid borders or patches of Silver Thyme are excellent for drawing a visitor's attention. Set plants 6–8 in. apart and thin or trim as necessary to prevent criss-crossing branches. Its pink or rose flowers are very petite and in good-sized patches are becoming, especially when they can also contribute their fragrance to the garden. Ornamental herbs that seem to be natural companions to Silver Thyme in a mixed border or perennial bed are *Potentilla, Alchemila alpina* and 'Nutmeg' Scented Geranium.

In the kitchen garden Silver Thyme should be seen cavorting in the strawberry bed, its shiny form poking around in the verdant pasture like a contented Guernsey. Its lack of symmetry is unimportant here and the color contrast is remarkable. If the bed is composed of everbearing varieties the Thyme also assists in pollination.

T. 'Wedgewood English' is a hybrid adorned with a blue-green streak down the center of each dark green leaf. The actual markings are not apparent from even a few feet but the overall color of the herb is shifted to blue-green. It has an agreeable French Thyme aroma. Propagation of branches with crisp or larger markings is advisable.

A mound of 'Wedgewood' Thyme has a habit similar to Silver Thyme, growing 6–10 in. high but spreading much more rapidly, forming a healthy mound to 18 in. wide in a season from a well-rooted clump. It is enhanced by close association with ornamental herbs such as 'Curly Girl' Rue, *Santolina neapolitana* and 'Silver Mound' Artemisia.

The Bush Thyme from which Spanish Origanum Oil is derived is *T. capitatus*, Conehead Thyme or Corido. It grows with a very stiff, upright posture and has showy lavender flowers borne in large globes on 8–10 in. high, thickly foliaged bushes. Corido is the only member of the subgenus of *Thymus*, Coridothymus. Except for the arrangment of flowers, it resembles to some extent the herb Za'atar, *Thymbra spicata* in habit and fragrance. The odor of Corido is distinctly Thyme-like but with a rich camphoraceous note. It is not hardy below 20°F. Corido is a good herb in rockeries and in formal knots and parterres. In the kitchen garden it can be paired with Summer Savory or German Camomile in a border. The flowers, arriving in May, usually last several weeks and will continue to emerge throughout the summer.

Plants sold as *T. hyemalis* or German Winter Thyme are invariably French Thyme or 'Orange Balsam' Thyme. True *T. hyemalis* has smaller leaves than French Thyme and a pink-purple flower. Flannery indicates that neither this species nor *T. adamovicii* are presently in cultivation in North America. The latter is substituted by Winter Savory.

Exceedingly popular are Lemon Thyme, *T.* × *citriodorus*, and its cultivar, Golden Lemon, *T.* × *c.* 'Aureus'. These two could be either a Creeping or Bush Thyme because their habits vary considerably. In general, consistent pruning will control the runaway nature of Lemon and Golden Lemon Thyme and they will form moderately dense mounds from 8–10 in. high.

They are hybrids of garden origin (a cross between *T. vulgaris* and *T. pulegioides*) and contain the chemicals geraniol for a spicyness and geranial and neral for the lemony note. Lemon Thyme is a pleasant, enjoyable hybrid but fails two basic criteria to be a good ornamental herb in the landscape. First, it does not form a compact mound, tending to become scraggly in midsummer. Too much pruning is required to keep it in shape. Second, the Golden Lemon cultivar does not maintain a uniform variegation; many branches are totally green, and the gold color washes out in summer. Propagating only the finest color does not eliminate the reversion back to dark green. Like Silver Thyme, Golden Lemon Thyme will exhibit a dark red margin on leaves near the tip of the branches during late winter months. This color change is uneven; often only a single branch is involved.

The flavor and fragrance of the Lemon Thymes are their only redeeming features. It is an engaging spice that can and should substitute for French Thyme. The camphoraceous note is absent in cooked dishes and a tangy citrus flavor takes over. It is particularly good in rice, potato salad, cheese spread, or salad dressing. Dry Lemon Thyme slowly at low temperature to preserve the lemon scent.

Other than the kitchen garden or dooryard garden confined to a narrow perimeter bed, the Lemon Thymes are useful only as a ground cover of limited size for rocky slopes or rock gardens or perhaps in an arrangement wrapped up in drifts of Creeping Thymes.

Mastic Thyme, *T. mastichina*, is a 10–16 in. shrub that has an atypical Thyme flower. It exhibits a very decorative, fuzzy, white inflorescence. Even on close inspection it is furry to the touch and creamy yellow. It would be more attractive, perhaps spectacular, if it had a flower color other than white, nevertheless it is an ornamental shrub with a pleasing spicy aroma. There is a faint citrus note that is apparently related to its cineole or linalool content. Distinct chemotypes are recognized. Its oil, called Spanish Marjoram Oil, is used in meat sauces and soup mixes. These are the identical uses of Mastic in the kitchen, along with Summer Savory and Sweet Marjoram, all of which influence one another positively. Combine Mastic Thyme with 'Krishna' Basil, Garlic, Black Pepper and Coriander for a superb spicy marinade mix (add to Cream Sherry and a teaspoon of Tarragon vinegar).

T. 'Broadleaf English', or English Thyme, is a shiny, dark green shrub with a very dense, attractive habit. It forms a 12–18 in. mound. Larger specimens have been reported but severe cold weather usually takes its toll on branch ends so that a heavy pruning is required every spring. The better, or more often, 'Broadleaf English' is trimmed the hardier it will be in cold areas.

'Broadleaf English' has a mild Thyme aroma with an herbaceous and spicy note like that of 'Oregano-scented' Thyme. It is not equivalent to French Thyme and in the kitchen it can be used where you would use French Thyme but a new flavor is the result. For heartily spiced sauces, meats, stuffings and dressings, 'Broadleaf English' does not leave a tangy aftertaste and can transform a beef gravy into something new.

A border of 'Broadleaf English' provides a striking green contrast in knots and parterres. Its glabrous (glossy) foliage truly outshines other herbs and is on par with Germander, Box, Myrtle, and Holly as a high gloss border. Light colored ground covers reinforce this effect. White sand, rock chips, or oyster shell are recommended.

A solid, neatly trimmed border is possible in warmer climates. Space plants about 12 in. and be sure to prune them heavily the first 2 years to ensure strong main branches. It is a rapidly growing but short-lived perennial herb, often no more than 5–6 years, before the unkempt, old age look sets in. Then the main branches droop and begin to root as the crown dies. Division is the best method to propagate 'Broadleaf English' Thyme as only female plants are known.

Propagation of Thyme by seed is a difficult matter because many of the choice cultivars do not produce seed true to type. Many bear only female flowers and if viable seed is recovered, it is from cross-pollinization. The cultivar will not win the battle of genetic codes. As a rule-of-thumb, in any cross-pollination the Thyme with the stronger thymol (French Thyme) scent will win. That does not mean all of the seed will be of that species, but likely to be the highest percentage and new cultivars and hybrids are always a possibility. Cuttings are therefore the most effective method of propagating Thyme as it ensures the identity of the herb and selection for superior traits can be done at a faster and more reliable rate.

The last Bush Thyme to be discussed is Garden Thyme, *T. vulgaris,* and its cultivars. Garden Thyme is highly polymorphic, that is showing considerable diversity. Most significant is its chemical diversity, which is evident in the herb's odor and flavor. The species has been divided into many chemical races (chemotypes and chemovars or cultivars) based on this chemistry. There are four chemical races of T. *vulgaris* cultivated by home gardeners: 'Narrow Leaf French' (thymol) with a warm, spicy aroma; 'Orange Balsam' (terpineol) with a fragrance of orange peels; 'Fragrantissimus' (geraniol) has the odor of the Rose Geranium; and 'Bittersweet' (carvacrol) with a Savory or "tar-like" odor. As many as seven distinct chemical races are recognized, although thymol is the main ingredient and is extracted for commercial use in pharmaceutical preparations, perfumes, and flavorings. Thymol is a mildly toxic chemical, and used as an antifungal agent in medicinals. Thymol has been shown to retard the growth of the virulent fungi *Fusarium, Verticillium* and *Botrytis.* This is undoubtedly the factor responsible for the observation that a decoction of French Thyme in water (plus a dollop of dish soap) sprinkled onto a seed flat prevents damp-off.

All of the *T. vulgaris* cultivars are essentially identical. Morphological variants include

Plate 11

The bright orange stigmas of Saffron are one of the world's most costly spices. This patch emerges from a bed of Black Mint that has already been pruned for the winter and mulched.

Masterwort, *Angelica atropurpurea,* in the center of a knot garden.

Looking into the Grey Garden at Fall City Herb Farm.

Sweet Bay sentinel in center of Shakespeare Garden, Fall City Herb Farm.

A fragrant respite in formal style. While the apples are in pre-pink stage Lovage, Sweet Cicely and Sweet Woodruff revel in the warm mid-spring sunshine conjuring their scents to entertain anyone whether seated or passing by. From the gardens of Fall City Herb Farm. (See Chapter 3, A Walk.)

Kitchen Garden replica of 17th century design. Foreground triangle contains Purple Cabbage. Triangle with Calendulas contains French Thyme, Orange Thyme and Sweet marjoram borders. Winter Savory, Borage and Lettuce share a triangle with pole beans in back and a hub of Chives is surrounded with Lemon Balm, Lemon Basil and Sweet Basil.

Plate 12

Formal checkerboard or "squares" arrangement of Medicinal Herb Garden, University of Washington, Seattle, WA.

Checkerboard garden design used extensively in monasteries during the Dark Ages. This four acre retreat is at the University of Washington and contains hundreds of medicinal and ornamental herbs. Reprinted by permission of Eric Hoyte.

Square of a single herb in a formal checkerboard design. Common Giant Fennel, *Ferula communis.* Medicinal Herb Garden, University of Washington, Seattle, WA.

Raised rectangular herb-stuffed bed of dooryard design.

Wild planted triangle of a kitchen garden includes pole beans in center, cucumbers ramble beneath, Southernwood at apex, Italian Parsley and Basil form the borders with self-sown Dill emerging here and there.

A path winds between squares in a formal design that forms a wild corner with tall herbs and small trees as a back border. Herbs in foreground are Sweet Fennel and Prickly Comfrey. Lovage rises behind. Medicinal Herb Garden, University of Washington, Seattle, WA.

Plate 13

fragrant patch of Chives in a raised bed.

Serpent Garlic or Rocambole shares its fascinating curves within a fragrant bed of Roses in a colorful border. St. Joseph's Church, Chehalis, WA.

cumber flavored Salad Burnet snuggles up to a Lady's Mantle
a colorful perennial bed in the garden of Michele Nash,
ercer Island, WA.

Russian Comfrey with an entourage of Chives in a square of a kitchen garden. This Comfrey has smaller, wrinkled leaves and prominent clusters of purple flowers for a more ornamental display than Common Comfrey.

Red flowering Comfrey. Beautiful crimson bells make this variety a valuable informal garden perennial herb.

Plate 14

A dooryard garden containing over one hundred species of herbs.

A low screen of Tansy (right), Wormwood (center) and Honesty.

Nurtured into a formal pose by the gate are two handsome patches of Fernleaf Tansy, each flanked by Chives. Also visible are white-flowering Garlic Chives (center). At Fall City Herb Farm.

Curly Parsley decorating a perimeter bed in dooryard garden.

Arrow-leaved Good King Henry in a perimeter bed displayed with early flowering perennial Primrose and Camas. Pansies and Poppies join the flowery fracas later.

A formal square of blooming Caraway in its second year is displayed at the Medicinal Herb Garden, University of Washington, Seattle, WA.

flat-topped mounds, compact bushes less than 10 in. high, and any combination in between. Leaf size, shape, and color will also vary. Of most importance to gardeners in cold climates is that hardiness will vary as well. It is imperative that gardeners purchase Thyme plants from an outdoor nursery that is located in a climate similar to their own. Care should always be used to propagate hardier cuttings each spring to improve the overall hardiness of the future crop.

'Narrow Leaf French' Thyme is a familiar and legendary herb. This is the French Thyme of culinary, medicinal, and ornamental value even today. Its warm, tangy or spicy aroma is one of the most exciting fragrances in the plant world. It is one of those herbs that embarrasses many a cook who is caught sniffing the spice bottle behind the kitchen door. Imagine now adding to its lingering scent an overtone of oranges or roses. They could be in your garden.

French and 'Orange Balsam' Thyme and less commonly, 'Fragrantissimus' are available from most herb growers. 'Bittersweet' is restricted to private collections. It should become available in the near future. All are available at plant sales sponsored by herb and rare plant or garden clubs.

For all practical purposes, *T. vulgaris* is not a formal border herb. Although it can be neatly trimmed, it has an unfortunate characteristic one would call middle-age spread. Both advanced age (3–6 yrs) and its propensity to survive cold winters at the expense of its crown cause a nice, symmetrical French Thyme to flatten out and eventually lose its central branches.

The death or drooping from old age of one or more plants in formal hedges causes unsightly gaps. Small groups of 3–4 plants nurtured as hedges in the vegetable garden or in containers make easy the task of repairing damage. In the event of diseased plants, remove those plants on either side of the dead one as well. Remove the soil and replace it with fresh. Depending upon the time of year new material is inserted, it will meld completely with the old hedge by fall. In any case, plants to be used as replacements should be root-pruned each spring and replanted to be sure they will survive when needed the most. As long as healthy plants are provided fertilizer (liquid) and sufficient water about ⅓ of the root ball can be removed without the need to prune foliage. In fact most woody herbs do better during and after transplanting if foliage is not pruned. Apparently there is some control of root growth that originates in the juvenile foliage and pruning may actually reduce transplant success. Research indicates that for best results plants should be watered 24 hours before transplanting, and uprooted and moved during the morning hours.

Thymes may be used to create fascinating informal borders that take advantage of a wide range of scents as well as distinct colors of foliage and flowers. Although all are quite fragrant, the Bush Thymes do need some stimulation or a high concentration of plants to be fragrant from afar. Using it as a frame enhances its ability to scent an area. Fragrant beds of Roses, Carnations, and many popular annuals enveloped by an informal or contemporary styled Thyme frame yield a generous amount of perfume at a distance. The Lemon, Orange, and French Thymes and richly scented Roses are excellent companions.

Thyme flowers must not be overlooked. They contribute significantly to the overall Thyme fragrance and color of the garden. Flower characteristics should be part of the original design plan. [Table 8, Flowering Periods for a Selection of Thymes may be used to select species for your Thyme feature in order to yield either a concurrent or continuous display of garden magic.]

It is also important to remember that trimmed plants are more commonly employed because the juvenile foliage has a more pleasant fragrance. One or two trims, once early in the spring and again after flowering is enough to keep Thyme healthy and youthful.

Table 8
Flowering Periods for a Selection of Thymes

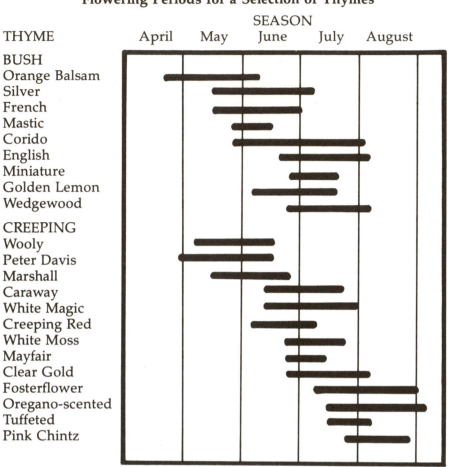

Of major importance to the Thyme grower is the care of the soil. It is one of the few herbs that is truly choosy. In colder climates, frost heave uproots small woody plants like Thyme, leaving the roots high and dry. This stress may cause death and surely encourage disease. In warmer climates, moisture can be fatal if lower branches rest too long on damp soil. Roots from branches that rest on the ground penetrate the soil some distance, anchoring the herb, awaiting the signal to begin a new life, as feeder roots. Excessive moisture here may cause their demise. Both conditions are recognizable when large inner branches wither and die after 2–3 years.

The solution is two-fold. First, Thyme enjoys a sandy or rocky soil, a soil composed of half sand and half garden soil of average richness. An addition of limestone chips or oyster shell is beneficial in areas of highly acidic soils, i.e., areas with high rainfall. Secondly, there must be a layer of inert material on the surface of the soil. A sand layer one inch deep 1) creates a quick drying surface that thwarts disease formation, and 2) inhibits frost action; if the plant is heaved upwards by frost the sand layer will protect the plant from being severely stressed by exposure. This sand layer significantly improves the chances of self-layering branches. Many will automatically root. With a moist sandy layer these branches form healthy root masses that are easily removed without damage and can be planted in the garden where they are to grow, rather than requiring nurturing for a month or more in a rich spot to develop a good root system.

The very nature of a formal or contemporary feature which often uses inert ground covers for balancing and accenting is a boon to the Thymes so they flourish there with little attention. Sand, oyster shell, pea gravel, or finely chipped rock materials are the recommended ground covers with Thyme. Avoid organic mulches, except perhaps in the driest areas. Where an organic soil conditioner is applied, dig it in, then apply to the soil surface an inorganic cover.

The Bush Thymes may be trimmed in spring or after flowering to as much as 50% of their height, or a light pruning amounting to less than 1 in. of material. In the formal setting heavily pruned hedges of Thyme will grow rapidly, requiring a light trim periodically to keep them neat. An informal, untrimmed hedge may only require removal of flower stalks and a light trim in the fall. Heavy pruning should not be done in late summer as insufficient time remains for the plant to put on a healthy protective canopy of evergreen foliage. Not just Thyme, but many woody evergreen herbs require a dense mound of foliage to protect their main branches and crown from extremely cold weather, and particularly from the desiccation of dry winter winds.

The Bush Thymes suggest many exciting possibilities in the formal garden. Their neat mounding and malleable forms are versatile for features commonly using evergreens such as conifers. Their resemblance is worth exploiting in arrangements where the larger conifers are paired with other highly ornamental cultivars and species of the Bush or Creeping Thymes. They are frequently paired with Winter Savory, its variety Pygmy, Dwarf Lavender, Dwarf Sage, Hyssop, the Santolinas and Germanders, Myrtle, Rue, and Miniature Roses. Yet these same combinations can be enjoyed in informal or wild garden rockeries, contemporary features, and in slender sun-baked borders in perennial beds. Other herbs for the miniature border or evergreen/herbaceous perennial bed that combine well with Bush Thymes are Bush Basil, Dwarf Feverfew, American Pennyroyal, *Origanum microphyllum*, 'Krishna' Basil, Chives and other low-growing Alliums, Fringed or Roman Wormwood, Silver Horehound, Indian Borage, or potted, dwarfed topiary and bonsai arrangements.

Some ornamental plants that are choice neighbors for Bush Thymes are *Sedum*, *Sempervivum*, 'Silver Mound' *Artemisia*, Cactus, Dwarf Snapdragons, Creeping Speedwell, ornamental grasses, Clove Pinks, Lotus, Birdsfoot Violet, and many mounding or tuffeted rockery and alpine plants. Examples of compact features include Golden Lemon Thyme in a sea of all-seasons Crocus for year round color, including clumps of Saffron for winter beauty, or among a field of isolated mounds of Forget Me Not, Lobelia, and Ageratums.

In the kitchen very little Thyme is needed to spice any dish, generally only ¼–½ tsp. of fresh or dried leaves is adequate. This is fortunate since very little is harvested from a single plant each year. One fully grown English Thyme, the largest of all, will yield about ½ c. of dried leaves. The microwave oven is perhaps the easiest method to dry Thyme. Set it on *defrost* and use 4–5, 3 minute bursts or until reasonably dry. If the flowers are included it dilutes the thymol aroma but is pleasant and sweetly aromatic.

Thyme is a spice that is included in a dish to make the nose twitch and the tongue tingle. It's exciting. There is no other word. It is not a spice to use alone so mix it with a sweet herb and a spicy one. Combinations recommended are: Thyme, Sweet Marjoram and Ginger; Thyme, Oregano and Orange Mint; or Thyme, Cumin and Bay. Tomato sauces, rice and gravies benefit from Thyme.

CHEESE SAUCE

1 c. grated cheddar or mozarella cheese	1 tsp. Honey
½ tsp. powdered Thyme	1 Tbsp. Butter
1 tsp. powdered Sweet Marjoram	¼ tsp. Ginger

Melt cheese slowly while stirring in herbs, honey and butter. Serve over your favorite steamed vegetable or biscuits.

An all-time favorite fragrant herb is Rosemary, *Rosmarinus officinalis.* It is one of the herbs most widely used by cooks as well as perfumers and decorators, yet grown in relatively few gardens. The neglect lies in the unwillingness of gardeners to nurture Rosemary in a container, as it is unfortunately a southern-minded herb. It is restricted to about Zone 7 with protection.

Rosemary is an exemplary performer as a fragrant border herb and should occupy a spot near a bench or chairs in a sheltered site in the landscape. It may also be situated adjacent to a patio door or frequently opened window where its luring scent can be appreciated on a hot sultry afternoon from a cool perch indoors. Its fragrance is best when at least four plants are used as a hedge in the landscape.

Many varieties and cultivars are available. From *R. officinalis* var. *officinalis* comes 'Logee Blue', 'Blue Spire' and 'Majorca', while forma *albiflorus* of this variety (often sold as 'Albus') is the only white-flowering Rosemary and one of the hardier forms.

The variety *angustifolius* gives us pine-scented Rosemary and 'Beneden Blue' as a cultivar, both of which are excellent for detailed topiary and bonsai. This variety includes forma *erectus* or upright Rosemary, with a narrow columnar habit suitable for container arrangements and topiary. This forma is frequently sold as 'Jessop's Upright' or 'Pyramidalis'.

The variety *rigidus* supplies the cultivar 'Tuscan Blue', an extremely hardy, handsome and fast growing Rosemary. From this variety comes forma *roseus,* including the delightful pink-flowered cultivars 'Majorca Pink' and 'Pinkie'. Although Rosemary's flowers are not its most spectacular attribute and add little to the overall fragrance, they are nevertheless charming.

Cultivars with an upright habit develop a denser, neater hedge while the open or pendulous forms (including the Prostrate Rosemarys discussed in Chapter 2) are useful for espaliered walls and borders. Any Rosemary may be supported by foundation walls (by wall nails, staples or ties), fences or trellises.

In the formal garden, a hedge of Rosemary is far more appealing when it is allowed to grow with only minimal trimming, providing a large boundary within the landscape. Its pendulous branches, waving dreamily in the breeze, soften the overall rigidity of a geometric design. The dark green Rosemarys are more effective as a background in designs where foliage colors are to be accented. 'Tuscan Blue', and white-flowering have the darkest green leaves.

There is no reason why Rosemary cannot be enjoyed in any ornamental garden: try it trimmed to exacting proportions among other pruned evergreens and conifers in the contemporary landscape; allow it to drape or hover over walks from a perch on a rock wall above; let it stand alone in stark, twisted habit on colored or raked gravels; use it to balance or accent forested backgrounds of Tamaracks, Pines and Firs; provide bold contrast to Bamboo or Rhododendrons; or nurture it into a playful accent in shrubbery borders of Tamarisk, Willow-leaf Pear, Everlasting, Heather and Lavender.

One way to enjoy its flowers is to use it potted or planted among the medicinals in a dooryard garden where the tiny blue flecks emerge continually during the cooler months where they can join a succession of other simple flowered herbs such as yellow-speckled Rue, snow-flecked Creeping Savory, and the blushing pinks of Wooly Betony and *Origanum microphyllum.*

In those regions where Rosemary is a container candidate only, the *standard* should be used in formal settings. Grown like a small tree resembling a lollipop, a single trunk supports a ball of neatly trimmed foliage on top. A Rosemary standard is made by staking a young start and removing lower branches in the fall until the desired trunk height is reached. The more upright forms of Rosemary should be chosen but because the standard may always need a stake for support, they are not mandatory. White-flowering, pine-scented, 'Tuscan blue', Upright and 'Majorca Pink' are good candidates.

When the desired trunk height is reached, branching is then encouraged. Initially, any new branches at that point are pruned back to a few inches to force more branching in order to form a dense cluster atop the trunk. Some lower branches may require tying down to form a more spherical shape if desired. The young standard is pruned heavily the first 2–3 years after the ball is formed on top. Once the desired shape is achieved, only a light trimming is needed to maintain a neat appearance throughout the year. Rosemary standards are choice formal plants, either in decorative pots or planted in the garden for the season, one on either side of a gate or standing as heralds at both ends of long beds of prize flowers.

If Rosemary, or any southern plant, is grown in a northern climate and is to be planted outdoors for the summer, there are a few steps that should be taken to protect them. Near the end of the season, but a safe period before the first frost, plants that are to be brought indoors must be uprooted, root pruned and potted, then left outdoors. As the first frost date approaches, the plant is moved to greenhouse or garage, then, if desired or necessary, weaned to the temperature of the home. Pots should be placed in large drain pans filled with gravel that is kept wet to ease the transition to a new temperature and humidity regimen.

Incana Santolina or Lavender Cotton, *Santolina chamaecyparissus*, is an accent herb used extensively in parterre and knot gardens as a frame or border and as a low hedge-like ground cover. Labeled "Incana" for its soft silvery foliage, it always provides a downy face to the world, while its cousin, *S. viridis*, always appears brilliantly green and shimmering in sunlight. Like Rosemary, Santolina's aroma is reminiscent of pine woods on a hot summer day.

Santolina forms a low hedge, from 8–24 in. depending on species and cultivar, and can be dense enough to support a book and a cup of tea, the ideal fragrant herb to rest and read beside. Excellent for topiary, Santolina borders may also be shaped into wave or zigzag patterns. The smaller compact cultivar, 'Pretty Carrol', may be shaped into nearly spherical bushes, spotlighting an area with fragrant silver balls. A number of cultivars are useful as cottony ground covers that need little maintenance. Trim and neat for accenting sun-drenched steps, patios and formal entrances, the low-growing cultivar 'Nana' is only a few inches high. It spreads slowly but is a tough herb. For less formal borders, Santolina must be allowed to ramble out of the garden onto walks and steps, sidle up a fence, poke through slats, or envelope a cul-de-sac and its reading bench.

Santolina chamaecyparissus can grow to 30 in. and is often used on steep hills or uneven slopes encircling formal designs. Lavender is often mixed into hillsides of Santolina. This combination of purple and gold flowers set off by light green-grey foliages, and announced from a distance by their fragrance, is an unforgettable experience.

S. viridis, the gleaming Green Santolina, should be mixed with its cottony cousins in a 1:3 or 1:4 ratio for contrast. This species should be used among flowering shrubs and evergreens that are in need of a contrasting ground cover. Camelias, bush Honeysuckles, Brooms, Heathers, and Eryngiums are particularly well suited growing on slopes surrounded by a shimmering green expanse of *S. viridis*. Together, they blanket the ground with a gently rolling surface resembling a calm sea. *S. viridis* is a hardy ornamental for austere arrangements in contemporary features accompanied by only creepers such as Sempervivum, Sedum or Thyme and colorful inert ground covers.

The names Incana and Lavender Cotton, by which Santolina is often referred, are old names alluding to the grey fuzzy appearance of *S. chamaecyparissus*—the species name refers to its cypress-like foliage. Perhaps more deserving of either name is *S. neapolitana*, whose white, feathery foliage almost resembles blue-green cotton-wool. *S. neapolitana* grows to 16 in., is less firm in texture and prone to damage, but significantly more ornamental. Display it beside Lady's Mantle, Geum, Coral Bells and the purple foliages of Red Japanese Maple and Opal Basil in informal beds.

As a formal hedge, Santolina requires patience, for it is a slow grower. It needs ample water during the summer and a rich loam to prevent damage from frost action and crown rot in winter. Santolina is not hardy below 0°F. so should be covered with fresh straw, pine boughs, or dry leaves during cold snaps below zero. In the first year, the plants should not be trimmed but allowed to spread. By the second or third year, plants separated by 12–15 in. will have grown together, so shaping and pruning are in order. For a Santolina hedge that has its back to a fence or masonry wall, prune the unseen side to encourage a dense growth of foliage and provide adequate spacing from the wall. The tops should be lightly pruned to keep it advancing with stronger wood and denser habit. In a sprawling informal border, Santolina may be grown with no trimming at all, aside from snipping away dying or damaged branches or flowers when they turn brown in the fall.

Santolina may be used as a repellent in linen closets and as a strewing herb, tossed to the floor to be trampled underfoot. Its pleasant pine scent is particularly useful in washwaters and as air freshening bouquets in the home. Bundles of Santolina, Southernwood, and Pennyroyal branches bound together and hung in doorways will provide a cool, clean odor for several weeks whenever brushed or shaken.

Santolina's curiously serrated foliage dries easily. The dried branches are often sprayed or dyed to use in wreaths. All the Santolinas contribute a late summer treat of countless, yellow, button flowers that bob on slender stems several inches above the foliage. They are in the form of a firm dense "button" that has been popular for decorative uses for many centuries. The Incana Santolinas all produce a yellow to dark yellow "button" that adorns the silvery bushes for up to 3 months, through mid-summer into late fall. The flowers of *S. viridis* are lemon-yellow and flower production is prolific. These larger buttons on long, lax stems are quite showy. Flowers are cut and dried, then painted or left a natural yellow-brown, if picked early, and dark brown or black if left on plants until winter, for use in ornamental arrangements with other dried herbs and flowers.

Hyssop, *Hyssopus officinalis,* has been foremost on the list of strewing herbs since man discovered it. Hyssop, Greek for aromatic, has a sharp camphoraceous fragrance, most pleasant when the herb is kept trimmed. Ever popular for the formal hedge, Hyssop is a versatile herb for minute detail in knot and parterre designs. Long borders with a generous amount of Hyssop become highly fragrant plantings, particularly when allowed to bloom. A mixture of Hyssop and Thyme in a hedge within a tidy knot garden yields a rich and delectable aroma. Excellent combinations include Hyssop and a selection of Thymes such as Moroccan, 'Orange Balsam', Golden Lemon or Silver.

Hyssop's willingness to be pruned down to 6 in. and its hardiness in poor soils make it a choice material for topiary and manicured borders. The small 12–18 in. bushes need continuous trimming, however, or they become unkempt. A variety sometimes called Dwarf Hyssop, is smaller, growing to only 10–12 in., more compact and superior for detail in parterres and knots.

Hyssop may self-sow. Plants from seed bloom by the second year. Cuttings will bloom the same year. The flowers are deep blue, pink and white. The blue flowers are nothing clever and unless Hyssop is grown for culinary uses or as a flowering ornamental, they should be trimmed off for a neater appearance. The pink, 'Rosea', red, 'Rubra' and white, 'Alba' and 'Grandiflora', cultivars are dense and showy, however, and highly recommended. Informal and wild gardens display the white and pink forms best and drifts of all three, within a carpet of flowering annuals, creates a parade of color in summer and a warm evergreen expanse in winter. Golden Hyssop, with golden speckles, is an interesting feature.

Only in the last several centuries has Hyssop been a popular topiary herb. It has been, however, a medicinal plant, a culinary spice, a disinfecting and deodorizing wash water and a strewing herb. The pine fragrance of blue Hyssop is due to the chemical pinene, which is a constituent of, and has an odor resembling, turpentine. There is also a sharp lemony note due to terpenes in young foliage. The young tops and flowers are picked and dried, then sprinkled onto fresh hot bread with sweet butter, on toast with honey, over salads, and for smoking beef or pork on the barbeque. Other varieties and cultivars do not have as remarkable a fragrance as blue Hyssop for most uses.

Southernwood, Old Man, or Lad's Love, *Artemisia abrotanum,* is a popular landscape herb today because it is hardy, has a light green foliage, and a sweet citrus and camphor scent. Southernwood cultivars include 'Tangerine', 'Lemon' and 'Camphor', each alluding to the scent of the foliage. The familiar Wormwood-like fragrance of Southernwood is a result of thujone, but the sweet aromatic notes that are dominant are variously from borneol and camphor (Camphor Southernwood). Also present is the camomile scent of azulene and the floral aroma of farnesol.

A near relative to Wormwood, but with a sweeter fragrance and more finely divided foliage, Southernwood grows in a 3–5 ft. upright mound. In the landscape, its wispy ever-green foliage is a special treat as an excellent light colored background for dark-hued flowers, particularly blues and purples. Because the height of Old Man can be maintained from 18 in. up by pruning, either a middle or low range contrasting border is possible. Southernwood lends itself to further use because it has no soil preferences, therefore, is easily mixed and matched with more temperamental ornamentals.

Southernwood's soft green cast makes it an excellent *transition herb,* used to begin and end plantings, to identify groupings within larger designs, or inserted periodically into borders to provide relief from monotonously long borders of widely mixed species. It is flowerless only in far northern latitudes, otherwise producing a standard artemisia bloom of yellow-green, rayless flowers in late summer that is delightfully fragrant and invaluable for weaving into scented baskets and wreaths.

In mild climates, Southernwood should be pruned heavily 2–3 times a year to encourage new growth and stronger branches. In northern climes, where temperatures fall below 0°F, Southernwood should be pruned to 6–8 in. in late fall. This insures a dormant period. Southernwood allowed to grow through moderate winters may not recover well from a late winter or early spring cold snap.

Cultivated as a trim hedge in formal gardens, Southernwood should be kept pruned to a dense smooth appearance, which is easily accomplished with constant light top pruning. Figure 8 is an example using Southernwood as a central feature of a simple formal garden. The borders here are pruned to 30 in. and adjoin narrow low borders along the inside edge of the turf runway. Easily sown fragrant annuals, Opal Basil, Sweet Basil, Mignonette and spring and fall bulbs are suggested companions. Large ornate containers with dazzling flower arrangements open and close this feature.

Southernwood can be substituted for conifer evergreens or join them in many arrangements, their fir-like habit pleasing as an accent or contrast. This dual role as ever-green and fragrant ornamental makes it a superb herb for the contemporary landscape. Give it the center stage cast against a weeping Hemlock or dwarf Spruce, an assortment of Creeping Thymes and Birdsfoot or Trailing Violets. For an informal or wild setting let its un-trimmed long, pendulous, bottle-brush branches droop onto a surrounding ground cover of Pineapple or Ginger Mint, Lawn Camomile or Dwarf Monarda in partial shade, or in the sun, looking over a miniature look-alike, 'Silver Mound' Artemisia or *Santolina neapolitana.*

Old Man's fragrance has guaranteed it a place in every bouquet and nosegay for centuries. Easily dried, it may be used in fragrant wreaths and bouquets. Old Man is an excellent hot-tub herb and sachet for bathing water, especially when combined with Pineaple Mint and Costmary. Southernwood has been used for thousands of years as a smoking wood for preserving and flavoring meats such as lamb and veal. Branch shavings or trimmings may be mixed with a little grated or dried orange or lemon peel and tossed onto hot coals of a barbeque brazier to add a delicate flavor to anything from veal chops to hamburgers.

Garden Rue, *Ruta graveolens,* may someday prove to be an effective medicine, as it has been touted for over two-thousand years, but its disagreeable taste and foul odor will not endear it to many gardeners. Color and shape are its virtues today. Its diminutive knobby foliage is a charming addition in the garden and in dried arrangements.

Garden Rue, the Herb-of-Grace, has enjoyed a reputation as an analgesic, repellent, counterpoison, ward against witches and evil magic, and an effective repellent of insects. Rue, as a strewing herb or in wash water, thwarts the onslaught of fleas brought into the home by pets. Diluted in water, Rue's odor becomes sweet. This strange chemistry comes about because one of Rue's constituents is methylanthranilate, one of the secret constituents responsible for Jasmine's alluring character. This chemical is detected by our noses even in extremely small concentrations, so while the less pleasing methylnonyl ketone, an almost fishy scented chemical, is diluted out, the rich floral scent of Jasmine flirts with our nose just at the limit of detectability.

Rue is an evergreen perennial best used as a contrasting foliage in a grey garden, or as a medium border behind colorful flowers. *Ruta graveolens* provides a blue-green foliage. The cultivar, 'Curly Girl', has a blue foliage. A variegated form, 'Variegatus', yields a white or yellow or light blue-green, while Fringed Rue, or *Ruta chalapensis,* provides a change in leaf texture, with a teardrop shape instead of round leaf. Graced throughout the summer and fall with dazzling yellow flowers, Rue's ½ in. propellor-like flowers are borne on long cymes, and may be trimmed for a neater appearance.

Growing from 18–36 in., depending on cultivar and species, Rue should be grown in spots protected from heavy rains and wind, which cause its semi-woody branches to droop. Branches can be tethered to one another from within, so as not to be noticeable, to prevent branches from falling to the ground. Although Rue is evergreen, extended sub-zero weather will burn it. It is a very slow-growing herb from seed or cuttings, taking 2 years or more to establish itself. Afterward, it may be heavily trimmed each spring and fall and still return to full height by mid-summer. Branches will become woodier and sturdier if they are left unpruned, but foliage becomes thin. Fall pruning in colder climates and late winter pruning in warm climates is recommended.

As a frame for small gardens, Rue may be pruned to less than 12 in., and as a border for formal landscapes it should be cut back to 6 in. from the ground each spring to encourage regrowth for a denser hedge. Rue is an excellent herb for the bonsai enthusiast. The branches on old, heavily pruned plants become gnarled and thick set, with little knots of misty blue foliage starting up from the oddest places. Small standards of Rue are delicate and pleasing to the eye and often used in parterres with other topiary, mounded or hemispherically trimmed herbs. Rue has also been used to form animals and other caricatures.

Rue's evergreen habit lets it mix with conifers in winter gardens. Winter gardens generally combine evergreen and herbaceous perennials or annuals for a total metamorphosis throughout each season. Evergreens ensure a winter season garden. The bluish hue of Rue is best paired with dark green Salad Burnet and Incana Santolina for a small evergreen contemporary garden. Dwarf Sage, Dwarf Lavender, Germander and Dwarf Myrtle are several companions for Rue in a formal knot or mixed border in an informal landscape. The rugged features of an old Rue, its leaves no longer covering all its branches, makes a beautiful specimen plant in a rock garden or rocky area in any landscape.

Although Germander, *Teucrium chamaedrys,* had been a vital component in electuaries (antidotes), its greatest claim to fame was its rediscovery as the perfect minihedge during the horticultural renaissance in Northern Europe during the 16th and 17th centuries. The search for hardy, slow-growing dwarf or compact evergreens was narrowed to only a few herbs, Rosemary, Lavender, Hyssop, Santolina and Box. When the Germanders were discovered, *T. chamaedrys* and a dwarf form, *T. chamaedrys* v. *prostratus,* half the size of the species, soon became the most popular.

Chamaedrys in Greek means "at the ground", indicating a low-growing or dwarf plant. Its glossy, evergreen leaves and dense habit make it a choice knot herb. It does require mulching in cold climates. A blanket of dry straw and conifer boughs can be used in areas with sub-freezing winds, which tend to desiccate Germander's thick succulent leaves. The Germander hedge has no equal. To some extent its thick, glossy, dark green leaves give it an almost plastic appearance, for a bright and distinct border. It is easily trimmed and propagated and has virtually no pests. Hedges as low as 6 in. are possible, yet even at its fullest height, as much as 24 in., Germander keeps its dense habit. The dwarf form is less manageable because of its procumbent habit, but it too exhibits dense growth for a shiny green mat only a few inches high. Dwarf Germander is not suitable for areas with foot traffic. The best application of Germander is in the mixed evergreen border in formal and informal gardens or with other evergreens in contemporary designs and to brighten for a dull lifeless corner with Creeping Red Thyme, *Cerastium tomentosum,* and Roman Camomile.

T. chamaedrys is essentially odorless, on rare occasion being sour or herbaceous smelling. Any scented Germander is likely to be *T. canadense,* American Germander, or Wood Sage, which may become a 3 ft. shrub, and has much larger, light green leaves, with hoary undersides. It, too, may be cultivated at only a fraction of its natural height for a superb hedge. Another fragrant Germander is *T. massiliense,* which grows to 12 in., with showy grey tomentose leaves and pink flowers. The fragrance of both is somewhat floral or vanilla-like, frequently with a sour note.

Other Germanders include *T. pyreniacum,* a flowering ornamental and herbaceous perennial with glabrous, green leaves and flower spikes of white and purple to 8 in. *T. fruiticans,* Tree Germander, is often sold as Silver Germander. It is a large shrub. Its thick green leaves have downy undersides, partially downy above, and very heavily downed stems. The overall appearance is a silvery green compact shrub of sparkling beauty that is further enhanced by large sky-blue flowers with exceptionally long and delicate stamens. *T. flavum* has thick, leathery, green leaves and yellow flowers. It forms an 18–24 in. firm, compact mound when grown in rockeries and on poor sandy or rocky soil. *T. marum,* Cat Thyme, forms a 12 in. dense mound of soft, downy, light blue-green leaves and huge 1–2 in. purple flowers for an extra treat on this very handsome compact Germander. *T. scorodonia,* Wood Sage or Wood Germander, is a hardy, 1 ft. tall rhizomatous shrub with dark green leaves that are rugose (wrinkled and pitted like Garden Sage). Wood Sage bears a profusion of bright yellow flowers with long delicate exerted stamens. Also called Garlic Sage, it has a pleasant camphoraceous odor and has been used as flavoring in ale. *T. polium* has been referred to as Golden Germander because of the thick, golden hairs covering the stems of some plants. It has slim, dark green leaves and white or red flowers. The stem hairs may also be white or light green. From a distance, this Germander takes on a two-tone color from the leaves and the fuzzy golden or white stems. *T. montanum* looks somewhat like a creeping Rosemary. Its 12 in. branches spread laterally over the ground to form a low mat that is moderately effective as a ground cover in high traffic areas. Its best use is in rockeries or along paths bordered by a rock wall, growing where the wall meets the pavement. Its cream colored flowers are not spectacular. *T. aroanium* is similar to *T. montanum,* forming a dense, very desirable ground cover as a procumbent shrub up to 8 in. high, but spreading by tip-rooting. Its dark green leaves have densely wooly undersides and somewhat so above. These tiny hairs capture the dew and give it the shimmering appearance in the morning sun.

Water is an important element in formal gardens and often the main feature. The pond was a vital component of any homesite in the past as a source of irrigation water for gardens. A spring or well was joined with a small dipping pool beside it as either a stone-walled reservoir or a mud-bottomed depression. The latter, called mint pools, were common in monasteries. They were large enough for raising fish as well as many aquatic herbs, the most valuable of which were the Mints; Water Mint, *Mentha aquatica;* Spearmint, *M. spicata,* and others.

Herbs easily cultivated in ponds and streams include *Veronica beccabunga;* Water Eryngo, *Eryngium aquatica;* Water cress, *Nasturtium officinale;* Pond lily, *Nymphaea odorata;* and the Water Lotus, *Nolumbo.* On the banks or in moist soils near seeping pools, many other herbs may be grown. In the shade try Cuckoopint, *Arum maculatum;* Blood Root, *Sanguinaria canadensis;* Columbine, *Aquilegia;* Colt's Foot, *Tussilago farfara;* Goldenseal, *Hydrastis;* Jack-in-the-Pulpit, *Arisaema triphylum;* Lady's Mantle, *Alchemilla;* and the Maidenhair fern, *Adiantum.* In sunny spots grow the Marshmallow, *Althea officinalis;* Asparagus; Dragonwort, *Polygonum bistortoides;* Blazing Star, *Lyatris spicata;* Boneset, *Eupatorium perfoliatum;* Bryony, *Bryonia alba;* Great Burnet, *Sanguisorba;* Dropwort and Meadow sweet, *Filipendula* spp; Nasturtiums, *Tropaeoleum majus;* the Pitcher plants, *Saraccenia;* Pokeweed, *Phytolacca;* Horsetail, *Equisetum;* Cattail, *Thyphus;* and Marsh Marigolds, *Caltha palustris.* Some popular culinary herbs that prefer damp soils near ponds include Lemon Balm, Chervil, Catnip, Burnet, Lovage, Mints, Monarda, Sweet Cicely, Angelica, and Sweet Flag. In this chapter we will discuss the last two, Angelica and Sweet Flag.

Angelica archangelica is a water-loving herbaceous biennial, though often perennial, growing in lush, tropical-looking clumps. With its roots near a plentiful source of water Angelica may be grown in a sunny spot, though it grows best in partial shade in moist soils. In the formal setting, a clump of Angelica should join mahogany or purple flowering Monarda and huge scarlet and yellow poppies near a pond's edge. The same clump will appear less formal when arranged with cattails, yellow iris, and the Marsh Marigold, all with their feet in a few inches of water.

A handsome formal setting for Angelica in the absence of water is a clump of 3–5 plants set in a circle within a surrounding ring of Lavender. In its fall colors, and especially in its waning days during the summer of its second year, Angelica's satiny, yellow leaves are a beautiful and delicate display against the grey-green Lavenders with their deep purple flower spikes. This feature should be one of the four squares of a "quad", a cloister garden arrangement discussed in Chapter 4.

Angelica frequented the ponds of medieval gardens, grown as a ward against evil. "Angelica, that happy counterbane", Du Bartas wrote in 1641, was an invaluable antidote to poisons and magic. A medicinal salve called Eau de Arquebusade, developed in the 16th century, included Angelica tops and seed mixed with Mint, Wormwood, and the oils of Rosemary and Juniper. Friar's Balsam and Balsam Traumatic are two medicinal salves made with Angelica for use as wound antiseptics. The bitter, herbaceous fragrance of Angelica is due in part to phellandrene and archangelicin (an isomer of coumarin).

Other uses of Angelica include candies made by boiling the seeds, roots, and young stems in thick sugar syrup until they become translucent. They are rolled in powdered or colored sugar crystals and stored. The flowering umbels are used in decorations.

Other species of Angelica are found wild in many parts of the northern hemisphere. *A. atropurpurea,* Purple Angelica or Masterwort, has purple-tinged stalks and dark green leaves for a more glamorous look, and *A. sylvestris,* American or Wood Angelica, is a taller species with enormous umbels and is a very hardy perennial. An Asian species, *A.*

polymorpha var. *sinensis,* is a powerful medicinal called Dong Quai and used as a laxative, stimulant and tonic for menstrual cramps.

The biennial nature of Angelica, an *Umbelliferae,* is variable so *A. archangelica* clumps may survive in moderate climates for several years. Removal of umbels improves the chances of survival, but robs the landscape of a very beautiful and delicate globe of seeds from 4–8 in. in diameter. Angelica self-sows readily in moist soils. The seeds, dropped from June to July, will germinate that season and by fall, become a healthy plant. It is recommended that self-sown plants be allowed to remain in a seed bed and transplanted in early spring as the viability of Angelica seed is extremely limited. Fresh frozen seed should be used if at all possible, since spring germination of last year's seed is very poor.

Sweet Flag, *Acorus calamus,* is another herb that is candied. Slices of the peeled spicy root are treated in the same manner as Angelica, providing a gingery treat once called Shaker Candy. The Iris-like leaves smell faintly of lemons and have been a popular strewing herb for centuries, and a refreshing fragrant weaving material for baskets, wreaths and door mats.

Both the leaves and the roots of Sweet Flag contain camphene, pinene, and eugenol, which contribute some of the spicy fragrance. A chemical asarone, also found in the roots of Wild Ginger, gives the sweet, spicy taste so prized in the root of both of these herbs. Extracts containing asarone are called Asarabaca Camphor.

Sweet Flag is different from the Flags of the *Iris* genus in that its flower is a cigar-like object, similar to the Cattail but jutting out from halfway up the plant at an angle like a rude pointing finger. In partial shade *Acorus* will do well in moist garden soil. In the sun, it must have its roots in a shallow pond. *Acorus calamus* includes two forms: a cultivar, 'Variegatus', with yellow-striped leaves, and, *Acorus c.* var. *angustifolius,* with thin, grassy leaves. Another species, *A. gramineus,* or Grassy-leaved Sweet Flag, has three cultivars, a dwarf form, 'Pusillus', which is commonly used in terrariums and only a few inches high, and two white-striped cultivars, 'Alba Variegatus' and 'Variegatus'.

Heralding in the New Year with yellow, orange, purple, and scarlet are two wondrous herbs, the rare and precious Saffron, peeking through a light snow cover, and high above it and us is Witch Hazel. Both are fragrant herbs though their scent is so fleeting one would scarcely notice save for a vast carpet of one and a copse of the other. These two herbs frequent the winter garden, formal or otherwise, joining evergreens and other winter-blooming shrubbery.

Crocus sativus, the Saffron Crocus, is a type of Winter Crocus. Saffron's lily-like flowers of lavender or purple are adorned with striking orange or crimson stigmas that emerge late fall to mid-winter. They vanish after lasting only a day or two, leaving a grassy tuft that remains throughout winter, disappearing just before summer. "Gems and incense bow before them" exclaimed Fortunatus, bishop of Portiers, circa. A.D. 565.

Grown for garden color and fragrance, Saffron is best in a garden where it is planted with an evergreen or other ground cover of 2–4 in. in height. It requires a sandy soil and full sun. Areas partially shaded by deciduous trees in summer may be equally suitable where Saffron may share a spot with Wild Ginger or Violets. In the landscape the rich, herbaceous odor of Saffron, classified as "ambrosaic", can only be sensed from mass plantings within the bounds of a windbreak and adjacent to a sun-warmed path. Such is needed to deflect chilly winter winds that rob the little crocus of its perfume.

In a formal landscape, Saffron is planted in a quantity large enough for its fragrance to be enjoyed. One or two dozen is a good culinary supply, but for perfume, a gardener needs borders 30 ft. or more long and 1 ft. wide, hemmed in by evergreens, such as the inner border along Southernwood in Figure 8. Annual herbs may be grown along the same swath the remainder of the year.

Saffron requires dividing every 3–4 years or blooming will be adversely affected. The plants are lifted in the spring when foliage has died back. The corms are divided, held in a cool dry spot for several weeks, and then replanted. They will bloom again by late fall or mid-winter.

Saffron has been a highly priced commodity for centuries. Though it has lost its appeal of late and Calendula and Safflower petals are substituted for it in commerce, in the past it was protected by rigid laws. Stealing Saffron, a vital export, resulted in death. Early in the 16th century it was spirited away from the Mideast to England by a clever and opportunistic pilgrim. He had hidden a small corm in the hollow handle of his staff. Two centuries of a highly profitable Saffron market followed, with England producing some of the finest Saffron available in Northern Europe.

Rich, golden soups and sunny, yellow breads are the reward for harvesting the bright orange and scarlet stigmas of the Saffron flower. One has to be quick—before rain and wind destroy them. Three stigmas per flower is all the harvester may expect. This is a sufficient amount of Saffron for recipes calling for a yellow hue in foods such as puddings, gravies, cheeses, yogurt and sauces.

The major constituents of Saffron are crocin and picrocrocin, both yellow-red dyes. The term picro means "bitter". The unique spicyness of Saffron is, therefore, best enjoyed by combining it, powdered, with honey, then eaten as a spread or dried and crumbled and used as sunny sprinkles on desserts and salads. Saffron has been employed as a dye for robes, scarves, and other linen. A fragrant, golden ink is easily made by mixing powdered Saffron and egg white.

GOLDEN GARBANZO SOUP

1 can Garbanzo beans
Boullion (chicken) or stock
1 c. chopped ham
1 chopped green pepper
2 Tbsp. butter
½ tsp. Saffron "threads"
2 tsp. Lovage
¼ c. chopped Chives
1 tsp. Fennel
¼ tsp. Savory

Simmer for ½ hour.

—Millie Adams

The other winter-blooming herb, Witch Hazel, *Hamamelis virginiana,* is a large, hardy shrub, growing to 30 ft. in the wild, but cultivars generally grow less than 15–20 ft. in the garden. It is a shade-tolerant shrub, growing best as an understory plant in hardwood copses. The fragrant flowers of Witch Hazel are a rare treat, blooming during the coldest, darkest days of the year, from mid-December to the end of February. The profusion of ragged, strap-shaped, yellow flowers appear to be purposefully decorating a leafless tree. Highly fragrant when in bloom, it is a centerpiece for the winter garden surrounded, perhaps, by a low ground cover of evergreen Wild Ginger, Hellebore, Sweet Woodruff, Saffron, and other fall Crocus, for an open woods effect. A waist-high ground cover of Sword fern, Sweet Cicely, Rhododendrons, and for summer color, Lilies, gives an ancient virgin world atmosphere.

In the formal landscape, Witch Hazel is included in the borders of flowering shrubs and trees. As a large shrub it is on par with many dwarf flowering trees. It is also placed in high visibility locations in groupings, such as the end of a long path against a background of evergreens. Several other species and cultivars are available and superior to American Witch Hazel, *H. virginiana*: Chinese Witch Hazel, *H. mollis*, with bright yellow, highly fragrant flowers whose foliage turns deep yellow in autumn; *H. mollis* 'Pallida', exhibits crowded clusters of ocher-yellow flowers; Japanese Witch Hazel, *H. japonica*, with greenish yellow flowers; *H. × intermedia*, 'Arnold's Promise', a cross between *H. mollis* and *H. japonica*, sports 1½ in. dark yellow flowers; the cultivar 'Diana', of the same cross, produces a generous cluster of red flowers from early February on. This cultivar has a yellow and red autumn foliage of exquisite beauty. *H. vernallis* responds to warm spells, blooming much earlier in the South and Pacific Northwest, with light yellow flowers. This species is the smallest of the Witch Hazels, growing to only 6 ft., and useful pruned into a formal hedge or screen. *H. virginiana* is frequently used as the root stock upon which other species are grafted for hardier, fast-growing characteristics.

The bark of, and less often, the leaves, of Witch Hazel are used today medicinally as an astringent for topical relief of inflammation from insect bites, bruises, and muscle ache. One of the active components is gallic acid. Pond's Extract of Witch Hazel is still widely used for minor aches and pains.

Chapter 3 / SECTION 3

A Walk
Through a Formal Garden

The garden through which we are going to stroll is formal. Had we never seen a formal garden, the landscape before us would momentarily baffle our senses. (Fig. 28)

Thematic is a safe description of this grand garden. Its formality is based on a geometric design popular several centuries ago. Yet, in some way it still reflects the basic sensibilities of contemporary design. It compartmentalizes the landscape by "functions" and ministers to each with a thematic garden. The theme here is herbs, the place, Fall City Herb Farm. In it is a richly herbed patch divided into a quad. A wide fragrant median of Creeping Thyme separates the halves and allows for better viewing of each quarter. Entertainment may be the rule in contemporary landscaping, the feature garden rendered superficial, but this garden is simply an exciting and extravagant garden adventure. It is, then, undoubtedly formal.

KEY 1 Rosemary *Rosmarinus officinalis* 'Tuscan Blue'
2 Scented Geranium *Pelargonium limoneum*
3 Apple *Malus* sp.
4 Southernwood *Artemisia abrotanum*
5 Fern Leaf Tansy *Tanacetum vulgare* 'Crispum'
6 Valerian *Valeriana officinalis*
7 Lovage *Levisticum officinale*
8 Sweet Cicely *Myrrhis odorata*
9 Sweet Woodruff *Gallium odorata*
10 Red flowering Comfrey *Symphytum officinalis* 'Coccineum'
11 Rose Campion *Dianthus caryophyllus*
12 Wooly Betony *Stachys byzantina*
13 Dwarf Catnip *Nepeta mussinii*
14 Lavender *Lavandula angustifolia*
15 *Santolina chamaecyparissus*
16 *Eryngium* Sea Holly
17 Dwarf Carnation *Dianthus*
18 Yarrow *Achillea clypeolata*
19 Roman Wormwood *Artemisia arborescens*
20 Beach Wormwood *Artemisia stellerana*
21 Dwarf Sage *Salvia officinalis* 'Nana'
22 Silver Sage *Salvia argentea*
23 Bed straw *Gallium verum*
24 St. John's Wort *Hypericum*
25 Safflower *Carthamus tinctorius*
26 *Coreopsis*
27 Woad *Isatis tinctoria*
28 Cornflower *Centaurea cyanus*
29 Dyer's Camomile *Anthemis tinctoria*
30 Lady's Mantle *Alchemilla vulgaris*

31 Saffron *Crocus sativa*
32 White Moss Thyme *Thymus praecox* ssp. *articus* 'White M
33 Cr. White Thyme *Thymus pulegioides* 'Foster flower'
34 Golden Lemon Thyme *Thymus* × *citriodorus* 'Aureus'
35 Cr. Red Thyme *Thymus pulegioides* 'Kermesinus'
36 Wooly Thyme *Thymus praecox* ssp. *articus* 'Languinosus'
37 French Thyme *Thymus vulgaris*
38 English Thyme *Thymus* 'Broadleaf English'
39 Dill *Anethum graveolens*
40 Summer Savory *Satureja hortensis*
41 Winter Savory *Satureja montana*
42 Sweet Basil *Ocimum basilicum*
43 Coriander *Coriandrum sativum*
44 Sage *Salvia officinalis*
45 Leeks *Allium porrum*
46 Tarragon *Artemisia dracunculus* 'Sativa'
47 Good King Henry *Chenopodium bonus-henricus*
48 Bible Leaf *Balsamita major*
49 Sweet Marjoram *Origanum majorana*
50 Rosemary *Rosmarinus officinalis*
51 Garlic *Allium sativum*
52 Poppies *Papaver orientale*
53 Wormwood *Artemisia absinthum*
54 Calendula *Calendula officinalis*
55 Rue *Ruta graveolens*
56 Lemon Balm *Melissa officinalis*
57 Pansy *Viola tricolor*
58 Sweet Bay *Laurus nobilis*
59 COTTAGE GARDEN, flowers
60 KITCHEN GARDEN, herber

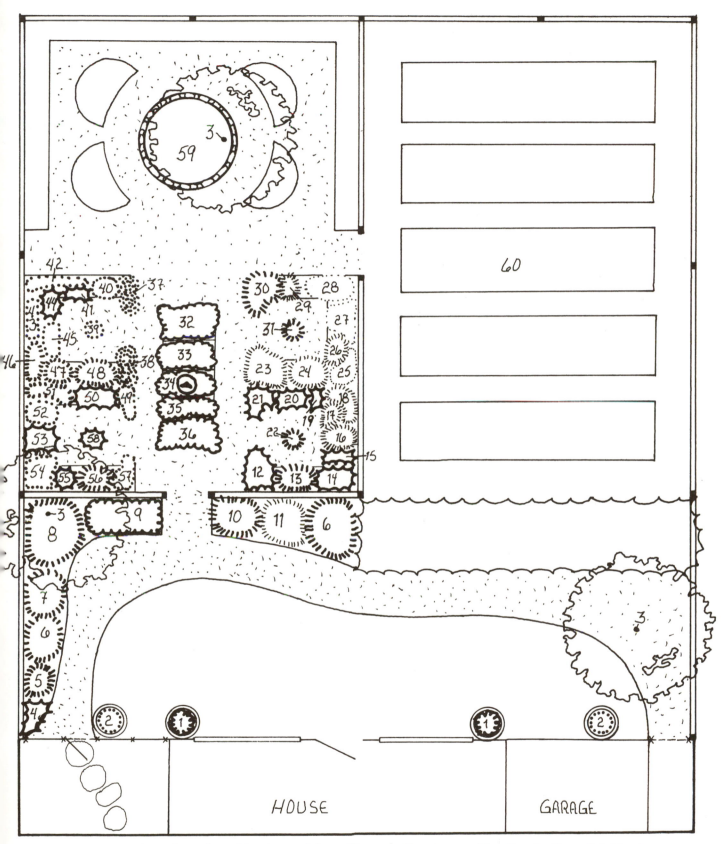

Fig. 28. Today's formal yard landscaped for utility as well as beauty. The Quad of beneficial herbs follows a Walk through a Formal Garden. Adapted from gardens of Fall City Herb Farm, Fall City, WA.

The medieval or monastic formal gardens were not only beneficial but beautiful. Yet they provided something else: instruction. Arrangements of herbs were lessons in art and nature. Some designs reflected botanical compatibilities and plant requirements, others human needs and desires: medicinals, foods, dyes, and scents. The garden we are touring offers five lessons: Grey Herbs, Dye Herbs, Kitchen Herbs, Shakesperean Herbs, and Creeping Thymes.

As we enter the garden the aromas of 2½ score of herbs enrich our understanding of the lives of our ancestors as well as our views of man's most precious plants. Now we are faced with a choice. As we decide which garden is to be our first lesson, we feel as if we are experiencing our birthday or Christmas. We are surrounded by 5 packages, each gaily wrapped with fragrant and colorful foliages, packages of common herbs, in a scheme so intriguing we are helpless to do anything but enter and learn.

Our first choice is the shimmering world of the Grey Garden. It is a monument to nature's unique talent for outfitting her herbs to survive both summer's dog days and the frigid madness of a mountain side. Tiny hairs, the "tomentose" or fuzzy coat that makes leaves grey, forestall the effects of dessication by the vicious claws of either heat or cold. All we care on the other hand is to be allowed to stoop and pet them, to feel their silvery fur. Most impressive is the concierge at the entrance of this garden, the huge and comical Lamb's Ears. By night, they become the downy beds for sprites and faeries. And lo, if you dry enough of them, a fine fragrant pillow stuffing this Wooly Betony will make.

Grey-green mounds of Dwarf Catnip studded with royal blue flowers sprawl beside the Betony. Our inquisitive fingers tell us how soft they are despite their rugose appearance. That fragrance! That is not ordinary Catnip. The strong clove odor is overwhelming and our imagination scrambles to redesign our own garden with a border of this herb.

In the very center of this quarter stands a lone sentinel of Silver Sage, *Salvia argenteus*. Like Clary Sage its mucilaginous seeds are used in eye preparations. Ornamentally, it has an oooh-provoking, silvery-furred rosette of leaves that we gladly fall to our knees before to stroke and fondle.

Like Jekyll and Hyde, a gentlemanly old Lavender, and a gnarled and twisted Incana Santolina stand side-by-side. The pale grey foliage of the latter and the grey-green of the Lavender are an apt backdrop for the purple and blue wands of the fragrant Lavender flowers and the ochre, malodorous buttons of the Santolina. They are inseparable and in many formal gardens their combined ornamental nature is relied upon to create a fragrant and colorful garden hedge.

Tucked between a troupe of Clove Pinks and Gilliflowers, *Dianthus caryophyllus* 'Dwarf' and *D. × allwoodii* (crosses of the old fashioned garden Pinks and perpetual flowering Carnations) are the misty blue and silver flowers of Sea Holly looking like spiral-armed galaxies dashing willy-nilly through the heavens. The Gilliflowers are dazzling neighbors in crimson and hot pink and with a fragrance as thrilling as a spice shop. Hidden behind are the grey, feathered branches from which arise several bright yellow flowers of Yarrow, *Achillea clypeolata*. These laybys for bees shine forth from the background like huge, gold doubloons hidden in this silver-stuffed treasure chest.

Two ornamental Artemisias, Fringed Wormwood and Beach Wormwood, are strange but wonderful tokens of nature's idiosyncratic leaf design. The first are like fern fronds and sea green, the latter dead-ringers for oak leaves of downy white. As we pass out of the Garden of Greys, hundreds of slim grey-green lancettes of Dwarf Sage slash out at our ankles.

On to the Dye Plant Garden. At its gates we are scrutinized by two creeping herbs of totally opposite character. On the right are countless tiny rosettes of Cleavers or Bedstraw—a near relative of Sweet Woodruff. On the left are the scalloped, sea shell-like leaves of Lady's

Plate 15

A dense patch of Wild Marjoram scents this end of the garden, joined by Roman Camomile which grovels at our feet ever desirous of being crushed and smelled.

Tropical Oregano snatches many second glances in this spot sharing the limelight with Incana Santolina and Dwarf Snapdragons.

Indian Borage, *Coleus amboinicus*, (center) is an entertaining herb from the tropics that resembles a thick-leaved Catnip (left-center) but smells exactly like Oregano. Here it is flanked by Greek and Golden Sage.

Bible Leaf (center) has extremely large and fragrant leaves excellent as book marks. Here they drape onto the path where they are likely to be crushed, sending a breath of minty freshness throughout the garden.

haring a garden. A frog lounges on a felty Wooly Betony leaf. reeping Savory lies to the left.

Using an informal perennial border and kitchen garden behind as transition from lawn to forest. Tall herbaceous herbs and vegetables appear to draw neighboring trees into the picture. The garden of Judy Zugish, Marysville, WA.

Plate 16

An herbaceous screen of Lovage hides service yard (far right) and pulls in neighboring trees to create feeling of seclusion within a forest.

Southernwood is often used as a transition plant and can accent both light and dark front border herbs in the ornamental garden. Garden of Judith Zugish, Marysville, WA.

Perennial bed utilising *Santolina viridis* as a transitional plant in a long bed parallel to a driveway. It is joined by Lavender, Dwarf Feverfew and Garlic, in the garden of Michele Nash, Mercer Island, WA.

The dry bed in this mead not only gives access but provides balance and naturalness in native stone. Creeping Thyme, Camomile, Violets, English Pennyroyal, Saffron, Wild Ginger, Mallows, Miner's Lettuce and many fall and winter bulbs are combined in this front yard that never needs mowing.

Shady spots in many gardens need light, brightly colored herbs. Here even from a distance Golden Mint and an ornamental *Artemisia* put some sparkle into this dark spot beside the boathouse at the home of Michele Nash, Mercer Island, WA.

Plate 17

...ittany, *Origanum × hybridum,* resembles Cretan Dittany
...ut is hardier.

Russian Oregano with showy flowers and dark green foliage (blooming center) and 'Krishna' Basil (far right) in purple splendor share a fragrant spot near an inviting turf seat covered with Caraway Thyme.

...lian Oregano (right) and Greek Oregano (left) in a raised bed
... a dooryard garden growing with Salad Burnet and Creeping
...olden Thyme.

A slow spreading but delicious mound of Golden Oregano in garden of Michele Nash, Mercer island, WA.

...ormal bed at home of Mary Medalia, Seattle, WA. with Sweet
...ely blooming in its shady bed beneath a tree providing fern-
...e background for colorful flowers and evergreens.

Shade-loving Violas share this spot with an assortment of bulbs and an albino Hosta.

Plate 18

Petite whorls of Sweet Woodruff create a fascinating shade-tolerant ground cover that is speckled with white flowers throughout the spring. Medicinal Herb Garden, University of Washington, Seattle, WA.

Lemon Balm in informal perennial border in garden of Gail Shilling, Bellevue, WA.

Beautiful scene of Chervil in bloom in spring from a winter planting in formal arrangement at Medicinal Herb Garden, University of Washington, Seattle, WA.

The exquisite coloration of Variegated Lemon Balm makes it a choice ornamental for the informal and contemporary herb garden. From the garden of John Eccles, Winlock, WA. It is shown here in comparison to the species.

A luscious verdant ground cover of Chervil in early summer surrounding a selection of *Monarda*.

Front border of light green Garden Sage is a good contrasting herb to dark evergreen back border ornamentals such as Rhododendrons.

Mantle. Flowers cling to her, like globs of lemon-yellow cotton-candy, spilling their sweet fragrance into the air. Again our minds sketch out a new design for our overburdened garden at home. The Bedstraw, *Gallium tinctorium* and *G. verum,* dyes come in reds and greens and golds while Lady's Mantle provides more verdant greens.

St. John's Wort, *Hypericum,* hidden beneath its yellow flowers, gives the expert dyer greys and golds while *Coreopsis* and Safflower yield yellow-oranges and rusty reds. Safflower, *Carthamus tinctorius,* is also a substitute for Saffron in color, but not in fragrance. A Saffron patch enjoys centerstage, its thin grassy tufts withered and brown this time of year. In late autumn its delicate purple flower will emerge, offering up to man 3 scarlet stigma that not only have been used to dye yellow the robes of kings and the doillied hankies of princesses, but bouillabaisse and breads as well, all with just a hint of ambrosia to entertain the nose.

The blue dye herbs, Woad, *Isatis tinctoria,* and Cornflower, *Centaurea cyanus,* stand back to back and crowd into a clump of Dyers Camomile, *Anthemis tinctoria,* which yields khaki and gold. This thicket of flowers around us in spikes, daisies, and plumes makes us feel as if we've accidentally ventured into a wild garden. Such a profusion of blooms however appears perfectly in place in its quadrant of this formal garden.

As we depart this exotic meadow we must dodge the median of Creeping Thymes. Magenta and rose flowers of 'Kermesinus' and 'Languinosus' grace the far end near the Grey Garden and the whites of 'Fosterflower' and 'White Moss' adorn the plots before us. A glorious frenzied mound of Golden Lemon Thyme encircles a sundial with a colorful lichen integument.

The kitchen Herbs interest us and we gaze fondly at the assemblage before us as if they were all family. French Thyme and 'English Broadleaf' Thyme lounge at the entrance. Good King Henry and Leeks are for pottage. Savory is the bean herb. Basil and Coriander tingle the nose and spice a pasta. Costmary is for the bottom of a cake tin to impart a minty freshness. Fennel is for a tea and condiment, Dill and Tarragon for salad dressings and gravies, and Sage for Thanksgiving dressing or the gamemeat sausages at Christmas. This garden smells like a gourmet's busy kitchen with the ovens abaking, pots aboiling, and chopped fresh greens addressing the air with tangy, herbaceous aromas that make mouths water and tongues tingle in excitement.

Our final adventure is the Shakespeare Garden where we will learn how the Bard used herbs. To him, herbs were for the pen, not the palate.

Decorating the entrance of this idyllic garden is Sweet Marjoram, one of the herbs that was favored for its zesty contribution to the dreadfully dull fare of the day. From this came the Bard's observation that a good woman was the "Sweet Marjoram of the Salad". Yet, if she fit into the class of the most bitter of herbs, Rue, she was "rather, of the Herb-of-Grace".

Rue also came to be used like Rosemary for funerals and fond fare-thee-wells. It was a celebrative herb and hallowed. One could send salutations to the bereaved with a sprig of Rue. So it came to be written, by he who wrote so well,

> "Rue—here shortly shall be seen,
> In the remembrance of a weeping Queen."

For herbs that accompanied memoirs and welcome reminiscences

> "There's Rosemary, that's for remembrance;
> May you, Love, remember;
> And there is Pansies, that's for thoughts."

The pansies scamper near the Lemon Balm in a partially shaded spot. Their confederate colors brighten the garden.

The Sweet Bay in the center patch sings a silent soliloquy warning:

" 'Tis thought the King dead: [when]
The Bay trees in our country are all withered."

An awesome thicket of poppies reflecting the colors of the pansies reminds us of this death which, according to the Bard, was "a sleep" that not even the poppy could conceive.

We can't miss the overstuffed patch of golden Calendulas and are reminded that

"The Marigold that goes to bed with the sun
With him rises weeping."

Like many daisied flowers, the Calendula draws in its petals at dusk and unfolds them at dawn dripping with dew.

Uncaringly stoic about dew drops or death is Wormwood, its silvered, filligreed leaves fidgeting in the wind. The exceptionally acrid taste of this herb gave reason for the woman scorned to let her rancorus tongue curse,

"Thou ravisher, thou traitor . . .
Thy sugar'd tongue to bitter Wormwood taste."

Since all is well that ends well, we'll end with a great dark green gathering of Lemon Balm. The oil of this herb was once so prized it was used to anoint kings. Its true lemon scent and renowned repellent charms encouraged the belief that an ointment of Balm bestowed security, desirability, and authority to a new king. Can you imagine the splendor of such a coronation? Fragrant flower petals flowed like flood waters and court chairs were given to the scour "with the juice of Balm and every precious flower".

The oil of Balm was a powerful talisman.

"Not all the water in the rough, rude sea
Can wash the Balm off from an anointed king."

It was unfortunate then that Richard II later lamented upon his regal misfortune, "With mine own tears I washed away my Balm". Tsk, tsk.

It was the formal garden—knot, parterres, and mazes—that inspired Shakespeare to wax so eloquently about the herbs of his day. They were used in a language all their own then, when few could pick up a pen and write a letter. Herbs and flowers were sent instead, symbols of thoughts and intentions, desires and hopes. The language of flowers is a lost art but we can still enjoy the art of the formal garden and admire those herbs that guided the hearts and tongues of romantics and lovers, artisans, philosophers, and bards. Measure for measure, the most sage advice the Bard left us—to improve our delivery when lecturing on herbs—was to

"Eat no onions nor garlic,
For we are to utter sweet breath."

Chapter 4 / SECTION 1

The Beneficial Formal Garden

Beauty is not the only reason for designing and planting a formal garden. In the past, gardens that supported a household were constructed using basic geometric patterns, depending upon square or rectangular beds and parallel rows. We know very little of primitive man's first gardens but some archaeological data has revealed that formal, as opposed to wild, patterns were employed, perhaps because of the guarantee that an organized garden would yield more. Food crops were cultivated under less strenuous conditions than ornamentals, given a full sun exposure, ample water and subjected to less competition.

The formal gardens discussed in this chapter are those that were used for the cultivation of beneficial herbs and food crops. The garden design that has re-emerged periodically since the beginning of man's agricultural awareness is the *checkerboard* form, while small cottage yards, whether in town or in farming districts, were suited to the compact *door yard* design. Across many centuries, in colonial stockade and castle keep alike, *kitchen* gardens were used for grains and root crops and *physicks* were employed by physicians.

The design of these gardens was quite subtle when beneficial herbs were placed for show and color and the whole balanced with the home and landscape. Creative use of foliage habits and hues more than flowers was made, but the latter are certainly not avoided. Herbs such as Sage, Thyme, Salad Burnet, Horehound, Caraway, the Savories, Sweet Cicely, Parsley, Calendula, Chervil, Lovage, Cumin and Anise were found in these gardens. Although a pond or water channel was frequently incorporated into these gardens, rarely were artifacts such as statues or ornate urns used, except for the most formal of situations.

The *kitchen garden* included pottage (for soup and stew) herbs, root crops and salad plants, along with a few annual culinary herbs and the major bulk foods such as potatoes, corn and beans. Even in such a utilitarian garden, pleasing designs were commonplace. (Fig. 29) They were patterned on a square format, which was advantageous to the gardener because it simplified maintenance and harvesting. Large squares were generally subdivided by either an X or cross access path, or composed of two or more concentric squares. Today, the kitchen garden has taken on leaner lines and been reduced to the simplest of form. We do not think of our vegetable patch as a garden that is part of the landscape, yet it can be. The delightful formal patterns used in the past can easily become a part of any landscape.

The herbs in these gardens are arranged by height, foliage color and special groupings of the most ornamental varieties. Central patches of each square may display tall ornamental plants; purple or yellow Wax Beans, Cardoon, Asparagus, Corn, Sorghum, Red Orach or fruit trees and trellised vines. The outer border of each square is the domain of the low ornamentals; Strawberries, Gourds, Red Cabbage, Bell and Red Peppers. Perimeter beds, those just inside the fence that surrounds all the squares of the kitchen garden, support vines, espaliered trees, berries or flowering herbs to be used for their fragrance or for dried

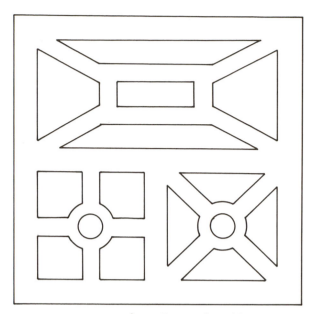

Fig. 29. The kitchen garden. Variations of the Quad from the Dark Ages are efficient and handsome. They were popular during the colonial period in American history.

arrangements, such as Lavender, Yarrow, Monarda, Tansy, Elecampane and Wormwood. Annual herbs are useful as borders. Herbs such as Borage, Coriander, Fennugreek and Calendula are grown for their flowers, which attract pollinators to the garden, while others, such as Dill, Basil and Savory, are grown as companion plants, herbs that protect neighboring garden plants from insect pests.

Perennials are not at all unwelcome in the kitchen garden. One of the advantages of the formal design is that compartmentation allows for differential treatment of plots of herbs. Thus perennial herbs such as Strawberries, caneberries and vines may be tended separately. Certain biennial herbs such as Cardoon, Artichoke and tuber crops like Jerusalem Artichoke, Alliums and Sweet Flag may be grown for their ornamental habits as well.

A garden design that was used extensively by monks was the checkerboard ("squares") pattern, as in Plate 12. Behind massive monastery walls, after the fall of the Roman Empire, the greatest works of herbal medicine were copied and abridged, and all manner of herbs were cultivated with care, keeping herbalism alive during the Dark Ages. Others followed suit during the Medieval centuries, using "squares" to grow herbs vital to life. These gardens were groupings of equidistant square beds, although rectangles were also used. Beds were not raised until after the 9th century, influenced by Charlemagne's successful gardens which employed this new concept. In ornamental use, squares were exhibited in groups of four, called "quads", or within a Hortus Conclusus. The entire garden was framed by a hedge or fence. Turf seats often replaced surrounding hedges, providing a fragrant respite. Quads were generally leisure spots that displayed wild flowers as well as more useful salad and pot herbs. Herbs naturalized into the quads were Lilies, Buttercups, Daisies, Sorrel, Salad Burnet, Camomile, Thyme, Dandelion, Plantain, Strawberry and Violets. When these gardens were allowed to overgrow, they became a "mead", a spot of wildness amidst the rampant formality of the day.

An entire landscape composed of squares, the *checkerboard* design, common in monasteries in the Dark Ages, creates a comfortable setting that encourages a lazy random stroll. It never pressures the viewer. From any point in the garden it is evident that everything is accessible and waiting to be discovered and pondered, not hiding, intending to surprise, as is often the rule in other landscape conceptions. Landscaped in a checkerboard pattern, a garden provides a long, leisurely walk in a small area. Herbs are its essential theme, including those that are valuable only as ornamentals. They too are part of the rich history of this garden form.

Here and there, a square may be paved or spilling over with a low ground cover. Upon it may be an inviting bench, or a clutch of potted houseplants basking in the summer sun. At least one, possibly more squares may be occupied by pools: a shallow one for reflecting a pleasant vista, a deep one for ornamental fish and aquatic herbs. The squares may be large and accommodate many herbs in simple arrangements that accent foliage themes. This is the basic plan of the monastic cloister garden. Or the squares may be small, each containing a single herb. The physician's herber was of this design. (Fig. 31)

Fig. 31. The physician's herber from the Dark Ages transformed into the average backyard raised bed garden. A small knot or formal sits to the left out of sight.

Physick gardens contained medicinal herbs and used, primarily, the squares format. As early as the 10th century, medicinal herbs and flowers were being separated from other beneficial herbs to facilitate their widely different cultural needs. The advent of ornamentality after the 15th century transformed the physician's herber. One of the most popular designs was the pie or circular shaped herber, that came to be termed a diver. (Fig. 32 and 33). It was used to cultivate diverse species of physick (medicinal) herbs in wedge-shaped beds, each dedicated to a specific cultural regimen. In many instances, over 100 different types of herbs were grown, significantly more than any other garden form. The hub of the diver was typically topiary, a dipping well or fountain, statue or sundial. The diver evolved over the centuries to include slices for other beneficial herbs including dye herbs, culinary and decorative herbs.

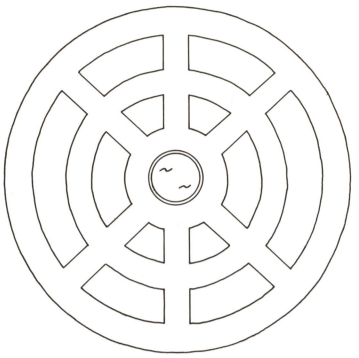

Fig. 32. A large diver for cultivation of medicinal or other beneficial herbs in a design popular during the early Medieval period.

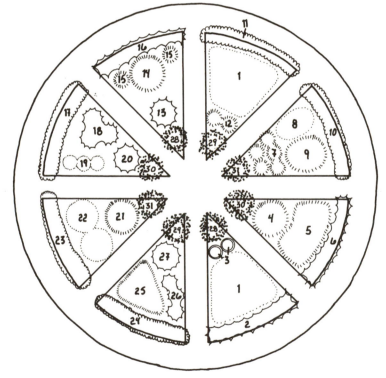

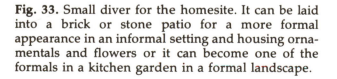

Fig. 33. Small diver for the homesite. It can be laid into a brick or stone patio for a more formal appearance in an informal setting and housing ornamentals and flowers or it can become one of the formals in a kitchen garden in a formal landscape.

KEY
1 German Camomile *Chamomilla recutita*
2 Dwarf Sage *Salvia officinalis* 'Nana'
3 potted Dittany *Origanum dictamnus*
4 Good King Henry *Chenopodium bonus-henricus*
5 Bible Leaf *Balsamita major*
6 Cr. Winter Savory *Satureja pilosa*
7 Chives *Allium schoenoprasum*
8 Calendula *Calendula officinalis*
9 Pineapple Mint *Mentha suavelolens*
10 Cr. Red Thyme *Thymus praecox* 'Coccineus'
11 Cr. Gold Thyme *Thymus* 'Clear Gold'
12 Dwarf Feverfew *Chysanthemum parthenium*
13 Golden Sage *Salvia officinalis* 'Aurea'
14 Yarrow *Achillea* 'Fire King'
15 Curly Parsley *Petroselinum crispum*
16 Dwarf Lavender *Lavandula angustifolia* 'Nana'
17 Roman Camomile *Chamaemellum nobile*
18 Oregano *Origanum vulgare*
19 Sweet Marjoram *Origanum majorana*
20 Salad Burnet *Sanguisorba minor*
21 Saffron *Crocus sativus*
22 Basil *Ocimum basilicum*
23 Caraway Thyme *Thymus herba-barona*
24 Hyssop *Hyssopus officinalis*
25 Black Mint *Mentha* × *piperita var. vulgaris*
26 Golden Oregano *Origanum vulgare* 'Aureum'
27 Southernwood *Artemisia abrotanum*
28 Silver Thyme *Thymus* 'Argenteus'
29 Golden Lemon Thyme *Thymus* × *citriodorus* 'Aureus'
30 Orange Thyme *Thymus vulgaris* 'Orange Balsam'
31 French Thyme *Thymus vulgaris* 'Narrow Leaf French'

The small compact *door yard* garden became the realm of the herbalist. (Fig. 34) Herbal medicine was laced with myth, magic and religion and though often effective, it was actively suppressed by the physicians, who were healers with some academic education in anatomy and basic medical science. During the reign of Henry VIII, herbalists in England were elevated to a status equal to physicians. Their expanding need for medicinals was satisfied by growing their own materials in a personal herber around their dwelling.

The herbalist's garden was small, generally only the front garden of a tiny cottage. Virtually all of the available space was used for cultivating herbs. Vines and espaliered plants covered the perimeter fence as well as the house itself. Just a few steps from the door were living remedies for the treatment of aches and pains of the "Augue" and childbearing, skin care ointments, hair rinses, wound dressings and poultices, potions for depression, cosmetics and secret electuaries for expelling demons, witches and malevolent fairies.

The garden frequently contained rectangular raised beds parallel to one another 2–4 ft. wide, though not so wide they were unmanageable. The raised bed technique was popular for the growing of beneficial herbs because of the ease of amending soils with sand, limestone, compost or any necessary combination that influenced the yield of finicky herbs. Wooden planks and rocks were the most common materials for the supporting sides. Brick and preformed concrete blocks are used today. Wood is not a recommended material because of its cost and short life. Treated wood should never be used in beneficial herb gardens. If wood is truly desired, cedar is the only one recommended. Depending on the height to which the beds are raised they can also double as sitting benches.

Raised beds solved other gardening miseries such as poorly drained or rocky, sandy, organically poor soils. They drain more quickly in spring and after heavy rain or flooding, allowing planting to begin earlier than in ground level gardens. Many more species of plants can be grown in raised beds, particularly those sensitive to poorly drained or acidic conditions.

In the dooryard garden all manner of herbs could be grown as well as the necessary medicinals, including spices, vegetables, fragrant herbs for purifying air or sweetening medicines, and decorative herbs to both cheer the spirits inside the home, or as strips of flowers encircling and enlivening the landscape. Surrounding the garden and home was a waist-high stone, wattle or mud and straw fence. Pathways were constructed of brick, stone or turf and supported many naturalized herbs for a soft and fragrant stroll.

Herbs here were displayed according to their foliage characteristics. Habit and color were used to accent prominent features of herbs that are the most ornamental. Flowering herbs such as Monarda, Calendula, Camomile, Lilies, Poppies, Tansy, Foxglove, White Mugwort, Meadowsweet, Pansies and Yarrow were used to create fascinating patterns of color within beds or as borders along the garden's perimeter.

The checkerboard and door yard designs can become a complete landscape. Into the regular pattern of square and rectangular beds are incorporated shrubbery and trees, shaded fern gardens and even dwarfed specimens for entertainment.

Themes can be woven by the use of limited categories of herbs, such as medicinals, dyes or particular foliage colors or heights. Moods can be controlled by the use of construction materials or the choice of plants. The use of brick or cut stone enhances the formality of a garden, rounded stones, wooden beams and old brick can be used for a rustic appearance, and a modern appearance can be had with the use of preformed concrete "stonework" and paving. The higher a bed is raised the more informal is the feeling it evokes, although it is also possible to invoke a less formal mood with beds that are flush with the paths by encouraging ground covers to spill out of their beds. Include fern and woodsy habitats or thickets of brushy herbs around the perimeter or wild patches by selecting a few squares off in one corner of the landscape to grow tall, flowering herbs and wildflowers through which paths

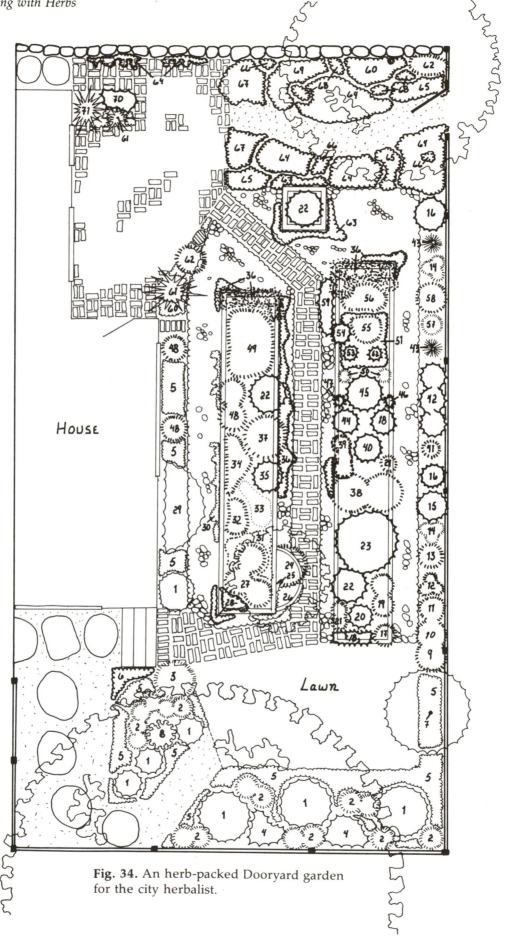

Fig. 34. An herb-packed Dooryard garden
for the city herbalist.

may run entirely hidden.

The kitchen and physick gardens today are essentially "formals" that are incorporated into other landscapes or displayed as featured gardens. Tying other landscape forms together with them requires the "formal" to be transformed by sharing some of the dominant elements featured in the landscape. They can be enclosed, becoming the Hortus Conclusus, so they can exhibit their formality more freely. This device ties it into the whole theme but its strict geometric nature keeps it a disconnected whole, a feature to be investigated and enjoyed.

However the beneficial formal garden is employed, it awakens much interest in visitors and can be an entertaining and educational focal point in any landscape and a mark of pride for the gardener.

KEY

1 Sword Ferns *Polystichum* spp.
2 Maidenhair Fern *Adiantum pedatum*
3 Bladder-Fern *Cystopteris fragilis*
4 Lenten Rose *Helleborus*
5 Oxalis and Bleeding Heart
6 Pineapple Mint *Mentha suaveolens*
7 Holly *Ilex*
8 Elderberry *Sambucus*
9 Fern Leaf Tansy *Tanacetum vulgare* 'Crispum'
10 Yarrow, Red & white *Achillea* cv's
11 Feverfew *Chrysan. parthenium*
12 Yarrow yellow *Achillea* 'Moonshine'
13 Golden Oregano *Origanum vulgare* 'Aureum'
14 Primrose *Primula* spp.
15 Variegated Sage *Salvia officinalis* 'Tricolor'
16 Rue *Ruta graveolens*
17 Basil-Thyme *Acinos arvensis*
18 Roman Camomile *Chamaemellum nobile*
19 Anise-hyssop *Agastache foeniculum*
20 Oregano *Origanum vulgare*
21 Dwarf Catnip *Nepeta mussinii*
22 Sage *Salvia officinalis*
23 Wooly Betony *Stachys byzantina*
24 Sweet Cicely *Myrrhis odorata*
25 Hazelnut *Corylus cornuta*
26 *Ajuga reptans*
27 *Angelica archangelica*
28 Applemint *Mentha* × *vilosa* var.
29 *Rhododendron* 'Jean Marie'
30 Creeping Charlie *Glechoma hederacea*
31 Chervil *Anthriscus cerefolium*
32 Beach Wormwood *Absinthum stellerana*
33 Pansies/Anemonies/Day lily
34 Lime Mint *Mentha* × *piperita* var. *citrata*
35 Greek Sage *Salvia fruticosa*
36 Creep. Golden thyme *Thymus* 'Clear Gold'
37 Bible Leaf *Balsamita major*
38 Cr. Savory *Satureja pilosa*

39 Basil (Cinnamon/Camphor/Thrysiflora)
40 Golden Sage *Salvia officinalis* 'Aurea'
41 Dropwort *Fillipendula vulgaris*
42 Hyssop (red/white/blue) *Hyssopus officinalis*
43 Miniature Roses
44 Lavender Cotton *Santolina chamaecyparissus*
45 Salad Burnet *Sanguisorba minor*
46 Indian Borage *Coleus amboinicus*
47 Tropical Oregano *Poliomintha longiflora*
48 Lemon Balm *Melissa officinalis*
49 Orange Mint *Mentha* × *piperita* var. *citrata*
50 Snapdragons, dwarf *Antirhinum* 'Floral Carpet'
51 Corsican Mint *Mentha requeinii*
52 Dwarf Sage *Salvia officinalis* 'Nana'
53 *Santolina neapolitana*
54 Dwarf Lavender *Lavandula angustifolia* 'Nana Atropurpurea'
55 Saffron *Crocus sativus*
56 Black Mint *Mentha* × *piperita* var. *vulgaris*
57 Shasta Daisy *Chrysanthemum maximum*
58 Good King Henry *Chenopodium bonus-henricus*
59 Cr. Rosemary *Rosmarinus officinalis* var. *prostratus*
60 Violet (wh) *Viola cornuta*
61 Arborvitae *Thuja orientalis*
62 Lovage *Levisticum officinale*
63 Lawn Camomile *Chamaemellum nobile* 'Trenague'
64 Violets/R. Camomile/Montia/Sw Woodruff
65 Cr. Thyme, *Thymus pulegioides* 'Foster flower'
66 Florists' Violet *Viola odorata*
67 Cr. Thyme, *Thymus pulegioides* 'Oregano-scented'
68 English Pennyroyal *Mentha pulegium*
69 Sweet Woodruff *Gallium odorata*
70 Southernwood *Artemisia abrotanum*
71 *Juniperus communis*

Chapter 4 / SECTION 2

Herbs for a Kitchen Garden

Each of these four formal gardens could contain every herb known and used. We will limit our discussion here to those herbs that are the most difficult to fit into the landscape. A few are prolific weeds that may become a nuisance. This group includes Comfrey, Tansy, Salad Burnet, and Sorrel. Others tend to be weedy in appearance no matter how much effort is spent in siting and cultivating them—Parsley, Caraway, Summer Savory, and Tarragon. The classical favorites, Calendula, Horehound, and Chives are included here.

Let's discuss the classical herbs first. This group contains Calendula, Chives, and Horehound. They have been used by man for over 3,000 years for both medicinal and culinary uses.

Chives, *Allium schoenoprasum,* has always been an enormously popular herb. It is a member of the Onion family. It grows with a tuft of hollow, grass-like leaves and is commonly used fresh in salads and soups. They are hardy in any soil and relatively pest-free, easily propogated and versatile in culinary use. To harvest, simply cut to 1–2 in. from the ground. Chives can be stored, either dried (in a moderately warm oven, 90–110°F) or as a butter.

CHIVE BUTTER

Add 2 Tbsp. of dried, powdered Chives to ½ c. of Margarine.
Bring to a boil for 3–5 minutes.
Turn into mold and store in refrigerator for up to 6 months.

If filtered, the green-colored margarines make a tasty dip or spread and can be used to baste chicken or as an oil in Chinese stir-fry dishes. The small bulbs harvested in early summer are often pickled and used as a condiment or for a sweet and tart oniony paste for crackers and chips.

Above all, Chive grows well in a container as a house plant during winter months when virtually all edible garden greens are dormant in northerly latitudes. For this reason, they have been a vital dietary complement for many centuries, able to provide necessary vitamins and minerals even in winter.

Chives are another misunderstood fragrant herb that must be grown in large masses to be discovered for what they are, a sweet, floral-scented herb with faint oniony highlights. Very rich, well-drained soils manured heavily 2–3 times per year are important for a full floral scent. Applications of phosphorus or wood ashes after each blooming period will boost subsequent blooming the same season. If calcium is added, it should be in the form of a sulfate, for this Onion prefers an acid soil in which to bloom to its fullest.

Their fragrance can contribute much to tiny scented gardens, their sweetness apparent when they are in bloom. They provide a spot of amusement no matter where they grow as their buoyant balls of lavender fluff bob about gaily on long, sturdy stems. A dozen 6 in. wide clumps will yield a hint of their mouth watering aroma throughout the garden on a rainy day. Chives grow so slowly that frequent uprooting and dividing is not necessary. Give Chives enough room to spread for a few years before dividing and replanting. Clump widths should be 6–9 in. and the distance between clumps from 15–18 in. As the rows broaden with time, the more fragrant the garden becomes.

The sleek vertical lines of a clump of Chives make a notable feature. A 3 year old clump of the North American native Chive, *A. s.* var. *sibiricum* can produce 12–16 in. leaves and scapes from 18–24 in., with flowers up to 2 in. in diameter. They are excellent in the landscape for small-scale vertical balance, such as in a mead or rockery or as a massed planting to balance tall conifers. This reed-like habit also allows them to appear as an expected component of marshes and muddy wallows, down among the Buttercups and Marigolds, so use them in any and every water feature. Here they should join ornamental grasses, Iris, Sweet Flag, and other Alliums.

Established clumps are a bold feature of lavender and dark green. This contrast is responsible for Chives being used more often than any other herb as a transition planting in the informal border or as a fiery burst of color in the contemporary garden. Borders of Chives can be used to form intricate scroll work in formal patterns such as the parterre and maze. They are easily cared for and the twice yearly show of countless, lavender maces jutting from some convoluted design is simply spectacular.

These borders are more entertaining when clumps are spaced rather than planted as a solid border. Varying this sequence,—e.g., 2 closely spaced clumps, then 3, with a double space between each group,—is arresting. The white flowering Garlic Chive, *Allium tuberosum,* and yellow-flowering *A. molly* or *A. flavum* may be substituted in a border for additional color and balance when framing a small circular garden in which fragrant annuals are snugly set. In addition, the white blossoms of Garlic Chives have a spicy or rose-like scent.

A single clump of Chives can be a vital component in a contemporary feature, with ball-shaped Bush Thymes and silvery sea urchin-like Clove Pinks scuttling around and about them. One large clump or several spaced closely for a mass effect, becomes a beacon, drawing the eye back to one point in the garden. At this focal point, they can accent statuary, a dipping well, rock features, or a planter in formal and other designs, or reign over a kitchen garden as its hub. In contemporary and dooryard settings, play them alongside their narrow leaved companions such as Sage, Lavender, Santolina, Bush Thyme, or Savory. Other plants Chives seem to enjoy as companions include the Yucca, Lilies, Snowdrops, Crocus, Salad Burnet, medium-height Yarrows and Veronica Incana.

Some of the hundreds of other members of the Onion family are quite ornamental and valuable as edible herbs. Most are relegated to the kitchen garden. These herbs include Rocambole or Serpent Garlic, Welsh Onions, Leeks, Egyptian Onions, and the Giant Alliums. The early showing Wild Onions grow into long-leaved clumps before most other perennials show and bloom in nodding clusters of white, pink and blue. They are safe for part shade and quite delicious. The larger varieties are all best grown as borders around taller crops such as Corn, Sorghum, Okra, and Pole Beans, or with a low front border of Dill, German Camomile, or Monarda for a surprise. A few of the Alliums, including Serpent Garlic, Elephant Garlic, and Egyptian Onion, have ornamental flowering characteristics that are quite handsome when massed together, forming the hub in a kitchen garden with lower growing herbs and vegetables, or as a feature garden in a contemporary landscape.

The Giant Allium, *Allium gigantium,* is one of the tallest Onions, at 4–5 ft., producing large 6 in. wide fragrant umbels and a fist-sized bulb. Although the fragrance of any Allium is strong and often obnoxious to the uninitiated nose, once in bloom, the Giant Allium's flower's sweet, honey-scent combines with the oniony aroma of the foliage, yielding a fragrance less appreciated than it should be. The lavender to pink globes bobbing about on a breezy day are a comical sight, resembling an alien forest such as described in C. S. Lewis' *Out of the Silent Planet.* "And on the summit, a grove of trees as man had never seen, their smooth columns were taller than a cathedral spire on earth, and at their tops, they grow rather into flower than foliage, large as a summer cloud." Other Giant Alliums which make entertaining garden plants, although not always as fragrant, are *A. flatunence,* light violet, from 3–5 ft., and *A. rotundum,* red-purple, to 3 ft.

Like Chives, these huge bulbs need high nitrogen levels for good growth, finest color, and best flavor. A thick application of manure in the spring and fall and just before flowering is recommended. The Giant Allium forms a modest screen when planted in successive rows. Bulbs should be staggered and set 6–8 in. apart in all directions. 4–5 rows are necessary. The Giant Allium is cultivated for food in Southeast Asia and India. The umbels can be dried to use in striking arrangements.

Another renowned perennial herb is White Horehound, *Marrubium vulgare,* the stuff of cold lozenges and tongue-tingling candies. Although it is a bitter herb (marrub meaning bitter), Horehound has been a favorite cold remedy for centuries. The mucilagenous material contains not only an antibacterial agent but also soothes the throat.

HOREHOUND LOZENGE OR CANDY

Make a decoction of 1 c. of Horehound leaves and ½ c. water.
Filter and add 2 c. sugar, ⅓ c. of honey.
Cook over low heat to 330°F on a candy thermometer.
Pour onto a cookie sheet or into candy molds.
Cut the candy on a cookie sheet when it is still warm.
Roll the pieces in powdered sugar and wrap individually in plastic and store.
For flavors, add ½ c. leaves of desired herb to the decoction or add commercial flavorings after the candy is cooled and just before pouring into the molds.

Horehound masquerades as a hoary (tomentose), round-leaved Mint. It is grey-green or light green and included in gardens for foliage contrast. Silver Horehound, *M. incanum,* has whitened leaves, denser, showy, snow white flower clusters and a more compact habit. Both grow upright like Mint, rising from 12–16 in. Flowers form fuzzy wads at each leaf node and are white and odorless, although quite popular with bees. It spreads quickly unless corraled. It is not a hardy herb, particularly in rich or clay soils, so is best grown in a poor, dry, sandy, or rocky soil. It grows rapidly from seed so may be treated as an annual and cultivated in a kitchen garden or dooryard where a box will confine it. Its fascinating grey, warty foliage may be displayed with patches of dainty flowers such as Dianthus, Camomile, Feverfew, and Phlox, or in a perennial garden as a ground cover alone, or with wildflowers such as the California Poppy, and Toad-flax.

Horehound makes an exceptionally showy border along a dark colored paving or asphalt driveway, thriving in the heat produced by these surfaces. Tall screen plants should be displayed behind it, especially those with spires, such as Delphiniums, Fraxinella, and Lupine. Herbs such as Fern Leaf Tansy and Lovage can be paired behind for contrast, or an *Artemisia* for a ghostly grey border against perhaps a dark stained fence or background of conifers. It also makes a fine ground cover for rocky slopes and poor soil.

The Calendula, or Pot Marigold, *Calendula officinalis* is an ancient flower, once cultivated and worshiped by the Egyptians. It's always there to greet you, displaying its cheerful rays of sunshine every day of the year when you step out into the garden. Its huge, bold green spatula-shaped leaves accent the 1–3 in. yellow, gold, or orange daisies. This little flower has a very special name, Calend, the word from which calendar comes. It was given to the herb for its uncanny habit of sending up a new bloom every month for the entire year. They act as if they were a short-lived perennial, flowering indefinitely wherever and whenever weather permits. The simplest is a small, yellow-orange flower, though many cultivars exist, including bronze and red hues. An annual in Northern climates, the Calendula can handle light frosts and gentle snowfalls. The seeds may be sown where they are to grow. They are fast-growing, very hardy in any soil, and pest-free if kept dry. Overhead watering causes mildew, so for best results, a soaker hose should be used. In the kitchen garden, a hub of Calendulas creates a cheerful, sunny center, attracting bees, therefore, improving pollination and yields from other plants in the garden.

The Calendula is the workhorse of the flowering ornamental herbs. It is used frequently in masses in every landscape form and perfect for a solid color border of exquisite beauty. Its borders are a bit sloppy for formal applications, so if used for such, should be shaped into circular or square patterns centered within a dense border of lower or similar height herbs. Rather large masses are fine in palatial grounds where thick, lush outside borders of Lemon Balm, Rue, or Santolina may be used, but for small garden features the Calendula, growing to 24 in., can be too large. Heavy rain or wind, pummel them to the ground in a nasty mess which still grows and blooms, but in an embarrassing posture. So unless they are grown in full sun and trimmed back when young—they can be pruned at any time—they will need support. They are not at all shy of poor soils. Especially beautiful in the informal and wild landscapes, drifts of Calendulas should be scattered before a verdant background, so as to appear like golden raindrops catching the sun.

Calendula petals contain saponins, chemicals that can both soothe a sore throat or create suds when shaken in water. Saponins are active in forming oil and water emulsions, contributing to the usefulness of Calendula's reputed use as a hair wash and in cooking, to impart smoothness to a soup. The golden petals, which contain significant amounts of vitamin A, may be used to enliven soups, broths, breads, butters, and candies. They are floated on punch or sugared for a treat. Calendula petals are easily dried at a medium temperature, 90–110°F, or they may be preserved in oil. Forgive me, but it does invite a variation on the adage, "One man's soap is another man's soup."

CALENDULA PETALS IN OIL

In a ½ pint jar, add ¼ c. vegetable oil and fill to top with petals, pressing them down regularly into the oil. Add oil to the top. Add 3 thinly sliced garlic cloves and stir.

Seal and keep in the refrigerator. Lasts for 2 weeks. Freeze for longer storage. An ideal method of storage is in an icecube tray. This form is excellent for Chinese stir-fry cuisine, dips, and for salad dressings.

If ice cubes are used, allow at least 24 hours for the mix to cure before transferring it to an icecube tray or the freezer. Separate the cubes and wrap individually in plastic and place in freezer containers. Use 1–2 cubes as necessary in a recipe.

HERB RICE

For each cup of rice, add 1 cube or 2–3 Tbsp. dried Calendula while cooking.

Add flowers of 1 umbel of Fennel (or of Sweet Cicely during early spring) and 1 Tbsp. of whole fresh or dried leaves of Chervil, Sweet Cicely, Tarragon, and Salad Burnet, 4 Tbsp. chopped Chives, 1 tsp. Boullion, (chicken in poultry dishes or beef for beef or pork dishes) and 4 Tbsp. butter or margarine. If an herb butter is used, a Fennel or Chive butter is recommended.

Serve with breast of chicken or beef cubes and for a vegetable, creamed corn or candied pumpkin squares.

This is a meal children will love.

An unusual and indispensible salad herb is Garden Burnet, *Sanguisorba minor.* It has the distinct flavor of cucumbers. *S.minor* ssp. *minor,* or Burnet, is frequently substituted but is nonetheless a valuable cucumber-flavored green herb that, like Salad Burnet, is available to us all year round in a delightful evergreen form. Young leaves picked in spring and fall are more tender and recommended for salad use, while all may be dried for use in cheese dips or cream sauces and soups. During summer months harvest only from first-year plants. Provide them with plenty of moisture in the summer to prevent bitterness.

SALAD BURNET DIP

Use plenty of leaf material for a full cucumber flavor. Be sure leaves are not bitter.

Strip from branches 1 cup of Salad Burnet leaves and chop in blender with a little oil and ¼ clove of Garlic. Fold into sour cream or non-dairy dressing in the amount desired. Allow to stand 4 hours in refrigerator before serving.

Salad Burnet is an evergreen perennial growing in a fascinating rosette pattern like the spokes of a wheel. It resembles a diminutive, dark green, frozen water fountain. The tiny, ½ in. leaves are sharply serrated and arrayed in odd numbers along the branches. It is quite handsome when grown on a layer of white crushed rock with Golden Lemon Thyme, Horehound, and variegated Mints. Its graceful habit is enhanced by combining it in a grey garden or surrounding it by Golden Oregano.

Salad Burnet makes a poor border herb and should be used as a single specimen planting or ground cover. As an annual, Burnet keeps a very low profile, less than 6 in. It can be used to create fascinating spider-like patches in a rock garden or a sparsely planted contemporary feature. As a perennial, Burnet develops an 18–24 in. fountain-like form with long, drooping tentacles tipped with fuzzy, knobby balls. These flowers are small, ½–1 in. capsules that display hundreds of tiny bright red filaments emerging like the many arms of a sea anemone. The flowering stems and fruits are not of exceptional beauty and may be removed to improve the neatness of the herb and to avoid spreading throughout the garden. It will self-sow profusely, spreading rapidly like a weed so needs controlling. Because of its ornamental appearance, however, it is an excellent self-sowing ground cover. As an annual, each plant requires a space about 18 in. in diameter and as a perennial, to 30 in.

An isolated community composed of several Salad Burnet plants in informal, wild or contemporary landscapes is recommended. It should be grown as an annual in a kitchen garden, in rows or as the points of a pentagram, the center of which is filled with Calendula.

Salad Burnet has two larger relatives, Japanese Burnet, *Sanguisorba obtusa,* 12–18 in., and *S. tenuifolia,* 3–4 ft., with larger leaves and fuzzy white, pink or rose, bottle-brush flowers of considerable ornamental value. Their leaves have no culinary use. They are best used sown in a wild landscape with Salad Burnet for size and flower color contrast or alone in a contemporary feature or wild garden.

An herb with a history as a medicinal in the Americas is Great Burnet, *Sanguisorba officinale,* which resembles the Salad Burnet except for its large, 3–5 ft. size. Canadian Burnet, *Sanguisorba canadense,* sports large, 3–4 in., bottle-brush flower spikes which extend out from the plant on 2 foot long stalks bending gracefully towards the ground. All of the Burnets have been used as fodder and medicine for centuries.

Another fodder and medicinal herb, although better known, is Comfrey, *Symphytum officinale.* This herbaceous perennial is a noxious weed so care must be taken to carefully confine a planting to prevent its spread, both by seed and by root pieces, such as when it is transplanted or improperly composted. Broad, 12–18 in. long leaves of Comfrey make it a spectacular plant in any garden, its lush, dark green clumps mimicking lush, tropical undergrowth. The pink, purple, yellow, and red flowers are a favorite of bees. We, too, may enjoy the sugary nectar of Comfrey flowers in salads or as a sweetener in herbal teas and candies.

In the kitchen garden, Comfrey is cultivated in large clumps in the center of the squares. There it will benefit the garden with a flowering display in May and June, and again in the fall, attracting pollinators. Comfrey may also be used as a border if carefully controlled while larger species act as a screen. In unconfined plantings, Comfrey combines well with tall, large-leafed plants such as Poppies, Hollyhocks, Elcampane, Hosta, and Iris.

Comfrey thrives in a moist soil and may be grown in partial shade. A poor, dry soil will help control it. Plantings are improved by a soil covering of crushed rock or bark. To stop Comfrey from spreading below ground, plant it in partially buried barrels or bury 10 in. boards around the plant.

The leaves and roots of Comfrey, or Knitbone, are used medicinally in a poultice (whole leaves applied to sore spot and covered by a warm, moist towel) to cure muscle aches and sprains. The active material is allantoin, which promotes wound healing. Comfrey is useful as a fodder and highly valued as a compost material because of its rapid growth and high mineral content.

In addition to a variegated form of Common Comfrey, *S. officinale* 'Variegatum', with leaves margined in white, red-flowering Comfrey, *S. o.* 'Coccinceum' and Yellow flowering 'Aureum', several other decorative species include: Prickly Comfrey, *Symphytum asperum,* primarily a fodder plant growing to 6 ft. which has flowers that change from rose to blue as they mature; *S.* × *uplandicum,* a cross of Common and Prickly Comfrey, called Russian Comfrey, is more ornamental with heavy flower clusters and also grows to 6 ft. with rose flowers changing to purple.

Another rampantly spreading herb is Garden Tansy, *Tanacetum vulgare.* Tansy is a tall, slim plant with feathery pine green foliage. The oily and herbaceous fragrance of its foliage becomes apparent to passersby, particularly on hot summer afternoons. A clump of Tansy takes little time to develop and needs no care other than occasional staking or tying together of its heavy bright gold button flowers in late summer. (Garden Tansy should not be confused with Tansy Ragwort, *Senecio jacobea,* a toxic weed.) An ornamental cultivar, *T. vulgare* 'Crispum', has fern-like leaves and is usually listed as Fern-leafed Tansy. It is a smaller variety, growing to no more than 3 ft., with the same sunny yellow flowers but a penetrating camphoraceous odor.

Fern-leafed Tansy is definitely more useful as an ornamental herb than the species. It develops a sturdier, denser habit with its dark green, filigreed leaves pointing downward and lying flat against one another. A large clump will stand alone and to some extent it can be molded into shape by pruning and by tying up with twine. The leaves remain on the lower portions of the plant for a very neat, pert appearance.

Tansy's hardiness makes it a choice plant for a screen. As a thick screen, Tansy should, at a minimum, be allowed to spread to a 12 in. wide clump. This provides a moderately dense hedge. The dark green foliage makes an excellent background for medium or low borders of yellow or white flowers. The oily scent of Tansy mixes well with spicy and floral scents of Clove Pinks and Roses. Handsome, fragrant borders can be created with light green or grey fragrant companions such as Wormwood, Carnations, Blue Sage and Valerian.

Tansy achieved a long list of accomplishments during the Dark Ages and for many centuries afterwards. It was an important herb for food during fast days. Tansies, or egg and flower concoctions using Tansy as an ingredient or simply egg and Tansy alone, were valuable foodstuffs for the peasants of medieval Europe. Today its flowers and foliage are valued highly for ornamental use only.

Note: Both Garden Tansy and the previously discussed herb, Comfrey, are no longer recommended as a food because they contain toxic chemicals like those found in Tansy Ragwort which can seriously harm or kill grazing animals. At present this warning is posted on a guilt by chemical association as no clinical research has been done to support or refute it.

One of the most useful herbs, but which has a weedy appearance, is Parsley, *Petroselinium crispum.* Parsley is one of the most widely used fresh green herbs, as a main course garnish at home, in restaurants, and as bright green flakes in hundreds of prepared foods. Parsley is noted for its high vitamin C content and has been used by man for so many millenia it does not now exist as an uncultivated natural species. Both the root and the leaves are useful in virtually all foods. The fresh greens are used in salads as garnishes in gourmet dishes and as pottage. Easily and rapidly dried by high temperature, 110–140°F, in an oven, Parsley keeps its green color and high mineral and vitamin content for an exceptionally long period. Parsley flakes are also used in soups, potato and egg salads, meats, stews, and vegetable dishes.

Fresh Parsley may be deep fried for a spicy, crunchy treat or as an excellent stir-fry vegetable in Oriental dishes, adding a bright green when pea pods and broccoli are not used or when seasonally unavailable. Crinkly or curly forms, *P. crispum* var. *crispum,* tend to be bitter but a rich soil and ample water will guarantee a refreshing spicy and herbaceous flavor. The spicy notes in Parsley are provided by turpenes and pinene.

Italian Parsley, also called Flat-leafed Parsley, *P. crispum* var. *neapolitanum,* has flat, serrated leaves which are larger and sweeter tasting, much more suitable for pottage or as a green coloring in butter, sauces, and cheeses. It is a tall, rangy herb, not at all suitable to ornamental use except perhaps in a wild garden, tucked into a screen of Dill and Yarrow, or grown with Lovage and Angelica.

Flat-leafed Parsley is used with butter and cheese to make a peppery, bright green spread for crackers and a hot dip for chips. For a tongue-tingling Parsley dip, combine 1 c. of fresh Parsley leaves, ¼ c. of Lovage leaves, and 1 clove of Garlic, with 1 Tbsp. of Tarragon vinegar in a blender. Fold into sour cream or non-dairy dressing. The dip may be used immediately but best flavor is achieved after standing several hours or overnight.

For fresh herbs, cut plants as near the ground as possible, removing only as many stems as needed. Plants trimmed heavily in mid-summer will regrow by late fall for a second crop. In warmer climates, Parsley will grow throughout the year and go to seed the following summer. For culinary purposes, only the first year growth is used. Seed from one plant is

Plate 19

A colorful feature and transition herb is Golden Sage. Here it shares a slender evergreen perennial bed with Rue, Caraway Thyme (blooming), German Camomile and a backborder of Garden Sage and Oregano (right).

Variegated Sage adorned in cream and pink creating a colorful feature in this dooryard perimeter bed along with a pink flowering Lavender (right), Oregano, Scarlet Poppy and a clump red flowering Florist's Violet.

Mound of Red Sage in garden of John Eccles, Winlock, WA.

Formal garden of red-hued herbs including Za'atar, *Thymbra spicata*, (center) with a coat of pink flowers, Melon Sage, *Salvia erisiana*, with crimson trumpets and a Gilliflower or Dwarf Carnation. Creeping Red Thyme and pink flowered Lime Mint reside at opposite ends of this feature just out of sight.

Silver Sage with chalk-white flowers at Medicinal Herb Garden, University of Washington, Seattle, WA.

Plate 20

Informal landscape. Home and gardens of Michele Nash, Mercer Island, WA.

A border of Golden Oregano, Chives and Silver Thyme. On the patio Creeping Thymes cascade over the walls. Garden of Michel Nash, Mercer Island, WA.

A garden on fire with red-orange Calendulas, Dahlias, Roses and Nasturtiums. Calendulas form the theme in all the interconnected gardens on this homesite in Chehalis, WA.

Small island garden dividing lawn area from kitchen garden at home of Judith Zugish, Marysville, WA.

A fragrant seat by one of three Rosemarys which play an important role in tying together the separate parts of this contemporary landscape. From the gardens of Angelo Pellegrini, Seattle, WA.

Plate 21

patch of early spring color juts
to the path. Sweet Cicely and
uga (bottom) contrast each
her in color and texture.

ound at one side of street
trance that is colorful and
agrant using 'Hidcote'
avender, Wooly Betony and
nny Toadflax.

stere perennial feature
gering into a backyard,
ludes neatly clipped hedges of
nch Thyme, Chives, Oregano,
lendula and Garden Sage.
lor and vertical contrast is
ovided by Rose Campion and
isies. It is an excellent example
an edible landscape from the
rdens of Gail Shilling,
llevue, WA.

Isolated entrance feature with Golden Sage, Lavender, fruit tree, Curly Parsley as a ground cover
and evergreens at home of Michele Nash, Mercer Island, WA.

Edible landscape. Perennial bed with Garden Sage, Giant Alliums, Garlic, Strawberries as a
ground cover, Rhubarb, fruit trees and many ornamentals in garden of Michele Nash, Mercer
Island, WA.

Incana Santolina growing merrily
among the Strawberries in an
edible landscape by Michele
Nash, Mercer Island, WA.

Plate 22

Costmary with a profusion of little daisies in mid-June. This species is also known as the Camphor Plant because of its strong camphor odor.

Hops as a ground cover.

Young Variegated Hop clinging to a rock wall.

The stately flowering portion of Common Giant Fennel, an imposing herb in any garden feature. The Marshmallow, *Althea officinalis*, shares this square at the University of Washington, Medicinal Herb Garden, Seattle, WA.

French Cardoon feature in formal square at Medicinal Herb Garden, University of Washington, Seattle, WA.

Bee Balm, *Monarda didyma* 'Cambridge Scarlet', in formal featur at University of Washington, Medicinal Herb Garden, Seattle, WA.

more than sufficient for the home. A variety, Turnip-rooted Parsley, *P. c.* var. *tuberosum,* is grown for its large edible roots.

Japanese Parsley, *Cryptotaenia japonica,* is an *Umbelliferae* resembling Italian Parsley. It is, however, lower in stature with a more pleasing taste and aroma that is popular in salads and Oriental cuisine. It grows well in partial shade but is best grown as an annual in the kitchen garden. As a perennial herb it grows to 18–24 in. in a slowly spreading clump. Honewort, *C. canadensis,* is a North American species often substituted.

As landscape ornamentals the curly forms of Parsley are choice. They make dense, 12–14 in. wide borders from 8 to 14 in. high in a number of green, dark green, and red hued varieties. When closely packed, they will merge to form a neat and admirable border. A high contrast planting of Curly Parsley may be used in formal arrangements to encircle specimen plants. In centuries past, Parsley was used to form the intricate scrollwork in knot gardens or parterres. Grown as an annual, little effort is needed to maintain it as a border. Single plants of Curly Parsley make a fine addition in a mixed border and may be used as transition plants for the beginning and ending of borders of flowering companions or interspersed in a long border in repeated fashion to break monotony and introduce motion. Today, the curly varieties are used as a border in informal and kitchen gardens and as isolated clumps of bold green contrast to greys in contemporary features.

It is important to remember that Curly Parsley purchased from a garden center may be last year's crop. In that case, as a biennial herb, it will not form a pleasant ornamental bush but a twiggy, thin form that will soon go to seed and die. Plant all Parsley from seed for guaranteed results. Parsley is not an ornamental herb in its second year and is less useful for culinary purposes as well.

Parsley is an extremely hardy herb, relatively pest-free and easily propogated by seed. It has been said that Parsley is slow to germinate but with the advent of good potting soils and hotbeds, fresh seeds that have been pre-soaked 24 hours will germinate in 7–21 days. Parsley seed fertility declines rapidly so use it fresh, no more than one year old. Purchased seed requires 3–4 weeks to germinate and longer as the seeds age. Sow all borders where they are to grow.

French Sorrel, *Rumex scutatus,* is strictly a kitchen garden herb used as a companion to corn, grains and tall vegetables. Its succulent leaves are used as Spinach in soups and as a boiled vegetable. It is highly valuable for both its mineral and vitamin content in early spring well before other pot herbs are available. Several culinary varieties are available so gardeners are advised to try more than one. Sorrel will spread if allowed to go to seed; cultivate only one or two plants for seed production. It requires full sun and a rich, moist garden soil. The useful life of a Sorrel patch is from 6–10 years.

French Sorrel may be used in large arrangements as a self-sowing ground cover that is hardy and quick to spread. Its 12 in. bold green to yellow-green growth is a fine accent for large grey herbs and around dark evergreen shrubs. Sorrels have been used in knot gardens as borders and in parterres to fill large areas.

Common Garden Sorrel, *Rumex acetosa,* is a perennial broad-leafed plant growing to 24 in. with reproductive spikes to 3 ft. The green leaves are arrow-shaped and from 4–6 in. long. 'Bellville' is a prominent and tasty cultivar. French Sorrel, *R. scutatus,* is a smaller species from 12–18 in. with arrow-shaped leaves but of a more oval form and better flavor. Other species include common weeds: Patience Dock, or Spinach Dock, *R. patientia,* growing to 6 ft., with 12 in. leaves; Red Sorrel or Sheep Sorrel, *R. acetosella,* a low, 6–12 in. rampantly spreading, but edible weed, with reddish flower spikes; and *R. crispus,* Curly Dock, which is used medicinally.

Looking considerably like a creeping form of Sorrel is Good King Henry, *Chenopodium bonus henricus,* an old-fashioned pot herb. In fact, the similarity, most noticeable in their inflorescence, reveals their distant relationship. Its dark green, arrow-shaped leaves are quite tasty and an excellent Spinach substitute in a hardy perennial package. This member of the goosefoot family has more ornamental potential in the garden than its annual relatives Lamb's Quarters, *C. album,* and Strawberry Blite, *C. capitatum.* Its low height, 6–12 in., and moderate spreading rate make it a useful front border herb in a mixed arrangement accompanying dark green or ruby-stained lettuce and chard or with Silver Sage and Meadow Clary for a wild ornamental effect. A grouping of Good King Henry with low Alliums or other herbs and ornamental plants with a strong vertical habit in a small area give the most pleasing arrangement.

Caraway, *Carum carvi,* is a weedy carrot-like biennial. In the first year, Caraway may be used as a low, 8–12 in. border. Its feathery, pine green foliage is excellent in salads and soups, having a discernible anise scent and flavor. Young, 2–4 in. seedlings may be eaten whole in salads and soups. The roots of first year plants are sweet and tasty either raw in salads or steamed. In stir-fry recipes the finger-thick roots of older plants add a crunchy sweetness which may substitute for water chestnuts. The second year, Caraway will grow rapidly to 2–3 ft., its insignificant white-flowered umbels developing (by early June) the popular Caraway seeds, used in bakery goods, sausages, and cheeses.

If a small row or plot is planted for its greens the first year, Caraway may be transplanted to another location such as a kitchen garden or wild garden for seed production, which is quite unornamental. Caraway seed must be allowed to ripen on the plants, which require tying or support. The tiny, brown seeds, borne Dill-like, are sweet and have a strong Anise flavor, much prized by gardeners, for it is easier to grow Caraway, a biennial that is hardy in cold climates, than Anise, the seeds of which may not even ripen. Predominant fragrant constituents in Caraway are carvone, carvacrol, cuminal, and limonene, the same chemicals found in Cumin and Coriander. Caraway seed is a complementary spice to Coriander, Cumin and Ginger and not as widely used in meat dishes as it should be. Crush it to release its essence. To fully enjoy the flavor of Caraway seed, use it in Chili or spaghetti sauce, with meat balls in a rich Basil sauce or with honey and Lovage on baked chicken.

MEAT BALLS

3 pounds ground beef	1 Tbsp. Lovage
2 pounds pork sausage	2 Tbsp. Caraway seed, crushed
1 c. oatmeal	1 Tbsp. Oregano
2 eggs	1 tsp. Savory
2 Tbsp. sugar	1 tsp. Basil

Combine ingredients. Make into 60 balls. Bake in oven at 350°F for 45 minutes. Place in a sauce and simmer for two hours.

TOMATO SAUCE

3 cans tomato sauce	1 Tbsp. Lovage
2 Tbsp. Caraway seed, crushed	1 Tbsp. Oregano
1 tsp. Coriander seed, crushed	1 tsp. Fennel
1 tsp. Basil	

Combine the ingredients and simmer for one hour, then add precooked meat balls. Add ½ c. brown sugar 45 minutes before serving.

For a pasta dish without tomato sauce, drench noodles in Lemon Basil butter and sprinkle with fresh, chopped Chives, Fennel, and Lovage leaves and serve with hot meat balls.

Caraway is easily dried by hanging the plants upside down in a paper bag to dry, The seeds are shaken loose and stored in airtight jars. They retain their flavor for several years. To hasten ripening and protect the seed heads from dust, paper bags may be tied over the plants in the garden. Any seeds that fall off early will be trapped in the bag. After no more than 1–2 weeks, the tops are cut and bags inverted and hung in a dry location for storage. There is an annual form of caraway that is grown commercially. It is planted in early spring and harvested in late fall. Another variety of Caraway is grown for its plump, tender Anise and Carrot flavored root.

As with all *Umbelliferae* mentioned in this text, the umbel from which the Caraway seeds are removed is valuable in decorative arrangements and may be used to make an ornamental ball resembling a sea urchin. To design a *gossamer sphere:* 1. Remove all seeds from the umbel gently so as to leave the fine hairs on the tips of the branchlets, or, 2. Trim all umbel branchlets to 1–2 in. by folding together and pruning. 3. Attach fishing line to the head of a pin and insert into the end of one branch. 4. Bend the tip of the pin to secure. 5. To the stems of each new umbel added use a dab of glue on stems in the center and connect the branchlets like the spokes of a wheel. 6. When complete, coat the hub with extra glue and spray the sphere with a paint fixative, spray paint or lacquer.

Summer Savory, *Satureja hortensis,* is a delightfully fragrant herb. It is also an unsavory, weedy looking thing and although Winter Savory, *Satureja montana,* its relative, is a great herb for borders in neat trimmed lines, Summer Savory, an annual, is best used in a kitchen garden or wild garden and grown for its culinary virtues.

Due to its lax habit and spindly growth, it is best suited to mass plantings in the wild garden, protected from foot traffic, but nevertheless bisected by paths, where its rich, spicy, camphoraceous scent may be relished and its tiny, fragrant, pink flowers appreciated. Or plant this thin little waif as a low border herb in the dooryard or kitchen garden where it will droop over a path, ever ready to emit its rich aroma when brushed.

Under the best of conditions, Summer Savory forms a 12–16 in. dark green or black stained bush. Its meager habit makes it hard to find it a home in the ornamental landscape. To keep their bush forms sturdy, plants must be allowed adequate light and ample space or they become spindly and will topple in the first heavy rain. It must be cultivated in full sun and rich soil. A patch of Summer Savory 30–50 sq. ft. will scent an entire garden.

The culinary value of Summer Savory exceeds that of its relative, Winter Savory. Unless it is grown separately in a vegetable or culinary herb garden where whole plants are harvested and dried, clippings may be taken from an ornamental garden any time through bloom. Summer Savory has a mellow camphoraceous aroma composed of thymol and carvacrol, a scent reminiscent of Oregano Thyme. It is excellent in hardy potato or meat soups, bean stews, chili, egg and cheese omelets, sausage and tangy sauces for the barbeque or broiler. Poultry and lamb may be smoked to a sharp, sausage-like flavor with 2–3 c. of Savory spilled onto the hot coals then covered to allow meat to smoke for 30 minutes.

CHILI BEANS

4 quarts water

Add: 4 c. pinto beans   2 Tbsp. chili
       6 large tomatoes   1 Tbsp. Lovage
       1 large green pepper   4 Cloves of Garlic
       1 tsp. beef bouillon   1 tsp. Fennel seed
       2 Tbsp. Chive butter   ½ tsp. Ginger
       2 Tbsp. Summer Savory   ½ c. maple syrup

Simmmer 3–4 hours until beans are cooked but firm.

Tarragon's weediness has been forgiven for centuries. It's an herb no gourmet would be without and so it is grown, groomed and harvested no matter if it does try to fall all over the ground and screw itself into a tangled web both above and below the ground. The entanglement of roots is the source of its ancient name, Dracunculus, for the serpentine mess that must be lifted and divided before it constricts itself. Its Hyssop-like leaves are nothing to look at but once dried have a flavor and fragrance that simply cannot be described. Sweet, cool and ethereal come close, without resorting to a comparison with another herb, the most common of which is Licorice.

This 2–3 ft., herbaceous ragamuffin must be grown where it can be staked to prevent it from touching the earth. It needs a spacious plot of top quality soil that is half sand or otherwise very well drained. Oyster shell and bonemeal are recommended as well as a good organic fertilizer in early spring and again in mid-summer. A fall mulch is not necessary and on poor soils will only accelerate decay. An annual lifting and root pruning is advisable in heavy soils.

About one cup of dried leaves is possible from an average Tarragon plant. It dries quickly, 2–3 hours at low temperature and in only a few minutes in a microwave. Tarragon is very different fresh and dried. The biting, anesthetic activity of fresh Tarragon, due perhaps to methoxycinnaminaldehyde, rapidly loses ground to ocimene, myrcene, methylchavicol and phellandrene as it dries. Tarragon sweetens a vinegar and performs a vital service for Tartar Sauce as we know it and is "one of the perfumery of spicy furniture of our sallots" as Sir John Evelyn noted in 1693. Fresh, dried, as a vinegar or wine, Tarragon adds a different flavor in each case to a dish. Its special virtue must be taken advantage of. Use it in a Sweet Rice recipe or with buttered vegetables such as carrots, coles and baked or candied squash. A butter of Tarragon is very strange and delicate, superb for a basted bird or for buttered noodles with bits of mild pork sausage. German potato salad demands a Tarragon vinegar and a tart mayonnaise sandwich spread is made with it and a pinch of dried Lovage and Thyme.

There are two types of Tarragon: Russian Tarragon, *Artemisia dracunculus,* and the popular and almost legendary French Tarragon, *A. d.* 'Sativa'. The former is nice but not the real thing. The Russian form can be grown from seed, and although it is hardier it is exceptionally weedy and does not have the bite and heady aroma so cherished in the French. French Tarragon can only be propagated by root divisions or cuttings.

Confine French Tarragon to the kitchen garden. Experiment with it elsewhere. It may join in an herbaceous perennial bed but keep it far to the back and never near the dripline of trees. Under an eve in partial shade is a possibility but expect a smaller harvest. Give it a long border in the kitchen garden, at least 4 plants, and allow it to neighbor with a perennial border of Gooseberry or Blueberry behind it and Strawberry before it. Every year divide and root prune ¼ of your plants to freshen them.

Chapter 4 / SECTION 3

A Walk Through a Formal Dooryard Garden

Touring a dooryard garden is a romantic experience. It conjures visions of storybook scenes. Before us is a quaint homestead, its eaves and gingerbread cloaked in gnarled vines, its dooryard garden thick with simples. (Fig. 34) Through squinted eyes we can almost see Hansel and Gretel frolicking among the herbs and spices that are used by the Wicked Witch for all her cakes and candies. Her medicinal and magical herbs for aches and incantations are there, portents of the awesome power of the one who wields them well. The landscape's medieval marks, formality and herbalism, remind us of castles and queens, kings and conquests. Here we will find all manner of healing herbs.

Before us is an old wooden gate, buttressed by thorny twisting briars. Beyond is an imposing garden, at first glance wild and free, but on closer inspection there is a suggestion of some power at work, cordoning these herbs into an unnatural, but handsome habitat for edification and introspection. No one comes to greet us; perhaps that is best. We were told that all the herbs were labeled. We were also told that in this tiny garden, 20 × 40 ft. are 140 different species, varieties, and cultivars of herbs. We enter and find ourselves on a cobblestone path, with herbs spilling and writhing from every nook and cranny available.

A grinning black grimalkin, eyeing us contemptuously from her perch on a honeysuckled porch rail, eerily reminds us of the old woman we spoke to on that very spot a week ago. She informed us that from this garden she could extract all she would need for "sauces and seasonings, syrups, scents and pretty condiments, bugbane and air freshener, robegarde and dye, for salves and syrupy simples, an herb for everything from childbirth to extreme unction." In a sense a dooryard garden is a little like visiting your pharmacist, grocery and health food store all at the same time.

There seems to be no beginning and certainly no end before us. The best place to start is with our nose. We sense a multitude of herbaceous odors but one or two nearby are minty and fresh. Since it had rained only an hour before, the scents of Mint, Camomile, Sage, and Lemon Verbena have taken wings about us. The purple leaves of Black mint emit a fragrance of mouthwatering menthol that summons visions of gum and penny candy while its neighbor, Pygmy Savory, exudes a rich camphoraceous aroma. It is flanked on either side by an equally fragrant but reclusive species of the same genus, Creeping Savory, that swarms over the side to the cobblestones below. Reaching out from its station on the cobblestone walk to catch hold of the Savory is pine-scented Rosemary. In late summer, the slender branches of both entwine while displaying their Sunday best, sapphire blue and pink-white flowers.

Now a strong apple-scent finds its way to our nose. We look down to discover we have trod upon some Roman Camomile. Draped to the stony path below, it waves its feathery tendrils and tiny, white daisies deliberately in our path. Bumping or stepping on it brings the scent of hot apple-cider to our nose. We back away, believing we have hurt it, but remember the saying "Like a Camomile bed, the more it is trodden, the more it will spread". Its neighbor is a dark green mound of Basil Thyme, which boasts a minty, Thymish scent and hosts of pink flowers, growing from long, drooping flower stalks like many rows of little bells.

A delicate wooly grey Greek Sage rests comfortably in a raised bed nearby. Anemones and Creeping Thymes share its box. This Sage has an ornamental character that resembles Horehound, with fuzzy, warped leaves and a stance that reminds us of their close alliance with the Mint family. Either Greek Sage or Blue Sage may be combined as a powder with Caraway Thyme, Rosemary, Mint, and baking soda for a tongue-tingling herbal tooth cleanser.

Sliding between the box and two long, parallel, raised beds we see the countless herbs that we were promised would be here. Hollow cylinders of drain tile provide support for the raised beds as well as a secure home for precious specimens or rampant spreaders. Many contain creeping herbs such as a Golden Thyme with a 2 in. high habit and light green leaves. There is Wild Thyme, *Thymus pulegioides,* with tiny, dark green leaves spreading in a ½ in. thick mat; Caraway Thyme, *T. herba-barona;* a Thyme called Brittanicus, *T. praecox;* and Red-flowering Thyme, *T. praecox* ssp. *arcticus* 'Coccineus', with tiny, dark green, needle-like leaves. Draping over the edge to the cobbles below are Creeping Savory, Roman Camomile, and *Ajuga.* These low mats are for sitting, a modest, but fragrant padding, in a fashion that has not been common for nearly 500 years.

The beds around us contain splendid colors. Snapdragons peek out from just about anywhere, without rhyme or reason, adding charm and color to nonflowering ornamental herbs such as a globe of Lavender Cotton, Bible Leaf, with spade-sized leaves, a dense bush of Golden Lemon Thyme, a patch of fragrant Eau de Cologne or Orange Mint, and spidery mounds of Creeping Savory. Crimson and gold Nasturtium flowers peek from among Mint and Angelica. Perky white and lime-green clusters of Dwarf Feverfews dot the landscape, accenting patches of Lemon Balm, Peppermint, Applemint, Oregano, and Sweet Cicely.

Snug within the confines of the boxes are all kinds of Sages and Basils. Most striking are the sky-blue flowers of Blue Sage, which are born in Monarda-like whorls, one above the other. It has blunt, spatula-shaped leaves with a refreshing lemony tang and is one of the most beautiful Sages. A cheery, yellow Golden Sage shares a cramped site with a Lemon Catnip and the most diminutive member of this genus, a Dwarf Sage, Dwarf Lavender, Pink Hyssop, and *Santolina* 'Nana', emerge from an emerald carpet of Corsican Mint. A hedge of Chives impedes the progress of this tiny creeping Mint on one side and a bumbling, fountain-like Burnet spreads its cucumber-flavored foliage in its path on the other.

The exceedingly long and slender rugose leaves of Mealy Cup Sage, *Salvia farinacea,* reach out from under two tall, spade-leafed, ornamental *Salvia, S. guarantica* and *S. mexicana,* while the wispy branches of Bog Sage, *S. uliginosa* confront them all, dangling over and through the patch willy-nilly. Below is the creeping, Lobelia-like form of Canyon Sage, *Salvia lycoides,* with tiny blue flowers. In late fall they produce a dramatic display with enormous plumes and spikes of blue and purple as well as serving up a fall treat of nectar to hummingbirds and bees.

Two long rows on either side of the middle of the box house a vast assortment of Oreganos, for color and charm and culinary delight. White and pink flowers strike out in graceful arcs from emerald, pine, and grey-green Marjoram foliages. On closer inspection we find Italian and Greek Oregano, Sweet Marjoram, and Pot Marjoram. A single plant of any is enough for a year's supply in any gourmet's kitchen. The cast includes Russian Oregano with dark green leaves, red-stained stems, and a surplus of pink powderballs and *Origanum microphyllum,* with dazzling, neon-pink flowers decorating what appears to be a miniature Money Plant whose silver baubles are actually leaves no bigger than an "O". The luxuriant frosted form of Cretan Dittany graces a small, cedar pot nestled in a grove of bushy 'Spice' Basil while a clump of Golden Oregano tries to outdo its neighbor, Golden Sage, a few feet away. A sample of each of the Oreganos reveals that their aroma is as different and as delicate as rare French perfumes.

Adding to the confusion are two odd herbs that reside in small clay pots sunk into the warm soil. Strange, succulent leaves on one and thick, rubbery leaves on the other remind us of tropicals. A sample under the nose tells us they are both Oregano, not Oregano by botanical nomenclature, but chemical. Because of their carvacol content these two herbs, Indian Borage, *Coleus amboinicus* and *Poliomintha longiflora,* are grown and used in Zone 9 to the tropics as Oregano substitutes. Both are beautiful and exotic herbs for the ornamental garden.

The far end of the box is overstuffed with a grey conglomeration of Lamb's Ears and Garden Sage. Called Lamb's Ears because of their soft, furry texture and size, the leaves are sweet, smell faintly of apples and are used in medicinal teas for soothing sore throats. This duo of Betony and Sage displays blushing pink and ice blue flowers for 3 months throughout summer, attracting every flying creature known. "On new moon nights, other flying things may come", warns our host who has been stalking us for several minutes. "Ye should pluck this" she says, swooping down with one hand to find a sprig of Rosemary. "Wave it about thee, so, then never you mind, they'll flee any of Mary's yarbs they will." Mary's herbs are numerous here; Pot Marigolds, Rosemary, Costmary, etc., and reputed to turn away evil spirits.

Colorful red blooms and a spicy scent nearby lead us to a Rose Geranium intertwined in the branches of the Sage and Betony. Blue, clove-scented flowers draw our attention as well, down to where the frogs and the snails creep. Clumps of grey-green Dwarf Catnip send wispy branches into the moist comfort of the Sage but grow more thickly toward the edge of the box, their lake-blue flowers cascading down in a continual show throughout the summer and into fall. Wild and free at the end of the box is a thick patch of Organy or Wild Marjoram. Its tall pink and white plumes of everlasting, fragrant flowers decorate this end of the bed.

The opposite bed sits in partial to full shade. In it dwell the sleepers, herbs that excel in the early spring or late fall, when the trees do not hide them from the sun. A triumvirate of Angelica, rising magestically over a ground cover of Applemint and seedling Chervil, dresses one end of this garden. A mat of purple and mocha *Ajuga* glides out from under the Angelica as well and down and around the trunk of a small Hazelnut, where a handsome, pea-green patch of Sweet Cicely governs. In early spring this scene is flecked with *Crocus, Eranthis,* and *Hyacinth.* A frail waif of Red Fennel pokes its sheepish head skyward, trying to eke out a living in this shady neighborhood. Its attempts to withdraw fail, thanks to its dashing rust-red appearance. Spilling out into the open, the dainty, filigreed leaves of the tender Chervil encounter an orgy of colors: here golden Calendulas, hot pink Nepetella and magenta and yellow Snapdragons fight for the sunlight with sky-blue, purple, and gold Heartsease Pansies.

As though planted for comic relief, a patch of Bible Leaf, with huge heavenward-pointed leaves appears indignant at the unabashed display of color around them. Those near the edge of the bed have given up hope and fall limp over the brink where they are sacrificed underfoot, releasing a wonderful minty aroma. Bible Leaf, placed here to balance the Lamb's Ears across the path, is combined with its neighbor, Orange Mint, for a tangy tea to clear the head. Hiding behind is Lemon Balm, a great, dark green mound with citronella-scented leaves of rugose character. An effective bugbane (insect repellent) when rubbed on the skin, Lemon Balm also provides a lemon twist for teas and tarts, potpourries, and herb pillows. Yet another citrus scent catches our attention here. A large patch of Orange Mint with purple-marked foliage resembles the odor of an overripe orange rind, at once sweet and bitter. It is a perky flavoring with honey in a strong black tea, or with honey, Camomile and roasted Chickory. The more familiar foliage of Peppermint shows itself, confined in a cylinder for a tidy appearance and to control spreading. The strong menthol flavor of this Mint can effectively numb the mouth and gums and its refined oil functions as an oral anesthetic today.

Our host beckons us to sit and rest beside her a moment upon a fragrant seat of Creeping Golden Thyme. Her ancient but sturdy hand plucks a cat-faced Pansy with whiskers of white and yellow. She kisses it fondly and begins her monologue on the healing value of the herbs around us.

"The Violets, they be for the bowels and scurvy, Angelica for the airs and innards. For blood pressure there be Chervil and Parsley. For the gout, Pennyroyal and Betony. Use Camomile and Sage for the cleaning of hair, and Cleavers and Comfrey for the skin. For bruises bathe with Thyme, for pains 'tis best to use a poultice of Witch Hazel. Horehound's to soothe the throat, and Fennel to stay the appetite. There is Milfoil for sores of the mouth and Mint for toothache, a Lavender bath for calming muscles, Valerian to calm the nerves, and Dill to lull thee to sleep. Here too be Wormwood, a scourge to vexing serpents, Boneset for breaks, Betony for wounds, and Mallows for birthing."

A clump of Lovage, lush and caressable, lounges in the shade before us. Creeping Charlie creeps about our heels, hugging the base of our herb seat, its oval leaves buoyed up on tiny stems complementing the cobblestones above which they seem to float. Here and there Violets and isolated shocks of flowerless Lawn Camomile extrude themselves from between the cobbles, while far to the other side of the yard is an entire mead composed of Violets and Camomile. There they join Creeping Thyme, Anemones, Wild Ginger, English Pennyroyal, Miner's Lettuce, and Mallows. On the opposite side of the yard is a forest of large Swordfern, Christmas Rose, Wood Sorrel, Elderberry, Lungwort, Solomon Seal, Jack-in-the-pulpit, Wild Strawberry, and Trilliums, all of which dwell in the dark shade of Old Man Walnut.

A perimeter bed along the fence is occupied by an odd assortment of ornamental herbs. Curly Parsley, its crisp green leaves gnarled into infinity, is a perky counterpart to a patch of arrow-leafed Good King Henry, *Chenopodium bonus-henricus.* Miniature Roses and ruby-red rag Poppies decorate this bed of dwarf and diminutive herbs, including Rue, Golden Lemon Thyme, Silver Thyme, red, white, and blue Hyssop in trim 10 in. tussocks, blue-bearded *Salvia viridis*, Dwarf Feverfew, Dropwort, 'Opal' Basil, 'Bush' Basil, Variegated Sage, Ariculas, with exotically fragrant yellow bells, and a youthful pink 'Rosea' Lavender snuggling up to an elderly Dwarf Lavender. The herbs rise in height as the bed confronts the forest beneath the Walnut. 'Moonshine' and 'Fireking' Yarrow, and a double-flowered Fever-few press against a screen of Tansy that abuts a Wormwood-collared American Holly.

This dooryard garden is a wondrous place to think, a place to ponder the histories of the great Herbalists of centuries past and examine their herbs, and a place to be alone, with the hummingbirds and goldfinches, flickers and robins, squirrels, moles, mice, frogs, snakes, snails, ladybugs, and damselflies. They, too, find it their dooryard garden.

Chapter 5 / SECTION 1

Informal Landscape

The dawning of informal gardens in the 18th century was a reaction to the extreme formalism of the preceding landscaping tradition. Formal gardens had been appreciated for their beauty and craftsmanship. They were an art form whose reign endured throughout the Middle Ages and the Renaissance, influenced more by the simpering minions of the courts than the gardeners who often deplored the contrived and unnatural creations dictated by courtly convention and fashion. Dynastic rivalry, self-indulgence, the desire to be considered fashionable and correct all fueled the self-appointed arbiters of taste, who seem to be able to fasten on the arts and cultural patterns in every era, including our own, ultimately drove formal garden design to the insufferable and unpalatable. Coupled with other historical developments a new view of nature and man emerged, which was reflected in the naturalistic garden.

The naturalistic mood was created with casual arrangements of trees and plants in their natural form, set around a centerpiece of lawn. The softening of formal lines required the substitution of flowering shrubs and small trees for squared hedges. The vertical lines of stately, towering topiary shifted to the use of large trees and tall perennials and herbs. Woodlands were substituted for the surrounding impenetrable border. Perennial flower beds evolved into features that melded meadows (the lawn) with forests (the woodland), flowing in a sinuous rather than straight, rigid geometric line. Impromptu rock outcroppings and restful meads of naturalized wildflowers provided subtle, earthy cues about the intended naturalness of this landscape. Foundation plantings arising from the house stretched into and blended with the landscape to endow the home with a sense of peaceful isolation.

Serenity is the word that best defines the mood of the informal landscape. Its casual style and quiescent atmosphere were favored by the ambitious, for it is a landscape that is designed to entertain during those cherished moments of relaxation away from the challenging undertakings of a hard-driving, commercial civilization.

We will deal with the use of herbs in five basic and distinct environs of the informal landscape: 1) woodlands, 2) borders of herbaceous perennials, 3) the lawn and mead, 4) rock gardens, and 5) foundation plantings.

Woodlands as the background make an informal landscape impressive, not the expansive lawn. Rising stark and magestic just out of reach beyond borders of dazzling shrubs and perennials, a forest or woodland is where visitors begin their survey. The massed vertical lines of trees immediately steal their attention, while individual groupings sustain the pleasure of viewing and stimulate curiosity and interest in examining the landscape more closely. Although a single tree dominates its immediate environment, all the trees within a design must be composed so that the garden and residence are brought together, balanced and accented one by the other.

A good rule of thumb in selecting trees is that their eventual size should be no higher than the shortest width of the property. Slender, high-story evergreens toward the back of the wooded area give an impression of an endless forest. Deciduous trees set well apart provide filtered shade, essential for many woodland wildflowers and ground covers. Native species should be included for their hardiness and to repeat natural patterns of growth seen in the vicinity.

Vital to a natural appearance is an understory of shade-tolerant species of trees, shrubs, and herbaceous perennial herbs with distinctive foliage and flowers. Shrubs should fill the boundary between woodland and meadow for a smooth transition to the lawn. This thickened perimeter of the wooded area reinforces the image of dense forest. Small properties, forced to rely on only one or a handful of trees, particularly require perennial borders and flowering shrubs to create the sense of a woodland setting. Metropolitan lots can often take advantage of tree scenes beyond the property line. Tying them into the view as if no boundary exists gives the impression of a forest without.

A few valuable shade-tolerant trees include: the American pawpaw (*Asimina triloba*), which bears an edible, banana-flavored fruit; the *Styrax japonica,* a fragrant summer flowering tree which is the source of Storax, a vital component in incense; the graceful and fragrant flowering Willow, *Itea virginica;* some flowering plums; and the Wild Cherry. The Hazelnut, *Corylus* spp., is shade-tolerant with beautiful fall color and a late winter display of plump yellow catkins, as is the flowering May Tree, or Hawthorne, *Crataegus* spp., an old favorite of the Druids, who surrounded their dwellings with barriers of it, which they called the "haege thorn", a hedge of thorns. Flowering Dogwoods, *Cornus* spp., Persimmon, Holly, American Beech, and California Bay are other suggestions. Visit an arboretum to acquaint yourself with the true form and habit of trees suitable as understory trees in your region.

Some useful understory shrubs include: Witch Hazel, *Hamamelis* spp., which are discussed in Chapter 3; *Skimmia,* or Mountain Ash, with exceptional fall colors and berry clusters; the fragrant winter and early spring blooming *Viburnum fragrans,* and the evergreen summer-blooming *V. davidii;* or the summer-blooming Blueberry and Whortleberry, *Vaccinium* spp., with gold and crimson fall colors, complemented by a prolific yield of edible berries. Understory shrubs for dry, rocky woodlands include Snowberry or Coralberry, *Symphoricarpos* spp. and Fragrant Sumac, *Rhus aromatica,* and for wet or boggy regions the evergreen Oregon Grape, *Mahonia* spp. and Huckleberry, *Vaccinium ovatum.*

As the woodlands open to fields and meadows, wide borders of tall herbs and low shrubs thrive in this cool, damp, and protected site along the forest front. The microclimate of constant humidity and moderated temperatures encourages the development of these thickly foliaged bands, made up of a variety of herbaceous perennials which, with their large leaves and dense habits, intercept all the sun they can to form thick screens. Their foliage disappears in winter, providing an unobstructed view into the woodlands, where wildflowers, bulbs, and colorful, clambering ground covers abound.

Herbaceous perennials commonly used in a similarly designed landscape are those that are noted for their sudden spring beauty and their self-maintaining habits. Densely planted borders of herbaceous perennials inhibit the spread of weeds since established beds emerge early in spring and proceed quickly to a dense covering. Progressive seasonal display is necessary and may well include drifts of Tansy, Peonies, Mugwort, Fennel, Yarrow, Valerian, Sweet Cicely, Chrysanthemums, Lovage, Angelica, Poppies, and Monardas. Few annuals are employed unless they may be seeded directly and ignored thereafter. The self-sowing annuals include German Camomile, Borage, Calendula, Dill, and Coriander.

Ornamentally foliaged herbs such as Lemon Balm, Horehound, and other genera in the Mint family, such as Dead Nettle, *Lamium,* and Archangel, *Lamiastrum,* as well as the Mints

Fig. 35. The essence of a mountain meadow with sharply focused ridges penetrating a sloping lawn surrounded by sparse but colorful shrubby vegetation.

KEY

1 Douglas Fir *Psuedotsuga menziesii*
2 Roman Camomile *Chamaemellum nobile*
3 German Camomile *Chamomilla recutita*
4 *Valeriana officinalis*
5 *Angelica atropurpurea*
6 Lovage *Levisticum officinale*
7 Azalea

8 *Lamium* 'Silver Beacon'
9 Fragrant Sumac *Rhus aromaticus*
10 Tree Roses
11 Blueberry *Vaccinium ovatum*
12 Red flowering Thyme *Thymus pulegioides* 'Kermesinus'
13 Pink Chintz/Caraway Thyme *Thymus praecox, T. herba-barona*
14 Wildflowers (Campanula/Camas etc.)

themselves, are delightful herbs despite their modest floral displays. Even relatively drab herbs, such as the salad herbs, may be used to good effect. Carrots, Sorrel, Rocket, Good King Henry, Chervil, Spinach, Skirrets, and Parsley are examples. Candidates for borders that twist in and out of the sunshine are such shade-tolerant herbs as Lovage, Angelica, Fennel, White Mugwort, Sweet Cicely, Tansy, and Monarda.

In the informal landscape an imitation of this natural border, suggesting a succession from meadow to forest, is attained using wide perennial beds situated between a centerpiece of lawn and the forest background. Borders should be as wide as possible: at a minimum no less than 2 ft., to which an additional 1–2 ft. for every 10 ft. of open lawn should be added.

The decorative curves of an informal boundary need not be laid out as a series of gentle arcs but should be laid out in keeping with the natural scene intended. A garden designed to recall a steep mountainous landscape will have a few slim conifers penetrating the property in long, narrow, parallel processions representing the steep slopes that end abruptly in alpine meadows. In this case, herbaceous borders are narrow and filled with many flowering species of low to medium height herbs and a few tall plants. See Figure 35. Marshy meadows have gently rounded boundaries and wide swaths of a very wide selection of herbaceous species, as in Figure 36, while relatively flat forests on prairie margins may be replicated by an isolated tree around which flows a narrow strip of lawn wedged between deciduous woodlands. Here the dense herbaceous foreground is composed of relatively few species, as in Figure 37.

A multitude of landscaping possibilities can be found in nature. Use holidays to pursue and appraise them for inspiration and models. Make your summer excursions an investigation in which the flora and georgraphy of the area visited is pursued as conscientiously as are your recreational activities. In lieu of visiting, careful reading of pictorial texts of geographical regions of the world are useful, as are maps and books on geography.

As borders winnow around the edge of the yard, abrupt changes in foliage patterns may occur, particularly between special features. The task of blending becomes a challenge. Blending involves the use of *transition plantings* that form a smooth bond between widely different plant habits and textures. The transition plants used may be of an entirely different genus or simply a different form of the same species. The latter choice tends to accentuate the novelty of the featured forms and gives a sense of movement to the border.

Where paths move into the woodland, the informal border should present an open, uncluttered appearance deriving from a ground cover or low-creeping or mat-forming herb (Fig. 38). The ground cover will follow the path into the woods so should be chosen to thrive in full sun as well as partial shade. This effect is reminiscent of an animal trail. Deer, etc. commonly browse at the edges of a forest. Wherever a path leads out of the forest, the vegetation is heavily browsed. The junction is marked by stunted trees and densely foliaged ground covers. Light penetrates further inward here because the tall screening plants have been eaten so ground covers eventually spread into the forest along the path.

One of the most vital features of an informal landscape is the lawn. It recalls a meadow. Lying comfortably beyond the forest's edge it suggests both seclusion and security, the demesne of deer and elk. Uncluttered and unadorned by ornamentation, a well-mown lawn is a relaxing scene, satisfying from every point of view. Owing to the amenable color green, the informal lawn is in essence a major transitional planting drawing the entire landscape together around it. It is a special design domain suggesting relaxation and contemplation, where viewing is the primary concern.

The lawn must not be thrown into confusion by criss-crossing paths, statuary, furniture, or potted plants. It is a gently sloping or rolling surface that may, on large grounds,

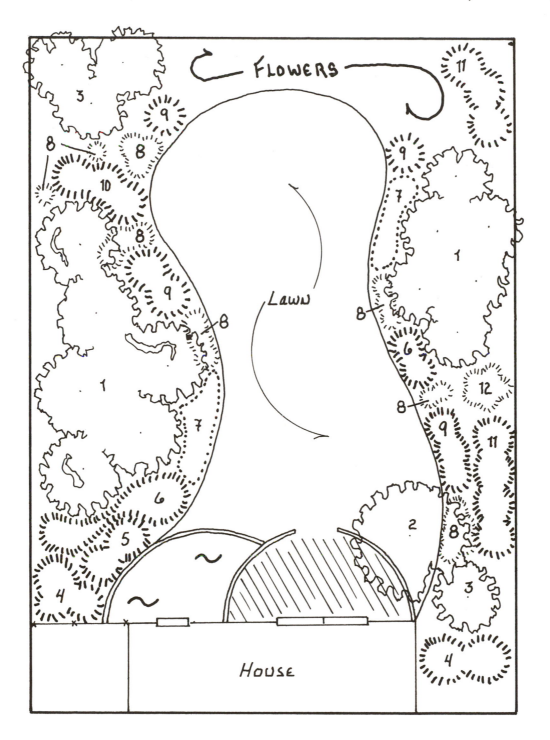

Fig. 36. The temperate meadow thick with small deciduous trees and flowery herbaceous plants.

KEY

1 Hoary Alder *Alnus rugosa*
2 Quaking Aspen *Populus tremuloides*
3 Hawthorne *Crataegus* sp.
4 Bee Balm *Monarda didyma*
5 *Angelica atropurpurea*
6 Golden Mint *Mentha* × *gracilis* var. *variegata*
7 *Calendula officinalis*
8 Tree Roses
9 Lemon Balm *Melissa officinalis*
10 *Valeriana officinalis*
11 Lovage *Levisticum officinale*
12 Violets *Viola* spp.

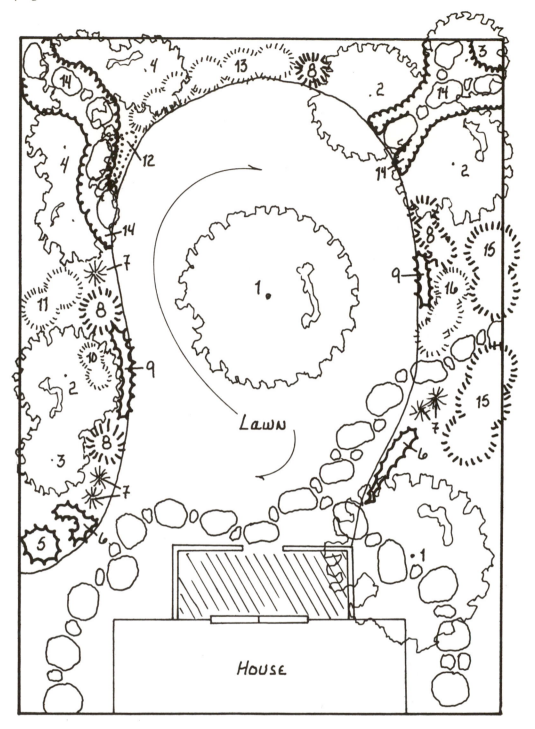

Fig. 37. The prairie meadow with large lawn, central tree and crowded perimeter with well spaced trees and a wide variety of plants crowded into every cranny.

KEY

1 White Oak *Quercus alba*
2 Sugar Maple *Acer saccharum*
3 Hawthorne (white) *Crataegus* sp.
4 Hawthorne (red) *Crataegus* sp.
5 Lavender *Lavandula angustifolia*
6 Golden Sage *Salvia officinale 'Aurea'*
7 Fragrant Sumac *Rhus aromatica*
8 *Valeriana officinalis*
9 Dwarf Sage *Salvia officinalis 'Nana'*
10 Primroses *Primula* spp.
11 *Astilbe* spp.
12 German Camomile *Chamomilla recutita*
13 Lupine/Nigella
14 Sweet Woodruff *Gallium odorata*
15 Lovage *Levisticum officinale*
16 Meadow Clary/Clary Sage *Salvia pratensis, S. sclarea*

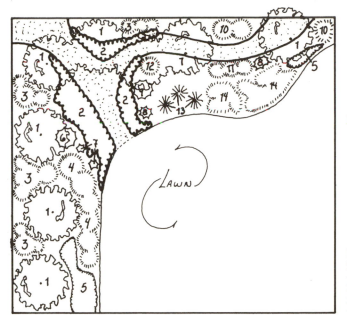

Fig. 38. Deertrail effect on pathway
at its junction from meadow into a forest.

KEY
1 Fl Cherry *Prunus*
2 Roman Camomile *Chamaemellum nobile*
3 Ornamental Grass
4 Peony *Paeonia* spp.
5 Lamium 'Silver Beacon'
6 Southernwood *Artemisia abrotanum*
7 'Silver Mound' *Artemisia frigida*
8 *Santolina neapolitana*
9 Lavender *Lavandula angustifolia*
10 *Valeriana officinalis*
11 Elecampane *Inula helenium*
12 Sweet Cicely *Myrrhis odorata*
13 Roses
14 Perennial flowers

include mounds bedecked with naturalized bulbs and wildflowers. Along its perimeter, near walks or the tree line, where perennial beds are absent, naturalized plants may again be used as transitional plantings to draw attention to and enhance the notion of a succession of plant forms, from the simple blade of grass to the lofty tree.

On larger home sites the landscape can be partitioned into two parts: One the lawn; the other a flowery mead. The mead is a region where low grasses, wildflowers, and herbs comprise the lawn. Shade-tolerant herbs used in naturalized meads include Sweet Woodruff, Variegated Creeping Charlie, Primroses, *Oxalis,* Wintergreen, Roman Camomile, *Ajuga,* English Pennyroyal, Violet, Yerba Buena, Corsican Mint and Wild Ginger. Herbs for sunny meads include Yarrow, Creeping Yarrow, Creeping Savory, Roman Camomile, English Daisy, Creeping Thyme, and Wooly Betony. Held under control by intense competition, even some weeds can be tolerated in such sanctuaries: Dandelions, Mallows, Creeping Charlie, Speedwell, Dead Nettle, and Miner's Lettuce.

The mead is a quiet zone composed to remove one's thoughts from the present and project oneself into a setting where flowers flow ankle deep around an ancient sitting bench. Quiet zones hidden among the trees, barren of all but ground covers, are designed to evoke the feeling of a timeless void within a vast forest.

The mead need not share its domain with turf grasses. A mixed ground cover devoid of grass has much to recommend it. In this case, adjoining turf should be discouraged from encroaching by installing a boundary; e.g., a path, a raised stone outcropping, a low fence or hedge, etc.

The informal landscape makes great demands of the plantings around the home itself. Foundation plantings must be congruous with the casual, unstructured nature of the informal grounds. Some suggestions: 1) vines, which cloak the home in green, thereby blending the contrasting structure with the natural world; 2) low contrast shrubbery placed in disconnected clumps about entrance walks or flowing away from the corners of the home at an angle, Figure 39; and 3) trees, planted as a small copse to one side of, but connected to the house, Figure 41.

Homes once displayed a foundation garden called the "goose foot", comprising a group of a few to several raised beds projected at angles away from one side of the house.

Fig. 39. Melding home with perimeter border using a foundation bed and island of low growing evergreen or shrubby herbs.

KEY
1 'Silver Beacon' *Lamium*
2 Wooly Betony *Stachys byzantina*
3 'Long Leaf Gray' *Thymus*
4 'Linear Leaf Lilac' *Thymus*
5 Dwarf Sage *Salvia officinalis* 'Nana'
6 Lavender *Lavandula angustifolia* 'Hidcote'
7 Dwarf Lavender *Lavandula angustifolia* 'Nana Atropurpurea'
8 *Juniper horizontalis*

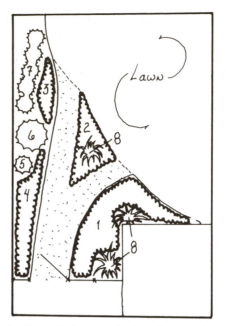

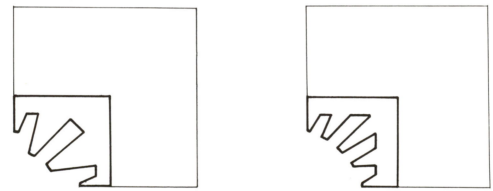

Fig. 40 A & B. Examples of the Goosefoot. Originally an informal design for melding the homesite with an informal landscape it evolved into a formal with the geometric rigidity shown here and contained beneficial herbs.

The outside beds were half the length of those between, giving the impression of a goose's webbed foot. (Figures 40 A & B). In fact, the design represented, in miniature, the forest as it advances into a meadow. It functioned as a mirror image of the wooded grounds at the periphery of the landscape, drawing the home and landscape together (Figure 41). The "goose foot" often replaced the knot as a "formal" garden, and was planted in beneficial herbs.

The rock garden came into its own with the advent of informal landscaping. The unstructured appearance of a rock outcrop appealed to gardeners who wanted their informal gardens to exhibit more rugged natural settings. Borders were cut into hillsides to yield solid rock faces or mounds were thrown up over rock debris and dilapidated brick or stone walls. Forested sites were scoured down to bedrock and streams diverted or formed from springs to cascade through new rocky beds. If at all possible, waterfalls were constructed. A quiet pool and trickling rivulet tucked within the woodland setting helped to isolate the scene in the imagination. Its solemn singsong sounds accompanied by the rustling of trees and the chattering of birds helped deaden urban noise.

Small clumping, mounding, or mat-forming herbs are chosen and planted as features along rocky crags. Dwarf and alpine Saxicoles, plants that thrive in rocky soil, are commonly used. Herbs such as *Alchemilla alpina*, Pygmy Savory, Creeping Savory, Winter

Plate 23

A wild walk with flowers and herbs on both sides including Garden Sage, Thyme and Rosemary. Calamint issues from the cracks in the path for a minty treat in the garden of Angelo Pellegrini, Seattle, WA.

Anise-Hyssop, a wild patch in a kitchen garden at home of Judith Zugish, Marysville, WA.

A truly wild display in a corner of a horse arena including the three common adventitious herbs found in the wild, Catnip, Feverfew and German Camomile. Home of Judith Zugish, Marysville, WA.

Walk leading from porch through wild yard where many species of Violets, Creeping Thymes and Camomiles share their niche with wild things such as Mallows and Miner's Lettuce. English Pennyroyal creeps out of the garden between bricks yielding mint-scented airs whenever stepped upon.

Plate 24

Drifts of French Thyme (right) and Wooly Thyme (left) among Iris on a sloping perimeter bed at the Medicinal Herb Garden, University of Washington, Seattle, WA.

Even in partial shade Borage performs mightily as a wild herb.

The magnificent Elecampane with sunny, spidery flowers on 6 ft. plants in the garden of Mary Medalia, Seattle, WA.

'Coronation Gold' Yarrow rises magestically in the same border as Elecampane. An assortment of gold-hued herbs dress this slim entrance-way border in the garden of Mary Medalia, Seattle, WA.

Lady's Mantle in bloom spilling her fragrant yellow cottony flowers at our feet.

An intimate relationship between Black Cumin, Lupine, Feverfew and other herbs and ornamentals graces this wild patch.

Fig. 41. The true informal Goosefoot. A large foundation planting with a small grove of trees and dense herbaceous cover for melding the home with the surrounding informal landscape.

KEY
1 Grey Birch *Betula populifolia*
2 Golden Creeping Thyme *Thymus* 'Clear Gold'
3 *Juniperus horizontalis*
4 Southernwood *Artemisia abrotanum*
5 Foxglove *Digitalis* spp.
6 Elecampane *Inula helenium*
7 *Valeriana officinalis*
8 Sweet Cicely *Myrrhis odorata*
9 Coral Bells *Heuchera sanguinea*
10 Lemon Balm *Melissa officinalis*

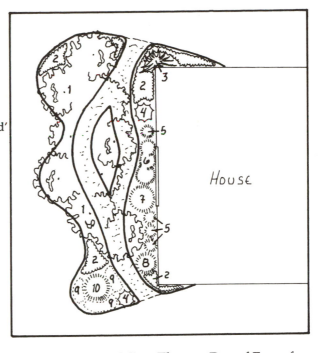

Savory, *Santolina* 'Nana', Dwarf Lavender, Violets, Corsican Mint, Thyme, Dwarf Feverfew, German and Roman Camomile, English Daisy, Saffron, Hyssop, and Wooly Betony are some of the obvious choices.

Ground covers are an essential element in any informal landscape. They are used to meld the subunits of the landscape. The use of ground covers softens junctions and boundary lines of paths by providing a uniform background. Ground covers displaying a marked color or foliage difference are chosen to accent featured plants. They can be used to veil a sunny knoll in somber hues or radiate a spectrum of color in gloomy recesses. In the contemporary landscape the ground cover becomes a feature itself with ornamental foliages and flowers exhibited along a hillside or path.

A mingling of various ground covers should be treated like any other mixed perennial planting, with forethought as to the overall texture. In expansive arrangements of many ground covers it is recommended that they be unified using "drifts". A drift is a clump of identical plants arranged in a variety of shapes that are combined with other groupings or drifts of other plants. Upon viewing a garden with drifts, the eye, seeing the undulating shapes, responds to the notion of movement. A collection of drifts is appealing to the eye because of the sense of motion.

A ground cover is also used to mask unwanted sections of the landscape with a uniform texture. A rocky or uneven terrain can be transformed by the gentle touch of a ground cover into a rolling sea of green. Cloaked in creeping herbs such as Hops, Wooly Betony, Roman Camomile, Creeping Germander, Creeping Rosemary, or Thyme, an area of poor soil becomes an asset instead of an eyesore in the landscape.

The herbs we will examine in detail in this chapter are all either shade-tolerant or shade-loving plants. For the most part, they are vital herbs for the preparation of elegant cuisine. Those that like total shade, at most a filtered shade (a site of shifting light intensity beneath the trees where neither sun nor shade dominates for more than an hour at a time), are Sweet Woodruff, Wintergreen, and Wild Ginger. Others grow preferentially in partial shade (part of the day in shade and part in sun): Sweet Cicely, Violet, and Chervil. Still others require a sunny environment but will tolerate some shade during the day: Lemon Balm, Oregano, Catnip, and Sage.

Chapter 5 / SECTION 2

Herbs for an Informal Garden

The hardiest, most easily cared for of the popular herbs is Oregano. It is an excellent ornamental herb with many applications, from thick borders and fluffy mounds to a dense ground cover of dark green or golden yellow, for steps and walks, creeping along low retaining walls, or tucked between the stones in rock walls. Oreganos thrive in sun-baked nooks and crannies, spreading quickly. The flower has a sweet, desirable floral scent and the delicious scent of its foliage reminds one of rich dishes of spaghetti or the stuffing in hot plump game hens.

The Oreganos are a confusing genus, with many common names for each species and some species quite variable in size, leaf shape, and flower color. The genus *Origanum* contains herbs that are called both Marjoram and/or Oregano. The major species available include Sweet Marjoram, *O. majorana;* Pot Marjoram or Rigani, *O. onites;* Wild Marjoram or Oregano, *O. vulgare* ssp. *vulgare;* Italian Oregano, *O. v.* ssp. *hirtum;* Russian Oregano, *O. v.* ssp. *gracile;* Golden Oregano, *O. v.* 'Aureum' and 'Golden Creeping'; Hop Marjoram or Dittany of Crete, *O. dictamnus;* and *O. microphyllum.*

The showiest of all Oreganos, excellent for both ornamental and culinary needs are Dittany, *O. dictamnus;* Wild Marjoram, *O. vulgare;* and *O. microphyllum.* They have larger flower clusters, often larger corollas, and longer blooming periods.

Except for *Origanum vulgare* the members of this genus should be considered tender perennials and either mulched heavily or brought indoors for the winter. During winter indoors, they should be kept dry, watering infrequently, and placed in a sunny, but cool location. An alkaline soil is necessary for the Oreganos to flourish, as they are susceptible to wilt in acid soils. They will grow in a poor soil as well as a rich loam, but it should be sandy for a dry root zone. The Oreganos also need organic fertilizer or they become bitter and herbaceous. Chemical fertilizer will cause both lax spindly foliage and poor fragrance for their oils are not properly stored when growing too rapidly, resulting in poorer keeping quality of the dried product.

The stronger Oreganos of *O. vulgare* contain carvacrol and thymol as the main aromatic ingredients, as well as linalyl acetate for a sweet note. Sweet Marjoram, Dittany, and Italian Oregano contain significant amounts of geraniol, eugenol, and a unique selection of the sharp, sweetly ethereal turpenes for a pleasantly floral scent.

All of the Oreganos are equally useful as a culinary spice. It is fortunate that the flavorful and fragrant virtues of all the Oreganos are reasonably equal because incorrect substitution occurs regularly when ordering any of the Oreganos, whether as seed or live plants. The finest are Italian Oregano, Dittany, and Sweet Marjoram. Wild Marjoram has a strong thymol aroma, at times medicinal. Greek and Italian are chemovars and vary only in that Italian is sweetly scented, but the robust Greek Oregano aroma is a pleasant one, nonetheless.

The fuzzy, grey, oval leaves of Hop Marjoram or Dittany makes it a dainty addition among bold green compact herbs in an informal border or contemporary perennial bed. Its bright pink flowers are ½ in. long and nearly everlasting, contrasting with their grey foliage. The name Hop Marjoram is derived from the Hop flower likeness of its flower head, which of course means very little to most people today. If we were to be a bit imaginative we could better describe them as miniature cabbages with tiny pink flowers poking out from among the leaves.

Dittany forms a small 12 in. compact plant whose showy nature is accentuated in a rock garden in any landscape or as a small grouping, accompanied by dark green or yellow-green ground cover such as Creeping Golden Thyme, 'White Moss' Thyme, Corsican Mint, or Caraway Thyme for added aroma. From a distance the blooms of Dittany are difficult to see so the grey, wooly foliage is the feature that is visible and must be planned around. Dittany should be planted no closer than 12 in. to prevent damp conditions from killing leaves. In wet climates, damp soil is best controlled by a sand layer or other inert ground cover. Plants kept in pots should be cut back in late spring or when transplanted to the garden to assure healthy, strong wood for a bushier habit.

The hybrid, *O. × hybridum*, a cross of *O. dictamnus* and *O. siphylem*, is a hardier, Dittany-like herb except that the flower stems are less showy and prone to be floppy. Branches, too, tend to be lax, but in close groupings their appearance is similar. *O. microphyllum* is another Dittany-like Oregano, with tiny, 1/16–1/8 in. ovalish leaves that are grey-green, but not fuzzy. This Oregano has pink, Dittany-like flowers and splendid foliage, making it a delightful herb for contrast in a Thyme rockery or among dwarf herbs and ornamentals.

Less showy, but an excellent ground cover in a perennial garden are the various subspecies of *O. vulgare*. The flowers are spectacular, especially their fragrance, so a large area of at least 30–50 sq. ft. should be planted to enjoy them. The flowers vary from white to red-purple. A subspecies with purple stems and bracts called Russian Oregano, *O. v.* ssp. *gracile*, is more ornamental and has a deep green foliage for a bold appearance. Its fragrance is similar to Italian Oregano except for a sharp tangy note. All the subspecies of *O. vulgare* form a copious mound in 2–3 years. A single full grown plant will produce more material for culinary use than anyone could ever use. For borders, they should be spaced 12–18 in. apart in full sun. First year cuttings should be pruned to encourage bushier growth. Flower stalks should be pruned in late summer. They dry easily and are everlasting.

As a winter ground cover, some subspecies of *O. vulgare* spread in dark green or golden mats up to 2 in. high and can be planted close so there is no semblance of single plants. Flower production is less rubust, but a dense and beautiful ground cover is created. Thin clumps to 24 in. on center to produce heavy flower harvests. Italian Oregano develops a more bush-like habit significantly more useful in arrangements and decoratively as bonsai, although it may be decidious in Zones 6 and 7, the limit of its range. *O. vulgare* subspecies *vulgare*, *gracile* and *viride* usually remain evergreen, even through subzero weather. Cold winds are a significant factor in placing Oregano in the garden. In extremely cold climates it should be given a sheltered position, along a fence or protected by an evergreen hedge. Full sun is required to produce the best fragrance from foliage or flowers, but all will grow well in partial shade that receives afternoon sun.

The foliages of two cultivars, *O. v.* 'Aureum' and 'Golden Creeping' have a yellow tint. The latter has a lower growing habit and is superb as a bright, colorful ground cover. Both are good border and pathway herbs where a bright color is needed to liven the scene and they are most beautiful along red brick walks or raining down terraces of dark stone. Both grow well in partial shade.

Pot Marjoram, *O. onites*, resembling Sweet Marjoram, is more strongly flavored and hardier, though it must still be considered a tender perennial in Zone 7. The seed from packets labelled Pot Marjoram are commonly Sweet Marjoram or a hybrid *O. majoricum*, and purchased plants of Wild Marjoram are often *O. onites*.

As a culinary flavor and fragrance plant, Oregano is more widely used around the world than any other herb. It has many forms, and not everyone employs herbs from the Oregano genus for the uses previously discussed. Other herbs that are commonly substituted are Za'atar, *Thymbra spicata*; Indian Borage or Spanish Thyme, *Coleus amboinicus*; Puerto Rican Oregano, *Poliomintha longiflora*; and Mexican Oregano, *Lippia graveolens*. There are oregano-scented herbs represented by the Thyme genus, as in *T. pulegioides* 'Oregano-scented' and Corido, *T. capitatus*; several species of Lippia and Lantana; a species of American Pennyroyal *Hedeoma floribundum*; *Monarda citriodora* var. *austromontana*; and many others. Plants that contain the chemical carvacrol yield the fragrance of Oregano but not entirely the same flavor or keeping quality. *Lippia graveolens* does not have the best oregano scent, being more herbaceous. *Thymbra spicata* has a strong camphoraceous note, excellent storage life, and is in fact a common constituent of the spice Oregano we buy at the grocery store. Oregano Thyme dries well and can be made sweeter by including its flowers, but in either case its storage life is shorter than true Oregano. The thick fleshy leaves of *Coleus amboinicus* are difficult and time consuming to dry. It gives off a pleasantly sweet oregano scent but does not retain this scent for long in storage. These herbs are all for southern gardens or containers and can be remarkably entertaining in any feature.

As a culinary spice Oregano is a facilitator, capable of enhancing the fragrance and flavors of other herbs. The large variety of terpenes in the essential oils of both the Oregano and Marjoram are available to give a boost to concentrations of such chemicals also found in many herbs that are culinary companions to Oregano: Cardamom, Basil, Thyme, Savory, Coriander, Caraway, Cumin, and Ginger. These herbs combine well in tomato sauces, thick soups, gravies, and beef stews. The sweet or floral constituents of Oregano or Marjoram enhance the flavor of herbs such as Ginger, Coriander, Dill, Caraway, Bay, Monarda, Rose, Blue Sage, Lemon Thyme, and Lemon or 'Spice' Basil. Combinations of these herbs are used in salad dressings, stuffings, veal and lamb stew, gravies, and thin broth soups.

An excellent recipe for Oregano is a *GIBLET STEW*.

Braise 1–2 pounds of chicken gizzards (whole) in 3 Tbsp. Basil butter. Add 1 c. stock or boullion and the following ingredients:

¼ c. Sherry	1 Tbsp. Oregano
2 garlic cloves	1 tsp. Chives
1 Tbsp. Lovage	1 tsp. Fennel

Combine the ingredients and simmer for 3 hours until the juices are browning, then add 1 c. water, reheat to boil, and serve as a soup with noodles.

A delicious *POTATO PATTY* is made with Sweet Marjoram.

Grate 4–6 potatoes. Add the following ingredients:

4 Tbsp. Calendula	1 tsp. Thyme
2 Tbsp. Sweet Marjoram	1 tsp. Lovage
1 Tbsp. Fennel	1 tsp. salt

Butter a baking pan or grill and form patties to ⅜ in. thickness. Cook at 425° for 20–25 minutes.

Another recipe for Sweet Marjoram is *SALMON CROQUETTES.* The ingredients include:

2–3 pounds canned or precooked Salmon	1 Tbsp. Fennel
3–4 medium mashed (chunky) potatoes	1 Tbsp. Lovage
3–4 carrots, mashed	1 Tbsp. Chives
2 eggs	1 Tbsp. Caraway seed, (crushed)
3 Tbsp. Sweet Marjoram	1 Tbsp. sugar

Mix all ingredients. Roll into 1 in. balls and flour with a mixture of ¾ c. barley or rye flour, 2 Tbsp. sugar, 1 tsp. salt, 1 Tbsp. Chinese Five Spice.

Deep fry for 3–5 minutes. Serve hot with fresh fruit and a salad.

Catnip, *Nepeta cataria,* famous for its erotic effect on cats, is an easily cultivated ornamental herb. All the Catnips are herbaceous perennials, hardy and eager to spread willy-nilly unless corraled. Best used as ground covers or thick drifts in perennial borders, Catnip's grey-green to green, serrated foliage becomes dense when plants are nipped regularly throughout the growing season. Catnip has a dainty, lavender to pink-spotted flower that is quite pretty, though so small that it is virtually invisible in a richly herbed garden.

Catnip's herbaceous, faintly citrus or "musty mint" scent is not as universally pleasing to people as it is to cats. The chemical attractant responsible has been aptly named, nepetalactone, and much research is underway concerning it. Citral, carvacrol and geraniol contribute a spiciness to its odor. A medicinal tea is brewed with Catnip that is sweet and peppery, used for the relief of sore throat or to ease the burning, scratching feeling of an insect bite. It is also reputed to make one sleepy. The chemical nepetalactone is similar to the active principle in Valerian which can promote sleep. It is best mixed with Camomile, which is also an anodyne, or pain reliever, and with Caraway seed as a flavor enhancer.

Two dwarf forms are available that provide a colorful flower display for an ornamental landscape effect. *N. mussinii,* often called Persian Catnip, rarely grows more than 12–14 in. high. *N. × faassenii,* which cannot produce fertile seed, grows 18–24 in. high. Both have a profusion of purple or deep blue flowers than remain for a long period. They are as hardy as the species, but superior as a ground cover and border herb. The flowers are prominent due to the smaller leaf size and 6 in. long spikes, thick with flowers. The foliage of both smell strongly of cloves and the flowers like cinnamon.

Lemon Catnip, *N. cataria* var. *citriodora,* has a pleasant lemon fragrance and is certainly a good substitute for the species in a medicinal tea. However, no research has indicated whether this variety can indeed be substituted for the species as a medicinal plant. It is a far more pleasantly scented Catnip for a fragrant patch in full sun or partial shade.

Any soil will suffice for Catnip. Tall, large-leafed plants will develop in manured garden soil, with a more pleasant citrus odor—rich soils generally tend to bring out the sweeter aspects and scents of herbs. The cultivars of catnip smell strongly no matter where they reside. Poor soils are equally suitable and it is just this soil type that they were intended to adorn. The flowering of the cultivars changes little with the addition of either manure or chemical fertilizer and they will grow well under alkaline conditions. They are herbaceous, although in protected spots an early frost will not hurt them. In late spring or early summer plants should be pruned to a uniform shape, whether that is a flat top in a closely spaced ground cover area or a hemisphere for individual plants, to encourage a dense growth and improve fragrance.

Catnip combines well with Monarda, Anise Hyssop or Korean Mint, Pineapple Sage, Feverfew, and Horehound in a small area for an enjoyable garden feature with bold colors.

Dwarf Catnips are quite frequently used with evergreens as an entrance theme or as colorful borders for long driveways against a background of darker evergreens.

Sweet Cicely, *Myrrhis odorata,* could very well be called the Licorice plant, for its flavor and scent are identical and as satisfying as commercial Licorice from the root of *Glycyrrhiza.* The ferny fronds of Sweet Cicely are a welcome sight in early spring. It has only a 2–3 month resting period, from November to February, depending on the extent to which the ground is frozen, but it often emerges in mid-February and lasts until Christmas. In cold regions, it will not usually emerge until the ground is thawed, in early to mid-spring. Sweet Cicely's sweet smelling flowers, ofttimes blooming through a light cover of snow, are a delicious treat for visitors strolling through the garden. The seeds ripen nearly 3 months later. They turn from green to shiny black, although they may be picked earlier to improve the appearance of the planting. If the seed is to be used in floral arrangements leave it on the plant to ripen to a hard ebony form that is quite handsome. A highly fragrant oil is pressed from the ripe seeds and was used as furniture polish in the 18th and 19th centuries to protect wood and to provide a licorice-scented finish. The oil that is expressed may be mixed with any paste wax for easier, more even application.

The light green, fern-like branches of Sweet Cicely are a delightful addition in the shady parts of the garden. It will spread slowly by reseeding and prefers a moist spot in the drip-line of trees or around ponds, even in full sun. It usually grows from 12–16 in. and can be used as an accent for tall or ungainly herbs such as Lovage, Angelica, and dwarf fruit trees or shrubs. A ground cover of Sweet Cicely and Turk's Cap Lilies spilling out of the shade under a group of hemlocks or evergreen oaks appears as a primeval forest, untouched and uncluttered by civilization. In isolated clumps it may be surrounded by a low ground cover such as Creeping Charlie, *Ajuga,* Sweet Woodruff, or *Oxalis,* and low-growing wildflowers in a small feature garden where it could be enjoyed for itself.

Sweet Cicely is a good ground cover, following paths into and out of the woodland, as it is tolerant of full and part shade, or full sun if provided with enough water. It is easily propagated by root divisions and seed, however the seed must be sown fresh and in late summer, or from fresh frozen seed in early spring, germinating in about 2 months. Sweet Cicely is not too picky about soils provided there is ample moisture. However, organic soils, such as leaf mold, encourage it to spread faster and self-sown seeds germinate better.

The flavor and scent of Sweet Cicely is probably composed of Anise-like constituents such as fenchone and anethole, common among many of the *Umbelliferae.* As a culinary spice it imparts more fragrance to a dish than flavor unless it is cooked for only a short period or used as a garnish in hot stir-fry or vegetable dishes. Experiment with Sweet Cicely in the kitchen. Use it with cooked vegetables such as carrots, sweet potatoes, rutabaga, and kohlrabi. For Sweet Carrots, slice or dice 3–4 c. of carrots and just cover with water. Add 1 Tbsp. Sweet Cicely, 1 tsp. Sweet Marjoram, ¼ tsp. salt, and 1 Tbsp. honey and cook to desired tenderness.

A delicious Oyster Stew is made with Sweet Cicely. The ingredient list includes:

OYSTER STEW

1 c. water plus chicken boullion	1 Tbsp. Sweet Cicely
3 Tbsp. butter	2 Tbsp. Calendula
1 Tbsp. Chive butter	1 tsp. Basil
1 Tbsp. honey	1 tsp. Lovage
¼ c. Sherry	½ tsp. Oregano

Combine the ingredients and simmer for 10 minutes, then add 3 sliced tomatoes, simmer for 10 minutes more, then add 1 green pepper, diced, and 1–2 pounds oysters. Simmer for 8–10 minutes after bringing it to a boil. Serve with crackers.

In woodland settings and in long perennial borders, Violets, *Viola* spp., are a choice border or ground cover. As a border, they spread only diffidently onto adjacent lawns, choosing rather to droop lazily over the edges, creating an appealing transition, not marred by a trench or small vertical guard placed to prevent the grass from moving into the garden. *Viola odorata,* often called the Florist's Violet, has a fragrance that can only be appreciated in large areas; at least 100 sq. ft. is required. Filtered shade within woodlands is a prime location for a fragrant patch. Plants should be spaced 8–10 in. They will grow to form 12 in. clumps with 2 in. flowers on stems from 6–10 in. long. The large leaves of *Viola odorata* combine well in mixed plantings with Wild Ginger, Wintergreen, Anemones and an occasional Jack-in-the-pulpit.

The Violet should be present in drifts of at least one dozen clumps. Overrunning by other plants should be controlled. In the wild, Violets are generally found in large masses where they are in control, holding other plants at bay because of their thick canopy of foliage that inhibits invaders from below by denying them light. Healthy Violet masses will stay weed-free. Bare patches due to dying or pest-riddled plants are quickly filled by small, slow-growing, self-sown plants that were hiding below in the darkness.

Small clumps of Violets do well on very steep, shady banks where they mix with small ferns and mosses. Some of the native species of *Viola* are very easily naturalized into the cracks of stone paths and are very hardy and pestfree, providing many different colors of flowers, from white to yellow, blue, and grey. Two species provide very ornamental foliage, the Lance-leaf Violet, *Viola lanceolata,* which has long, narrow leaves, and *Viola pedata,* the Bird's Foot Violet, whose leaves extend out like the fingers of a hand. The latter is one of the Violets that will grow in full sun in a rockery and blooms very early in the spring.

The Violet is an excellent salad herb because it is an early spring plant that is high in vitamin C. Use it sparingly however as both the flower and the foliage are good laxatives. The Violet scent in the flowers consists of two chemicals, ionone and irone (both of which occur in the root of the Florentine Iris, or Orris Root, the source of a perfume fixative).

A relative of Summer Savory and a fine ground cover is the herb Yerba Buena, *Satureja douglasii.* Its fragance is fleeting, most noticeable on a hot summer afternoon, but as a shade tolerant ground cover it is excellent. Growing from 2–4 in. it is a camphoraceous and fruity or Mint-scented creeper that needs a rich woodland setting and filtered sunlight for best appearance. It makes a fine tea.

Lemon Balm, *Melissa officinalis,* is a favorite garden herb because of its lemony scent and flavor and its hardy, no-nonsense growth habit. Lemon Balm contains two lemon-scented chemicals, citral and citronellal. The latter is an effective insect repellent when brushed on the skin. The tea of Lemon Balm is a fair representation of lemon and is best used to improve real lemonade or substitute for a lemon twist in a cup of green or a good Jasmine tea.

The light green to green foliage of Lemon Balm varies with the amount of sun; the shadier the site, the lighter the green. However, a good iron-rich fertilizer will reverse this fading. Lemon Balm looks its best only when a healthy green. A variety sold as Variegated Balm or Golden Balm is available and quite attractive for borders along hot, sunny paths or around a partially shaded patio.

Lemon Balm will grow in all soils, in full sun or shade, but it does prefer a moist environment. It will reseed itself and naturalize in lawns. In an herbaceous border it will form slowly-advancing clumps 12–14 in. high. In partial shade it should be trimmed back in early summer to 8–10 in. or less to force it to branch and thicken. Clumps 2–4 years old exhibit the best ornamental form. It may be useful to cultivate it in a separate garden for transplanting to the feature site in fall for a more impressive display. Older clumps forming woody centers that are sparsely foliaged should be divided and replanted.

In the full sun, this bush-like neatness is perfect with evergreen features in perennial beds, as a trim border in formal or informal gardens, or as a featured planting in single ornamental clumps, contrasted with dark green background foliage or variegated ground covers such as the spicy-scented Creeping Charlie, *Glechoma hederaceae* var. *variegata,* in partial shade, or Creeping Golden Thyme in the sun. It arrives early in the spring to add a new dimension to a feature garden when joined by Dittany and Golden Oregano in a conifer arrangement or surrounded by a field of white Violets and spring bulbs.

Lemon Balm is not an easy herb to dry and should be dried slowly at a low temperature. In most cases, air or microwave drying is recommended. The latter will preserve the green foliage color better. It may be used as a strewing herb, in a bouquet as an insect repellent, or made into a syrup or powdered and used in puddings and other sweet desserts. The name, Melissa, means bee, stemming from its use in attracting bees to hives and its use as a honey plant.

In northerly latitudes an herb called Wild Ginger, genus *Asarum,* grows in the wilder parts of woodlands. It is unrelated to the tropical Ginger, *Zingiber.* Like true Ginger, however, Wild Ginger roots are the source of a tangy, spicy flavoring for candies, spice cakes, and some meat dishes. Dried roots are powdered and used as a substitute for true Ginger. Wild Ginger is a moist woods dweller that creeps along the ground, sending up an occasional heart-shaped glossy green leaf. Its purple and brown flowers are almost never seen, for they hide under the forest litter where they are pollinated by browsing beetles.

A number of species exist; some are evergreen and a few are variegated. The largest is a deciduous species, *A. canadense,* with 3–6 in. wide glossy green leaves that stand up on 10 in. high stems. Two evergreen species, *A. europeum* and *A. caudatum,* have 3–5 in. leaves and stand up to 6 in. high. Two species with light green mottling of the leaves are *A. virginicum* and *A. shuttleworthii.* They bloom late spring to early summer and have 1–3 in. leaves, up to 8 in. high. The most ornamental Wild Ginger is *A. hartwegii* that has white-mottled, 3–5 in. leaves on stems up to 8 in. high.

Wild Ginger is a superb ground cover in full or partially shaded areas with rich moist soils. Moisture is imperative and a thick cover of leaf litter or mulch is necessary for it to thrive and spread. It grows slowly but is very hardy. Rocky, shaded areas that have been amended with pockets of peat moss, leaf mulch, or rich loam are excellent. With time, a dense dark green cover is formed.

The informal landscape offers many sites where Wild Ginger may frolic with Anemones, Violets, and native forest wildflowers. A lone clump of fern looming from behind an aging statue or handsome tree trunk is brought into focus and subdued by a rich carpet of Wild Ginger surrounding the scene. The quiet zone nestled in a small woody setting is best carpeted with Wild Ginger. The shifting shadows of surrounding trees provide enough shade to keep the leaves from burning, but enough sun to guarantee a gorgeous, emerald ground cover.

The roots of Wild Ginger are harvested in early spring, dried, and stored whole. They are easily candied but are usually ground, powdered, or peeled into shavings for use in cooking. In general, a greater quantity is required when Wild Ginger is substituted for commercial Ginger. Meat dishes can be vastly improved with the liberal use of Ginger root.

BEEF CUBES

2 lbs. beef cubes braised in 3 Tbsp. Fennel butter	1 Tbsp. Lovage
1 c. stock	1 tsp. Basil
½ c. Sherry	1 Bay leaf
6, 2″ pieces of Wild Ginger root (or 1 tsp. Ginger)	1 tsp. Sweet Cicely

Simmer until juices brown (approx. 2 hrs.) then add ½ c. water, 3 Tbsp. honey, and ½ c. Sherry and simmer for 1 hour. Serve over rice.

The Teaberry, or Wintergreen, *Gaultheria procumbens,* is another forest dweller with shiny, dark green leaves. It resembles strawberry to some extent but with leathery, bristled leaves. Small, urn-shaped, white flowers bowing bell-like beneath the canopy of leaves become bright, orange-red berries in the fall. The berries have the unmistakable odor and taste of the oil of Wintergreen. It contains the compound methyl salicylate, which is a form of the analgesic, aspirin, used for topical pain relief from the itch of insect bites and minor muscle aches.

Wintergreen is relatively slow growing, prefers a moist, acid soil composed of considerable leaf litter or peat moss, and will tolerate a sandy soil. It will, however, grow in regular garden soil, but much more slowly and may not be as hardy. The foliage may exhibit a slight reddish color in some soils. It combines well with the beautiful Bunch Berry, *Cornus canadense,* and Wild Ginger. Because it does not grow over 8 in. high it should be combined with slow-growing, ground-hugging herbs that are not invasive.

A related species, *Gaultheria hispidula,* the Creeping Snow Berry, grows to only 2–3 in. high in moist, acid soils. It is even slower-growing and has a white fruit. Both are very hardy herbs, evergreen through the coldest of winters, and have been used to reclaim strip-mined land.

A medicinal tea made from Teaberry is just that, medicinal in odor and flavor. The leaves are fermented for 24–36 hours in canning jars by pouring boiling water over a jar filled with leaves. The liquid is then strained and diluted as needed. (Fermentation allows an enzyme to free the active chemical, methyl salicylate, thus imparting both the analgesic and Wintergreen fragrance to the mixture. This fragrance is in the native state, and the berries do occasionally taste medicinal.)

Sweet Woodruff, *Galium odorata,* with its zillions of glossy, green whorls, is a pleasant smelling herb and a hardy ground cover. This distant relative of Cleavers and Bedstraw is an old ale herb, with the fragrance, when dried, of new mown hay. The chemical responsible is coumarin, which is characterized by a sweet, herbaceous aroma. Although Sweet Woodruff can be used in herbal teas to enhance the aroma it is not recommended because it has very powerful blood thinning properties that can be dangerous. Use it as a strewing herb and in dried arrangements for ornamentation with a summertime fragrance. It is also used as a fixative in potpourri and perfume.

May wine could not be what it is without Sweet Woodruff, nor should any evergreen forested landscape be without it. The glossy, green leaves, resembling the spokes of a bicycle wheel, are a curious sight. Nodding in the breeze beneath the boughs of conifers, Woodruff's whorls bear an uncanny resemblance to the lofty trees above. This complementary texture and its preference for dark, dry woods and acid soil make Woodruff one of the choicest ground covers among conifers and a perfect contrast beneath large Rhododendrons in an evergreen woodland.

Woodruff spreads rapidly in moist, friable soils, even into the dense shade. In early spring a patch of flowering Woodruff is adorned with countless, tiny, white flowers which last for about a month. Woodruff is a fragile herb and cannot handle foot traffic. Paths can be worn into a patch, however, Woodruff constantly clamoring into the open space, its journey repeatedly foreshortened by the treading of feet. A natural effect is created in a wooded site in this way. An imitation of a deer trail can be created by using ferns and low shade-tolerant underbrush placed along the path at corners and junctions with Woodruff filling the spaces between.

Because it is a shade-loving herb it is suited to forested homesites where a green lawn is desired but grasses are not successful. Prepare the soil as you would for a lawn and plant rooted cuttings 12 in. on center. Keep it moist until plants show healthy signs of spreading then fertilize 2–3 times per year. Iron should be used to maintain a rich dark green.

Wildflowers and bulbs do not balk at this benign ground cover so stock it with many resplendent varieties. Woodruff's dark green compliments light hues and is especially companionable with rayed flowers, shaggy petalled flowers, herbs with clusters of small flowers borne in umbels, or herbs with broad spathes such as Jack-in-the-Pulpit and Skunk Cabbage. It can also share a wooded site with culinary herbs such as Sweet Cicely, Lovage, Wild Ginger, Roman Camomile, Chervil, English Pennyroyal, and Saffron.

Sweet Woodruff is one of the more ornamental ground covers for a contemporary landscape. Its leaf whorls can be cleverly repeated in building architecture, such as octagonal or spoked clerestory windows and transoms, or in yard furniture, patio designs, and fences that employ, for example, a wheel pattern or fleur-de-lis.

An interesting and remarkably practical use for Sweet Woodruff is soaking up automotive oil resulting from spills or leakage in the garage. Traditionally, straw or lawn grass is used, but Sweet Woodruff soaks up the oil just as effectively but with a fresh hayfield fragrance that overpowers the oily odor.

Chervil *Anthriscus cerefolium,* one of the "fine herbs", is a highly fragrant, annual *Umbelliferae.* The leaves, seeds, and roots of Chervil all taste and smell of Licorice, resulting from the fenchone and anethole content. Green seeds are used as condiments or as a sweetener in candy, cakes, and pastries. The unripe seeds straight from the garden are one of nature's most exquisite condiments and are a complement to the already legendary flavor of Chervil foliage.

A shady spot is required to fully enjoy the licorice fragrance of Chervil. Damp forest litter such as the rich soils of Hemlock, Fir, and Oak leaf mulches are best and here healthy stands will reseed themselves. It is important to cover at least 100 sq. ft. with Chervil alone to be able to enjoy its scent. A patch grown only for seed measuring 3×3 ft. should produce enough seed to cover 100 sq. ft. Chervil should be sown evenly over the area and not be vital for early summer appearances when it bolts to seed. The fine, white mist of tiny flowers is priceless and only enjoyed in mass plantings.

Chervil's bright foliage is a welcome shade of green, and best used in filtered sun in a wooded recess. A setting of ferns, Hellebore and *Oxalis,* in a wooded stretch, seeded generously with Chervil and criss-crossed by wood-chip foot paths, is an enchanting forest. Shafts of sunlight flashing here and there glint off the glossy Chervil leaves, suggesting the flitting activity of wood fairies. In the forest setting, Chervil is a good ground cover around and under a closely planted grouping of ferns or large evergreen shrubs such as Rhododendrons.

Chervil may be grown nestled under other herbs such as Angelica or Fennel. It does not combine well with dense, evergreen ground covers such as the Violas due to poor germination and pests hidden under their leaves. Thin ground covers are recommended, such as Tea Berry or Strawberry. Its fall color makes it valuable for replacing waning annuals in early autumn or in herbaceous beds to fill in for winter-slumbering herbs such as Mints, Monarda, and Wood Sorrel.

Chervil has a short growing season, although both a spring and fall planting is possible in most climates. A spring planting will go to seed by summer. For this reason, Chervil must be joined with other ground covers or considerable background foliage. Exposure that is part shade early in the season and stands in considerable sun by mid-summer, such as on the northwest side of the home, is best. When ripening in full sun the stems darken as they age in the hot summer sun, eventually turning a russet or a purple color and very attractive for dried arrangements. In late fall, Chervil is best planted in full sun exposures or among deciduous woods where fall and winter sunlight can penetrate to keep green plants nourished and the ground warm. As long as the surface of the ground does not freeze solid, Chervil will survive a winter. Chervil is frost-hardy and may grow through cold snaps as low as 0°F. This statement is conditional, for it depends upon the gardener's willingness to propagate plants using seed from preceding years. Many of the *Umbelliferae* are frost-tolerant but gain considerable hardiness if the seed is saved from year to year rather than purchased.

Although Chervil will grow to 18 in., in the process of setting seed it generally maintains a low profile, from 6–10 in. Young plants of Chervil should be harvested regularly to keep them small and producing new growth, which is the only fresh foliage that should be used. Older leaves become bitter quickly, particularly in sunny locations. Chervil is a very sweet herb and should be added to salads fresh and is a must as a sweetener in rice puddings or soups and as a garnish on potatoes and vegetable dishes. A sweet garnish of fresh Chervil sprinkled on vegetable dishes and potato or egg salads adds flavor and fragrance rarely experienced even in the finest restaurants. Vegetables are pleasantly flavored when cooked with Chervil. The following Sweet Carrot and Chicken recipes are excellent dishes to discover the power of Chervil.

SWEET CARROTS

3 c. sliced carrots
1 tsp. Sweet Marjoram
2 Tbsp. fresh chopped Chervil
1 Tbsp. honey
¼ tsp. salt
2 Tbsp. butter

Boil in enough water to cover until desired firmness is reached.

CHICKEN BREAST

1 chicken breast, boned
¼ c. broth
1 Tbsp. Sherry or white wine
1 clove Garlic
½ tsp. Lovage
3 Tbsp. Chervil, chopped
½ thinly sliced green pepper

In baking pan add chicken, broth, wine, and garlic. Sprinkle with herbs and arrange green pepper diagonally over chicken. Cover. Bake at 325° for 45 minutes. Serve with fresh fruit and garlic toast.

Two unrelated herbs, American Sweet Cicely or Sweet Chervil, *Osmorhiza* ssp., and Tuberous Chervil, *Chaerophyllum bulbosum,* are often confused with Chervil. The root of the latter is a popular sweet vegetable in Europe.

Garden Sage, *Salvia officinalis,* is undoubtedly one of the most widely grown herbs, not for its culinary use, which is of course part of the attraction, but more for its ability to grow well anywhere. Although Sage is hardier when grown in a rocky alkaline soil, it satisfies millions of gardeners by growing wherever it is planted.

Garden Sage displays three distinct phases each year. In the first, it is a fast growing perennial that may be treated as a deciduous plant in the colder climates, therefore becoming part of the perennial herbaceous border. In early spring, it adds grey or silver-green foliage to the scene.

Secondly, its mid-summer display of blue flowers are a special treat for both the gardener and hummingbirds. Rising half again the height of the plant, the flower stalks bear a dense coat of large, blue flowers and either purple or light green bracts. As the flowers fade, the bracts often give a second display for a month or more, with reddish purple stalks now providing the color.

The evergreen nature of Sage is its third feature that can be enjoyed far into the winter season in warmer climates. Sage will keep its leaves through severe frosts but at the expense of its vigor the following spring. When snow cover stays it is time to prune the Sage, both to protect the branches from snow breakage, so inviting disease, and from desiccating winds that kill young branches, often splitting them, thus tearing into healthy wood below, and again, possibly introducing decay and disease.

The light, grey-green, rugose (pitted and bumpy) leaves of Sage are enjoyably fuzzy and highly fragrant. It is an aroma that constantly brings to mind a fine sausage or turkey dressing. Sage inspires many visitors because it is so rewarding to rub the velvety leaves between the fingers, releasing its aroma to the air. It is an herb which provides instant gratifaction and wonderful memories.

The strong scented chemical in Sage, thujone, is also present in the *Artemisia* such as Sage Brush, and can delay the putrefaction of meat. Thus, plants containing it are used to spice prepared meats in the form we call sausage. Garden Sage, however, also contains some pleasantly scented chemicals such as eucalyptol and borneol for a pure camphoraceous odor, and pinene for a tangy note. It also contains uracilic acid, also found in the waxy coating on apples, that displays some antibacterial activity.

Because Sage is a borderline evergreen in cold climates, it may require cutting back in fall. Strong main branches must be nurtured so the plants are not killed by sub-zero weather. A plant cut back for the first 3 years to 6–8 in. in fall will last many years if it is continually pruned in the same fashion. It will better tolerate partial shade if pruned this way. In warmer climates, flower stalks should be removed as they wane near the end of the summer. Avoid the crew-cut; instead cut them back at least two leaf nodes from the flowering portion of the stem in order to stimulate new growth and to encourage further flowering the remainder of the year. Prune again in the spring to whatever height is desired.

Sage's claim to fame as an ornamental herb is also due to its grey color, which remains relatively constant throughout the year. As a grey herb it is used to brighten up a dark, drab corner in the midst of evergreen conifers, add sparkle to a semi-shady niche overgrown with blue and gold annuals and wildflowers, or as the centerpiece of a grey garden. Historically, grey gardens were composed of the herbs Sage, Lavender, Wormwood, Incana Santolina, Horehound, and Dittany. Many more possibilities have been amassed to our greater benefit: Wooly Lavender; Wooly Betony; Curry Plant; Silver Sage; Beach, Fringed and Roman Wormwood and many more *Artemisia*; 'Silver Beacon' Lamium; *Origanum microphyllum*; Silver Thyme; and Cardoon. Other grey-foliaged ornamentals used today include Everlasting, *Helichrysum lanatum*; *Veronica incana*; *Senecio* 'White Diamond'; Carnations; Wormseed, *Artemisia maritima*; *Cineraria maritima*; New Zealand Mountain Daisy, *Celmisia spectabilis*; and *Anthemis cupaniana*.

Sage blends well with other large-leaved or tall mat-forming herbs such as Costmary, Lamium, Wooly Betony, and Lady's Mantle. Its flowers add special charm among these lesser beauties yet their fragrances contribute equally to scent the air, yielding mixtures of camphor and mint, lemon, apple, or spice. It is a tough herb that should be located on well travelled paths where passersby will come into contact with its foliage. Highly fragrant ground covers scooting out from around it and under the feet add to the effect. Creeping

Thyme, Corsican Mint, and Lawn Camomile are preferred.

For borders of Sage set plants 24 in. apart. Sage is an open, airy herb in any case and closer spacing down to 18 in. will not significantly thicken a border but rather confound the herb's ability to get sufficient light and nutrients to stay healthy. The informal border is recommended. Dead plants are easily replaced and only a fall pruning is necessary. Keep borders under 24 in. wide. Unfettered, Sage will grow to 36 in. or more but tends to suffer during cold winters and in damp conditions. The shorter, pruned hedge develops stronger wood and denser habit for better winter protection and remains more manageable.

Because of its numerous cultivars, Garden Sage can fulfill many dreams of the rockery enthusiast, providing grey and gold, lavender, and magenta, white and sundry greens; something for every spot. A pocket of sandy chalky soil is heaven for Sage and it will look its best when only a few large gnarled old branches emerge from a warty stump to droop lackadaisically into the path of pedestrians. Whenever it is brushed or jostled it releases its delicious odor for us inspiring dreams of plump, hot sausages.

For a strange, but simple ornamental grey garden in the contemporary landscape, use a centerpiece of a single Cardoon, several Garden Sage flowing away in a teardrop shape from it, and a surrounding cover of Snow-in-summer, *Cerastium tomentosum*. In the perennial border use it as a transition plant and match it up with Scarlet Bee Balm or Crimson Geraniums and thick-set clumps of Shasta Daisy and white Alpine Poppies. In the fragrant garden, a massive planting about a reading bench can refresh the air and clear the harried mind, preparing it for deeper concentration.

Garden Sage is sometimes sold as Dalmation Sage, but this label refers more to a spice mixture imported from the Dalmation coast of Yugoslavia and Albania than it does to *S. officinalis*. The spice contains a combination of Garden and Greek Sage and hybrids in between. Garden Sage has numerous ornamental cultivars, and other Sages of the *Salvia* genus offer extensive variations so let us discuss them individually beginning with the cultivars of Garden Sage.

Dwarf Sage is a cultivar of Garden Sage which makes a snappy border on hot exposed banks or driveways. Rarely growing more than 10 in. high, it has a small, narrow leaf with a grey-green color, essentially a miniature of the species, but tends to pale after blooming before the new growth in late summer. Dwarf Sage is the recommended variety for planters and arrangements of live herbs often used in the kitchen and to adorn the porch, where they are easily accessible. It is a slow-growing, undemanding herb with a true Sage flavor and aroma, often superior during late summer.

Another fine container variety is Golden Sage which is available in two cultivars, *S. officinalis* 'Aureus' and 'Icterina'. Because they are slower growing they do not outgrow other plants in a small arrangement. They have a slight citrus scent if grown in well-limed soils and are fine culinary substitutes for the species. 'Icterina' is variegated—yellow or gold margin and wide green veins—and forms a low 14–18 in. dense mound that is a pastel yellow-green from a distance. 'Aureus' is an unvariegated form with entirely yellow leaves. 'Icterina' is one of the hardiest of the Garden Sages, remaining evergreen in areas to −10°F. The dense habit is a major factor in its survival.

Golden Sage is understandably the most popular cultivar of Garden Sage. It can put a touch of warmth into any garden, particularly in a wintry scene with dark green, evergreen Azaleas blooming in early and late winter, or with grey herbs having colorful flowers such as *Santolina neapolitana; Anthemis cupaniana;* or the Newfoundland Mountain Daisy, *Celmisia spectabilis*. The gold foliage goes well with purple or red hued herbs such as 'Opal' or 'Krishna' Basil or complementing a crimson Blueberry in the fall.

Variegated Sage, or Tricolor Sage, *S. o.* 'Tricolor', a fascinating, scintillatingly patterned Sage, with dabs of cream, pinegreen, and purple, and Red Sage, *S. o.*

'Purpurascens', with entirely red-purple leaves, are both lanky, weak herbs that must either be grown in a poor, chalky, dry soil in full sun or be constantly nipped in the bud to force them to bush. It is unlikely that either will winter over unless so treated, but they are alluring ornamentals, particularly in evergreen settings, with Thymes and/or conifers. They quickly develop root rot in areas other than those with dry, chalky soil. A mixture of oyster shell or dolomite chips and sand should be added to an equal amount of soil, thereby giving them the medium required. They are best combined with other drought-and alkaline-tolerant herbs such as Dwarf Lavender, Creeping Rosemary, Dittany, Savory, and Thyme. Variegated Sage is best displayed against a dark green background provided either by conifers or broadleafed evergreens. Red Sage can be cradled in a recurved border of Italian Oregano or flanked by Golden Oregano for added color. Red Sage is recommended as contrast in grey gardens or among light colored foliages. Both are suitable alternates for Garden Sage in the kitchen.

Greek Sage, *S. fruticosa*, has wide, blunt, fuzzy leaves with a wavy margin and a pair of small lateral lobes snuggled up to the base of the larger terminal leaf, forming an arrowhead shape. Its flowers are pale lilac and arrive in late spring and continue all summer. This species constitutes more than half of the Sage purchased as a spice because of its exceptional Sage flavor and fragrance. There are a few subspecies, and crosses of Greek and Garden Sage are common. In growth and habit treat it like a Garden Sage but remember that it is not hardy below 20°F and must be brought indoors—where it is a delightfully fragrant plant throughout the winter—or kept in a cold frame or greenhouse and pruned regularly.

Blue Sage, *S. clevelandii*, very closely resembles Garden Sage in overall shape and habit, but its flower is exceptionally beautiful. Twinned China-blue flowers are borne in large, 2 in., Monarda-like whorls on long stems. They are a special treat for hummingbirds, as are all Sage flowers. They are an exotic addition in any garden and can be easily combined in perennial beds with Daisies and Monardas. Its slim, lanceolate leaves mix with many smaller leaved ornamentals as well.

Although it may be used wherever you would place Garden Sage in the landscape, it is not hardy below 10°F, so should be potted in the fall and brought in for a stint out of the weather. While Garden Sage can easily flourish in partial shade, Blue Sage must grow in full sun for fullest blooming. It may grow larger than Garden Sage, however it should be kept pruned to a more compact size; 18–24 in. is recommended for improved flowering and better winter protection when it can remain outside. This small size also facilitates transplanting to a pot for wintering over in a greenhouse or the home.

The 2–3 in. long, ¼–½ in. wide, butter knife-shaped leaves of Blue Sage have a very strong and pleasant citrus aroma. It is a more pleasant, less camphoraceous species that is superior to Garden Sage for stuffings and potato salad or beans. It has a lasting, lemony scent and flavor that can appreciably transform the common Sage-spiced dish into a special treat.

Clary, *S. sclarea*, and Silver Sage, *S. argentea*, are biennial herbs that provide two shows for the price of one. For their first year their unique foliage is attractive by itself. Silver Sage has thick, downy leaves that rest on the ground and appear to be encased in spider webs. These fascinating hoary rosettes can dot a perennial bed among non-invasive ground covers or grace a potted arrangement with 'Opal' Basal and Variegated Lemon Balm. The following spring an 18 in. branched spike of white flowers adorns the little, fuzzy, mother plant. Clary, on the other hand, forms a modest pile of large, delightfully fragrant, grey leaves—excellent contrast in any perennial bed and a fabulous contemporary feature herb. In the second year it rockets forth with a tall spike of blue flowers. Clary has a variety, *S. s.* var. *turkestaniana*, with a prolific display of pinkish white flowers. If you want to entertain your palate, or have brave guests, two enjoyable uses of Clary leaves include hiding them whole inside pancakes or substituting them for cabbage leaves and stuffing with mildly spiced pork or veal.

Pineapple Sage, *S. elegans,* is true to its name in flavor and fragrance and is definitely an elegant herb in the ornamental garden. Its large, dark green leaves are a perfect background for its scarlet flowers. Pineapple Sage must be pruned to force it to bush or it will shoot straight up 3 ft. or more. In the latter habit it is used in the informal landscape as a tall screen or back border and allowed to shoot up with Tansy, Yarrow, and numerous other ornamental *Salvias* for late summer color. Or it may be pruned to a 12–18 in. bush, joining German Camomile, Golden Oregano, and 'Opal' Basil for a remarkably colorful, fragrant, and beneficial feature garden in the contemporary landscape. It is not hardy below 30°F.

Meadow Sage, *S. pratensis,* has a habit similar to Silver Sage but with large, green, ground-hugging leaves. Its leaves were once used in ales and as a pot herb. Dozens of flower spikes, decorated in violet or navy blue, writhe, like the many serpents on Medusa's head, above this tough little perennial Sage. Use it, as its name suggests, in wild garden meadows among other low-growing herbs with strong vertical habits. Let it surround taller herbs, its many purple arms begging at the feet of a mixed feature of White Mugwort and Valerian, or waving in triumph while surrounding a centerpiece of 'Coronation Gold' Yarrow and Elecampane.

There are countless other ornamental Sages, any of which have beautiful flowers or fragrant foliage, or both, including the crimson flowering fruit-scented Sage, *Salvia dorisiana;* Texas Sage, *S. coccinea,* which also has a fruity-scented foliage and a quick, annual habit; or the blue or purple flowering *S. guarantica, S. mexicana,* Bog Sage, *S. uliginosa,* and Canyon Sage, *S. lycoides.* Virtually none of these are hardy below 30°F and many succumb to temperatures around 36–38°. Treat them as annuals. They are fast-growing and many are prolific fall-blooming ornamentals, each possessed of its own virtue that must be experimented with to be appreciated fully.

Chapter 5 / SECTION 3

A Walk Through an Informal Garden

The postman told me that it was far easier to get to the house I was seeking by water than by land. (Fig. 42) It is also true that the best way to enjoy an informal garden is to approach it in an informal way. With this advice to guide us, we will now stop paddling our canoe and let it glide up onto the lawn, not up to the boat dock, for as I said, we will arrive informally and disembark on the lawn to refresh ourselves in the cool shade of a willow tree.

A mystical kingdom looms before us, rising up into the mist that seems to have snagged itself on the trees farther up the slope. A modern-day castle, a masterpiece of wood and glass hiding among the trees, peers down tolerantly at us through all its windows, silently mindful of our approach. Flowery mats of Thymes and Sedums spill across the hillside. The faint, woodsy aromas of turpentine and spice exite our nostrils. A silver lining of red, ripe Roses across the top suggest to us that the summit is not far off and perchance we will find our way up there later.

The lawn beneath our feet is soft and firm, like green suede cloth pulled taut over a drum. Our footfalls make no sound as we move to the center of the yard. From here, it is less than a few paces in any direction to the surrounding flower beds. As gardeners, we may reflect on how much an informal garden is an arena, where as victors in our struggle to conquer we stand in the center of our creation and watch nature shift and vie for space in the grandstands around us.

This is a somber crowd we are gazing upon, a group of no nonsense plants that provide the patron with more than a pretty face, a kingdom of mystical herbs that even the burden of centuries of toil could not weaken. Marching upslope along the pathway leading to the house is a column of culinary herbs. A bright bundle of Golden Oregano is a fitting standard bearer followed by a clump of Silver Thyme, a silver epaulet on every leaf. Coming behind, tall and proud, are Chives, with great, shocking purple maces held high. A dark green swath of Caraway Thyme, trying hard to keep up, is prodded from behind by a hundred silvery lance-leaves of a Dwarf Sage. Bringing up the rear in an uncontrolled cabaret are the white and purple blossoms of 'White Moss' and Wooly Thymes swarming over the ground. A few overzealous strands plunge over the escarpment to the patio below.

Majestic evergreen shrubs and dwarf conifers hug the escarpment as well. They appear to be stalking the hillside, their mantis-like forms crouching behind their downslope prey. Their prey includes an Old Man, *Artemisia abrotanum,* or two, hardy evergreen com-

Fig. 42. Informal landscape. Gardens of Michele Nash, Mercer Island, WA.

KEY
1 Cr. Thyme *Thymus pulegio* 'Foster Flower'
2 'Silver King' *Artemisia ludoviciana* var.
3 Dwarf Feverfew *Chrysanthemum parthenium* 'Selaginoides'
4 Barberry *Berberis thunbergii* 'Atropurpurea Nana'
5 *Sedum* spp.
6 Wooly Thyme *Thymus praecox* ssp. *articus* 'Languinosus'
7 *Fushia magellanica* Evergreen Fuschia
8 Kurume Azalea
9 Dwarf Mugo Pine *Pinus* spp.
10 *Tsuga mertensia*
11 Sweet Cicely *Myrrhis odorata*
12 Wood Sorrel *Oxalis acetosella*
13 Violets *Viola cornuta*
14 Cr. Red Thyme *Thymus praecox* ssp. *articus* 'Coccineus'
15 Caraway Thyme *Thymus herba-barona*
16 Chive *Allium schoenoprasum*
17 Silver Thyme *Thymus* 'Argenteus'
18 Golden Oregano *Origanum vulgare* 'Aureum'
19 Dwarf Sage *Salvia officinalis* 'Nana'
20 Weeping Hemlock *Tsuga* spp.
21 *Euonymous*
22 Golden Lemon Thyme *Thymus* × *citriodorus* 'Aureus'
23 Southernwood *Artemisia abrotanum*
24 *Viburnum fragrans*
25 'White Moss' Thyme *Thymus praecox* ssp. *articus*
26 Sweet Woodruff *Gallium odorata*
27 Strawberry *Fragaria* sp.
28 Weeping Willow *Salix babylonica*
29 Red Leaf Maple *Acer palmatum* 'Atropurpurea'
30 *Santolina viridis*
31 Azalea
32 *Heuchera sanguinea*
33 *Armeria maratima*
34 San Jose Juniper
35 Painted Daisy *Chrysanthemum coccineum*
36 Violets/Wild Ginger
37 Elecampane *Inula helenium*
38 Sword Fern *Polystichum* spp.
39 Primrose *Primula* spp.
40 *Ajuga*
41 *Primula aricula*
42 *Eremurius*
43 Ornamental Grass *Festuca ovina* 'Glauca'
44 Black Hellebore *Helleborus niger*
45 *Iris* spp.
46 Variegated Flowering Dogwood *Cornus florida* 'Welchii'
47 Peppermint *Mentha* × *piperita*
48 Corsican Hellebore *Helleborus corsicus*
49 Basil-Thyme *Acinos arvensis*
50 Golden Mint *Mentha* × *gracilis* var *variegata*
51 Roses
52 Oregon Grape

petitors with rapidly growing branches that resemble bottle-brushes emerging wrong side out of a bucket.

Immediately before us, shades of red and yellow clamber around like a challenging army preparing for a charge uphill. Their handsome prince in purple robes, an *Acer palmatum* 'Atropupureum', perched by the patio, directs his armies and confers with his generals: a ghostly tuft of *Festuca ovina*, a gold baubled, silver-chested Incana Santolina and an elegant crimson braided Coral Bell, *Heuchera sanguinea*. Scattered camps of Wild Marjoram, with flowering Mother-of-Thyme and other exotic Creeping Golden and 'Tuffeted' Thymes join the ornamental evergreens adorning this garden.

A great finger of forest swoops down to the far right. Swarms of Evening Primroses, *Oenothera tetragona*, Swordferns, and fragrant Ariculas decorate the forest front. Here an inviting Ajuga-cloaked path, its entrance marked by a clump of maroon *Aremuria*, disappears into a dense tangle of Pfitzers and Primroses. Nearby, pink everlasting bouquets of Golden Oregano and the yellow and violet flowers of Oregon Grape and Barrenwort, *Epimedium grandiflorum*, dance around a boulder under the watchful eyes of a pink-flowering Dogwood. Some Basil Thyme, a youthful pair of glossy-leaved Corsican Hellebore, *Helleborus corsica*, and a soft golden yellow Ginger Mint, all dew-covered and sleepy-eyed, reside in the shade of the boathouse.

In the left-hand garden are a few familiar herbs; Wild Thyme, Wooly Thyme and Lemon Thyme, creeping wildly in unrestricted glee with their neighbors, a clump of Chives, a petite mound of Dwarf Feverfew, a back border of Strawflowers, *Helichrysum bracteatum*, and espaliered Pyracantha.

Near the patio is a young Willow, *Salix babylonica*, with Sweet Cicely, Violets and purple-eyed *Oxalis* flourishing in the filtered shade beneath its lazy branches. Two exotic ornamentals also decorate this spot: an evergreen Kurume Azalea, 'Hi No Mayo', and a splendid, hardy *Fuschia magelanica* spreading to form a small hedge.

What lies beyond? What is above the trees? After ascending the slope up to the ridge of Roses we saw from below, we can see that alongside the house is a forest path, dense with undergrowth; shade tolerant shrubs, ferns, Sweet Woodruff, Violets and Wild Ginger reign here with countless wildlings lifting their haughty flowered heads through the forest litter.

Our journey is cut short however. Alas, viewing the grand gardens above will not be an opportunity we will get today, for the guard has picked up our scent. With the baying of Brindle behind us, we scamper back to our canoe, grab up a paddle, and push off. As we drift away, the magical kingdom melts into the mist and vanishes.

Chapter 6 / SECTION 1

The Contemporary Landspace

The contemporary landscape could be described as an artist's impressionistic interpretation of a formal garden. Both employ geometric patterns to compartmentalize the homesite into separate gardens and separate functions. Each compartment, whether for lounging, play, entertaining, or dining, is a distinct element in the landscape highlighted by a small feature garden. This is analogous to the formal landscape, with parterres in one place, a fountain and pool in another, and an enclosed courtyard nestled against the home.

The contemporary landscape is intended to be visually nondemanding. While formal gardens are strict geometric puzzles, and plant materials are grown to perform according to the design, the contemporary design organizes natural features and plant forms into an uncomplicated relationship. It exhibits the least textural contrast of any design style, very few species are displayed and one species is used repetitively to form the theme.

In the formal landscape, visitors are aware that it is the gardens they have come to enjoy, other pursuits aside. Not so in the contemporary landscape. The various divisions are designed to encompass functions that are active, being centered around recreation, rather than passive, such as the solely ornamental parterres and fountains. The extensive use of inert ground covers in lieu of turf throughout the landscape makes it a foregone conclusion that the contemporary homesite is definitely intended for one or more nonviewing functions.

The entertaining or eyecatching aspect of a contemporary feature is that it is oriented either asymmetrically within a compartment and/or as a simple, asymmetrical design. (Figs. 43 and 44) Asymmetry and simplicity are vital, asymmetry for visual interest and simplicity to maintain a subdued presence. Because the feature is not located in the center or all the way around the edge of the space provided, it is understood to be an accent only.

Much of the asymmetry in a contemporary landscape is kept in balance by large areas of bark, mulch, or gravel used for ornamental purposes. Methods of controlling horizontal balance include the introduction of wide paths, the use of curving or angular lines and striking repetitive patterns, and broad, stone-paved patios and courtyards. Vertical components are satisfied by a few trees or small clumps of tall ornamental herbs. Emphasis is placed on their unique stature and branching habits, not exlusively on foliage characteristics, although showy autumn colors are desired.

A multitude of inert and organic materials are available to provide the balance for asymmetry in the contemporary landscape. They should be chosen according to their task: coarse fill for paths and balancing blocks of broad-leafed and robust herbs; fine, earthy mulches for a warm, moody or expressive garden blanket; colored fill for small, visually intense features; sand for visual stability in well harmonized arrangements; and pea gravel for a monotonous background where the barest hint of life is desired.

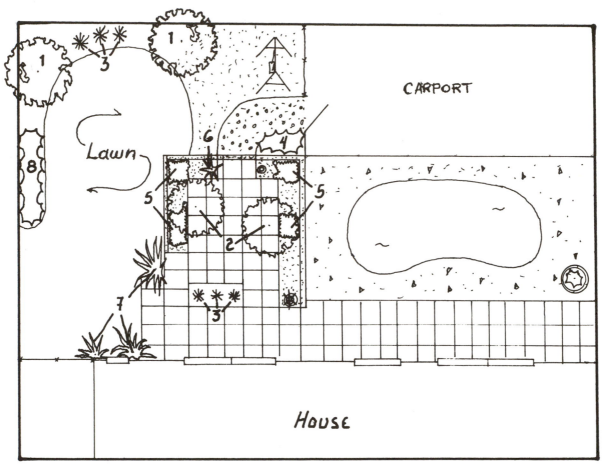

Fig. 43. Spanish style landscape shows the details of contemporary design; compartmentation, assymetry and minimal use of vegetation.

KEY

1 Dwarf Apple *Malus*
2 Pear *Pyrus communis*
3 Roses
4 Southernwood *Artemisia abrotanum*

5 Cr. Thyme, Caraway/'Pink Chintz' *Thymus herba-barona, T. praecox ssp. articus* cv.
6 *Yucca gloriosa*
7 Pftzer 'Aurea' *Juniperus × media*
8 *Eleagnus pungens*

Fig. 44. Looking into the courtyard of Fig. 43 we can see the simplicity and naturalness that converts a geometric pattern into contemporary styling.

The inert category includes rock (from sizes as small as sand to boulders), brick, concrete, and cinders or flyash. The advantage of inert materials is their longevity and cleanliness. A gravel path may last decades if weeds are controlled. The types of rocks used are numerous but include basalt, limestone, granite, quartzite (crystal rock), shale, and sandstone. Other inert materials of local origin may include beach sand (with shells), beach shells, oyster shells, pumice, travertine (hot springs rock formations of unusual character), and volcanic ash.

Organic materials include mulches (leaves, grass, hay, pine needles, manure, compost, and recycled wastes), lumber products (planks, posts, railroad ties), and wood by-products (sawdust, wood chips, bark). Organic and wood by-products mulches are generally used in herbaceous beds, doubling as soil improvers. Well composted vegetable material is the best mulch while bagged manure is a close second, although not as economical. Wood chips, bark, and nut shell wastes are generally spread over polyethylene when used on paths or in feature gardens to inhibit decay. Rounds, the butt end of a log removed before milling, and posts or ties cut in sections make long-lived paths with a woodsy or rustic appearance. Some composts include mushroom culture media and municipal sewage or land fill materials of organic nature that have been specifically composted for sale. Recycled organic wastes include nut shells, beer hops, beet and corn silage, or other vegetable waste from processing plants and sediments from clarifying or sedimentation ponds (pollution control devices in the food industry).

Grass, whether it be Kentucky Blue, Zoysia or Pachysandra, is an important living ground cover for its color contrast, balancing effect and influence on the microclimate of a homesite. Other ground covers are handsome, ornamental or perhaps more clever, but grass can cool a garden in the summer, warm it on cool evenings, control humidity and hold down dust in a way that no non-living ground cover can. Don't ignore it because it doesn't sound like a clever idea. Use it to lessen the burden of maintaining a large area where existing ground covers are simply not up to your expectations. Consider using grass for paths. A path carpeted with a cool spongy grass is kind to the weary-footed and ornamental in a landscape with little or no lawn.

Let's examine some popular garden uses and the gardens that accompany them.

In the contemporary landscape, the kitchen garden is displayed as mounds with herbs planted in a series of arcs, concentric circles (maze-like) or as part of the entire landscape. This latter design features herbs and food plants as ornamental borders and specimens in what is called an edible landscape. Many vegetable crops can be used ornamentally in herbaceous perennial beds. Borders may be composed of Carrots, Curly Parsley, Lettuce (dozens of shapes, sizes, and hues exist, the most ornamental being the old European varieties variegated with purple, red, and dark green), Salad Burnet, Beets, Spinach, and the highly ornamental Kohlrabi and Kales. Screens of Peas, Pole Beans, espaliered Tomatoes, Corn, Red Orach, and Sorghum (an excellent wild bird seed) are productive and entertaining. Isolated features of Purple Cabbage, Brussel Sprouts, Asparagus, Artichoke, Cardoon, and the Purple Okra, with huge, yellow flowers are exciting additions to any landscape. Ground covers include potatoes or the pot herbs, Good King Henry and the ornamental, but edible Strawberry Blite, *Chenopodium capitatum,* which resembles Lamb's Quarters but with a blushing pink sheen on new leaves and a deep red spike of seeds in fall (a treat for many meadow birds), or the Squashes with all manner of fascinating edible gourds. A number of cultivated grains can be displayed in controlled clumps, to add character to the edible landscape, in addition to supplying bird seed for a family pet or wild birds. The most ornamental include Bearded Wheat, *Triticum aestivum;* Barley, both 6- *Hordeum vulgare* and 2-row *H. distichon;* Oats, *Avena sativa;* Millet, *Panicum miliaceum;* and Sorghum.

The putting green (Fig. 45) is formed by a small, oval section of turf (Bent Grass cut to ⅛th in. with a reel mower) forming a flattened mound surrounded by sand pits and evergreen shrubbery. Immediately edging the green is a ground cover of low contrast Wooly Thyme that flows naturally down the sandy slopes of the sand pits, in which are featured a stately Yucca and several barrel-chested Bush Thymes. Around the periphery are Incana Santolina and Lavender, forming a fragrant hedge.

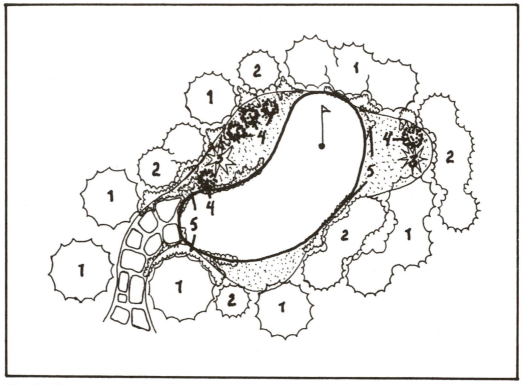

Fig. 45. Compartmentation for recreational endeavors allows the isolated garden, such as this golf green to become part of the landscape in much the same way the parterre does in a formal landscape.

KEY

1 Lavender *Lavandula angustifolia*
2 *Santolina chaemecyparrissus*
3 *Yucca gloriossa*
4 Silver Thyme *Thymus* 'Argenteus'
5 Cr. Red Thyme *Thymus praecox* ssp. *articus* 'Coccineus'

A clover leaf outdoor entertainment or meeting area (Fig. 46) for business-at-home, uses a warm, red or toasty, yellow-brown, brick patio, partitioned by slender austere beds. A rich, natural mulch with deep, earthy tones and odors helps emphasize the garden's simplicity. It is a garden that can't get in the way of mingling crowds. Creepers and evergreens are used because of their crisp, no nonsense appearance. A slope is generated by mounding a 3 ft. berm the north side. A hollow formed around the trees gives the impression of a deep forest, and while the partitions on the north side are mounded to 12 in. in the center to suggest ridges, the south side is mounded to 6 in. or less so the effect of a slope is more pronounced. The pond and lush foliage of the water feature create a limited but none-the-less relaxing scene.

A small circular concrete pad at the side of a garage becomes a fenced basketball court (Fig. 47). One tall Arizona Cypress and low Junipers, that can take the thump of a ricocheting ball, are blended here with a silver carpet of Wooly Betony for a rough, tough garden needing virtually no maintenance. As Wooly Betony creeps onto the pavement and paths it naturalizes the atmosphere of this recreational space. Hops or any other espaliered

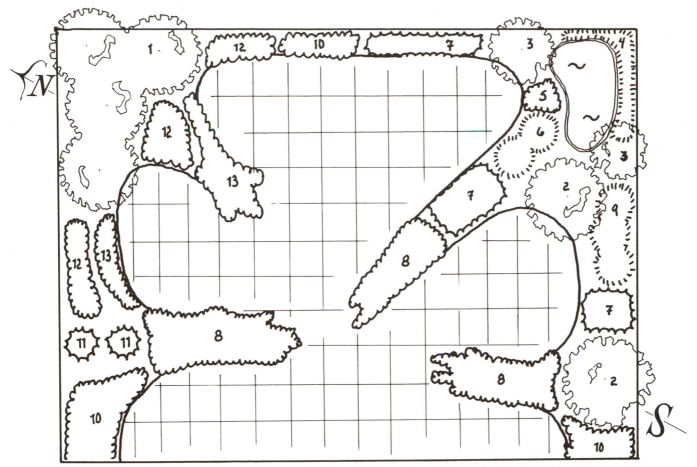

Fig. 46. The patterned patio is popular in contemporary design and this one functionally encompasses a major portion of the homesite.
KEY
1 Grey Birch *Betula populifolia*
2 Dwarf Apple *Malus* spp.
3 *Viburnum fragrans*
4 Coyote Mint *Monardella villosa*
5 Golden Lemon Thyme *Thymus citriodora* 'Aureus'
6 *Angelica archangelica*
7 Wooly Betony *Stachys byzantina*
8 Wooly Thyme *Thymus praecox* ssp. *articus* 'Languinosus'
9 Lovage *Levisticum officinale*
10 Silver Thyme *Thymus* 'Argentea'
11 Greek Sage *Salvia fruticosa*
12 Oregano Thyme *Thymus pulegioides* 'Oregano-scented'
13 Red Flowering Thyme *Thymus pulegioides* 'Kermesinus'

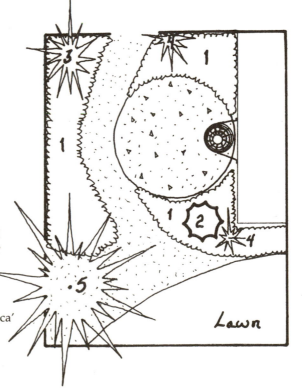

Fig. 47. The basketball court landscaped to be fit and frugal is increasingly popular for recreationally active families.
KEY
1 Wooly Betony *Stachys byzantina*
2 Lavender *Lavandula angustifolia* 'Rosea'
3 Arizona Cypress *Cupressus glabra* 'Glauca'
4 Cr. Juniper *Juniperus horizontalis*
5 Serbian Spruce *Picea omorika*

ornamental planted along the cinder block wall reduces both the glare and the air temperature.

Hops, low creeping Junipers, Red Japanese Maple, and Creeping Thyme create a grand entrance theme for a small front yard (Fig. 48). A few large clumps of basalt loom like denizens of the deep, lurking in the dark green sea of Hops. Variegated Hops provide a lightening effect, imitating frothy waveforms wherever necessary. The walkway of sandstone with paving blocks set well apart and separated by oyster shells and sand, gives the impression of a beach. Swaths of colorful green Thymes creep over this sandy beach or peek from soil pockets in the rocks like seaweeds.

Do not forget that one of the attributes homeowners must consider when designing a garden is minimal care. Because the contemporary landscape uses fewer plant materials and fewer species but more inert ground covers in wide open areas it requires much less effort to maintain than any other landscape, leaving more time for recreation and relaxation.

Herbs ideal for the contemporary landscape include ground covers of Costmary, Wooly Betony and Hops, magnificently flowered towers of Monarda, *Agastache*, and Cardoon, and the majestic, exotic herbs Sweet Bay, Lemon Verbena and Giant Fennel.

Fig. 48. A metropolitan homesite may be small but can be converted by a ground cover of Hops and a few evergreens to a comfortable and clever landscape.

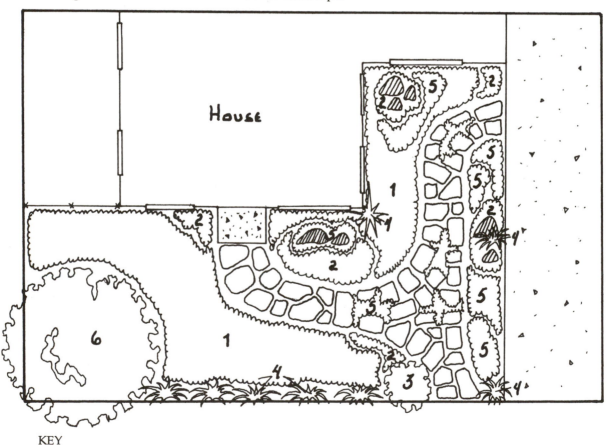

KEY
1 Hop *Humulus lupulus*
2 Variegated Hop *Humulus japonica* var. *variegata*
3 Red Leaf Maple *Acer palmatum* 'Atropurpurea'
4 Creeping Juniper *Juniperus horizontalis*
5 Cr. Golden Thyme *Thymus* 'Clear Gold'
6 Maple *Acer saccharum*

Chapter 6 / SECTION 2

Herbs for a Contemporary Landscape

A luscious, green carpet of Costmary, *Balsamita major,* capping a sunny mound near a hot patio is an attractive and irresistible minty treat within the contemporary landscape. There are two forms: Camphor Plant and Bible Leaf. Camphor Plant has silver-grey to grey-green leaves and a strong camphor aroma closely resembling Wormwood. Its taste is extremely bitter. It forms a low growing mound 12–18 in. high and in mid-summer is covered in tiny white daisies. Bible Leaf is a tastier culinary version of Costmary. It has satiny green leaves with a refreshing minty fragrance and taste. There is still some bitterness, but in a tangy salad with vinegar and oil dressing it is unnoticeable. This form grows to 30 in. and has tiny, yellow-green button flowers in late summer. While Camphor Plant is a shimmering ornamental and covered in swarms of daisies, Bible Leaf's flower stalks if left unchecked are weedy and unnecessary. They should be removed to bolster the growth of large handsome specimens of leaves which may grow to be 12 in. long and 3 in. wide. It is this habit that is pleasing to the eye in an arrangement and most certainly a centerpiece for much conversation.

Costmary is a quick-spreading, herbaceous perennial that is very hardy. It emerges in spring and grows rapidly into a green carpet. Leaves that hang into paths release their minty aroma when brushed. Costmary cannot be tread upon; the succulent leaves are damaged easily. Young leaves point skyward, but eventually bend earthward as they mature, whereupon they overlap each other, completely blanketing the ground and virtually excluding all light beneath, eliminating weeding.

Bible Leaf, once known as Alecost, was a prominent bitter flavoring for ales in the Middle Ages, and a popular nosegay herb because of its fragrant ornamental leaf. The keeping quality of its perky, minty scent made it a good book marker. The name Bible Leaf evolved from its use in Bibles to mask their musty odor. Costmary also provided a refreshing whiff during overly long sermons.

The large decorative leaves of Costmary are attractive in small contemporary arrangements with Garden Sage and purple-tinged Mints. Their combination of aromas is a bonus. In partial shade, a clump of Costmary surrounded by Lemon and Nutmeg Scented Geraniums and an edible ground cover of Nasturtiums is a colorful ornamental feature for the herbaceous perennial garden.

Costmary should be a neighbor to only large-leafed plants as it will obscure the beauty of the mini-leafed plants such as Thyme, Savory or Rosemary. Accent the Costmary feature with fragrant herbs and colorful flowers instead. Examples for contemporary features include Borage, a few dark red Himalayan Poppies surrounded by a carpet of California Poppies, or a patch of Costmary, Wooly Betony and Golden Sage, is a joyous mixture. Other large-leafed, herbaceous perennials that go well with Costmary are Elecampane and Comfrey.

The fragrant leaves of Costmary can be dried in either a flower press or between the pages of a book. The book should be placed flat in a dry location and other books or some heavy object placed on top. Glossy pages should be avoided as they absorb moisture too slowly and leaves may discolor. After 1 week the leaves should be turned over or moved and pressed again for another week. They may be used in arrangements or as fragrant book marks. A musty old book is given a refreshing lift by pressing several Costmary leaves between its pages. This procedure is not recommended for valuable texts since some warping of the pages may occur.

Costmary can be used in a fresh green salad or a combination shredded cabbage and flavored gelatin salad. In the same fashion as Bay, Costmary can be added as a whole leaf covering a baking fish, in beans or some cream sauces and placed on the bottom of a cake tin to impart a minty freshness to white cake.

Wooly Betony, *Stachys byzantina,* is a strangely lovely herb, valuable for its relentless but alluring habit of carpeting the ground with a great grey mat of fuzzy "Lamb's Ears". The common name, Lamb's Ears, aptly describes the large, 3–6 in. long, 2 in. wide, and ⅛ in. thick, densely wooly leaves. Its shimmering, silver flower spikes are flecked with pink blooms for up to 2 months, all the while attracting billions of bees and hummingbirds.

Wooly Betony is little used other than an ornamental, but its faint apple scent and flavor make it a pleasant and attractive salad herb or sweetener in a tea. The sweetness is due to betonicine, a chemical also found in Yarrow. Wooly Betony is not cultivated as a medicinal source of betonicine. The species, Betony, *Stachys officinalis,* is cultivated for medicinal purposes. It has an attractive flower spike and large green leaves. Of great repute, and valued above most, if not all, other herbs as a healing herb, Betony lost favor quickly in the last century. Betony, from the Celtic meaning a "head herb", makes a flavorful tea taken to alleviate headache or migraine. It has also been used as an astringent in minor cuts, thus its name, Woundwort.

Wooly Betony provides a bright, dense ground cover in poor soils or on rocky slopes. It will spread quickly. For large areas in a rocky feature, it is a splendid herb to take up space, demanding little, including water. An established clump of Wooly Betony is drought resistant. It is an attractive herb which should be planted where it is highly visible so that frequent visitations to it by hummingbirds may be enjoyed. In the past, Wooly Betony was allowed to sprout between the paving stones, much like a weed, and enjoyed by sitting around or over it. It is an excellent foundation planting, in full sun or partial shade and will draw attention to a dark colored home or provide contrast for arborvitae and broadleaf evergreens that surround a home or parade along the driveway.

Wooly Betony is very hardy and evergreen to about Zone 5. It does not handle foot traffic well, but if it borders a pathway, as from a patio door to poolside, or down steps to a parking area, it should be allowed to amble where it sees fit. It will attempt to venture onto the path. To keep it neat remove any crushed leaves and branches. It will try again, and again, and again. Few other flowers compete successfully with Wooly Betony since it overtakes any open space quite rapidly. Fast-growing, self-sowing annual wildflowers such as California Poppy, Toadflax, etc. are beautiful with Wooly Betony. If the garden becomes clogged with the herb, remove a square foot of Wooly Betony here and there and reseed the wildflower.

As a clump of Wooly Betony ages it tends to produce fewer and fewer flower stalks from the center—analogous to a fairy ring, the flowering part is always on the outside edge of the circle—so it may not be appealing to a gardener. The flowering stalks form on new stems as they advance. To produce flowering throughout the patch, it must be thinned. Completely remove portions down to bare earth to allow new branches to advance into the open spaces. The best way to maintain a Wooly Betony patch is to remove the flowering branches all the way back to their roots, pulling with them some of the lateral shoots to provide enough open space for regrowth in the spring. There is a flowerless cultivar, 'Silver Carpet', which grows more slowly, forming a tight rosette of silver wooly leaves that can be used for sparkling accents in herbaceous perennial gardens or in rockeries.

Wooly Betony is primarily used in dried arrangements where its silver-wooly appearance is much appreciated. The leaves are easily dried at high temperature and a whole branch can be dried and hung for use later, snapping the leaves off as they are needed. Dried and pulverized Wooly Betony is used to add some sweetness to orange-spiced and Camomile teas.

The Hop, *Humulus lupulus*, is a rather gregarious vine that always wants to grow into or around another plant, shrub, or tree, rather than on a fence, where we would like it. Unlike the grape, which uses its coiling tendrils to anchor itself, the Hop is extremely sticky, due to tiny hairy hooks that cling tenaciously to anything from tree bark to concrete.

The Hop is famous for its major role in bringing medieval ale manufacturing out of the doldrums. Hops were originally used to leaven and improve bread. Because of its powerful antibacterial activity (the chemical humulon is responsible) bread was better and stayed fresh longer. Frequently, bread was used to initiate fermentation in alcohol. When it was discovered that Hop-leavened bread could significantly increase the alcohol content of a fermented beverage the hop beer industry was born. Two chemicals provide a spicy note—farnescene and myrcene.

In the garden today, the Hop is an unbeatable ground cover. One seed planted in late spring will eventually cover about 50 sq. ft. The Hop should also be grown and featured alone as a climbing plant. It will easily scale anything in its path, although a bare concrete wall is somewhat of a barrier. In the rockery, control it by planting only enough plants to cover a designated area in a single year. Although it generally branches, it should be forced to do so with a machete or pruning shears. Poor soil will slow its growth, but essentially it is a superb ground cover for areas such as this, where a low cover is needed quickly. In the contemporary landscape, the Hop is a good ground cover for service areas to beautify a refuse can collection, coal bin, wood shed, a fence around a well house, along an entrance walk, or for a garden without grass. Although it does not handle foot traffic it grows quickly enough to regrow after minor damage from an occasional stroll through a patch. For the landscape without a lawn, the Hop has advantages that no inert fill such as bark or rock can match—reducing heat buildup around the home. A living ground cover reduces the air temperature 10°F or more, as compared to soil or most inorganic ornamental materials.

In Northerly latitudes it is often grown as an annual although plants can live and produce hops (the female flowers) for up to 10 yrs. The species *H. lupulus* is the most hardy and is an herbaceous perennial to about Zone 5. An extraordinary species, Variegated Hop, *H. japonica* var. *variegata* has enormous, maple-like leaves to 10 in. wide that are lime-green splashed with white. No two are alike.

Hop tea is an effective medicinal treatment for sore throats and by virtue of its antibiotic activity can cure Strep throat. It is generally combined with other throat remedies and strongly flavored since it has an astringent and strongly bitter taste.

Hop vines are often woven into arrangements. Their white, fluffy, cone-shaped flowers and fan-like leaves are an interesting counterpart to solid forms such as Cattail and Teasel. The variegated variety provides more contrast since its flowers are often pink and its vine red, not to mention the spatter-painted leaves, for the ultimate in a contrasting effect. They are easy to grow and have few pests.

There is a strange, but entertaining genus of the *Umbelliferae* family, *Ferula*. Of most interest are Common Giant Fennel, *Ferula communis,* and Asafetida, *Ferula assa-foetida.* "Giant" is certainly apropos since they both resemble a 12–15 ft. Fennel plant. The stalk, like Bamboo, may be over 2 in. in diameter. As such, they are definitely eye-catching, if not imposing herbs. These herbaceous perennials grow much less gargantuan as annuals, forming handsome dark green bushes early in the spring, resembling huge, glossy green piles of fishing line. Their foliage has a pleasant Dill/Fennel odor.

Asafetida is used medicinally and in the kitchen. When the plant is 2–3 years old the flowering stalk is cut off at the ground in early summer. The sap emerging from the stump is collected, dried, and rolled into balls. It has a spicy, garlic and vanilla odor and among other uses, is incorporated into Worcestershire sauce. This sap contains disulfides with pesticidal properties. It has been used to repel garden varmints such as rabbits and deer, and is used by veterinarians to prevent bandage chewing.

In the contemporary landscape, let Giant Fennel be itself, perhaps encircled by another tall herb such as the Marshmallow, *Althea officinalis,* Hollyhocks, Lupines, Delphiniums, Yucca or ornamental grasses.

Cardoon, *Cynara cardunculus,* is a relative of the Artichoke, *C. scolymus.* Both belong to the thistle family although Cardoon is one of the largest and certainly the most ornamental of all, growing into a silvery, fern-like plant, with leaf stalks 2–4 ft. long. The upper part of the stalk is thick and fans out, resembling a large, grey Dandelion leaf. The leaf margins of French Cardoon have tiny, ½–1 in. needles that are wicked looking. The spineless form is more popular in the kitchen garden for obvious reasons.

Cardoon's satiny, silver-blue, thistle-like leaves make a choice contrast in contemporary gardens, growing with Himalayan Poppies, Kniphofia, and surrounded by a carpet of 6–10 in. wildflowers. It can also be used as a major vertical component in an arrangement of low rotund evergreens, neatly trimmed for maximum contrast. A procession of 'Moonshine' or 'Fireking' Yarrow and 'Opal' Basil winnowing in and out among the plants adds color and charm.

Used ornamentally in the kitchen garden, a group of Cardoon should be the central feature, surrounded by purple cabbage and peppers. In either a kitchen or contemporary landscape, Cardoon is a fascinating screen which combines well with tall-spiked flowers, particularly Clary and Delphiniums. Ornamental plants with large, dark green leaves make a striking contrast with the large, silvery leaves of Cardoon. In any garden where Cardoon will be used as a screen it should be accompanied by Fennel and purple Okra for an extremely entertaining and beneficial border.

When grown as a culinary staple, Cardoon is treated like Celery; that is bound and wrapped with black plastic or burlap to blanch stems for better flavor and crispness. It should be planted in rills, or shallow troughs, for more efficient watering and to assist in banking earth up around the main stalk as it grows. Its large, purple flowers are displayed in a hair-raising shock of petals atop a globe-shaped bud. The buds resemble, and are eaten like, an Artichoke. The Artichoke is essentially a step beyond Cardoon in that most of the herb's vegetative production, and hence the culinary attraction, has been confined to the bud. It is also a unique and handsome herb for the contemporary kitchen garden. Cardoon requires full sun and a rich loam for the finest flavor, but it will grow virtually anywhere there is sufficient moisture. Poor soils or limited water reduce its normal 5–6 ft. height to 3–4.

For wild gardens, Cardoon's erect silvery stature is a bold vertical component in a setting with Tansy, Lupine, Poppies, Valerian and Yarrow.

The Monardas are an enjoyable and rewarding ornamental genus of herbs. Their variously scented foliage and brightly colored, spider-like flowers are two excellent reasons for growing this handsome native American herb. The *Monarda* genus encompasses such delightful herbs as Lemon Mint, Oswego Tea, Horse Mint, Mountain Balm, Wild Bergamot and Bee Balm. The herb sold as Mountain Mint is not *Monarda* but from the closely related genus, *Monardella*.

The major species of concern is *M. didyma*, Oswego Tea or Bee Balm. This herb was originally popular among early American colonists as a tea substitute. The leaves are often wilted and fermented for varying periods before being brewed as a hot beverage. There are at least a dozen cultivars in various hues of red, including 'Cambridge Scarlet', 'Violet Queen', 'Salmonea', 'Mahogany', 'Alba' and a dwarf form, 'Granite Pink' growing to only 10 in. Many of the cultivars available may belong to *M. × media* which is a hybrid of *M. clinopodia*, *M. didyma* and *M. fistulosa*. The hybridization has been only to the benefit of gardeners. Monarda is one of the most ravishingly beautiful flowers in the herb world.

The flowers of *M. didyma* are about 2, but often 3, in. wide in rich, moist soils and sunny spots. It grows to 4 ft. in a nettle-like fashion. Its 4 in. long, serrated leaves are pleasantly aromatic; a mixture of herbaceous, spicy and camphoraceous scents. Its fragrance and flavor is the result of the chemicals thymol (of which *Monarda didyma* is a commercial source) and the oregano-scented carvacrol. Its spicy notes come from eucalyptol and cymene. Frequently a small flower appears out of the top of the one below. Such is the habit of many herbs of the Mint family—repeated vertilicasters—but not with the show of these uninhibited, crimson spiders, one atop the other.

The tea of this herb is mildly stimulating. For a hot beverage it should be mixed with some Lemon Balm or Camomile. Honey should not be used as a sweetener as it spoils the mild flavor of the tea, particularly the apple aroma of Camomile.

The Monardas may be cut back early to force a low, bushy growth. Every three to four years they must be divided and replanted. No shade and plenty of water are required for the best and most fragrant flowering. The better the quality of the flower, the more useful as a coloring agent, both in culinary applications and in cosmetics. Popular with American Indians, Bee Balm was highly regarded as a cosmetic herb, the flowers used on the face and skin as a rubefacient. The leaves were woven as bracelets and worn on the arms and legs, symbolic of age and status as well as in a practical fashion as a deodorant. From the diary of John McCowan comes this description of his meeting in 1872 with an Indian brave. "A handsome brave came first, with the painted tin horse hanging down from his neck to his naked bronze breast, skunk fur around his ankles, hawk's feathers on his head, and a great bunch of sweet smelling Monarda on one arm to set him off the more." The Blackfeet called this flower "Young Man".

Wild Bergamot, *M. fistulosa*, resembles Bee Balm in most respects, but its leaves are often hairy and the flower is usually lavender. *M. fistulosa* f. *albescens* has a white flower and a variety, *M. f.* var. *menthefolia*, spicy scented leaves.

Dotted Mint or Horse Mint, *M. punctata*, is shorter, growing to 3 feet, and much branched. Its repeated vertilicasters have led to a less frequently used common name, Twin Flower, recalling the superimposition of 2 or more spidery flowers arising one out of the other, much as in *M. didyma*, though more regular. They are small, 1¼ in. yellow flowers spotted with purple. Horse Mint is a hardy species, tolerant of dry, sandy soils.

A species sold as Lemon Mint is really Western Balm, *Monardella odoratissima*. Both are named for their strong citrus scents. Western Balm, or Mountain Mint, is an 18–24 in. perennial forming a densely branching mound of small, slightly pubescent leaves and large 2 in. rose flowers. It is a very hardy Western U.S. native. Its small, 18 in. compact habit makes it an especially ornamental Monarda in herbaceous perennial borders. The leaves are strongly aromatic and make a good, citrus-flavored tea. Lemon Mint is more properly the annual, often biennial, *Monarda citriodora*, with pink flowers spotted purple. It is rarely available, Western Balm being substituted, which has a more ornamental value in any case.

The genus *Monardella* contains another ornamental species that is often offered as *Monarda*. Coyote Mint, *M. villosa*, is an 18 in. hardy perennial with a decumbent habit, akin to the creeping Thymes. The stems hug the ground, rising only at the tips. It forms a dense ground cover displaying many small 1 in. rose-purple flowers throughout the summer into fall. It is also a Western U.S. native.

In the contemporary garden, the taller Monardas are excellent for features or borders in partial shade. They are enhanced by a ground cover of Columbine, Primroses, Sweet Cicely and small ferns. Also in the contemporary setting make a small corner garden featuring Monarda, Elecampane and a front border of German Camomile backed by tall spiked flowers such as white Delphiniums or Hollyhocks.

The Giant Hyssops, *Agastache* spp., are an enjoyable group of herbs from the Mint family. They all closely resemble the Mints, with an especially ornamental, fragrant flower spike and aromatic leaves that give off a minty or spicy and herbaceous odor. Pulegone and menthone are two mint-scented chemicals common in the Giant Hyssops. They make fine teas and good ornamental herbs in herbaceous perennial borders.

Korean Mint, or Wrinkled Giant Hyssop, *A. rugosa*, and Anise-Hyssop, *A. foeniculum*, are the most ornamental and fragrant. Anise Hyssop, also called Blue Giant Hyssop, has an exceptionally fragrant foliage and can be distinguished from substitutions based on that characteristic. Substitutions include the common native American species Purple Giant Hyssop, *A. scrophulariifolia* and Nettle-Leaf Giant Hyssop, *A. urticifolia*.

In the landscape the *Agastache* should be clumped in small groups of 3–6 plants. Do not surround them with tall materials that will hide their handsome shape. Well-spaced plants spread outward to 18 in. and become relatively dense, particularly if pruned in early summer. A 3–4 in. pink or purple spike graces the plant for 2 months or more to make a remarkable display. The flower spike is dense and firm and keeps its color and fragrance on drying.

Combine *Agastache* with light green or grey herbs such as ground covers of Wooly Betony, Santolina, yellow-green Junipers, Silver Thyme or Wooly Lavender. An enticing display for a small garden might include 2 clumps, each containing 5 plants of Korean Mint, 1 of Shasta Daisy, 3 Dwarf Feverfew, and a smattering of deep blue Pansies. The gaily blooming patch is a spot of summer color year after year.

Full sun and rich soil are required for best flavor and fragrance, but *Agastache* will grow in any soil and in partial shade. They are a favorite plant of the bees and hummingbirds. A few species of Giant Hyssop are grown commercially to produce honey. These include *A. mexicana*, or Mexican Giant Hyssop, to 2 ft. with showy red flowers, and *A. cana*, Mosquito Plant, with large pink flowers that bloom for a long period of time.

A popular herb that must be grown in containers throughout most of the northern latitudes is Sweet Bay, *Laurus nobilis*. Sweet Bay is most widely cultivated for its culinary value. Although Bay is a tree, it may grow as a multi-branched shrub, especially if it has been frozen back once or twice. Temperatures below 28°F will damage youthful growth, but only extended freezing of the ground will kill it. As a potted herb the bushy habit is considerably more ornamental and provides more leaf area than otherwise possible. The sweet, spicy notes so cherished are captured only by a mid-to-late-summer harvest when the levels of Bay's aromatic chemicals are peaking.

Sweet Bay leaves are thick and tough and can take considerable abuse in high traffic areas where its fragrant pine-green leaves may flaunt themselves on paths and porches near sitting benches. It was once a popular topiary medium because of its quick regrowth and dense habit after pruning. The species is often called Grecian Laurel, but the two other types of Bay are atypical and more ornamental. A sweet and exceptionally fragrant Sweet Bay is the forma *angustifolius* or narrow-leaved Bay. The forma *crispa* has crinkled leaves which are large and dark green and have an undulating margin for an entertaining appearance. The narrow-leaved form is hardier and significantly more valuable in the kitchen.

In the contemporary landscape, Sweet Bay may be planted out in the garden for the summer and then repotted in late summer, to be brought indoors for the winter. If care is taken to assure its survival each fall it makes a beautiful, brilliant green standard. When trimmed, Sweet Bay should be joined with other low-growing trimmed herbs such as Thyme, Germander and Santolina in a very small garden. Sweet Bay is often trimmed as a formal hedge in southerly climates and can become a large tree from 20–40 ft.

Sweet Bay is a popular aromatic herb used as part of a fragrant wreath or Yule log for the fireplace. The soothing, spicy aroma of Bay, composed of eucalyptol, eugenol and methylchavicol, permeates the room. Bay is also used as a flavoring, particularly in meat dishes and commercially in baked goods. The berries are edible and quite sweet and are used to flavor soft drinks; however, it rarely flowers or sets fruit in northerly climates.

A culinary substitute for Sweet Bay is Oregon Myrtle or California Laurel, *Umbellularia californica* (not to be confused with *Myrica californica*, California Wax Myrtle). It is a handsome, slow-growing, broad-leaved evergreen tree. In the landscape it takes on a shrubbery form with a summer treat of white flowers. The leaf is several times the size of Sweet Bay and is of a stronger, more camphoraceous aroma. California Laurel is used in dishes exactly as the legendary Sweet Bay but sparingly as it is stronger. The berries have a bitter, minty taste when green and in fact contain a fair amount of menthol. The chemical umbellulone gives the foliage its strong camphoraceous note.

Lemon Verbena, *Aloysia triphylla*, is another herb that should be grown in a tub or ornamental container in cold climates and brought indoors for the winter. It is valued for its pleasant lemon fragrance and profusion of lemon scented flowers. It is truly a wondrous herb. Its fresh lemon scent is so pure the tongue is deceived into a sensation of tartness. In a tea its lemony contribution is welcome and possibly superior to lemon juice due to the absence of acidity. Lemon Verbena does not discolor a black tea as does lemon juice, and yet adds a strong lemon flavor and aroma. The chemical contributions from its oil to flavor and scent include citral, myrcene and citronellal.

Lemon Verbena leaves should be dried carefully. They rapidly lose their fragrance if dried quickly and with much heat. It is best to freeze them to retain the natural flavor. They can be preserved for a short time in sugar or an alcohol solution for culinary uses and in almond oil, wax or lard for cosmetic applications, simply to add a pleasant lemon fragrance to products. As it is essentially an evergreen in tropical climates it can be enjoyed year-round if nurtured in a greenhouse during the winter. To maintain it through northern winters it must be grown in a greenhouse at 55–60°F. Water, fertilizer and misting should be continued frequently. At mid-point of winter prune to 6–8 in. and decrease maintenance until early spring. Cuttings are taken from spring growth and can put on 18–24 in. of growth in one season, so prune repeatedly for a dense vigorous habit that is more useful in an ornamental garden.

There are a number of useful species in the *Lippia* genus which are related to Lemon Verbena and are categorically called the Verbenas: Licorice Verbena, *L. alba,* is a glossy green, anise- and vanilla-scented herb; Mexican Oregano, *L. graveolens* and *L. origanoides,* both strongly scented by the chemical carvacrol; Sweet Herb, *L. dulcis,* an exceedingly sweet herb popular for centuries in Central America; and dozens of others with fragrant leaves and decorative flowers from cream to purple. They will not generally survive a cold snap below 30°F but are easily planted back into the garden each spring after being sheltered indoors for the winter. They are all shrubs, and should be pruned heavily before being brought indoors and kept dry through the winter. Some may be deciduous.

In the contemporary landscape, the Verbenas may be used as a fragrant centerpiece in a small garden with other fragrant plants, particularly the Scented Geraniums, Basils and Sages, for a delightfully fragrant garden. Keep them accessible for caressing in areas where entertaining or a considerable amount of foot traffic occurs and wandering hands are commonplace. In southerly climates it may attain 8–10 ft. though it is best to trim it into a 3–4 ft. hedge surrounding patios and along entrance walks or as a centerpiece in a courtyard near a doorway or sitting area.

The flower of Lemon Verbena is cream-colored and deliciously fragrant, unequalled for adding both sweetness and lemon tang in a good orange pekoe tea. Other Verbenas have lavender flowers with exotic sweet and spicy scents. Their secret is not preservable except by freezing so enjoy their simple beauty.

Note: Many tropical plants have not undergone the scrutiny of Old World herbs and have been less clearly defined. Presently, Lemon Verbena is most often classified as being within the *Aloysia* genus. Older references place it in the *Lippia* genus. *Lippia alba* and *L. origanoides* have also been classified within the *Lantana* genus, a group of popular and highly fragrant houseplants.

A Walk Through a Contemporary Garden

The contemporary landscape we will visit belongs to a large family. (Fig. 49) The yard is designed to meet a variety of expectations. An enormous sandbox provides the 3–12 year old crowd with ample entertainment: enough sand for the largest castles possible, a swing set, picnic table and tether ball pad. The lawn is petite, just right for the teenagers to soak up the sun and mowed close enough for Dad to get in his putting practice. The brick patio is spacious and partly covered. It plays a role in entertaining not only friends but also business associates. The greenhouse is Mom's, and off-limits to all but her garden club cohorts. The kitchen garden is a conspiracy, a vegetable patch turned entertainer, with color and texture and charm all its own. This landscape paints a significant contemporary picture.

We enter this contemporary domain by the side entrance passing through a side yard that has been designed as a miniature basketball court (See Fig. 47). The ground cover is exclusively Wooly Betony. A few conifers and a large sweet-smelling Lavender imbues this site with a rugged, wild feeling.

The great, grey, board gate opens and a peaceful land lays beyond. Through the branches of a dwarf apple tree we can see a most beautiful kitchen garden. A hedge of golden down catches our eye in an instant. This telltale sign of fall is a back border of Asparagus which has turned and its autumn color is a dazzling backdrop to knobby-kneed Brussel Sprouts and a few remaining Artichokes with their delicious tophats gone to fluff. Parchment brown shocks of corn, countless scarlet fingers of Cayennes hanging from frost blackened bushes, and swollen purple cabbages also decorate this garden, a feature garden of vegetables.

As we move into the yard over a sun-warmed ground cover of red-brown bark, pastel-green clumps of fresh herbs are evident beneath each of the fruit trees. Like one another, yet not, they are Sweet Cicely and Chervil, and likely they will remain green for weeks to come, succumbing only to heavy snow. Their anise foliage provides sweetness in a long list of dishes that can be enjoyed almost all year.

The feathery, bronze figure of a clump of Red Fennel can be seen hiding behind the tree. Our host tells us that in summer it is only the centerpiece for a trio of purple herbs, which included to its left a circle of Purple Okra, which grew to almost 7 ft. and aside from lemon-yellow trumpets their enormous 6–8 in. pods are a special treat in Gumbos. On the right was a double row of Opal Basil bordering the lawn releasing a clove and citrus fragrance on hot afternoons.

Across the lawn is a vermillion hedge of autumn-dressed Blueberries jutting out

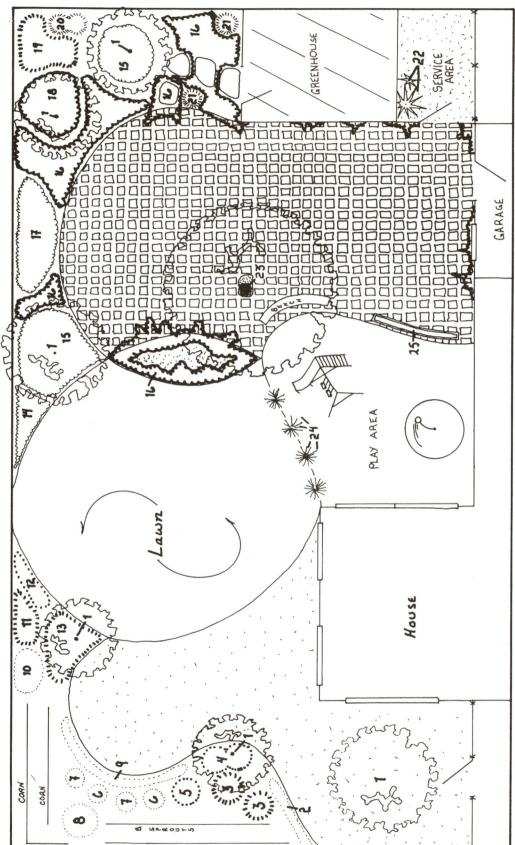

Fig. 49. The contemporary homesite—a valuable recreational facility that fulfills the basic needs of all the family members in many ways. Coordinating these needs into a landscape can be a challenge.

KEY
1 Dwarf Apple *Malus*
2 Ruby Chard
3 Lovage *Levisticum officinale*
4 Chervil *Anthriscus cerefolium*
5 *Calendula officinale*
6 Red Cabbage *Brassica oleracea* var. *rubra*
7 Red Pepper *Capsicum*
8 Scarlet Runner Beans *Phaseolus* spp.
9 Lettuce *Lactuea* spp.
10 Purple Okra
11 Red Fennel *Foeniculum vulgare* 'Rubrum'
12 Opal Basil *Ocimum basilicum* 'Dark Opal'
13 Sweet Cicely *Myrrhis odorata*
14 Hops, Variegated *Humulus japonica* var.
15 Wild Ginger *Asarum hartwegii*
16 Caraway Thyme *Thymus herba-barona*
17 Strawberry *Fragaria* spp.
18 Violets *Viola* spp.
19 Pineapple Mint *Mentha suaveolens*
20 Shasta Daisy *Chrysanthemum maximum*
21 Ornamental Grass *Festuca ovina*
22 Arborvitae *Thuya occidentalis*
23 Japanese Walnut *Juglans seiboldiana*
24 Blueberry *Vaccinium corymbosum*
25 planter, annuals

from the corner of the house to intercept an amber-yellow Walnut that is just now shedding its spiny capsules of sweetmeats. The chocolate-brown paving of the patio is such a complementary color it is evident it was chosen to emphasize the autumn colors around us.

Creeping Golden Thyme, its minute pine-green foliage with swatches of rich yellow, decorates the entrance way to this entertainment area. Bright red berries of espaliered Pyracanthas, scarlet and white berries of Wintergreen, juicy, blood-red fruits of everbearing Strawberries all combine in a small but breathtaking scene.

The enormous white-stained, maple-like leaves of a Variegated Hops run along the fence in the recesses behind the trees, while cream-spotted patches of Pineapple Mint frolic at its feet. A few white and gold Violets, Anemones and other fall flowers poke their shy heads skyward under the cover of the dwarf apples.

Creeping Thymes and Creme-de-Menthe Mint scamper everywhere on this patio unfettered by a gardener's demands and seemingly unaffected by feet. Their verdant hues are a vivid, provocative contrast to the chocolate brick beneath them.

A wafer-thin veil of dark green creeping Thyme has overflowed some stepping stones, revealing little of the path to the greenhouse. It is enough however to lure anyone along. On this cold autumn afternoon, spying on the herbs within is not possible as the panes are fogged with condensation. Our host glides up beside us and between nervous glances over his shoulder he draws the door ajar for us to see inside. A fragrant rush of humid air tickles our chilly nose and recipes dash through our minds as we take tally of the herbs within: Sweet Basil, Marjoram, Parsley and Summer Savory revel in beds, their feet warmed by cables of heat. So too are Rosemary, Lemon Verbena, Blue Sage and two exotic Lavenders, French and Spanish, lounging in cedar tubs awaiting their cues to entertain guests either in the house or on the patio when weather permits. Other ornamentals and houseplants share the confines of this small but ample greenhouse.

As we depart it is evident again from a single glance across the yard that fall is not forgotten in this landscape and indeed it is plainly part of the scheme. What of the other seasons? Perhaps we will return in the spring to see for ourselves what is revealed.

Chapter 7 / SECTION 1

The Wild Landscape

In late spring or early summer, millions of pilgrims venture to the mountains and secluded valleys of the wilderness to witness one of nature's greatest wonders—wildflowers. In an endless procession, these insignificant herbs emerge and bloom in boundless profusion, to the awe and delight of everyone. Rare is the heart without envy for, as any homeowner or gardener knows, wildflowers are fickle worts, bowing to no man's fancy.

The wild garden, one with an endless display of flowers and gay foliages throughout most of the growing season, is the most difficult landscape to design and maintain. This is so because the natural forces that govern where and how plants grow are complex. In our tiny little lots, the power of these laws suddenly become evident. What we desire and can offer is all too frequently incompatible with natural rules.

The solution is for the gardener to be more thoroughly knowledgeable of the needs and niches of hundreds of plants. These are not herbs to be sown and abandoned to the unnatural circumstances surrounding man's houses. Because the garden is by no means a natural thing, it is not uncommon for Mother Nature's laws to be carelessly avoided or misapplied. Limitations of space, moisture levels, soil constituents, light exposures, the length of the annual growth cycle, temperature, winds, and on and on must be fine-tuned to prevent death. In most cases, we can circumvent disaster through knowledge and with extended care. Because the wild garden is a rapidly evolving, highly competitive and complex community with which to work, this care cannot be remedial or after the fact, but rather academic and preventative. Our understanding and knowledge must be deep and broad enough that we are capable of seeing the trouble spots where nature's power diminishes our vision of wilderness.

To provide a starting point let us think of a natural garden, one that is designed according to the principles of permaculture. Here, many of the plants and their relationships in the landscape are indigenous or adventitious. They have grown so long in the area to become naturalized. This strong, natural component in the design is appealing because there is no sudden boundary separating the garden and the home in it from the real world. But this does not suggest simply letting the wild things at the margins in and leaving them alone. This is after all a human habitation and must be organized—designed—with the needs, wishes, and hopes of its inhabitants in mind. So selection of plants and their placement relative to one another requires the intervention of the inhabitant's mind and hand. From this intervention unique elements can be incorporated to create garden features.

On the other hand, a wild garden is an imaginary meadow, a richly robed reproduction of a refuge found once in a wilderness far, far away, living now in the mind of the gardener.

In essence, the wild garden takes its cues from the informal landscape. The mead and quiet zones within the forest and its deep herbaceous borders are excerpted from the informal picture and are drawn with a new and different emphasis into a setting where they are dominant features. Naturalized wildflowers, bulbs, and herbs dominate the landscape. The forest is only suggested and lawns are limited to scattered patches of ornamental grass or herb-choked stone walks.

The wild landscape becomes an enchanted mead suitable for inner reflection and a serene abode not found in other landscape forms. Sitting on a tuffet among waist or shoulder high flowers banishes all thoughts of the corporeal world from the mind. Amidst a thicket of flowers, extravagant alien colors, and all fashion of flowers and foliages, we can expect to meet, if not come to terms with, life's underlying meaning. This is a place where we are at ease, entering into conversation with ourselves and with nature.

Many centuries ago, cloistered monks used this same garden, dedicated to silence and prayer. If this garden was large it was called a "Field of Paradise", if it was small, the "Hortus Conclusus", a minute garden designed expressly as the place for meditation. (Fig. 50)

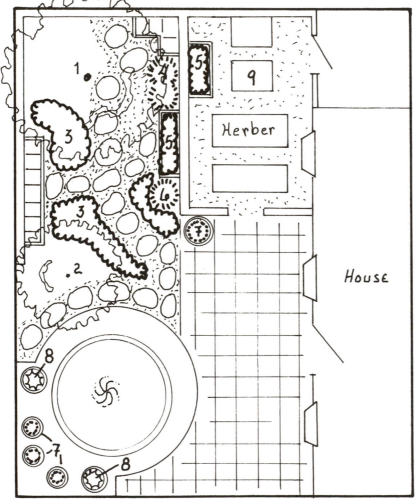

KEY
1 Elm *Ulmus*
2 Golden Rain Tree *Laburnum anagyroides*
3 Violets *Viola* spp.
4 Valerian *Valeriana officinalis*
5 Caraway Thyme *Thymus herba-barona*
6 Variegated Lemon Balm *Melissa officinalis* var. *variegata*
7 potted fragrant annuals
8 Rosemary standard *Rosmarinus officinalis*
9 Herber

Fig. 50. For the metropolitan garden two ancient wild designs hark from the Dark Ages. The enclosed garden filled with flowering plants galore is the Hortus Conclusus (see Fig. 12) and the open garden drawing nigh to the patio contains many wildflowers and bulbs and is called the Field of Paradise. Both follow in the monastic tradition, the former a place of solitude where the flowers for the altar and celebrations were cultivated and the latter a place for tranquil strolling or lounging.

Encompassed by trellises of twining espaliered herbs such as Blackberry, Rose, Grape, Honeysuckle, Hop, and Jasmine, the Hortus Conclusus was a secluded spot from which the herbs and flowers necessary for altar decorations and celebrations were derived. Indeed a celebration is the perfect description of a wild garden.

So how do we create this unworldly world? The natural laws must not be flagrantly violated. When we do break them, two forces must intervene to keep chaos at bay: knowledge that we have broken the law, and therefore, what we must do to compensate, and physical effort.

To understand wild garden design we must first understand the wilderness environments where wildflowers are the predominant flora: temperate and alpine meadows and forest glades.

The temperate meadow (Fig. 51) is home to the robust herbaceous perennials of tall

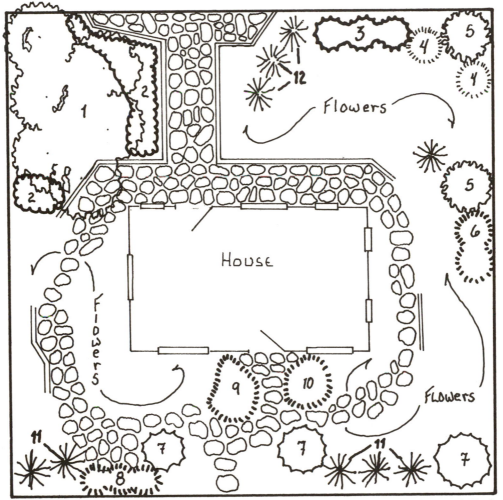

Fig. 51. The temperate meadow is an exciting medium for the wild landscape full of herbaceous perennials of tall rangy or spreading habits and small trees and shrubs. The semi-walkway and wall are reminiscent of aged paths, conveying timelessness yet contributing to the form of the design.

KEY
1 Chinquapin *Castanea pumila*
2 Violets, Primroses
3 Sage *Salvia officinalis*
4 Maltese Cross *Lychnis chalcedonica*
5 *Viburnum fragrans*
6 *Valeriana officinalis*
7 Oregon Grape *Mahonia aquifolium*
8 Lovage *Levisticum officinale*
9 Orange Mint *Mentha* × *piperita* var. *citrata*
10 Black Mint *Mentha* × *piperita* var. *vulgaris*
11 Roses
12 Buckthorn *Ceanothus americanus*

dense habit. Evergreens are not uncommon here. Because water and nutrients are not limited, many species can compete even though patterns change from year to year as one species overtakes another. Red, yellow, and white are the predominant colors and daisies, plumes and spikes, are the more common flower arrays. The temperate meadow requires a sloping or uneven terrain. It may be divided by a stream either real or abstract as in a dry bed. A pond or rock outcrop provides the basis for a feature garden and widely different plant types.

The alpine meadow (Fig. 53) should feature a limited number of dwarf or low plants, to 12 in., scattered in equally distributed groupings with taller, medium height evergreens as the background. On mountain slopes, evergreens act as microclimate modifiers, abating winds and therefore, the chill factor; they hold top soil and therefore, moisture. They must be the background from which the meadow originates and flows into the homesite. Rocks are common, either as outcrops, protruding abruptly from the ground, with little or no soil at the sides to cover or soften their strong vertical lines, or as stone fields, rocks littered over the surface in a random, runaway fashion. Alpine gardens may contain grasses or none at all, being defined instead by scree, loose rock chips in irregular heaps, characteristic of landslide materials. They are often terraced on steep slopes or narrow valleys and littered with mounds of large rocks.

Woodland wildflowers are the embodiment of the Sylvans, legendary beings of enchanted forests. Flower-filled glades are transformed into a grand arena of sprightly music and dance at the touch of the waxing moon on a clear night. Mists and underbrush, of course, prevent our viewing these events. We can prepare for it by sowing an assortment of sylvan seeds; herbs such as Violets, Wood Sorrel, Camomile, Pansies, Creeping Thyme, Corsican Mint, Saffron, and Dwarf Monarda, and weeds such as Miner's Lettuce, Foamflower, Mallows, Solomon Seal, Buttercup, Blazing Star, Anemone, and wildflowers by the hundreds.

Sylvan wildflowers should be ankle or knee deep, and as thickly set as possible. Deciduous or evergreen backgrounds of small trees and shrubbery (copse) or a thicket of medium-sized trees (spinney) are recommended. Some flowers must overflow into the forest and the garden should be interrupted by a stream bed, whether real or false, which doubles as the site of a pathway. For the most part, sylvan flowers are shade tolerant and enjoy the filtered shade beneath widely spaced deciduous trees. Herbs and wildflowers able to grow in partial shade to full sun may be used as long as sufficient sunlight is made available. Because the garden itself can be perceived as an open and gloriously sunny glade, surrounded on the periphery by trees, plants requiring full sun can be enjoyed. (Fig. 52). Rich soils and moisture make the woodland meadow a thriving world for every imaginable wildflower.

There are four features to consider in designing a wild garden: rocks, trees, water, and topography. Rocks are used to break monotony, add feature gardens, or provide access, such as with a path. They may be a memory of more than a score of geologic features, scree, outcrops, tallus, glacial deposits, or man-made features such as walls, cairns, and ruins. Trees provide balance, shade, and perspective; i.e., making a scene appear closer at hand or farther away than it actually is. Water is soothing and imparts peacefulness but provides humidity, water for irrigation, and in the case of a stream bed an access route. Topography is the lay of the land: rolling, steep, rugged, or flat.

The meadow is a rapidly evolving environment that is home to many kinds of flowers, vines, dwarf trees, shrubs, and grasses. It is a total picture we wish to design, not just put in plants. Many evergreen shrubs are unsurpassed for year-round beauty, such as Azaleas and Oregon Grape. Small ornamental trees, including Mountain Ash and Conifers, are useful. Vines such as Jasmine and Grape are easily naturalized over exposed rocks and

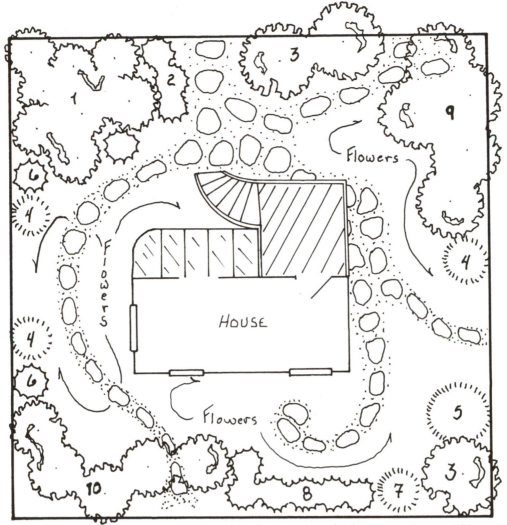

Fig. 52. The open glade, fashioned after the sun drenched retreats deep within a forest, is seemingly surrounded by small trees and large shrubs, in a sense isolated. A drybed path provides accesss and contributes to the natural artistry of the landscape but is far from lifeless and home to creeping herbs and clumps of ornamental grasses.

KEY
1 Mtn. Ash *Sorbus sargentiana*
2 Southernwood *Artemisia abrotanum*
3 Flowering Cherry *Prunus triloba* 'Flore pleno'
4 *Valeriana officinalis*
5 Bee Balm *Monarda didyma*
6 Variegated Holly *Ilex aquifolium* 'Golden Queen'
7 Meadow Rue *Thallictum aquilegifolium*
8 'Puget Blue' Buckthorn *Ceanothus imperssus*
9 *Viburnum fragrans*
10 Lilacs *Syringa vulgaris*

along walls where naturally occuring weeds such as Bryony, Morning Glory, or brambles thrive. And finally, grasses. Most of what we see immediately is grass, Field Grass or Canary Grass and countless others that compete vigorously for limited space. Ornamental grasses must be substituted in our gardens. Their visual effect far surpasses ordinary grass and the challenge of incessant weeding is less likely to become a torture so we can more enjoy the product of our toil. Grasses do not produce more seed than any other plant but they are remarkably fertile and grow rapidly to maturity, so choose the most ornamental: Fescue, *Phalaris*, Zebra Grass, Quaking Grass, Cloud Grass, etc. Many are useful decorative materials and provide winter forage for birds. A well-balanced wild garden will preferentially draw meadow birds to it because familiar foods are available. In the garden a variety of grasses and herbs with large and small seeds will attract more species of birds than an excess of any one type. Determine your local species of birds and plant to their needs if you wish to attract them.

Both perennial and annual herbs are found in meadows. Most early spring flowers are perennials while a large number of the summer-blooming plants are annuals, which continue to germinate until the first frost. Herbs blooming in the late summer or early fall, surviving the frosts and even gentle snowfalls, are predominantly perennials.

All of these assembled plants provide a plethora of textures and habits but they do not appear in nature in a random fashion, growing whenever their seed is given life, nor should they in our gardens. Each plant species occupies a specific "niche". In ecological terms, a "niche" can be defined as the role played by a specific plant type within its immediate surroundings. Tall herbs tend to accumulate more tall species around them because they deprive lower plants of sunlight. Only a tall herb can successfully compete. Evergreen shrubs are dense so they can keep other species from invading their territory. They tend to produce rounded mounds in regions of poor soil where only grasses or low herbs will grow. However, they are usually shade-tolerant so during their life any tall herbs or small trees successfully maturing beside them will not severely stress them. Meadow trees are fast growing, able to survive some shade during early years, when they might be overtaken by tall herbs, and many are able to produce their own nitrogen. Surround the garden with these and the meadow's edge is complete.

The textures created by these natural processes are fairly consistent over a period of time. We will find in any meadow an overall smooth appearance that flows gently into taller and taller herbs as well established clumps survive and push outward. There is little abruptness on a meadow. Tall plants should not jut unceremoniously from a low ground cover. Smooth transitions are important in the wild garden to accentuate contrasting colors and foliage textures.

The last matter of concern in the wild garden design is the manner in which plants propagate. The first realization that species of plants grew in drifts was derived from extensive studies of the natural meadow environment. Be sure to apply this principle to the arrangement of wildflowers. The drift emphasizes a downhill procession in the wild garden. It also recalls the directional dispersal of the plant type. Plant communities can move slowly, as old plants die, younger ones further ahead continue on while adjacent species move in. Thus the colony progresses, albeit slowly and erratically. For the same reason, a species will not always be spread uniformly throughout a meadow and will succeed better as a clump than as a lone plant. Meadow flowers are invariably found as clumps of a few to hundreds of the same species. How many clumps and where is governed by environmental restrictions—i.e., soil type, moisture or acidity—and is up to the gardener.

It is important to remember that water in the wild garden will imply to the well travelled visitor tall herbs and dense thickets. Meadow streams are rarely unobstructed unless soil is virtually absent, or the stream is intermittent so life cannot survive the summer months. A stream bed in a wild garden must reflect this natural pattern. If it is to be used as a dry bed, a path and access way, it must be inhabited by low, hardy and possibly evergreen herbs. With water available, taller herbs will need to be nurtured there or nature will do it for you.

A number of tall and ungainly herbs are suited to the wild landscape. The majority are annuals. Three, Dill, Anise, and Cumin, are *Umbiliferae,* members of the Dill Family. Three others, Borage, Sesame, and Fennugreek are popular for their use as sprouts. The perennials include Mugwort, Elecampane, and Yarrow, three very decorative herbs. Another perennial, Lovage, has been a pot herb, valuable since antiquity. In one fashion or another, these herbs reveal themselves most satisfactorily in the wild garden.

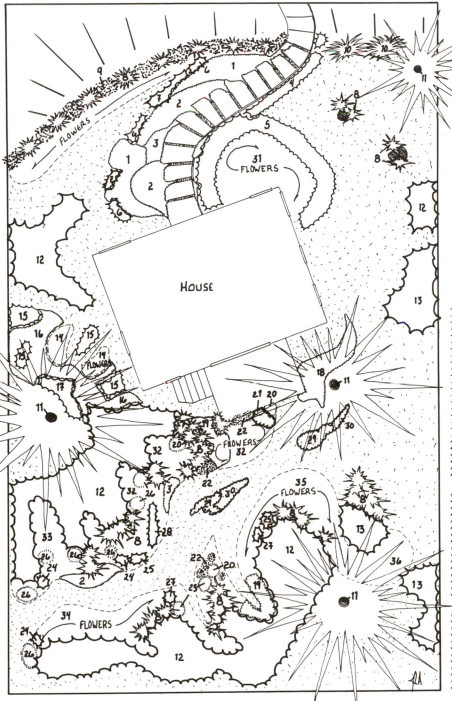

KEY

1 Oregano Thyme *Thymus pulegioides* 'Oregano-scented'
2 Cr. Red Thyme *Thymus pulegioides* 'Kermesinus'
3 'White Magic' Thyme *Thymus pulegioides*
4 Dwarf Lavender *Lavandula angustifolia* 'Nana Atropurpurea'
5 Compact Lavender *Lavandula angustifolia* 'Compact'
6 *Santolina* 'Nana'
7 *Santolina neapolitana*
8 Heather *Erica* spp.
9 Silver/French/Gold Lemon Thyme
10 *Juniper horizontalis*
11 Redwood *Sequoia semperviren*
12 Azalea/Oregon Grape
13 Rhododendron
14 Primroses *Primula* spp.
15 Black Hellebore *Helleborus niger*
16 Violets/Creeping Charlie
17 Wild Ginger *Asarum canadense*
18 Pearlwort *Sagina procumbens*
19 Lady's Mantle *Alchemilla* spp.
20 Golden Oregano *Origanum vulgare* 'Aureum'
21 Corsican Mint *Mentha requeinii*
22 Golden Lemon Thyme *Thymus* × *citriodorus* 'Aureus'
23 Chive *Allium schoenoprasum*
24 Dwarf Sage *Salvia officinalis* 'Nana'
25 Golden Sage *Salvia officinalis* 'Aurea'
26 *Alliums*
27 'Rosea' Lavender *Lavandula angustifolia*
28 *Hyssopus officinalis*
29 Cr. Winter Savory *Satureja pilosa*
30 Lawn Camomile *Chamaemellum nobile* 'Trenague'
31 Daisy Garden
32 Avens/Pansies/Eng. Daisy/Coral Bells
33 Lupine/Alliums/Campanula
34 CA poppy/Alliums/Wildflowers
35 Chinese Lantern/Lupine/Nigella
36 Lupine/Foxglove/Everlasting

Fig. 53. The wild alpine retreat, like Fig. 35, is a stark contrast of basic elements. A few large trees and ravines of exposed rock shape the design. Tuffeted, mounded and creeping herbs and low evergreen shrubbery dominate the site for year round entertainment. Rivulets of flowers splash into every nook and cranny for that wild tousled look.

Chapter 7 / SECTION 2

Herbs for the Wild Landscape

The most commonly cultivated herb of the *Umbelliferae* is the family's namesake, Dill, *Anethum graveolens.* This rapidly growing, self-sowing annual is popular in the kitchen garden, where its use for pickling and seasoning is paramount. Yet beyond its utilitarian value, Dill's pungent, spicy aroma is a delightful addition in the wild garden to the many floral and aromatic scents that abound there. Dill provides a dilute pervasive odor that accentuates other spicy aromas from herbs such as Rosemary, Southernwood, Basil, Roses, Sweet Peas, and Mints. Many late-flowering fragrant annuals and perennial ornamentals are highlighted by the catchy familiar scent of dill. If a small patch is planted, it makes enough of a come-on to attract attention without spoiling the overall fragrance or the view.

In enriched garden soils with plenty of moisture, Dill rises from 3–5 ft., producing large fragrant umbels bearing the seeds that are vital components in pickling recipes. Under poor conditions, Dill should not be expected to exceed 12–18 in., and if planted late, bolts to seed, producing little foliage. The deep blue-green of Dill's feathery foliage is attractive in groupings of light green or silver foliaged plants.

In the wild garden, Dill should be composed into long sinuous drifts that wind among many isolated clumps of Day Lily, Yarrow, Artemisias, German Camomile and Poppies. Add as many tall ornamental fragrant flowers such as Carnations and Roses as needed, where their scents will collide in a pleasant fashion. On a hot summer day, or after a rainstorm, the refreshing pungency of Dill's familiar pickle aroma becomes a prevalent scent in the garden.

More than one type of Dill is available. Garden Dill, *Anethum graveolens,* is often sold in a reputedly dwarf form, which rarely performs as such in good gardens. This variety variously sold as 'Bouquet' or Dwarf still grows to 3 ft. under excellent circumstances. If a dwarf is desired, mid-summer sowing of seed will suffice to reduce the height of Dill. Indian Dill, *A. sowa,* is often desired for its more fragrant foliage and larger seeds. Both will self-sow with little assistance and may cross-pollinate with a few other *Umbelliferae,* occasionally losing both the fine fragrance and flavor. Wild, self-sown Dill is not always as flavorful as it is fit, therefore, save seed only from plants grown in ideal conditions, where cross species pollination does not occur. Dill, Fennel, Queen Anne's Lace, and other *Umbelliferae* all bloom about the same time and may potentially cross, with adverse results.

Dill is, of course, most popular in the kitchen garden. It may be grown as a tall back-border or screen or as a tall massed planting of at least 6–12 plants. It should be grown only in full sun in the best soils. In a dooryard garden or a garden used to cultivate herbs for ornamental purposes, Dill can be grown with Yarrow, Tansy, and Feverfew in a perimeter bed.

The foliage of Dill is excellent in soups and salads. Fresh green seed is also used. The sharp, concentrated Dill flavor needs getting used to, so seeds should be used sparingly. The name, Dilla, is from the old Norse, "to lull", and the seed is used in a nerve-calming tea famous as a sleepy-time drink for children. The seeds themselves may be used and mixed into a soft candy or peanut butter, or given in a spoonful of corn or maple syrup. Dillweed, as the foliage is called, is used in cooking fish and poultry, particularly in stuffings and sauces. For a tangy dip:

TANGY DIP

½ c. Dill weed
¼ clove Garlic (crushed)
1 Tbsp. Lemon Basil butter
6–8 oz. sour cream or non-dairy
    dressing

Combine herbs and puree in blender, then fold into dressing. Allow 2–3 hours before using.

The lower leaves of Anise, *Pimpinella anisum*, like Coriander, are fanlike while the upper ones are divided and feathery. But while Coriander releases its fragrance from only a gentle touch, Anise is a treat only for the tongue. In full bloom, a large patch carries only a faint suggestion of its delicate flavor so cherished in cookies, cakes, and candies. The Anise cookie is a traditional favorite Christmas season gift, as is the liqueur, Anisette.

Anise is a quick-growing annual which has a longer ripening period than other *Umbelliferae* and requires hot weather to produce an abundance of seed. It grows from 12–18 in. high, although in northerly latitudes, when sown from seed, it rarely grows over 12 in. The plants are not sturdy and are susceptible to wind and heavy damage from rain.

In the wild garden, Anise should be tucked away in a thick drift between other herbs for protection. It can be used as a border and should be planted with a 6–8 in. spacing between plants to ensure a dense, uniform appearance. A kitchen garden is probably the best home for Anise, as it requires a very high quality soil and much care for weeding and protection from wind and rain.

The entire Anise plant is edible. The roots may be chopped into salads and vegetable dishes. The leaves are used fresh in rice and stir-fry cuisine and recommended in green salads and potato salads. The seeds may be eaten as a condiment before or after dinner or used in potato or lettuce salads, puddings, and desserts. Crushed green or dried seeds are extracted in any liqueur to add flavor. The strong extract is called Anisette and is added to other drinks or used over crushed ice or ice cream.

CHICKEN ORIENTAL

1 Tbsp. sesame oil

Add: 1 crushed Garlic clove
      1 Tbsp. crushed Anise seed

Fry thin strips from chicken breast and add:

1 Tbsp. Sherry
Sliced green and red peppers
Mushrooms
Slices of Caraway or Lovage root
1 tsp. Lovage
1 Tbsp. fresh chopped Parsley

Simmer ingredients to desired tenderness and serve with hot rice.

Anise seeds are equally enjoyable green (unripened) and may be harvested and frozen for future use. In short-season climates, it is difficult to thoroughly ripen Anise. Seeded directly into the garden it requires 4 or more months to ripen. In warm climates, rain just as the seeds ripen will ruin them. The green seeds and flowering tops and leaves are parts of the Anise plant that the grower of Anise should learn to use in cooking. They can be dropped into a sugar syrup and crystallized, made into sticks or patties, and then chocolate-covered.

Cumin, *Cuminum cyminum,* finds itself at home in a wild garden. Resembling Dill but growing only 12–18 in., it has white or pink flowers with a spicy odor to the foliage. Its spicy seed is cherished for taco and curry spice and is used in Central American and Indian cuisine.

As a culinary spice, Cumin imparts more odor than taste. The pungent camphoraceous odors of pinene, cymene, and dipentene are mellowed by heavy, spicy aromas of anisealdehyde and cuminal, which can create a sensation of taste from a deep whiff. These penetrating odors are allies to those of Chili powder, Coriander, Black Pepper, and Ginger, which are frequently combined in recipes because of their synergistic effect. Adding Fennugreek and Turmeric, we have the basic ingredients of curry powder. Children will love this recipe for a sweet taco meat that uses no sugar.

SWEET TACO MEAT

2 pounds hamburger
1 6 ounce can tomato paste
1 tsp. beef boullion
1 Tbsp. Cumin
1 Tbsp. Sweet Marjoram
1 Tbsp. Sweet Cicely
1 chopped green pepper
1 tsp. Lovage
6 cloves Garlic

Cumin is an expensive spice and is worth cultivating properly. It is grown as an annual and like Anise, requires a long, hot summer for ripening. It should be broadcast in thick rows or in drifts like Dill. It likes to be transplanted or sown into warm, 70°F soil. If started indoors, use a larger pot than for Dill as its longer growing season is often a result of an inadequate root system, the result of growing in a cool climate. Irrigating with water which has been held in containers will benefit since tap water can be 20 to 30°F below air/soil temperatures, essentially slowing the growth of Cumin. A row or patch of Cumin containing one dozen plants will yield, under good circumstances, more than enough seed. Less than 1 tsp. of seed is called for in most instances and a single plant will produce about 2 Tbsp. of seed. Unripened seed of Cumin often tastes like Caraway seed.

Black Cumin, *Nigella sativa,* or *Bunium persicum,* are spicy seeds used like Cumin. They have a sharp, peppery taste and odor with a hint of orange rind. The former is also called Roman Coriander or Black Caraway. Its seeds were once used as a condiment like Fennel and Caraway seed. Curries and hot, spicy S.E. Asian cuisine still employ this spice and its relative, Love-in-a-Mist, *N. damascena,* which has become an ornamental border flower. Experiment with this spice in taco meat, sparingly in stir-fry dishes or in a zippy vinegar and oil dressing with White Pepper, Garlic and Sweet Marjoram.

The seed pods of *Nigella* are prized for their unique and attractive nature, valuable in dried arrangements. They resemble a golden rosehip entwined or suspended within a collar of looped threads. Both are easily cultivated annuals suitable for informal or wild garden borders or preferably, mass plantings in sunny areas. Love-in-a-Mist, also called Wild Fennel, has several colorful cultivars.

Another herb rarely grown in the home garden today is Fennugreek, *Trigonella foenum-graecum.* Quite common in health food stores or on nutrition counters in grocery stores, Fennugreek seed is a popular sprout herb with a pleasant, nutty or maple-like odor. Next to Poppy seed, Fennugreek has one of the highest nutrient levels of all the cultivated herbs and figures into many balanced diets and herbal treatments.

The most precious gift of this herb is only seen in the wild garden, its profusion of extremely fragrant, Sweet Pea-like flowers. This semi-bushy leguminous herb with clover-like leaves will grow from 12–18 in. tall and produce long, slim pods with flat seeds. It is easy to grow in moist fertile soils and germinates in 5–7 days. It will reseed with some success from late plantings and can be sown very early in the spring, from April to mid-July but grows poorly on wet soils. It is a good cover crop (green manure) if enough seed is available. Because it is leguminous, it will not rob the soil of nitrogen. It is often grown with silage to act as an insect repellent in the dried hay.

Young leaves of Fennugreek can be eaten in salads but tend to be bitter and, therefore, are included in soup and stews. Fennugreek seed may be used like sesame seed on breads and in rolls or as sprouts in salads or in oriental stir-fry cuisine. An imitation maple syrup is made from the oil of Fennugreek seed. Recent medical research has found that Fennugreek is an excellent biological source of diosgenin, a precursor of progesterone, a sex hormone used extensively in the treatment of menstrual problems. Its primary medicinal use has been in poultices and salves because of its mucilaginous nature and the detergent (antibiotic) properties of its saponins.

The large, pink flowers of Sesame, *Sesamum orientale,* with their long blooming periods, are this herb's main value to the gardener in most climates. If plants are hot-house grown and set out in mid-April or early May in Zones 7–10, Sesame will produce seed by late August or mid-September. Heat is imperative and like Cumin, Sesame should be irrigated with warm water in cool climates for best results. The 3 ft. tall, unbranched plants of Sesame begin blooming after 1–2 months and continue blooming higher up the plant as it grows and adds height. Seeds form on the lower portion and must be harvested before frost or rain is imminent. A small harvest can usually be expected. The legendary phrase "Open Sesame" is perhaps derived from the habit of the Sesame seed to open explosively, throwing seeds in every direction. Sesame has such an extended ripening period, however, it may never produce seed in northern climates so this occurrence is rarely observed. Sesame seeds are a major southern European agricultural crop, harvested for use as flour, cooking oil, and heating oil. Animal fodder is recovered as a by-product of the sesame oil industry.

Halva is a sweet condiment made from the Sesame seed and honey. By adding seeds of Caraway, Anise, Fennel, or Sweet Cicely, an Anise or Licorice flavor is imparted to the Halva.

HALVA

3 c. Sesame seeds
¼ c. Anise seed or 1 tsp. extract
1 tsp. Sesame oil
½ c. honey
1 Tbsp. Almond extract

Blend into a paste and refrigerate

In the wild garden, Sesame's long pink flowers are bright, cheerful, and endearing. Crowded clumps or drifts of Sesame with plants separated by 6–10 in. are recommended. It makes an excellent background plant. The large green leaves and attractive, unbranched stalks are a useful vertical component in garden design. It combines well with Mugwort and Borage for a garden full of autumn colors. An ornamental grass such as Quaking Grass surrounding a clump of Sesame provides fall contrast that is pleasing visually for the tan rattles of the grass that huddle around the blooming Sesame, and acoustically from hundreds of tiny quaking castanets.

Borage, *Borago officinalis,* is a mighty herb from its beginning as a large seed and seedling to a dense tower of prickly stems and leaves that spread 3 ft. in all directions on massive succulent branches. Huge, bristled leaves like plate-armour hang down defying anyone to trespass or reach in and pluck it from the earth. A few may be allergic to these bristles, but for all they are quite nettlesome in any case and ofttimes remain behind in the hand. As bristly as they are, these huge leaves are nutritionally valuable pottage, cooked and eaten like spinach. Generally, the tender leaves of young plants not yet in flower are utilized.

The most relished use of Borage, however, is in its seedling stage. Plucked from loose, fertile soil, deeply sown seeds will provide long, crisp, juicy stems. These sprouts and the newly opened leaves, are virtually indistinguishable from the taste and texture of cucumbers. Plants that matured in vegetable gardens provide ample self-sown seed in the spring for sprouts. As the soil warms, the sprouts come up from ever deeper levels in the soil. There never seems to be an end to them. They will continue to emerge well into summer. They should not be treated as an uninvited guest but edible weeds, plucked regularly for salads, soups, and dips. They should be picked before the secondary leaves have developed significantly but older sprouts in very fertile circumstances are equally tasty. Sprouts last 3–4 days held in a wet towel at 45°F. Add ¼ c. of sprouts per person to a hot stir-fry dish as it is served or as a side dish with hot buttered mushrooms and green peppers for a unique taste of cucumber in a combination not otherwise possible.

The flowers, too, are a culinary treat. Plucked by pulling on the hub of the flower, the little, blue star can be dipped in egg-white and then sugar for a sparkling decoration on cakes and cookies, or eaten as a condiment or in place of sugar cubes for sweetening beverages. Borage's flowers are frequently used to decorate a huge bowl of punch, their starry, sky-blue shapes floating daintily on flavored, sparkling waters. Borage reputedly brings happiness and courage to everyone and is a grand herb for use as confetti at weddings.

Borage can become a very large plant, with prickly leaves 12 in. long and massive stems to 2 in. in diameter—a gargantuan herb guarding its flock of delft-blue flowers. These humble little blue stars, with faces forever gazing down, are the plant's only redeeming feature in the landscape. They should never be taken too seriously, however. The sky-blue haze they impart to a hedge of Borage is soothing to the eye and the buzzing of the unbelievable number of bees further accentuates the tranquilizing affect. Because of its masses of nectar-rich flowers, Borage has been called the "bee plant". Its deep root is a boon to gardeners used effectively in the poorest soils to break up clay or hard pan. It is rampantly self-sowing but does not germinate in cold soil, although raised beds or cold frames may encourage sprouting earlier in the spring. Borage is a hardy annual which can be sprouted indoors, hardened off, and planted in the garden well before the last frost in early spring. Plants grown in full sun and well-drained soil can withstand several degrees of frost. Hardy plants self-sown for many years can produce offspring hardy to 20°F in wet climates. Dampness and moisture facilitate cold hardiness, because water on leaves insulates them from cold snaps.

In the wild garden, Borage is best used as a background herb blended with other large-leaved herbs such as Comfrey, Elecampane, White Mugwort, or Calendula. The kitchen garden is undoubtedly the home of Borage but it is equally admirable in a wild or informal garden, used in sentry-like positions, at corners, the top of a mound, the center of a colorful patch of wildflowers, or at the very edge of a forest, where it may self-sow its way slowly into the forest over the years.

A misty hedge or screen placed well back in a wild or informal garden can be made using Borage, White Mugwort, Sweet Fennel, and Yarrow. This gives a grey-green background throughout the year and a late summer through fall display of colors; the white of Mugwort, the blue of Borage, and red, yellow, or white of Yarrow.

In the kitchen garden, Borage is a companion to vegetables that are dependent upon bees for pollination. Use it as a central theme in a square divided four ways, with each plot containing Bush Beans, Squash, Tomatoes, and Peppers. Purple Cabbages, Chives, or flowering Kales in blues and lavenders set all around a clump of Borage is also pleasing to the eye. A tight ring of Pepper plants with bright green and red fruits contrasting with the hazy blue flowers of Borage they encircle is an attractive display.

Of the four perennials discussed in this chapter, Lovage, Mugwort, Elecampane, and Yarrow, Lovage, or the Maggi plant, *Levistium officinale,* is the least showy. Being of the Dill family, its flowers, born in umbels, are not spectacular and should be discouraged, as they rob the herb of vigor during long, dry summers. It is, however, a hardy, herbaceous perennial resembling Celery in habit and flavor. The leaves are used rather than the stems which, like Bamboo, are hollow and stringy. Although Lovage prefers wet, clay soil it will thrive in any moist soil from full sun to full shade. Minus its ungainly flowering umbels it is a handsome, tropical looking herb that has some landscape value.

In the wild garden, Lovage provides a dense screen or background for low flowering perennials and annuals. Emerging early in the spring, it brings life and color to the garden long before other ornamental perennials. In either the wild or informal landscape, Lovage does well as an understory herb along woodsy walks that wander in and out of sun and shadow. Its lush growth suggests a tropical origin and enhances such a vision in a water feature, along with Angelica, ornamental grasses, and Bamboo.

For a contemporary feature, enjoin the odd charms of Lovage, variegated Comfrey, Elecampane, and Monarda. This garden can be in the shade a few hours of the day if necessary, or in full sun if plenty of moisture is provided. Red or yellow flowering Comfrey can be substituted for variegated Comfrey. In the contemporary landscape, Lovage is an excellent herbaceous hedge.

In most any garden, Lovage is best used as a screen, along open borders. A mature, healthy clump of Lovage produces a 4–6 ft. barrier that fully obscures sights and muffles sounds. It may be cut back to the ground at any time to clear the way for other flowering ornamentals nearby and will emerge again as healthy and dense as before. It is a pleasant privacy screen for secluded informal walks or cul-de-sacs.

The hardiness of Lovage is one of its virtues, growing in any zone and any soil. Under excellent conditions, Zones 7–10, its flower stalks will climb to 10 ft. The large, celery-like leaves emit a refreshing, but sharp herbaceous aroma on hot days, or whenever brushed. If allowed to bloom, the tiny, inconspicuous yellow-white flowers smell sweetly floral, reminiscent of honeysuckle. As the seeds swell and ripen, they become more decorative, eventually turn a toasty hue and are a favorite of many wild birds. Those that fall to the ground germinate readily in 14–21 days to produce a healthy plant by fall. Lovage seed, as in many *Umbelliferae,* is extremely short-lived. It is recommended that it be frozen for use for the following year. Since Lovage is easily divided as it matures, it is seldom necessary to collect the seed. A portion of the root may be severed from a clump and planted in a cool moist spot to produce a more robust plant more rapidly than from seed.

As a mature plant, a Lovage clump will yield about 30–40 spears, like Asparagus.

These spears are a nutritious, early spring vegetable and partly responsible for Lovage being an invaluable herb for several millenia. Although relatively uncommon in gardens today, Lovage was well known to the Greeks and brought to Northern Europe and England with the Roman armies. It is cultivated today as a commercial crop for the manufacture of tobaccos and perfumes.

LOVAGE SPEARS

Harvest 6 spears per person, 4 in. long
Sprinkle with lemon juice and ¼ c. chopped Chervil or Sweet
Cicely (early spring herbs)
Steam and serve as a vegetable, or in a sauce of Romano or Mozarella cheese
to which has been added Thyme and 2 Tbsp. of Sherry

Lovage seeds are certainly useful in cooking and impart the same flavor as the foliage. They require long, low heat cooking times for tenderizing and will add a sharp, tangy taste when crushed in the mouth. They can be ground to a flour as needed after the ripened seeds have been dried and stored. Because of the prolific production of seed, Lovage flour can be a useful food source during winter to complement wheat and other flours in biscuits and rolls.

The root of Lovage may be washed and peeled down to the pith, which is a soft, white, spongy material that can be steamed or deep-fried and eaten as a vegetable side dish, used cooked or raw in salads, or in stir-fry dishes. An aromatic oil is extracted from the root, used in perfumes and beverages. The pith can also be candied. As young plants, leaf stalks can be blanched by shielding them from the sun with a burlap cover. This should be done only with early spring foliage, as older foliage becomes stringy.

The leaves of Lovage have a tangy or peppery Celery-like flavor, which once used, is never left out of a recipe again. Soups, rice, potato and egg salad, seafood, meat stews, tomato sauce, and chili dishes are vastly improved with the liberal addition of dried Lovage. The high vitamin and mineral value of Lovage can be tapped in this flavorful way. The leaves are easily dried at high temperature, 140°F or air-dried by hanging and storing in paper bags in a dry, cool, storage room. Both the green color and the flavor are retained on drying.

LOVAGE SOUP

1 c. of chicken broth per person	1 Tbsp. Calendula
¼ c. of chopped onion per cup of broth	¼ tsp. Oregano
	1 tsp. Parsley
¼ c. chopped fresh Lovage	¼ tsp. Basil
1 diced carrot	

The exquisite spidery flowers of Elecampane, *Inula helenium*, are reason enough to include it in every garden. This herbaceous perennial produces several blooms or one large bloom if all the competing buds are pruned off. Its 3–4 in., yellow hued flowers gently swaying atop a 6 ft. stem are as ornamental as any popular show flower such as Dahlias or Chrysanthemums. Flowers can be as wide as 5–6 in. while the herb itself may grow to 10 ft. and produce enormous leaves 6–8 in. wide and 24 in. long—a truly gigantic herb in the average garden setting. In poor soil or partial shade, Elecampane grows only 2–5 ft. high with leaves up to 18 in. long.

Ornamental effect is best exploited as a small feature in a contemporary landscape with 1–2 clumps of Shasta Daisy, Rudbekia, and a ground cover of Costmary, bordered by English Daisies. This arrangement provides a procession of Daisy-like flowers from early spring through fall.

In the wild landscape, the huge, yellow daisy of Elecampane, carried aloft throughout July and August, is best joined by Yarrow combined with a carpet of California Poppies, Marguerites, Narcissus and Calendulas for a sunny garden from the last frost to the first. If several Elecampanes are grouped together they should be spaced 2–3 ft. and should not be grown within a ground cover unless it is non-invasive and not a climber. Violets, Creeping Charlie, Sweet Woodruff, Yerba Buena, and Corsican Mint are recommended for partial shade with Sword Fern and Solomon's Seal.

The imposing form of Elecampane is a valuable vertical component in herbaceous perennial borders. This function is best employed in a wild garden containing few shrubs or trees. In such a garden a sizeable clump of Elecampane will create a focal point in the back of the garden. Rising magestically out of a crowd of Bee Balm, Chrysanthemums, and Dahlias, the impression of a hill can be created,—the rising herbs' heights drawing the eye upward as if such a mound actually existed.

The young leaves of Elecampane have been used as a pot herb although the camphor-scented root is the most desirable product. Crisp, fresh slices are used in salads, deep-fried, or boiled and mashed like potatoes. The starch in Elecampane does not create problems for diabetics and has been powdered and used as a sweetener in bread and tea.

Will the real Mugwort please stand up? There are three herbs from the genus *Artemisia* referred to as Mugwort; Common Mugwort, *Artemisia vulgaris;* White Mugwort, *A. lactiflora;* and Western Mugwort, *A. ludoviciana.*

Common Mugwort, *Artemisia vulgaris,* is a ghastly weed. It is, however, a nutritional pot herb with a mild herbaceous scent and flavor, not at all unpleasant or camphoraceous, like many Artemisias, though not nearly as pleasant as Tarragon, *A. dracunculus.* Common Mugwort is distinguished by dark green leaves with downy, white undersides and a purple-striped stem. It is grown strictly in the kitchen garden as a pot herb. Common Mugwort has little ornamental value, even in a wild garden, and can be a serious problem if allowed to go to seed or its perennial roots to become established.

White Mugwort, *A. lactiflora,* from China, is a smaller species than Common Mugwort but similar in appearance except that it does not have stripes on the stem nor white undersides on its leaves. Also called Ghost Wormwood, it is cultivated as a fragrant ornamental. The fragrance of its foliage is similar to Common Mugwort but harbors a bitterness when eaten. The flower's fragrance is reminiscent of Camomile and Southernwood.

White Mugwort is a semi-hardy perennial that requires full sun and a fertile soil for best production of flower blooms. The blooms develop in late summer and last into the fall months. They are usually cut just after opening and dried for use in dried arrangements for their everlasting color and fragrance.

A White Mugwort screen, planted to provide a barrier at the edge of a wild or informal garden, succeeds well. On misty mornings in late summer and far into the fall months, its appearance suggests a band of ghosts sneaking along the back of the bed, their huge, white heads hung secretively down. As easy to grow as any Artemisia, it rises gracefully from 3–6 ft. and long into fall is topped with dense, creamy white blooms. For a screen, it should be planted in full sun and the plants set in 2–3 rows, 18 in. apart with plants set 18–24 in. apart. Its plain green exterior and simple Eiffel Tower-shape are enhanced by low spreading companions with bright flowers and foliage such as Dwarf Monarda or a clump of ornamental Sage such as *Salvia viridis* or *Salvia dorisiana.* In a contemporary garden White Mugwort should be featured with pink and white Poppies and surrounded by a selection of ornamental Thymes, in particular Moroccan and Peter Davis.

Western Mugwort, *A. ludoviciana,* is a native North American herb. A handsome, silver-leaved, Wormwood-like herb, it is used only as an ornamental. It is a hardy, evergreen perennial, available in garden centers. A cultivar, 'Silver King', *A. ludoviciana* var. *albula,* is more commonly cultivated and grows from 2–4 ft. in dry soils in full sun.

Yarrow, *Achillea millefolium,* is the common weed, Milfoil. It is a beautiful perennial in the wild or informal garden. Various flower colors and degrees of filigreed foliage make it a versatile herb in the ornamental garden. The flowers and foliage are excellent for dried arrangements. It is commonly grown as a valuable addition to the mead and used medicinally as an astringent for the cessation of bleeding or soothing the pain of a small cut or toothache.

There are Yarrows from 2 in. to 6 ft. tall, all with tiny, ¼ in. flowers that form flat heads (corymbs) from the size of a quarter to a dinnerplate. Most of the Yarrows do not produce a prominent odor, though a few, under some circumstances, have a spicy aroma similar to Camomile. In fact, the same chemicals present in Camomile, azulene and chamazulene, are also found in Yarrow. *A. moschata* and *millefolium* also contain a small amount of eucalyptol for a camphoraceous note and the sweetener, betonicine. The tea of Yarrow, once a treatment for bleeding ulcers and toothache, is not at all unpleasant, if the herb is grown in fertile soil, full sun, and very young leaves are harvested in early spring. Known by many native peoples as the "wound herb", Yarrow was given the genus name *Achillea* because it was believed that Achilles first employed this herb to heal his soldiers. It can also be used for an astringent in a rinse for oily skin.

Yarrow, or Thousand Leaf, is an herb with a thousand names as well. It is an ancient plant brought in on the hooves of cattle that were driven into Europe from Central Asia by primitive man. Its use in staunching the flow of blood both internally and externally has earned it many handles on the battlefield, including Knight's Milfoil and Soldier's Wort, and to the cabinet maker, Carpenter's Weed. Its popularity in magic potions won it the name Devil's Nettle, its flavor, Old Man's Pepper, and in brewing a heady ale, Field Hops.

All of the Yarrow species are hardy, rewarding herbs, each with just the right character for a particular occasion. *A. millefolium* can be both a 2 ft. column of dark green capped with white or an exceptionally hardy, dark green lawn in poor, dry soil where grass will not grow. For that reason, it is one of the finest mead herbs, planted in those spots where traffic is heaviest and soil is poor. It must have a well drained location and can be mowed from ¾–1 ½ in.

Common Yarrow, *A. millefolium,* represents the white, red, or pink forms of Yarrow. 'Fireking' and 'Cerise Queen' are cultivar names with *rubra* and *rosea* as varieties. Their foliage is dark green, exceptionally filigreed and most grow from 18 in.–3 ft.

A. filipendulina and some crosses of that species and *A. clypeolata* (*A. taygeta*) are the yellow-hued Yarrows; the 4–6 ft. 'Coronation Gold', the diminutive 18 in. 'Moonshine', and giant flowered 'Gold Plate' with flowers as wide as 8–10 in. *A. clypeolata* has charming soft grey leaves, perfect in a grey garden, and grows to only 18 in. with 2 in. wide, lemon-yellow flowers.

A. tomentosa and *A. chrysocoma,* the creeping Yarrows, are mead herbs forming low-growing mats from 2 in. for *A. t.* 'Nana', up to 6–8 in. for other species and varieties.

As single plants or in large drifts, Yarrow is a natural wild or informal garden herb. Its value is in its ability to provide vertical balance in a colorful and simple way. The small yellow flowers of 'Moonshine' emerging crisply erect from a patch of dainty Sweet Cicely in semi-shade provide a bold and attractive asymmetry for a sylvan glade or contemporary feature. Other tall herbs such as Teasel, *Eryngium* and Cattail are often found in gardens with Yarrows cultivated both for their decorative uses and vertical contrast. In the kitchen garden, tall, slim

Yarrows join Sunflowers and Jerusalem Artichokes in sunny central patches.

Contemporary gardens have not seen much use of Yarrow due to its rangy habits. Two exceptions are the red, and diminutive white Yarrows such as *A. ptarmica* 'The Pearl', tucked into a mixed ground cover of Wormwood or Western Mugwort and Horehound or Santolina for a contemporary feature that appears cool and composed. Tall, yellow 'Gold Plate' Yarrow can be featured with Elecampane in a closeknit patch offset in a field of orange and white Poppies.

Long, solid color borders of Yarrow are a fashionable use of this flower in formal gardens, while mixed borders in informal gardens combine 2 or more species of Yarrow and Valerian, Foxglove, Fern-leaf Tansy, White Mugwort, or Elecampane. Their hardy, profusely blooming nature has given them a reputation as trustworthy, colorful border plants. There are many flower colors to choose from: light yellow to white to cream, dark yellow, orange, pink, and red. Yarrow is also at home as a tall border or screen along the back of a bed, its foliage providing a dark green background for light colored flowers or ornamental foliages.

Chapter 7 / SECTION 3

A Walk
Through a Wild Garden

Tucked among the Redwoods up a coastal draw somewhere along the endless warm Pacific beach was Wildhaven. (Fig. 53) I came upon it a while back but never drew a map. A few steps hidden by scrub and a name carved into driftwood were sufficient to suggest more. Searching again with a more serious eye I could see Heathers and Thymes wrestling above on the brink of a ledge, each trying to force the weaker over. My nose was quick to ascertain what other pleasures grew up there: Sage, Lavender, Savory and Camomiles in great swatches no doubt. So with the breeze off the land and the ebbing ocean at my back I bravely ascended the steps which wound steeply upward out of the sight of the ever-curious sea.

The first dozen or so steps were obviously flotsam, lashed together with ship's chain and anchored in concrete. Apparently the sea plays roughly even this far above the berm. A mixed hedge of Dwarf Lavender and Heather scampers along the path beside me. On one side the border becomes a wall that rises steeply, inviting the Lavender to drape down from several feet above. Dew and perfume drip from thousands of deep blue magic wands.

On the other side the landscape dips back toward the sea. Creeping Thymes charge out from the edge of the path, plying their way across the landscape and eventually piling up in frothing fury before a border of silver-grey *Santolina* 'Nana' and *S. neapolitana,* which slow, but do not stay, the advancing Thyme. A pinch of the white flowered Thyme tells my nose it is the lemon-scented 'White Magic' and a pinch of the other reminds me of 'Oregano-scented' Thyme, one of my favorites.

The Heathers and Thymes I saw from the beach play beyond in the far garden, the two separated by a wide swath of fist-sized river rock. Silver, French and Golden Lemon Thymes battle it out with a dozen red-haired Heathers while a girdle of golden Alyssums hold fast the inside edge, keeping them from invading the rocky access area.

Reposing beneath a heavy load of flowered sod and staring sullenly upon this landscape is an earth home. A decorative wreath adorns the door. Peeking through a window to see if anyone responds to my knocking, I see a wealth of wreaths, swags and dried arrangements laying about inside. The owner is apparently an artist of sorts, herbs and dried plants her medium.

A rocky path leading to the right around the house and upslope passes a large patch of Azaleas that engulfs the side yard, diverting traffic down into the Heather and Thyme or up into a shady nook. Lounging in the shade of a Redwood are Black Hellebore, *Helleborus niger;* Wild Ginger; and thousands of Violets. This, rich dark green carpet is all aglitter from a few filtered sunbeams. Wedged between two islands of Corsican Hellebore is a bed of Primroses robed in elegant habiliments of gold and crimson and royal blue. Invading from above is a sheet of Violas and Variegated Creeping Charlie, *Glechoma hederacea* var. *variegata.*

The rocky path winds around to a patio in the backyard that opens up and up and up. I can just see the tops of two parallel ridges that have entered this property. They have been flattened to make room for scores of Azaleas and some Oregon Grape. Between the ridges is a stone-filled gully that allows access to the rich beds on their flanks. These beds have become the home of many perennials, evergreens and wonderous little alpines. Heathers and Campanulas are a strong theme, while herbs such as Pygmy Savory, Dwarf and Golden Sage, Bush and Creeping Thymes, neatly trimmed Lavender and Red and White 'Grandiflora' Hyssop fill in between banks of ornamental ground covers. The fragrance of a few want to lull me into an effortless sleep: Lady's Mantle shaking her huge yellow plumes at my feet filling the air with a floral-scented magic potion; Corsican Mint cavorting between the gully stones sending waves of menthol upward; 'White Moss' Thyme giving up its crisp thymol aroma; and little raggedy-mop tufts of Creeping Savory are making me hungry with the aroma of smoked meats at Christmas.

These beds are host to innumerable sorts of ornamental herbs and alpine plants. I can see Mountain Avens, *Geum montana*; Soapwort, *Saponaria ocymoides*; Tomentil, *Potentilla arbuscula* and *P. nepalensis* with yellow and scarlet flowers; Fairy Thimbles, *Campanula pusilla*, scattered everywhere; and strings of yellow Alliums, *Allium flavum*, like the colored beads of a necklace, striking across the wash again and again, vanishing near the top in an orange-red sea of California Poppies, *Eschscholzia californica*. Dwarf Sage and Dwarf Lavender are accompanied by a few Bluebells, *Campanula carpatica*; a white muffler of Snow-in-Summer, *Cerastium tomentosum*; and Spiderwort, *Tradescantia virginiana*.

A broad elevated bed in the center of the landscape boasts a dozen or more annual herbs and ornamentals, undoubtedly used for the dried arrangements I saw through the window. There are slender drifts of fire-orange *Lupine*; Love-in-a-Mist, *Nigella damascena*; Chinese Lanterns, *Physalis alkekengi*; and Honesty, *Lunaria biennis*. They are joined by herbs such as Coriander, Cinnamon Basil, Summer Savory and Dill for a banquet of fragrances, and more Bluebells and California Poppies for exotic color.

The ridge tops are swarming with knee-high Azaleas all dressed in their Sunday finery, blossom prints of pink, snow white, vermillion and royal purple. The gentle arms of three matronly Redwoods hover lovingly over these little mountain children and offer soothing contrast to the stark rocky earth that is the common ground in this landscape. Though harsh, this rocky expanse is not sterile but teaming with minute things: quick clumps of blue-fingered *Campanula zoysii*; luscious patches of Corsican Mint; paper-thin mats of red and pink flowering Creeping Thyme; and a clump of Heather with a collar of Lawn Camomile.

Rounding the back of the home, the rocky path is carpeted in Pearlwort, *Sagina subulata*. The yard slopes steeply back to the beach. A small grey garden clings to the front corner of the house affording the inhabitants a scene of uncluttered beauty through two windows that face the garden. From inside only a flowered meadow, a stately Redwood and the distant sea can be seen. Within the ring of Lavender are Painted Daisies, *Pyrethrum rosea*; Gazanias in bold golden sunset colors; cloud-white New Zealand Mountain Daisies, *Celmisia coriacea*; and sky-blue Mountain Knapweed, *Centaurea montana* joining in a scene of artistic design. Dozens of dwarven Canterbury Bells, *Campanula medium* 'Dwarf', dance among the daisies, and the silvery, pink-speckled spikes of Wooly Betony jut upward from everywhere inside, trying to outdo the blue splendor of the highly ornamental ring of 'Twickle Purple' Lavender.

A duo of Heather and sitting stones in the middle of the wasteland beyond the grey garden is an inviting reststop from which to admire this wilderness retreat. True, it is only a suggestion of wilderness. It is an imaginary world created by the wild imagination of its designer. It is fitting it should be neighbor only to a Redwood forest and the sea.

APPENDICES

APPENDIX I

Physical Characteristics of Ornamental Herbs & Herb Culture

KEY

BOTANICAL NAME: the binomial used is the one that is most commonly accepted today.

LIFE CYCLE

A = annual
B = biennial
D = deciduous
E = evergreen
H = herbaceous
P = perennial
S = semi

NATURAL HEIGHT because plant materials come from sources world wide, there is a significant variation in the height of a species; many species themselves are polymorphic as well and vary considerably.

HABIT

UP, *upright*, inverted pyramid, tall and thin
BU, *bushy*, implies a spherical or hemispherical shape
MAT, *mat-forming*, implies a spreading herb (mint-like) or a creeper that will continue to spread unless corralled.
SHB, *shrub*, like bushy, but grows from a main stem and does not root along branches to any great degree.
CL, *clumping*, very slowly spreading herbs (chive-like) that form dense central patches with time.
TR, *tree*
VN, *vine*

FOLIAGE TEXTURES: thin, dense, coarse, fine and feathery (as seen from a distance of several feet.
COLOR: GN=green, DGN-dark green, BGN-blue green, YGN=yellow green, GY=grey, PUR=purple (or red stained on dark green), YonGN=variegated.

BLOSSOM	SEASON: W=winter, SP=spring, SM=summer, F=fall. COLOR: BLU=blue, R=red, PUR=purple, LAV=lavender, RO=rose, Y=yellow, PK=pink, W=white, BRN=brown, GN=green, O=orange, CRM=cream, MAG=magenta. *showy flowers.
SUN EXPOSURE	FS=full sun, PS=part sun, SH=shade.
GERMINATION	d=days, wk=weeks, yr=years (seed germination data is provided as a *range* because seed can be very old, thus lengthening germination, and many plants do vary considerably depending upon the ripening conditions). Brackets [] indicate rooting period for cuttings.
PROPAGATION	S=seeds, SS=self sows, D=root or crown division, L=layering, C=cutting, B=bulb, BLT=bulblet.
SOIL MOISTURE	WD-well drained (the most common, implies good drainage and is used when no other specific soil moisture level is recommended) M=moist AQ=aquatic (which includes all soils in and around a pond) DR=drought resistant.
SOIL TYPE	G=garden (herb is not choosy), R=rich, S=sandy, L=limed, A=strongly acid
PESTS	The few pests noted here are derived from texts on commercial culture of ornamentals, not word of mouth. Unless otherwise noted, pests listed under the first entry in each genus may be considered common to the entire genus. The following is a guide that provides the cure for what ails your herb, as noted in the tables or as you may have discovered. Be absolutely sure of the pest first or the cure will be wasted and useless.

STERILIZE SOIL: root rot, crown gall, stem rot, crown rot, nematodes

REMOVE & DESTROY LEAVES: leaf spot

DESTROY PLANTS: crown gall, stem rot, smut, virus, stalk borer, wilt, rust

DORMANT OIL/LIME SULFUR: leaf gall aphid, scale

WETTABLE SULFUR: powdery mildew, blight

BORDEAUX: anthracnose, severe leaf spot, blight

LYE SOAP: aphids

MALATHION: white fly, severe scale, psyllids

ZONES	Like other characteristics of herbs the zone in which they can survive is quite variable. Herbs may be purchased from many zones where they have been acclimatized, and do better or worse as the case may be in your garden. I advise you to experiment and talk with gardeners in your immediate area to find out what they can grow—get a cutting from them, if at all possible. This is very important in cold climates.

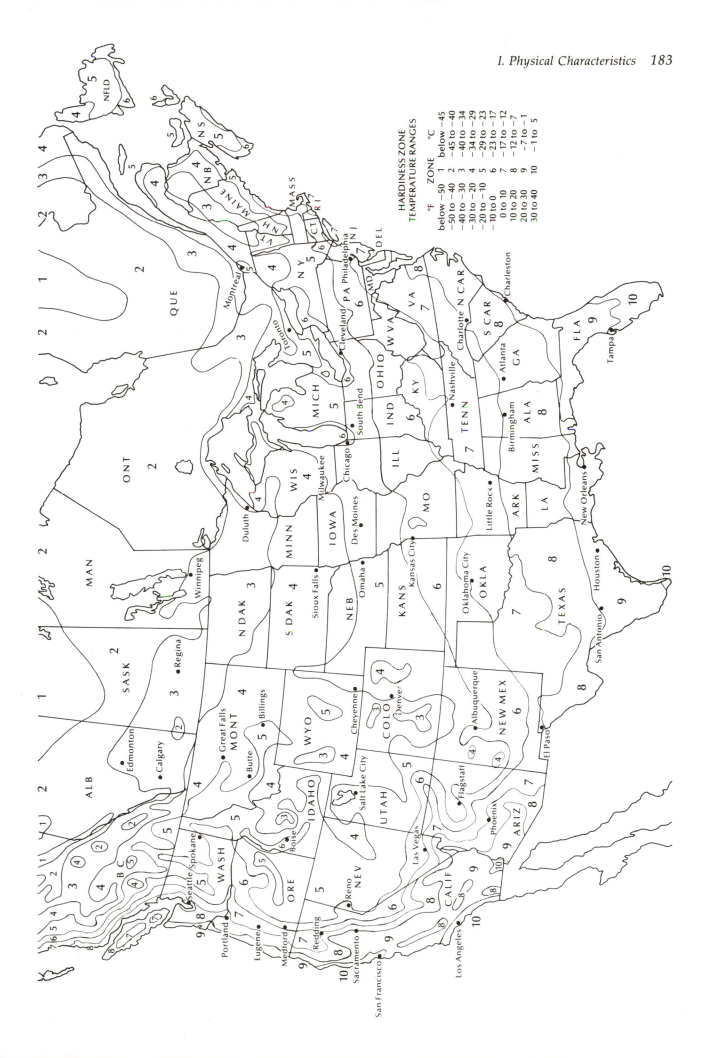

HARDINESS ZONE
TEMPERATURE RANGES

°F	ZONE	°C
below −50	1	below −45
−50 to −40	2	−45 to −40
−40 to −30	3	−40 to −34
−30 to −20	4	−34 to −29
−20 to −10	5	−29 to −23
−10 to 0	6	−23 to −17
0 to 10	7	−17 to −12
10 to 20	8	−12 to −7
20 to 30	9	−7 to −1
30 to 40	10	−1 to 5

BOTANICAL NAME	LIFE CYCLE	HEIGHT	HABIT	FOLIAGE TEXTURE	FOLIAGE COLOR	BLOSSOM SEASON	BLOSSOM COLOR	SUN	PROPAGATION	GERMINATION	SOIL MOISTURE	SOIL TYPE	INSECTS	DISEASE	ZONE
Achillea clypeolata Yarrow	HP	12"	CL	fine/dense	GY	SM	Y*	FS	D		WD	G			
A. filipendulina Yarrow	HP	1–1½'	CL	fine/dense	GYGN	SM	Y*	FS	D		WD	G		rust	4–9
A. millefolium Yarrow	HP	2–3'	UP	fine/dense	DGN	SM	W/R/PK*	FS	D/S	4–6wk	DR	G		crown gall stem rot	2–10
A. tomentosa 'Nana' Creeping Yarrow	HP	2–4"	MAT	fine/dense	DGN	SM	Y	FS-PS	D/L	[8wk]	WD	S			6–9
Acinos arvensis Basil-Thyme	HP	10–16"	CL	coarse/dense	DGN	SM	PK	FS	S/C/D		M	G			3–10
Acorus calamus Sweet Flag	HP	3–6'	UP	grassy/thin	GN	SM	BRN	FS-PS	D		AQ	R			3–9
A. gramineus Grass-leaved Sweet Flag	HP	18"	UP	grassy/thin	GN	SM	BRN	PS	D		AQ	R			5–10
Agastache cana Mosquito Plant	HP	18–30"	UP	coarse/thin	DGN	SM	RED*	FS	S/D		WD	G			6–10
A. foeniculum Anise Hyssop	HP	2–4'	UP	coarse/thin	DGN	SM	BLU*	FS	S/D	1–2wk	WD	G			4–9
A. rugosa Korean Mint	HP	2–3'	UP	coarse/thin	DGN	SM	PUR	FS	S/D/C	1–2wk	WD	G		mildew, rust leaf spot	6–9
A. scrophulariifolia Purple Giant Hyssop	HP	2–4'	UP	coarse/thin	DGN	SM	ROSE	FS	S/D		WD	G			4–9
Alchemilla vulgaris Lady's Mantle	HP	12–18"	MAT	coarse/dense	LGN	SM	Y*	FS-PS	C/D/S	3–4wk	WD	G			3–8
Allium ascalonicum Shallot	A	12"	CL	grassy/thin	DGN	SM		FS	B		WD	R		mildew root rot	A
A. flavum	HP	10–15"	CL	grassy/thin	DGN	SM	Y*	FS	D/S	3–4wk	WD	R			4–9
A. giganteum	HP	4–5'	UP	coarse/thin	DGN	SM	ROSE*	FS	D/S	4–8wk	WD	R		mildew	6–10

Name	Type	Height	Habit	Texture	Color	Season	Flower	Light	Soil	Prop.	Moist.	Prop.	Pest	Disease	Zones
A. s. var. *ophioscorodon* Rocambole	A/P	12"	UP	grassy/thin	GN	SM		FS	B/BLT		WD	R		mildew root rot	3–9
A. schoenoprasum Chive	HP	10–18"	CL	grassy/thin	DGN	SP/F	ROSE*	FS-PS	D/S	2–4wk	M	R		white mold	3–10
A. s. var. *sibirica*	HP	18–24"	UP	grassy/thin	DGN	SP/F	ROSE	FS-PS	D/S	2–3wk	WD	G			2–9
A. tuberosum Garlic Chive	HP	1–2'	CL	grassy/thin	DGN	SM	W*	FS	D/S	2–4wk	WD	R			3–10
Aloysia triphylla Lemon Verbena	D/EP	3–6'	SHB	fine/thin	GN	SM	W	FS	C/L/S	[6wk]	WD	R		leaf spot crown gall	8–10
Althea officinalis Marshmallow	HP/B	2–3'	UP	coarse/thin	GN	SM	PK/W*	FS	S/SS	2–3wk	WD	G		rust anthracnose	2–10
Anethum graveolens Dill	A	3–5'	UP	feathery/thin	DGN	SM	Y	FS	S/SS	2–3wk	WD	G		leaf spot	A
A. sowa Indian Dill	A	3–5'	UP	feathery/thin	DGN	SM	Y	FS	S/SS	2–3wk	WD	G		virus	A
Angelica archangelica Angelica	HB	3–5'	UP	coarse/thin	GN	SP	GN-W*	PS	S,SS	2–4wk	M-W	R	leaf miner	leaf spot	2–10
A. atropurpurea Masterwort	HB	4–6'	UP	coarse/thin	GN-PR	SP	GN*	FS-PS	S,SS	2–4wk	M-W	R		rust	3–9
A. sylvestris Wood Angelica	HB/P	4–6'	UP	coarse/thin	GN	SP	GN*	FS-PS	S,SS	2–4wk	M-W	R		rust	2–10
Anthriscus cerefolium Chervil	A	1–2'	UP	fine/thin	GN	SM	W	PS-SH	S/SS	1–2wk	M	R	leaf miner		2–9
Artemisia abrotanum Southernwood	EP	3–5'	BU	feathery/dense	LGN	SM	Y	FS	C/L		WD	G		root rot	4–9
A. absinthum Wormwood	EP	1–3'	BU	fine/dense	GYGN	SM	Y	FS-PS	L/D/S	4–6wk	DR	G		rust	4–9
A. arborescens	EP	2–3'	BU	fine/dense	GY	SM	BRN	FS	C/L		WD	G			4–9
A. dracunculus Russian Tarragon	HP	2–3'	UP	fine/thin	GN	SM	Y	FS-PS	S/D	3–4wk	M	R,S		root rot	4–8
A. dracunculus 'Sativa' French Tarragon	HP	3–5'	UP	fine/thin	DGN	SM	Y	FS	D/C	[10wk]	M	RS		root rot	6–8
A. frigida 'Silver Mound'	HP	8–12"	MAT	feathery/dense	GY	SM	Y	FS	D		WD	S		crown rot	3–9

BOTANICAL NAME	LIFE CYCLE	HEIGHT	HABIT	FOLIAGE TEXTURE	FOLIAGE COLOR	BLOSSOM SEASON	BLOSSOM COLOR	SUN	PROPAGATION	GERMINATION	SOIL MOISTURE	SOIL TYPE	PESTS INSECTS	PESTS DISEASE	ZONE
A. lactiflora White Mugwort	HP	3–5'	UP	fine/dense	DGN	F	Y-W*	FS	D/S		WD	R	slug	mildew root rot	7–10
A. lanata Silver Mound	HP	6–8"	MAT	feathery/dense	GY	SM	Y	FS	D		WD	S		crown rot	3–9
A. ludoviciana Western Mugwort	EP	2–3'	UP	fine/thin	GY	SM	Y	FS	D		DR	G			4–9
A. l. var. albula 'Silver King'	EP	1–2'	UP	fine/dense	GY	SM	Y	FS	D/L		WD	G			5–9
A. pontica Roman Wormwood	SEP	2–3'	BU	feathery/dense	GYGN	SM	Y	FS	C/L/S	[8wk]	WD	G		root rot	6–10
A. stellerana Beach Wormwood	DP	12–18"	MAT	coarse/dense	GY	SM	Y	FS-PS	L/C	[6wk]	DR	S		white mold	3–9
A. vulgaris Common Mugwort	HP	4–6'	UP	fine/thin	DGN	SM	R-BRN	FS	S/D	2–3wk	DR	G			2–10
Asarum canadense Wild Ginger	EP	8–12"	MAT	coarse/dense	DGN	SP	PUR-BRN	SH	D		M	RA		leaf spot	5–8
A. europeum Wild Ginger	EP	4–6'	MAT	coarse/dense	DGN	SP	BRN	SH	D		M	RA			6–8
A. hartvegii Wild Ginger	EP	4–8'	MAT	coarse/dense	Won DGN	SP	PUR-BRN	SH	D		M	RA			6–8
A. virginicum Wild Ginger	EP	6–8"	MAT	coarse/dense	LGNon DGN	SP-SM	PUR	SH	D		M	RA		rust	4–8
Borago officinalis Borage	A	2–3'	BU	coarse/dense	DGN	S-F	BLU	FS-PS	S/SS	5–7d	DR	G		leaf spot	ALL
Calendula officinalis Calendula	A	1–2'	UP	coarse/dense	GN	SP-F	Y/O*	FS	S/SS	5–7d	DR	GL		cab. looper virus	ALL
Calamintha nepeta Calamint	HP	12–18"	MAT	coarse/thin	GN	SM	PK	FS-PS	S/L/C		M	R			4–9
Chamomilla recutita German Camomile	A	15"	BU	fine/dense	LGN	SP-F	W*	FS-PS	S/SS	2–3wk	DR	G		mildew rust	ALL
									S	2–3wk	M	P		stem rot	3–9

Name	Type	Height	Habit	Texture	Foliage	Form	Flower	Light	Prop.	Germ.	Moist.		Pests	Diseases	Zone
C. n. cv. Rayless Chamomile	SEP	4–6″	MAT	feathery/thin	LGN	SM	Y(rayless)	PS	D/S	5–10d	M	R			7–10
C. n. 'Trenague' Lawn Camomile	EP	1–3″	MAT	feathery/dense	LGN	None	—	FS-PS	D		M	R			6–10
Chenopodium bonus henricus Good King Henry	HP	12–16″	MAT	coarse/dense	DGN	SM	BRN	FS	S/D	2–3wk	WD	R		leaf spot	3–9
Chrysanthemum balsamita Camphor Plant	HP	18″	MAT	coarse/dense	GY	SP	W*	FS-PS	D/L	[8wk]	M	G	slug		3–10
Balsamita major Costmary	HP	1–3′	MAT	coarse/dense	GN	SM	Y-GN	PS	D		M	R	slug	leaf spot	3–10
Chrysanthemum parthenium 'Selaginoides' Dwarf feverfew	HP	10–12″	BU	coarse/dense	YGN	SM-F	W*	FS-PS	S/D	1–2wk	WD	G		mildew	4–9
C. p. 'DoubleBonnet'	HP	18–24″	BU	coarse/dense	YGN	SM-F	W*	FS	S/D	1–2wk	WD	G			4–9
Coleus amboinicus Indian Borage	EP	1–3′	UP	coarse/thin	GN	SM	LAV*	FS	C	[6wk]	M	R			9–10
Coriandrum sativum Coriander	A	2–3′	UP	fine/thin	DGN	SM	W-PK	FS	S/SS	1–2wk	WD	R			4–10
Crocus sativus Saffron	HP	12–16″	CL	grassy/thin	DGN	W	PUR*	FS-PS	B/S	8–10wk	WD	SL		dry rot	7–10
Cryptotaenia japonica Japanese Parsley	HP	18″	UP	coarse/thin	GN	SM	YGN	PS	S	2–6wk	M	R			2–9
Cuminum cyminum Cumin	A	12″	UP	fine/thin	DGN	SM	PK	FS	S	1–2wk	WD	R			6–10
Cynara cardunculus Cardoon	HB	3–6′	UP	coarse/thin	GY	SM	ROSE*	FS	S	1–3wk	M	R		crown rot leaf spot	4–10
Ferula assa-foetida Asafetida	HP	6–12′	CL	feathery/dense	DGN	SM	Y	FS	S/D		M	R			8–10
F. communis Giant Fennel	HP	5–10′	CL	feathery/dense	DGN	SM	Y	FS	S/D		M	R			8–10
Filipendula ulmaria Meadowsweet	HP	2–4′	UP	coarse/thin	DGN	SM	Y-W*	FS-PS	S/D		M	R		mildew rust	2–9
F. vulgaris Dropwort	HP	1–2′	CL	fine/thin	DGN	SM	W-CRM	FS	S/D		M	R			2–9

BOTANICAL NAME	LIFE CYCLE	HEIGHT	HABIT	FOLIAGE TEXTURE	FOLIAGE COLOR	BLOSSOM SEASON	BLOSSOM COLOR	SUN	PROPAGATION	GERMINATION	SOIL MOISTURE	SOIL TYPE	PESTS INSECTS	PESTS DISEASE	ZONE
Foeniculum vulgare ssp. *vulgare* var. *azoricum* Finocchio	A	2–3'	UP	feathery/thin	DGN	SM	Y	FS	S	3–6wk	M	R			2–10
F. v. ssp. *v.* var. *dulce* Sweet Fennel	HP	3–6'	UP	feathery/thin	DGN	S-F	Y	FS-PS	S/SS	2–4wk	M	R	aphid	stem rot	3–9
F. v. ssp. *v.* 'Rubrum' Bronze Fennel	HP	3–4'	UP	feathery/thin	RED-GN	S-F	Y	FS	S/SS	1–2wk	M	R	aphid		3–9
Galium odorata Sweet Woodruff	HP	4–8"	MAT	fine/dense	DGN	SP	W	PS-SH	S/D/L	2mo.	M	RA		leaf spot rust, mildew	3–9
Glechoma hederaceae Creeping Charlie	HP	2–8"	MAT	feathery/dense	DGN	SM	Y	PS-SH	S/D		M	RA		mildew	7–10
G. h. var. *variegata*	HP	2–6"	MAT	coarse/dense	Won-DGN	SP-SM	BLU	PS-SH	D		M	R		mildew	2–9
Gaultheria hispidula Creeping Snowberry	SEP	2–3"	MAT	coarse/thin	DGN	SP	W	SH	D/L		WD	RA		leaf spot	4–9
G. procumbens Wintergreen	EP	4–6"	MAT	coarse/thin	DGN	SM-F	W/PK	SH	D/L		WD	RA		leaf spot	4–9
Hamamelis japonica Japanese Witch Hazel	DP	20'	SHB	coarse/thin	DGN	W-SP	Y*	PS-SH	C/G		WD	R		mildew	4–9
H. mollis Chinese Witch Hazel	DP	20'	SHB	coarse/dense	DGN	W-SP	Y-O*	PS-SH	C/G		WD	R			3–9
H. vernalis	DP	6'	SHB	coarse/dense	DGN	SP	Y*	PS-SH	S/C		M	R			4–9
H. virginiana Witch Hazel	DP	15'	SHB	coarse/thin	DGN	W	Y*	PS-SH	C/S	2yr	M	R	leaf gall aphid	leaf spot	2–9
Hedeoma pulegioides American Pennyroyal	A	10–16"	BU	fine/thin	GN	SM	BLU	FS	S/C		M	R			4–9
Helichrysum italicum Curry plant	EP	1–2'	BU	fine/thin	GY	SM	Y	FS	S/C	[6wk]	WD	SL			6–10
					DGN	F	GN	FS	S	1-2wk	WD	C		mildew	5–10

Name		Height	Form	Texture	Foliage	Size	Flower	Light	Prop.	Time	Drainage		Pest/Disease		Zone
variegated Hop				dense	GN										
Hyssopus officinalis Hyssop	EP	8-16"	BU	fine/dense	DGN	SM	B/W/PK	FS	S/C	1-3wk	WD	G		nematode	2-10
Inula helenium Elecampane	HP	4-6'	UP	coarse/thin	DGN	SM	Y*	FS-PS	S/D	6-8wk	M	R		mildew	2-10
Jasminum humile	EP	20'	SHB	coarse/thin	GN	F	Y	FS	C		WD	R		leaf spot	5-10
J. officinalis Poet's Jasmine	DP	30'	VN	fine/dense	DGN	SM-F	W	FS-PS	C		WD	R	scale	blossom blight	5-10
J. sambac Arabian Jasmine	EP	15'	VN	coarse/thin	GN	SP-F	W*	FS	C	[10wk]	WD	R			7-10
Laurus nobilis Sweet Bay	EP	40'	TR	coarse/dense	DGN	SM	Y	PS	C	[16wk]	WD	R	psyllid	leaf spot	8-10
Lavandula angustifolia ssp. *angustifolia* English Lavender	EP	3-5'	SHB	fine/dense	GYGN	SM	LAV*	FS	S/C/L	2-3wk	DR	S		root rot nematode	2-10
L. a. ssp. *a.* 'Munstead' 'Hidcote' 'Mitcham Gray'	EP	1½-2'	SHB	fine/dense	GYGN	SM	PUR*/PK	FS	C/L		DR	S			3-10
L. a. ssp. *a.* 'Nana Atropurpurea' 'Nana Alba'	EP	12-18"	SHB	fine/dense	GYGN	SM	PUR/W	FS	C/L		DR	S			3-10
L. a. ssp. *a* 'Compacta' 'Twickle Purple' 'Irene Doyle'	EP	2-3'	SHB	fine/dense	GYGN	SM	LAV	FS	C/L	[8wk]	DR	S			3-10
L. dentata French Lavender	EP	2-4'	SHB	fine/thin	GY	SM-F	LAV	FS	C		WD	S			8-10
L. latifolia Spike Lavender	EP	3-4'	SHB	fine/dense	GYGN	SM	PUR	FS	C/L		DR	S			4-10
L. lanata Wooly Lavender	EP	2-3'	SHB	fine/dense	W	SM	PUR	FS	C/L		WD	S			8-10
L. multifida Fringed Lavender	EP	2-3'	SHB	feathery/dense	GYGN	SM-F	PUR	FS	S/C		WD	S			8-10
L. stoechas Spanish Lavender	EP	3-5'	SHB	fine/dense	GYGN	SM-F	PUR*	FS	S/C/L	3-4wk	DR	S			7-10
L. viridis	EP	2-3'	SHB	fine/dense	GYGN	SM	Y	FS	C		WD	S			8-10

BOTANICAL NAME	LIFE CYCLE	HEIGHT	HABIT	FOLIAGE TEXTURE	FOLIAGE COLOR	BLOSSOM SEASON	BLOSSOM COLOR	SUN	PROPAGATION	GERMINATION	SOIL MOISTURE	SOIL TYPE	PESTS INSECTS	PESTS DISEASE	ZONE
L. × intermedia Lavandin	P	3–4′	SHB	fine/dense	GYGN	SM	LAV	FS	C/L		WD	S			ALL
Levisticum officinale Loveage	HP	4–6′	CL	coarse/dense	GN	SM	Y	FS-SH	S/D	2–3wk	M	R	leaf miner	crown rot	9–10
Lippia alba Licorice Verbena	EP	2–4′	SHB	coarse/thin	DGN	SM	W	FS	C/L	[6wk]	WD	R			9–10
L. graveolens Mexican Oregano	EP	4–6′	SHB	coarse/thin	DGN	SM	CRM	FS	C/L		WD	R			7–10
Marrubium vulgare Horehound	EP	1–2′	MAT	coarse/thin	GY	SM	W	FS	S/C	2–3wk	WD	S			2–9
Melissa officinalis Lemon Balm	HP	18–30″	BU	coarse/dense	GN	SM	W	FS-SH	S/D/C	2–3wk	M	R	cutworm		2–9
M. o. var. variegata Variegated Balm	HP	12–18″	BU	coarse/dense	YonGn	SM	W	FS	C/D	[4wk]	M	R			2–9
Mentha aquatica Water Mint	HP	1–2′	MAT	coarse/dense	DGN	SM	ROS	FS-PS	D/C/S	[4wk]	M-AQ	R			
M. cervina Holt's Pennyroyal	HP	2–3″	MAT	fine/thin	GN	SM	BLU	FS	S/D/C		WD	G		mildew wilt	
M. × gracilis var. variegata Ginger Mint	HP	12–16″	MAT	coarse/dense	YonGN	SM	PK	FS	C/D	[4wk]	M	R			4–9
M. × piperita Peppermint	HP	2–3′	MAT	coarse/dense	GN	SM	LAV	FS-PS	C/D/S	3–4wk	M	R		anthracnose wilt	2–9
M. × p. var. citrata Orange Mint	HP	16–18″	MAT	coarse/dense	P-DGN	SM	LAV	FS-PS	S/D/C		M	R			4–9
M. × p. var. piperita, 'Mitcham'	HP	1–2′	MAT	coarse/dense	DGN	SM	ROS	FS-PS	D/C	[4wk]	M	R		rust resistant	4–9
M. × p. var. vulgaris Black Mint	HP	1–2′	MAT	coarse/dense	PUR	SM	LAV	FS-PS	C/D		M	R		rust resistant	4–9
M. pulegium English Pennyroyal	EP	1–2′	MAT	coarse/dense	GN	SM	PK*	FS-SH	S,SS/D		M	G			6–10
M. pulegium var.	HP	2–3′	MAT	coarse/	LGN	SM		FS-PS	D/C		M	G			6–10

Species	Type	Height	Habit	Texture	Leaf Color		Flower Color	Light	Soil	Germination	Water	Prop.	Pests	Disease	Zone
M. spicata Spearmint	HP	1–2'	MAT	coarse/thin	GN	SM	LAV	FS-PS	S/C/D	[4wk]	M	R		rust	2–9
M. suaveolens **Pineapple Mint**	HP	18"	MAT	coarse/dense	WonLGN	SM	W	FS	C/D	[6wk]	M	R			3–9
M. s. var. Round-leaved Mint	HP	1–2'	MAT	coarse/dense	DGN	SM	LAV	PS-SH	C/D/C		M	R		rust mildew	2–9
M. × *villosa* var. Applemint	HP	2–3'	MAT	coarse/thin	LGN	SM	W/PK	FS-SH	S/D/C		M	G			3–9
Monarda didyma Bee Balm	HP	3–4'	UP	coarse/thin	DGN	SM	R/W/PK*	FS-PS	S/C/D	2–6wk	M	R	stalk borer	crown rot	2–9
M. d. 'Granite Pink' Dwarf Monarda	HP	10–12"	MAT	coarse/dense	DGN	SM	PK*	PS	S/C/D	1–4wk	M	R		leaf spot rust	2–9
M. fistulosa Wild Bergamot	HP	3–4'	UP	coarse/thin	DGN	SM	ROS/LAV*	FS-PS	S/D/C	2–6wk	M	R		mildew wilt	3–9
M. punctata Dotted Mint	HP	18"	BU	coarse/dense	GN	SM	Y	FS	S/D	4–6wk	D	S			3–9
Monardella odoratissima Western Balm	HP	18–24"	CL	coarse/thin	GN	SM-F	ROS*	FS-PS	D/S		WD	R			2–9
M. villosa Coyote Mint	HP	12–18"	MAT	coarse/dense	DGN	SM-F	ROS*	FS-PS	D/S	1–2wk	WD	R			2–9
Myrrhis odorata Sweet Cicely	HP	18–24"	CL	feathery/dense	LGN	SP	W*	PS-SH	S/D	2–3m	M	R			2–9
Nepeta cataria Catnip	HP	2–4'	UP	coarse/thin	GYGN	SM	W/PK	FS-PS	S/C/D	1–3wk	WD	G		leaf spot	2–9
N. c. 'Citriodora' Lemon Catnip	HP	2–3'	UP	coarse/thin	GYGN	SM	W/PK	FS	C/D	[6wk]	WD	R			6–9
N. × *faassenii* Catmint	HP	1–2'	MAT	coarse/dense	GY	SM	VIO*	FS-PS	C/D	[8wk]	WD	G			2–9
N. mussinii Dwarf Catnip	HP	12"	MAT	coarse/dense	GYGN	SM	BLU*	FS	S/D	1–2wk	WD	G			2–9
Ocimum americanum Lemon Basil	A	12"	BU	fine/thin	LGN	SM	W	FS	S	1–2wk	WD	R			9–10
O. basilicum Sweet Basil	A	1–2'	BU	coarse/dense	GN	SM	W	FS	S	5–7d	WD	R	beetles		9–10
O. b. 'Bush'	A/SP	12"	BU	fine/dense	LGN	SM	W	FS	S/C	1–2wk	WD	G			9–10

BOTANICAL NAME	LIFE CYCLE	HEIGHT	HABIT	FOLIAGE TEXTURE	FOLIAGE COLOR	BLOSSOM SEASON	BLOSSOM COLOR	SUN	PROPAGATION	GERMINATION	SOIL MOISTURE	SOIL TYPE	PESTS INSECTS	PESTS DISEASE	ZONE
O. b. 'Dark Opal'	A	18″	BU	coarse/ dense	PUR	SM	PK*	FS	S/C	5–7d	WD	G			9–10
O. b. 'Thyrsiflora'	A/SP	12″	BU	coarse/ dense	PUR-GN	SM	PK*	FS	S/C	1–2wk	WD	G			9–10
O. canum Hoary Basil	A/SP	2–3′	UP	coarse/ thin	DGN	SM	W	FS	S/C	2–3wk	WD	R			9–10
O. kilimandscharicum Camphor Basil	A/SP	2–4′	UP	coarse/ thin	GN	SM	W	FS	S/C/L	2–3wk	WD	G			9–10
O. sanctum 'Sri' Holy Basil	A/SP	1–2′	UP	coarse/ thin	GN	SM	W	FS	S/C/L	1–4wk	WD	G			9–10
O. s. 'Krishna' Purple Holy Basil	A/SP	1–2′	UP	coarse/ thin	PUR	SM	PK	FS	S/C/L	1–4wk	WD	R			9–10
O. 'Spice' Spice Basil	A	15″	BU	coarse/ dense	PONGN	SM	PK	FS	S/C	5–7d	WD	R			9–10
Origanum dictamnus Dittany of Crete	EP	8–12″	BU	coarse/ dense	GY	SM	PK*	PS	C/D	[4wk]	WD	SL			9–10
O. × *hybridum* Dittany	EP	12–18″	BU	coarse/ thin	GY	SM	PK	FS	C/L		WD	SL			8–10
O. majorana Sweet Marjoram	A/SP	12–18″	MAT	coarse/ dense	GYGN	SM	W	FS	S/D/L	1–2wk	WD	R			8–10
O. microphyllum	EP	12–18″	BU	fine/ dense	GY	SM	PK*	FS	S/D/L	[4wk]	WD	S			7–10
O. onites Pot Marjoram	A/SP	1–2′	MAT	coarse/ thin	GYGN	SM	W	FS	S/D		WD	G			7–10
O. vulgare ssp. *vulgare* Oregano	EP	18–24″	MAT	coarse/ dense	DGN	SM	W/PUR	FS	D/C/S	1–2wk	WD	GL			6–10
O. v. ssp. *gracile* Russian Oregano	EP	18–24″	MAT	coarse/ dense	PURGN	SM	PK*	FS	S/D/L	2–4wk	WD	G			4–10
O. v. ssp. *hirtum* Italian Oregano	SEP	18–24″	BU	coarse/ dense	LGN	SM	W	FS	C/D	[6wk]	WD	GL			8–10
O. v. 'Aureum' Golden Oregano	EP	12–18″	MAT	coarse/ dense	YGN	SM	W	FS	D/L		WD	G			6–10

Name	Type	Height	Form	Texture	Foliage	Flower	Color	Exp.	Soil	Prop.	Water		Insect	Disease	Zone
Perovskia atriplicifolia Russian Sage	EP	2–4'	BU	fine/thin	GYGN	SM-F	BLU	FS	S/C		WD	G			5–9
Petroselinum crispum var. *crispum* Curly Parsley	HB	12–18"	BU	coarse/dense	GN	SM	YGN	FS	S,SS	1–2wk	WD	G		leaf spot, stem rot	2–10
P. c. var. *neapolitanum* Italian Parsley	HB	2–3'	UP	coarse/thin	GN	SM	YGN	FS	S,SS	1–2wk	WD	R	leaf miner	leaf spot	2–10
Phlomis fruticosa Jerusalem Sage	EP	2–4'	BU	coarse/dense	GYGN	SM	Y*	FS	S/D		WD	GL		leaf spot	6–10
Pimpinella anisum Anise	A	12–18"	BU	fine/dense	DGN	SM	W	FS	S	1–2wk	WD	R			5–10
Reseda officinalis Mignonette	A/B	1–2'	CL	coarse/thin	GN	SP-F	Y*	FS	S	5–10d	WD	R		leaf spot	3–9
Rosmarinus officinalis var. *officinalis* Rosemary	EP	4–6'	BU	fine/dense	DGN	SP-F	BLU/W	FS	S/C/L	4–6wk	WD	GL		root rot	8–10
R. o. var. *angustifolius* Upright Rosemary	EP	3–4'	BU	fine/dense	DGN	SM	BLU	FS	C/L	[10wk]	WD	S			8–10
R. o. var. *prostratus* Creeping Rosemary	EP	12–18"	MAT	fine/dense	DGN	SM-F	BLU	FS	C/L	[12wk]	WD	SL			7–10
R. o. var. *rigidus* 'Tuscan Blue' 'Majorca Pink'	EP	3–4'	BU	fine/dense	DGN	SM	BLU	FS	C/L	[12wk]	WD	GL			8–10
Rumex acetosa Garden Sorrel	HB	2–3'	CL	coarse/dense	GN	SM	BRN	FS	S,SS	1–2wk	M	R			3–9
R. scutatus French Sorrel	HB	12–18"	CL	coarse/dense	GN	SM	BRN	FS	S,SS	1–2wk	M	R		leaf spot, rust	3–9
Ruta chalapensis Fringed Rue	SEP	2–3'		fine/dense	BGN	SM	Y	FS	S/C/L	4–6wk	WD	GL			7–10
R. graveolens Rue	SEP	1–2'	BU	fine/dense	BGN	SM	Y*	FS-PS	S/C/L	4–6wk	WD	GL			6–10
R. g. 'Curly Girl'	SEP	12–18"	BU	fine/dense	BGY	SM	Y	FS	C/L	[12wk]	WD	GL			6–10
R. g. var. *variegata*	SEP	1–2'	BU	fine/dense	WonBGY	SM	Y	FS	C/L	[15wk]	WD	GL			
Salvia argentea Silver Sage	B/HP	3–6"/18"	CL	coarse/thin	GY	SP	W	FS	S/SS	5–10d	WD	GS	stalk borer	stem rot	7–10

BOTANICAL NAME	LIFE CYCLE	HEIGHT	HABIT	FOLIAGE TEXTURE	FOLIAGE COLOR	BLOSSOM SEASON	BLOSSOM COLOR	SUN	PROPAGATION	GERMINATION	SOIL MOISTURE	SOIL TYPE	PESTS INSECTS	PESTS DISEASE	ZONE
S. clevelandii Blue Sage	EP	3–5'	BU	coarse/thin	GYGN	SM	BLU*	FS	C/L	[8wk]	WD	GL			8–10
S. dorisiana	EP	2–3'	BU	coarse/dense	LGN	SM-F	R*	FS	C/L/D	[6wk]	WD	RL			7–10
S. elegans Pineapple Sage	EP	3–5'	UP	coarse/thin	DGN	SM-F	R*	FS	C/L		WD	RL			8–10
S. fruticosa Greek Sage	EP	2–3'	BU	coarse/thin	GY	SM	LILAC	FS	C/L/S	2–3wk	WD	GL			8–10
S. officinalis Garden Sage	EP	2–3'	BU	coarse/thin	GYGN	SM	BLU*	FS-PS	S/L/C	1–2wk	WD	GL	stalk borer	stem rot rust	3–9
S. o. 'Aurea' Golden Sage	EP	12–18"	BU	coarse/dense	YGN	—	—	FS	C/L	[12wk]	WD	GL			2–10
S. o. 'Icterina' Golden sage	EP	12–18"	BU	coarse/dense	YonGN	—	—	FS	C/L	8wk	WD	GL			2–10
S. o. 'Nana' Dwarf Sage	EP	12"	BU	coarse/dense	GYGN	SM	BLU*	FS-PS	C/L	[8wk]	WD	GL		rust	4–10
S. o. 'Purpurascens' Red Sage	EP	12–18"	BU	coarse/thin	PUR	—	—	FS	C/L	[10wk]	WD	GL			8–10
S. o. 'Tricolor' Variegated Sage	EP	12–18"	BU	coarse/thin	W&P on DGN	—	—	FS	C/L	[6wk]	WD	GL			8–10
S. pratensis Meadow Clary	EP	1–3'	CL	coarse/thin	DGN	SM	PUR	FS	S,SS	1–2wk	WD	R			4–10
S. scalarea Clary	HB	2–5'	UP	coarse/thin	GY	SM	W/PK	FS-PS	S,SS		WD	GL			6–9
S. uliginosa Bog Sage	EP	3–4'	UP	coarse/thin	GN	SM-F	BLU*	FS	C/D		WD	GL			7–10
S. viridis Annual Clary	A	12–18"	CL	coarse/dense	VIO/PK ON DGN	SM	PUR/PK*	FS	S/SS	1–2wk	WD	GS			4–10
Sanguisorba canadense Great Burnet	HP	2–4'	CL	coarse/thin	DGN	SM	W	FS	S/D	2–4wk	WD	G			2–8
S. obtusum	HP	1–2'	CL	coarse/thin	DGN	SM	PK*	FS	S/D	2–4wk	M	G			4–8

Name	Type	Height	Habit	Texture/Density	Leaf Color	Size	Flower	Light	Soil	Germ.	Moisture	Prop.	Pests/Disease	Zone
Santolina chamaecyparissus Lavender cotton	EP	1–3'	SHB	fine/dense	GY	SM	Y*	FS-PS	C/L	[12wk]	M	S	crown rot	6–10
S. c. 'Nana' Dwarf Santolina	EP	8–12"	MAT	fine/dense	GY	SM	Y*	FS	C/L	[12wk]	M	S		6–10
S. neapolitana Fringed Santolina	EP	12–18"	SHB	fine/dense	GY	SM	Y*	FS-PS	C/L	[10wk]	M	S		7–10
S. virens Green Santolina	EP	18–24"	SHB	fine/dense	GN	SM	Y*	FS	C/L	[8wk]	M	S		3–9
Satureja douglasii Yerba Buena	HP	1–3"	MAT	coarse/dense	DGN	SP/F	W/PUR	PS-SH	S/L		M	RA		7–9
S. hortensis Summer Savory	A	12–18"	BU	fine/thin	DGN	SM	PK	FS	S	1–2wk	WD	R		ALL
S. montana Winter Savory	EP	6–16"	BU	fine/dense	DGN	SM	W/PK	FS	S/C/L	3–4wk	WD	G	mildew	4–9
S. m. ssp. *pygmaea* Pygmy Savory	EP	6–8"	BU	fine/dense	DGN	SM	W	FS	C/L	[6wk]	WD	G		4–9
S. pilosa Creeping Savory	DP	4–10"	MAT	fine/thin	DGN	SM	W	FS	S/L/C	2–3wk	WD	S		6–9
Sesamum indicum Sesame	A	3–4'	UP	coarse/thin	GN	SM-F	W/R*	FS	S	1–2wk	WD	R	leaf spot	4–10
Solidago odorata Fragrant Goldenrod	HP	2–4'	CL	coarse/dense	GN	SM-F	Y	FS	S/D		DR	GS	leaf spot, rust, mildew	4–9
Stachys byzantina Wooly Betony	EP	12–18"	MAT	coarse/dense	GY	SM	PK/RO	FS-PS	S,SS/L	1–2wk	DR	G		3–9
S. b. 'Silver Carpet'	EP	6"	CL	coarse/dense	GY	—	—	FS-PS	D	[6wk]	WD	G		4–9
S. officinalis Betony	HP	2–3'	UP	coarse/thin	GN	SP	ROSE*	FS	S	1–2wk	WD	G	leaf spot mildew	3–9
Symphytum officinale Comfrey	HP	3–5'	CL	coarse/dense	DGN	SM	LAV/R/Y	FS-SH	S/D	1–2wk	M	G	leaf spot	2–10
S. × *uplandicum* Russian Comfrey	HP	3–6'	CL	coarse/dense	DGN	SM	RO/PUR	FS	S/D	1–2wk	M	G		2–10
Tanacetum vulgare Garden Tansy	HP	3–5'	CL	feathery/dense	DGN	SM	Y*	FS-PS	S,SS/D	3–4wk	WD	G		2–9
T. v. 'Crispum' Fern Leaf Tansy	HP	3–4'	CL	feathery/dense	DGN	SM	Y*	FS	S/D	3–4wk	WD	G		2–9

BOTANICAL NAME	LIFE CYCLE	HEIGHT	HABIT	FOLIAGE TEXTURE	FOLIAGE COLOR	BLOSSOM SEASON	BLOSSOM COLOR	SUN	PROPAGATION	GERMINATION	SOIL MOISTURE	SOIL TYPE	PESTS INSECTS	PESTS DISEASE	ZONE
Teucrium chamaedrys Germander	EP	1–2'	SHB	fine/dense	DGN	SM	ROSE	FS	S/C/L	[12wk]	WD	G		rust	2–9
T. c. 'Prostratum' Creeping Germander	EP	6–8"	MAT	fine/dense	DGN	SM	ROSE	FS	C/L	[12wk]	WD	G			4–9
T. fruticans Silver Germander	EP	18–24"	SHB	fine/dense	GY	SM	BLU*	FS	C/L		WD	G			8–10
T. marum Cat Thyme	EP	12–18"	SHB	fine/dense	GY	SM	PK*	FS	S/C		WD	G			4–9
T. scorodonia Wood Sage	EP	8–10"	SHB	fine/dense	DGN	SM	Y	FS	S/C		WD	G			8–10
Thymbra spicata Za'atar	EP	12–16"	BU	fine/dense	DGN	SM	PK*	FS	S/C		WD	G			4–9
Thymus 'Argenteus' Silver Thyme	EP	8–10"	SHB	fine/dense	W on DGN	SM	PK	FS	C/L		WD	SL			5–9
T. 'Broadleaf English' English Thyme	EP	1–2'	SHB	fine/dense	DGN	SM	ROSE	FS	C/L		WD	S			8–10
T. brousonetti Moroccan Thyme	EP	10–12"	SHB	fine/thin	GN	SP-SM	PK*	FS	C/L		WD	S		root rot	4–10
T. caespititius 'Tuffet' Tuffeted Thyme	EP	to 3"	CL	fine/dense	LGN	SM	ROSE	FS	S/D/L		WD	S			9–10
T. camphoratus Camphor Thyme	EP	4–6"	SHB	fine/dense	DGN	SM	ROSE	FS	C		WD	S	mealy bug		8–10
T. capitatus Corido	EP	8–10"	SHB	fine/dense	DGN	SP-S	LAV	FS	S/C		WD	SL	mealy bug	root rot	9–10
T. carnosus	EP	4–6"	SHB	fine/thin	DGN	SM	W	FS	S/C		WD	S			6–10
T. × *citriodorus* 'Aureus' Golden Lemon Thyme	EP	8–12"	SHB	fine/thin	Y on DGN	SP-SM	PK	FS	C	[6wk]	WD	SL			6–10
T. 'Clear Gold' Transparent Thyme	EP	8–10"	MAT	fine/thin	YGN	SM	LAV	FS-PS	C/L		WD	S		root rot	

Thyme

Name														
T. herba-barona Caraway Thyme	EP	1–4"	MAT fine/dense	DGN	SM	ROSE	FS	S/C/L	[9wk]	WD	S			3–9
T. leucotrichus Peter Davis Thyme	EP	3–4"	MAT fine/thin	GYGN	SP	ROSE*	FS	C/L		WD	S			6–10
T. 'Linear Leaf Lilac' Marshall Thyme	EP	3–8"	MAT fine/dense	GYGN	SM	LAV*	FS	C/L	[12wk]	WD	S			4–10
T. 'Long Leaf Gray'	EP	3–6"	MAT fine/thin	GYGN	SP-S	LAV*	FS	C/L		WD	S			3–9
T. mastichina Mastic Thyme	EP	10–16"	SHB fine/dense	GYGN	SP-S	W	FS	S/C/L		WD	S			8–10
T. praecox ssp. *arcticus* Wild Thyme	EP	2–4"	MAT fine/dense	DGN	SM	PUR	FS	S/L/C	4–6wk	WD	SL			1–9
T. p. 'Coccineus' Crimson Thyme	EP	1–3"	MAT fine/dense	DGN	SM	R*	FS	S/L/C	[9wk]	WD	S			4–9
T. p. 'Languinosus' Wooly Thyme	EP	to 1"	MAT fine/dense	GY	SM	ROSE	FS	L/C	[9wk]	WD	SL			2–9
T. p. 'Mayfair'	EP	to 1"	MAT fine/dense	YonDGN	SM	ROSE	FS	L/D	[6wk]	WD	SL			4–9
T. p. 'Pink Chintz'	EP	to 1"	MAT fine/dense	YonDGN	SM	ROSE	FS	L/D	[6wk]	WD	SL			2–9
T. p. 'White Moss'	EP	to ½"	MAT fine/dense	GN	SM	W	FS	L/D	[6wk]	WD	SL			2–9
T. pulegioides Mother-of-Thyme	EP	4–10"	MAT fine/thin	DGN	SM	LAV	FS-PS	S/L/C	3–4wk	WD	C	cut worm	root rot	6–10
T. p. 'Fosterflower' Creeping White Thyme	EP	4–6"	MAT fine/thin	DGN	SM	W	FS-PS	L/C	[4wk]	WD	S	cut worm		6–10
T. p. 'Gold Dust' Creeping Gold Thyme	EP	8–10"	MAT fine/thin	YonDGN	SM	ROSE	FS	C/L		WD	W		root rot	7–10
T. p. 'Kermesinus' Creeping Red Thyme	EP	6–8"	MAT fine/thin	DGN	SM	MAG*	FS	C/L		WD	S			6–10
T. p. 'Oregano-scented' Oregano Thyme	EP	6–10"	MAT fine/dense	DGN	SM	LAV*	FS-PS	L/C	[4wk]	WD	S	cut worm		6–10

BOTANICAL NAME	LIFE CYCLE	HEIGHT	HABIT	FOLIAGE TEXTURE	FOLIAGE COLOR	BLOSSOM SEASON	BLOSSOM COLOR	SUN	PROPAGATION	GERMINATION	SOIL MOISTURE	SOIL TYPE	PESTS INSECTS	PESTS DISEASE	ZONE
T. vulgaris French Thyme 'Orange Balsam' 'Fragrantissimus'	EP	12–18"	SHB	fine/dense	DGN	SM	W/PK	FS	S,SS/C/L	4–6wk	DR	SL			2–9
T. v. 'Miniature' Dwarf Thyme	EP	4–6"	SHB	fine/dense	GYGN	—	—	FS	C	[10wk]	WD	SL			4–9
T. 'Wedgewood'	EP	4–6"	MAT	fine/dense	BGN	SM	W	FS	C/L	[6wk]	WD	S			4–10
T. zygis	EP	6–8"	SHB	fine/thin	DGN	SM	LAV	FS	S/C		WD	S			6–10
Trigonella foenum-graecum Fennugreek	A	18–30"	UP	fine/thin	DGN	SM	W/PK	FS	S	5–10d	M	R			3–9
Valeriana officinalis Valerian	HP	3–6'	UP	fine/thin	DGN	SP-SM	W/PK	PS	S/D		M	R		crown rot rust	2–9
Viola odorata Florist's Violet	HP	4–8"	CL	coarse/dense	DGN	SP-SM	PUR/W/R*	SH-PS	S,SS/D	1–2wk	M	RA	cut worm slug	crown rot root rot	4–9
V. canadensis	HP	8–10"	CL	coarse/dense	DGN	SP-SM	W*	PS-SH	S,SS/D	5–10d	M	RA	cut worm	rust leaf spot	2–9
V. lanceolata Lance-leaf Violet	HP	6–10"	CL	coarse/thin	DGN	SP-SM	W*	PS	S,SS/D		AQ	RS			4–9
V. pedata Bird's-foot Violet	HP	4–6"	CL	fine/dense	DGN	SP	PUR/LAV*	FS-PS	S/D	1–2wk	WD	GS			2–9
V. tricolor Pansy	HP	6–10"	CL	coarse/dense	DGN	SP-F	PUR/Y	FS-PS	S/SS	5–10d	WD	G	slug cutworm		4–9

Landscape Uses & Herbal Uses of Ornamental Herbs

Columns Scent–Pond fall under **LANDSCAPE USES**; columns Tea–Medicinal fall under **HERBAL USES**.

HERB (Common Name)	Scent	Bee Herb	Flowers	Bonsai	Shade	Ground Cover	Hedge	Screen	Border	Potted	Rockery	Pond	Tea	Salad	Spice	Smoking	Pottage	Companion	Dried Material	Fragrance	Confection	Strewing	Repellent	Medicinal	ORIGINS
Angelica		X			X							X		X	X	X								X	Eurasia
Anise									X					X	X	X					X				S. Europe
Anise Hyssop		X	X						X					X	X	X		X	X	X	X				N. Amer.
Asafetida		X							X	X					X										S.E. Asia
Basil, Bush	X								X	X	X			X	X	X									
Basil, Camphor									X	X												X			E. Afr.
Basil, Cinnamon	X								X		X			X	X	X		X	X	X	X				
Basil, Crinkled									X						X						X				
Basil, Lemon									X	X				X	X	X					X	X			N.W. India
Basil, Sacred	X								X	X				X	X	X	X	X	X	X	X				S.E. Asia
Basil, Spice		X							X	X	X			X	X	X					X	X			garden
Basil, Sweet	X	X							X	X				X	X	X		X			X				ancient
Basil, Thyrisflora		X							X	X	X				X						X	X			India
Basil, Tree										X					X							X	X		
Basil—Thyme	X	X	X						X		X			X	X	X						X			Eurasia
Bay, Sweet				X	X	X	X								X		X	X	X	X	X				Med.
Bay, California															X				X	X	X				W. USA
Bedstraw					X			X											X						
Bee Balm		X	X	X				X	X				X						X	X	X	X	X		E. USA
Betony		X							X	X				X									X		
Betony, Wooly		X				X				X	X		X						X						Turkey/SW Asia
Bible Leaf	X		X	X												X	X	X		X	X	X			Eurasia
Borage		X	X	X					X					X							X				Eur./N. Afr.
Burnet, Great		X						X	X																
Burnet, Japanese		X							X	X															

HERB COMMON NAME	LANDSCAPE USES												HERBAL USES												ORIGINS
	Scent	Bee Herb	Flowers	Bonsai	Shade	Ground Cover	Hedge	Screen	Border	Potted	Rockery	Pond	Tea	Salad	Spice	Smoking	Pottage	Companion	Dried Material	Fragrance	Confection	Strewing	Repellent	Medicinal	
Burnet, Salad					X	X			X				X	X			X		X						Eurasia
Calamint	X				X				X					X	X	X	X					X	X	X	S. Eur/Med.
Calendula		X							X	X	X		X	X				X			X				S. Europe
Camomile, German	X	X	X		X	X	X		X									X	X	X	X	X		X	Europe
Camomile, Lawn	X				X	X	X	X														X			
Camomile, Roman	X	X			X	X	X	X	X													X	X	X	Eurasia
Camomile, Dyer's			X					X											X						
Caraway								X						X	X	X	X	X	X		X				Europe
Cardoon		X						X	X						X			X	X						S. Europe
Catnip			X						X					X								X	X	X	Eurasia
Catnip, Lemon									X	X				X							X				
Catnip, Dwarf	X	X		X					X		X							X	X		X				Iran
Chervil					X	X								X	X	X		X				X	X		
Chive		X	X						X	X	X	X		X	X		X	X	X					X	Eurasia
Chive, Garlic		X							X	X	X			X	X			X	X					X	China
Clary		X							X	X							X				X			X	S. Europe
Clove Pink	X	X							X	X	X								X	X	X	X			
Comfrey		X	X		X	X	X	X									X							X	Eurasia
Coriander	X								X					X	X	X	X	X	X		X				S. Europe
Corido		X				X			X	X	X						X					X			Med./E. Asia
Costmary	X	X				X				X										X	X		X	X	Eurasia
Creeping Charlie					X	X			X	X	X							X			X				Europe
Cumin									X						X	X					X				Med.
Curry Plant	X	X		X					X	X	X			X	X	X	X		X	X	X				S. Europe
Dill	X	X							X	X				X	X	X	X	X	X			X	X	X	
Dittany		X							X	X	X			X	X	X		X	X		X				Greece/Crete
Dong Quai		X	X							X								X	X	X				X	China
Dropwort		X	X						X															X	
Egyptian Onion																			X						
Elecampane		X	X						X								X	X	X					X	C. Asia
English Daisy																									
Fennel	X		X					X	X					X	X	X	X	X	X					X	S. Europe
Fennugreek		X	X		X										X	X	X	X			X		X	X	S. Eur/Asia
Finocchio									X						X		X								
Garlic		X							X	X					X	X	X	X	X				X	X	
Geranium, Scented	X								X	X	X			X	X	X			X	X	X	X			S. Afr.
Germander, Wall		X		X	X	X													X						Europe
Germander, Silver		X		X	X	X												X	X						Asia
Giant Allium		X							X	X									X						W. Med.
Ginger, Wild					X	X						X			X	X	X				X	X			N. hemisph.
Goldenrod, Fragrant		X							X				X						X	X	X	X			
Good King Henry						X								X			X								

| | LANDSCAPE USES | | | | | | | | | | | | HERBAL USES | | | | | | | | | | | | |
COMMON NAME	Scent	Bee Herb	Flowers	Bonsai	Shade	Ground Cover	Hedge	Screen	Border	Potted	Rockery	Pond	Tea	Salad	Spice	Smoking	Pottage	Companion	Dried Material	Fragrance	Confection	Strewing	Repellent	Medicinal	ORIGINS
Hop						X		X					X						X		X			X	N. hemisph.
Horehound		X						X	X				X						X		X			X	S. Europe
Hyssop	X	X	X	X		X			X	X	X					X					X	X			S. & E. Europe
Indian Borage	X								X	X						X	X		X						S.E. Asia
Jasmine, Poet's	X		X		X		X	X												X	X				W. China
Jasmine, Arabian	X		X					X					X							X	X	X			
Lady's Mantle	X		X	X	X				X										X						
Lamb's Quarters									X					X			X								N. hemisph.
Lavender, Dwarf		X	X						X	X	X								X	X					
Lavender, English	X	X	X			X	X	X	X	X									X	X			X	X	Med.
Lavender, French	X		X			X	X	X	X	X									X	X					S. Spain
Lavender, Spanish			X						X	X	X								X	X					W. Med.
Lavender, Wooly			X						X	X	X								X	X					S. Spain
Lavender Cotton			X			X	X		X	X	X									X			X	X	Spain/N. Afr.
Leek									X					X	X		X								
Lemon Balm	X	X			X				X	X			X	X	X			X	X	X	X	X	X		S. Europe
Lovage					X				X	X			X	X	X	X	X	X			X	X			E. Europe
Love-in-a-Mist		X			X				X	X					X				X	X					
Lungwort		X	X	X		X																			
Mallows			X	X										X	X		X		X						
Marjoram, Pot									X	X					X		X								SE Eur/Turkey
Marjoram, Sweet									X	X	X			X	X	X	X	X			X	X			SW Asia/N. Afr.
Marshmallow					X			X	X	X											X		X		
Marsh Marigold			X	X										X			X								
Masterwort		X	X							X									X	X					Bulgaria
Meadow Clary		X	X		X				X									X	X						Eurasia
Meadow Sweet	X	X			X				X	X									X				X		Eurasia
Mignonette	X	X							X	X									X						
Mint, Apple	X	X			X	X							X	X							X	X			S. Europe
Mint, Black	X	X	X		X								X	X				X	X	X	X		X		England
Mint, Corsican	X				X	X				X	X										X				Corsica
Mint, Coyote	X	X	X		X														X						W. USA
Mint, Curly	X									X	X										X				
Mint, Dotted	X	X							X		X								X		X				C. USA
Mint, Ginger	X					X				X	X		X		X						X	X			
Mint, Korean	X	X	X										X						X		X	X			
Mint, Mountain	X	X				X			X				X						X						N. Amer.
Mint, Orange	X	X	X		X	X				X	X		X	X				X	X	X	X				
Mint, Pepper	X	X											X								X	X		X	garden
Mint, Pineapple	X	X				X				X	X		X								X	X			
Mint, Round-leaved	X	X	X		X	X							X	X							X	X			N. hemisph.
Mint, Spear	X	X				X							X								X	X			ancient

Columns under **LANDSCAPE USES**: Scent, Bee Herb, Flowers, Bonsai, Shade, Ground Cover, Hedge, Screen, Border, Potted, Rockery, Pond.
Columns under **HERBAL USES**: Tea, Salad, Spice, Smoking, Pottage, Companion, Dried Material, Fragrance, Confection, Strewing, Repellent, Medicinal.

HERB COMMON NAME	Scent	Bee Herb	Flowers	Bonsai	Shade	Ground Cover	Hedge	Screen	Border	Potted	Rockery	Pond	Tea	Salad	Spice	Smoking	Pottage	Companion	Dried Material	Fragrance	Confection	Strewing	Repellent	Medicinal	ORIGINS
Mint, Stone	X					X																X			E. No. Amer.
Mint, Water	X		X		X	X							X							X	X	X	X		
Mugwort, Common						X									X		X								Europe
Mugwort, Western						X													X						C & W USA
Mugwort, White	X		X			X	X												X	X					China
Oregano	X	X	X			X			X	X					X	X	X		X						Eurasia
Oregano, Golden						X				X							X								garden
Oregano, Italian	X				X				X	X	X		X	X	X	X	X		X	X	X	X	X		SE Europe
Oregano, Mexican									X						X		X								C. Amer.
Origanum microphyllum			X						X	X					X						X				
Pansy			X			X			X	X	X		X					X						X	
Parsley, Curly									X	X	X			X	X			X			X				Eurasia
Parsley, Italian									X					X	X	X		X	X						Eurasia
Parsley, Japanese					X				X					X	X	X	X	X							N. Amer./Siberia
Pennyroyal, Engl.	X	X	X		X	X			X	X									X	X		X			Europe
Pennyroyal, Amer.	X								X	X	X											X			N. Amer.
Pennyroyal, Holt's	X					X					X		X									X			E. No. Amer.
Pineapple Weed						X											X			X	X				N. Amer.
Rocambole		X							X	X				X	X			X	X	X					
Rosemary	X		X				X	X	X	X	X		X		X	X			X	X	X	X	X	X	Med.
Rosemary, Creeping	X					X			X	X													X	X	
Rue		X	X		X				X	X	X							X	X			X	X		S. Europe
Saffron		X	X						X	X	X		X		X							X	X		Turkistan
Sage, Bog		X							X	X								X							
Sage, Canyon		X			X				X	X															W. USA
Sage, Blue	X	X	X			X			X	X	X		X	X	X	X			X	X	X	X	X		
Sage, Dwarf		X	X			X			X	X	X		X		X	X			X	X		X	X		
Sage, Garden	X	X	X	X		X	X		X	X			X		X	X		X	X			X	X	X	Spain/Asia Minor
Sage, Golden	X								X	X	X		X		X	X						X			
Sage, Greek	X	X	X			X			X	X			X		X	X						X	X		
Sage, Pineapple		X											X	X	X										Mexico
Sage, Red									X	X	X		X		X	X			X	X					
Sage, Silver			X						X	X	X							X						X	
Sage, Tricolor									X	X	X		X		X	X			X	X					
Sage, Wood		X							X									X							Europe
Santolina		X		X	X		X		X										X						Med.
Santolina, Green		X		X	X		X												X						
Savory, Creeping	X	X				X			X																
Savory, Pygmy					X				X	X	X						X								
Savory, Summer	X								X					X	X	X					X				Med.
Savory, Winter	X	X					X		X	X							X					X			Med.

| HERB / COMMON NAME | LANDSCAPE USES | | | | | | | | | | | | HERBAL USES | | | | | | | | | | | | ORIGINS |
	Scent	Bee Herb	Flowers	Bonsai	Shade	Ground Cover	Hedge	Screen	Border	Potted	Rockery	Pond	Tea	Salad	Spice	Smoking	Pottage	Companion	Dried Material	Fragrance	Confection	Strewing	Repellent	Medicinal	
Sesame		X							X				X	X							X				Africa
Shallot									X				X	X	X										
'Silver King'									X										X						
'Silver Mound'						X				X	X								X						
Skirrets													X				X								China
Sorrel									X								X								Eurasia
Southernwood	X					X	X	X	X									X	X	X	X		X		SE Europe
Sweet Cicely	X		X			X	X		X	X			X	X	X	X		X	X	X	X	X			Europe
Sweet Flag	X				X								X	X			X		X	X	X	X		X	N. hemisph.
Sweet Woodruff																									
Tansy, Garden	X	X	X			X	X													X	X	X	X		Eurasia
Tansy, Fern Leaf		X				X	X	X												X		X	X		
Tarragon													X	X	X	X	X				X				
Thyme, Camphor	X				X		X		X												X				Portugal
Thyme, Caraway	X	X	X		X				X	X			X	X	X							X	X		Corsica, Sard.
Thyme, Cat		X				X			X	X	X							X							W. Med.
Thyme, Creeping Golden						X				X			X	X											
Thyme, English		X				X			X	X			X	X											garden
Thyme, French	X	X	X			X	X		X	X	X		X	X	X			X	X	X	X	X	X	X	W. Med.
Thyme, Golden Lemon						X			X	X			X	X	X						X	X			
Thyme, Lemon						X			X	X			X	X	X						X				garden
Thyme, Marshall		X	X			X			X	X			X								X				
Thyme, Mastic		X				X			X	X	X		X												Spain/Portug.
Thyme, Miniature						X			X	X	X		X												USA
Thyme, Moroccan		X	X			X			X	X	X		X									X	X		Morocco
Thyme, Mother of	X	X	X		X	X				X			X	X	X							X	X	X	Europe
Thyme, Orange	X		X			X	X		X	X	X		X	X	X			X	X	X	X	X	X		Europe
Thyme, Oregano	X	X	X		X	X				X			X	X	X										Europe
Thyme, Peter Davis		X	X			X			X	X			X									X			Balkan Pen
Thyme, Red-flowering		X	X			X				X			X												
Thyme, Silver		X	X			X	X		X	X	X		X	X	X										garden
Thyme, Tuffeted		X				X			X	X	X		X												Portu/Azores
Thyme, Wedgewood		X				X				X			X	X											USA
Thyme, White-flowering		X	X		X	X				X			X	X	X							X	X		Europe
Thyme, 'White Moss'						X				X															
Thyme, Wild	X	X	X			X			X	X			X												Europe
Thyme, Wooly		X				X				X															
Thymus zygis		X					X		X	X	X		X									X			Spain/Portug.
Valerian	X	X	X						X	X		X								X	X				Eurasia

COMMON NAME	LANDSCAPE USES Scent	Bee Herb	Flowers	Bonsai	Shade	Ground Cover	Hedge	Screen	Border	Potted	Rockery	Pond	HERBAL USES Tea	Salad	Spice	Smoking	Pottage	Companion	Dried Material	Fragrance	Confection	Strewing	Repellent	Medicinal	ORIGINS
Verbena, Lemon	X	X					X	X	X	X			X		X	X		X	X	X	X	X			Chile
Verbena, Licorice		X						X	X								X		X	X	X	X			C & S Amer.
Violet, Florist's	X	X		X	X			X	X	X				X			X		X	X	X			X	Eurasia/Afr.
Wild Bergamot		X	X					X	X				X						X		X				E. No. Amer.
Wild Fennel		X						X	X	X					X	X			X		X				
Wintergreen		X			X	X					X		X						X	X	X			X	E. N. Amer.
Witch Hazel	X	X	X	X	X	X	X												X					X	
Wormwood	X			X	X	X		X	X							X	X					X	X		Europe
Wormwood, Beach					X	X				X									X						
Wormwood, Roman								X	X	X									X						S. Europe
Yarrow		X			X		X	X					X						X					X	N. hemisph.
Yarrow, Creeping		X			X					X									X						
Yerba Buena	X		X	X									X	X	X						X				N. America
Za'atar			X				X	X	X	X							X		X	X			X	X	Turkey/E. Afr.

Appendix III

Dictionary of Latin Names

(deriv.) derived from; (ref.) refers to

acetosa	bitter	caespititius	mounded, sod
acetosella	vinegar salt	calamint	excellent mint
achillea	Achilles (name)	calamus	reed-like
agastache	crowded ear of grain (ref fl.)	calendula	calendric (ref. fl)
ajuga	not yoked (ref. fl.)	campanula	bell-shaped
albus	white	candicans	white, hoary
alchemilla	alchemist's herb	canum	grey, hoary
allium	garlic-like, pungent	capitatus	headed
althea	Althaea (name)	cardunculus	thistle-like
anethum	Anethon (Gk.)	carnosus	fleshy
angelica	angelic	carvi	Karawaya, Arabian
angustifolius	narrow	caryophyllus	clove-like
anthemis	flower	caudatum	of woodlands
anthriscus	Thrace (deriv.), rejoice	cerefolium	waxy-leaved
aquilegia	eagle's claws (ref. fl)	chalapensis	fringed (ref. fl)
arborescens	tree-like	chamaecyparissus	ground cypress
archangelica	Archangel Michael	chamaedrys	on the ground
argenteus	silver	chamaemellum	ground apple
aroanium	furrowed	chenopodium	goosefoot
artemisia	Artemis, elegant	chrysanthemum	golden flower
arvensis	field grown, cultivated	citriodorus	lemon scented
ascalonicum	Syrian (deriv.)	coccinea	scarlet-colored
atropurpureum	dark purple	coleus	sheath
aureus	golden	communis	common
balsamita	balsam-like	coreopsis	bug-like (ref. fruit)
basilicum	royal, princely	coriandrum	bug-like (ref. odor)
bellis	pretty	corsicus	Corsica
borago	rough	cotula	small cup
byzantina	Byzantium (city)	crispum	curly
		crocus	Krokos, Gk.
		cryptotaenia	hidden band
		cumin	Kumino, Gk.

cyanus — blue
cyminum — cyme bearing
cyparissus — cypress-like

damascena — Damascus (city)
dictamnus — Mount Dict (Crete)
didyma — twinned
dentata — toothed
douglasii — David Douglas (explorer)
dracunculus — serpentine, little dragon

elegans — elegant

farinacea — starchy, mealy
ferula — cane or fennel-like
fillipendula — thread-like and pendulous
fistulosa — hollow
flavum — yellow
florepleno — double flowered
floridus — flowery
foeniculum — hay-scented
foenum-graecum — Greek hay
foetida — bad odor
fragrantissimus — very fragrant
fructifera — fruitful
frutescens — bushy, shrubby
fruticans (fruticosa) — bushy, shrubby

gallium — curdles milk, cheese renning
gentilis — of the family
glacialis — icy
glaucus — blue-green, grey
gracilis — slender
gramineus — grass-like
grandiflorum — large flowered
graveolens — strong scented
gaultheria — Francois Gaultier

hamamelis — apple tree-like
hedeoma — sweet smelling
hederacea — ivy-like

helleborus — to injure, poison
hirtum — hairy, rough
hortensis — of gardens
humilis — dwarf
humulus — earthy
hyssop — aromatic herb

inula — helenium (deriv.)

jasmine — Yasmin, Persian

labiatae — lipped
lactiflora — milk white flower
lanata — wooly
languinosus — wooly
lanicaulis — wooly stem
latifolia — broad-leaved
lavandula — to wash
leucotrichus — white haired
lovage — Liguria (city) (deriv.)
lupulus — wolf-like

majorana — greater
marrubium — bitter (Hebrew)
melissa — of bees
mentha — Minthe (name)
micans — sparkling
millefolium — thousand leaved
mollis — soft
monarda — Nicolas Monardes
monardella — dimin. Monarda
moschata — musk-like
multifida — parted many times
myrrhis — myrrh like

nana — little
neapolitana — of Naples
nepeta — Nept (city)
niger — black
nitens — blooming
nitidus — flourishing, luxuriant
nobilis — noble, famous
nudiflorum — naked flower

obtusum	blunt, rounded
ocimum	to smell
odorata	fragrant
officinalis	medicinal
origanum	joy of the mtn., mtn. beauty
oxalis	sour
panonicus	Panonicus
patens	spreading
patiencia	enduring
pedata	footed
pedemontana	mountain walker
petroselinum	mountain celery
pilosa	covered with hair
pimpinella	bipinnula (deriv.)
piperita	pepper-like
plumosus	feathered
pontica	Pontus (city)
poterium	claret cup herb (deriv.)
praecox	early, ripe before time
pratensis	of meadows
primula	early
prunella	prune colored (ref. fl.)
ptarmica	feathery, comb-like
pulchellum	very pretty
pulegioides	pennyroyal-like
pulegium	fleabane
punctata	dotted, spotted
purpurascens	purple
repens	creeping
requienii	to rest upon
reseda	to soothe
rosmarinus	delights in sea spray (der.)
rotundifolia	round leaved
rugosa	wrinkled
ruta	to set free, cure
rutilans	red
salvia	save
sambucifolia	elder-leaved
sanctum	holy, sacred
sanguisorba	blood staunch
sativus	cultivated
schoenoprasum	rush leek
sclarea	clear eye (deriv.)
scutatus	buckler-shaped, shielded
semperflorens	ever blooming
sinensis	chinese
solidago	to make whole, heal
spicata	ear of corn (ref. fl.)
stachys	ear of grain (ref. fl.)
stellerana	bright, shining
stoechas	Stoechade Is.
sylvestris	of woodlands
symphytum	unite, bring together
tanacetoides	tansy-like
tanacetum	immortal (ref. fl.)
teucrium	Tucer (name)
thracicus	Thrace (country)
thymbra	savory, Thymbra (city)
thymus	incense, fumigate
thyrsiflora	spirally wound fl.
tinctoria	dyer's herb
tomentosa	densely wooly
trigonella	three angled fl.
tuberosum	tuberous
ulmaria	elm-leaved
urticifolia	nettle-leaved
valerian	to be in health
vera	true
verbena	sacred herb, Vervain (deriv.)
vernalis	of spring
verum	true
villosa	soft and hairy
viola	Ione, Gk. (deriv.)
viridis	green
vulgaris	common
zygis	yoked, joined

Bibliography

This bibliography is provided to help you in your search for information on herbs or their use in the ornamental garden. Books that may give more detailed medicinal data are preceded by (M). Books that may be useful for garden design information are preceded by (D). Any book that constitutes a reference guide is marked with (R).

ANDERSON, E., *Plants, Man and Life* (52)

ARBER, A., *Herbals: Their Origin and Evolution* (32)

BAILEY, L. H., *How Plants Get Their Names* (Dover 63)

(R)_____ , *Hortus III, Manual of Cultivated Plants* (76)

(D)BILES, R., *The Complete Book of Garden Magic* (47)

(D)BIRDSEYE, C. & E., *Growing Woodland Plants* (51) (Dover 72)

(D)BROOKLYN BOTANIC GARDENS, *Herbs and Their Ornamental Uses* (83)

_____ , *Dye Plants and Dyeing* (64)

BROWN, D., *Encyclopedia Botanica* (78)

BROWN, A., *Old Man's Garden* (38)

BROWNLOW, M., *Herbs and the Fragrant Garden* (57)

(M)BUCHMAN, D., *Herbal Medicine* (79)

(R)BOERNER BOT. GAR., *Herb Information Handbook*, Ed. R. Wrensch (75)

(D)CHATTO, B., *The Damp Garden* (84)

CLARKSON, R., *Herbs and Savory Seeds* (72)

_____ , *The Golden Age of Herbs and Herbalists* (40) (Dover 72)

_____ , *Green Enchantment* (44)

_____ , *Magic Gardens* (39)

_____ , CLARKSON, R., *Herbs: Their Culture and Uses* (42) (71)

CONROW, R. & HACKSEL, A., *Herbal Pathfinders* (79)

(R)CRACKER, L. & SIMON, J. Eds., *Herbs, Spices, and Medicinal Plants*, Vol. I (85)

(D)CRISP, SIR FRANK, *Medieval Gardens* (33)

(D)CROCKETT, J., *Encyclopedia of Gardening*

(D)_____ , *Landscape Gardening*

CROW, W., *Occult Properties of Herbs* (69)

DARAH, H., *The Cultivated Basils* (80)

DIOSCORIDES, *The Greek Herbal* (34)

FITZPATRIC, F., *Our Plant Resources* (64)

(R)FLANNERY, H., *A Study of the Taxa of Thymus Cult. in the U.S.* (82) (monograph)

(D)FLEMING, L. & GORE, A., *The English Garden* (79)

(D)FOLEY, D., *Ground Covers for Easier Gardening* (61) (Dover 72)

FOSTER, G., *Herbs for Every Garden* (73)

FOX, H., *Gardening with Herbs for Flavor and Fragrance* (33) (Dover 70)

_____ , *The Years in My Garden* (53)

GARLAND, S., *Complete Book of Herbs and Spices* (80)

(D)_____ , *The Herb Garden* (84)

(D)GESSERT, K., *The Beautiful Herb Garden* (82)

GIBBONS, E., *Stalking the Healthful Herbs* (66)

_____ , *Stalking the Wild Asparagus* (69)

(D)GILBERTIE'S. & SHEEHAN, L., *Herb Gardening at its Best* (82)

(D)GIVENS, H., *Landscape it Yourself*

GORDON, L., *A Country Herbal* (85)

_____ , *Green Magic-Flowers, Plants & Herbs in Lore & Legend* (77)

GRANT, J., *Designing a Garden*

_____ , *The Fragrant Garden*

GREENAWAY, K., *The Language of Flowers* (1884 reprnt)

GRIEVE, M., *A Modern Herbal* (31) (Dover 71)

GRIMM, W., *Home Guide to Trees, Shrubs and Wildflowers* (70)

HALL, D., *The Book of Herbs*

HARRISON & MASEFIELD, *Oxford Book of Plants*

(R)HARRINGTON, H. & DURRELL, L., *How to Identify Plants* (57)

(D)HARVEY, J., *Medieval Gardens* (83)

(R)HAY, R. & SYNGE, P., *The Color Dictionary of Flowers and Plants* (82)

HAYES, E., *Spices and Herbs, Lore and Cookery* (61)

HEALY, B., *A Gardener's Guide to Plant Names* (72)

HEDRICK, U., *Sturtevant's Edible Plants of the World* (19) (Dover 72)

HEFFERN, R., *The Herb Buyer's Guide*

HVASS, E., *Plants that Feed and Serve Us* (73)

(D)IREYS, I., *Small Gardens for City and Country*

(D)_____ , A., *How to Plan & Plant Your Own Property* (75)

JACOB, D., *A Witches Guide to Gardening* (65)

JONES, D., *The Herb Garden* (72)

(M)KADANS, J., *Modern Encyclopedia of Herbs* (70)

KAMM, M., *Old Time Herbs for Northern Gardens* (38) (Dover 71)

(M)KLOSS, J., *Back to Eden* (39) (75)

(M)KROCHMAL, A. & C., *Guide to the Medicinal Plants of the US* (73)

KRUTCH, J., *The Gardener's World*

LATHROP, N., *Herbs, How to Grow, Select and Enjoy* (80)

LEHNER, E. & J., *Folklore and Odysseys of Food and Medicinal Plants* (62)

LEIGHTON, A., *Early American Gardens—For Meate or Medicine* (70)

(D)LEIGHTON, A., *American Gardens in the Eighteenth Century* (76)

(M)LEUNG, A., *Chinese Herbal Remedies*

LEVY, J., *Herbal Handbook for Everyone* (66)

LOWENFELD, C., *Herb Gardening: Why and How to Grow Herbs* (71)

_____ , & BACK, P., *Herbs, Health and Cookery* (67)

(M)LUST, J., *The Herb Book* (74)

(R)MARINO-RODRIGUEZ, M., *Plants and Plant Products, FAO Bul. 25-1* (83)

(R)MATHEWS, D., *Travel Guide to Herb Shops, Farms and Gardens* (83)

(R)_____ , *Herbs by Mail* (83)

MATHEWS, W., *Mazes and Labyrinths* (22) (Dover 72)

MELTZER, S., *Herb Gardening in Texas* (83)

(M)MERCK INDEX, 10th ED., *An Encyclopedia of Chemicals, Drugs and Biologicals* (83)

(R)MORTON, J., *GoldenGuide to Herbs and Spices* (77)

_____ , *Major Medicinal Plants*

NEHRING, A. & I., *Picture Book of Perennials* (64) (77)

(R)NUTRITION SEARCH INC., *Nutrition Almanac* (73)

(M)PARK DAVIS CO., *Manual of Theraputics* (10)

(R)OLIVER, P., *The Herb Gardener's Resource Guide* (83)

PELLEGRINI, A., *The Food Lover's Garden* (70)

(R)PIRONE, P., *Diseases and Pests of Ornamental Plants* (70)

PRUTHI, J., *Spices and Condiments*

RANDOLPH, V., *Ozark Magic and Folklore* (47)

REPPERT, B., *A Heritage of Herbs* (76)

RHODE, E., *A Garden of Herbs* (69) (Dover 83)

(M)ROBERTS, B., *Characteristics of Selected Controversial Nutrition Products,* Table I (83)

RODALE PRESS, *Rodale Herb Book* (74)

_____ , *Encyclopedia of Organic Gardening* (78)

ROSE, J., *Herbs and Things: Jeanne Rose's Herbal* (72)

SANDERSON, L., *How to Make Your Own Herbal Cosmetics* (79)

SAUNDERS, C., *Edible, Useful Wild Plants of the US and Canada* (20) (Dover 76)

(M)SCHAUNBERG, P., *Guide to Medicinal Plants*

SCOBEY, J. & MEYERS, N., *Gifts from your Garden* (75)

SILVERMAN, M., *A City Herbal*

(R)SIMON, J. CHADWICK, A. & CRACKER, L. *Herbs—An Indexed Bibliography, 1971–80* (84)

SIMMONS, A., *Herbs to Grow Indoors* (69)

_____ , *Herb Gardening in Five Seasons* (69)

(R)SIMONSEN, J., *The Terpenes, VOL. I–IV* (47)

SINGLETON, E., *The Shakespeare Garden* (31)

SQUIRES, M., *The Art of Drying Plants and Flowers* (58)

STUART, M., Ed., *The Encyclopedia of Herbs and Herbalism* (79)

(D)SUNSET BOOKS, *Lawns and GroundCovers* (81)

(D)SWANSON, F. & RADY, V., *Herb Garden Design* (84)

SWANSON, F., *How to Grow Herbs* (82)

(D)TALOUMIS, G., *Container Gardening Outdoors* (72)

TANNAHILL, R., *Food in History* (73)

TAYLOR, N., *Fragrance in the Garden* (53)

(R)TETENYI, P., *Infraspecific Chemical Taxa of Medicinal Plants*

TIEDJENS, V., *The Vegetable Encyclopedia and Gardening Guide* (43)

(D)TINKEL, K., *Rooftop Gardening*

(D)TIPPING, Ed., *Gardens Old and New*

TUCKER, A., *Potpourri, Incense and Other Fragrant Concoctions* (72)

(M)TYLER, V., *The Honest Herbal* (81)

(R)UPHOFF, J., *Dictionary of Economic Plants* (68)

WEBSTER, H., *Herbs, How to Grow and Use Them* (39)

(M)WEINER, M., *Weiner's Herbal-Guide to Herb Medicine* (80)

WESTCOTT, C., *Plant Disease Handbook* (71)

(M)WHEELWRIGHT, E., *Medicinal Plants and Their History* (35) (Dover 74)

WHITLOCK, S. & RANKIN, M., *Dried Flowers, How to Prepare Them* (62) (Dover 72)

WILDER, L., *The Fragrant Path* (32)

YANG, L., *The Terrace Gardener's Handbook* (75)

General Index and Cross Reference

Included in this comprehensive index is a cross reference for the many common names of herbs, as well as a listing of over 650 species and cultivars. Page numbers or listings preceded by the letter **C** indicate *Chemical,* and by the letter **F** a *Food* or culinary use of the herb. An **R** indicates a *Recipe* in which the specific herb is used. A species name enclosed by brackets implies a change and is followed by one that is more accepted. The names of the major herbs are bold-faced; page numbers indicating primary reference information are also bold-faced.

Absinthe (Wormwood)
Achillea (Yarrow)
  ageratum (Maudlin)
  chrysocoma 179
  clypeolata 90, **174**
  filipendulina (Yarrow, Fern-leaf)
    'Coronation Gold'
    'Gold Plate'
  millefolium 174
    'Cerise Queen' 174
    'Fire King' 174
    var. *rosea* 174
    var. *rubra* 174
  moschata (Yarrow, Musk)
  ptarmica (Sneezeweed)
    'The Pearl' 175
  taygeta
    'Moonshine'
  tomentosa
    'Nana' 174
Acinos thymoides (Savory, Alpine)
Acorus (Flag, Sweet)
  calamus
    var. *angustifolius* (Flag, Sweet)
    'Variegatus' (Flag, Striped Sweet)
  gramineus (Flag, Grass-leaved Sweet)
    'Albo Variegatus' 85
    'Variegatus' 85
    'Pusillus' (Flag, Dwarf Sweet)

  [*japonicus* var. *variegatus*]—*A.c.* 'Variegatus'
F Additives, Herbs as 29
Agastache (Hyssop, Giant)
  [*anethiodora*]—*A. foeniculum*
  cana (Mosquito Plant)
  foeniculum (Anise-Hyssop)
  mexicana (Hyssop, Mexican Giant)
  rugosa (Mint, Korean)
  scrophulariifolia (Hyssop, Purple Giant)
  urticifolia (Hyssop, Nettle-leaf Giant)
Air currents, Landscaping with 23–25
Alchemilla (Lady's Mantle)
  alpina 122
F Alcohol extracts Tab. 4, 28
Alecost (Bibleleaf)
Alehoof (Creeping Charlie)
Alexanders (Masterwort)
C Allantoin 105
C Allelopathic 25
Allgood (Good King Henry)
C Allicin Tab. 3
Allium 77, 94, 108, 177
  ampeloprasum (Garlic, Elephant)
    var. (Garlic, Levant)
  ascalonicum (Shallot)
  cepa var. *viviparum* (Onion, Egyptian)

  flavum 42, **101**, 177
  giganteum (Allium, Giant)
  karataviense 42
  moly 42, **101**
  porrum (Leek)
  pulchellum 42
  sativum (Garlic)
    var. *ophioscorodon* (Garlic, Serpent)
  schoenoprasum (Chive)
    var. *sibiricum* (Chive, Giant)
  scorodoprasum (Sand Leek)
  tuberosum (Chive, Garlic)
Allium, Giant (*Allium giganteum*) 23, **101–102**; PL. 21
Aloysia (Verbena)
  [*citriodora*]—*A. triphylla*
  triphylla (Verbena, Lemon)
Alpine gardens 162; Fig. 53
Alpine herbs 177
Althea officinalis (Marshmallow)
Al-Zahafaran (Saffron)
[*Amaracus*]—*Origanum*
  [*tomentosus*]—*Origanum dictamnus*
C Anethol Tab. 3, 34, 41, 132
Anethum graveolens (Dill)
  sowa (Dill, Indian)
Angelica (*Angelica archangelica*) **84–85**, 106, 112, 113, 116, 118, 128, 132, 171
  American (Angelica, Wood)
  Purple (*Angelica atropurpurea*) 84; PL. 11

Wood (*Angelica sylvestris*) 84
Angelica
    acutiloba (Toki)
    archangelica (Angelica)
    atropurpurea (Angelica, Purple)
    polymorpha var. *sinensis* (Dong
        Quai)
    sylvestris (Angelica, Wood)
[*Angelica levisticum*]—*Levisticum
    officinale*
[*Angelica officinalis*]—*Angelica
    archangelica*
Anise (*Pimpinella anisum*) Ch-Tab.
    3, F 28, 93, 164, **167–168**, R
    167, 169
Anise-Hyssop (Hyssop, Blue
    Giant)
Anise Root (Finocchio)
Anise, Star (*Illicium verum*)
F Anisette 167
Anthemis
    cotula (Mayweed)
    cupaniana 33, 134, 135
    tinctoria (Camomile, Dyers)
    [*Anthemis nobile*]—*Chamaemellum
        nobile*
Anthriscus cerefolium (Chervil)
Antimicrobial activity 29, 40, 48,
    74, 81, 102, 134, 149, 169
Aquatic herbs 84
Archangel (*Lamium album*)
    Yellow (*Lamiastrum galeobdolon*)
C Archangelicin 84
C *Artemisia* 22, 102, 166
    abrotanum (Southernwood)
    absinthium (Wormwood,
        Common)
    annua (Wormwood, Sweet)
        'Camphor'
        'Lemon'
        'Tangerine'
    arborescens (Wormwood,
        Fringed)
    campestris (Southernwood,
        Field)
    dracunculus (Tarragon, Russian)
        'Sativa' (Tarragon, French)
    frigida (*A.f.* 'Silver Mound') **41,**
        52, 73, 77, 81
    genipi (Silver Mound)
    glacialis (Silver Mound)
    lactiflora (Mugwort, White)
    lanata (Silver Mound) PL. 6
    ludoviciana (Mugwort,
        Western)
        var. *albula* (Silver King
            Artemisia)
    maratima (Wormseed)
    [*pedemontana*]—*A. lanata*
    pontica (Wormwood, Roman)
    [*redowskii*]—*A. dracunculus*
        'Sativa'
    [*spicata*]—*A. genipi*
    stellerana (Wormwood, Beach)
    vulgaris (Mugwort, Common)

Artichoke (*Cynara scolymus*) 94,
    143, 150, 155
    Jerusalem 94, 175
Asafetida (*Ferula assa-foetida*) 146,
    150
Asarabaca (Ginger, Wild)
Asarabaca Camphor 85
C Asarole Tab. 3
C Asarone
Asarum (Ginger, Wild)
    canadense 130
    caudatum 130
    europeum (Ginger, European)
    hartwegii 130
    shuttleworthii 130
    virginicum 130
C Ascorbic acid (preservative) 28
Asparagus 143, 155
Attractant scents 25, 127
Attracting
    Birds 143, **163,** 171
    Hummingbirds 134, 148, 152
    Pollinators 27, 148, 152
C Azulene Tab. 3; 34, 81, 174

Balm
    Bee (*Monarda didyma*) 84, **151,**
        173; PL. 22
        Pony (*Monarda pectinata*)
    Canary (*Cedronella canariensis*)
    Field (Creeping Charlie)
    Golden (Balm, Variegated
        Lemon)
    Lemon (*Melissa officinalis*) 17,
        20, 22, 53, 54, 91, 92, 103,
        112, 114, 116, **129–130;** Ch-
        Tab. 3; F 28; PL. 2, 9, 11, 18
    Mountain (*Monarda* or
        Pycnanthemum)
    Stinking (Pennyroyal,
        American)
    Variegated Lemon (*Mellisa
        officinalis* var. *variegata*) **129,**
        136; PL. 18
    Western (*Monardella
        odoratissima*) 151
Banks, Landscaping 148, 149, 162
F Barbeque 38, 81, 82, 109
Basil (*Ocimum*) Figs. 17, 18; 18, 20,
    23, 27, **44–46,** 63, 91 154,
    166; F 28–29, 108, 126; R 43,
    108, 130
    'Broad-leaved Sanctum' (Basil,
        'Spice')
    Bush (*O. basilicum* var.
        minimum) **45, 46,** 49, 63, 67,
        77; PL. 7
    Camphor (*O.
        kilimandscharicum*) 45, 46
    'Camphor' (*O. canum* cv.) **45,**
        46; PL. 7
    Cinnamon (*O. canum basilicum*)
    'Cinnamon' (*O. canum*) 46, 48,
        63, 177; PL. 1, 7

'Citriodorum' (*O. basilicum* cv.)
    45
Crinkled (*O. basilicum*
    'Crispum')
'Crispum' (*O. basilicum* cv.) 45,
    46, 47
'Dark Opal' (*O. basilicum* cv.)
    45, 46, 47, 53, 63, 67, 80, 81,
    135, 136, 137, 150, 155; PL.
    2, 7, 8
Dwarf (Basil, Bush)
Hoary (*O. canum*) 45
Holy (Basil, Sacred)
'Italian' (*O. basilicum* cv.) 45
'Krishna' (*O. sanctum* cv.) 14, **45,**
    46, 47, 63, 67, 77, 135; F 29; R
    74; PL. 17
Krishna Tulsi (*O. sanctum*
    'Krishna')
Lemon (*O. americanum*) 45, 47,
    63; F 29; R 167; PL. 7, 11
Lemon (*O. basilicum*
    'Citriodorum')
'Lemon' (*O. canum* cv.) **45,** 46
'Lettuce Leaf' (*O. basilicum* cv.)
    45, 46, 47; PL. 7
'Licorice' (*O. canum* cv.) **45,** 46,
    48
'Minimum' (Basil, Bush)
Opal (Basil, 'Dark Opal')
Picolo Verde (Basil, Bush)
Purple (Basil, 'Dark Opal')
Purple Sacred (Basil, 'Krishna')
Sacred (*O. sanctum*) 44, **45**
'Silver Fox' (*O. b.* var. *minimum*
    cv.) 45, 67
Small-leaved (Basil, Bush)
'Spice' (*O.* 'Spice') 45, 46, 67,
    113; F 126; PL. 7
'Sri' (*O. sanctum* cv.) 45, 46
'Sri Tulsi' (Basil, 'Sri')
Sweet (*O. basilicum*) 45, 63, 81;
    R 172; PL. 8, 11, 12
'Thyrsiflora' (*O. basilicum* cv.)
    45, 46
Tree (*O. gratissimum*) 45, 46
Tulasi (Basil, Sacred)
Basil-Thyme (*Clinopodium
    calamintha*) 112, 140
Basil, Wild (*Clinopodium vulgare*)
Basketball court, Landscaping 144,
    146; Fig. 47
F Baste 28, 100, 110
Bay
    California (Laurel, California)
    Sweet (*Laurus nobilis*) 63, 70,
        92, 146, **152–153;** F 77, 126;
        R 130; PL. 11
    Sweet (*Magnolia virginiana*) 37
Bayberry (*Myrica pennsylvanica*)
Bay Rum (*Pimenta racemosa*)
Bean herb (Savory)
F Bean stew/soup 91, 109, 136, **148;**
    R 86
Bedstraw (*Galium verum*) 90, 91

Dyer's (*Galium tinctorium*) 90,
91
F Beef cubes R 130
Bee herbs 35, 47, 72, 94, 103, 105,
170
Bee plant (Borage)
C Benzyl esters/acetate Tab. 3; 48
Bergamot, Oil of (*Citrus aurantium*
var. *bergamia*)
Bergamot, Wild (*Monarda fistulosa*)
151
C Betonicine 148
Betony (*Stachys officinalis*) 148
Wooly (*S. byzantina*) 13, 39, 46,
66, 77, 90, 113, 121, 123, 134,
144, 146, **148–149**, 152, 155,
177; PL. 9, 21
'Silver Carpet' (*S. b.* cv.) **149**
Bible Leaf (Costmary)
C Bisabolol (isomer of Farnescene)
Tab. 3
F Biscuits 44, 172
F Blanched stems 150, 172
F Blends, herb 28–29
Bloodwort (Burnet, Great)
Boneset (*Eupatorium perfoliatum*)
Bonsai **58**, 82, 125
Borage (*Borago officinalis*) 13, 94,
116, 148, 164, **170–171**; F
164; PL. 11, 24
Indian (*Coleus amboinicus*) 77,
113; F 126; PL. 15
Borago officinalis (Borage)
Borders **4**, 22–23
C Borneol Tab. 3; 32, 38, 40, 72, 81,
134
F Breads 44, 103, 169, 172, 173
Breezway 23–25; Fig. 5 A–C
F Broths 103, 126
Bugbane 114
Bugloss (Borage)
Burnet (*Sanguisorba*) 84, 105
Canadian (*S. canadense*)
Evergreen (Burnet, Great)
Garden (Burnet, Salad)
Great (*S. officinale*) 84, **105**
Japanese (*S. obtusa*) 105
Salad (*S. minor*) 82, 93, 94, 100,
101, **104–105**, 143; R 104;
PL. 13, 17
F Butters Tab. 4; 10, 28–29, 43, 103,
106, 110; R 100, 109, 130

C Cadinene (isomer of azulene)
Caespitose **31**, 205
F Cake 10, 91, 132, 148, 167
Calamint (*Calamintha nepeta*) 17,
23, **37**; F 28–29; PL. 6, 23
Lesser (*C. n.* ssp. *nepeta*) 37
Calamintha nepeta (Calamint) 17,
23; F 28, 29
ssp. *glandulosa* (Nepetella) **37**,
113
ssp. *nepeta* (Calamint, Lesser)
[*officinalis*]—*C. n.* ssp. *glandulosa*

sylvatica 37
Calamus (Flag, Sweet)
Calendula (*Calendula officinalis*)
13, 92, 93, 94, 97, 100, **103**,
105, 113, 116, 170, 173; F 85;
R 43, 63, 103, 104, 126, 128,
172; PL. 1, 11, 20, 21
Caltha palustris (Marigold,
Marsh)
Camomile 40, 44, 66, 97, 102, 162
Dyer's (*Anthemis tinctoria*) 33,
91
German (*Chamomilla recutita*)
14, 18, 20, 23, 28, **33–35**, 47,
48, 52, 73, 114, 116, 123, 137,
152, 166; F 28, 114, 149, 151;
Ch-Tab. 3; PL. 2, 19, 23
Hungarian (Camomile,
German)
Lawn (*Chamaemellum nobile* cv.)
18, 20, 23, **33–35**, 45, 81, 114,
135, 177; Ch-Tab. 3
Roman (*Chamaemellum nobile*)
18, 20, 23, **33–35**, 83, 112,
121, 123, 132; Ch-Tab. 3; PL.
1, 2, 15, 16
Roumanian (Camomile,
German)
Stinking (Mayweed)
'Trenague' (Camomile, Lawn)
C Camphene 38, 41, 49, 72
C Camphor 25, 32, 38, 40, 45, 81;
Tab. 3
Camphor plant (*Chrysanthemum
balsamita*) **147**, 173; PL. 22
F Candy 10, 28, 84, 103, 105, 130,
132, 167, 172; R 102
Candy Plant (Fennel)
F Canned food, spicing 44
Caraway (*Carum carvi*) 63, 93,
108–109; F 126, 169; R 108,
167; Ch-Tab. 3; PL. 14
Black (Cumin, Black)
Cardamom 126
Cardoon (*Cynara cardunculus*) 93,
94, 134, 143, 146, **150**
French 150; PL. 22
Carpenter weed (Yarrow)
Carum carvi (Caraway)
[*Carum petroselinum*]—
Petroselinum crispum
C Carvacrol Tab. 3; 74, 108, 109, 113,
124, 127, 151, 153
C Caryone Tab. 3; 32, 35, 108
Catmint (*Nepeta faassenii*) 127
Catnip (*Nepeta cataria*) 20, 28, 84,
127–128; PL. 23
Dwarf (Catmint or Catnip,
Persian) 20, 33, 66, 90, 113,
127; PL. 2, 9
Lemon (*N. c.* 'Citriodora') 127
Persian (*N. mussinii*) 33, **127**
C Cedral Tab. 3
[*Cedronella cana*]—*Agastache cana*
[*mexicana*]—*A. mexicana*

Chamaemellum nobile (Camomile,
Roman)
var. *florepleno* (Camomile,
double flowered) 33
'Trenague' (Camomile, Lawn)
C Chamazulene Tab. 3; 174
Chamomilla recutita (Camomile,
German)
suaveoleus (Pineapple Weed)
C Chavicol Tab. 3
Checkerberry (Wintergreen)
Checkerboard 93, **94–95**; PL. 12,
14, 22
F Cheese 10, 28, 86, 106, 108; Tab. 4
Herb Tab. 4; 28
Sauce R 77
Spread 73
Chenopodium album (Lamb's
Quarters)
bonus henricus (Good King
Henry)
capitatum (Strawberry Blite)
Chervil (*Anthriscus cerefolium*) 18,
28, 29, 84, 113, 118, **132–
133**, 155; F 28–29; R 104,
133, 172; PL. 7, 18
Chervil,
Japanese Wild (*Cryptotaenia
japonica*)
Sweet (*Osmorrhiza longistylus*)
133
Tuberous (*Chaerophyllum
bulbosum*) 133
F Chicken 49, 108, 109; R 43, 126,
137, 167
F Chili 32, 108, 109, 172; R 110
F Chips, tortilla R 39
Chive (*Allium schoenoprasum*) 20,
29, 42, 63, 77, **100–101**; F 29,
109; R 39, 43, 44, 86, 100,
104, 110, 126, 127, 128; PL.
6, 8, 9, 11, 13, 14, 20, 21
Garlic (*A. tuberosum*) 42, **101**;
PL. 14
Giant (*A. schoenoprasum* var.)
Chinese (Chive, Garlic)
Oriental (Chive, Garlic)
[*Chrysanthemum balsamita* var.
tanacetoides]—*Balsamita
major*
*Chrysanthemum
balsamita* (Camphor Plant)
cinerariaefolium (Dalmation
Pyrethrum)
parthenium (Feverfew)
'Double Bonnet'
'Selaginoides' (Feverfew,
Dwarf)
Cilantro (Coriander)
C Cineole (isomer of eucalyptol)
Cinnamon Ch-Tab. 3
C Cinnamonaldehyde Tab. 3
C Citral Tab. 3; 45, 127, 129, 153
C Citronellal Tab. 3; 129, 153
Clary (Sage, Clary)

Meadow (Sage, Meadow)
Cleavers (*Galium* spp.)
Clinopodium
   calamintha (Basil-Thyme)
   vulgare (Basil, Wild)
Cloister garden (Checkerboard)
Clove Ch-Tab. 3
Coleus amboinicus (Borage, Indian)
   [*aromaticus*]—*C. amboinicus*
Colored earths (Fill)
F Coloring, food 86
Comfrey (*Symphytum*) 100, **105,**
   148, 170; Ch-106
   Common (*S. officinale*) 105
   Garden (Comfrey, Common)
   Prickly (*S. asperum*) 105; PL. 12
   Red-flowering (*S. o. cv.*) **105,**
     171; PL. 13
   Russian (*S. uplandicum*) 105;
   PL. 13
   Variegated (*S. o. cv.*) **105,** 171
   Yellow-flowering (*S. o. cv.*) 105
Companion plants 94
Compost 105
Confetti 170
Container gardening 23, 35, 38, 48,
   56, **58,** 70, 157; PL. 3
Contemporary Landscaping 11,
   141–158; Figs. 43–49; PL. 6,
   20
F Cookies 29, 167
F Cooking with herbs 26
   Coriander (*Coriandrum sativum*)
     13, 14, 44, **46–48,** 54, 94, 116,
     167, 177; F 90, 108, 126, 168;
     R 74, 108
   Roman (Cumin, Black)
Corido (*Thymus capitatus*) 71, **73;**
   Tab. 8
Coridothymus 73
[*Coridothymus capitatus*]—*Thymus*
   capitatus
Cosmetic herbs 151, 153
Costmary (*Balsamita major*) 20, 82,
   91, 112, 113, 134, 146, **147–**
   148; PL. 15
Costmary (Camphor Plant)
Cottage garden Fig. 28
C Coumarin Tab. 3; 131
Courtyard Figs. 23, 43, 44
Cowslip (Marigold, Marsh)
F Cream sauce 148
Creeping Charlie (*Glechoma*
   hederacea) 114, 121, 173
   Variegated (*G. h.* var. *variegata*)
     121, 130, 176
Creeping Snowberry (*Gaultheria*
   hispidula) 131
C Crocin 86
Crocus sativus (Saffron)
Crocus, winter (Saffron)
   'Cashmirianus' (Saffron,
     Kashmir)
F Croquettes 127
Cryptotaenia canadensis

(Honewort)
   japonica (Parsley, Japanese)
Culantro (*Eryngium foetidum*)
Cultivar 4
Cumin (*Cuminum cyminum*) Ch-
   Tab. 3; 93, 164, **168;** F 77,
   108, 126
Cumin, Black 168
   Bunium persicum 168
   Nigella sativa **168,** 169
C Cuminal 108, 168; Ch-Tab. 3
[*Cunila mariana*]—*Cunila*
   origanoides
Cunila origanoides (Mint, Stone)
Curry 168
Curry plant (*Helichrysum*
   angustifolium ssp. *siitalicum*)
   49, 134
C Cymene Tab. 3; 151, 168
Cynara cardunculus (Cardoon)
   scolymus (Artichoke)

Dalmation Pyrethrum
   (*Chrysanthemum*
   cinerariaefolium)
Dalmation Sage 135
Damp off, prevention of 41, 74
Decoction 29
F Decorating (cakes etc.) 10, 132,
   170
Decumbent 31
F Deep fried 106, 172, 173
Deer (animal) trail 118, 131; Fig.
   38
Design transfer 65; Fig. 21; Tab. 7
F Desserts 86, 130, 167
Dictamnus (Dittany of Crete)
Dictamnus fraxinella (Gas Plant)
Dill (*Anethum graveolens*) 13, 47,
   91, 106, 116, 164, **166–167,**
   177; F 126; PL. 12
   'Bouquet' (Dill, Dwarf)
   Dwarf (*A. graveolens*)
   Indian (*A. sowa*) 166
   Suwa (Dill, Indian)
Dillweed R 167
C Diosgenin 169
Dip 100; R 44, 104, 167
C Dipentene 168
C Disulfides 150
Dittany (*Origanum hybridum*) 125;
   PL. 17
   American (Mint, Stone)
   Cretan or Crete (Dittany of
     Crete)
   Maryland (Mint, Stone)
Dittany of Crete (*Origanum*
   dictamnus) 39, 46, 72, 113,
   124, **125,** 130, 134, 136
Diver **95;** Figs. 32, 33
Dock
   Curly (*Rumex crispus*) 107
   Patience (*Rumex patientia*)
   Spinach (Dock, Patience)
Dog Fennel (Mayweed)

Dong Quai (*Angelica polymorpha*
   var. *sinensis*) 85
Doorways 4
Dooryard garden 11, 93, **97;** Fig.
   34; PL. 12, 14
Dracunculus (Tarragon)
Drift 4
Driveways, Landscaping 20, 34;
   PL. 2, 16
Dropwort (*Fillipendula vulgaris*)
Drought tolerant herbs 136
Drybed 162
Drying herbs Tab. 4; 29
   Air 29
   Microwave 29
   Oven 29
   Temperatures 29
Dye herbs 86, 90–91; Fig. 28

Earth Apple (Camomile)
Edible, Landscaping (see indiv.
   veget.) 143; PL. 21
F Egg Salad 106, 172
Elder, Spotted or Striped (Witch
   Hazel)
Elecampane (*Inula helenium*) 94,
   105, 137, 148, 152, 164, 170
   171, **172–173,** 175; PL. 24
   Dwarf (*I. ensifolia*)
English Daisy (*Bellis perennis*) 121
   123
   [*nervosum*]—*E. pulchellum*
Entrance way 20; Fig. 2
Eranthemum pulchellum (Sage,
   Blue)
Espalier 4, **58,** 78
Essences 17
Estrade **58;** Fig. 10 A–C
Estragon (Tarragon)
C Eucalyptol 25, 38, 40, 74, 134, 151,
   Tab. 3
Eucalyptus, Lemon (*Eucalyptus*
   maculata var. *citriodora*) 17
C Eugenol 124; Tab. 3
Everlasting, White-leaved (Curry
   Plant)

C Farnescene 149; Tab. 3
C Farnesol 81; Tab. 3
Fastigiate 71
Fat hen (Good King Henry)
Felon herb (Mugwort, Common)
C Fenchone 40, 41, 132; Tab. 3
Fennel (*Foeniculum vulgare*) 17, 18,
   20, 22, 23, **41–44,** 49, 53, 91,
   116, 118; F 28, 109, 169; R
   86, 104, 108, 110, 126, 127;
   Ch-Tab. 3
   Bitter (Fennel, Wild)
   Bronze (*F. v.* ssp. *v.* 'Rubrum')
     42, 113, 155
   Florence (Finocchio)
   Red (Fennel, Bronze)
   Roman (Fennel, Sweet)
   Sweet (*F. v.* ssp. *v.* var. *dulce*) **42,**

171; R 43; PL. 3, 12
  Wild (*F. v.* ssp. *v.* var. *vulgare*) 42
Fennel, Common Giant (*Ferula communis*) 150; PL. 12, 22
  Giant (Asafetida)
  Wild (Love-in-a-Mist)
Fennel Flower (Cumin, Black— *Nigella*)
Fennugreek (*Trigonella foenum-graecum*) 94, 164, 168, **169**
Ferula assa-foetida (Asafetida)
  communis (Fennel, Common Giant)
Feverfew (*Chrysanthemum parthenium*) 48, 63, 102, 127, 166; PL. 1, 23
  'Double Bonnet' 114
  Dwarf 46, 50, 66, 77, 114, 123, 140, 152; PL. 8, 16
  'Selaginoides' (Feverfew, Dwarf)
Filipendula
  [*hexapetala*]—*F. vulgaris*
  ulmaria (Meadowsweet)
  vulgaris (Dropwort)
Fill **63–64**, 66, 67–68; Tab. 5, 6
Filtered shade 4, **123**
Finocchio (*Foeniculum vulgare* ssp. *v.* var. *azoricum*) 42; R 42
F Fish 10, 43, 148, 167; R 127
Flag (*Acorus* spp.)
  Dwarf Sweet (*A. gramineus* 'Pusillus') 85
  Grassy-leaved Sweet (*A. gramineus*) 85
  Striped Sweet (*A. calamus* 'Variegatus') 85
  Sweet (*A. calamus*) 84, **85**, 94, 101; PL. 8
F Flavors
  Anise 108, 109, 167, 169
  Carrot 109
  Celery 171
  Cucumber 112, 170
  Lemon 112, 129
  Licorice 128, 132, 169
  Pineapple 137
Flea bane (Pennyroyal or Rue)
F Flowers 154, 168, 170
  Flybane (Dill)
  Fodder 105
Foeniculum
  [*dulce*]—*F. vulgare* ssp. *vulgare* var. *dulce*
  vulgare (Fennel)
    ssp. *vulgare*
    var. *azoricum* (Finocchio)
    var. *dulce* (Fennel, Sweet)
    var. *vulgaris* (Fennel, Wild)
    'Rubrum' (Fennel, Bronze)
"Formal" garden 4, **55**, **61**, 99, 122; Fig. 40 A–B
Formal lndscp. 11, **55–92**, 93; Figs. 7–28, 40 A–B
Foundation planting 115, **121**; Fig.

1, 39, 40 A–B, 41; PL. 20
Foxglove (*Digitalis*) 42, 97
Fragrances 17, **25–27**; Tab. 3
  Ambrosaic 85
  Anise 17, 153, 155
  Apple 25, 33, 112
  Camphor 25, 40, 45, 46, 50, 81, 147, 173
  Camphoraceous 25, 34, 37, 38, 40, 47, 73, 80, 105, 109, 129, 151, 153, 168
  Caraway 17, 32
  Celery 171
  Cinnamon 46, 127
  Citronella 114
  Citrus 36, 40, 47, 53, 72, 74, 81, 114, 127, 136, 151
  Clove 44, 45, 127
  Ethereal 124
  Fishy 82
  Floral 40, 48, 82, 83, 100, 124, 126, 171
  Fruity 33, 40, 48, 129, 137
  Garlic 150
  Ginger 36, 44, 45
  Grass/Hay 131
  Herbaceous 34, 74, 83, 105, 127, 131, 151, 152, 171, 173
  Honey 35, 53, 102
  Lemon 17, 32, 45, 46, 54, 72, 73, 81, 127, 129, 136, 153, 154, 176
  Licorice 44, 46, 128, 132
  Lime 25; Tab. 3
  Maple syrup 169
  Medicinal 40, 124, 131
  Menthol 114
  Mint 17, 25, 35, 112, 129, 147, 152, 153
  Nutty 169
  Oily 105
  Oniony 100, 102
  Orange 54, 74, 75, 114
  Oregano 113, 126, 151, 153
  Pickle 166
  Pine 40, 81
  Pineapple 17, 50, 137
  Resinous 72, 74
  Rose 74, 75, 101
  Spicy 25, 32, 34, 38, 40, 45, 47, 49, 50, 73, 74, 75, 77, 106, 109, 127, 138, 149, 151, 152, 154, 166, 168, 174
  Thyme 72, 74, 112, 124
  Turpentine 81, 138
  Vanilla 53, 83, 150, 153
  Waxy 47, 50
  Wintergreen 131
Fragrant lndscp. **17–54**; Figs. 1–6
Framing (with fragrant herbs) 20
Freezing herbs 27; Tab. 4
Frost heave 76
Frost tolerance 133
Furniture polish 128

Galium
  aparine (Cleavers)
  odorata (Sweet Woodruff)
  tinctorium (Bedstraw, Dyer's)
  verum (Bedstraw)
C Gallic acid 87
Garden Heliotrope (*Valeriana officinalis*) 23, 42, **48–49**, 53, 106, 116, 137, 150, 175; PL. 1
Garden Myrrh (Sweet Cicely)
Garlic (*Allium sativum*) Ch-Tab. 3; R 74, 103, 106, 110, 133, 167, 168
  Bavarian (Garlic, Serpent)
  Elephant (*A. ampeloprasum*)
  Giant (Serpent)
  Levant (*A. ampeloprasum* var.)
  Serpent (*A. sativum* var. *ophioscorodon*) 101; PL. 13
Garlic, Society (*Tulbaghia, violacea*)
Garlic Bush (*Adenocalymna alliaceum*)
F Garnish 86, 106, 133
Gates, lndscp. 20; Fig. 3
Gaultheria
  fragrantissima (Wintergreen, Indian)
  hispidula (Snowberry, Creeping)
  procumbens (Wintergreen)
C Geranial 43
C Geraniol Tab. 3; 40, 73, 74, 124, 127
Geranium, Scented (*Pelargonium*) 17, 18, 23, 29, 53, 72, 147, 154
Germander (*Teucrium chamaedrys*) 38, 63, 70, 74, 77, 82, **83**, 153; PL. 10
  American (*T. canadense*) 83
  Dwarf (*T. chamaedrys* 'Prostratum') 33, 71, **83**, 123
  Fragrant (*T. massiliense*) 83
  Golden (*T. polium*) 83
  Greek (*T. aroanium*) 83
  Silver (*T. fruticaus*) 83
  Tree (Germander, Silver)
  Wall (Germander)
  Wood (*T. scorodonia*) 83
Gill-over-the-Ground (Creeping Charlie)
Gilliflowers **23**, 90
Ginger (*Asarum* spp.) 130; PL. 16
  Wild (*A. canadense*) 130
  European (*A. europeum*) 130
Ginger (*Zingiber*)
Glabrous 74
Glechoma hederaceae (Creeping Charlie)
  var. *variegata* (Creeping Charlie, Variegated)
Glycyrrhiza (Licorice)
Goldenrod, Fragrant (*Solidago odorata*) 53
Golfgreen 144; Fig. 45

Good King Henry (*Chenopodium bonus henricus*) 91, **107–108**, 114, 118, 143; PL. 14
Goosefoot garden **121–122**; Fig. 40 A–B, 41
Gossamer sphere 109
Gow choy (Chive, Garlic)
Grass, Lemon (*Cymbopogon*) 17
    Ornamental 163
    Pudding (Pennyroyal, English)
F Gravies 28, 43, 74, 77, 86, 91, 126
Green manure 169
F Green Tea 48, 129
Grey herbs 90, 134; Fig. 28; PL. 11
F Grilled meat 38
Ground Apple (Camomile)
Ground covers 22–23, **123**
    Colored 63
    Inert 63–64, 77, **141, 143**
    Living **143**
    Organic 64, **141, 143**
Ground Ivy (Creeping Charlie)
F Guacamole R 44

Hair rinse 34, 103
F Halva 169
Hamamelis (Witch Hazel)
    intermedia 87
    'Arnold's Promise' 87
    'Diana' 87
    japonica (Witch Hazel, Japanese)
    mollis (Witch Hazel, Chinese)
    'Pallida'
    vernalis 87
    virginiana (Witch Hazel, American)
Harvesting herbs 27
Hazelwort (Ginger, European)
Heartsease (Pansy)
Hedeoma
    floribundum (Oregano, Mexican)
    pulegioides (Pennyroyal, American)
    [*Hedeoma longiflora*]—*Poliomintha longiflora*
Hedge 23, 78, 153, 154
Helichrysum
    angustifolium (Curry Plant)
    bracteatum (Strawflower)
    lanatum 41, 134
Herb 3–4, 9
Herb of Grace (Rue)
Herb of War (Lavender)
Herb pillow 17, 90, 114
Herbaceous perennial 116
Herber (Physick)
    circular (Diver)
    square/rect. (Kitchen garden)
Hindheal (Tansy, Garden)
Honewort (*Cryptotaenia canadensis*) 107
F Honey Ch-Tab. 3; 86, 108, 152

Honeysuckle (*Lonicera* spp.) 20, 53, 161
Hop (*Humulus lupulus*) Ch-Tab. 3; 123, 144, 146, **149**, 161; PL. 22
    Variegated (*H. japonica* var. *variegata*) 50, 146, **149**, 157; PL. 22
Hop, Wild (*Bryonia dioica*)
Horehound
    Black (*Ballota nigra*)
    Silver (*Marrubium incanum*) 77, **102**
    Water (*Lycopus*)
    White (*Marrubium vulgare*) 93, 100, **102**, 104, 116, 127, 134, 175
Horseheal (Elecampane)
Hortus Conclusus **60**, 94, 99, 160; Figs. 12, 50
Hot organ tea (Pennyroyal, English)
Hot tub herbs 82
C Humulon 149
Humulus
    japonica var. *variegata* (Hop, Variegated)
    lupulus (Hop)
Hyssop (*Hyssopus officinalis*) 80; PL. 2, 7
    Blue (Hyssop) 20, 38, 63, 70, 77, **80–81**, 83, 114, 123; Ch-Tab. 3
    Dwarf (Hyssop) 80
    'Golden' (*H. o.* cv.) 80
    'Grandiflora' (*H. o.* cv.) 80
    Pink (*H. o.* 'Rosea') 80
    Red (*H. o.* 'Rubra') 80
    White (*H. o.* 'Alba') 80
Hyssop, Giant (*Agastache* spp.) 146, **152**; PL. 23
    Blue (*A. foeniculum*) 17, 66, 127, **152**; F 28
    Fragrant (Hyssop, Blue Giant)
    Mexican (*A. mexicana*) 152
    Nettle-leaf (*A. urticifolia*) 152
    Purple (*A. scrophulariifolia*) 152
    Wrinkled (*A. rugosa*) 17, 127, **152**

F Ice cream 167
F Ices 10, 167
Inula helenium (Elecampane)
    ensifolia (Elecampane, Dwarf)
Incense 38, 40, 44
Informal Landscape 115–139; Figs. 27, 35–39, 41, 42; PL. 20
Infusion 29
Ink, Saffron 86
C Ionone 129; Tab. 3
C Irone 129; Tab. 3

Jasmine (*Jasminum* spp.) 20, 23, **48**, 54, 129, 161, 162
    Angel Wing (Jasmine,

    Confederate)
    Arabian (*J. sambac*) 48
    Confederate (*J. nitidum*)
    Italian (*J. humile* 'Revolutum')
    Japanese (*J. mesnyi*)
    Pinwheel (*J. gracilimum*)
    Poet's (*J. officinalis*) 48
    Revolutum (*J. humile* cv.)
    Royal (*J. grandiflorum*) 48
    Sambac (Jasmine, Arabian)
    Star (*J. multiflorum*)
Jasmine
    Cape (*Gardenia jasminoides*)
    Carolina (*Gelsemium*)
    Madagascan (*Stephanotis floribunda*)
Jasminum
    gracilimum (Jasmine, Pinwheel)
    grandiflorum (Jasmine, Royal)
    humile 'Revolutum'
    mesnyi (Jasmine, Japanese)
    multiflorum (Jasmine, Star)
    nitidum (Jasmine, Confederate)
    nudiflorum
    odoratissimum 48
    officinalis (Jasmine, Poet's)
    polyanthus 48
    sambac (Jasmine, Arabian)
Jessamine (Jasmine)
Johnny-jump-up (Violet, yellow fls.)

Kale 43, 47, 63, 71
Kesso (Valerian, Japanese)
Kitchen garden **93–94**; Figs. 28, 29, 49; PL. 8, 11, 12, 15
Knitbone (Comfrey)
Knot garden 61–65; Tab. 7; Figs. 13–20; PL. 8, 11
    Closed 62
    Open 62

Labyrinth (Maze)
Lad's Love (Southernwood)
Lady's Mantle (*Alchemilla*) 84, 90, 134, 177; PL. 8, 10, 13, 24
F Lamb 43, 82, 109, 126
Lamb's Ears (Betony, Wooly)
Lamb's Quarters (*Chenopodium album*) 108, **143**
Lamium 'Silver Beacon' 134
Lamwick (*Phlomis lychnitis*)
Landscaping (see indiv. category)
Lantana 154
Laurel
    Bay (Bay, Sweet-*Laurus*)
    California (*Umbellularia californica*) 153
    Mountain (*Kalmia latifolia*)
Laurus nobilis (Bay, Sweet)
    f. *angustifolia* **152**; F 153
    f. *crispa* 152
    ['Undulata']—f. *crispa*
Lavandin (*Lavandula intermedia*) 39

Lavandula (Lavender)
  angustifolia (Lavender, English)
    ssp. *angustifolia*
      'Alba' 39
      'Compacta' **39**, 63; PL. 3
      'Gray Lady' 39
      'Hidcote' **39**, 40
      'Irene Doyle' **39**, 40
      ['Jean Davis']—*L. a.* ssp. *a.*
        'Rosea'
      'Lodden Blue' 39
      'Mitcham Gray' 39
      'Munstead' 39
      'Nana Alba' 39
      'Nana Atropurpurea' 39
      'Rosea' **39**, 66; PL. 19
      'Twickle Purple' **39**, 40, 177
    [buchii]—*L. pinnata* var. *buchii*
    [canariensis]—*L. multifida* var.
      canariensis
  dentata (Lavender, French)
  [hybrida]—*L. intermedia*
  intermedia (Lavandin)
'Dutch' 39
'Grappenhall' 39
'Grosso' 39
'Hidcote Giant' 39
  lanata—(Lavender, Wooly)
  latifolia—(Lavender, Spike)
  multifida—(Lavender, Fringed)
  [officinalis]—*L. a.* ssp. *a.*
  [pedunculata]—*L. stoechas* ssp.
    pedunculata
  pinnata 39
  stoechas—(Lavender, Spanish)
    ssp. *pedunculata* 39
    ssp. *stoechas* 'Alba' 39
  [vera]—*L. angustifolia*
  viridis—(Lavender, Yellow-
    flowering)
Lavender (*Lavandula*) 14, 18, 20,
  39–40, 41, 63, 70, 78, 83, 84,
  90, 94, 101, 144, 155, 176,
  177; PL. 10, 16, 21
  'Alba' (*L. angustifolia* ssp. *a.* cv.)
    39
  Dwarf (*L. a.* ssp. *a.* 'Nana
    Atropurpurea') 23, 77, 112,
    123, 136, 176, 177; PL. 6
  English (*L. angustifolia*) 39, 63,
    66; Ch-40
  French (*L. dentata*) **39**; Ch-40
  Fringed (*L. multifida*) 39
  'Hidcote' (*L. a.* ssp. *a.* cv.) 39; PL.
    21
  'Munstead' (*L. a.* ssp. *a.* cv.) 39
  Spanish (*L. stoechas*) 39; PL. 6, 9
  Spike (*L. latifolia*) **39**; Ch-40
  Stoechade (Lavender,
    Spanish)
  Topped (Lavender, Spanish)
  Wooly (*L. lanata*) **39**, 134, 152
  Yellow-flowering (*L. viridis*)
Lavender Cotton (Santolina,
  Incana)

Lawn 118
Leek (*Allium porrum*) 91, 101
F Lemonade 129
Levisticum officinale (Lovage)
Licorice (*Glycyrrhiza*)
[*Ligusticum levisticum*]—*Levisticum*
  officinale
Ligusticum scoticum—(Lovage,
  Scotch)
C Limonene 32, 40, 41, 49, 108; Tab.
  3
C Linalool 40, 47, 74; Tab. 3
Lion's Tail (*Agastache cana*)
Lippia 153
  alba (Verbena, Licorice)
  [*citriodora*]—*Aloysia triphylla*
  dulcis—(Sweet Herb)
  graveolens—(Oregano,
    Mexican) 153
  micromeria—(Thyme, False)
  origanoides—(Oregano,
    Mexican) 153
  psuedo-thea (Brazilian Tea)
F Liqueur 167
Living screen 4, 23, 25; PL. 16
[*Lophanthus anisatus*]—*Agastache*
  foeniculum
Louisa, Herb (Verbena, Lemon)
Lovage (*Levisticum officinale*) 13,
  54, 84, 93, 102, 106, 116, 118;
  F 28, 108, 109, 110; R 43,
  106, 108, 110, 126, 127, 130;
  PL. 11, 12, 16
Lovage, Black (*Smyrnium*
  olisatrum)
  Scotch (*Ligusticum scoticum*)
Love-in-a-Mist (*Nigella damascena*)
  168–169, 177; PL. 23
Lungwort (*Pulmonaria officinalis*)
C Lynalyl acetate 124

Madderwort (Wormwood,
  Common)
Maggi plant (Lovage)
Mallows 114, 121, 162
F Maple syrup, Imitation 169
Marguerite (Camomile, Dyer's)
Marigold
  Marsh (*Caltha palustris*) 84,
    101; PL. 8
  Pot (Calendula)
[Majorana]—*Origanum*
  [hortensis]—*Origanum majorana*
  [onites]—*Origanum onites*
Marjoram (*Origanum* spp.)
  Annual (Marjoram, Sweet)
  Golden (Oregano, Golden)
  Creeping (Oregano,
    Creeping Golden)
  Hop (Dittany of Crete)
  Knotted (Marjoram, Sweet)
  Pot (*Origanum onites*) 112, 124,
    125–126
  Sweet (*Origanum majorana*) 63,
    91, 112, **124**, 126; F 28, 74,

  77; R 43, 44, 77, 126, 127,
  133, 168; PL. 11
  Syrian (*Origanum syriacum*)
  Wild (*Origanum vulgare* ssp.
    vulgare) 63, 113, 124, **125**,
    126, 140; PL. 1, 15, 19, 21
  Winter (Oregano, Italian)
  Winter Sweet (Marjoram,
    Wild)
Marrubium
  incanum (Horehound, Silver)
  vulgare (Horehound, White)
Marshmallow (*Althea officinalis*)
  84, 150; PL. 22
Mary's herbs 113
Mass planting 22; Fig. 4
Master of the wood (Sweet
  Woodruff)
Masterwort (Angelica, Purple)
Mat-forming 23, 122
[*Matricaria chamomilla*]—
  Chamomilla recutita
  [*matricarioides*]—*Chamomilla*
    suaveolens
  [*recutita*]—*Chamomilla recutita*
Maudlin (*Achilla ageratum*)
Mayweed (*Anthemis cotula*) 33, 34
Maze 59, 61, **70**; Figs. 7, 11, 27
Mead 5, 30, 32, 33, **121**, 174
Meadow 116, 118; Figs. 35–38, 51,
  52, 53
Meadowsweet (*Fillipendula*
  ulmaria) 23, 84, 97
F Meatballs R 108, 109
Medicinal Herb Garden 14; PL. 12
Melissa officinalis (Balm, Lemon)
  var. *variegata* (Balm, Variegated
    Lemon)
Mentha (Mint)
  aquatica (Mint, Water)
    var. *crispum* (Mint, Curly)
  arvensis (Mint, Corn)
  [cardiaca]—*M.* × *gracilis*
  cervina (Pennyroyal, Holt's)
  [crispa]—*M. aquatica* var.
    crispum
  [gentilis]—*M.* × *gracilis*
  × *gracilis*—(Mint, Red)
    var. *variegata* (Mint, Golden)
  longifolia (Mint, Horse)
  [× *niliaca*]—*M.* × *rotundifolia*
  × *piperita* (Mint, Pepper)
    var. *citrata* (Mint, Orange)
    'Lime'
    'Lemon'
      var. *piperita* 'Mitcham'
      var. *vulgaris* (Mint, Black)
  pulegium (Pennyroyal, English)
    var. *gibraltarica* (Pennyroyal,
    Hoary)
  requeinii (Mint, Corsican)
  [rotundifolia]—*M. suaveolens*
  × *rotundifolia* (Mint, Round-
    leaved)
  spicata (Mint, Spear)

[*spicata* 'Crispii' or 'Crispata'] —
M. *aquatica* var. *crispum*
suaveolens var. *variegata* (Mint,
Pineapple)
[*sylvestris*] —*M. longifolia*
[*tomentosa*] —*M. longifolia*
villosa var. *alopecuroides* (Mint,
Apple)
[*viridis*] —*M. spicata*
Menthe coq (Costmary)
Menthella (Mint, Corsican)
[*Menthella requienii*] —*Mentha
requienii*
C   Menthol 25, 35, 36, 153; Tab. 3
Mercury (Good King Henry)
C   Methoxycinnamonaldehyde 110
C   Methylanthranilate 48
C   Methylchavicol 110
C   Methylcinnamate 45
C   Methylepijasmonate 25; Tab. 3
C   Methylnonylketone 82
C   Methylsalicilate 131; Tab. 3
Metropolitan gardens 67; Figs. 23,
48, 50
Microwave (Drying herbs)
Mignonette (*Reseda odorata*) 23, 81
Milfoil (Yarrow)
Mint (*Mentha* spp.) 18, 20, 23, 35–
37, 63, 84, 104, 132, 147, 166;
F 28–29; PL. 23
Apple (*M. villosa* var.) **35, 36,**
52, 63, 112, 113
Bergamot (Mint, Orange)
Black (*M.* × *piperita* var.
vulgaris) 36, 52, 111; PL. 11
'Black Mitcham' (*M.* × *piperita*
var. *piperita*) 35
Corn (*M. arveusis*)
Corsican (*M. requienii*) 23, **35,
36–37,** 45, 52, 71, 112, 121,
123, 125, 135, 157, 162, 173,
177; PL. 5, 10
Creme de Menthe (Mint,
Corsican)
Curly (*M. aquatica* var. *crispum*)
52; PL. 8
Eau de Cologne (Mint,
Orange)
Egyptian (Mint, Spear)
English (Mint, Spear)
Field (Mint, Corn)
Flea (Pennyroyal, English)
Gibraltar (Pennyroyal, Hoary)
Ginger (Mint, Golden)
Golden (*M.* × *gentilis* var.
variegata 'Golden') 35, **36,**
40, 52, 81; PL. 1, 16
Grapefruit (Mint, Round-
leaved)
Horse (*M. longifolia*) 52
Japanese (*M. arvensis* var.
piperascens)
Lamb (Mint, Pepper)
'Lemon' (*M.* × *piperita* var.
citrata cv.) 36

'Lime' (*M.* × *piperita* var. *citrata*
cv.) **36,** 53
'Murray Mitcham' (*M.* ×
piperita var. *p.* cv.) 35
Orange (*M.* × *piperita* var.
citrata) 35, **36,** 63, 112, 113; F
77, 114; PL.3
Pepper (*M.* × *piperita*) 52, 112;
Ch-25, Tab. 3; PL. 3
Pineapple (*M. suaveolens* var.
variegata) **35, 36,** 50, 52, 81,
82, 157; PL. 5; Ch-Tab. 3
Red (*M.* × *gracilis*)
Round-leaved (*M.* ×
rotundifolia)
Scotch (Mint, Red)
Silver (*M. longifolia* var.) 35
Spear (*M. spicata*) 36, 52, 84
'Todd Mitcham' (*M.* × *piperita*
var. *p.* cv.) 35
Water (*M. aquatica*) 36, 84; PL. 8
White (*M.* × *piperita* var.
officinalis)
Wooly (Mint, Apple)
Mint
Coyote (*Monardella villosa*) 152
Dog (Basil, Wild)
Dotted (*Monarda punctata*) 151
Korean (Hyssop, Wrinkled
Giant)
Lemon (*Monarda citriodora*) 151
Licorice (Hyssop, Wrinkled
Giant)
Mountain (Balm, Western)
Mountain (*Picnanthemum
virginianum*)
Squaw (Pennyroyal,
American)
Stone (*Cunila origanoides*)
Wood (*Blephilia hirsuta*)
Mint Bush (*Prosanthera
rotundifolia*) 17
Mint Geranium (Costmary)
Mint Shrub (*Elsholtzia stauntonii*)
F   Mixed drinks 28
Monarda spp. 12, 84, 94, 97, 116,
118, 127, 132, 135, 146, **150–
152,** 171, 173; F 126; PL. 18
austromontana (Oregano)
citriodora (Mint, Lemon)
clinopodia
[*coccinea*] —*M. didyma*
didyma (Balm, Bee)
'Granite Pink' 66, 81, **151,**
162, 173
fistulosa (Bergamot, Wild)
f. *albescens* 151
var. *menthifolia* 151
× *media* 151
[*menthifolia*] —*M. f.* var.
menthifolia
pectinata (Balm, Pony Bee)
punctata (Mint, Dotted)
russeliana
Monarda, Dwarf (*Monarda didyma*

'Granite Pink')
Monardella spp. **151–152**
odoratissima (Balm, Western)
villosa (Mint, Coyote)
Monastic garden (Checkerboard)
Mosquito plant (*Agastache cana*)
152
(Pennyroyal, American)
(Pennyroyal, English)
Mounding 31, 122
Mugwort (*Artemisia* spp.) 116, 164,
170, **173**
Common (*A. vulgaris*) 173
Fragrant (Mugwort, White)
Western (*A. ludoviciana*) 173,
174, 175
White (*A. lactiflora*) 23, 42, 52,
54, 97, 118, 137, 170, 171,
173, 175
C   Myrcene 41, 110, 149, 153; Tab. 3
Myrrhis odorata (Sweet Cicely)
Myrtle
California Wax (*Myrica
californica*)
Oregon (Laurel, California)
Sweet (Flag, Sweet)

Nard, Celtic (*Valeriana celtica*) 48
Nasturtiums 84, 112
Wild (Ginger, European)
Naturalizing 115, 121
Nep (Catnip)
Nepeta
cataria (Catnip)
'Citriodora' (Catnip,
Lemon)
× *faassenii* (Catmint)
'Six Hills Giant'
mussinnii (Catnip, Dwarf)
nepetella
C   Nepetalactone 127
Nepetella (*Calamintha nepeta* ssp.
glandulosa)
(*Nepeta nepetella*)
C   Neral 73
Niche 164
Nigella
damascena (Love-in-a-Mist)
sativa (Cumin, Black)
F   Noodles 109, 110
F   Nutty 108

C   Ocimene 40, 41, 110
Ocimum spp. (Basil)
americanum (Basil, Lemon)
basilicum (Basil, Sweet)
'Citriodorum'
'Crispum'
'Dark Opal'
'Italian'
'Lettuce Leaf'
'Thyrsiflora'
var. *minimum* (Basil, Bush)
'Silver Fox'
canum (Basil, Hoary)

'Anise'
'Camphor'
'Cinnamon'
'Lemon'
'Licorice'
kilimandscharicum (Basil,
Camphor)
sanctum 'Sri' (Basil, Sacred)
'Krishna' (Basil, Purple
Sacred)
'Spice' (Basil, Spice)
F Oil paste 27–29, 100; Tab. 4; R 103,
169
Old Man (Southernwood)
Old Woman (Wormwood, Beach)
Olitory (Fragrant lndscp)
F Omelette 49, 106, 109
Onion, Egyptian (*Allium cepa* var.
viviparum) 101
Oregano (*Origanum* spp.) 12, 63,
112, **124–126;** F 77; R 43,
108, 126, 128, 172; Ch-Tab.
3, 124
Golden (*O. vulgare* 'Aureum' or
'Golden Creeping') 46, 63,
66, 67, 104, 113, 124, **125,**
130, 136, 137, 138, 140; PL.
17, 20
'Greek' (*O. v.* spp. *hirtum* cv.)
112; PL. 17
Italian (*O. v.* ssp. *hirtum*) 112,
124; PL. 17
Russian (*O. v.* ssp. *gracile*) 113,
124, **125;** PL. 17
Showy (Oregano, Russian)
Trailing (*O. v.* ssp. *v.*
'Compactum Nanum')
'Tythantum' (Oregano,
Russian)
Oregano (*Monarda austromontana*)
Oregano, Cuban
(*Plectranthus caerulea*)
(*Poliomintha longiflora*)
Oregano, Mexican
(*Hedeoma floribundum*) 37
(*Lippia graveolens*) **126**
Oregano, Puerto Rican (Borage,
Indian or *Lippia graveolens*)
Oregano, Rocky Mountain
(*Brickellia* spp.)
Oregano, Spanish (*Plectranthus
caerulea*)
Oregano, Tropical (*Poliomintha,
Plectranthus,* and *Coleus
amboinicus*) 113; PL. 15
Oregano, Virgin Island (Borage,
Indian)
Oregano Maru (*Origanum
syriacum*)
Organy (Marjoram, Wild)
Origanum spp. (Oregano)
dictamnus (Dittany of Crete)
[*heracleoticum*]—*O. vulgare* ssp.
hirtum 'Greek'
× *hybridum* (Dittany)

[*hirtum*]—*O. v.* ssp. *hirtum*
majorana (Marjoram, Sweet)
× *majoricum* **126**
[*maru*]—*O. syriacum*
microphyllum 46, 49, 71, 72, 77,
78, 113, 124, **125,** 134
onites (Marjoram, Pot)
syphylum **125**
syriacum (Oregano Maru)
[*tytthanthum*]—(*O. v.* ssp.
gracile)
vulgare 124, 125
ssp. *gracile* (Oregano,
Russian)
ssp. *hirtum* (Oregano,
Italian)
'Greek' (Oregano,
Greek)
ssp. *viride* 125
ssp. *vulgare* (Marjoram,
Wild)
'Aureum' (Oregano,
Golden)
'Compactum Nanum'
(Oregano, Trailing)
'Golden Creeping'
(Oregano, Golden)
[var. *prismaticum*]—*O. v.* ssp.
gracile
Orris root Ch-125
Oswego Tea (Balm, Bee)
Overwintering tender perennials
79
F Oyster Stew R 128

F Pancake 136
Pansy (*Viola tricolor*) 97, 113, 152,
162
Parsley (*Petroselinum*) 93, 100,
106–107, 118; R 167, 172
Broad-leaf (Parsley, Italian)
Curly (*P. crispum* var. *crispum*)
63, 71, **106,** 114, 148; PL. 14,
21
Flat-leaved (Parsley, Italian)
Italian (*P. crispum* var.
neapolitanum) **106;** R 106;
PL. 12
Turnip-rooted (*P. crispum* var.
tuberosum) 107
Parsley, Chinese (Coriander)
Japanese (*Cryptotaenia japonica*)
107
Parterre 61, **66–70;** Figs. 21–26
Compartmented 67; Fig. 26
Cutwork 67; Fig. 26
Embroidery 67
English 67; Fig. 25
Partial shade 5, 123
F Pasta 47, 91
F Pastries 28–29, 132
Path materials 55
Paths 20, 22, 55, 97
Patios 20, 22, 60; Fig. 46
Pennyroyal 9, 17, 18, 23, **36–37,** 52

American (*Hedeoma pulegioides*)
17, **37,** 52, 77
English (*Mentha pulegium*) 36,
37, 52, 80, 114, 121, 132; Ch-
Tab. 3; PL. 5, 16, 23
Hoary (*Mentha pulegium* var.
gibraltarica) 37
Holt's (*Mentha cervina*)
Mock (Pennyroyal, American)
Wild (Balm, Western)
Perimeter beds 93, 114; Fig. 39
Permaculture 159
Petroselinum crispum (Parsley)
var. *crispum* (Parsley, Curly)
var. [*latifolia*]—*P. c.* var.
neapolitanum
var. *neapolitanum* (Parsley,
Italian)
var. *tuberosum* (Parsley, Turnip-
rooted)
[*hortense*]—*P. crispum*
[*Peucedanum graveolens*]—*Anethum
graveolens*
Pharmacognosy 14
C Phellandrene 84, 110; Tab. 3
C Phenyl acetic acid Tab. 3
Phlomis fruticosa (Sage, Jerusalem)
lychnitis (Lamwick)
Phu (Valerian)
Physicks 13, 93, **95–96;** Figs. 31,
32; PL. 12
F Pickling 166
C Picrocrocin 86
F Pie 44
Pimpernel (Burnet)
Pimpinella anisum (Anise)
Pineapple Weed (*Chamomilla
suaveolens*) 33
C Pinene 25, 38, 40, 41, 47, 49, 71, 81,
106, 134, 168; Tab. 3
Pinks, Clove 20, 40, 46, 77, 90, 101,
106
C Piperitone 35; Tab. 3
F Pizza 47
Plectranthus caerulea (Oregano,
Cuban or Spanish)
Poliomintha longiflora (Oregano,
Tropical)
Pollinators 25, 27, 47
Polymorphic 5, 31
Ponds 11, 84, 93, 122; Figs. 9, 46;
PL. 8
Poppies 84, 92, 97, 105, 114, 116,
135, 148, 150, 166, 173, 175,
177; F 169
F Pork 43, 136
F Potato
Patty R 126
Salad 73, 106, 110, 133, 136,
167, 172
Soup 109
[*Poterium sanguisorba*]—
Sanguisorba minor
[*obtusum*]—*Sanguisorba obtusa*
F Pot herbs 43, 91, **93,** 106, 107, 108,

137, 164, 170, 173
Potpourri 5, 17, 48, 114
F Poultry 109, 167
Preservation **26–29**, Tab. 4
Primrose 20, 121, 140, 152, 176
Evening 140
Procumbent 23, **31**
Prostrate 30
F Pudding 43, 86, 130, 167
Pudding grass (Pennyroyal,
English)
C Pulegone 35, 37, 152; Tab. 3
F Punch 28, 103, 170

Quad 5, 84, 94; Figs. 28, 29
Queen of the Meadow (Meadow
Sweet)

Raised bed 94, **97**, 121; PL. 12
Repellants
Animal 25, 150
Insect 27, 37, 38, **41**, 80, 82, 114,
130, 169
Reseda odorata (Mignonette)
F Rice 43, 54, 73, 77, 104, 110, 133,
136, 167, 172
F Rice pudding 43, 133
Rocambole (Garlic, Serpent)
Rooftop gardens 58–60; Fig. 11
F Roots 107, 108, 109, 167, 173
Rose 40, 75, 106, 166; F 126; Ch-
Tab. 3
Rosemarinus officinalis (Rosemary)
var. *angustifolius* (Rosemary,
Pine-scented)
'Beneden Blue' 78
f. *erectus* (Rosemary,
Upright)
var. *officinalis* 78
'Blue Spire'
'Logee Blue'
'Majorca'
f. *albiflorus* (Rosemary,
White-flowering)
var. [*procumbens*]—*R. o.*
var. *prostratus*
var. *prostratus* (Rosemary,
Creeping)
'Golden Prostrate'
'Huntington Carpet'
'Kenneth Prostrate'
'Lockwood de Forest'
var. *rigidus* 78
'Tuscan Blue
f. *roseus* (Rosemary, Pink-
flowering)
'Majorca Pink'
'Pinkie'
var. [*rupestris*]—*R. o.* var.
prostratus
[*tennuifolius*]—*R. o.* var.
angustifolius
Rosemary (*Rosmarinus officinalis*)
PL. 20, 23
Albus (Rosemary, White-

flowering)
Columnar (Rosemary,
Upright)
Creeping (*R. o.* var. *prostratus*)
123
'Jessops Upright' (Rosemary,
Upright)
'Miss Jessop' (Rosemary,
Upright)
Pine-scented (*R. o.* var.
angustifolius) **78**, 79, 111
Pink-flowering (*R. o.* var. *rigidus*
f. *rosea*) 78
Prostrate (Rosemary,
Creeping)
Pyramidalis (Rosemary,
Upright)
Trailing (Rosemary, Creeping)
Upright (*R. o.* var. *angustifolia* f.
erectus) 78
White-flowering (*R. o.* var.
officinalis f. *albiflorus*) **78**, 79;
PL. 8
Rosemary
Bog (*Andromeda* spp.)
Marsh (*Ledum palustre*)
Rue (*Ruta* spp.) 13, 63, 66, 70, 77,
78, **82–83**, 91, 103, 114; PL.
10, 19
Corsican (*R. corsica*) PL. 10
Fringed (*R. chalapensis*) 82
Garden (*R. graveolens*) **82–83**
Variegated (*R.g.* 'Variegatus')
82
Rue
Goat's (*Galega officinalis*)
Meadow (*Thallictrum* spp.) 42,
49, 54
Rugose 5
Rumex (Sorrel)
acetosa (Sorrel, Garden)
acetosella (Sorrel, Red)
crispus (Dock, Curly)
patientia (Sorrel, Patience)
scutatus (Sorrel, French)
Ruta (Rue)
chalapensis (Rue, Fringed)
corsica (Rue, Corsican)
graveolens (Rue, Garden)
'Curly Girl' 73, **82**
'Variegatus'

Sachet 5, 17, 48
Safflower (*Carthamus tinctorius*) F
85; 90
Saffron (*Crocus sativus*) 77, **85–86**,
123, 132, 162; R 86; PL. 11,
16
Kashmir (*C.s.* 'Cashmirianus')
Saffron, American (Safflower)
False (Safflower)
Sage (*Salvia* spp.) 13, 18, 20, 93,
101, **133–137**, 147, 154
Anise (*S. guaranitica*) 112, **137**
Baby (*S. microphylla*)

Blue (*S. clevelandii*) 42, 67, 106,
112, 136, 157, 176; F 126
Bog (*S. uliginosa*) 112, 137
Canyon (*S. lycoides*) 112, 137
Clary (*S. sclarea*) 41, 108, **136**,
150
Cleveland (Sage, Blue)
Dwarf (*S. officinalis* 'Nana') 46,
66, 67, 71, 77, 90, 112, **135**,
138, 176, 177; PL. 5
Fruit-scented (*S. dorisiana*) 137,
173; PL. 19
Garden (*S. officinalis*) 41, 48, 91,
113, **133–135**, 148; F 29; Ch-
Tab.; PL. 3, 5, 9, 18, 19, 21, 23
Golden (*S. o.* 'Aureus' or
'Icterina') 46, 54, 66, 112,
113, **135**, 176; PL. 15, 19, 21
Greek (*S. fructicosa*) 112, 135,
136, PL. 15
Meadow (*S. pratensis*) **137**
Mealy Cup (*S. farinacea*) 112
Mediterranean (Sage, Greek)
Melon (Sage, Fruit-scented)
Mexican (*S. mexicana*) 112, **137**
Mexican Bush (*S. leucantha*)
Muscatel (Sage, Clary)
Ornamental Tricolor (*S. viridis*)
114, 173
Pineapple (*S. elegans*) 127, 137;
F 28
Purple (Sage, Red)
Red (*S. o.* 'Purpurascens') 67,
135; PL. 19
Scarlet (Sage, Texas)
Silver (*S. argentea*) 41, 67, 90,
108, 134, **136**, 137; PL. 19
Texas (*S. coccinea*) 137
'Tricolor' (*S. o.* 'Tricolor') 67,
135; PL. 19
Tri-lobed (Sage, Greek)
Variegated (Sage, 'Tricolor')
Sage
Blue (*Eranthemum pulchellum*)
Garlic (*Teucrium scorodonia*)
Jerusalem (Lungwort)
Jerusalem (*Phlomis fruticosa*)
Russian (*Perovskia atriplicifolia*)
41
White (Mugwort, Western)
Wood (Germander, American)
F Salad 10, 13, 38, 81, 105, 106, 108,
110, 133, 147, 148, 166, 167,
169, 173
Dressing 28, 73, 86, 91, 126; R
168
Gelatin 148
F Salmon R 127
F Salt, herb 29; Tab. 4
Salvia spp. (Sage)
argentea (Sage, Siver)
clevelandii (Sage, Blue)
coccinea (Sage, Texas)
dorisiana (Sage, Fruit-scented)
elegans (Sage, Pineapple)

farinacea (Sage, Mealy Cup)
fruticosa (Sage, Greek)
guaranitica (Sage, Anise)
[*horminum*]—*S. viridis*
leucantha (Sage, Mexican Bush)
lycoides (Sage, Canyon)
mexicana (Sage, Mexican)
microphylla (Sage, Baby)
officinalis (Sage, Garden)
    'Aureus' (Sage, Golden)
    'Icterina' (Sage, Golden)
    'Nana' (Sage, Dwarf)
    'Purpurascens' (Sage, Red)
    'Tricolor'
pratensis (Sage, Meadow)
[*rutilans*]—*S. elegans*
sclarea (Sage, Clary)
    var. *turkestaniana* 136
[*triloba*]—*S. fruticosa*
uliginosa (Sage, Bog)
viridis (Sage, Ornamental
    Tricolor)
    'Violacea'
F Sandwich spread 28, 86, 100, 110;
    R 106
Sanguinary (Yarrow)
Sanguisorba (Burnet)
canadense (Burnet, Canadian)
minor (Burnet, Salad)
    ssp *minor* (Burnet)
obtusa (Burnet, Japanese)
officinalis (Burnet, Great)
tenuifolia (Burnet, Ornamental)
    105
    'Alba'
    'Rosea'
Santolina (*Santolina* spp.) 13, 63,
    77, **79–80**, 83, 90, 144, 175
    Dwarf (*S. chamaecyparissus*
    'Nana') 46, 66, 71, **79**, 112,
    123, 176; PL. 2, 5
    Fringed (*S. neapolitana*) 42, 53,
    73, **79**, 81, 135, 176; PL. 8, 10
    Green (*S. viridis*) 46, **79–80**; PL.
    1, 16
    Incana (*S. chamaecyparissus*) 33,
    79–80, 82; PL. 1, 9, 10, 15, 21
Santolina
    chamaecyparissus (Santolina,
        Incana)
        'Nana'
        'Pretty Carrol'
    ericoides
    neapolitana (Santolina, Fringed)
    viridis (Santolina, Green)
C Saponin 103, 169
Satureja spp. (Savory)
    douglasii (Yerba Buena)
    hortensis (Savory, Summer)
    montana (Savory, Winter)
        var. *pygmaea* (Savory,
        Pygmy)
    pillosa (Savory, Creeping)
[*Satureja origanoides*]—*Cunila
    origanoides*

F Sauces 28, 74, 86, 106, 109, 126; R
    108
Savory (*Satureja* spp.)
    Creeping (*S. pillosa*) **37–38**, 78,
        111, 121, 122, 176; F 126; PL.
        2
    Pygmy (*S. m.* ssp. *pygmaea*) **38**,
        71, 77, 111, 122, 177; PL. 6
    Summer (*S. hortensis*) 47, 73,
        90, 100, **109**, 177; F 28–29,
        44, 74; R 86, 108, 110
    Winter (*S. montana*) 20, **37–38**,
        63, 77, 109, 122, 136; PL. 8,
        11
Savory, Alpine (*Acinos thymoides*)
Saxicoles 122
[*Scandix cerefolium*]—*Anthriscus
    cerefolium*
F Seafood 172
F Seeds 43, 47, 91, 108, 128, 132, 166,
    167, 168, 169, 170, 172; R
    169
    Sesame (*Sesamum orientale*) 164,
    169–170; R 169
Shade-tolerant shrubs 116
    trees 116
F Shaker candy 85
Shakespearean herbs 91–92; Fig.
    28; PL. 11
F Side dish 172; R 42, 170
Side yard lndscp. 144–145; Fig. 47
Simples 5
Skirrets (*Sium sisarum*) 118
F Smoking 38, 81, 82, 109
Snakeroot (Ginger, Wild)
Sneezewort (*Achillea ptarmica*)
Solidago odorata (Goldenrod,
    Fragrant)
    Sorrel (*Rumex* spp.) 100, **107**, 118
    French (*R. scutatus*) 107
    Garden (*R. acetosa*) 107
    Patience (*R. patientia*) 107
    Red (*R. acetosella*) 107
    Sheep (Sorrel, Red)
F Soup 10, 28–29, 42, 74, 91, 103,
    106, 108, 109, 126, 133, 167,
    172; R 43, 86, 172
    Southernwood (*Artemisia
    abrotanum*) 18, 20, 42, 52, 63,
    80, **81–82**, 138, 166; PL. 1, 2,
    12, 16
    'Camphor' 81
    'Lemon' 54, **81**
    'Tangerine' 81
F Spaghetti sauce 32
Spanish Marjoram Oil 74
Spanish Origanum Oil 73
F Spears 171; R 172
Speick (Nard, Celtic)
Sport 5, 12
F Sprouts 164, 169, 170
Squares, garden 93–94; PL. 12, 14,
    22
Stachys (Betony)
    byzantina (Betony, Wooly)

    'Silver Carpet'
    [*lanata*]—*S. byzantina*
    officinale (Betony)
C Standard 5, 20, **58**, **78**, 153
C Starch 173
F Steamed vegetable 172, 173
Steps 20
F Stew 28–29, 106
F Stewed meat 10, 32, 38, 74, 106,
    109, 126, 172
St. George's Herb (Valerian)
Stickadove (Lavender, Spanish)
F Stir-fry 28, 29, 100, 106, 108, 167,
    168, 169, 170, 172
Storing herbs 27
Strawberry 72, 93, 94, 110, 132; PL.
    21
Strawberry Blite (*Chenopodium
    capitatum*) 143
Strewing herbs 5, 18
F Sugared 29, 84, 103, 168, 170; Tab.
    4
    Sweet Cicely (*Myrrhis odorata*) 17,
    18, 53, 84, 93, 112, 113, 116,
    118, 128, 132, 140, 152, 174;
    F 28, 69; R 104, 128, 130,
    172; PL. 11, 17, 21
Sweet Herb (*Lippia dulcis*) 153
Sweet herbs 18
    Sweet Woodruff (*Galium odorata*)
    86, 121, **131–132**, 140, 173;
    PL. 11, 18
F Sweetener 170, 173
Symphytum (Comfrey)
    asperum (Comfrey, Prickly)
    officinale (Comfrey, Common)
        'Argenteum' (Comfrey,
        Variegated)
        'Coccineum' (Comfrey,
        Red-flowering)
    × *uplandicum* (Comfrey,
        Russian)
F Syrup 29, 130; Tab. 4

F Taco filling R 168
Tanacetum vulgare (Tansy, Garden)
    'Crispum' (Tansy, Fern-leaf)
    Tansy (*Tanacetum*)
    Fern-leaf (*T. v.* 'Crispum') 42,
        54, 102, **105**, 175; PL. 14
    Garden (*T. vulgare*) 23, 50, 97,
        100, **105–106**, 114, 116, 118,
        137, 150, 166; PL. 14
    Tarragon (*Artemisia*) 100, **110**; F
        28; R 104, 106
    French (*A. d.* 'Sativa') 90, **110**; F
        27; R 74
    Russian (*A. dracunculus*) 110
Tarragon, Mexican (*Tagetes lucida*)
F Tartar sauce 110
F Tarts 114
F Tea 13, 28, 29, 34, 48, 91, 105, 113,
    114, 127, 129, 131, 148, 149,
    151, 152, 153, 154, 167, 173
F Teabags 28

C Terpenes 40, 47, 81, 106, 124
C Terpinene 47; Tab. 3
C Terpineol 74
C Terpinyl acetate 72
Teucrium (Germander)
   aroanium (Germander, Greek)
    [*aureum*]—*T. polium*
   canadense (Germander,
    American)
   chamaedrys (Germander)
    'Prostratum' (Germander,
    Dwarf)
   flavum 83
   fruticans (Germander, Tree)
  marum (Thyme, Cat)
   massiliense (Germander,
    Fragrant)
   montanum 83
   polium (Germander, Golden)
   pyreniacum 83
   scorodonia (Germander, Wood)
Thematic gardens 13; Fig. 28
C Thujone 40, 81, 134; Tab. 3
Thymbra spicata (Za'atar)
Thyme (*Thymus* spp.) 20, 30–33,
   38, 40, 70, **75–77**, 93, 123,
   136, 138, 153, 174, 176; F
   28–29, 110, 126; R 126, 172
  Broad Leaf English (T. 'Broad
   Leaf English') 71, **74**, 77, 91;
   Tab. 8; PL. 9
  Bush 49, 63, **71–77**, 80, 101,
   144, 177
  Camphor (T. *camphoratus*) **71–
   72**
  Caraway (T. *herba-barona*) 17,
   32, 112, 125, 138; PL. 17, 19
  Coconut (T. *praecox* ssp.
   arcticus)
  Conehead (Corido)
  Creeping 23, **30–33**, 45, 81, 91,
   112, 114, 121, 157; PL. 2, 16,
   20, 23
   Golden (T. 'Clear Gold' or T.
    pulegioides 'Gold Dust') 31,
    112, 114, 125, 130, 140, 157;
    PL. 3, 4, 10, 17
   Red (T. *praecox* × ssp. *arcticus*
    'Coccineus') **31**, 112
  Cretan (Corido)
  Crimson (T. *p.* 'kermesinus') 31,
   32; PL. 4
  Davis (T. *leucotrichus*) **31–32**,
   33, 174; Tab. 8
  Dwarf (Thyme, Miniature)
  English (T. 'Broad-leaf English')
  French (Thyme, Narrow-leaf
   French) 29, 91, 176; F 74; R
   77; Ch-Tab. 3
  Garden (Thyme, French)
  German Winter (T. *hyemalis*)
   71, **73**
  'Gold Eagle' (Thyme, Golden
   Lemon)
  Golden (T. 'Doone Valley')

Golden Dwarf (T. 'Clear Gold')
'Golden King' (Thyme, Golden
  Lemon)
Golden Lemon (T. × *citriodorus*
  'Aureus') 46, **73**, 77, 80, 91,
  104, 112, 114, 176; Tab. 8;
  PL. 9
Greek (Thyme, French)
Greek Gray (Thyme, French)
Hall's Wooly (Thyme, Wooly)
Languinosus (Thyme, Wooly)
Lemon (T. × *citriodorus*) 17, 71,
  73, 140; F 126
Marshall (T. 'Linear Leaf Lilac')
  31, **32–33**; Tab. 8
Mastic (T. *mastichina*) 71, **73–
  74**; Tab. 8
'Mayfair' (T. *praecox* ssp. *a.* cv.)
  31; PL. 4
Miniature (T. *vulgaris*
  'Miniature') **71**, 72; Tab. 8;
  PL. 9
Mitcham Gray (Thyme,
  French)
Moroccan (T. *brousonetti*) **31–
  32**, 80, 174; Tab. 8
Mother of (T. *pulegioides*) 30,
  140
'Narrow-leaf French' (T. *v.* cv.)
  29, 71, 73, **74–75**, 91, 176; F
  74; R 77; Tab. 8; PL. 5, 9, 10,
  11, 21, 24
Nutmeg (Thyme, Caraway)
of the Ancients (Corido)
Orange (T. *v.* 'Orange Balsam')
'Orange Balsam' (T. *v.* cv.) 73,
  74–75, 80; Tab. 8; PL. 11
Oregano (Thyme, Oregano-
  scented)
'Oregano-scented' (T.
  pulegioides cv.) **31–32**, 176; F
  74, 126; Tab. 8; PL. 5
Peter Davis (Thyme, Davis)
Red-flowering (T. *pulegioides*
  'Kermesinus') **31–32**, 83, 91;
  Tab. 8
Silver (T. 'Argenteus') 39, 71,
  72, 80, 114, 134, 138, 152,
  176; Tab. 8; PL. 9, 20
Silver Lemon (Thyme, Silver)
Silver Queen (Thyme, Silver)
Tiny (Thyme, Tuffeted)
Tuffeted (T. *caespititius* 'Tuffet')
  31, 140; Tab. 8
Wedgewood (T. 'Wedgewood
  English') 71, **73**; Tab. 8
White-flowering (T. *pulegioides*
  'Foster Flower' and 'White
  Magic')
'White Magic' (T. *pulegioides* cv.)
  31–32, 176; Tab. 8
'White Moss' (T. *praecox* ssp. *a.*
  'White Moss') **31**, 71, 125,
  138, 177; Tab. 8; PL. 4, 5, 20
Wild (T. *praecox*) 30, 112, 140;

  PL. 4
  Wooly (T. *praecox* ssp. *a.*
   'Languinosus' or 'Hall's
   Wooly') **31**, 71, 91, 138, 140;
   Tab. 8; PL. 2, 20 24
  Yellow Transparent (T. 'Clear
   Gold')
Thyme
  Cat (*Teucrium marum*) 83
  False (*Lippia micromeria*)
  Spanish (Borage, Indian)
  Water (*Elodea* spp.)
Thyme Oil 72
C Thymol 32, 74, 109, 124, 151; Tab.
  3
Thymus (Thyme)
  adamovicii 73
  [*angustifolius*]—*T. vulgaris*
   'Narrow-leaf French'
  'Argenteus' (Thyme, Silver)
  [*azoricus*]—*T. caespititius*
  'Broad-leaf' (T. 'Broad-leaf
   English')
  brousonetti (Thyme, Moroccan)
  caespititius (Thyme, Tuffeted)
  camphoratus (Thyme,
   Camphor)
  capitatus (Corido)
  carnosus 71, **72**
  × *citriodorus* (Thyme, Lemon)
   'Aureus' (Thyme, Golden
   Lemon)
   'Clear Gold' (Thyme, Golden
   Creeping)
  [*creticus*]—*T. capitatus*
  'Doone Valley' (Thyme,
   Golden)
  [*drucei*]—*T. praecox* ssp. *arcticus*
  [*fragrantissimus*]—*T. vulgaris*
   'Fragrantissimus'
  [*glabrous loveyanus*]—*T.* 'Long
   Leaf Gray'
  herba-barona (Thyme,
   Caraway)
  hyemalis (Thyme, German
   Winter)
  [*lanicaulis*]—*T.* 'Long Leaf Gray'
  leucotrichus (Thyme, Davis)
  'Linear Leaf Lilac' (Thyme,
   Marshall)
  'Long Leaf Gray' 31, **32–33**; PL.
   5
  [*marshallianus*]—*T.* 'Linear Leaf
   Lilac'
  mastichina (Thyme, Mastic)
  [*micans*]—*T. caespititius*
  [*nitidus*]—*T. richardii* ssp.
   nitidus
  nummularius 32
  'Nutmeg' (Thyme, Caraway)
  [*pannonicus*]—*T.* 'Linear Leaf
   Lilac'
  praecox (Thyme, Wild)
   ssp. *arcticus*
    'Coccineus' **31**, 112

'Hall's Wooly' (Thyme, Wooly)
'Languinosus' (Thyme, Wooly)
'Mayfair'
'Pink Chintz' **31**; Tab. 8; PL. 4
'White Moss'
[*psuedolanguinosus*]—*T. praecox* ssp. *a.* 'Languinosus'
pulegioides (Thyme, Mother of)
['Albus']—*T. p.* 'Foster Flower'
'Foster Flower' **31–32**, 91; Tab. 8
'Gold Dust' **31–32**
'Kermesinus' (Thyme, Crimson)
'Oregano-scented'
'White Magic'
richardii ssp. *nitidus* 71
serpyllum 32
[*skorpilii*]—*T. praecox* ssp. *skorpilii*
[*thracicus*]—*T.* 'Long Leaf Gray'
vulgaris (Thyme, French)
'Bittersweet' 74–75
'Fragrantissimus'
'Miniature' (Thyme, Miniature)
'Narrow Leaf French' (Thyme, French)
'Orange Balsam' (Thyme, Orange)
'Wedgewood English' (Thyme, Wedgewood)
zygis 72
Tisane 5
Toki (*Angelica acutiloba*)
F Tomato sauce 77, 172
Tomentose **90**, 102
Tooth cleanser 112
Topiary 5, 56, **58**, 77, 81, 82, 95
Transition herb 35, **81**, 118; PL. 16
Transplanting (to indoors) 79
Trigonella foenum-graecum (Fennugreek)
Tulasi (Basil, Sacred)
Turf seat 23, 33–34, 94, 112, 114; Figs. 11, 12, 50; PL. 3
Turmeric (*Curcuma Longa*) 168

C Umbeliferone (isomer of coumarin) Tab. 3
Umbelularia californica (Laurel, California)
C Umbelulone 153
C Uracilic acid 134

Valerian (*Valeriana*)
Dwarf (*V. arizonica*) 49
Elder-leaved (*V. sambucifolia*) 49
Indian (*V. wallichii*) 48
Japanese (*V. officinalis* var.

latifolia) 48
Marsh (*V. dioica*) 49
Valeriana (Valerian)
arizonica (Valerian, Dwarf)
celtica (Speick)
dioica (Valerian, Marsh)
mexicana **48**, 49
officinalis (Garden Heliotrope)
var. *latifolia* (Valerian, Japanese)
sambucifolia (Valerian, Elder-leaved)
sitchensis **48**, 49
wallichii (Valerian, Indian)
Valerian
American (*Cypripedium calceolus*)
Red (*Centranthus ruber*)
Valerianic acid/ether 49
Variety (nomenclatural) 5
Veal 82, 126, 136
Vegetables 32, 42, 43, 106, 108, 110; R 132
Vegetables (fresh) 42, 100, 133, 167, 172, 173
Vegetables (ornamental) 143
Verbena
Lemon (*Aloysia triphylla*) 17, 37, 53, 146, **153–154**, 157; F 27, 28, 29; PL. 3
Licorice (*Lippia alba*) 153
Vermifuge 41
Vinegar 28, 110; Tab. 4
Viola (Violets)
lanceolata (Violet, Lance leaf)
odorata (Violet, Sweet)
pedata (Violet, Bird's foot)
tricolor (Pansy)
Violet (*Viola* spp.) 85, 91, 114, 121, 123, **129**, 130, 132, 140, 157, 162, 173, 176; PL. 2, 16, 17, 23
Bird's foot (*V. pedata*) 40, 77, 81, **129**
Florist's (Violet, Sweet)
Lance leaf (*V. lanceolata*) 129
Sweet (*V. odorata*) 20, 23, 114, **129**; F 29; Ch-Tab. 3
Violet, German (*Exacum affine*)
Volatiles 5, 25–27

Weaving material 81, 85
Wild lndscp. 159–177; Figs. 50–53; PL. 24
Windbreak 23–25
Window box 23
F Wine 110, 131
Winterbloom (Witch Hazel)
Winter garden 85
Wintergreen (*Gaultheria procumbens*) 121, 129, **131**, 132, 157; Ch-Tab. 3
Indian (*Gaultheria fragrantissimus*)
Witch Hazel (*Hamamelis* spp.) 85,

86–87
American (*H. virginiana*) 86
Chinese (*H. mollis*) 86
Japanese (*H. japonica*) 86
Woodruff (Sweet Woodruff)
Wormseed (*Artemisia maratima*)
Wormwood (*Artemisia* spp.)
Beach (*A. stellerana*) 40, **41**, 46, 90, 134; PL. 7
Common (*A. absinthum*) 13, 20, **40–41**, 50, 63, 92, 94, 106, 114, 134, 175; PL. 6, 14
Field (*A. campestris*)
Fringed (*A. arborescens*) 77, 90, 134
Ghost (Mugwort, White)
Indian (Mugwort, Common)
'Lambrook Silver' (Wormwood, Common)
Roman (*A. pontica*) **41**, 77, 134
Sweet (*A. annua*)
Woundwort (Yarrow)
Wreath 49, 80, 81, 153

Yarb (herb) 113
Yarrow (*Achillea* spp.) 94, 97, 101, 106, 116, 121, 137, 150, 164, 166, 171, **174–175**; Ch-148
'Cerise Queen' (*A. millefolium* cv.) 174
'Coronation Gold' (*A. filipendulina* cv.) 137, **174**; PL. 23, 24
Creeping (*A. tomentosa*) 121, **174**
Fern-Leaf (*A. filipendulina*) 174
'Fire King' (*A. millefolium* cv.) 114, **174**
'Gold Plate' (*A. f.* cv.) **174**
'Moonshine' (*A. taygeta* cv.) 114, **174**
Musk (*A. moschata*)
Red-flowering (*A. millefolium* var.) 48, 54, **174**
Sweet (*A. ageratum*)
White-flowering (*A. millefolium*)
Yellow-flowering (*A. f.* cultivars)
Yerba Buena (*Satureja douglasii*) 121, **129**, 173
F Yogurt 86
Yule log 153

Za'atar (*Thymbra spicata*) 73; F 126; PL. 19
Zingiber (Ginger)

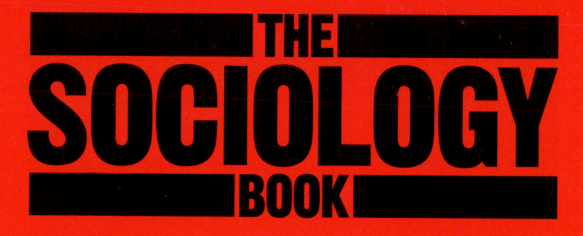

THE SOCIOLOGY BOOK

Penguin
Random
House

DK LONDON

SENIOR EDITOR
Sam Atkinson

SENIOR ART EDITOR
Amy Child

EDITORS
Alexandra Beeden
Miezan van Zyl

MANAGING EDITOR
Esther Ripley

MANAGING ART EDITOR
Karen Self

PUBLISHER
Liz Wheeler

ART DIRECTOR
Phil Ormerod

**ASSOCIATE
PUBLISHING DIRECTOR**
Liz Wheeler

PUBLISHING DIRECTOR
Jonathan Metcalf

JACKET DESIGNER
Laura Brim

JACKET EDITOR
Claire Gell

**JACKET DESIGN
DEVELOPMENT MANAGER**
Sophia Tampakopoulos

**SENIOR PRODUCER,
PRE-PRODUCTION**
Luca Frassinetti

SENIOR PRODUCER
Gemma Sharpe

ILLUSTRATIONS
James Graham

DK DELHI

JACKET DESIGNER
Dhirendra Singh

SENIOR DTP DESIGNER
Harish Aggarwal

MANAGING JACKETS EDITOR
Saloni Singh

original styling by

STUDIO8 DESIGN

produced for DK by

COBALT ID

ART EDITORS
Darren Bland, Paul Reid

EDITORS
Diana Loxley, Marek Walisiewicz,
Christopher Westhorp

First published in Great Britain in
2015 by Dorling Kindersley Limited,
80 Strand, London, WC2R 0RL

2 4 6 8 10 9 7 5 3 1
001 - 187530 - July/2015

Copyright © 2015
Dorling Kindersley Limited
A Penguin Random House Company

A CIP catalogue record for this
book is available from
the British Library.

ISBN: 978-0-2411-8229-1

Printed and bound in China by
Leo Paper Products Ltd

A WORLD OF IDEAS:
SEE ALL THERE IS TO KNOW

www.dk.com

CONTRIBUTORS

CHRISTOPHER THORPE, CONSULTANT EDITOR

Our co-consultant and contributor Christopher Thorpe is a sociologist with an interest in social theory, cultural sociology, and British representations of Italy. He has a doctorate in sociology from the University of Aberdeen, Scotland, and is co-editor of the journal *Cultural Sociology*, author of several academic articles, and co-author of *An Invitation to Social Theory* (2012).

CHRIS YUILL, CONSULTANT EDITOR

Our co-consultant and contributor Chris Yuill is a sociologist and lecturer at Robert Gordon University, Aberdeen, Scotland. His interests include the social dimensions of health, both in the community and the workplace, and what makes for a successful urban space. He is a former committee member of The British Sociological Association and has written several books, including *Understanding the Sociology of Health: An Introduction* (2011)

MITCHELL HOBBS

A lecturer in the department of media and communications at the University of Sydney, Australia, Mitchell Hobbs has a doctorate in media sociology from the University of Newcastle, Australia. He is co-author of *Communication, New Media and Everyday Life* (2011); author of several national and international studies on global media, cultural flows, and political communication; and has worked in a communications role for former Australian prime minister Julia Gillard.

MEGAN TODD

A senior lecturer in social science at the University of Central Lancashire, England, Megan Todd has a doctorate in sociology from the University of Newcastle, England. Her research interests include gender, sexuality, and violence. She has contributed chapters on intimacies and violence in various publications and is currently writing a textbook on sexualities.

SARAH TOMLEY

A writer, editor, and psychotherapist, Sarah Tomley has contributed to many books on the social sciences, including *The Philosophy Book* (2011) and *The Psychology Book* (2012) in DK's Big Ideas series.

MARCUS WEEKS

A writer and musician, Marcus Weeks studied philosophy and worked as a teacher before embarking on a career as an author. He has contributed to many books on the arts and popular sciences, including various titles in DK's Big Ideas series.

6

CONTENTS

10 INTRODUCTION

FOUNDATIONS OF SOCIOLOGY

20 A physical defeat has never marked the end of a nation Ibn Khaldun

21 Mankind have always wandered or settled, agreed or quarrelled, in troops and companies Adam Ferguson

22 Science can be used to build a better world Auguste Comte

26 The Declaration of Independence bears no relation to half the human race Harriet Martineau

28 The fall of the bourgeoisie and the victory of the proletariat are equally inevitable Karl Marx

32 Gemeinschaft and Gesellschaft Ferdinand Tönnies

34 Society, like the human body, has interrelated parts, needs, and functions Émile Durkheim

38 The iron cage of rationality Max Weber

46 Many personal troubles must be understood in terms of public issues Charles Wright Mills

50 Pay to the most commonplace activities the attention accorded extraordinary events Harold Garfinkel

52 Where there is power there is resistance Michel Foucault

56 Gender is a kind of imitation for which there is no original Judith Butler

SOCIAL INEQUALITIES

66 I broadly accuse the bourgeoisie of social murder Friedrich Engels

68 The problem of the 20th century is the problem of the colour line W E B DuBois

74 The poor are excluded from the ordinary living patterns, customs, and activities of life Peter Townsend

75 There ain't no black in the Union Jack Paul Gilroy

76 A sense of one's place Pierre Bourdieu

80 The Orient is the stage on which the whole East is confined Edward Said

82 The ghetto is where the black people live Elijah Anderson

84 The tools of freedom become the sources of indignity Richard Sennett

88 Men's interest in patriarchy is condensed in hegemonic masculinity R W Connell

90 **White women have been complicit in this imperialist, white-supremacist capitalist patriarchy** bell hooks

96 **The concept of "patriarchy" is indispensable for an analysis of gender inequality** Sylvia Walby

MODERN LIVING

104 **Strangers are not really conceived as individuals, but as strangers of a particular type** Georg Simmel

106 **The freedom to remake our cities and ourselves** Henri Lefebvre

108 **There must be eyes on the street** Jane Jacobs

110 **Only communication can communicate** Niklas Luhmann

112 **Society should articulate what is good** Amitai Etzioni

120 **McDonaldization affects virtually every aspect of society** George Ritzer

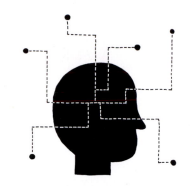

124 **The bonds of our communities have withered** Robert D Putnam

126 **Disneyization replaces mundane blandness with spectacular experiences** Alan Bryman

128 **Living in a loft is like living in a showcase** Sharon Zukin

LIVING IN A GLOBAL WORLD

136 **Abandon all hope of totality, you who enter the world of fluid modernity** Zygmunt Bauman

144 **The modern world-system** Immanuel Wallerstein

146 **Global issues, local perspectives** Roland Robertson

148 **Climate change is a back-of-the-mind issue** Anthony Giddens

150 **No social justice without global cognitive justice** Boaventura de Sousa Santos

152 **The unleashing of productive capacity by the power of the mind** Manuel Castells

156 **We are living in a world that is beyond controllability** Ulrich Beck

162 **It sometimes seems as if the whole world is on the move** John Urry

163 **Nations can be imagined and constructed with relatively little historical straw** David McCrone

164 **Global cities are strategic sites for new types of operations** Saskia Sassen

166 **Different societies appropriate the materials of modernity differently** Arjun Appadurai

170 **Processes of change have altered the relations between peoples and communities** David Held

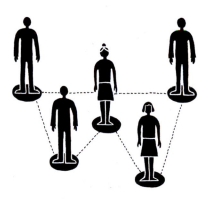

CULTURE AND IDENTITY

176 The "I" and the "me"
G H Mead

178 The challenge of
modernity is to live
without illusions and
without becoming
disillusioned
Antonio Gramsci

180 The civilizing process is
constantly moving
"forward" Norbert Elias

182 Mass culture reinforces
political repression
Herbert Marcuse

188 The danger of the future
is that men may become
robots Erich Fromm

189 Culture is ordinary
Raymond Williams

190 Stigma refers to an
attribute that is deeply
discrediting
Erving Goffman

196 We live in a world
where there is
more and more
information, and less
and less meaning
Jean Baudrillard

200 Modern identities are
being decentred
Stuart Hall

202 All communities are
imagined
Benedict Anderson

204 Throughout the world,
culture has been
doggedly pushing
itself centre stage
Jeffrey Alexander

WORK AND CONSUMERISM

214 Conspicuous consumption
of valuable goods is a
means of reputability
to the gentleman
of leisure
Thorstein Veblen

220 The Puritan wanted to
work in a calling; we
are forced to do so
Max Weber

224 Technology, like art, is a
soaring exercise of the
human imagination
Daniel Bell

226 The more sophisticated
machines become, the
less skill the worker has
Harry Braverman

232 Automation increases
the worker's control
over his work process
Robert Blauner

234 The Romantic ethic
promotes the spirit
of consumerism
Colin Campbell

236 In processing people,
the product is a state
of mind Arlie Russell
Hochschild

244 Spontaneous consent
combines with coercion
Michael Burawoy

246 Things make us just as
much as we make things
Daniel Miller

248 Feminization has had
only a modest impact
on reducing gender
inequalities
Teri Lynn Caraway

THE ROLE OF INSTITUTIONS

254 Religion is the sigh of the oppressed creature
Karl Marx

260 The iron law of oligarchy
Robert Michels

261 Healthy people need no bureaucracy to mate, give birth, and die
Ivan Illich

262 Some commit crimes because they are responding to a social situation Robert K Merton

264 Total institutions strip people of their support systems and their sense of self Erving Goffman

270 Government is the right disposition of things
Michel Foucault

278 Religion has lost its plausibility and social significance Bryan Wilson

280 Our identity and behaviour are determined by how we are described and classified
Howard S Becker

286 Economic crisis is immediately transformed into social crisis
Jürgen Habermas

288 Schooling has been at once something done to the poor and for the poor
Samuel Bowles and Herbert Gintis

290 Societies are subject, every now and then, to periods of moral panic
Stanley Cohen

291 The time of the tribes
Michel Maffesoli

292 How working-class kids get working-class jobs
Paul Willis

FAMILIES AND INTIMACIES

298 Differences between the sexes are cultural creations
Margaret Mead

300 Families are factories that produce human personalities
Talcott Parsons

302 Western man has become a confessing animal
Michel Foucault

304 Heterosexuality must be recognized and studied as an institution
Adrienne Rich

310 Western family arrangements are diverse, fluid, and unresolved
Judith Stacey

312 The marriage contract is a work contract
Christine Delphy

318 Housework is directly opposed to self-actualization Ann Oakley

320 When love finally wins it has to face all kinds of defeat
Ulrich Beck and Elisabeth Beck-Gernsheim

324 Sexuality is as much about beliefs and ideologies as about the physical body
Jeffrey Weeks

326 Queer theory questions the very grounds of identity Steven Seidman

332 DIRECTORY

340 GLOSSARY

344 INDEX

351 ACKNOWLEDGMENTS

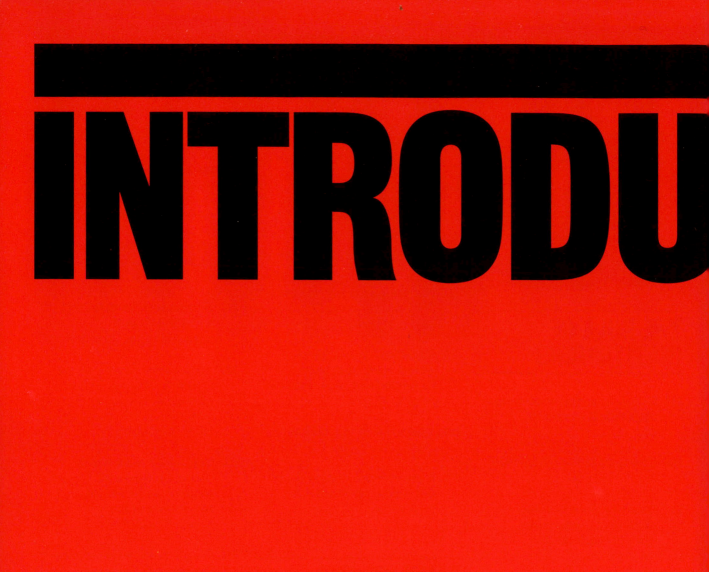

INTRODU

Humans are social creatures. Throughout our evolution, from our days of foraging and hunting animals, we have tended to live and work in social groups, which have become progressively larger and more complex. These groups have ranged from simple family units, through clans and tribes, villages and towns, to cities and nation states. Our natural inclination to live and work together has led to the formation of civil societies, which have been shaped by the increasing breadth of our knowledge and sophistication of our technology. In turn, the nature of the society we live in influences our social behaviour, affecting virtually every aspect of our lives.

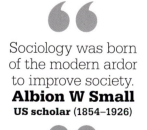

Sociology was born of the modern ardor to improve society.
Albion W Small
US scholar (1854–1926)

Sociology is the study of how individuals behave in groups and how their behaviour is shaped by these groups. This includes: how groups are formed; the dynamics that animate them; and how these dynamics maintain and alter the group or bring about social change. Today, sociology's scope ranges from the theoretical study of social processes, structures, and systems, to the application of these theories as part of social policy. And, because societies consist of a collection of individual people, there is an inevitable connection between the structures of society as a whole and the behaviour of its individual members. Sociologists may therefore focus on the institutions and organization of society, the various social groupings and stratifications within it, or the interactions and experiences of individuals.

Perhaps surprisingly, sociology is a comparatively modern discipline. Although philosophers in ancient China and ancient Greece recognized the existence of civil society, and the benefits of social order, their concern was more political than sociological – how society should be organized and governed, rather than a study of society itself. But, just as political

philosophy emerged from these civilizations, sociology appeared as a result of profound changes in Western society during the Age of Enlightenment.

There were several aspects to these changes. Most noticeably, technological advances had provided the machinery that brought about the Industrial Revolution, radically changing methods of production and creating prosperous industrial cities. The traditional certainties based on religious belief were called into question by the philosophy of the Enlightenment. It was not only the authority of the Church that was undermined by this so-called Age of Reason: the old order of monarchies and aristocracies was under threat, with demands for more representative government leading to revolutions in America and France.

Society and modernity
A new, modern society was created from the Age of Enlightenment. Sociology began to emerge at the end of the 18th century as a response to this transformation, as philosophers and thinkers attempted to understand the nature of modernity and its effects on society. Inevitably, some simply

bemoaned the erosion of traditional forms of social cohesion, such as the family ties and community spirit found within small, rural societies, and the shared values and beliefs offered by a common religion. But others recognized that there were new social forces at work, bringing about social change with a potential for both social order and disorder.

In keeping with the spirit of the Enlightenment, these early social thinkers sought to make their study of society objective, and create a scientific discipline that was distinct from philosophy, history, and politics. The natural sciences (physics, chemistry, astronomy, and biology) were well established, and the time was ripe for the study of humans and their behaviour.

Because of the nature of the Industrial Revolution and the capitalism that it fostered, the first of the new "social sciences" to emerge was economics, pioneered by Adam Smith's *An Inquiry into the Nature and Causes of the Wealth of Nations*, better known as *The Wealth of Nations*, in 1776. However, at the same time, the foundations of sociology were also being laid, by philosophers and theorists such as Adam Ferguson and Henri de Saint-Simon, and

in the early part of the following century by Auguste Comte, whose scientific approach to the study of society firmly established sociology as a distinct discipline.

Following in Comte's footsteps came three ground-breaking sociologists, whose different approaches to the analysis and interpretation of social behaviour set the agenda for the subject of sociology in the 20th century and beyond: Karl Marx, Émile Durkheim, and Max Weber. Each identified a different aspect of modernity as the major factor in creating social order, disorder, and change. Marx, a materialist philosopher and economist, focused on the growth

> "
> Human nature is... unbelievably malleable... responding accurately and contrastingly to contrasting cultural traditions.
> **Margaret Mead**
> "

of capitalism and the subsequent class struggle; Durkheim on the division of labour brought about by industrialization; and Weber on the secularization and rationalization of modern society. All three have had an enthusiastic following, influencing sociology's major schools of thought to the present day.

A social science

Sociology was a product of the Age of Reason, when science and rational thinking began to reign supreme. Early sociologists were therefore anxious that, for their discipline to be taken seriously, their methods should be seen to be rigorously scientific – no mean feat, given the nature of their subject: human social behaviour. Comte laid the ground rules for the new "science" of sociology, based on empirical evidence in the same way as the natural sciences. Marx, too, insisted on approaching the subject scientifically, and Durkheim was perhaps the first to gain acceptance for sociology as a social science in the academic world.

To be scientific, any research method must be quantitative – that is to say, have measurable results. Marx and Durkheim could point to facts, figures, and statistics to back up their theories, but others »

maintained that social research should be more qualitative. Weber especially advocated an interpretive approach, examining what it is like to live in modern society, and the social interactions and relationships that are necessary for social cohesion.

Although this viewpoint was initially dismissed by many as unscientific, in the latter half of the 20th century sociology has become increasingly interpretive, with a methodology that includes a combination of quantitative and qualitative research techniques.

Social reform

For many sociologists, sociology is more than simply the objective study of society, and the quest to analyse and describe social structures and systems. Sociological theories, like theories in the natural sciences, have practical applications, and can be used to improve the society in which we live. In the 19th century, Comte and Marx saw sociology as a way of understanding the workings of society in order to bring about social change. Marx famously said, "The philosophers have only interpreted the world, in various ways. The point, however, is to change it", and his many

followers (sociologists as well as political activists) have taken this to heart.

Durkheim, who was nowhere near as politically radical as Marx, made great efforts to have sociology accepted as an academic discipline. To gain the approval of the authorities, he had to demonstrate not only the subject's scientific credentials, but also its objectivity, especially in light of the political unrest that had existed in Europe for more than a century following the French Revolution. This somewhat "ivory tower" approach, divorced from the real world, dominated sociology for the first part of the 20th century, but as sociologists gradually adopted

> ❝
> The function of sociology, as of every science, is to reveal that which is hidden.
> **Pierre Bourdieu**
> ❞

a more interpretive stance, they also advocated sociology as a tool of social reform.

This was particularly noticeable among sociologists with a Marxian perspective and others with a left-wing political agenda. After World War II, sociologists, including Charles Wright Mills and Michel Foucault, examined the nature of power in society and its effects on the individual; the ways in which society shapes our lives, rather than the way we shape society, and how we can resist these forces. Even in more mainstream sociology, the mood was changing, and the scope of the subject broadened from the academic study of society as it is, to include practical applications informing public policy and driving social change. In 1972, Howard Becker, a respected US sociological theorist, wrote: "Good sociology... produces meaningful descriptions of organizations and events, valid explanations of how they come about and persist, and realistic proposals for their improvement or removal."

Institutions and individuals

As a reflection of the increased emphasis on the relevance of sociology, the subject gained greater acceptance, and even

popular interest, in the second half of the 20th century, and as more thinkers turned their attention to social issues, so the scope of sociology broadened. Evolving from the traditional study of the structures and systems of modern society, and the forces of social cohesion and causes of social disorder, it began to examine the connections between these areas and the interactions of individuals and social groups.

A century or so ago sociologists were divided into those who approached the subject on a macro level (looking at society as a whole and the institutions that it is constituted of), and those who approached it on the micro level – focusing on the individual's experience of living within a society. While this distinction still exists to an extent, sociologists now recognize that the two are closely connected and many concentrate their work on groups that fall between these two approaches – social classes; ethnic, religious, or cultural groups; families; or groups that are defined by gender or sexual orientation.

Sociology has also responded to the accelerating pace of change. Since World War II, many social conventions have been challenged, and new social norms have taken their place. In the Western world the civil rights and women's movements have done much to address racial and gender inequalities, and sociological theories have also helped change attitudes to sexuality and family life. Here, as Zygmunt Bauman advises, "The task for sociology is to come to the help of the individual. We have to be in service of freedom."

The global age

Technological innovations have arguably brought about social changes comparable to – or more far-reaching than – those wrought by the Industrial Revolution. Increased automation and computerization, the rise of the service industries, and the growth of consumer society have all contributed to the shape of society many of us live in today. While some sociologists see this as a continuation of the process of modernity, others believe we are now entering a postmodern, post-industrial age.

Advances in communication and mobility have also made the world a smaller place. Sociologists have recently turned their attention to the importance of cultural and national identity and to the effects of globalization, especially on local communities. With new forms of communication – particularly the Internet and fast international travel – have come entirely new social networks. These do not depend on face-to-face contact, but bring together individuals and groups in ways that were unimaginable even 50 years ago. Modern technology has also provided sociology with a sophisticated means of researching and analysing the evolution of these new social structures. ∎

> The real political task in a society such as ours is to criticize the workings of institutions that appear to be... both neutral and independent... to criticize and attack them... so that one can fight against them.
> **Michel Foucault**

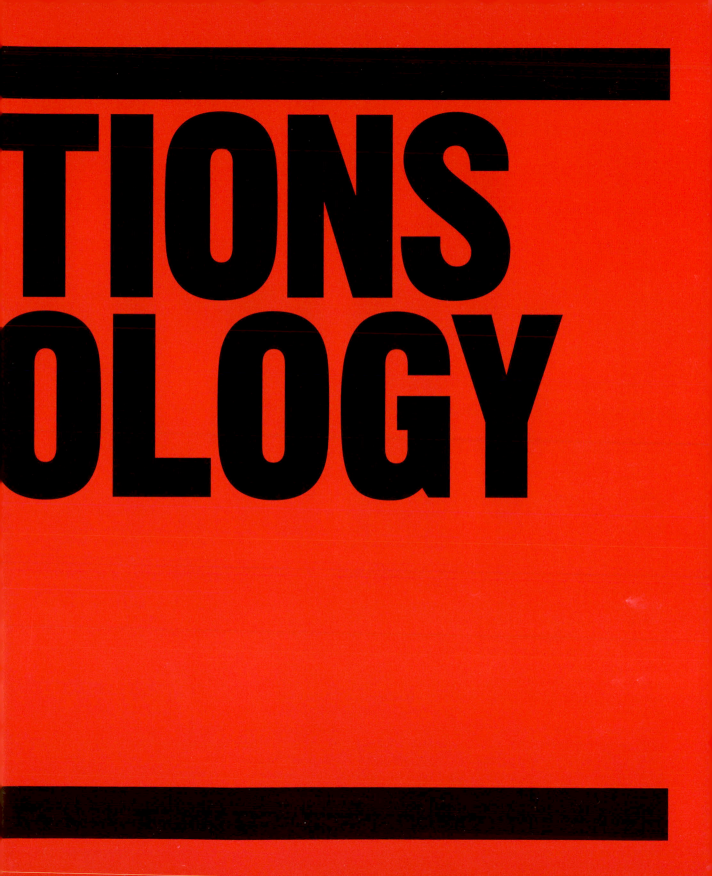

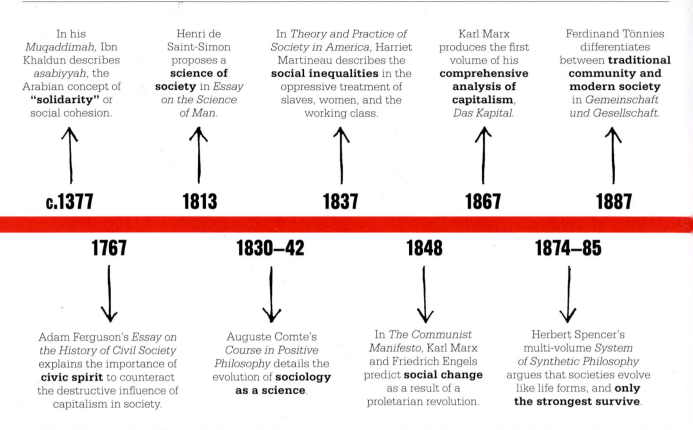

In his *Muqaddimah*, Ibn Khaldun describes *asabiyyah*, the Arabian concept of **"solidarity"** or social cohesion.

Henri de Saint-Simon proposes a **science of society** in *Essay on the Science of Man*.

In *Theory and Practice of Society in America*, Harriet Martineau describes the **social inequalities** in the oppressive treatment of slaves, women, and the working class.

Karl Marx produces the first volume of his **comprehensive analysis of capitalism**, *Das Kapital*.

Ferdinand Tönnies differentiates between **traditional community and modern society** in *Gemeinschaft und Gesellschaft*.

c.1377   **1813**   **1837**   **1867**   **1887**

1767   **1830–42**   **1848**   **1874–85**

Adam Ferguson's *Essay on the History of Civil Society* explains the importance of **civic spirit** to counteract the destructive influence of capitalism in society.

Auguste Comte's *Course in Positive Philosophy* details the evolution of **sociology as a science**.

In *The Communist Manifesto*, Karl Marx and Friedrich Engels predict **social change** as a result of a proletarian revolution.

Herbert Spencer's multi-volume *System of Synthetic Philosophy* argues that societies evolve like life forms, and **only the strongest survive**.

Sociology did not establish its credentials as a discipline until the 20th century, but its many strands of thought, approaches, and fields of study had evolved from centuries of work by historians and philosophers.

Although the first recognizably sociological study was made by Ibn Khaldun in the 14th century, the pioneers of sociology as we know it today only began to emerge from the late 18th century, when society underwent a sea-change in Western Europe: Enlightenment ideas were replacing traditional beliefs, and the Industrial Revolution was transforming the way that people lived and worked. These observers identified social change being driven by forces that became known as "modernity", which included the effects of industrialization and the growth of capitalism, and the less tangible (but no less significant) effects of secularization and rationality.

A social science

Modern society was the product of the Age of Reason: the application of rational thought and scientific discoveries. In keeping with this mood, the pioneers of sociology, such as French philosopher Henri de Saint-Simon and his protégé Auguste Comte, sought to provide verifiable evidence to support theories. Comte believed that not only could the forces of social order be explained by rules similar to the laws of physics and chemistry, but that applied sociology could bring about social reform in the same way as applied sciences had led to technological advances.

Like Comte, Karl Marx believed that the purpose of studying society is not simply to describe or explain it, but also to improve it. He was just as keen to be scientific, but chose as his model the new science of economics, identifying capitalism as the major factor of modernity driving social change.

Almost a century before Marx, the Scottish philosopher Adam Ferguson had warned of the threat to traditional social cohesion posed by the self-interest of capitalism, and both Harriet Martineau and Marx's colleague Friedrich Engels described the social injustices of industrialized capitalist society in the mid-19th century. Another pioneer sociologist, Ferdinand Tönnies, echoed Ferguson's ideas with his description of two very different forms of social cohesion

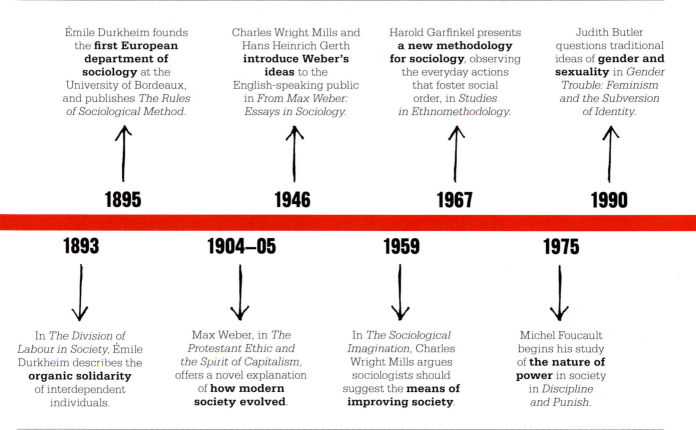

Émile Durkheim founds the **first European department of sociology** at the University of Bordeaux, and publishes *The Rules of Sociological Method*.

Charles Wright Mills and Hans Heinrich Gerth **introduce Weber's ideas** to the English-speaking public in *From Max Weber: Essays in Sociology*.

Harold Garfinkel presents **a new methodology for sociology**, observing the everyday actions that foster social order, in *Studies in Ethnomethodology*.

Judith Butler questions traditional ideas of **gender and sexuality** in *Gender Trouble: Feminism and the Subversion of Identity*.

1895   **1946**   **1967**   **1990**

1893   **1904–05**   **1959**   **1975**

In *The Division of Labour in Society*, Émile Durkheim describes the **organic solidarity** of interdependent individuals.

Max Weber, in *The Protestant Ethic and the Spirit of Capitalism*, offers a novel explanation of **how modern society evolved**.

In *The Sociological Imagination*, Charles Wright Mills argues sociologists should suggest the **means of improving society**.

Michel Foucault begins his study of **the nature of power** in society in *Discipline and Punish*.

in traditional and modern societies – a concept variously interpreted by many subsequent sociologists.

Towards the end of the 19th century, sociology proved itself as a field of study distinct from history, philosophy, politics, and economics, largely thanks to Émile Durkheim. Adopting Comte's idea of applying scientific methodology to the study of society, he took biology as his model. Like Herbert Spencer before him, Durkheim saw society as an "organism" with different "organs", each with a particular function.

An interpretive approach

While Durkheim's objective rigour won him academic acceptance, not all sociologists agreed that it was possible to examine social issues with scientific methods, nor that there are "laws" of society to be

discovered. Max Weber advocated a more subjective – "interpretive" – approach. Whereas Marx named capitalism, and Durkheim industrialization, as the major force of modernity, Weber's focus was on the effects on individuals of rationalization and secularization.

A strictly scientific discipline was gradually supplanted by a sociology that was a study of qualitative ideas: immeasurable notions such as culture, identity, and power. By the mid-20th century sociologists had shifted from a macro view of society to the micro view of individual experience. Charles Wright Mills urged sociologists to make the connection between the institutions of society (especially what he called the "power elite") and how they affect the lives of ordinary people.

After World War II, others took a similar stance: Harold Garfinkel advocated a complete change of sociological methods, to examine social order through the everyday actions of ordinary people; while Michel Foucault analysed the way power relations force individuals to conform to social norms, especially sexual norms – an idea taken further in Judith Butler's study of gender and sexuality.

By the end of the century, a balance had been found between the objective study of society as a whole and the interpretive study of individual experience. The agenda had been set by a handful of ground-breaking sociologists, and their various methods are now being applied to the study of society in an increasingly globalized late-modern world. ∎

A PHYSICAL DEFEAT HAS NEVER MARKED THE END OF A NATION

IBN KHALDUN (1332–1406)

IN CONTEXT

FOCUS
Solidarity

KEY DATES
c.622 The first Islamic state is established in Medina.

c.1377 Ibn Khaldun completes *Muqaddimah* (or *Prolegomena*), the introduction to his history of the world.

1835 Volume 1 of Alexis de Tocqueville's *Democracy in America* describes how the association of individuals for mutual purpose benefits political and civil society.

1887 Ferdinand Tönnies writes *Gemeinschaft und Gesellschaft* (*Community and Society*).

1995 Robert Putnam explains the concept of social capital in his article "Bowling Alone", expanded into a book in 2000.

1996 Michel Maffesoli's *Du Nomadisme* continues his study of neo-tribalism.

The group dynamics of how some societies come to flourish and take over others fascinated Ibn Khaldun, the Arab philosopher and historian. He is best known for his ambitious multi-volume history of the world, the *Kitab al-'Ibar*, especially the first part called the *Muqaddimah*. The *Kitab* is seen as a precursor of sociology because of its analyses of Berber and Arabic societies.

Central to Ibn Khaldun's explanation of the success of a society is the Arabic concept of *asabiyyah*, or social solidarity. Originally, *asabiyyah* referred to the family bonds found in clans and nomadic tribes, but as civilizations grew it came to mean a sense of belonging, usually translated today as "solidarity". According to Ibn Khaldun, *asabiyyah* exists in societies as small as clans, and as large as empires, but the sense of a shared purpose and destiny wanes as a society grows and ages, and the civilization weakens. Ultimately, such a civilization will be taken over by a smaller or younger one with a stronger sense of solidarity: a nation may experience – but will never be brought down by – a physical defeat but when it "becomes the victim of a psychological defeat... that marks the end of a nation".

This concept of the importance of solidarity and social cohesion in society anticipated many ideas of community and civic spirit in modern sociology, including Robert Putnam's theory that contemporary society is suffering from a collapse of participation in the community. ∎

The desert Bedouin tribes were cited by Ibn Khaldun in his theory of group dynamics, in which social and psychological factors contribute to the rise and fall of civilizations.

See also: Ferdinand Tönnies 32–33 ▪ Robert D Putnam 124–25 ▪ Arjun Appadurai 166–69 ▪ David Held 170–71 ▪ Michel Maffesoli 291

MANKIND HAVE ALWAYS WANDERED OR SETTLED, AGREED OR QUARRELLED, IN TROOPS AND COMPANIES
ADAM FERGUSON (1723–1816)

IN CONTEXT

FOCUS
Civic spirit

KEY DATES
1748 Montesquieu publishes
The Spirit of the Laws, arguing
that political institutions
should derive from the social
mores of a community.

1767 Adam Ferguson outlines
his views in his book *Essay
on the History of Civil Society*.

1776 With *The Wealth of
Nations*, Adam Smith pioneers
modern economics.

1867 Karl Marx analyses
capitalism in the first volume
of *Das Kapital*.

1893 Émile Durkheim
examines the importance of
beliefs and values in holding
society together in *The
Division of Labour in Society*.

1993 Amitai Etzioni founds
The Communitarian Network
to strengthen the moral and
social foundations of society.

Progress is both inevitable
and desirable, but we must
always be aware of the
social costs that might be exacted
as progress is made. Such was
the warning of the philosopher
and historian Adam Ferguson,
who was one of the "Select Society"
of Edinburgh intellectuals of the
Scottish Enlightenment, a group
that included the philosopher David
Hume and economist Adam Smith.

Ferguson believed, as did
Smith, that commercial growth is
driven by self-interest, but unlike
Smith he analysed the effects of
this development and felt it was
happening at the expense of
traditional values of cooperation
and "fellow-feeling". In the past,
societies had been based on
families or communities, and
community spirit was fostered
by ideas of honour and loyalty.
But the self-interest demanded by
capitalism weakens these values,
and ultimately leads to social
collapse. To prevent commercial
capitalism from sowing the seeds
of its own destruction, Ferguson

Man is born in civil society...
and there he remains.
Montesquieu
French philosopher (1689–1755)

advocated promoting a sense of
civic spirit, encouraging people
to act in the interest of society
rather than in self-interest.

Ferguson's criticism of
capitalism and commercialism
meant that his theories were
rejected by mainstream thinkers
such as Hume and Smith, but they
later influenced the political ideas
of Hegel and Marx. And because
he viewed the subject from a social
rather than political or economic
angle, his work helped to lay the
foundations of modern sociology. ■

See also: Ferdinand Tönnies 32–33 ▪ Karl Marx 28–31 ▪ Émile Durkheim 34–37 ▪
Amitai Etzioni 112–19 ▪ Norbert Elias 180–81 ▪ Max Weber 220–23

SCIENCE CAN BE USED TO BUILD A BETTER WORLD

AUGUSTE COMTE (1798–1857)

IN CONTEXT

FOCUS
Positivism and the study of society

KEY DATES
1813 French theorist Henri de Saint-Simon suggests the idea of a science of society.

1840s Karl Marx argues that economic issues are at the root of historical change.

1853 Harriet Martineau's abridged translation *The Positive Philosophy of Auguste Comte* introduces Comte's ideas to a wider public.

1865 British philosopher John Stuart Mill refers to Comte's early sociological and later political ideas as "good Comte" and "bad Comte".

1895 In *The Rules of Sociological Method*, Émile Durkheim seeks to establish a systematic sociology.

By the end of the 18th century, increased industrialization had brought about radical changes to traditional society in Europe. At the same time, France was struggling to establish a new social order in the aftermath of the French Revolution. Some thinkers, such as Adam Smith, had sought to explain the rapidly changing face of society in economic terms; others, such as Jean-Jacques Rousseau, did so in terms of political philosophy. Adam Ferguson had described the social effects of modernization, but no one had yet offered an explanation of social progress to match the political and economic theories.

See also: Harriet Martineau 26–27 ▪ Karl Marx 28–31; 254–59 ▪
Ferdinand Tönnies 32–33 ▪ Émile Durkheim 34–37 ▪ Max Weber 38–45; 220–23

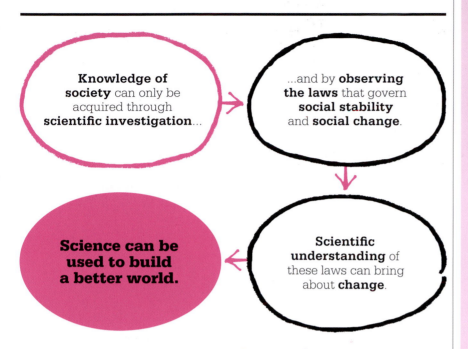

Knowledge of **society** can only be acquired through **scientific investigation**…

…and by **observing the laws** that govern **social stability** and **social change**.

Science can be used to build a better world.

Scientific understanding of these laws can bring about **change**.

Auguste Comte

Auguste Comte was born in Montpellier, France. His parents were Catholics and monarchists, but Auguste rejected religion and adopted republicanism. In 1817 he became an assistant to Henri de Saint-Simon, who greatly influenced his ideas of a scientific study of society. After disagreements, Comte left Saint-Simon in 1824, and began his *Course in Positive Philosophy*, supported by John Stuart Mill, among others.

Comte suffered during this time from mental disorders, and his marriage to Caroline Massin ended in divorce. He then fell madly in love with Clotilde de Vaux (who was separated from her husband), but their relationship was unconsummated; she died in 1846. Comte then devoted himself to writing and establishing a positivist "Religion of Humanity". He died in Paris in 1857.

Key works

1830–42 *Course in Positive Philosophy* (six volumes)
1848 *A General View of Positivism*
1851–54 *System of Positive Polity* (four volumes)

Against the background of social uncertainty in France, however, the socialist philosopher Henri de Saint-Simon attempted to analyse the causes of social change, and how social order can be achieved. He suggested that there is a pattern to social progress, and that society goes through a number of different stages. But it was his protégé Auguste Comte who developed this idea into a comprehensive approach to the study of society on scientific principles, which he initially called "social physics" but later described as "sociology".

Understand and transform

Comte was a child of the Enlightenment, and his thinking was rooted in the ideals of the Age of Reason, with its rational, objective focus. The emergence of scientific method during the Enlightenment influenced Comte's approach to philosophy. He made a detailed analysis of the natural sciences and their methodology, then proposed that all branches of knowledge should adopt scientific principles and base theory on observation. The central argument of Comte's "positivism" philosophy is that valid knowledge of anything can only be derived from positive, scientific enquiry. He had seen the power of science to transform: scientific discoveries had provided the technological advances that brought about the Industrial Revolution and created the modern world he lived in.

The time had come, he said, for a social science that would not only give us an understanding of the mechanisms of social order and social change, but also provide us with the means of transforming society, in the same way that the physical sciences had helped to modify our physical environment. »

He considered the study of human society, or sociology, to be the most challenging and complex, therefore it was the "Queen of sciences".

Comte's argument that the scientific study of society was the culmination of progress in our quest for knowledge was influenced by an idea proposed by Henri de Saint-Simon and is set out as the "law of three stages". This states that our understanding of phenomena passes through three phases: a theological stage, in which a god or gods are cited as the cause of things; a metaphysical stage, in which explanation is in terms of abstract entities; and a positive stage, in which knowledge is verified by scientific methods.

Comte's grand theory of social evolution became an analysis of social progress too – an alternative to the merely descriptive accounts of societal stages of hunter-gatherer, nomadic, agricultural, and industrial-commercial. Society in France, Comte suggested, was rooted in the theological stage until the Enlightenment, and social order was based on rules that were ultimately religious. Following the revolution in 1789, French society entered a metaphysical stage, becoming ordered according to

Comte identified three stages of progress in human understanding of the world. The theological stage came to an end with the Enlightenment at the end of the 18th century. Focus then shifted from the divine to the human in a metaphysical stage of rational thought, from which evolved a final stage in which science provides the explanations.

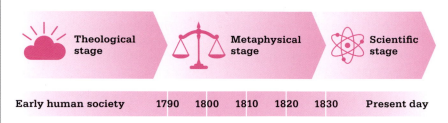

Theological stage	Metaphysical stage	Scientific stage

| Early human society | 1790 | 1800 | 1810 | 1820 | 1830 | Present day |

secular principles and ideals, especially the rights to liberty and equality. Comte believed that, recognizing the shortcomings of post-revolutionary society, it now had the possibility of entering the positive stage, in which social order could be determined scientifically.

A science of society

Comte proposed a framework for the new science of sociology, based on the existing "hard" sciences. He organized a hierarchy of sciences, arranged logically so that each science contributes to those following it but not to those preceding it. Beginning with mathematics, the hierarchy ranged through astronomy, physics, and chemistry, to biology. The apex of this ascending order of "positivity" was sociology. For this reason, Comte felt it was necessary to have a thorough grasp of the other sciences and their methods before attempting to apply these to the study of society.

Paramount was the principle of verifiability from observation: theories supported by the evidence of facts. But Comte also recognized that it is necessary to have a hypothesis to guide the direction of scientific enquiry, and to determine the scope of observation. He

divided sociology into two broad fields of study: "social statics", the forces that determine social order and hold societies together; and "social dynamics", the forces that determine social change. A scientific understanding of these forces provides the tools to take society into its ultimate, positive, stage of social evolution.

Although Comte was not the first to attempt an analysis of human society, he was a pioneer in establishing that it is capable of being studied scientifically. In addition, his positivist philosophy offered both an explanation of secular industrial society and the means of achieving social reform. He believed that just as the

Sociology is, then, not an auxiliary of any other science; it is itself a distinct and autonomous science.
Émile Durkheim

From science comes prediction; from prediction comes action.
Auguste Comte

sciences have solved real-world problems, sociology – as the final science and unifier of the other sciences – can be applied to social problems to create a better society.

From theory to practice

Comte formed his ideas during the chaos that followed the French Revolution, and set them out in his six-volume *Course in Positive Philosophy*, the first volume of which appeared in the same year that France experienced a second revolution in July 1830.

After the overthrow and restoration of monarchy, opinion in France was divided between those who wanted order and those who demanded progress. Comte believed his positivism offered a third way, a rational rather than ideological course of action based on an objective study of society.

His theories gained him as many critics as admirers among his contemporaries in France. Some of his greatest supporters were in Britain, including liberal intellectual John Stuart Mill, who provided him with financial support to enable him to continue with his project, and Harriet Martineau, who translated an edited version of his work into English.

Unfortunately, the reputation Comte had built up was tarnished by his later work, in which he described how positivism could be applied in a political system. An unhappy personal life (a marriage break-up, depression, and a tragic affair) is often cited as causing a change in his thinking: from an objective scientific approach that

The 1830 revolution in France coincided with the publication of Comte's book on positivism and seemed to usher in an age of social progress that he had been hoping for.

examines society to a subjective and quasi-religious exposition of how it should be.

The shift in Comte's work from theory to how it could be put into practice lost him many followers. Mill and other British thinkers saw his prescriptive application of positivism as almost dictatorial, and the system of government he advocated as infringing liberty.

By this time, an alternative approach to the scientific study of society had emerged. Against the same backdrop of social turmoil, Karl Marx offered an analysis of social progress based on the science of economics, and a model for change based on political action rather than rationalism. It is not difficult to see why, in a Europe riven by revolutions, Comte's positivist sociology became eclipsed by the competing claims of socialism and capitalism. Nevertheless, it was Comte, and to a lesser extent his mentor Saint-Simon, who first proposed the idea of sociology as a discipline based on scientific principles rather than

> The philosophers have only interpreted the world... the point is to change it.
> **Karl Marx**

mere theorizing. In particular he established a methodology of observation and theory for the social sciences that was taken directly from the physical sciences. While later sociologists, notably Émile Durkheim, disagreed with the detail of his positivism, and his application of it, Comte provided them with a solid foundation to work from. Although today Comte's dream of sociology as the "Queen of sciences" may seem naive, the objectivity he advocated remains a guiding principle. ■

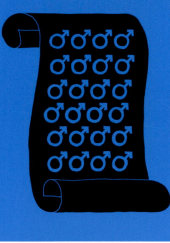

THE DECLARATION OF INDEPENDENCE BEARS NO RELATION TO HALF THE HUMAN RACE
HARRIET MARTINEAU (1802–1876)

IN CONTEXT

FOCUS
Feminism and social injustice

KEY DATES

1791 French playwright and political activist Olympe de Gouges publishes the *Declaration of the Rights of Woman and the Female Citizen* in response to the Declaration of the Rights of Man and of the Citizen of 1789.

1807–34 Slavery is abolished in the British Empire.

1869 Harriet Taylor and John Stuart Mill co-author the essay "The Subjection of Women".

1949 Simone de Beauvoir's *The Second Sex* lays the foundations for "second-wave" feminism of the 1960s–1980s.

1981 The United Nations Convention on the Elimination of All Forms of Discrimination Against Women (CEDAW) is ratified by 188 states.

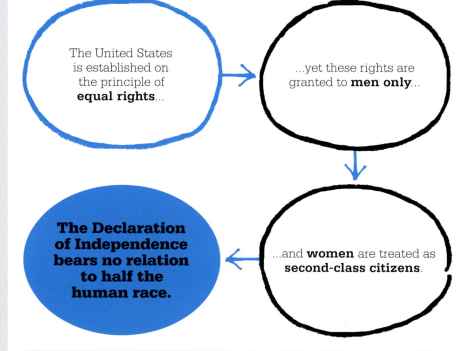

The United States is established on the principle of **equal rights**...

...yet these rights are granted to **men only**...

...and **women** are treated as **second-class citizens**.

The Declaration of Independence bears no relation to half the human race.

In 1776, the US Declaration of Independence proclaimed: "We hold these truths to be self-evident, that all men are created equal, that they are endowed by their Creator with certain unalienable Rights, that among these are Life, Liberty and the pursuit of Happiness." More than 50 years later, between 1834 and 1836, Harriet Martineau travelled around the USA and recorded a very different picture of US society. What she saw was a marked discrepancy between the ideals of equality and democracy, and the reality of life in the USA.

Before her visit, Martineau had made her name as a journalist writing on political economy and

See also: Judith Butler 56–61 ▪ R W Connell 88–89 ▪ Sylvia Walby 96–99 ▪
Teri Caraway 248–49 ▪ Christine Delphy 312–17 ▪ Ann Oakley 318–19

social issues, so on her travels she set down in book form her impressions of US society. Her *Theory and Practice of Society in America* went beyond mere description, however, for it analysed the forms of social injustice she came across there.

Social emancipator

For Martineau, the degree to which a society can be thought of as civilized is judged by the conditions in which its people live. Theoretical ideals are no measure of how civilized a society is if they do not apply to everybody. The supposed ideals of US society, notably the cherished notion of freedom, were "made a mockery" by the continued practice of slavery, which Martineau identified as the prime example of one section of society having domination over another.

Throughout her life, Martineau campaigned for an end to slavery in the USA, but she also applied her principles of what constitutes a civilized society to identify and oppose other forms of exploitation and social oppression, such as the unjust treatment of the working class in industrial Britain and the subjugation of women in the Western world.

Martineau highlighted the hypocrisy of a society that prided itself on liberty, yet continued to oppress women. This treatment was a particular affront because, as she pointed out, women were half the human race: "If a test of civilization be sought, none can be so sure as the condition of that half of society over which the other half has power." Unlike many of her contemporaries, however, Martineau did not merely campaign for women's rights to education or the vote, but described the ways in which society restricted women's liberty in both domestic and public life.

Martineau was well known in her lifetime, but her contribution to the development of sociology was not recognized until recently. Today, however, she is regarded as not only the first woman to make a methodical study of society, but also the first to formulate a feminist sociological perspective. ∎

The Continental Congress adopted its highly moral plan for government on 4 July 1776. But Martineau questioned whether social virtues were possible in a society characterized by injustice.

Harriet Martineau

Harriet Martineau was born in Norwich, England, the daughter of progressive parents who ensured she had a good education. She showed an early interest in politics and economics, and after the death of her father in 1825 made a living as a journalist. Her success as a writer enabled her to move to London, and in 1834–36 to travel around the USA. On her return to England, she published a three-volume sociological critique of the USA. Her experiences there confirmed her commitment to campaigning for the abolition of slavery and for the emancipation of women.

Although profoundly deaf since her teenage years, Martineau continued working and campaigning until the 1860s. She had by this time moved to the Lake District, where, housebound by ill health, she died in 1876.

Key works

1832–34 *Illustrations of Political Economy*
1837 *Theory and Practice of Society in America*
1837–38 *How to Observe Morals and Manners*

THE FALL OF THE BOURGEOISIE AND THE VICTORY OF THE PROLETARIAT ARE EQUALLY INEVITABLE

KARL MARX (1818–1883)

IN CONTEXT

FOCUS
Class conflict

KEY DATES
1755 Genevan philosopher Jean-Jacques Rousseau identifies private property as the source of all inequality.

1819 French social theorist Henri de Saint-Simon launches the magazine *L'Organisateur* to promote his socialist ideas.

1807 Georg Hegel interprets historical progress in *The Phenomenology of Spirit*.

1845 In *The Condition of the Working Class in England in 1844*, Friedrich Engels describes the division of capitalist society into two social classes.

1923 The Institute for Social Research is founded and attracts Marxist scholars to the University of Frankfurt.

I n the mid-19th century, Europe was characterized by political instability that had begun with the French Revolution. The insurrectionary spirit spread across the continent, and there were attempts to overthrow and replace the old order of monarchies and aristocracy with democratic republics. At the same time, much of Europe was still coming to terms with the changes in society created by industrialization. Some philosophers had explained the problems of the modern industrial world in political terms, and offered political solutions, and others such as Adam Smith looked to economics as both the cause of the

See also: Auguste Comte 22–25 ▪ Max Weber 38–45 ▪ Michel Foucault 52–55 ▪ Friedrich Engels 66–67 ▪ Richard Sennett 84–87 ▪ Herbert Marcuse 182–87 ▪ Robert Blauner 232–33 ▪ Christine Delphy 312–17

problems and the answer to them, but there had been little research into the social structure of society.

Between 1830 and 1842, the French philosopher Auguste Comte had suggested that it was possible, and even necessary, to make a scientific study of society. Karl Marx agreed that an objective, methodical approach was overdue and was among the first to tackle the subject. Marx did not set out, however, to make a specifically sociological study, but rather to explain modern society in historical and economic terms, using observation and analysis to identify the causes of social inequality. And where Comte saw science as the means of achieving social change, Marx pointed to the inevitability of political action.

Historical progress

In Marx's time, the conventional explanation of the development of society was of an evolution in stages, from hunting and gathering, through nomadic, pastoral, and agricultural communities to modern commercial society. As a philosopher, Marx was well aware of this idea of social progress and the economic origins of industrial society, but developed his own interpretation of this process.

His primary influence was the German philosopher Georg Hegel, who had proposed a dialectic view of history: that change comes about through a synthesis of opposing forces in which the tension between contradictory ideas is resolved. Marx, however, viewed history as the progression of material circumstances rather than ideas, and took from Hegel the dialectical framework, while

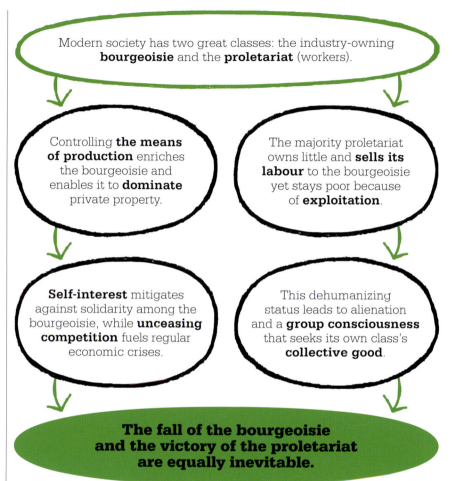

Modern society has two great classes: the industry-owning **bourgeoisie** and the **proletariat** (workers).

Controlling **the means of production** enriches the bourgeoisie and enables it to **dominate** private property.

The majority proletariat owns little and **sells its labour** to the bourgeoisie yet stays poor because of **exploitation**.

Self-interest mitigates against solidarity among the bourgeoisie, while **unceasing competition** fuels regular economic crises.

This dehumanizing status leads to alienation and a **group consciousness** that seeks its own class's **collective good**.

The fall of the bourgeoisie and the victory of the proletariat are equally inevitable.

dismissing much of his philosophy. He was also influenced by French socialist thinkers, such as Jean-Jacques Rousseau, who laid the blame for inequality in civil society on the emergence of the notion of private property.

Marx offered a new approach to the study of historical progress. It is the material conditions in which people live that determine the organization of society, he said, and changes in the means of production (the tools and machinery used to create wealth) bring about socio-

economic change. "Historical materialism", as this approach to historical development came to be known, provided an explanation for the transition from feudal to modern capitalist society, brought about by new methods of economic production. Under feudalism, the nobles had controlled the means of agricultural production, as owners of the land that the peasants or serfs worked. With the machine age a new class, the bourgeoisie, emerged as owners of a new means of production. As technology »

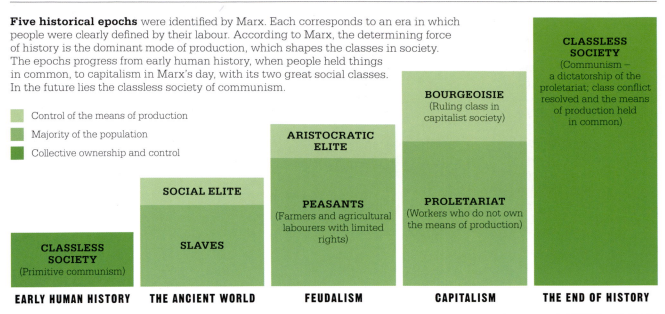

Five historical epochs were identified by Marx. Each corresponds to an era in which people were clearly defined by their labour. According to Marx, the determining force of history is the dominant mode of production, which shapes the classes in society. The epochs progress from early human history, when people held things in common, to capitalism in Marx's day, with its two great social classes. In the future lies the classless society of communism.

- Control of the means of production
- Majority of the population
- Collective ownership and control

CLASSLESS SOCIETY
(Primitive communism)

EARLY HUMAN HISTORY

SOCIAL ELITE

SLAVES

THE ANCIENT WORLD

ARISTOCRATIC ELITE

PEASANTS
(Farmers and agricultural labourers with limited rights)

FEUDALISM

BOURGEOISIE
(Ruling class in capitalist society)

PROLETARIAT
(Workers who do not own the means of production)

CAPITALISM

CLASSLESS SOCIETY
(Communism – a dictatorship of the proletariat; class conflict resolved and the means of production held in common)

THE END OF HISTORY

became more prevalent, the bourgeoisie challenged the nobles and brought about a change to the economic structure of society. The opposing elements of feudal society contained the seeds of the capitalist society that replaced it.

Karl Marx's prediction of a communist revolution became a reality in 1917 – it did not, however, take place in an advanced industrial nation as he had anticipated, but in Tsarist Russia.

Marx maintained that, as he and Friedrich Engels put it in *The Communist Manifesto*, "the history of all hitherto existing society is the history of class struggles". Whereas feudalism had been characterized by the two classes of nobles or aristocracy and peasants or serfs, modern industrial society had created a bourgeoisie class of capitalists, which owned the means of production, and a proletariat class, which worked in the new industries.

Class conflict

Tension and conflict between the classes in society was inevitable, according to Marx. Therefore, just as feudalism had been replaced, so too would capitalist society and the dominant bourgeoisie. He believed that the proletariat would one day control society, having overthrown the system that had brought it into existence.

It is the method of production of material necessities, Marx argued, that determines the social structure of capitalist society: the

classes of capital and labour. Capitalists obtain their wealth from the surplus value of goods produced, in the factories they own, by the labour of the workers. The proletariat, on the other hand, own almost nothing, and in order to survive have to sell their labour to the bourgeoisie.

The relationship between the classes is exploitative, enriching the owners of capital and keeping the working class poor. In addition, the unskilled nature of the work in factories and mills contributes to a feeling of dehumanization, and alienation from the process of production, which is aggravated by the threat of unemployment when production exceeds demand.

Over time, however, oppression fosters a class-consciousness in the proletariat – a realization that together the working class can organize a movement for its collective good. The inherent self-interest of capitalism tends to prevent such a development among the bourgeoisie, and constant competition leads to more and more frequent economic crises. The increasing solidarity of the working class, and weakening of the bourgeoisie, will in time allow the proletariat to take over control of the means of production and bring about a classless society.

A key contribution

Marx's analysis of how capitalism had created socio-economic classes in the industrial world was based on more than mere theorizing, and as such was one of the first "scientific" studies of society, offering a comprehensive economic, political, and social explanation of modern society. In the process, he introduced several concepts that became central to later sociological thinking, particularly in the area of social class, such as class conflict and consciousness, and the notions of exploitation and alienation.

His ideas inspired numerous revolutionaries, and at one stage in the 20th century around a third of the world's population lived under a government espousing Marxist principles. But not everyone agreed with the Marxian division of society into classes defined by their economic status, nor the idea that social change is the inevitable result of class conflict. In the generation following Marx, both Émile Durkheim and Max Weber, who along with Marx are often cited as the "founding fathers" of modern sociology, offered alternative views in reaction to his.

Durkheim acknowledged that industry had shaped modern society, but argued that it was industrialization itself, rather than capitalism, that was at the root of social problems.

Weber, on the other hand, accepted Marx's argument that there are economic reasons behind class conflict, but felt that Marx's division of society into bourgeoisie and proletariat on purely economic grounds was too simple. He believed that there were cultural and religious as well as economic causes for the growth of capitalism, and these were reflected in classes based on prestige and power as well as economic status.

Although Marx's influence on sociology in the Western world waned during the first half of the 20th century, the members of the so-called "Frankfurt School" of sociologists and philosophers (including Jürgen Habermas, Erich Fromm, and Herbert Marcuse) remained notable adherents to his principles. After World War II, with the advent of the Cold War, opinion became even more divided. In the USA in particular, Marxist theory of any type was largely discredited, while in Europe, especially France, a number of philosophers and sociologists further developed Marx's social ideas.

Today, as new technology is once again transforming our world, and at the same time people are becoming conscious of a growing economic inequality, some of Marx's basic ideas have begun to be revisited by social, economic, and political thinkers. ∎

> 66
> [Marx is] the true father of modern sociology, in so far as anyone can claim the title.
> **Isaiah Berlin**
> **Russo-British philosopher (1909–1997)**
> 99

Karl Marx

Regarded as one of the "founding fathers" of social science, Karl Marx was also an influential economist, political philosopher, and historian. He was born in Trier, Germany, and at his lawyer father's insistence, he studied law, rather than the philosophy and literature he was interested in, at the University of Bonn, and later at Berlin. There he developed his interest in Hegel, and went on to gain a doctorate from the University of Jena in 1841.

After becoming a journalist in Cologne, Marx moved to Paris, where he developed his economic, social, and political theory, collaborating with Friedrich Engels. In 1845 the pair co-wrote *The Communist Manifesto*. Following the failure of the revolutions in Europe in 1848, Marx moved to London. After the death of his wife in 1881, his health deteriorated, and he died two years later, aged 64.

Key works

1848 *The Communist Manifesto*
1859 *A Contribution to the Critique of Political Economy*
1867 *Das Kapital, Volume 1*

GEMEINSCHAFT AND GESELLSCHAFT

FERDINAND TÖNNIES (1855–1936)

IN CONTEXT

FOCUS
Community and society

KEY DATES

1651 English philosopher Thomas Hobbes describes the relationship between man's nature and the structure of society in *Leviathan*.

1848 In *The Communist Manifesto*, Karl Marx and Friedrich Engels set out the effects of capitalism on society.

1893 Sociologist Émile Durkheim outlines the idea of social order maintained by organic and mechanical solidarity in *The Division of Labour in Society*.

1904–05 Max Weber publishes *The Protestant Ethic and the Spirit of Capitalism*.

2000 Zygmunt Bauman introduces the idea of "liquid modernity" in an increasingly globalized society.

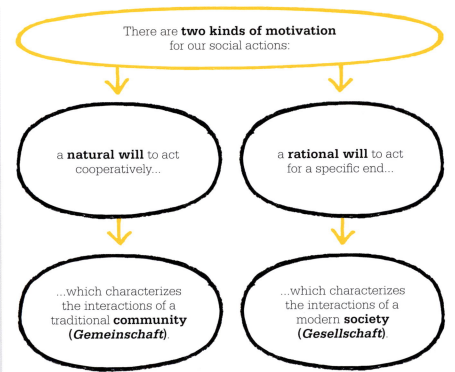

There are **two kinds of motivation** for our social actions:

a **natural will** to act cooperatively...

a **rational will** to act for a specific end...

...which characterizes the interactions of a traditional **community** (*Gemeinschaft*).

...which characterizes the interactions of a modern **society** (*Gesellschaft*).

Towards the end of the 19th century, a number of thinkers turned their attention to the social implications of modernity, and in particular the growth of capitalist industrial society. Among them were Émile Durkheim, Max Weber, and Ferdinand Tönnies, widely regarded as founding fathers of sociology. Tönnies' major contribution to the discipline was his analysis of contrasting types of social groupings in his influential *Gemeinschaft und Gesellschaft*, published in 1887.

See also: Adam Ferguson 21 ▪ Émile Durkheim 34–37 ▪ Max Weber 38–45 ▪ Amitai Etzioni 112–19 ▪
Zygmunt Bauman 136–43 ▪ Karl Marx 254–59 ▪ Bryan Wilson 278–79 ▪ Michel Maffesoli 291

In this book, his magnum opus, Tönnies points out what he sees as the distinction between traditional rural communities and modern industrialized society. The former, he argues, are characterized by *Gemeinschaft*, community, which is based on the bonds of family and social groups such as the church. Small-scale communities tend to have common goals and beliefs, and interactions within them are based on trust and cooperation.

Triumph of "will"

In large-scale societies such as modern cities, the division of labour and mobility of the workforce have eroded traditional bonds. In place of *Gemeinschaft* there is *Gesellschaft*, association or society. Relationships in such societies are more impersonal and superficial, and based on individual self-interest rather than mutual aid.

The two extremes of *Gemeinschaft* and *Gesellschaft* exist to a greater or lesser extent in every social grouping, but Tönnies argued that the ethos of

Gemeinschaft by its very essence is of an earlier origin than its subject or members.
Ferdinand Tönnies

capitalism and competition had led to a predominance of mere association in the industrial society in which he lived.

At the root of Tönnies' theory was his idea of "will" – what motivates people to action. He distinguished between what he called *Wesenwille*, "natural will", and *Kürwille*, "rational will". *Wesenwille*, he said, is the instinctive will to do something for its own sake, or out of habit or custom, or moral obligation. This is the motivation that underlies the

social order of *Gemeinschaft*, the will to do things for and as a part of the community. On the other hand, *Kürwille* motivates us to act in a purely rational way, to achieve a specific goal, and is the type of will behind decisions made in large organizations, and particularly businesses. It is *Kürwille* that characterizes the *Gesellschaft* of capitalist urban society.

Despite his Left-leaning politics, Tönnies was seen as an essentially conservative figure, lamenting modernity's loss of *Gemeinschaft*, rather than advocating social change. Although he had gained the respect of fellow sociologists, his ideas had little influence until many years later. Tönnies' theory, along with his work on methodology, paved the way for 20th-century sociology. Weber further developed Tönnies' notions of will and motivation to social action, and Durkheim's idea of mechanical and organic solidarity echoed the contrast between *Gemeinschaft* and *Gesellschaft*. ∎

Ferdinand Tönnies

Ferdinand Tönnies was born in North Frisia, Schleswig (now Nordfriesland, Schleswig-Holstein, Germany). After studying at the universities of Strassburg, Jena, Bonn, and Leipzig, he was awarded his doctorate at Tübingen in 1877.

In his postdoctoral studies in Berlin and London, Tönnies' interest shifted from philosophy to political and social issues. He became a private tutor at the University of Kiel in 1881, but an inheritance allowed him to focus on his own work. He was also a co-founder of the German

Sociological Society. Because of his outspoken political views, he was not offered a professorship at Kiel until 1913. His Social Democratic sympathies, and a public denunciation of Nazism, led to his removal from the university in 1931, three years before his death, aged 80.

Key works

1887 *Gemeinschaft und Gesellschaft*
1926 *Progress and Social Development*
1931 *Introduction to Sociology*

SOCIETY, LIKE THE HUMAN BODY, HAS INTERRELATED PARTS, NEEDS, AND FUNCTIONS

ÉMILE DURKHEIM (1858–1917)

IN CONTEXT

FOCUS
Functionalism

KEY DATES
1830–42 Auguste Comte advocates a scientific approach to the study of society in his *Course in Positive Philosophy*.

1874–77 Herbert Spencer says society is an evolving "social organism", in the first volume of *The Principles of Sociology*.

1937 In *The Structure of Social Action*, Talcott Parsons revives the functionalist approach in his action theory.

1949 Robert K Merton develops Durkheim's idea of anomie to examine social dysfunction in *Social Theory and Social Structure*.

1976 Anthony Giddens offers an alternative to structural functionalism in *New Rules of Sociological Method*.

S ociology was only gradually accepted as a distinct discipline, a social science separate from philosophy, in the latter half of the 19th century. The intellectual atmosphere of the time meant that for sociology to be recognized as a field of study, it had to establish scientific credentials.

Among those who had studied philosophy but been drawn to the new branch of knowledge was Émile Durkheim, who believed that sociology should be less of a grand theory and more of a method that could be applied in diverse ways to understanding the development of modern society. Now regarded as one of the principal founders of

See also: Auguste Comte 22–25 ▪ Karl Marx 28–31 ▪ Max Weber 38–45 ▪
Jeffrey Alexander 204–09 ▪ Robert K Merton 262–63 ▪ Herbert Spencer 334

Humankind has evolved from gathering in small, **homogeneous communities** to forming large, **complex societies**.

⬇

In traditional society, religion and culture created a **collective consciousness** that provided **solidarity**.

⬇

In modern society, the **division of labour** has brought about increased **specialization** and the focus is more on the **individual** than the **collective**...

⬇

...and **solidarity** now comes from the **interdependence** of individuals with **specialized functions**.

⬇

Society, like the human body, has interrelated parts, needs, and functions.

Émile Durkheim

Born in Épinal in eastern France, Émile Durkheim broke with family tradition and left rabbinical school to follow a secular career. He studied at the École Normale Supérieure in Paris, graduating in philosophy in 1882, but was already interested in social science after reading Auguste Comte and Herbert Spencer.

Durkheim moved to Germany to study sociology. In 1887 he returned to France, teaching the country's first sociology courses at the University of Bordeaux, and later founded the first social science journal in France. He was appointed to the Sorbonne in 1902 and stayed there for the rest of his life, becoming a full professor in 1906. He felt increasingly marginalized by the rise of right-wing nationalist politics during World War I, and after his son André was killed in 1916, his health deteriorated and he died of a stroke in 1917.

Key works

1893 *The Division of Labour in Society*
1895 *The Rules of Sociological Method*
1897 *Suicide*

sociology, with Karl Marx and Max Weber, Durkheim was not the first scholar to attempt to establish the subject as a science; the earlier work of other thinkers inevitably influenced his own ideas.

Forging a scientific model

Auguste Comte had laid the foundations with his theory that the study of human society is the pinnacle of a hierarchy of natural sciences. And, because society is a collection of human animals, the idea grew that of all the natural sciences, biology was the closest model for the social sciences. Not everyone agreed: Marx, for example, based his sociological

ideas on the new science of economics rather than biology. But the appearance of Charles Darwin's theory of the origin of species provoked a radical rethink of many conventionally held ideas. This was especially true in Britain, where Darwin's work provided a model of organic evolution that could be applied to many other disciplines.

Among those inspired by Darwin was Herbert Spencer, a philosopher and biologist who likened the development of modern society to an evolving organism, with different parts serving different functions. His writing established the idea of an "organic" model for the social sciences. »

Durkheim argued that religions, especially long-established faiths such as Judaism, are fundamentally social institutions that give people a strong sense of collective consciousness.

Durkheim upheld Spencer's functional idea of separate parts serving a purpose and the notion that society was greater than the sum of its individual elements. And Auguste Comte's "positivism" (his belief that only scientific enquiry yields true knowledge) helped to shape the scientific methodology that Durkheim felt would reveal how modern society functions.

Durkheim focused on society as a whole, and its institutions, rather than the motivations and actions of individuals within society; above all, he was interested in the things that hold society together and maintain social order. He argued that the basis for sociological study should be what he called "social facts", or "realities external to the individual" that can be verified empirically.

Like the other pioneering sociologists, Durkheim tried to understand and explain the factors

> Is it our duty to seek to become a... complete human being, one quite sufficient unto himself; or... to be only a part of a whole, the organ of an organism?
> **Émile Durkheim**

that had shaped modern society, the various forces known as "modernity". But where Marx had associated them with capitalism, and Weber with rationalization, Durkheim connected the development of modern society with industrialization, and in particular the division of labour that came with it.

A functional organism

What differentiates modern society from traditional ones, according to Durkheim, is a fundamental change in the form of social cohesion; the advent of industrialization has evolved a new form of solidarity. Durkheim outlined his theory of the different types of social solidarity in his doctoral thesis, "The Division of Social Labour".

In primitive societies, such as hunter-gatherer groups, individuals do much the same jobs, and although each could be self-sufficient, society is held together by a sense of a common purpose and experience, and commonly held beliefs and values. The similarity of individuals in such

a society fosters what Durkheim called "collective consciousness", which is the basis of its solidarity.

But as societies grew in size and complexity people began to develop more specialized skills, replacing self-reliance with interdependence. The farmer, for example, relies on the blacksmith to shoe his horses, while the blacksmith relies on the farmer to provide his food. The mechanical solidarity, as Durkheim refers to it, of traditional society becomes replaced by an organic solidarity based not on the similarity of its individual members, but their complementary differences.

This division of labour reaches its peak with industrialization, when society has evolved to become a complex "organism" in which individual elements perform specialized functions, each of which is essential to the wellbeing of the whole. The idea that society is structured like a biological organism composed of distinct parts with specialized functions became a significant approach to sociology, known as functionalism.

The "social fact" – by which he meant a thing that exists without being subject to any individual will upon it – that Durkheim identifies as driving this evolution from mechanical to organic solidarity is the increase in "dynamic density", or population growth and concentration. The competition for resources becomes more intense, but with the increased population density comes the possibility of greater social interaction within the population itself, triggering a division of labour to more efficiently deal with its demands.

In modern society, the organic interdependence of individuals is the basis for social cohesion. But Durkheim realized that the division of labour that came with rapid industrialization also brought social problems. Precisely because it is built on the complementary differences between people, organic solidarity shifts the focus from the community to the individual, replacing the collective consciousness of a society – the shared beliefs and values that provide cohesiveness. Without that framework of norms of behaviour

A beehive is created by the division of labour of industrious insects. As well as producing a functioning whole, the bees maintain a symbiotic relationship with the flora of their environment.

people become disoriented and society unstable. Organic solidarity can only work if elements of mechanical solidarity are retained, and members of society have a sense of common purpose.

The speed of industrialization, according to Durkheim, had forced a division of labour so quickly on modern society that social interaction had not developed sufficiently to become a substitute for the decreasing collective consciousness. Individuals felt increasingly unconnected with society, and especially the sort of moral guidance that mechanical solidarity had previously given them. Durkheim used the word anomie to describe this loss of collective standards and values, and its consequent sapping of individual morale. In a study of patterns of suicide in different areas, he showed the importance of anomie in the despair that leads someone to take their own life. In communities where collective beliefs were strong, such as among Catholics, the suicide rate was lower than elsewhere, which confirmed for Durkheim the value of solidarity to the health of a society.

An academic discipline

Durkheim based his ideas on thorough research of empirical evidence, such as case studies and statistics. His major legacy was the establishment of sociology as an academic discipline, in the tradition of the positivist doctrine of Comte – that social science is subject to the same investigative methods as the natural sciences.

Durkheim's positivist approach was met with scepticism, however. Sociological thinkers from Marx onwards rejected the idea that something as complex and unpredictable as human society is

> Society is not a mere sum of individuals. Rather, the system formed by their association represents a specific reality which has its own characteristics.
> **Émile Durkheim**

consistent with scientific research. Durkheim also went against the intellectual mood of the time by looking at society as a whole rather than at the experience of the individual, which was the basis of the approach adopted by Max Weber. His concept of "social facts" with a reality of their own, separate from the individual, was dismissed, and his objective approach was also criticized for explaining the basis of social order but not making any suggestions to change it.

But Durkheim's analysis of society as composed of different but interrelated parts, each with its own particular function, helped to establish functionalism as an important approach to sociology, influencing among others Talcott Parsons and Robert K Merton.

Durkheim's explanations of solidarity were an alternative to the theories of Marx and Weber, but the heyday of functionalism lasted only until the 1960s. Although Durkheim's positivism has since fallen out of favour, concepts introduced by him, such as anomie and collective consciousness (in the guise of "culture"), continue to figure in contemporary sociology. ∎

THE IRON CAGE OF RATIONALITY

MAX WEBER (1864–1920)

Modern industrial society brought **technological and economic advances**.

But this was accompanied by **increased rationalization** and a **bureaucratic structure**...

...that imposed **new controls, restricted individual freedoms,** and **eroded community and kinship ties**.

Bureaucratic efficiency has stifled traditional interactions, trapping us in an "iron cage of rationality".

U ntil the latter half of the 19th century, the economic growth of the German states was based on trade rather than production. But when they made the shift to large-scale manufacturing industry, of the sort that had urbanized Britain and France, the change was rapid and dramatic. This was especially noticeable in Prussia, where the combination of natural resources and a tradition of military organization helped to establish an efficient industrial society in a very short time.

Germany's unfamiliarity with the effects of modernity meant it had not yet developed a tradition of sociological thought. Karl Marx was German by birth, but he based his sociological and economic ideas on his experiences of industrialized society elsewhere. However, towards the end of the century, a number of German thinkers turned their attention to the study of Germany's emergent modern society. Among them was Max Weber, who was to become perhaps the most influential of the "founding fathers" of sociology.

Weber was not concerned with establishing sociology as a discipline in the same way as Auguste Comte and Émile Durkheim in France, who sought universal "scientific laws" for society (in the belief, known as "positivism", that science could build a better world).

While Weber accepted that any study of society should be rigorous, he argued that it could not be truly objective, because it is the study not so much of social behaviour but of social action, meaning the ways in which individuals in society

See also: Auguste Comte 22–25 ▪ Émile Durkheim 34–37 ▪ Charles Wright Mills 46–49 ▪ Georg Simmel 104–05 ▪ George Ritzer 120–23 ▪ Max Weber 220–23 ▪ Karl Marx 254–59 ▪ Jürgen Habermas 286–87 ▪ Talcott Parsons 300–01

interact. This action is necessarily subjective, and needs to be interpreted by focusing on the subjective values that individuals associate with their actions.

This interpretive approach, also called *verstehen* ("understanding"), was almost the antithesis of the objective study of society. Whereas Durkheim's approach examined the structure of society as a whole, and the "organic" nature of its many interdependent parts, Weber sought to study the experience of the individual.

Weber was heavily influenced by Marx's theories, especially the idea that modern capitalist society is depersonalizing and alienating. He disagreed, however, with Marx's materialist approach and its emphasis on economics rather than culture and ideas, and with Marx's belief in the inevitability of proletarian revolution. Instead,

Weber synthesized ideas from both Marx and Durkheim to develop his own distinctive sociological analysis, examining the effects of what he saw as the most pervasive aspect of modernity: rationalization.

An "iron cage"

In arguably his best-known work, *The Protestant Ethic and the Spirit of Capitalism* (1904–05), Weber describes the evolution of the West from a society governed by tribal custom or religious obligations to an increasingly secular organization based on the goal of economic gain.

Industrialization had been achieved through advances in science and engineering, and the capitalism that accompanied it called for purely rational decisions based on efficiency and cost-benefit analysis (assessing the benefits and costs of projects). While the rise

The fate of our times is characterized... above all... by the disenchantment of the world.
Max Weber

of capitalism had brought many material benefits, it also had numerous social drawbacks; traditional cultural and spiritual values had been supplanted by rationalization, which brought with it a sense of what Weber called "disenchantment" as the »

The 1936 film *Modern Times* depicts actor Charlie Chaplin as an assembly-line worker subject to the dehumanizing effects of modernity and rationalization.

...the world could one day be filled with nothing but those little cogs, little men clinging to little jobs and striving toward bigger ones.
Max Weber

intangible, mystical side of many people's day-to-day lives was replaced by cold calculation.

Weber recognized the positive changes brought about by increased knowledge, and the prosperity that resulted from logical decision-making rather than the dictates of outdated religious authorities. But rationalization was also changing the administration of society by increasing the level of bureaucracy in all kinds of organizations. Having been brought up in Prussia, where well-established military efficiency became the model for the newly industrialized state, this development would have been especially noticeable to Weber.

Bureaucracy, Weber believed, was both inevitable and necessary in modern industrial society. Its machine-like effectiveness and efficiency is what enables society to prosper economically, which meant its growth in scope and power was apparently unstoppable. However, whereas the eclipse of religion meant that people were liberated from irrational social norms, a bureaucratic structure imposed a new form of control and threatened to stifle the very individualism that had led people to reject dogmatic religious authority. Many members of modern society now felt trapped by the rigid rules of bureaucracy, as if in an "iron cage" of rationalization. Moreover, bureaucracies tend to produce hierarchical organizations that are impersonal, and with standardized procedures that overrule individualism.

Dehumanization

Weber was concerned with these effects on the individual "cogs in the machine". Capitalism, which had promised a technological utopia with the individual at its heart, had instead created a society dominated by work and money,

> The fully developed bureaucratic apparatus compares with other organizations exactly as does the machine with the non-mechanical modes of production.
> **Max Weber**

overseen by an uncompromising bureaucracy. A rigid, rule-based society not only tends to restrict the individual, but also has a dehumanizing effect, making people feel as though they are at the mercy of a logical but godless system. The power and authority of a rational bureaucracy also affects the relationships and interactions of individuals – their social actions. These actions are no longer based on ties of family or community, nor traditional values and beliefs, but are geared towards efficiency and the achievement of specific goals.

Because the primary goal of rationalization is to get things done efficiently, the desires of the individual are subservient to the goals of the organization, leading to a loss of individual autonomy. Although there is a greater degree of interdependence between people as jobs become more and more specialized, individuals feel that

The German Chancellery in Berlin is the headquarters of the German government. The civil servants who work there are a bureaucracy tasked with implementing government policy.

their worth in society is determined by others rather than by their own skills or craftsmanship. The desire for self-improvement is replaced with an obsessive ambition to acquire a better job, more money, or a higher social status, and creativity is valued less than productivity.

In Weber's view, this disenchantment is the price modern society pays for the material gains achieved by bureaucratic rationalization. The social changes it causes are profound, affecting not only our system of morality but also our psychological and cultural makeup. The erosion of spiritual values means our social actions are instead based on calculations of cost and benefit, and become a matter more of administration than moral or social guidance.

Social actions and class

While Weber often despaired of the soulless side of modern society, he was not completely pessimistic. Bureaucracies may be difficult to destroy, but because they are created by society he believed they can also be changed by society. Where Marx had predicted that the

> ...what can we oppose to this machinery... to keep a portion of mankind free from this... supreme mastery of the bureaucratic way of life.
> **Max Weber**

Increased bureaucracy is, says Weber, a product of rationalization, providing society with a machine-like organization that promotes efficiency. However, to work within an administrative apparatus can lead to individual disenchantment: with little scope for personal initiative and creativity, a bureaucrat can feel their lot is one of monotonous and repetitive paperwork.

exploitation and alienation of the proletariat by capitalism would inevitably lead to revolution, Weber felt communism led to even greater bureaucratic control than capitalism. Instead, he advocated that within a liberal democracy, bureaucracy should only have as much authority as members of society are prepared to allow it. This is, he said, determined by the social actions of individuals as they try to improve their lives and their "life chances" (or opportunities).

Just as society had progressed from the "charismatic" authority of kinship ties and religion, through the patriarchal authority of feudal society, to the modern authority of rationalization and bureaucracy, so too individual behaviour had evolved from emotional, traditional, and value-based social actions to "instrumental action" – action

based on the assessment of costs and consequences, which Weber considered the culmination of rational conduct. In addition, he identified three elements of social stratification in which these social actions could be taken, affecting different aspects of a person's "life chances". As well as the economically determined social class, there is also status class based on less tangible attributes such as honour and prestige, and party class based on political affiliations. Together these help the individual to establish a distinct position in society.

A gradual acceptance

Weber's innovative perspective formed the foundation of one of the major approaches to sociology in the 20th century. By introducing the idea of a subjective, interpretive » examination of individuals' social actions, he offered an alternative to Durkheim's positivism by pointing out that the methodology of the natural sciences is not appropriate to the study of the social sciences, and to Marx's materialist determinism by stressing the importance of ideas and culture over economic considerations.

Although Weber's ideas were highly influential among his contemporaries in Germany, such as Werner Sombart and Georg Simmel, they were not widely accepted. He was regarded in his lifetime as a historian and economist rather than a sociologist, and it was not until much later that his work received the attention it deserved. Many of his works were only published posthumously, and few were translated until well after his death. Sociologists at the beginning of the 20th century felt antipathy towards Weber's approach because they were anxious to establish the

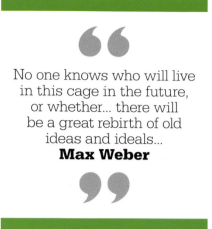

> No one knows who will live in this cage in the future, or whether... there will be a great rebirth of old ideas and ideals...
> **Max Weber**

credentials of sociology as a science; his notion of subjective *verstehen* and his examination of individual experience rather than of society as a whole was seen as lacking the necessary rigour and objectivity. And some critics, especially those steeped in the ideas of Marxian economic determinism, disputed Weber's account of the evolution of Western capitalism.

Nevertheless, Weber's ideas gradually became accepted, as the influence of Durkheim's positivism began to wane. Weber was, for example, an influence on the critical theory of the Frankfurt School, centred around Goethe University in Frankfurt, Germany. These thinkers held that traditional Marxist theory could not fully account for the path taken by Western capitalist societies, and so sought to draw on Weber's anti-positivist sociological approach and analysis of rationalization. Escaping the rise of Nazism, members of the Frankfurt School took these ideas to the USA, where Weber's insights were enthusiastically received, and where his influence was strongest in the period following World War II. In particular, American sociologist Talcott Parsons

attempted to reconcile Weber's ideas with the then dominant positivist tradition in sociology established by Durkheim, and to incorporate them into his own theories. Parsons also did much to popularize Weber and his ideas within US sociology, but it was Charles Wright Mills who, with Hans Heinrich Gerth, brought the most important of Weber's writings to the attention of the English-speaking world with their translation and commentary in 1946. Wright Mills was especially influenced by Weber's theory of the "iron cage" of rationality, and developed this theme in his own analysis of social structures, in which he showed that Weber's ideas had more significant implications than had previously been thought.

The rational gone global

By the 1960s, Weber had become mainstream, and his interpretive approach had all but replaced the positivism that had dominated sociology since Durkheim. In the last decades of the 20th century, Weber's emphasis on the social actions of individuals, and their relationship to the power exerted by a rationalized modern society, provided a framework for contemporary sociology.

More recently, sociologists such as British theorist Anthony Giddens have focused on the contrast between Durkheim's approach to society as a whole, and Weber's concentration on the individual as the unit of study. Giddens points out that neither approach is completely right or wrong, but instead exemplifies one of two different perspectives – the macro and micro. Another aspect of Weber's work – that of culture and ideas shaping our social structures

Franz Kafka, a contemporary of Weber, wrote stories depicting a dystopian bureaucracy. His work engages with Weberian themes such as dehumanization and anonymity.

The conditions within semiconductor fabrication plants, where workers wear masks and "bunny suits", are a visible symptom of rationalization and the stifling of human interactions.

more than economic conditions – has been adopted by a British school of thought that has given rise to the field of cultural studies.

Weber and Marx

In many ways, Weber's analysis proved more prescient than Marx's. Despite his dismissal of Marx's interpretation of the inevitability of historical change, Weber predicted the endurance, and global triumph, of the capitalist economy over traditional models as a result of rationalization. He also foresaw that a modern technological society would rely upon an efficient bureaucracy, and that any problems would not be of structure but management and competence: too rigid a bureaucracy would paradoxically decrease rather than increase efficiency.

More significantly, Weber realized that materialism and rationalization created a soulless "iron cage", and if unchecked would lead to tyranny. Where Marx had a vision of workers' emancipation and the establishment of a utopian communist state, Weber argued that in modern industrial society everybody's lives – those of both owners and workers – are shaped by the ongoing conflict between impersonal, organizational efficiency and individual needs and desires. And in recent decades, this has proved to be the case, as economic "rational calculation" has led to the eclipse of high-street sole traders by supermarkets and shopping malls, and the export of manufacturing and clerical jobs from the West to lower-wage economies worldwide. The hopes and desires of individuals have, in many cases, been contained by the iron cage of rationalization. ∎

Max Weber

Max Weber is one of the founding fathers of sociology, along with Karl Marx and Émile Durkheim. Born in Erfurt into a German middle-class intellectual family, Weber received his doctorate in 1888 and held professorial posts at the universities of Berlin, Freiburg, and Heidelberg. His knowledge of economics, history, politics, religion, and philosophy serve as the terrain out of which so much sociological thinking in these areas has developed and grown.

Although Weber's professional legacy remains outstanding, his personal life was a troubled one, and in 1897 he had a breakdown following the death of his father. In spite of his untimely death in 1920, at the age of 56, Weber's account of the role of religion in the rise of capitalism remains a sociological classic.

Key works

1904–1905 *The Protestant Ethic and the Spirit of Capitalism*
1919–1920 *General Economic History*
1921–1922 *Economy and Society: An Outline of Interpretive Sociology*

MANY PERSONAL TROUBLES MUST BE UNDERSTOOD IN TERMS OF PUBLIC ISSUES

CHARLES WRIGHT MILLS (1916–1962)

IN CONTEXT

FOCUS
The sociological imagination

KEY DATES
1848 In *The Communist Manifesto*, Karl Marx and Friedrich Engels describe progress in terms of class struggles, and depict capitalist society as a conflict between the bourgeoisie and proletariat.

1899 In *The Theory of the Leisure Class*, Thorstein Veblen suggests that the business class pursues profit at the expense of progress or social welfare.

1904–05 Max Weber describes a society stratified by class, status, and power in *The Protestant Ethic and the Spirit of Capitalism*.

1975 Michel Foucault looks at power and resistance in *Discipline and Punish*.

During the Cold War that developed after World War II, very few US sociologists openly adopted a socialist standpoint, particularly during the anti-communist witch-hunt that was known as McCarthyism. Yet Charles Wright Mills went against the grain; his most influential books criticized the military and commercial power elites of his time.

Wright Mills risked not only falling foul of the authorities during this "Red Scare" era of the 1940s and 1950s, but also rejection by mainstream sociologists. However, he was no apologist for Marxist ideology and instead presented a

See also: Karl Marx 28–31 ▪ Max Weber 38–45 ▪ Michel Foucault 52–55 ▪ Friedrich Engels 66–67 ▪ Richard Sennett 84–87 ▪ Herbert Marcuse 182–87 ▪ Thorstein Veblen 214–19

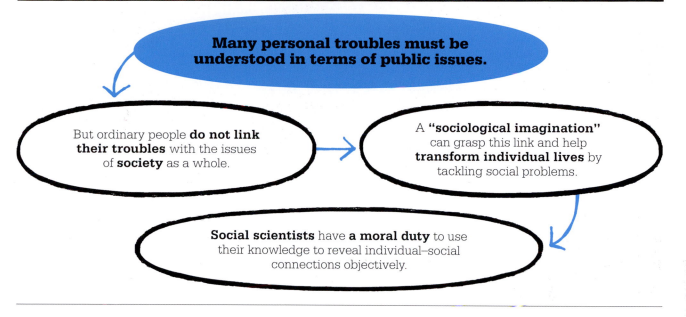

Many personal troubles must be understood in terms of public issues.

But ordinary people **do not link their troubles** with the issues of **society** as a whole.

A **"sociological imagination"** can grasp this link and help **transform individual lives** by tackling social problems.

Social scientists have **a moral duty** to use their knowledge to reveal individual–social connections objectively.

critique of the effects of modernity, pointing out what he saw as the complacency among his fellow intellectuals that had allowed the oppression of "mass society".

Wright Mills' maverick stance belied the firm foundations on which it was based. He had been a brilliant and uncompromising student of sociology, and especially admired the work of Max Weber, whose idea of rationalization inspired the central theme of his own social thinking.

Dehumanized society

For Weber, modern society was replacing traditional customs and values with rational decision-making in a dehumanizing process that affected not only the culture but also the structure of society. He noted that rational social organization is not necessarily based on reason, or for the welfare of all. Weber also provided Wright Mills with a more sophisticated notion of class than the simple

economic model proposed by Marx, introducing the elements of status and power as well as wealth.

With a thorough understanding of Weber's theories, and the belief that they were more radical than had been thought previously, Wright Mills set about applying them to his own analysis of the effects of rationalization in mid-20th century Western society.

He focused his attention first on the working class in the USA, criticizing organized labour for collaborating with capitalists and thus allowing them to continue to oppress the workforce. But his was not a Marxist attack on capitalism; he felt Marxism failed to address the social and cultural issues associated with the dominance of commercial industry.

Next, he examined the most obvious product of rationalization: the bureaucratic middle classes. He maintained that by the mid-20th century the US middle classes, alienated from the processes of

production, had become divorced from traditional values, such as pride in craftsmanship, and dehumanized by ever-increasing rationalization. In his view, they were now "cheerful robots" – finding pleasure in material things, but intellectually, politically, and socially apathetic – without any control over their circumstances.

The failure of the working class, and the inability of the middle class, to take control allowed »

Let every man be his own methodologist, let every man be his own theorist.
Charles Wright Mills

The collapse of the auto industry in Detroit, USA, brought ruin to the city, but many workers did not link their poverty to the actions of a power elite, which included union leaders.

society to be shaped by what Wright Mills called a power elite. This, he emphasized, was not necessarily an economic elite, but one that included military, political, and union leaders too. Whereas Weber had argued half a century earlier that rationalization meant that the business elite made the decisions, Wright Mills said that a new military–industrial ruling class had been created. He believed that this was a turning point marking the transition from the modern age to what he called a "Fourth Epoch". Rationalization, which had been assumed to produce freedom and social progress, was increasingly having the opposite effect.

This was not just a problem for liberal democracies, which now faced the prospect of being powerless to control social change, but also for the communist states in which Marxism had proved equally unable to provide a means of taking control. At the heart of the

Neither the life of an individual nor the history of a society can be understood without understanding both.
Charles Wright Mills

problem, according to Wright Mills, is the fact that ordinary people in "mass society" are unaware of the way in which their lives are affected by this concentration of political and social power. They go about their lives without realizing how the things that happen to them are connected to the wider social context. Each individual's troubles, such as becoming unemployed, or ending up homeless or in debt, are perceived as personal and not in terms of forces of historical change. As Wright Mills puts it, "They do not possess the quality of mind essential to grasp the interplay of men and society, of biography and history, of self and world" – the quality that he calls "the sociological imagination".

It was the lack of sociological imagination that was to blame for the emergence of the power elite. In *The Sociological Imagination*, published in 1959, Wright Mills turns his sights from society to sociology and the social sciences themselves. Because it is difficult for the ordinary person to think of their personal troubles

in terms of larger public issues, it is up to sociologists to enlighten, inspire, and instruct them – to provide essential knowledge and information.

What ought to be?
Wright Mills was highly critical of academic sociology of the time, which was, in his opinion, remote from everyday experience; more concerned with providing "grand theory" than becoming involved in social change. Wright Mills took the pragmatic view that knowledge should be useful, and felt that it was the moral duty of sociologists to take the lead. It was time, he said, for intellectuals to leave their ivory towers and provide people with the means of changing society for the better, and transforming their individual lives, by encouraging public engagement in political and social issues.

His attack on the social science establishment called into question the very notion of what sociology was about. At that time, social scientists were striving to be neutral observers, objectively describing and analysing social, political, and economic systems. But Wright Mills was calling for them to address the ways in which rationalization and the shift of social control to an elite were affecting people on an individual level too. The adoption of a sociological imagination implied a move from the objective study of "what is" to a more subjective answer to the question of "what ought to be?" He advocated that power should effectively be transferred to an intellectual elite.

A pioneering spirit

Unsurprisingly, Wright Mills' criticism of sociology was met with hostility and he became isolated from the mainstream. His interpretation of the changing nature of the class struggle was also largely dismissed. The conservative establishment also shunned him, rejecting his claims of a concentration of power in the military, business, and political elite, which was seen as a direct attack on the basis of Cold War policy in the West.

Nevertheless, the books and articles of Wright Mills were widely read, and became influential

Unemployment can lead to people blaming themselves for their situation. But a sociological imagination would, says Wright Mills, prompt such people to look to wider causes and effects.

outside the social science establishment. The philosophers and political activists who emerged from the period of McCarthyism were particularly attracted to his description of a power elite. Many of his ideas were adopted by the social movements of the US New Left (a term that Wright Mills popularized in his "Letter to the New Left" in 1960), which in turn paved the way for sociologists such as the German scholar Herbert Marcuse to adopt a New Leftist approach in the 1960s.

Wright Mills' ideas were, in many ways, ahead of their time, and his untimely death in 1962 meant that he did not live to see many of them gain general acceptance. His work foreshadowed the emergence of new socialist thinkers, especially in France, with the counterculture of the 1960s. Michel Foucault's emphasis on the notion of power bears a particularly strong resemblance to ideas that were first raised by Wright Mills.

Today, the so-called War on Terror, in the aftermath of the 9/11 attacks on the USA, and the disastrous financial crises of the early 21st century, have led to a growing realization that much of our everyday lives are shaped by wider social and historical issues. US urban policy analyst Professor Peter Dreier claimed in 2012 that Wright Mills would have loved the Occupy Wall Street movement against social and economic inequality. This example of ordinary people objecting to a power elite that they claim is controlling society and affecting their lives is the sociological imagination being exhibited in a campaign for social change. ∎

Charles Wright Mills

Fiercely independent and critical of authority, Charles Wright Mills attributed his unconventional attitudes to an isolated and sometimes lonely childhood because his family moved around frequently. He was born in Waco, Texas, USA, and initially studied at Texas A&M University, but found the atmosphere there stifling and left after his first year. He transferred to the University of Texas in Austin, graduated in sociology and gained a master's

degree in philosophy. An obviously talented, but difficult, student, he went on to study at the University of Wisconsin, where he fell out with his professors and refused to make revisions to his doctoral thesis. He was, however, eventually awarded his PhD in 1942. By this time, he had taken up a post at the University of Maryland, and with one of his doctoral supervisors, Hans Gerth, wrote *From Max Weber: Essays in Sociology.*

In 1945 Wright Mills moved, on a Guggenheim fellowship, to Columbia University, where he

spent the rest of his career. Although his outspoken criticism of the social science establishment saw him pushed out of the mainstream, he gained much popular attention. His career ended abruptly when he died of heart disease in 1962, aged only 45.

Key works

1948 *The New Men of Power: America's Labor Leaders*
1956 *The Power Elite*
1959 *The Sociological Imagination*

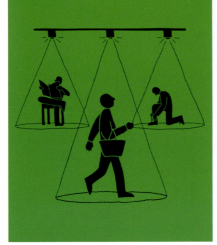

PAY TO THE MOST COMMONPLACE ACTIVITIES THE ATTENTION ACCORDED EXTRAORDINARY EVENTS
HAROLD GARFINKEL (1917–2011)

IN CONTEXT

FOCUS
Ethnomethodology

KEY DATES
1895 Émile Durkheim advocates a strict scientific methodology for the social sciences in *The Rules of Sociological Method*.

1921–22 Max Weber's methodological individualism is explained in *Economy and Society*, published posthumously.

1937 Talcott Parsons attempts to form a single, unified social theory in *The Structure of Social Action*.

1967 Harold Garfinkel publishes *Studies in Ethnomethodology*.

1976 Anthony Giddens incorporates ideas of Garfinkel's ethnomethodology into mainstream sociology in his book *New Rules of Sociological Method*.

The structure of society is not determined **"top down"** by a limited set of general rules.

⬇

Instead, the rules are built **"bottom up"**, from our small exchanges and interactions.

⬇

These rules can be seen in our **spontaneous behaviour** in everyday life, rather than in social structures and institutions.

⬇

Pay to the most commonplace activities the attention accorded extraordinary events.

In the 1930s, the US sociologist Talcott Parsons embarked upon a project of bringing together the various strands of sociology in a single, unified theory. His 1937 book *The Structure of Social Action* combined ideas from Max Weber, Émile Durkheim, and others, and attempted to present a universal methodology for sociology. In the years after World War II, Parsons' ideas gained him a significant number of supporters.

Among his admirers was Harold Garfinkel, who studied under Parsons at Harvard. While many of the followers were attracted by the idea of a "grand theory" of sociology, Garfinkel picked up on Parsons' idea of examining the roots of social order, rather than social change, and in particular his methods of researching the subject.

The workings of society
Parsons had suggested a "bottom up" rather than "top down" approach to analysing the foundations of social order. This meant that to understand how social order is achieved in society, we should look at micro interactions and exchanges rather than at social structures and institutions.

See also: Émile Durkheim 34–37 ▪ Max Weber 38–45 ▪ Anthony Giddens 148–49 ▪ Erving Goffman 190–95; 264–69 ▪ Talcott Parsons 300–01

This approach turned traditional sociological methodology on its head: until then, it had been thought that people's behaviour could be predicted by finding the underlying "rules" of society.

Garfinkel took the idea further, developing what amounted to an alternative to the conventional sociological approach, which he called ethnomethodology. The underlying rules of social order are built from the ways that people behave in reaction to different situations, and it is by observing everyday interactions that we can gain an insight into the mechanisms of social order.

New perspectives

One category of experimental methods Garfinkel advocated became known as "breaching experiments". These were designed to uncover social norms – the expected, but largely unnoticed, ways people construct a shared sense of reality. Breaching these norms – for example by asking his students to address their parents

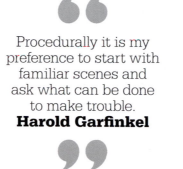

> Procedurally it is my preference to start with familiar scenes and ask what can be done to make trouble.
> **Harold Garfinkel**

formally as "Mr X" or "Mrs X" or to act as though they were lodgers – often provoked exasperation or anger, as the foundations of the social order were challenged.

Ethnomethodology not only offered an alternative method of social research, but also indicated a flaw in conventional methodology. According to Garfinkel, social researchers support their theories with evidence from specific examples, but at the same time

they use the theories to explain the examples – a circular argument. Instead, they should examine particular social interactions independently, and not set out to find an overall pattern or theory. He referred to jury deliberation and queueing as "familiar scenes" that we simply know how to organize intelligibly in recognizable ways. Any social setting, he argued, can "be viewed as self-organizing with respect to the intelligible character of its own appearances as either representations of or as evidences of a social order".

Garfinkel's approach was set out in *Studies in Ethnomethodology* in 1967. In an age when "alternative" ideas were popular, Garfinkel attracted a large following, despite his impenetrable writing style. His ideas were initially dismissed by mainstream sociologists, but by the end of the 20th century had become more generally accepted, perhaps not as an alternative to sociological methodology, but offering an additional perspective to the field of social order. ▪

Harold Garfinkel

Born in Newark, New Jersey, USA, Harold Garfinkel studied business and accounting at the University of Newark, then later took an MA at the University of North Carolina. At the same time, he began his writing career, and one of his short stories, "Color Trouble", was included in the anthology *The Best Short Stories, 1941*.

After noncombatant service in the army during World War II, he studied under Talcott Parsons at Harvard, where he

gained his PhD. He then taught at Princeton and Ohio State universities, before settling in 1954 at the University of California. Garfinkel retired in 1987, but continued to teach as an emeritus professor until his death in 2011.

Key works

1967 *Studies in Ethnomethodology*
2002 *Ethnomethodology's Program*
2008 *Toward a Sociological Theory of Information*

An orderly queue is a collectively negotiated, member-produced form of organization that is based on the unspoken rules of social interaction in a public space.

WHERE THERE IS POWER THERE IS RESISTANCE

MICHEL FOUCAULT (1926–1984)

IN CONTEXT

FOCUS
Power/resistance

KEY DATES
1848 Karl Marx and Friedrich Engels describe the oppression of the proletariat by the bourgeoisie in their book *The Communist Manifesto*.

1883 Friedrich Nietzsche introduces the concept of the "Will to Power" in *Thus Spoke Zarathustra*.

1997 Judith Butler's *Excitable Speech: A Politics of the Performative* develops Foucault's idea of power/knowledge in relation to censorship and hate speech.

2000 In *Empire*, Italian Marxist sociologist Antonio Negri and US scholar Michael Hardt describe the evolution of a "total" imperialist power, against which the only resistance is negation.

The power to maintain social order, or to bring about social change, has conventionally been seen in political or economic terms. Until the 1960s, theories of power usually fell into two types: ideas of the power of government or state over citizens; or the Marxist idea of a power struggle between the bourgeoisie and the proletariat. However, these theories tended to concentrate on power at the macro level, either ignoring the exercise of power at lower levels of social relations, or seeing it as a consequence of the primary exercise of power (or only of secondary importance).

See also: Karl Marx 28–31 ▪ Max Weber 38–45 ▪ Charles Wright Mills 46–49 ▪ Herbert Marcuse 182–87 ▪ Erich Fromm 188 ▪ Jürgen Habermas 286–87

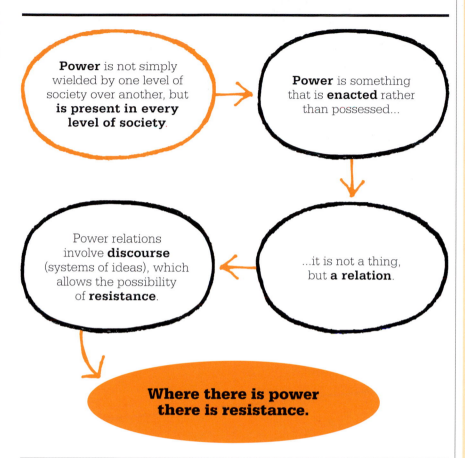

Power is not simply wielded by one level of society over another, but **is present in every level of society**.

Power is something that is **enacted** rather than possessed...

...it is not a thing, but **a relation**.

Power relations involve **discourse** (systems of ideas), which allows the possibility of **resistance**.

Where there is power there is resistance.

Michel Foucault

A brilliant polymath, influential in the fields of philosophy, psychology, politics, and literary criticism as well as sociology, Michel Foucault was often associated with the structuralist and post-structuralist movements in France, but disliked being labelled as such. He was born in Poitiers, France, and studied philosophy and psychology at the École Normale Supérieure in Paris. He taught in Sweden, Poland, and Germany in the 1950s, and received his doctorate in 1959. He lectured in Tunisia from 1966 to 1968 and when he returned to Paris was appointed head of philosophy at the University of Vincennes. Two years later, he was elected to the Collège de France as professor of "the history of systems of thought". He died in 1984, one of the first prominent victims of HIV/AIDS-related illness in France.

Key works

1969 *The Archaeology of Knowledge*
1975 *Discipline and Punish: The Birth of the Prison*
1976–84 *The History of Sexuality* (three volumes)

Michel Foucault, however, thought that in today's Western liberal societies, these approaches are an oversimplification. Power, he said, is not just exercised by the state or capitalists, but can be seen at every level of society, from individuals through groups and organizations to society as a whole. In his words, "power is everywhere, and comes from everywhere". He also disagreed with the traditional view of power as something that can be possessed and wielded, like a weapon. This, he says, is not power, but a capacity to exercise power – it does not become power until some action is taken. Power is therefore not something someone has, but something that is done to others, an action that affects the action of others.

Power relations

Instead of thinking of power as a "thing", Foucault sees it as a "relation", and explains the nature of power through examination of the power relations present at every level of modern society. For example, a power relation exists between a man and the state in which he lives, but at the same time, there are different forms of power relation between him and his employer, his children, the organizations to which he belongs, and so on. »

Foucault acknowledges that power has been, and continues to be, the major force in shaping social order, but describes how the nature of power relations has changed from medieval times to today. What he calls the "sovereign" exercise of power, such as public torture and executions, was the method that authority figures in feudal society used to coerce their subjects into obedience. With the advent of the Enlightenment in Europe, however, violence and force were seen as inhuman and, more importantly, as an ineffective means of exercising power.

Surveillance and control

In place of harsh physical punishment came a more pervasive means of controlling behaviour: discipline. The establishment of institutions such as prisons, asylums, hospitals, and schools characterized the move away from the notion of merely punishing to a disciplinary exercise of power: specifically, acting to prevent people from behaving in certain ways. These institutions not only removed the opportunity for transgression, but provided the conditions in which people's

conduct could be corrected and regulated, and above all monitored and controlled.

This element of surveillance is especially important in the evolution of the way power is exercised in modern society. Foucault was particularly struck by the Panopticon, the efficient prison design inspired by British philosopher Jeremy Bentham, with a watchtower that enabled continual observation of inmates. The cells, Foucault points out, are backlit to prevent inmates from hiding in shadowy recesses. Prisoners can never be certain of when they are under surveillance, so they learn to discipline their behaviour as if they always are. Power is no longer exercised by coercing people to conform, but by establishing mechanisms that ensure their compliance.

Regulating conduct

The mechanisms by which power is exercised, the "technology of power", have since become an integral part of society. In the modern Western world, social norms are imposed not so much by enforcement, as by exercising "pastoral" power, guiding people's

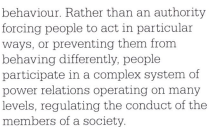

Foucault's *History of Sexuality*... warns us against imagining a complete liberation from power. There can never be a total liberation from power.
Judith Butler

behaviour. Rather than an authority forcing people to act in particular ways, or preventing them from behaving differently, people participate in a complex system of power relations operating on many levels, regulating the conduct of the members of a society.

This pervasive sort of power is determined by the control society has over people's attitudes, beliefs, and practices: the systems of ideas Foucault refers to as "discourse". The belief system of any society evolves as people come to accept certain views, to the point that

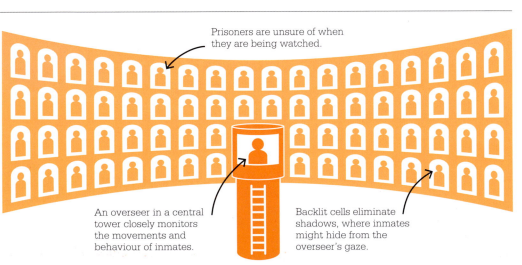

The Panopticon, designed by Bentham, is the supreme eye of power for Foucault. The circular space enables a permanent visibility that guides prison inmates to comply with their own disciplining and control. Foucault argues that not only prisons, but all hierarchical structures (such as hospitals, factories, and schools) have evolved to resemble this model.

Prisoners are unsure of when they are being watched.

An overseer in a central tower closely monitors the movements and behaviour of inmates.

Backlit cells eliminate shadows, where inmates might hide from the overseer's gaze.

A shepherd tending his flock is the analogy Foucault uses to describe "pastoral" power, whereby people are guided to act in certain ways and then allow themselves to be governed.

these views become embedded in that society, defining what is good and bad, and what is considered normal or deviant. Individuals within that society regulate their behaviour according to these norms, largely unaware that it is the discourse that is guiding their conduct, as it makes opposing thoughts and actions unthinkable.

Discursive regimes

Discourse is constantly reinforced, as it is both an instrument and an effect of power: it controls thoughts and conduct, which in turn shape the belief system. And because it defines what is right and wrong, it is a "regime of truth", creating a body of what is considered undeniable common knowledge.

Foucault challenged the idea that "knowledge is power", saying that the two are related more subtly. He coined the term "power–knowledge" for this relationship, noting that knowledge creates power, but is also created by power. Today, power is exercised by controlling what forms of knowledge are acceptable, presenting them as truths, and excluding other forms of knowledge. At the same time, accepted knowledge, the discourse, is actually produced in the process of exercising power.

Unlike the way power had traditionally been used to compel and coerce people to behave in a particular way, this form of power–knowledge has no immediately recognizable agent or structure. And because of its all-pervasive nature, it would appear to have

nothing specific that can be resisted. Indeed, Foucault points out that political resistance, in the form of revolution, may not lead to social change, as it challenges only the power of the state, but not the ubiquitous, everyday way in which power today is exercised.

However, Foucault argues that there is a possibility of resistance: what can be resisted is the discourse itself, which can be challenged by other, opposing discourses. Power that relies on complicity implies at least some degree of freedom of those subject to it. For the discourse to be an instrument of power, those subject to it must be involved in a power relation, and he argues that if there is a power relation, there is also a

possibility of resistance – without resistance, there is no need for the exercise of power.

The deployment of power

Foucault's concepts of power–knowledge and discourse are subtle and at the time were rejected by many scholars as speculative and vague. But his lectures and writings became enormously popular, despite the difficult concepts and his sometimes convoluted prose style. The ideas of power described in *Discipline and Punish* and *The History of Sexuality* gradually gained acceptance by some in the mainstream of sociology (if not among historians and philosophers), and eventually influenced the analysis of how discourse is used in society as an instrument of power in many different arenas.

The development of modern feminism, queer theory, and cultural studies owes much to Foucault's explanation of how norms of behaviour are enforced. Today, opinion is still divided as to whether his theories are the somewhat vague conclusions of poor research and scholarship or whether he should be considered one of the 20th century's most original and wide-ranging thinkers in the social sciences. ■

Discourse transmits and produces power; it reinforces it, but also undermines and exposes it.
Michel Foucault

GENDER IS A KIND OF IMITATION FOR WHICH THERE IS NO ORIGINAL

JUDITH BUTLER (1956–)

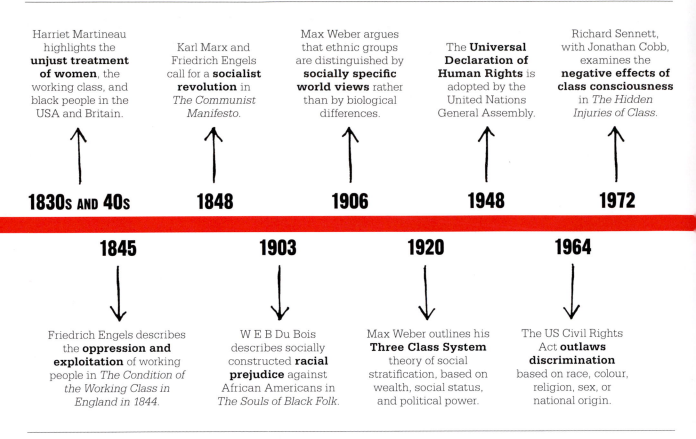

Harriet Martineau highlights the **unjust treatment of women**, the working class, and black people in the USA and Britain.

Karl Marx and Friedrich Engels call for a **socialist revolution** in *The Communist Manifesto.*

Max Weber argues that ethnic groups are distinguished by **socially specific world views** rather than by biological differences.

The **Universal Declaration of Human Rights** is adopted by the United Nations General Assembly.

Richard Sennett, with Jonathan Cobb, examines the **negative effects of class consciousness** in *The Hidden Injuries of Class.*

1830s AND 40s   **1848**   **1906**   **1948**   **1972**

1845   **1903**   **1920**   **1964**

Friedrich Engels describes the **oppression and exploitation** of working people in *The Condition of the Working Class in England in 1844.*

W E B Du Bois describes socially constructed **racial prejudice** against African Americans in *The Souls of Black Folk.*

Max Weber outlines his **Three Class System** theory of social stratification, based on wealth, social status, and political power.

The US Civil Rights Act **outlaws discrimination** based on race, colour, religion, sex, or national origin.

T he modernity that emerged from Enlightenment ideas and the technological innovations of the Industrial Revolution offered the promise not only of greater prosperity but also of a more just society. In Europe, at least, the absolute power of monarchs, the aristocracy, and the Church was challenged, and old dogmas were discredited by rational and scientific thought. At the same time, advances in technology brought mechanization to many trades and gave birth to new industries, increasing wealth and bringing hope of improvement to people's working lives.

Class consciousness
As the modern industrialized society became established, however, it became apparent that

it was not the utopian dream that had been expected. By the 19th century, many thinkers had begun to realize that this progress came at a cost, and that some of the promises had yet to be kept. Instead of becoming more just, modern industrial society had created new inequalities.

Among the first to study the new social order was Friedrich Engels, who saw the emergence of a working class, exploited by the owners of the mills and factories. With Karl Marx, he identified oppression of this class as the result of capitalism, which in turn fuelled and fed off industrialization.

Marx and Engels considered the social problems of industrial society in material, economic terms, and saw inequality as a division between the working class (the

proletariat) and the capitalist class (the bourgeoisie). Later sociologists also recognized that social inequality is manifested in a class system, but suggested that the stratification was more complex. Max Weber, for example, proposed that as well as economic situation, status and political standing also play a part. Perceptions of class and the issue of class consciousness became focuses for sustained sociological study of inequality, including the concept of "habitus", as explained by Pierre Bourdieu.

Racial oppression
While Engels and Marx concentrated on the economic disparity between the classes, others realized that it was not only the working classes that suffered social injustice. Harriet Martineau

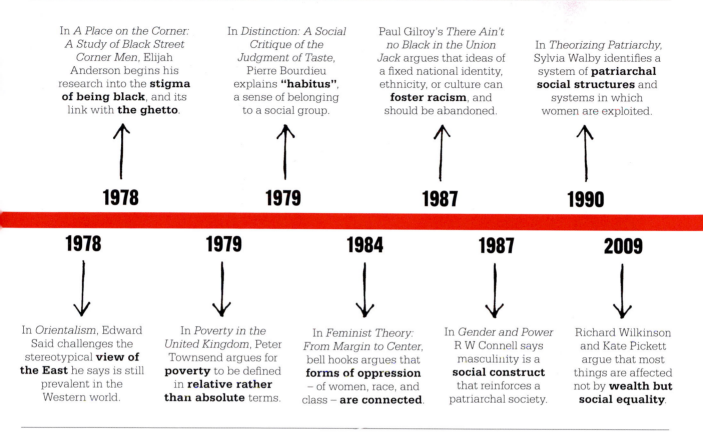

In *A Place on the Corner: A Study of Black Street Corner Men*, Elijah Anderson begins his research into the **stigma of being black**, and its link with **the ghetto**.

In *Distinction: A Social Critique of the Judgment of Taste*, Pierre Bourdieu explains **"habitus"**, a sense of belonging to a social group.

Paul Gilroy's *There Ain't no Black in the Union Jack* argues that ideas of a fixed national identity, ethnicity, or culture can **foster racism**, and should be abandoned.

In *Theorizing Patriarchy*, Sylvia Walby identifies a system of **patriarchal social structures** and systems in which women are exploited.

1978   **1979**   **1987**   **1990**

1978   **1979**   **1984**   **1987**   **2009**

In *Orientalism*, Edward Said challenges the stereotypical **view of the East** he says is still prevalent in the Western world.

In *Poverty in the United Kingdom*, Peter Townsend argues for **poverty** to be defined in **relative rather than absolute** terms.

In *Feminist Theory: From Margin to Center*, bell hooks argues that **forms of oppression** – of women, race, and class – **are connected**.

In *Gender and Power* R W Connell says masculinity is a **social construct** that reinforces a patriarchal society.

Richard Wilkinson and Kate Pickett argue that most things are affected not by **wealth but social equality**.

highlighted the gap between the Enlightenment ideal of equal rights and the reality of modern society. Her experiences in the USA, where she encountered slavery, showed that even in a democracy founded on ideals of liberty, some groups – women, ethnic minorities, and the working classes – were excluded from participation in shaping society. The connection she made with these various forms of oppression was re-explored by bell hooks some 150 years later.

Even when slavery was finally abolished, true emancipation was incomplete; the political exclusion of black people – by being denied the vote – persisted in the USA well into the 20th century. Black people in the USA and Europe also faced prejudices as a hangover from slavery and European colonialism

that have persisted to the present day. Sociologists such as W E B Du Bois examined the position of ethnic groups in predominantly white European industrial societies, and in the 20th century attention became focused on the connections between race and social inequality. Elijah Anderson began his study of black people and their association with the concept of "the ghetto"; Edward Said analysed negative Western perceptions of "the East"; and British sociologists such as Paul Gilroy sought to find ways of eradicating racism in modern multicultural societies.

Gender equality

Women likewise struggled for political suffrage, but even after this had been achieved they faced

injustice in societies that remained fundamentally patriarchal through the 20th century and up to the present day. It had taken "first-wave" feminism over a century to get women the vote, and the task of the second wave, starting soon after World War II, was to examine and overcome persistent social injustice based on gender.

Rather than simply addressing the economic and political factors underlying the continued oppression of women, Sylvia Walby suggested a comprehensive analysis of the social systems that maintain society's patriarchal structure, while R W Connell pointed out the prevalence of conventional perceptions – socially constructed forms – of masculinity that reinforce the concept of patriarchal society. ∎

I BROADLY ACCUSE THE BOURGEOISIE OF SOCIAL MURDER

FRIEDRICH ENGELS (1820–1895)

Living in England from 1842 to 1844, the German philosopher Friedrich Engels had seen, first-hand, the devastating effects of industrialization on workers and their children. The bourgeoisie, or capitalist class, he said, knowingly causes the workers' "life of toil and wretchedness... but takes no further trouble in the matter".

He claimed the bourgeoisie were turning a blind eye to their part in the early deaths of their workers, when it was within their power to change things, so he accused them of "social murder".

In the 1840s, England was seen as the workshop of the world; it enjoyed a unique position at the centre of the Industrial Revolution. Engels observed that it was

In the 1840s, **mortality in working class streets** in Manchester was 68 per cent higher than in those of the "first class".

↓

Bourgeois society condemned the workers to **unhealthy living conditions, insecure wages,** and **physical** and **mental exhaustion**.

↓

If society puts people in such a position that they die an **early and unnatural death**, it is murder.

↓

I broadly accuse the bourgeoisie of social murder.

See also: Karl Marx 28–31 ▪ Peter Townsend 74 ▪ Richard Sennett 84–87 ▪ Max Weber 220–23 ▪ Harry Braverman 226–31 ▪ Robert Blauner 232–33

undergoing a massive but silent transformation that had altered the whole of English civil society.

Industrialization had driven down prices, so hand-crafted work, which was more expensive, was less in demand; workers moved to the cities only to endure harsh conditions and financial insecurity. The industrialized, capitalist economy lurched from boom to bust, and workers' jobs could quickly disappear. Meanwhile, the bourgeoisie grew richer by treating the workers as disposable labour.

The legacy of industrialism

In Engels' first book, *The Condition of the Working Class in England in 1844*, he described the appalling way of life of the workers, or proletariat, in Manchester, London, Dublin, and Edinburgh, and found similar situations in all these cities. He reported filthy streets with pools of stagnant urine and excrement, filled with the stench of animal putrefaction from the tanneries. Widespread cholera outbreaks occurred, along with constant epidemics of consumption and typhus. Workers were packed into one-room huts or the cellars of damp houses that had been built along old ditches to save the house-owner money. They lived in conditions that defied all consideration of cleanliness and health, Engels said – and this in Manchester, "the second city of England, the first manufacturing city of the world".

The proletariat were worked to the point of exhaustion, wearing cheap clothing that gave no protection against accidents or the climate. They could buy only the food spurned by the bourgeoisie, such as decaying meat, wilted vegetables, "sugar" that was the refuse of soap-boiling firms, and cocoa mixed with earth.

When work disappeared and wages failed, even this meagre diet proved impossible, and many workers and their families began to starve; this caused illness and a continued inability to work, should work become available. Doctors were unaffordable, and very often entire families starved to death. The worker, Engels explained, could only obtain what he needed – healthy living conditions, secure employment, and a decent wage – from the bourgeoisie, "which can decree his life or death". He was insistent that this hugely exploitative, capital-owning class should therefore take immediate steps to change workers' conditions and stop its careless murder of an entire social class. ∎

Working-class families in England during the 1840s endured social deprivation, crippling financial instability, and terrible sickness due to the effects of industrial capitalism.

Friedrich Engels

Political theorist and philosopher Friedrich Engels was born in Germany in 1820. His father was a German industrialist who struggled with Engels' reluctance to attend school or work in the family business. As a teenager, he wrote articles under the pseudonym Friedrich Oswald, which gained him access to a group of left-wing intellectuals.

After working for a short time in a family factory in Manchester, England, he became interested in communism. In 1844 he travelled to Paris, where he met Karl Marx and became his colleague and financial sponsor. They jointly wrote *The Communist Manifesto*, and worked together until Marx's death in 1883, after which Engels completed the second and third volumes of *Das Kapital*, along with many books and articles of his own.

Key works

1845 *The Condition of the Working Class in England in 1844*
1848 *The Communist Manifesto*
1884 *The Origin of the Family, Private Property and the State*

THE PROBLEM OF THE 20TH CENTURY IS THE PROBLEM OF THE COLOUR LINE

W E B DU BOIS (1868–1963)

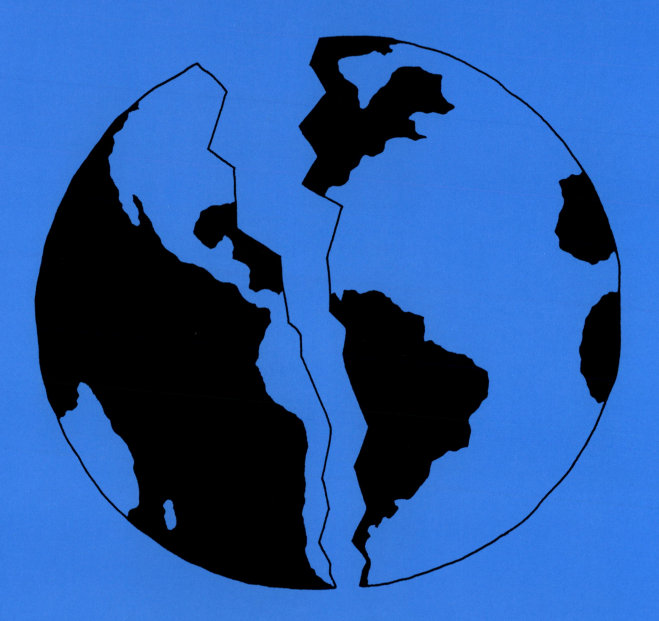

IN CONTEXT

FOCUS
Race and ethnicity

KEY DATES
1857 US Chief Justice Roger B Taney rules against a petition for freedom from enslaved Dred Scott, saying that blacks cannot be granted citizenship and therefore equal protection under the law because they are inferior to whites.

1906 Max Weber says that shared perceptions and common customs, not biological traits, distinguish ethnic groups from each other.

1954 The legal case of "Brown vs Board of Education" in the USA rules that establishing "separate but equal" schools for black and white children is unconstitutional.

1964 The Civil Rights Act outlaws public segregation and ends discrimination based on race, colour, religion, or sex.

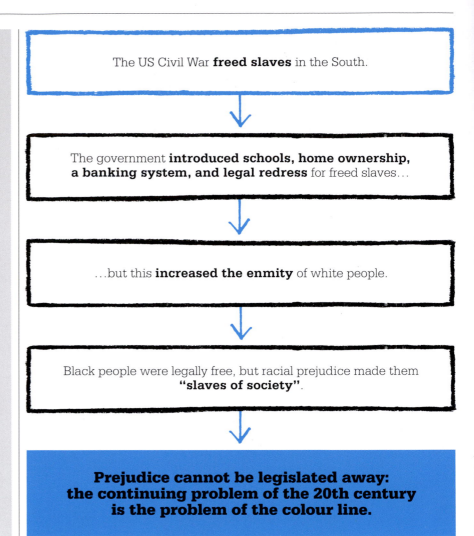

The US Civil War **freed slaves** in the South.

The government **introduced schools, home ownership, a banking system, and legal redress** for freed slaves…

…but this **increased the enmity** of white people.

Black people were legally free, but racial prejudice made them **"slaves of society"**.

Prejudice cannot be legislated away: the continuing problem of the 20th century is the problem of the colour line.

Towards the end of the 19th century, the US social reformer and freed slave Frederick Douglass drew attention to the continuing prejudice against black people in the USA. He claimed that although blacks had ceased to belong to individuals, they had nevertheless become slaves of society. Out of the depths of slavery, he said, "has come this prejudice and this color line", through which white dominion was asserted in the workplace, the ballot box, the legal courts, and everyday life.

In 1903, W E B Du Bois investigated the idea of the colour line in *The Souls of Black Folk*. A literary, sociological, and political landmark, it examines the changing position of African-Americans from the US Civil War and its aftermath to the early 1900s, in terms of the physical, economic, and political relations of black and white people in the South. It concludes that "the problem of the 20th century is the problem of the color line" – the continuing division between the opportunities and perspectives of blacks and whites.

Du Bois begins his study by pointing out that no white person is willing to talk about race explicitly, choosing instead to act out prejudice in various ways. But what they really want to know is this: "How does it feel to be a problem?"

Du Bois finds the question unanswerable, because it only makes sense from a white perspective – black people do not see themselves as "a problem". He then examines how this duality of perspective has occurred and gives the example of his first encounter with racism. While

See also: Harriet Martineau 26–27 ▪ Paul Gilroy 75 ▪ Edward Said 80–81 ▪ Elijah Anderson 82–83 ▪ bell hooks 90–95 ▪ Stuart Hall 200–01

at primary school, a new pupil refused to accept a greeting card from Du Bois, at which point "it dawned on me that I was different from the others".

He felt like them in his heart, he says, but realized that he was "shut out from their world by a vast veil". Initially undaunted, he says that he felt no need to tear down the veil until he grew up and saw that all the most dazzling opportunities in the world were for white people, not black people. There was a colour line, and he was standing on the side that was denied power, opportunity, dignity, and respect.

Identity crisis

Du Bois suggests that the colour line is internal too. Black people, according to him, see themselves in two ways simultaneously:

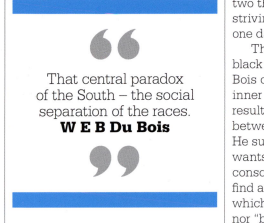

That central paradox of the South – the social separation of the races.
W E B Du Bois

through the reflection of the white world, which views them with amused contempt and pity, and through their own sense of self, which is more fluid and less well defined. These combine to form what Du Bois calls a double-consciousness: "...two souls,

two thoughts, two unreconciled strivings; two warring ideals in one dark body."

The unfolding history of the black person in the USA is, Du Bois claims, the history of this inner conflict, which itself is a result of the external, worldly battle between black and white people. He suggests that a black person wants to merge the double-consciousness into one state, and find a true African-American spirit, which does not Africanize America, nor "bleach his African soul in a flood of white Americanism".

The Freedmen's Bureau

How had black people become the "problem"? To try to explain this issue, Du Bois looks to the history of slavery in the USA and the turning point of the Civil War. »

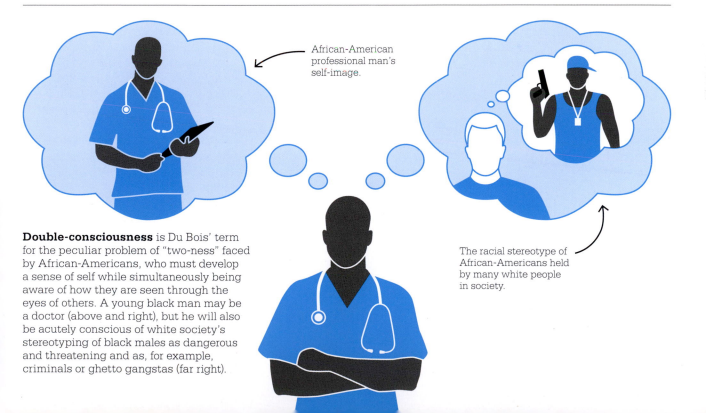

African-American professional man's self-image.

Double-consciousness is Du Bois' term for the peculiar problem of "two-ness" faced by African-Americans, who must develop a sense of self while simultaneously being aware of how they are seen through the eyes of others. A young black man may be a doctor (above and right), but he will also be acutely conscious of white society's stereotyping of black males as dangerous and threatening and as, for example, criminals or ghetto gangstas (far right).

The racial stereotype of African-Americans held by many white people in society.

Ulysses S Grant and his generals advance on horseback in the US Civil War. In 1868 the votes of a new black electorate were vital to Grant's election as Republican president.

According to him, slavery was the real cause of the war, which started in 1861. As the Union army of the northern states marched into the South, slaves fled to join it. At first, slaves were returned to their owners, but the policy changed and they were kept as military labour.

In 1863 slaves were declared free, and the government set up the Bureau of Refugees, Freedmen, and Abandoned Lands (also called the Freedmen's Bureau) to issue food, clothing, and abandoned property to the "flood" of destitute fugitive former slaves (men, women, and children). However, the Bureau was run by military staff ill-equipped to deal with social reorganization. The Bureau was also hampered by the sheer size of the task: the promise of handing over slave-driven plantations to former slaves "melted away" when it became clear that over 800,000 acres were affected.

One of the great successes of the Bureau was the provision of free schools for all children in the South.

Slavery is gone, but its shadow still lingers… and poisons… the moral atmosphere of all sections of the republic.
Frederick Douglass
US social reformer (c.1818–1895)

Du Bois points out that this was seen as a problem, because "the South believed an educated Negro to be a dangerous Negro". The opposition to black education in the South "showed itself in ashes, insult, and blood".

At the same time, the Bureau sowed division in legal matters. According to Du Bois, it used its courts to "put the bottom rail on top" – in other words, it favoured black litigants. Meanwhile, the civil courts often aided the former slavemasters. Du Bois describes white people as being "ordered about, seized, imprisoned, and punished over and over again" by the Bureau courts, while black people were intimidated, beaten, raped, and butchered by angry and revengeful (white) men.

The Bureau also opened a Freedman's Bank in 1865, to handle the deposits of former slave men and women. This initiative was hampered by incompetency, and the bank eventually crashed, taking the dollars of the freedmen with it. Du Bois says that this was the least of the loss, because "all the faith in saving went too, and much of the faith in men; and that was a loss that a nation which today sneers at Negro shiftlessness has never yet made good".

The Bureau had set up a system of free (non-slave) labour and ex-slave proprietorship, secured the recognition of black people as free people in courts of law, and founded common schools. The greatest failing of the Bureau was that it did not establish goodwill between the former masters and the ex-slaves; in fact, it increased enmity. The colour line remained, but instead of being explicit it now operated in more subtle ways.

Compromise or agitation?
Following the post-war period known as the Reconstruction, some of the newly won black rights started to slip away. A ruling in a US legal case (Plessy vs Ferguson, 1896) made segregation in public places permissible and set a pattern of racial separation in the South that lasted until Brown vs Board of Education, 1954. Anxiety caused by modernity also fuelled a rebirth of the Ku Klux Klan and its nativist white supremacism, accompanied by a rise in racist violence, including lynchings.

In 1895 the African-American politican Booker T Washington had given a speech now known as "the Atlanta Compromise". He suggested that black people should be patient, adopt white middle-class standards, and seek self-advancement by self-improvement and education to show their worth. By foregoing political rights in return for economic rights and legal justice, Washington argued that social change would be more likely in the longer term. This accommodating stance became the dominant ideology of the time.

Du Bois disagreed strongly, and in *The Souls of Black Folk* he said that while black people did not expect full civic rights immediately, they were certain that the way for a people to gain their rights "is not by voluntarily throwing them away". Du Bois had hoped to eliminate racism and segregation through social science, but he came to believe that political agitation was the only effective strategy.

Stretching the colour line

In 1949, Du Bois visited the Warsaw Ghetto in Poland, where two-thirds of the population had been killed during the Nazi occupation, and 85 per cent of the city lay in ruins. He was shocked by the experience, which he said gave him a "more complete understanding of the Negro problem". Faced with such absolute devastation and destruction, and knowing that it was a direct consequence of racist segregation and violence, Du Bois reassessed his analysis of the colour line and declared it a phenomenon that can occur to any cultural or ethnic group. In his 1952 essay for the magazine *Jewish Life*, "The Negro and the Warsaw Ghetto", he writes: "The race problem... cut across lines of color and physique and belief and status and was a matter of... human hate and prejudice." It is therefore not colour that matters so much as the "line", which can be drawn to articulate difference and hatred in any group or society.

Activist and scholar

Du Bois became one of the founder members of the civil rights organization, the National Association for the Advancement of Colored People (NAACP). His ideas were concerned with people of African descent everywhere, and during the 1920s he helped found the Pan-African Association in Paris, France, and organized a series of pan-African congresses around the world. However, at the time of writing about the African soul, in the early 1900s, he said that the conditions that were necessary to achieve a true and unified African-American spirit had not yet been reached.

Du Bois applied systematic methods of fieldwork to previously neglected areas of study. The use of empirical data to catalogue the details of black people's lives enabled him to dispel widely held stereotypes. For example, he produced a wealth of data on the effects of urban life on African-Americans in *The Philadelphia Negro* (1899), which suggests that rather than being caused by anything innate, crime is a product of the environment. His pioneering sociological research and thinking was a huge influence on later prominent civil rights leaders, including Dr Martin Luther King, Jr. Du Bois is recognized as one of the most important sociologists of the 20th century. ∎

W E B Du Bois

William Edward Burghardt Du Bois was a sociologist, historian, philosopher, and political leader. He was born in Massachusetts, USA, three years after the end of the Civil War.

After graduating from high school, Du Bois studied at Fisk University, Nashville, and the university of Berlin, Germany, where he met Max Weber. In 1895 he became the first African American to receive a PhD when he gained a doctorate in history at Harvard University. From 1897 to 1910 he was professor of economics and history at Atlanta University, and from 1934 to 1944 he was chairman of the department of sociology. In 1961 Du Bois moved to Ghana, Africa, to work on the *Encyclopedia Africana*, but died two years later. He wrote numerous books, articles, and essays, and founded and edited four journals.

Key works

1903 *The Souls of Black Folks*
1920 *Darkwater: Voices from Within the Veil*
1939 *Black Folk, Then and Now*

THE POOR ARE EXCLUDED FROM THE ORDINARY LIVING PATTERNS, CUSTOMS, AND ACTIVITIES OF LIFE
PETER TOWNSEND (1928–2009)

IN CONTEXT

FOCUS
Relative poverty

KEY DATES
1776 Scottish economist Adam Smith says the necessities of life include, "whatever the custom of the country renders it indecent for creditable people, even of the lowest order, to be without".

1901 British sociologist Seebohm Rowntree publishes *Poverty: A Study of Town Life*.

1979 Peter Townsend publishes *Poverty in the United Kingdom*.

1999 The UK government carries out the Poverty and Social Exclusion survey of Britain.

2013 French economist Thomas Piketty publishes *Capital in the 21st Century*, documenting extreme income inequality in 20 countries.

Poverty was defined by the social campaigner Seebohm Rowntree at the beginning of the 20th century as a state in which "total earnings are insufficient to obtain the minimum necessaries for the maintenance of merely physical efficiency". This is the "subsistence level" definition of poverty, which has been used by governments to determine the cost of a person's basic needs such as food, rent, fuel, and clothing.

Food banks in the UK have faced surging demand in recent years. They meet basic needs, but often include non-essential foodstuffs that are now considered normal for people to have.

However, in 1979 the British sociologist Peter Townsend said that "poverty" should be defined not in absolute terms, but in terms of relative deprivation. He indicated that every society has an average level in terms of living conditions, diet, amenities, and the type of activities people can participate in. Where an individual or family lacks the resources to obtain these, they are socially excluded from normal life, as well as being materially deprived. Other factors, such as poor skills or bad health, must also be taken into account.

Townsend – a leading campaigner who co-founded the Child Poverty Action Group – pointed out that there was an assumption that poverty had been steadily decreasing in affluent societies. But he drew attention to the increasing income gap between those at the top and lower levels of society, and said that when a country becomes wealthier, but income distribution is markedly uneven, the number of people in poverty is bound to increase. ∎

See also: Karl Marx 28–31 ▪ Friedrich Engels 66–67 ▪ Richard Sennett 84–87

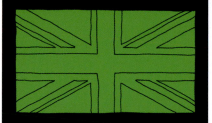

THERE AIN'T NO BLACK IN THE UNION JACK

PAUL GILROY (1956–)

IN CONTEXT

FOCUS
Racism

KEY DATES
18th–19th centuries
Biological-based ideas of race
are used to justify slavery
and colonialism.

1940s The Nazi party uses
"race" to justify political
inequality and introduces
ideas of "racial purity".

1950 UNESCO declares that
"race" is a social myth.

1970s Michel Foucault argues
that biological ideas of race,
linked with certain essential
traits, arose with colonialism.

1981 US sociologist Anne
Wortham publishes *The Other
Side of Racism*, identifying
five black movements that
prevent society from reaching
a position "beyond racism".

1987 Paul Gilroy publishes
*There Ain't No Black in the
Union Jack*.

I n his book *There Ain't No
Black in the Union Jack*,
British sociologist Paul Gilroy
focuses on racism in Britain in
the 20th century. He points out
that in the 1970s Britain worried
about its "national decline"
almost obsessively, and many
commentators ascribed this
to the "dilution of homogenous
and continuous national stock"
– specifically, Gilroy says, to the
arrival of black people in Britain.

Gilroy indicates that fixed
notions of nationality, such
as "Britishness", may not be
intentionally racist, but they have
racist consequences. In seeking
to define Britishness, 20th-century
writers always seemed to imagine
a white Britain – black people were
seen as permanent outsiders. They
were denied authentic national
membership on the basis of their
"race", and it was often assumed
that their allegiance lay elsewhere.

While accepting that the idea
of race has been a historical and
political force, Gilroy says that it
is no more than a social construct,
a concept created in society. Where
some sociologists have suggested
a discussion of "ethnicity" or
"culture" instead, Gilroy proposes
that we should abandon all of these
ideas. Whatever terms we use, he
says, we are creating a false idea
of "natural" categories by putting
disparate people into different
groups, leading to a division
between "them" and "us".

Raciology

According to Gilroy, all these types
of discussion leave us enmeshed
in what he calls "raciology" – a
discourse that assumes certain
stereotypes, prejudices, images,
and identities. Anti-racists find
themselves inverting the position
of racist thinkers, but are
nevertheless unable to displace
the idea of racism altogether. The
solution, Gilroy suggests, lies in
refusing to accept racial divisions
as an inescapable, natural force,
and instead developing "an ability
to imagine political, economic,
and social systems in which
'race' makes no sense". ∎

See also: Michel Foucault 52–55; 270–77 ∎ W E B Du Bois 68–73 ∎
Elijah Anderson 82–83 ∎ bell hooks 90–95 ∎ Benedict Anderson 202–03

A SENSE OF ONE'S PLACE

PIERRE BOURDIEU (1930–2002)

IN CONTEXT

FOCUS
Habitus

KEY DATES
1934 The essay "Body Techniques" by French sociologist and anthropologist Marcel Mauss lays the foundations for Pierre Bourdieu's re-elaboration of the concept of "habitus".

1958 Max Weber suggests that "a specific style of life can be expected from those who wish to belong to the circle".

1966 English historian E P Thompson says class is "a relationship that must always be embodied in real people and in a real context".

2003 US cultural theorist Nancy Fraser says that capitalist society has two systems of subordination – the class structure and the status order – which interact.

From Marx to Durkheim and Weber to Parsons, sociologists have been keen to determine how the social-class system is reproduced, in the belief that it is structurally bound to economics, property ownership, and financial assets.

But in the 1970s Pierre Bourdieu claimed, in *Distinction*, that the issue was more complex: social class is not defined solely by economics, he said, "but by the class habitus which is normally associated with that position". This concept was first discussed by the 13th-century Italian theologian Thomas Aquinas, who claimed that the things people want or like, and

See also: Karl Marx 28–31 ▪ Émile Durkheim 34–37 ▪ Friedrich Engels 66–67 ▪ Richard Sennett 84–87 ▪ Norbert Elias 180–81 ▪ Paul Willis 292–93

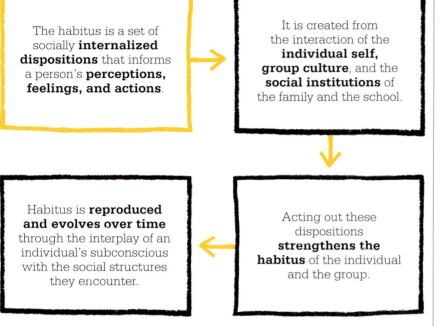

The habitus is a set of socially **internalized dispositions** that informs a person's **perceptions, feelings, and actions**.

It is created from the interaction of the **individual self, group culture**, and the **social institutions** of the family and the school.

Acting out these dispositions **strengthens the habitus** of the individual and the group.

Habitus is **reproduced and evolves over time** through the interplay of an individual's subconscious with the social structures they encounter.

the way they act, is because they think of themselves as a certain kind of person: each of us has a particular inclination, or habitus.

Bourdieu, however, develops the idea significantly. He defines habitus as an embodied set of socially acquired dispositions that lead individuals to live their lives in ways that are similar to other

Habitus is society written into the body, into the biological individual.
Pierre Bourdieu

members of their social-class group. An individual from one class will "know" that something is "pretentious" or "gaudy", whereas a person from another class will see the same thing as "beautiful" or "stunning". He suggests that a child learns these things from their family, and then from their school and peers, who demonstrate to the growing child how to speak and act, and so on. In this way, he says, "the social order is progressively inscribed in people's minds".

Class dispositions

While researching class divisions in France in the 1960s, Bourdieu noticed that people of the same class exhibited similar cultural values. The things they knew and valued, the way they spoke, their choice of clothes and decoration of the body, and their views on art, leisure, and entertainment

activities were all similar to one another. The French upper classes, he noted, enjoyed reading poetry, philosophy, and politics. They liked going to classic or avant-garde theatre, museums, and classical-music concerts; they enjoyed going camping and mountaineering.

Within the working classes, Bourdieu found that people liked reading novels and magazines, betting, visiting music halls and boutiques, and owning luxury cars. The choices were relatively limited and they were determined not by cost, but by taste. He realized that people who were members of a certain class, or "class fraction" (class subset), shared tastes because they shared dispositions, or "habitus". They had somehow come to like and dislike the same things. And this awareness of shared habitus gave them a distinct sense of place; they "fitted" into this or that class.

The construction of habitus is due neither to the individual nor the existing environment – it is created through the interplay of the subjective mind with the structures and institutions around him or »

Fox-hunting is a leisure pursuit that feels natural to some as a result of their habitus, or disposition. The same tendency makes other types of activity (such as karaoke) feel strange.

her. Individuals are born into a particular social-class group. Each is defined by a specific lifestyle, referred to by Bourdieu as the habitus of the group. Every social-class group has a group habitus that simultaneously defines, and differentiates it from, all the other group habitus in society.

The habitus of the group is also inscribed in the bodily dispositions and gestures of the individual. The social class of a person can be discerned from how they walk, talk, laugh, cry, and so on – from everything they do, think, and say. For the most part, because they are born and raised within a particular group habitus, individuals are generally unaware of the ways in which habitus both enables and restricts how they think, perceive, act, and interact with the world around them.

Habitus – as the embodiment of the dispositions of the wider group to which the individual belongs – provides people with a clear sense of the type of person they are and what it is that people like themselves should think and feel, as well as the manner in which they should behave.

Habitus gives individuals a unique "sense of one's place", because their internalized self perfectly matches the structure of their external world. But if they were to stray into the "fields" (institutions or structures) of a different class, they would feel like "a fish out of water", wrong-footed at every turn.

Forms of capital

Bourdieu maintains that the habitus of an individual is made up of different types and amounts of capital (economic, cultural, and social), which he redefined as "the set of actually usable resources and powers" that a person has.

Economic capital refers, quite simply, to monetary resources and property. A person's cultural capital is their capacity to play "the culture game" – to recognize references in books, films, and theatre; to know how to act in given situations (such as apt manners and conversation at the dinner table); to know what to wear and how; and even who "to look down your nose at". Because habitus defines a person within any situation as being of a certain class or class fraction, it is critical in delineating the social order.

Bourdieu says the habitus is often obvious through "judgments of classification", which are pronounced about a thing, such as a painting, but act to classify the person speaking. Where one person describes a painting as "nice", and another as "passé", we learn little about the artwork, but much more about the person and their habitus. People use these judgements deliberately to distinguish themselves from their neighbours and establish their class.

In addition to economic and cultural capital, people may have social capital – human resources (friends and colleagues) gained through social networks. These relationships give a sense of mutual obligation and trust, and may offer access to power and influence.

This idea of social capital can be seen in the success of social networking websites such as Facebook and LinkedIn, which provide ways for individuals to increase their social capital. Bourdieu also saw scholastic

Scientific observation shows that cultural needs are the product of upbringing and education.
Pierre Bourdieu

capital (intellectual knowledge), linguistic capital (ease in the command of language, determining who has the authority to speak and be heard), and political capital (status in the political world) as playing a part in class.

The class game

The class struggle, outlined so comprehensively by Marx, can be played out at an individual level using Bourdieu's terms. He says that an individual develops within relationships (the family and school), before entering various social arenas or "fields" (such as institutions and social groups), where people express and constantly reproduce their habitus. Whether or not people are successful in the fields they enter depends on the type of habitus they have and the capital it carries.

Every field has a set of rules that reflects the group habitus, to the extent that the rules seem "common sense" to them. People are recognized for their "symbolic capital" and its worth within the field. Their symbolic capital represents the total of all their other forms of capital, and is reflected as prestige, a reputation for competence, or social position.

Those who talk of equality of opportunity forget that social games… are not 'fair games'.
Pierre Bourdieu

During their lifetimes, people put their various forms of capital to work. They also "strategize", figuring out how to compete with each other for increased power and capital. The particular forms that these strategies can take are governed by habitus, and yet most people are not consciously aware of the extent to which their actions and choices in life are determined by these acquired dispositions.

The possibility of change

Because Bourdieu's idea of cultural capital rests so heavily on the constantly reproduced habitus, which is embedded in all of us, he seems quite pessimistic about the possibility of social mobility.

However, the habitus *is* open to change through different forces within the field. The interaction of institutions and individuals usually reinforces existing ideas, but it is possible for someone from a lower social class to gain cultural capital by, for instance, being sent to a "good" school. This might raise their economic capital – and their children, in turn, might be privately schooled and benefit from increased economic and cultural capital and a different habitus. So, for Bourdieu, all forms of capital are interrelated: people convert their economic capital into cultural and social capital in order to improve their life chances.

Bourdieu's habitus has had a major impact on sociological debate in the last few decades. More than any other idea, it captures the extent to which impersonal social structures and processes influence what are regarded as seemingly unique personal dispositions. In short, habitus brings together insights of a number of prominent thinkers in one compact and versatile concept. ∎

Pierre Bourdieu

Born in 1930 in a rural village in southwest France, Pierre Bourdieu was the only son of a postman. A teacher recognized his potential and recommended he go to Paris to study. After graduating from the prestigious École Normale Supérieure with a degree in philosophy, he taught at the University of Algiers during the Algerian Liberation War (1956–62).

While in Algeria, he undertook ethnographic studies that resulted in his first book, *The Sociology of Algeria* (1958). On his return to France he became Director of Studies at the École des Hautes Études en Sciences Sociales, Paris, and began an acclaimed career in social studies. He believed research should translate into action, and was involved in many political protests against inequality and domination. Bourdieu died in 2002.

Key works

1979 *Distinction: A Social Critique of the Judgment of Taste*
1980 *The Logic of Practice*
1991 *Language and Symbolic Power*

THE ORIENT IS THE STAGE ON WHICH THE WHOLE EAST IS CONFINED
EDWARD SAID (1935–2003)

IN CONTEXT

FOCUS
Orientalism

KEY DATES
1375 Chaucer refers to the Orient as the lands lying east of the Mediterranean.

Early 19th century French academic Silvestre de Sacy sets out the terms of modern Orientalism.

1836 Edward William Lane's book *Manners and Customs of the Modern Egyptians* becomes an important reference work for writers such as French novelist Gustave Flaubert.

1961 Franz Fanon writes about the dehumanizing forces of colonialism in *The Wretched of the Earth*.

1981 Sadik Jalal al-'Azm argues that Orientalism tends to categorize the West in the same way that Said says it packages the East.

The idea of "the Orient" evolved from Western colonial powers and is a politically dangerous and culturally biased idea that continues to infect Western views of the Eastern world. This powerful argument is made by Edward Said in his influential text, *Orientalism* (1978).

The concept of Orientalism, he says, works in two important ways: it presents the East as one homogenous region that is exotic, uncivilized, and backward; and at the same time, it constructs and fixes the West's idea of the East in a simplified, unchanging set of representations.

European "experts" (historians, scientists, and linguists) report on what **"the Orient"** is like, from their own perspective.

Their ideas are reduced still further into **stereotypes and representations that construct and fix Western views of "the East"** and its peoples...

...and fuel and **perpetuate Western fears** about the East, especially Arabs, as **dangerous and "other"**.

The Orient is the stage on which the whole East is confined.

See also: Michel Foucault 52–55 ▪ W E B Du Bois 68–73 ▪ Paul Gilroy 75 ▪ Elijah Anderson 82–83 ▪ Stuart Hall 200–01 ▪ Benedict Anderson 202–03 ▪ Stanley Cohen 290

Said explains that the idea of modern Orientalism arose when a French army led by Napoleon Bonaparte conquered Egypt in 1798. This conquest was significant because Napoleon took with him not only soldiers, but also scientists, philologists, and historians. These experts were given the job of recording and categorizing what they saw. In describing their experience of "the Orient" as objective knowledge, their words gained an unquestionable authority and influence in Europe.

Categorizing the East

However, as Said suggests, they were looking at the peoples around them through the lens of imperialist conquest. They saw themselves as the superior power and therefore as superior people. They drew an imaginary line between Us and Them, West and East, and began to define both sides in opposition to one another. Where the peoples of the East were perceived as irrational, uncivilized, lazy, and backward, those of the West were rational, civilized, hardworking, and progressive. The reports sent back to Europe by Napoleon's "experts" meant that the East was presented to Europeans in a highly packaged way; the East was explained by the West, and in the process moulded to suit the Europeans. This idea of what "Orientals" were like was appropriated and disseminated widely by literary figures such as Lord Byron, who romanticized the Orient but continued to emphasize its inalienable difference.

Perpetuating fear

The problem continues, Said says, because the idea of the Orient has prevented people in the West being able to view the East in all its complexity. The same repertory of images keeps arising: the Orient is seen as a place of mythical exoticism – it is the home of the Sphinx, Cleopatra, Eden, Troy, Sodom and Gomorrah, Sheba, Babylon, and Muhammad.

Orientalism is a framework used to understand the unfamiliar, says Said, but at the same time it tells

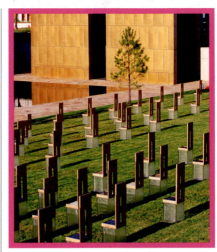

A memorial to victims of the bombing in Oklahoma, USA, in 1995. The attack was first blamed by media on "Muslims" and "Arabs" (the other), but was the work of a white American.

us that the peoples of the East are different and frightening. In this context, "the Arab" is viewed as a violent fanatic, and Western nations feel the need to protect themselves from "the infiltration of the Other". The challenge, he says, is to find a way of coexisting peacefully. ∎

Edward Said

Cultural theorist and literary critic Edward Said was the founder of post-colonial studies. Born in West Jerusalem during the British Mandate in Palestine, his father was a wealthy Palestinian-American of Christian faith, and Said went to private international schools in Lebanon, Egypt, and the USA. He later studied at Princeton and Harvard before becoming a professor of English Literature at Columbia University, where he taught until his death in 2003. Said wrote prolifically on a wide range of topics, including music and Palestinian issues.

Said stated that he was politicized by the Six-Day War of 1967 between Israel and its Arab neighbours, after which he became an important voice for the Palestinian cause, especially in the USA. In 1999 he founded an Arab-Israeli orchestra with the conductor Daniel Barenboim, in the belief that music transcends politics.

Key works

1978 *Orientalism*
1979 *The Question of Palestine*
1993 *Culture and Imperialism*

THE GHETTO IS WHERE THE BLACK PEOPLE LIVE
ELIJAH ANDERSON (1943–)

IN CONTEXT

FOCUS
The iconic ghetto

KEY DATES
1903 W E B Du Bois says the problem of the 20th century is the problem of the colour line.

Early 20th century Blacks migrate from the rural South to cities throughout the USA.

1920 Black political leader Marcus Garvey holds an international convention in Harlem, the traditionally black area of New York City.

1960s There is a "white flight" from areas in the USA where black people live, leading to "black ghettos".

1972 The Equal Employment Opportunity Act is passed in the USA.

1992 Riots take place in Los Angeles, USA, after police are filmed beating a black motorist, Rodney King, and then acquitted of his assault.

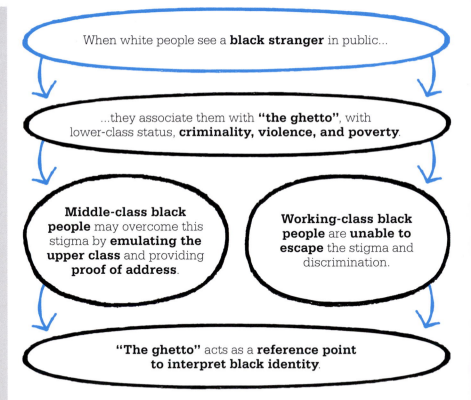

When white people see a **black stranger** in public...

...they associate them with **"the ghetto"**, with lower-class status, **criminality, violence, and poverty**.

Middle-class black people may overcome this stigma by **emulating the upper class** and providing **proof of address**.

Working-class black people are **unable to escape** the stigma and discrimination.

"The ghetto" acts as a **reference point to interpret black identity**.

In 2012, Elijah Anderson wrote "The Iconic Ghetto", which argued that many Americans associate the ghetto with a place where "the black people live". He said that to these same Americans, the ghetto symbolizes a lawless, impoverished, drug-infested, chaotic area of the city, ruled by violence. So when they think of "black people", they imagine them as immoral, drug-addicted, criminal "hoods", deserving of prejudice and discrimination.

See also: Michel Foucault 52–55 ▪ W E B Du Bois 68–73 ▪ Paul Gilroy 75 ▪
Edward Said 80–81

Working-class black people who live in impoverished areas are, says Anderson, routinely stigmatized and "demoralized by racism".

Anderson gives the example of a racist incident while he was on holiday in a "pleasant Cape Cod town full of upper-middle-class white vacationers". As he enjoyed a jog through the town, a middle-aged white man blocked the road with his car, and shouted "Go home!" to Anderson. Bemused, Anderson later questioned what the man meant, and realized that it was an order to "go home" to the ghetto. The institution of the ghetto is persistent, says Anderson, and it leads many to think that the black person's place is most often in the ghetto, not in middle-class society.

Iconic status

Most black people in America do not come from a ghetto, and legally they have access to the same schooling and job opportunities as white people. However, because "the ghetto" has reached iconic status, it operates as a mindset, and black people of all classes find themselves having to prove that they are not from the ghetto before they do anything else. Anderson says that middle-class black people do this by "speaking white" (mimicking the formal speech style of upper-middle-class whites), or demonstrating exceptional intelligence, manners, and poise. They deal with insults by laughing them off with friends, but in fact these small events, like Anderson's jogging incident, can make "the scales fall from one's eyes" and induce a feeling of having been a fool for believing that they fitted seamlessly into society.

Disproving the ghetto

Middle-class black people can work to disabuse others of this "assessment", Anderson says, but the problem for poorer black people is less easily solved. If they actually live in a ghetto, how can they distance themselves from all its associations? How do working-class black people signify that they are not violent drug-addicts, or in any way counteract the prejudice already operating against them?

Anderson points to the shooting of Trayvon Martin in 2012: the unarmed, innocent 17-year-old was shot dead by a neighbourhood-watch coordinator, who said Martin looked "out of place". This exposes the danger of many white people's belief that black people come from, and should remain in, "the ghetto", not white neighbourhoods.

According to Anderson, the idea that black people have a specific "place" in society (the "ghetto") persists in the imagination of white people. This is despite a black presence in every social class and neighbourhood. The iconic ghetto acts to continually stigmatize people with black skin, and treat them as "dangerous outsiders". ▪

Elijah Anderson

Elijah Anderson is one of the leading urban ethnographers in the USA. He was born on a plantation in Mississippi during World War II. His parents were originally sharecroppers who picked cotton, but after his father's experience of fighting as a soldier in Europe during the war, the family found the racism of the South intolerable and moved to Chicago and then Indiana, both in the north of the country.

Anderson studied sociology at Indiana University and then Chicago, where his dissertation on black street-corner men became his first book, *A Place on the Corner* (1978). He was Vice President of the American Sociological Association (ASA) in 2002, and has won many awards, including the ASA's Cox-Johnson-Frazier Award.

Key works

1990 *Streetwise*
1999 *Code of the Street:
Moral Life of the Inner City*
2012 "The Iconic Ghetto"

> The black man is treated as a dangerous outsider until he proves he is worthy of trust.
> **Elijah Anderson**

THE TOOLS OF FREEDOM BECOME THE SOURCES OF INDIGNITY

RICHARD SENNETT (1943–)

IN CONTEXT

FOCUS
Class inequality

KEY DATES
1486 Italian philosopher Giovanni Pico della Mirandola says that unlike animals, people search for meaning and dignity in life.

1841 In "Self-Reliance", US philosopher and essayist Ralph Waldo Emerson sees self-reliance as a moral imperative that enables individuals to shape their own destiny.

1960s French philosopher Jean-Paul Sartre says that a class society is a society of resources unfairly distributed because some people have arbitrary power.

1989 British academic Richard Hoggart says, "Every decade we swiftly declare we have buried class, each decade the coffin stays empty."

Sociologists and economists traditionally accepted the idea that social class was linked to money: as workers earned higher incomes and gained more possessions, they would move into the middle class and enjoy not just prosperity, but also an increased sense of dignity. But this concept was challenged when US sociologist Richard Sennett, in collaboration with Jonathan Cobb, investigated a paradox that seemed to afflict working-class people who moved into the middle class.

What Sennett discovered in his interviews with workers, as outlined in *The Hidden Injuries of Class,* published in 1972, was

See also: Friedrich Engels 66–67 ▪ W E B Du Bois 68–73 ▪ Pierre Bourdieu 76–79 ▪ Elijah Anderson 82–83 ▪
Georg Simmel 104–05 ▪ Samuel Bowles and Herbert Gintis 288–89 ▪ Paul Willis 292–93

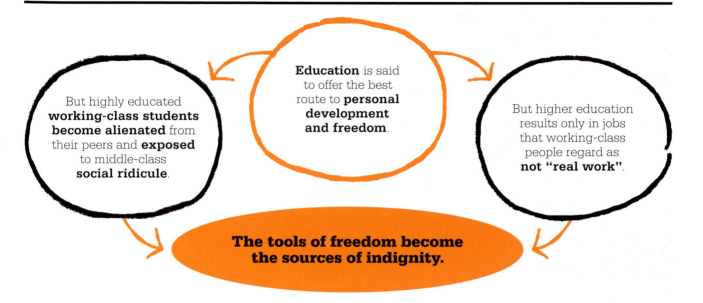

But highly educated **working-class students become alienated** from their peers and **exposed** to middle-class **social ridicule**.

Education is said to offer the best route to **personal development and freedom**.

But higher education results only in jobs that working-class people regard as **not "real work"**.

The tools of freedom become the sources of indignity.

that an increase in material power and freedom of choice was accompanied by a significant crisis in self-respect. In reaching for greater freedom, workers were being asked to use "tools", such as education, that left them feeling alienated and incapable.

Immigration and racism

To explain how this might be happening, Sennett looked first at the history of the working class in the USA. During the urbanization of the 19th century, rural workers moved from small farms to towns and then cities, which grew quickly under this sudden influx. In addition, most US cities had large enclaves of newly arrived European immigrants, from Ireland, Italy, Poland, and Greece,

for example. Here the old languages were spoken and cultural traditions were kept alive.

This mass immigration meant that industrialists soon realized that unskilled labour was cheaper than machine production. So they hired large numbers of immigrants

and switched the focus of their machinery to replacing the more expensive, skilled labour. Hostility arose towards the newcomers and there was a rise in racist attitudes.

A kind of "moral hierarchy" among nationalities soon gained widespread acceptance. Western »

Immigrants disembark from a ship in New York, USA, in the early 20th century. These "foreigners" were often used for cheap labour, which led to hostility from some US citizens.

The pyramid of achievement

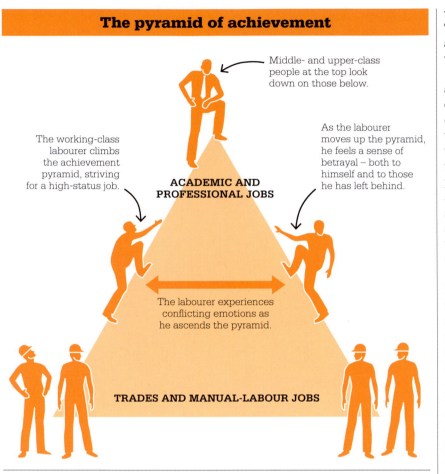

Middle- and upper-class people at the top look down on those below.

The working-class labourer climbs the achievement pyramid, striving for a high-status job.

As the labourer moves up the pyramid, he feels a sense of betrayal – both to himself and to those he has left behind.

ACADEMIC AND PROFESSIONAL JOBS

The labourer experiences conflicting emotions as he ascends the pyramid.

TRADES AND MANUAL-LABOUR JOBS

Europeans (apart from the Irish) were at the top of this hierarchy; they were seen as diligent, hard working, and skilled. However, at the opposite end of the scale, Sennett notes that "Slavs, Bohemians, Jews, and Southern Europeans… were accused of dirtiness, secretiveness, or laziness". The new immigrants found that they could depend only on their countrymen for support, so ethnic communities flourished.

But during the mid-20th century, US cities underwent urban renewal programmes that broke up the immigrant communities. Immigrant families were integrated into the larger society, which had different attitudes to social respect from their own. In the wider US society, higher educated, "cultured" people were treated with the most respect. An honest, hard-working man or woman who may have been highly regarded in the "old neighbourhood" was now viewed with disdain and suspicion for being ignorant and "foreign".

Education and failure

Sennett says that the working class was being challenged to become "cultured"; education seemed to be the way to acceptance and respect. However, there were several notable problems with this. First, to people who had always valued hard, physical labour, the "pen-pushing" jobs of the middle class were not considered "real work". These jobs were not worthy, so a worker could not view himself with respect while doing them.

In addition, although intellect and education were held in high esteem by the middle and upper classes, it seemed to the workers that "the educated" did nothing worth respecting; on the contrary, they were often seen to use their privileged position to cheat, lie, and avoid working, while at the same time commanding high salaries. How, therefore, could a worker aim to maintain his dignity and self-respect in this position?

The workers interviewed by Sennett use the word "educated" to stand for a range of experiences and feelings that move beyond pure schooling. Education's elevated status results from the fact that it is thought to increase rationality and develop the finest human capacities. But Rissarro, a shoeshine boy turned bank clerk, explains how this works differently across the social divisions. He believes that people of a higher class have the power to judge him because they are more "internally developed". Despite Rissarro's rise to professional employment, his

> **"** The educated… middle-class people… [with] the 'right' values stand out from a mass whose understanding… they believe inferior to their own. **"**
> **Richard Sennett**

middle-class colleagues look down on him, and he lacks respect for himself, because he feels that he is not doing "real work". He accepts society's admonitions to "better himself", but he feels like an imposter and is puzzled by his sense of discomfort. He believes that the only explanation is that there is something wrong with him.

Sennett maintains that workers tend to see their failure to fit in and achieve respect as personal failure, not as a condition of societal divisions and inequalities. He quotes James, a highly educated son of an immigrant, who sees himself as a failure, whatever he does. "If I really had what it takes," he says, "I could make this school thing worthwhile." On the other hand, if he "had the balls to go out into the world" and get a real job, that would earn him real respect. James holds himself responsible for not having more self-confidence and for having failed to "develop".

The political is personal

This conjunction of class and self is a uniquely US phenomenon, says Sennett, that is tied up with the prizing of "the individual". Success in IQ tests and schooling is seen as a way of freeing an individual from his or her social conditions at birth – everyone who truly has merit or intelligence will rise. This belief in equality of opportunity is at the heart of the American Dream.

Working-class children do not have the same opportunities as children from more affluent backgrounds, and those who strive to excel are seen as traitors. They are exiled from their peer groups, with a subsequent loss of self-worth. The tools of freedom are a source of indignity for them, both at school and at college, where they are looked down on for not knowing the rules and lacking in wider cultural knowledge. Their educational achievement exposes them not to respect but to disdain from the middle-class people around them and they suffer a sense of failure and alienation.

According to Scottish-American businessman Andrew Carnegie, the justice of industrial capitalism is that society will always reward "a man of talent". If a person is worthy of escaping poverty, he or she can do so. If he or she does not have the ability to "make it", however, what right does that person have to complain? As Sennett notes: in a meritocracy, if you fail, you have no merit. Failure to succeed is due to personal inadequacy. In this way the inequalities of class become hidden by the widespread "personal failures" of working people.

The Hidden Injuries of Class is a subtle and sensitive exploration of working-class lives that exposes how social difference can be made to appear as simply a question of character, competence, and moral resolve, when it is essentially a matter of inherited class. ■

Arthur Miller was a working-class boy who rose to become one of the leading US dramatists of the mid-20th century – he was, however, largely looked down upon by US critics.

Richard Sennett

Literary author and sociologist Richard Sennett was born in Chicago, USA, to parents with communist beliefs. Both his father and uncle fought as internationalists in the civil war in Spain. Sennett was brought up by his mother in one of the first racially mixed public housing projects.

Sennet studied cello at Juilliard, New York City, but a wrist operation in 1964 brought his musical career to an end. He began a career in sociology at Harvard University, and has taught at Yale and the London School of Economics (LSE). In the 1970s he co-founded The New York Institute for the Humanities with writers Susan Sontag and Joseph Brodsky. Sennett made his name with *The Hidden Injuries of Class*, which he wrote after spending four years researching with Jonathan Cobb. He is married to sociologist Saskia Sassen.

Key works

1972 *The Hidden Injuries of Class* (in collaboration with Jonathan Cobb)
1974 *The Call of Public Man*
2005 *The Culture of the New Capitalism*

MEN'S INTEREST IN PATRIARCHY IS CONDENSED IN HEGEMONIC MASCULINITY
R W CONNELL (1944–)

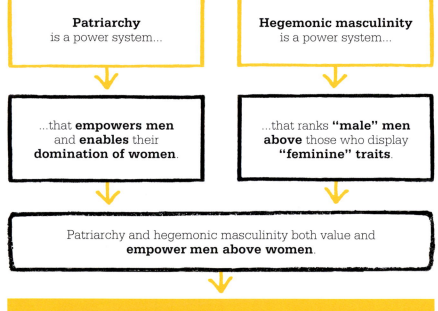

Patriarchy is a power system...

Hegemonic masculinity is a power system...

...that **empowers men** and **enables** their **domination of women**.

...that ranks **"male" men above** those who display **"feminine" traits**.

Patriarchy and hegemonic masculinity both value and **empower men above women**.

Men's interest in patriarchy is condensed in hegemonic masculinity.

It is often assumed that masculinity is a natural, biological state that cannot be altered. R W Connell claims, however, that it is not a fixed thing, but an acquired identity: there is no one pattern of masculinity that is found everywhere or over any extended period of time, and, she says, we should speak about masculinities, not masculinity, when exploring what it means to "be a man".

Masculinity also has multiple definitions within multicultural societies. In any one setting, such

See also: Harriet Martineau 26–27 ▪ Judith Butler 56–61 ▪ bell hooks 90–95 ▪ Margaret Mead 298–99 ▪ Adrienne Rich 304–09 ▪ Christine Delphy 312–317 ▪ Jeffrey Weeks 324–25 ▪ Steven Seidman 326–31

as a school or workplace, a particular form of masculinity will be seen as the "best" and most effective way to be a man.

This idea lies behind Connell's concept of hegemonic masculinity, which claims that in any time or place, different forms of masculinity are organized into a hierarchy. The dominant form – seen as the ideal masculinity and the one that others will be judged against – is the hegemonic form. It will constitute that society's idea of "manliness" and those few men who can embody this form of masculinity will be "the most honoured and desired".

Subordinate masculinity

Subordinated or marginalized forms of masculinity are those that deviate from the norm; men espousing these suffer humiliation, exclusion, and loss of privilege. When the masculine role moves towards a more "female" position (as in homosexuality), there is a corresponding loss of status and power. In this way, the patriarchal

position aligns with the hegemonic ideal in Western societies. As men reap significant benefits from maintaining dominance over women, their general interest and investment in patriarchy is formidable – it is what gives them social, cultural, and economic control. The closer a man's masculinity is to the hegemonic ideal, the more power he has.

Practising gender

Connell claims that the European/American hegemonic form, which is linked closely to the patriarchal ideal of the powerful, aggressive, unemotional male who will often use violence to get his way, is being extended across the world through processes of globalization. The media glamourizes the hegemonic ideal through its adulation of ruthless billionaire entrepreneurs and fighting fit, contact-sports stars.

Women are complicit in recognizing a hierarchy of masculinities, according to Connell. Their continued loyalty to

Most men find it difficult to be patriarchs... but they fear letting go of the benefits.
bell hooks

patriarchal religions and romantic narratives, and their perpetuation of gender expectations of children, sustains the power of the patriarchal ideal and the hegemonic masculinity associated with it. By describing masculinity within the terms of hegemony or hierarchy, Connell grants it a fluidity, which means that there is an opportunity for change. A move to establish a version of masculinity that is open to equality with women, she says, would constitute a positive hegemony. ∎

Exclusion of homosexual desire from the definition of masculinity is, according to Connell in *The Men and the Boys*, an important feature of modern-day hegemonic masculinity.

R W Connell

R W Connell was born in Australia in 1944 as Robert William ("Bob") Connell. A transsexual woman, Connell completed her transition late in life and took the first name of Raewyn. Educated in high schools in Manly and North Sydney, Connell went on to gain degrees from the universities of Melbourne and Sydney.

During the 1960s Connell was an activist in the New Left. She became one of the youngest people to attain an academic chair when she was appointed professor of sociology at Macquarie University, New South Wales, in 1976. Although best known for her work on the social construction of masculinities, Connell has also lectured extensively and written on poverty, education, and the northern hemisphere bias of mainstream social science.

Key works

1987 *Gender and Power*
1995 *Masculinities*
2000 *The Men and the Boys*

WHITE WOMEN HAVE BEEN COMPLICIT IN THIS IMPERIALIST WHITE-SUPREMACIST CAPITALIST PATRIARCHY

BELL HOOKS (1952–)

IN CONTEXT

FOCUS
**Feminism and
intersectionality**

KEY DATES
1979 The Combahee River
Collective, a black feminist
lesbian organization in the
USA, claims it is essential to
consider the conjunction of
"interlocking oppressions".

1980s US economist Heidi
Hartmann says that in the
"unhappy marriage" of Marxist
feminism, Marxism (the
husband) dominates feminism
(the wife), because class
trumps gender.

1989 US law professor
Kimberlé Crenshaw uses
"intersectionality" to describe
patterns of racism and sexism.

2002 German sociologist
Helma Lutz claims at least 14
"lines of difference" are used in
power relations, including age,
gender, skin colour, and class.

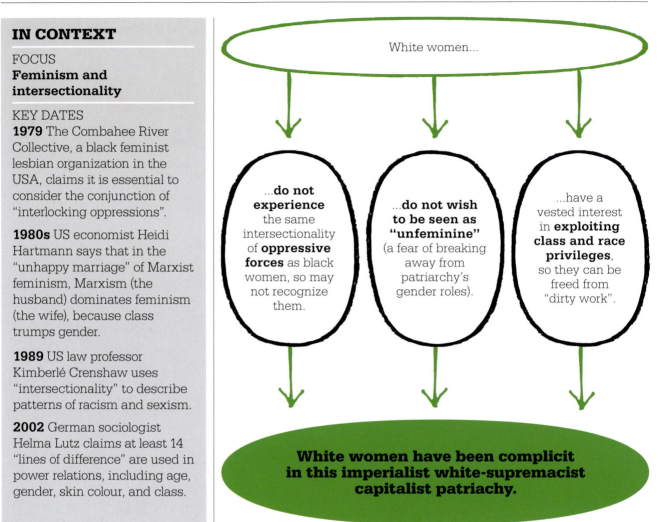

White women...

...**do not
experience** the same
intersectionality
of **oppressive
forces** as black
women, so may
not recognize
them.

...**do not wish
to be seen as
"unfeminine"**
(a fear of breaking
away from
patriarchy's
gender roles).

...have a
vested interest
in **exploiting
class and race
privileges**,
so they can be
freed from
"dirty work".

**White women have been complicit
in this imperialist white-supremacist
capitalist patriachy.**

The "second-wave" feminists of the 1960s to 1980s presented a far more formidable and thoroughgoing challenge to male domination than earlier feminists. Their broadening agenda included issues such as legal inequalities, sexuality, rape, the family, and the workplace.

But the US feminist bell hooks criticized the feminism of the 1980s in particular as representing the view of privileged white women. In *Feminist Theory: From Margin to Center*, published in 1984, she claimed that an emphasis on

women as the "sisterhood" masked what she saw as the "opportunism of bourgeois white women".

hooks says that the situation is more complicated than the second-wave feminists recognized. Worse still, these women helped maintain an intersecting network of oppressive forces that impacted the lives of working-class women of colour: white women have been complicit in perpetuating white patriarchal domination.

In 1989, US lawyer Kimberlé Crenshaw described the criss-crossing forces of oppression as

"intersectionality". She likened this to a place where traffic flows in four directions. Discrimination, like traffic, may flow in one direction or another. If an accident happens at an intersection, it could have been caused by cars travelling from any number of directions – sometimes from all directions. If a black woman is harmed because she is "at the intersection", this may have been caused by sex or race discrimination, or both.

As a lawyer, Crenshaw found that black women in the workplace were discriminated against on both

See also: Harriet Martineau 26–27 ▪ Karl Marx 28–31 ▪ Judith Butler 56–61 ▪ Friedrich Engels 66–67 ▪
Paul Gilroy 75 ▪ Elijah Anderson 82–83 ▪ R W Connell 88–89 ▪ Christine Delphy 312–17

Second-wave feminism of the 1960s to 1980s, with its emphasis on "sisterhood", is criticized by hooks as opportunistic and as representing the interests of middle-class white women.

counts – being black and female – but fell through a legal loophole. They were the last to be hired and the first to be laid off, but their employers denied this had anything to do with discrimination. When a case went to court, the judge ruled that they could not have been laid off because they were women, as other women still worked in the firm. Neither could the reason have

been their colour, as black men still worked there. The law could only deal with one or other form of oppression, not the two together.

Hierarchy systems

bell hooks was to take the idea of intersectionality still further. In *The Will to Change* (2004), she says: "I often use the phrase 'imperialist white-supremacist capitalist patriarchy' to describe the interlocking political systems that are the foundation of our nation's politics." The phrase is used to describe a set of systems that combine to situate people within the power hierarchies of society.

White supremacy is the assumed superiority of lighter-skinned or "white" races over others. While hooks acknowledges that "those who allow [racial] prejudice to lead them to hostile

acts are in the minority no matter the class standing of the neighbourhood", racial prejudice is still apparent in beliefs that a person is lazy, stupid, or more violent, for instance, because of their racial background. This form of stereotyping means that an Indian doctor or Hispanic teacher might be viewed as less competent than white Europeans.

Capitalism refers to the economic system that is characterized by private or corporate ownership of firms and goods, together with control over the prices, goods, and the labour force. It has an inherent hierarchy: those who own the means of production and control the labour force are privileged over the workers. hooks agrees with the US writer and prominent activist Carmen Vázquez, who she »

> It was clear to black women… that they were never going to have equality within the existing white-supremacist capitalist patriarchy.
> **bell hooks**

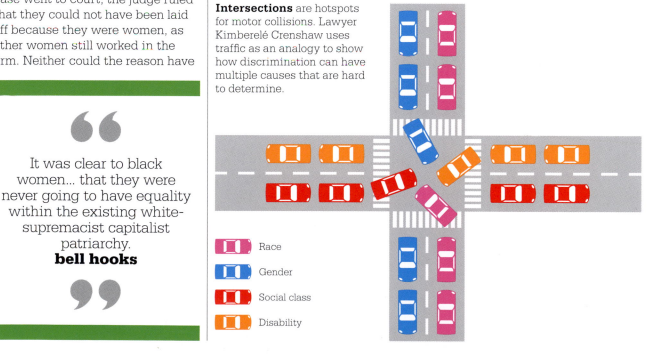

Intersections are hotspots for motor collisions. Lawyer Kimberelé Crenshaw uses traffic as an analogy to show how discrimination can have multiple causes that are hard to determine.

Race
Gender
Social class
Disability

quotes as saying that the "American capitalist obsession for individualism" means that "anything goes so long as it gets you what you want". Capitalism values money more than people, so the wealthy are seen as more important than the poor.

The attitudes encased in white supremacy and capitalism continue to cause problems, according to hooks. Imperialism and colonialism also remain relevant because, historically, non-white peoples and their countries' resources have been plundered and exploited by white supremacist capitalists in their pursuit of wealth.

The rules of patriarchy

hooks defines patriarchy as "a political-social system that insists that males are inherently dominating, superior to everything… and endowed with the right to dominate and rule over the weak and to maintain that dominance through various forms of psychological terrorism and violence." She says that of all the interlocking political systems we encounter, this is the one we learn the most about while growing up. In *The Will to Change*, hooks explains how she and her brother were schooled in the meaning of "patriarchy".

At church they were told God was a man and had created man to rule the world and everything in it. Women were created to obey and serve men. Men must be strong, provide for their family, strategize, and lead – they could also expect to be served. These are the patriarchal gender roles that are apparent in

> 66
>
> Only privileged women had the luxury to imagine working outside the home would provide them with an income… to be economically self-sufficient.
> **bell hooks**
>
> 99

every institution of a community, from families, schools, and sports arenas to courtrooms.

If challenged, these ideas may be reinforced through violence; but sometimes the cold stares or mockery of a group of peers is enough to pull someone back into behaviour more appropriate to their gender role. A crying boy or an angry girl may quickly become aware of having transgressed the gender roles that have been defined for them.

One of the most insidious things about patriarchy, hooks says, is that it is not spoken about, and we cannot dismantle a system as long as we are in "collective denial about its impact on our lives". Men rarely even know what the word "patriarchy" means – they don't use the term in everyday life, despite rigidly enforcing its rules while also suffering from them. Boys submit to the rule of the father just as girls do, and neither talks about what is happening to them.

The aim of feminism

This interlocking system, hooks says, means there is no sense in making "equality between the sexes" the goal of feminism. Since men are not equals among themselves in white supremacist, capitalist, patriarchal class structure, "which men do women want to be equal to?"

She notes that women in lower-class and poor groups, particularly black women, would not define women's liberation as equality with men, because men in their groups are also exploited and oppressed –

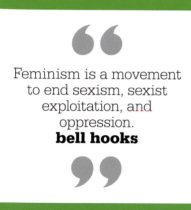

> Feminism is a movement to end sexism, sexist exploitation, and oppression.
> **bell hooks**

they too may lack social, political, and economic power. While these women are aware that patriarchy gives those men privileges, they tend to see exaggerated expressions of male chauvinism in their own group as stemming from a sense of powerlessness compared to other male groups.

The continuing effect of imperialist, white-supremacist, capitalist patriarchy is a complex "intersectionality" that must be examined in its totality of effect on women, if feminists are to improve the lives of all women. hooks claims that black women have been suspicious of the feminist movement since its inception. They realized that if its stated aim was equality with men, it could easily become a movement that would mostly improve the social standing of middle- and upper-class women. Privileged white women, hooks argues, have not been anxious to call attention to race and class privilege because they benefit from these; they could "count on there being a lower class of exploited, subordinated women to do the dirty work they were refusing to do".

Privilege and politics

Women with multiple social privileges (such as being white, heterosexual, and wealthy), may see a situation as demonstrating just one form of oppression, rather than the intersectionality of many different types of oppression. This may be due in part to ignorance, hooks suggests – in the town in which she grew up, black people frequently travelled to the white district to work, but white people did not visit her neighbourhood. They had no knowledge or experience of that world at all.

In addition, according to hooks, some women tend to shun identification with any political movement, especially one that is considered radical; or they do not wish to be associated with a "women's rights" movement of any form. This fear of being seen to join a movement that challenges male rights and behaviours has been inculcated into them from an early age through the influence of patriarchy, whose rules they continue to abide by and enforce.

Once we see that it is the system of patriarchy, and not men, that is the problem, we can then begin to find an answer, suggests hooks. She says that feminists must call attention to the diversity of women's social and political reality, and recognize that race and class oppression are also feminist issues. The feminist movement will then not solely benefit any specific group of women or privilege women over men. The real solution lies, hooks maintains, in changing the philosophical structures that underlie oppression. For this reason, feminism is a political movement, not a "romantic notion of personal freedom". ∎

---

bell hooks

US social activist and scholar Gloria Jean Watkins took the name of her maternal great-grandmother, Bell Hooks, as a pen name to honour her and to gain strength from her ability to "talk back". She uses lowercase letters to signal to the reader to focus on her ideas, rather than herself.

Born in 1952 in rural Kentucky, USA, her father was a janitor and her mother was a parent to their seven children. She went to a racially segregated school, but then attended an integrated high school, where she became acutely aware of differences in race and class. In 1973 hooks gained a degree in English from Stanford University, then took an MA and a PhD before becoming a professor of ethnic studies at the University of Southern California. Since writing her first book at the age of 19, she has published more than 30 books on different topics.

Key works

1981 *Ain't I a Woman?*
1984 *Feminist Theory: From Margin to Center*
2000 *Feminism is for Everybody*

THE CONCEPT OF "PATRIARCHY" IS INDISPENSABLE FOR AN ANALYSIS OF GENDER INEQUALITY

SYLVIA WALBY (1953–)

IN CONTEXT

FOCUS
Patriarchy

KEY DATES
1792 Mary Wollstonecraft, English advocate of women's rights, publishes *A Vindication of the Rights of Woman*.

1969 In *Sexual Politics*, US feminist Kate Millett says patriarchy is a universal power relationship that is all-pervasive and enters into all other forms of social divisions.

1971 Italian feminist Mariarosa Dalla Costa argues that women's unwaged labour is an essential part of the functioning of capitalism.

1981 In "The Unhappy Marriage of Feminism and Marxism", US feminist economist Heidi Hartmann suggests that the "dual systems" of capitalism and patriarchy oppress women.

In 1990, the British sociologist Sylvia Walby published *Theorizing Patriarchy*, a groundbreaking book that claims "patriarchy" is a highly complex phenomenon made up of many intersecting forces. Whereas earlier feminists had focused on identifying a single cause of patriarchy, linked to a particular historical era or culture, Walby defines patriarchy as "a system of social structures and practices in which men dominate, oppress, and exploit women". She claims there are six interacting structures: the family household, paid work, the state, male violence, sexuality, and cultural institutions. To examine

See also: Karl Marx 28–31 ▪ Judith Butler 56–61 ▪ bell hooks 90–95 ▪ Teri Caraway 248–49 ▪ Christine Delphy 312–17 ▪ Ann Oakley 318–19

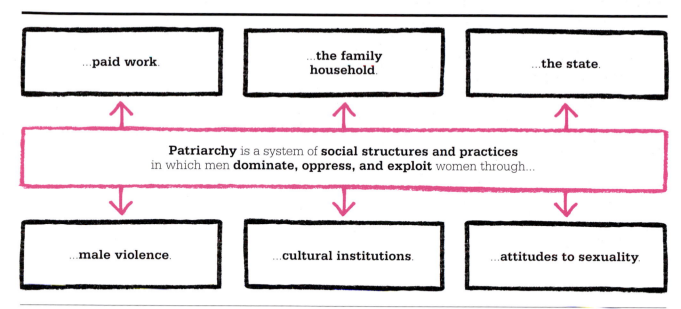

...paid work.

...the family household.

...the state.

Patriarchy is a system of **social structures and practices** in which men **dominate, oppress, and exploit** women through...

...male violence.

...cultural institutions.

...attitudes to sexuality.

these six structures, Walby looks back through the struggles and work of previous feminists.

First-wave feminism

Walby notes that the "first-wave" feminism of the 19th and early 20th centuries in Europe and the USA focused on the private, rather than public, nature of patriarchy. At this time, she says, married women were excluded from paid employment, so patriarchal domination occurred mainly within the family, where it was "the man in his position as husband or father who [was] the direct oppressor and beneficiary... of the subordination of women". The idea of "domesticity" intensified during this era. Middle-class women were confined to the private sphere; they were denied the right to vote, own property,

or to gain higher-level education, and violence by husbands was legally sanctioned.

The first-wave feminists addressed these issues on a legal level, but Walby maintains that the significant rights they won for women failed to eliminate all forms of inequality. This was because the family and the household continued to function effectively as

a "patriarchal mode of production". Patriarchy within the household is the first of Walby's six patriarchal structures; it undervalues the work of housewives (as unpaid labour), while apparently valuing them only within this role (this was women's "rightful place").

Walby points out that in Marxist terms, housewives are the producing class, while husbands »

Emmeline Pankhurst (1858–1928) was a militant, first-wave feminist who fought hard to advance women's basic rights and to secure married women the vote in the UK.

Women are not passive victims of oppressive structures. They have struggled to change both their immediate circumstances and the wider social structures.
Sylvia Walby

are the class that benefits "individually and directly" from women's unpaid labour.

Women within capitalism

By the 20th century, capitalism had become the dominant global economic model. As capitalism grew, women lost forms of work that had once been open to them (in textiles, for instance) through the growth of industrialization. They moved into a position that was disadvantaged in two ways: vertical segregation (being offered employment only in the lower grades of work) and horizontal segregation (being seen as suitable only for particular areas of work). For this reason, Walby proposes that "patriarchal relations in paid work", which give men the highest opportunities in jobs available and level of employment, constitute the second of the six structures that maintain patriarchy.

However, Walby notes that in the 20th century an interesting conflict began to arise between patriarchy and capitalism, because they had rival interests in the exploitation of women's labour.

As she says: "if women are working for capitalists they have less time to work for their husband."

Conflicts between patriarchy in the home and in the workplace have often been resolved through the intervention of Walby's third patriarchal structure: the state. For example, during World War II, British women were needed to work in munitions factories. The trade unions were unhappy about this and persuaded the UK government to introduce legislation (the Restoration of the Pre-War Practices Act 1942) to ensure that women would be removed from employment in factories at the end of the war. In this way women were moved to service the public or private arenas according to the needs of men, regardless of their own preferences.

In the West, the state has also intervened to enhance women's rights, such as the 1970 Equal Pay Act in the UK. However, many of the apparent gains have led to little change in practice, with women still earning less than men. Walby says that this is because the state is "a site of patriarchal relations", which is necessary to patriarchy as a whole. She notes that there have been important changes in state policy over the last 150 years but these also include some very significant limitations. "The state is still patriarchal as well as capitalist and racist", she says.

Male violence and sexuality

The fourth of Walby's six structures is male violence against women. Domestic violence includes controlling or threatening behaviour, and violence or abuse between intimate partners or family members. These intimate relationships are power-structured (as is the case with all of

patriarchy's six structures) and work through a set of arrangements whereby one person is controlled by another. Men's violence (or threatened violence) against women plays an important part in their continuing control and domination of women.

The fifth of the structures is sexuality. Walby says that societies prize heterosexual relationships above all others, in many cases seeing them as the only permissible option. Sexuality is a major area in which men exercise domination of women: they impose their ideas of femininity onto women and have constructed sexual practices that revolve around male notions of desire.

Walby points out that the second-wave feminists of the 1960s to 1980s looked at a wider range of "unofficial" inequities than the first-wave feminists. They queried sexuality, the family, the workplace, and reproductive rights – although some present-day, third-wave feminists have criticized them for "unfinished business". However, when oppressive laws on sexuality were abolished, some of the hard-won changes became traps for women. Sexual liberty led to the mainstreaming of pornography and

Male violence against women is sufficiently common and repetitive... to constitute a social structure.
Sylvia Walby

The automobile industry has a long history of using women as sex objects to sell cars (despite the deeply tenuous link to the product), positioning them as a focus of male fantasy and desire.

increased exploitation of women in prostitution, the sex industry, and human trafficking.

The last of Walby's six structures is culture; specifically, a society's cultural institutions. She claims that patriarchy permeates key social institutions and agents of socialization in society, including education, religion, and the media, all of which "create the representation of women within a patriarchal gaze". The world's religions, for example, continue to exclude women from the top positions and seem determined to restrict them to the "caring" rather than executive level – this, they say, is more "natural" for them. Women are thereby defined from a patriarchal viewpoint and kept firmly "in their place".

A shift to public patriarchy
The notions of private and public patriarchy are important for Walby in distinguishing other ways in which power structures intersect to affect women. She points out, for example, that British women of Afro-Caribbean origin are more likely to experience public patriarchy (finding it hard to gain

higher paid employment, for instance), while British Muslim women are more likely to experience higher levels of private patriarchy (affecting their abilities to leave the house or choose their preferred form of dress).

Since writing *Theorizing Patriarchy*, Walby has noted that while conventional "wisdom" sees the family as still central to women's lives, it has become less important. However, this has resulted, she suggests, in women working more, shifting them from the realms of private patriarchy into greater levels of public patriarchy. Women in the West are now exploited less by "individual patriarchs", such as their fathers and husbands, and more by men collectively, via work, the state, and cultural institutions.

Central to Walby's examination of patriarchy is her insistence that we see patriarchy neither as purely structural (which would lock women into subordinate positions within cultural institutions) nor as pure agency (the actions of individual men and women). She says that if we see patriarchy as fundamentally about structure, we are in danger of seeing women as passive victims. On the other hand, if we see women as locked into patriarchy through their own, voluntary actions, we may see them "as colluding with their patriarchal oppressors".

In *Theorizing Patriarchy*, Walby gives an account of patriarchy that explains both changes in structure (such as changes in the capitalist economy) and of agency (the campaigns of the three waves of feminism). She says major shifts must be made both within women themselves and by the society and cultures that surround them if we are to make meaningful progress. ∎

Sylvia Walby

Professor Sylvia Walby is a British sociologist whose work in the fields of domestic violence, patriarchy, gender relations, and globalization has found wide acceptance and acclaim. She graduated in sociology from the University of Essex, UK, in 1984, and went on to gain further degrees from the universities of Essex and Reading.

In 1992 Walby became the founding President of the European Sociological Association, and in 2008 she took up the first UNESCO Chair in Gender Research, to guide its research into gender equality and women's human rights. In the same year she was awarded an OBE for services to equal opportunities and diversity. Walby has taught at many leading institutions, including the London School of Economics (LSE) and Harvard University.

Key works

1986 *Patriarchy at Work*
1990 *Theorizing Patriarchy*
2011 *The Future of Feminism*

> 66
> When patriarchy loosens its grip in one area it only tightens it in other arenas.
> **Sylvia Walby**
> 99

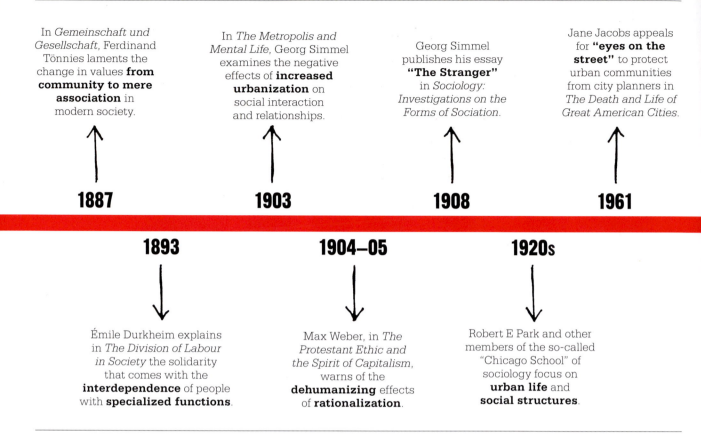

In *Gemeinschaft und Gesellschaft*, Ferdinand Tönnies laments the change in values **from community to mere association** in modern society.

In *The Metropolis and Mental Life*, Georg Simmel examines the negative effects of **increased urbanization** on social interaction and relationships.

Georg Simmel publishes his essay **"The Stranger"** in *Sociology: Investigations on the Forms of Sociation*.

Jane Jacobs appeals for **"eyes on the street"** to protect urban communities from city planners in *The Death and Life of Great American Cities*.

1887   **1903**   **1908**   **1961**

1893   **1904–05**   **1920s**

Émile Durkheim explains in *The Division of Labour in Society* the solidarity that comes with the **interdependence** of people with **specialized functions**.

Max Weber, in *The Protestant Ethic and the Spirit of Capitalism*, warns of the **dehumanizing** effects of **rationalization**.

Robert E Park and other members of the so-called "Chicago School" of sociology focus on **urban life** and **social structures**.

As prehistory's primitive human groups began to settle down in one place, the foundations of civilization were laid. From these early beginnings, humans increasingly lived together in larger and larger groups, and civilization grew further with the establishment of villages, towns, and cities. But for the greater part of human history, most people lived in rural communities. Large-scale urbanization came about only with the Industrial Revolution, which was accompanied by a huge expansion of towns and cities, and massive numbers of people migrating to work in the factories and mills that were located there.

Living in an urban environment became as much an aspect of "modernity" as industrialization and the growth of capitalism, and

sociologists from Adam Ferguson to Ferdinand Tönnies recognized that there was a major difference between traditional rural communities and modern urban ones. This alteration of social order was ascribed to a variety of factors by an assortment of thinkers: to capitalism by Karl Marx; to the division of labour in industry by Émile Durkheim; to rationalization and secularization by Max Weber. It was Georg Simmel who suggested that urbanization itself had affected the ways in which people interact socially – and one of the fundamental characteristics of modern living is life in the city.

Community in the city
Simmel examined not only the new forms of social order that had arisen in the modern cities, but also the

effects upon the individual of living in large groups, often separated from traditional community ties and family. Building upon his work, the so-called Chicago School of sociology, spearheaded by Robert E Park, helped to establish a distinct field of urban sociology. Soon, however, sociologists changed the emphasis of their research from what it is like to live in a city, to what kind of city we want to live in.

Having evolved to meet the needs of industrialization, the city – and urban life, with all its benefits and disadvantages – was felt by many sociologists to have been imposed on people. The Marxist sociologist Henri Lefebvre believed that the demands of capitalism had shaped modern urban society, but that ordinary people could take control of their urban environment,

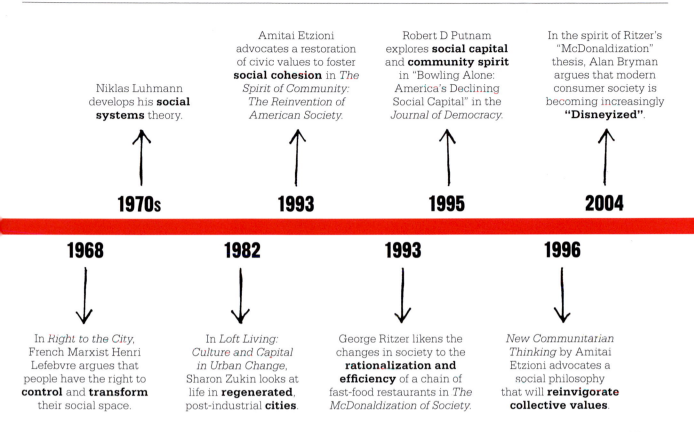

Niklas Luhmann develops his **social systems** theory.

1970s

Amitai Etzioni advocates a restoration of civic values to foster **social cohesion** in *The Spirit of Community: The Reinvention of American Society*.

1993

Robert D Putnam explores **social capital** and **community spirit** in "Bowling Alone: America's Declining Social Capital" in the *Journal of Democracy*.

1995

In the spirit of Ritzer's "McDonaldization" thesis, Alan Bryman argues that modern consumer society is becoming increasingly **"Disneyized"**.

2004

1968

In *Right to the City*, French Marxist Henri Lefebvre argues that people have the right to **control** and **transform** their social space.

1982

In *Loft Living: Culture and Capital in Urban Change*, Sharon Zukin looks at life in **regenerated**, post-industrial **cities**.

1993

George Ritzer likens the changes in society to the **rationalization and efficiency** of a chain of fast-food restaurants in *The McDonaldization of Society*.

1996

New Communitarian Thinking by Amitai Etzioni advocates a social philosophy that will **reinvigorate collective values**.

what he called their "social space". Similarly (but from a different political standpoint), Jane Jacobs advocated that people should resist the plans of urban developers and create environments that encouraged the formation of communities within the city.

In the late 20th century, several sociologists took up this idea of the loss of community in our increasingly individualized Western society. A communitarian movement emerged, led by US sociologist Amitai Etzioni, suggesting new ways to restore community spirit in what had become an impersonal society. Robert D Putnam also gave prominence to the idea of community in his explanation of "social capital", and the value and benefits of social interaction.

Not everyone agreed, however, that the answer to the social problems of urban life was a return to traditional community values. Niklas Luhmann pointed out that the problem today is one of communication between social systems that have become increasingly fragmented and differentiated. In the post-industrial age, with all its new methods of communication, new strategies for social cohesion need to be found.

Post-industrial cities
The nature of cities began to change in the late 20th century, as the manufacturing industries moved out or disappeared. While some cities became ghost towns, others became centres of the service industries. As working-class areas were gentrified, and

industrial buildings became desirable postmodern living spaces, the concept of modern metropolitan life became associated with prosperity rather than gritty industrialization.

This manifested itself not only in the transformation of urban living spaces, as described by Sharon Zukin in the 1980s, but throughout the postmodern social order. George Ritzer likened the efficiency and rationalization of the service industries to the business model pioneered by fast-food chain McDonalds, and Alan Bryman has noted how a US entertainment culture created by Disney has influenced modern consumerism. Modern urban society, having been created by industrialization, is now being shaped by the new demands of post-industrial commerce. ∎

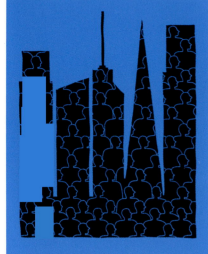

STRANGERS ARE NOT REALLY CONCEIVED AS INDIVIDUALS BUT AS STRANGERS OF A PARTICULAR TYPE
GEORG SIMMEL (1858–1918)

IN CONTEXT

FOCUS
Mental life of the metropolis

KEY DATES
19th century Urbanization begins taking place on a large scale in Europe and the USA.

From 1830 Nascent sociology claims to offer the means to understand the changes brought about in society by the Industrial Revolution.

1850–1900 Key social thinkers such as Ferdinand Tönnies, Émile Durkheim, and Karl Marx express concerns about the effect of modernization and industrialization on society.

From the 1920s Simmel's work on the impact of urban life influences the development of urban sociology in the USA by a group of sociologists, known collectively as the Chicago School.

The Industrial Revolution was accompanied in Europe and the USA by urbanization from the 19th century onwards. For many people this resulted in increased freedom as they experienced liberation from the constraints of traditional social structures. But in tandem with these developments came growing demands from capitalist employers for the functional specialization of people and their work, which meant new restrictions and curtailments of individual liberty.

German sociologist Georg Simmel wanted to understand the struggle faced by the city dweller in preserving autonomy and individuality in the face of these overwhelming social forces. He discovered that the increase in human interaction that was brought about by living and

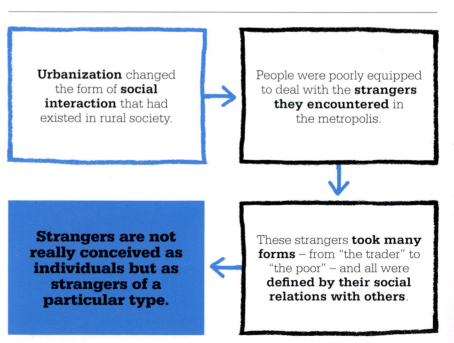

Urbanization changed the form of **social interaction** that had existed in rural society.

People were poorly equipped to deal with the **strangers they encountered** in the metropolis.

These strangers **took many forms** – from "the trader" to "the poor" – and all were **defined by their social relations with others**.

Strangers are not really conceived as individuals but as strangers of a particular type.

See also: Karl Marx 28–31 ▪ Ferdinand Tönnies 32–33 ▪ Émile Durkheim 34–37 ▪ Max Weber 38–45 ▪ Zygmunt Bauman 136–43 ▪ Thorstein Veblen 214–19 ▪ Erving Goffman 264–69 ▪ Michel Foucault 270–77

working in an urban environment profoundly affected relationships between people. He set out his findings in *The Metropolis and Mental Life*. Whereas in pre-modern society people would be intimately familiar with those around them, in the modern urban environment individuals are largely unknown to those who surround them. Simmel believed that the increase in social activity and anonymity brought about a change in consciousness.

The rapid tempo of life in a city was such that people needed a "protective organ" to insulate them from the external and internal stimuli. According to Simmel, the metropolitan "reacts with his head instead of his heart"; he erects a rational barrier of cultivated indifference – a "blasé attitude". The change in consciousness also leads to people becoming reserved and aloof. This estrangement from traditional and accepted norms of behaviour is further undermined by the money culture of cities, which reduces everything in the metropolis to a financial exchange.

> Through this anonymity...
> each party acquires an
> unmerciful matter-of-factness.
> **Georg Simmel**

Simmel says that the attitude of the metropolitan can be understood as a social-survival technique to cope with the mental disturbance created by immersion in city life – an approach that enables people to focus their energies on those who matter to them. It also results in them becoming more tolerant of difference and more sophisticated.

Space in the metropolis

Degrees of proximity and distance among individuals and groups were central to Simmel's understanding of living in a metropolis, and ideas about social space influenced one of his best-known concepts: the social role of "the stranger", which is set out in an essay in *Sociology*. In the past, he says, strangers were encountered only rarely and fleetingly; but urbanite strangers are not drifters – they are "potential wanderers". Simmel says that the stranger (such as a trader), or the stranger group (his example is "European Jews"), is connected to the community spatially but not socially; he or she is characterized by both "nearness and remoteness" – *in* the community but not *of* it.

The stranger was one of many social types described by Simmel, each becoming what they are through their relations with others; an idea that has influenced many sociologists, including Zygmunt Bauman. Erving Goffman's concept of "civil inattention", whereby people minimize social interaction in public – by avoiding eye contact, for instance – is also informed by one of Simmel's insights: his notion of the "blasé attitude". ▪

Georg Simmel

Born in Berlin in 1858 to a prosperous Jewish family, Georg Simmel is one of the lesser-known founders of sociology. He studied philosophy and history at the University of Berlin and received his doctorate in 1881. Despite the popularity of his work with the German intellectual elite, notably Ferdinand Tönnies and Max Weber, he remained an outsider and only gained his professorship at Strasbourg in 1914.

He developed what is known as formal sociology, which derives from his belief that we can understand distinct human phenomena by concentrating not on the content of interactions but on the forms that underlie behaviour. But it is his study of life in a metropolis that remains his most influential work, as it was the precursor to the development of urban sociology by the so-called Chicago School in the 1920s.

Key works

1900 *The Philosophy of Money*
1903 *The Metropolis and Mental Life*
1908 *Sociology*

THE FREEDOM TO REMAKE OUR CITIES AND OURSELVES
HENRI LEFEBVRE (1901–1991)

IN CONTEXT

FOCUS
The right to the city

KEY DATES
19th century Extensive urbanization takes place across Europe and the USA.

1848 Karl Marx and Friedrich Engels offer a critique of class inequalities in Western capitalist society in *The Communist Manifesto*.

1903 German sociologist Georg Simmel publishes *The Metropolis and Mental Life*.

From the 1980s According to British sociologist David Harvey and Spanish theorist Manuel Castells, cities serve the interests of capitalism and this affects the interaction of those who live there.

From the 1990s Lefebvre's concept of "right to the city" influences social movements across the world, including in the USA, France, Brazil, and the Philippines.

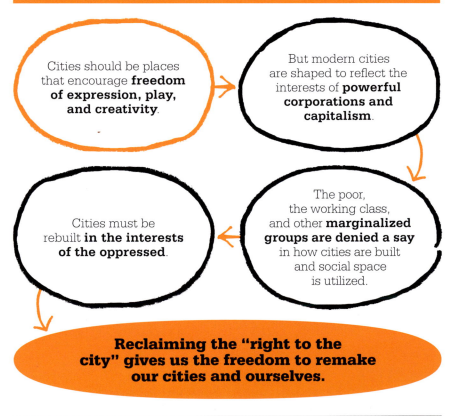

Cities should be places that encourage **freedom of expression, play, and creativity**.

But modern cities are shaped to reflect the interests of **powerful corporations and capitalism**.

The poor, the working class, and other **marginalized groups are denied a say** in how cities are built and social space is utilized.

Cities must be rebuilt **in the interests of the oppressed**.

Reclaiming the "right to the city" gives us the freedom to remake our cities and ourselves.

The city need not be seen as a concrete jungle – grimy, unpleasant, and threatening. For French sociologist and philosopher Henri Lefebvre, who dedicated most of his life to the study of urban society, it is an exciting and complex combination of power relationships, diverse identities, and ways of being.

Writing in the 1960s and 1970s, Lefebvre maintained that one of the most fascinating aspects of the city is not simply the people in it, but

See also: Karl Marx 28–31 ▪ Ferdinand Tönnies 32–33 ▪ Peter Townsend 74 ▪ Elijah Anderson 82–83 ▪
Georg Simmel 104–05 ▪ Jane Jacobs 108–09 ▪ Amitai Etizoni 112–19 ▪ Sharon Zukin 128–31 ▪ Saskia Sassen 164–65

Vast, impersonal malls serve the interests of consumer capitalism. The construction of such spaces often leads to the displacement of the area's original, working-class residents.

the fact that it is an environment that both reflects and creates society. Applying a Marxist perspective to his analysis, Lefebvre also says that urban spaces are shaped by the state and serve the interests of powerful corporations and capitalism. Parts of the city mirror the class relations contained within it: the opulence of some areas reveals the power and wealth of elites, while run-down inner-city areas and ghettos outside the centre indicate the displacement and marginalization of the poor, the working class, and other excluded groups.

Public and private

Many modern cities, for example, have become dominated by private spaces, such as shopping malls and office complexes, built in the service of capitalism. The loss of public space has severely restricted the arenas in which people can meet on an equal footing with others, so eroding their personal freedoms and stifling their means to satisfy their social and psychological needs. This can lead to serious social problems, such as crime, depression, homelessness, social exclusion, and poverty.

Considerable power is wielded by those who own and control urban spaces – architects, planners, "the merchant bourgeoisie, the intellectuals, and politicians", according to Lefebvre. But he believes that decisions about the exact nature of the urban environment – what takes place in it, how social space is built and used – should be open to all. Ordinary people should participate in creating a space that reflects their needs and interests – only by claiming this "right to the city" can major social issues be addressed.

Lefebvre's vision is of cities that pulse with life and are vibrant expressions of human freedom and creativity, where people can play, explore their creative and artistic needs, and achieve some form of self-realization. City streets should, he says, be designed to encourage this type of existence – they may be raw, exciting, and untamed but precisely because of this they will remind people that they are alive.

Lefebvre's demand for the right to the city is not simply a call for a series of reforms but for a wholesale transformation of social relations within the city, if not wider society – it is, in essence, a proposal for a radical form of democracy, whereby control is wrested from elites and turned over to the masses. This, he says, is only achievable by groups and class factions "capable of revolutionary initiative". ∎

Henri Lefebvre

Marxist sociologist and philosopher Henri Lefebvre was born in Hagetmau, France, in 1901. He studied philosophy at the Sorbonne, Paris, graduating in 1920. He joined the French Communist Party in 1928 and became one of the most prominent Marxist intellectuals in France. He was, however, later expelled by the Communist Party and became one of its fiercest critics. In 1961 he was appointed professor of sociology at the University of Strasbourg, before moving to Nanterre in 1965. Lefebvre was a prolific writer on a wide range of subjects. His work challenged the dominant capitalist authorities and as such was not always well received, but has gone on to influence several disciplines, including geography, philosophy, sociology, political science, and architecture.

Key works

1968 *Right to the City*
1970 *The Urban Revolution*
1974 *The Production of Space*

THERE MUST BE EYES ON THE STREET
JANE JACOBS (1916–2006)

IN CONTEXT

FOCUS
Urban community

KEY DATES
1887 Ferdinand Tönnies'
*Gemeinschaft und
Gesellschaft* stirs sociological
interest in the bonds of
community in urban society.

From the 1950s Inner city
neighbourhoods in Western
cities experience waves of
pressure from city planners.

2000 US sociologist Robert D
Putnam argues in *Bowling
Alone* that community values
have eroded since the 1960s.

2002 In *The Rise of The
Creative Class*, US sociologist
and economist Richard Florida
cites Jacobs as an influence on
his theories of creativity.

2013 Increased use of camera
surveillance in US cities
after 9/11 results in the
identification of suspects
wanted for the Boston
Marathon bombings.

A **good city street** has buildings that face outwards...

↓

...and a mix of **business** and **residential properties**.

↓

It needs a **steady traffic of people** on the sidewalks...

↓

...to increase **community and security**...

↓

...and **create activity** for people to watch and enjoy.

↓

There must be eyes on the street.

Jane Jacobs spent her working life advancing a distinct vision of the city – in particular focusing on what makes a successful urban community. Her ideas were formed from her observations of urban life in the neighbourhood of West Greenwich Village, New York, where she lived for more than 30 years.

Jacobs was opposed to the large-scale changes to city life that were occurring in New York during the 1960s, led by city planner and her arch-rival Howard Moses; these included slum-clearance projects and the building of high-rise developments. At the heart of her vision is the idea that urban life should be a vibrant and rich affair, whereby people are able to interact with one another in dense and exciting urban environments. She prefers chaos to order, walking to driving, and diversity to uniformity.

For Jacobs, urban communities are organic entities – complex, integrated ecosystems – that should be left to grow and to change by themselves and not be subject to the grand plans of so-called experts and technocrats. The best judges of how a city should be – and how it should

See also: Ferdinand Tönnies 32–33 ▪ Michel Foucault 52–55 ▪ Georg Simmel 104–05 ▪ Henri Lefebvre 106–07 ▪ Robert D Putnam 124–25 ▪ Sharon Zukin 128–31 ▪ Saskia Sassen 164–65

Jane Jacobs' vision of what a city street should be like is exemplified by this New York scene of vibrant urban life, with residential apartments, street-level businesses, and sidewalk bustle.

evolve – are the local residents themselves. Jacobs argues that urban communities are best placed to understand how their city functions, because city life is created and sustained through their various interactions.

Ballet of the sidewalk

Jacobs notes that the built form of a city is crucial to the life of an urban community. Of prime importance are the sidewalks. The streets in which people live should be a tight pattern of intersecting sidewalks, which allow people to meet, bump into each other, converse, and get to know one another. She calls this the "ballet of the sidewalk", a complex but ultimately enriching set of encounters that help individuals become acquainted with their neighbours and neighbourhood.

Diversity and mixed-use of space are also, for Jacobs, key elements of this urban form. The commercial, business, and residential elements of a city should not be separated out but instead be side by side, to allow for greater integration of people. There should also be a diversity of old and new buildings, and people's interactions should determine how buildings get used and reused.

Finally, urban communities flourish better in places where a critical mass of people live, work, and interact. Such high-density – but not overcrowded – spaces are, she feels, engines of creativity and vibrancy. They are also safe places to be, because the higher density means that there are more "eyes on the street": shopkeepers and locals who know their area and provide a natural form of surveillance. ▪

Jane Jacobs

Jane Jacobs was a passionate writer and urbanist. She left Scranton, Pennsylvania, USA, for New York in 1935, during the Great Depression. After seeing the Greenwich Village area for the first time she relocated there from Brooklyn – her interest in urban communities had begun. In 1944 she married, and moved into a house on Hudson Street.

It was when Jacobs was working as a writer for the magazine *Architectural Forum* that she first began to be critical of large top-down urban regeneration schemes. Throughout her life she was an activist and campaigner for her community-based vision of the city.

In 2007 the Rockefeller Foundation created the Jane Jacobs Medal in her honour to celebrate urban visionaries whose actions in New York City affirm her principles.

Key works

1961 *The Death and Life of Great American Cities*
1969 *The Economy of Cities*
1984 *Cities and the Wealth of Nations*

ONLY COMMUNICATION CAN COMMUNICATE
NIKLAS LUHMANN (1927–1998)

IN CONTEXT

FOCUS
Systems of communication

KEY DATES
1937 US sociologist Talcott Parsons discusses systems theory in *The Structure of Social Action.*

1953 Austrian philosopher Ludwig Wittgenstein's concept of language games is published posthumously and influences Luhmann's ideas on communication.

1969 *Laws of Form* by British mathematician George Spencer-Brown underpins Luhmann's ideas about structural differentiation.

1987 German sociologist Jürgen Habermas engages Luhmann in critical debate about systems theory.

2009 Luhmann's ideas are applied by Greek scholar Andreas Mihalopoulos in his analysis of the criminal justice and legal systems.

Modern society has **distinct social systems** (the economy, the law, education, politics, and so on).

These **systems give meaning to the world**, yet they consist not of people but of **communications**.

Each system processes activities and problems in its own distinctive way, so **cannot connect to other systems** without assistance.

Structural couplings enable **restricted communications** between the different communication systems.

Modernity's defining feature, according to German sociologist Niklas Luhmann, is advanced capitalist society's differentiation into separate social systems – the economic, educational, scientific, legal, political, religious, and so on. Luhmann argues that the term "society" refers to the system that encompasses all the other systems: society is, he says, the system of systems.

Individuals, Luhmann insists, are socially meaningless. Society's base element is not the human actor but "communication" – a term that he defines as the "synthesis of information, utterance, and understanding" arising out of the

See also: Max Weber 38–45 ■ Jürgen Habermas 286–87 ■ Talcott Parsons 300–01 ■ Herbert Spencer 334 ■ Alfred Schütz 335

activities and interactions, verbal and non-verbal, within a system. Luhmann argues that just as a plant reproduces its own cells in a circular, biological process of self-production, so a social system is similarly self-sustaining and develops out of an operation that possesses connectivity – emerging when "communication develops from communication". He likens communication to the structural equivalent of a chemical.

Structural couplings

Luhmann uses George Spencer-Brown's ideas on the mathematical laws of form to help define a system, arguing that something arises out of difference: a system is, according to this theory, a "distinction" from its environment. And, says Luhmann, a system's environment is constituted by other systems. For example, the environment of a family system includes other families, the political system, the medical system, and so on. Crucially, each individual system can only make sense of the

events – the activities and ways of communicating – peculiar to itself; it is relatively indifferent to what takes place in the other systems (and the wider society). So, for example, the economic system is functionally dedicated to its own interests and is uninterested in moral issues, except where these might have an impact on the profitability of economic activities and transactions – whereas moral concerns are of great consequence in, say, the religious system.

Luhmann identifies this lack of systems integration as one of the major problems confronting advanced capitalist societies. He identifies what he calls "structural couplings" – certain forms and institutions that help to connect separated systems by translating the communications produced by one system into terms that the other can understand. Examples include a constitution, which couples the legal and political systems, and a university, which couples the educational and, among others, economic systems.

Artists protest at BP's sponsorship of London's Tate Britain art gallery, reflecting the protesters belief that the system of corporate enterprise is not compatible with that of the art world.

"Structural coupling" is a concept that helps to account for the relationship between people (as conscious systems) and social systems (as communications).

Despite its extreme complexity, Luhmann's theory is used worldwide as an analytical tool for social systems. His critics say that the theory passes academic scrutiny, but operationally it fails to show how communication can take place without human activity. ■

Humans cannot communicate; not even their brains can communicate; not even their conscious minds can communicate.
Niklas Luhmann

Niklas Luhmann

Niklas Luhmann studied law at the University of Freiburg, Germany, from 1946 to 1949, before becoming a civil servant in 1956. He spent 1960 to 1961 on sabbatical at Harvard University, USA, studying sociology and administrative science, where he was taught by Talcott Parsons.

In 1966 Luhmann received his doctorate in sociology from the University of Münster and in 1968 he became professor of sociology at the University of Bielefeld, where he remained. Luhmann was the recipient of several honorary degrees, and in 1988 he was the winner of the prestigious Hegel Prize, awarded to prominent thinkers by the city of Stuttgart. He was a prolific writer, with some 377 publications to his name.

Key works

1972 *A Sociological Theory of Law*
1984 *Social Systems*
1997 *Theory of Society* (two volumes)

SOCIETY
SHOULD ARTICULATE
WHAT IS GOOD
AMITAI ETZIONI (1929–)

Communities rather than individuals are, says Etzioni, the elemental building blocks of society, and society comprises multiple, overlapping communities. People are therefore characteristically members of many different intersecting communities.

formations, such as families and schools, through macro formations, such as ethnic groups, religions, or nation-states.

Communities need not be geographically concentrated: for example, the Jewish community in New York is dispersed across the city but nevertheless maintains a strong sense of moral solidarity through core institutions such as synagogues and faith-based schools. Etzioni even counts online Internet-based communities as legitimate forms of community, provided that members are committed to, and share, the same values. Conversely, some classically conceived communities, such as villages, do not meet Etzoni's criteria if the aggregate of the people comprising the village are not bound by an obvious commitment to shared norms and values.

Communities are not always virtuous: some may be harsh and confining, or they may be founded on shared values that are far from ethical. Etzioni cites the example of an Afrikaaner village in South Africa whose members supported and colluded in lynching.

The communal society

Rather than just operating at the intellectual level, Etzioni proposes four aspects of how a communitarian society should be implemented and organized. He does this by identifying the core aspects of communitarian society and the functions each one plays in relation to the wider social whole.

The first aspect is what Etzioni calls the "moral voice" – the name given to the shared set of collectively assembled norms and values on which the interpersonal and moral conduct that binds community members is based. No society can thrive without a solid moral order, especially if reliance on state intervention in public matters is to be kept to a minimum. By identifying and establishing a moral voice, it is no longer necessary to rely on either individual conscience or law enforcement agencies to regulate the conduct of community members. When communities value certain behaviours – such as avoiding alcohol abuse and not speeding – anti-social behaviours are prevented, and tend to be curbed effectively.

Second is the "communitarian family". Bringing a child into this world not only obligates the parents to the child but the family to the community too. When children are raised poorly, the consequences must usually be faced not just by the family but by the entire »

Two-parent families, Etzioni claims, are far better equipped to undertake the job of rearing children than one-parent families, because it is a "labour intensive, demanding task".

School leavers should enrol for military service (as at these barracks in Germany in 2011), Etzioni argues, because it instils self-discipline and builds character and community spirit.

community. It is for this reason, according to Etzioni, that the procreation, and bringing up, of children should be considered a communitarian act. Etzioni argues that parents have a moral responsibility to the community to raise their children to the best of their ability; and the communities have an obligation to help them in their efforts. Communities should support and encourage, rather than stigmatize, parents who take a respite from work in order to spend time with their children.

> Education, particularly character formation, is the essential family task.
> **Amitai Etzioni**

Etzioni finds that the accumulation of evidence tends to support the important social role of the family, and observes: "It is no accident that in a wide variety of human societies (from the Zulus to the Inuits, from ancient Greece and ancient China to modernity), there has never been a society that did not have two-parent families." He argues that such a structure, or one that replicates its supportive parenting arrangements, is crucial to "reducing the parenting deficit" brought about by developments such as new career patterns, divorce, the growth in single parenthood, and increased individualism. As part of this, he says that society needs to limit the institutionalization of young children in day-care centres.

Etzioni's third principle sets out the functions of the "communitarian school". Schools should do far more than transmitting skills and knowledge to pupils. They should build upon the task of character formation initiated by parents to help lay the foundations for a stable

sense of self, of purposefulness, and the ability to control impulses and defer immediate gratification. In particular, the values of discipline, self-discipline, and internalization – the integration of the values of others into one's own sense of self – play a major role in the child's psychological development and wellbeing.

As part of his emphasis on self-discipline, Etzioni argues that all school leavers should undertake a mandatory year of national service. Doing so, he claims, would provide "a strong antidote to the ego-centred mentality as youth serve shared needs".

Fourth, and finally, Etzioni puts forward measures intended to counter the loss of traditional community while also serving as the basis on which to build new communities. These include changing what US sociologist Robert N Bellah termed "habits of the heart". Etzioni's measures include fostering a "community environment" in which thinking about our individual actions in

> The imbalance between rights and responsibilities has existed for a long time.
> **Amitai Etzioni**

terms of their consequences for the wider community becomes second nature; working out conflicts between individual career aspirations and goals and commitments to the community; redesigning the physical, lived environment in order "to render it more community-friendly"; and seeking to reinvest more of our personal and professional resources back into the community.

Criticisms

Etzioni's communitarianism is a response to a range of real concerns about the deterioration of private and public morality and shared values, the decline of the family, high crime rates, and civic and political apathy across US society.

Volunteers play an important part in thousands of organizations across North America and Western Europe, including community tree-planting projects in many neighbourhoods.

His vision of a more democratic, just, and egalitarian society is commended by scholars and commentators from a wide range of ideological positions. However, Etzioni's work has also drawn criticism. For example, some supporters of feminism object strongly to communitarianism as an attempt to undo women's economic liberation. They argue that a mother with a full-time job now spends more quality time with her children than the average homemaker did 30 years ago. Beatrix Campbell has accused the communitarians of a "nostalgic crusade", pointing out that the kind of mother they evoke did not exist.

US sociologist and political theorist Richard Sennett claims Etzioni's work fails to address the nature of political and economic power other than in the vaguest of terms, and does not provide a convincing account of what might motivate individuals to commit to

Today there is increasing interest among youngsters... in finding careers... [in which] you can combine 'making it' with something meaningful.
Amitai Etzioni

communitarian principles and values. If, as Etzioni claims, US culture is self-obsessed and overly individualistic, then he fails to provide an answer as to why anyone would choose to take on responsibility to a community that would make demands of them and potentially impinge upon their individual rights.

In spite of criticisms, many of the ideas at the heart of Etzioni's communitarianism have influenced governments. In his book *The Third Way,* British sociologist Anthony Giddens sees Etzioni's work as central to the framework of the political philosophy known as the Third Way, developed by former British prime minister Tony Blair. Etzioni's work appealed to the UK's New Labour government in two distinct ways: first, it provided middle ground between the political Left, with its overemphasis on the role to be played by the State, and the political Right, with its exaggerated support of the free market and championing of the individual; second, it presented the notion of citizenship as something that has to be earned through the fulfilment of shared expectations and obligations. ■

MCDONALDIZATION AFFECTS VIRTUALLY EVERY ASPECT OF SOCIETY

GEORGE RITZER (1940–)

IN CONTEXT

FOCUS
McDonaldization

KEY DATES
1921–1922 Max Weber's *Economy and Society*, which analyses the relationship between rationality and bureaucracy, is published in Germany.

1961 US entrepreneurs Richard ("Dick") and Maurice ("Mac") McDonald sell their pioneering fast-food burger business to Ray Kroc, who develops it worldwide.

1997 The sushi restaurant chain YO! Sushi opens in Britain, self-consciously using the McDonald's model.

1999 British sociologist Barry Smart edits *Resisting McDonaldization*, a wide-ranging collection of critical responses to Ritzer's McDonaldization thesis.

G erman sociologist Max Weber argued that a defining feature of the shift from traditional to modern society was the ever-growing number of aspects of life that were organized and enacted along rational, as opposed to emotionally oriented or value-laden, lines.

Developing Weber's ideas, US sociologist George Ritzer claims that the process has reached new levels in both North American and Western European culture, and is now manifested in unprecedented ways. According to Ritzer, author of the 1993 sociological classic *The McDonaldization of Society*, this "wide-ranging process of

See also: Karl Marx 28–31 ▪ Max Weber 38–45 ▪ Roland Robertson 146–47 ▪ Herbert Marcuse 182–87 ▪ Harry Braverman 226–31 ▪ Karl Mannheim 335

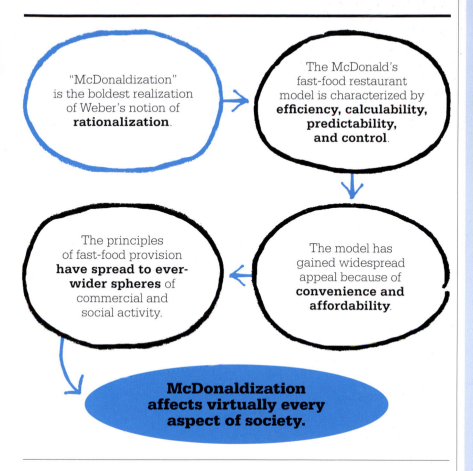

"McDonaldization" is the boldest realization of Weber's notion of **rationalization**.

The McDonald's fast-food restaurant model is characterized by **efficiency, calculability, predictability, and control**.

The principles of fast-food provision **have spread to ever-wider spheres** of commercial and social activity.

The model has gained widespread appeal because of **convenience and affordability**.

McDonaldization affects virtually every aspect of society.

George Ritzer

George Ritzer was born in 1940 in New York City, USA. His father drove a taxi and his mother worked as a secretary. Ritzer claims that his upbringing inspired him to work as hard as he could at his studies in order to distance himself from the often lowly standard of living that characterized his "upper lower-class" childhood.

Since 1974, George Ritzer has been at the University of Maryland, where he is now Distinguished University Professor. While the McDonaldization thesis is his best-known and most influential contribution to sociological theory, he is primarily a critic of so-called consumer society and has published prolifically across a wide range of areas.

Key works

1993 *The McDonaldization of Society: An Investigation into the Changing Character of Social Life*
1999 *Enchanting a Disenchanted World: Revolutionizing the Means of Consumption*
2004 *The Globalization of Nothing*

rationalization" is most clearly exemplified by the McDonald's fast-food restaurant chain.

The McDonald's way

Wherever you are in the world, a McDonald's restaurant never seems to be far away. In fact, there are around 35,000 restaurants in more than 100 countries around the globe. And no matter where that happens to be, there is a virtually flawless level of uniformity and reliability. This familiarity of experience is a definitive feature of McDonald's restaurants all over the world and it is directly attributable to the strong emphasis the McDonald's corporation places

on rationalization. Ritzer terms this development "McDonaldization", and claims that the tendencies and processes it refers to have infiltrated, and now dominate, "more and more sectors of American society as well as the rest of the world". He argues that McDonaldization has five main components: efficiency, calculability, predictability, control, and "the ultimate irrationality of formal rationality".

Efficiency refers to the bureaucratic principles employed by the corporation as it strives, from the level of organizational structure down to the interactions between employees and customers, to find »

A **McDonald's** next to Xi'an's historic Drum Tower. McDonald's opened its first outlet in China in 1990. By 2014, with 2,000 premises, it was China's second-biggest restaurant chain.

the optimum means to an end. For example, food preparation: burgers are assembled, cooked, and distributed in an assembly-line fashion because this is the most efficient way. Not only is this true in terms of the time taken to prepare food, but also the space necessary for doing so. Moreover, the physical layout of a McDonald's restaurant is designed in such a way that employees and customers alike behave in an efficient manner. A culture of efficiency is cultivated and maintained by staff adhering to a strict series of standardized norms, regulations, rules, and operational procedures.

Calculability refers to things that are counted and quantified; in particular, there is a tendency to emphasize quantity (the "Big Mac") over quality. Ritzer notes that many aspects of the work of employees at McDonald's are timed, because the fast-paced nature of the restaurant environment is intended to ensure maximum productivity.

Predictability affects the food products, restaurant design, and employee and customer interactions. Irrespective of the geographic setting, or the time of day or night, when customers enter a restaurant they want to know what to expect – and knowing what it is they want, where to find the menu, and how to order, they will be able to pay, eat, and leave.

Control is closely linked to technology. The machinery used to cook the food served in McDonald's restaurants dominates both employees and customers. The machines dictate cooking times, and so the pace of work for the employees; and the machines produce a uniform product so customers cannot specify how they would like their food to be cooked. Ritzer argues that – in time –

> ❝
> **McDonald's has become more important than the United States itself.**
> **George Ritzer**
> ❞

technologies that are more predictable and easier to control than people may come to replace employees entirely.

Finally, Ritzer assesses the costs of this otherwise beneficial rationalization. He acknowledges his debt to Weber in observing that, paradoxically, rational systems seem to spawn irrationalities and unintended consequences. The ultimate irrationality, Ritzer emphasizes, is the dehumanizing effects that the McDonald's model has on both employees and customers.

He notes that McDonald's employees work in mindless, production-line style jobs, often in cramped circumstances for little pay. There is virtually no scope for innovation and initiative on behalf of employees, either individually or collectively, resulting in worker dissatisfaction and alienation, and high staff-turnover rates.

The customers queue to buy and eat unhealthy food in what Ritzer describes as "dehumanizing settings and circumstances". Moreover, the speed of production and consumption in McDonald's restaurants means that, by definition, customers cannot be served high-quality food, which requires more time to prepare.

Principles of modernity

Ritzer argues that the sociological significance of these five principles of McDonaldization is their extension to an ever-greater number of spheres of social activity. In essence, the dominant cultural template for organizing all manner

> "
> Within sociology, theory is one of the least likely elements to be McDonaldized, yet it too has undergone that process, at least to some extent.
> **George Ritzer**
> "

of collective and individual actions and interactions is now shaped by efficiency, calculability, predictability, control, and rationalization costs.

This is an extension of Weber's argument that, once set in motion, the process of rationalization is self-perpetuating and proliferates until it covers virtually every aspect of social life. To remain competitive in the market, firms must adhere to the principles of rationality and efficiency being used by others. Ritzer cites a host of examples to substantiate his claims, including fast-food chains, such as Subway, and children's toyshops, such as Toys "R" Us. All of these corporations have self-consciously adopted McDonald's principles as a way of organizing their activities.

While Ritzer admires the efficiency and capacity to adapt to change demonstrated by the McDonald's fast-food chain since its inception in 1940, he is simultaneously wary of the

dehumanizing effects that the pursuit of rationalization can lead to. Echoing Weber's notion of the "iron cage", Ritzer argues that although McDonald's has assumed iconic status as a highly efficient and profitable Western corporation, the spread of its principles across an increasing number of spheres of human activity leads to alienation.

As a transnational corporation, McDonald's plays a significant role as a carrier of Western rationality. To this end, according to Ritzer, McDonaldization is one of the key elements of global cultural homogenization. However, critics of this position, such as British sociologist John Tomlinson, rebut this charge by using the concept of glocalization. Tomlinson acknowledges that McDonald's is a global brand, but points out that it does make allowances for local contingencies and contexts. An example of this is the adaptation of products to conform to local dietary conventions, such as including vegetarian burgers on menus in India.

Two decades after it first appeared, Ritzer's McDonaldization thesis remains as pertinent as ever, if not more so. Ritzer and others have continued to work to apply, recalibrate, and update it across a range of topics, including the sociology of higher education. A collection of essays edited by British social thinkers Dennis Hayes and Robin Wynyard, *The McDonaldization of Higher Education*, contains a range of arguments that draw upon Ritzer. For example, Hayes claims that the traditional value-base on which higher education was founded – from college to postgraduate university-level education – is rapidly being replaced by standardization, calculability, and so on. Furthermore, argues Hayes, the McDonaldization of higher education holds true for students as much as it does for academic institutions and staff because, increasingly, the former approach education with a rational mindset as a means to an end, rather than as an end in itself. ∎

YO! Sushi restaurants in the UK enhance McDonald's rationalization approach by making the creation and distribution of the food into an urban, Tokyo-style eating experience.

THE BONDS OF OUR COMMUNITIES HAVE WITHERED
ROBERT D PUTNAM (1941–)

IN CONTEXT

FOCUS
Social capital

KEY DATES
1916 The term "social capital"
is coined by US social reformer
L J Hanifan, and refers to
intangible things that count
in daily life, such as "good will,
fellowship, sympathy, and
social intercourse".

2000 Finnish sociologist
Martti Siisiäinen critically
compares Pierre Bourdieu and
Robert D Putnam's respective
concepts of social capital.

2000 The Saguaro Seminar at
Harvard University produces
"Better Together", a report
led by Putnam and a team of
scholars aimed at addressing
the "critically low levels" of
social capital in the USA.

2013 Dutch social thinker
Marlene Vock and others use
the concept of social capital in
"Understanding Willingness to
Pay for Social Network Sites".

A recurrent theme animating early social thinkers was the fear that modern society was eroding traditional forms of community life, social cohesion, and a shared sense of solidarity. As valid as those concerns about change were, the 19th century was also a great era of voluntarism, during which people cooperated and established many of the institutions – such as schools, missions for the poor, and charities – which we know today.

Social capital grows from **a sense of common identity** and shared values such as **trust, reciprocity, good will, and fellowship**...

...which help to create the **voluntary associations and civic institutions** that bind communities together.

But our lifestyles are increasingly individualized and we have **disengaged from public affairs**, and even friends and neighbours.

The bonds of our communities have withered.

See also: Karl Marx 28–31 ▪ Pierre Bourdieu 76–79 ▪ Richard Sennett 84–87 ▪ Jane Jacobs 108–09 ▪ Amitai Etizoni 112–19 ▪ Sharon Zukin 128–31

Putnam's Saguaro Seminar, founded in 1995, is named after the cactus that he regards as a social metaphor – "it takes a long time to develop, and then it serves lots of unexpected purposes".

However, by the late 20th century, the state had taken on many of these responsibilities and the civic connections that once unified people had gone into decline.

The social glue that binds together individuals and wider collectives is referred to as "social capital" by the US sociologist Robert Putnam, and is reproduced through voluntary associations and social and civic networks. Americans today are wealthier than in the 1960s, says Putnam, but at the cost of a shared sense of moral obligation and community.

Three different types of link make up this social capital: bonds, bridges, and linkages. Bonds are forged from a sense of common identity, including family, friends, and community members. Bridges extend beyond shared identity to include colleagues, associates, and acquaintances. Linkages connect individuals or groups further up or lower down the social hierarchy. Differences in the type of social capital binding people are important. For example, bonds with friends and family can help to secure a job, or provide a source of comfort at times of emotional need. But bonds can be restricting, too: in immigrant communities, bonds with fellow immigrants can hinder the formation of social bridges and linkages, which makes integration into wider society more difficult.

Civic engagement

Putnam's study *Bowling Alone* applies the concept of social capital to US society. He shows that the demise of traditional suburban neighbourhoods and the increasing solitude that commuters and workers face daily – listening to iPods, or sitting in front of computer screens – means that people are not just far less likely to engage with voluntary and community-based initiatives, but also to spend less time socializing with friends, neighbours, and family.

Putnam uses ten-pin bowling to illustrate his point: the number of Americans taking up the sport has increased, but the proportion who join a team is in decline. People are literally "bowling alone" because the traditional community values of trust and reciprocity have been eroded, which impacts negatively upon voluntary associations and civically oriented organizations, from parent/teacher associations (PTAs) to local council committees. Since Putnam set up the Saguaro Seminar initiative in 1995 to look into aspects of civic engagement, his concept of social capital has become vastly influential, and has been applied to a wide range of phenomena spanning neighbourhood quality of life and crime rates to voting behaviour and church attendance. ▪

Robert D Putnam

Robert David Putnam was born in 1941 in New York, USA, and raised in the small town of Clinton, Ohio. With a degree from the University of Oxford, UK, and a doctorate from Yale, he directs the Saguaro Seminar and is the Malkin professor of Public Policy at Harvard University.

In 1995 his article "Bowling Alone: America's Declining Social Capital" began a debate about civic engagement and Putnam was invited to meet with then US President Bill Clinton. Since then, with the article having become a book in 2000, his reputation has grown. In 2013 President Barack Obama awarded him the National Humanities Medal for his contributions to understanding and trying to ameliorate community life in the USA.

Key works

2000 *Bowling Alone: The Collapse and Revival of American Community*
2002 *Democracies in Flux*
2003 *Better Together* (with Lewis M Feldstein)

The core idea of social capital theory is that social networks have value.
Robert Putnam

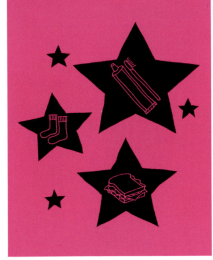

DISNEYIZATION REPLACES MUNDANE BLANDNESS WITH SPECTACULAR EXPERIENCES
ALAN BRYMAN

IN CONTEXT

FOCUS
Disneyization

KEY DATES
1955 Walt Disney opens the first Disneyland to the general public in California, attracting 50,000 visitors on its first day.

From the 1980s The term "globalization" is used increasingly to refer to the growing interconnectedness of the world.

1981 In *Simulacra and Simulation*, Jean Baudrillard says, "Disneyland is presented as imaginary in order to make us believe that the rest is real, whereas all of Los Angeles and the America that surrounds it are no longer real, but belong to... the order of simulation."

1983–2005 Disney parks are opened in Tokyo, Paris, and Hong Kong.

1993 US scholar George Ritzer publishes *The McDonaldization of Society*.

Walt Disney creates **Disneyland** and gradually begins to open branches **across the world**.

The organizational principles that underlie Disney's parks **influence modes of consumption** more broadly.

Everyday activities are **transformed into extraordinary events** that blur the distinction between reality and fantasy.

Disneyization replaces mundane blandness with spectacular experiences.

Modern consumer culture creates issues that have far-reaching implications. British professor Alan Bryman is interested in the impact that Disney theme parks have upon wider society and in how their model is influencing the ways in which services and products are made available for consumption.

Bryman argues that "Disneyization" lies at the heart of contemporary consumer society. The phenomenon is profoundly shaping our shopping experiences because, he says, the principles underlying the organization of such parks are increasingly dominating other areas: "Thus, the fake worlds of the Disney parks, which represent

See also: George Ritzer 120–23 ▪ Sharon Zukin 128–31 ▪ Jean Baudrillard 196–99 ▪ Arlie Hochschild 236–43

a non-existent reality, become models for American society." Furthermore, Disneyization is also occurring in the rest of the world.

Blurring fantasy and reality

Bryman identifies four aspects to Disneyization: theming, hybrid consumption, merchandizing, and emotional labour.

Theming involves drawing on widely recognized cultural sources to create a popular environment – for example, using rock music as the theme of Hard Rock Café.

Hybrid consumption refers to areas where different kinds of consumption become interlinked: airports and sports arenas, for example, become shopping malls.

Merchandizing involves the promotion and sale of goods with copyrighted images and logos. For example, literature and films such as the *Harry Potter* series or *Shrek* generate a plethora of products from t-shirts to video games.

The term "emotional labour" was coined by Arlie Hochschild in *The Managed Heart* to describe

a person altering their outward behaviour to conform to an ideal. In Disneyization this occurs where a job appears to become more of a performance, with a scripted interaction, dressing up, and the impression of having endless fun.

The effect of these processes is that they can transform everyday occurrences, such as shopping and eating, into spectacular and sensational events. At the same time, however, the tendency to repackage things in a sanitized format undermines the authenticity of other experiences and places.

The Buddha Bar has franchises throughout the world and is an example of Bryman's "theming" theory, whereby a cultural source – in this case, religion – is used to create a product or venue.

Ultimately this blurs the distinction between fantasy and reality. Bryman cites the fashion for trying to bestow character on somewhere by associating it with a well-known cultural totem, leading to England's Nottinghamshire becoming "Robin Hood Country" and Finland's Lapland "Santa Claus Land".

Bryman proposes Disneyization as a parallel notion to George Ritzer's McDonaldization, a process by which the principles of the fast food restaurant (McDonald's itself is merely a symbol) come to dominate more and more sectors of society. McDonaldization is grounded in the idea of rationalization and produces sameness. Theme parks echo this in several ways, but Disneyization is essentially about increasing the inclination to consume (goods and services), often through variety and difference. The popularity of theming and merchandizing suggests that Dizneyization has become an integral part of modern life and identity. ∎

Alan Bryman

British sociologist Alan Bryman is a professor of organizational and social research in the school of management at the University of Leicester, England. Prior to this he worked at the University of Loughborough for 31 years. Bryman is interested in methodological issues and different aspects of consumer culture. His specializations include combining qualitative and quantitative research methods; Disneyization and McDonaldization; and effective leadership in higher education. He is widely published in all three areas.

Bryman is unable to understand the disdain of fellow intellectuals for all things Disney; his love of the cartoons and parks has greatly inspired his academic work, which has become influential in both cultural and sociological studies.

Key works

1995 *Disney and his World*
2004 *The Disneyization of Society*

LIVING IN A LOFT IS LIKE LIVING IN A SHOWCASE

SHARON ZUKIN

IN CONTEXT

FOCUS
Gentrification and urban life

KEY DATES
1920s US sociologist Robert E Park coins the term "human ecology" and is a leading figure in establishing the "Chicago School" and its systematic study of urban life.

1961 Jane Jacobs' *The Death and Life of Great American Cities* is published, becoming one of the most influential post-war studies of urban environments.

1964 British sociologist Ruth Glass invents the word "gentrification" to describe the displacement of working-class occupiers by middle-class incomers.

1970s Artists begin to move into former factory buildings in Lower Manhattan, New York.

C ities are dynamic places of change and renewal for people, communities, ideas, and the built environment. Social thinkers have always been drawn to the study of urban life, especially during times of rapid change. The period of metropolitan growth from the 19th century onwards, the transformation of cities and the movement into suburbia that followed World War II, and changes in the structure of the urban village in the 1960s have all been the subjects of intense study.

Another such period occurred in the 1980s, when many cities in the Western world had been radically altered by the loss of manufacturing

See also: Georg Simmel 104–05 ▪ Henri Lefebvre 106–07 ▪ Jane Jacobs 108–09 ▪ Alan Bryman 126–27 ▪
Saskia Sassen 164–65

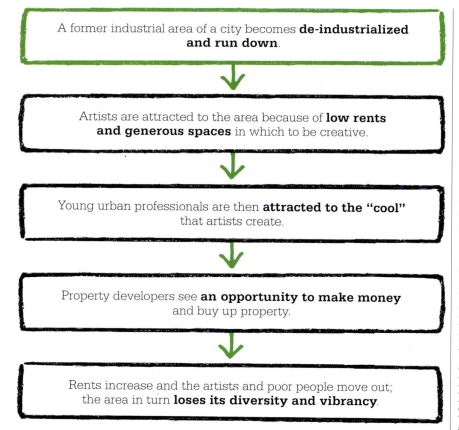

A former industrial area of a city becomes **de-industrialized and run down**.

Artists are attracted to the area because of **low rents and generous spaces** in which to be creative.

Young urban professionals are then **attracted to the "cool"** that artists create.

Property developers see **an opportunity to make money** and buy up property.

Rents increase and the artists and poor people move out; the area in turn **loses its diversity and vibrancy**.

to replace the mass production of modernism and the uniformity of suburban living with the individualization of a space once used for mass production (since many loft spaces had once been workshops or factories). In a loft, the privacy of the detached suburban house was replaced by a non-hierarchical layout that opens up "every area... to all comers". This space and openness creates an impression of informality and equality, transforming the loft into a "tourist attraction" or a showcase – a place that demands to be seen.

Urban regeneration

Zukin also closely examined the costs of urban regeneration and loft living. On the surface, the movement of people back into virtually abandoned districts appears to be a positive process, breathing new life into old buildings and places. However, Zukin questions this assumption, arguing that regeneration »

industries and the growing impacts of globalization. A new generation of scholars began to investigate inner-city decline, the processes of urban regeneration, and what gives somewhere its distinctive sense of place. Prominent among them has been Sharon Zukin, author of the influential 1982 work, *Loft Living*.

The meanings of space

Zukin moved into a loft – a former garment factory and artist's studio – in Greenwich Village, New York, USA, in 1975. She became interested in what these new residential spaces meant to their occupiers, and was particularly concerned by the impact that

their use as dwellings was having on long-established communities in New York.

Zukin reiterated the ideas of thinkers such as French philosopher Gaston Bachelard, who argued, in *The Poetics of Space* (1958), that a home was more than a space for living; it represented the "psychic state" of the inhabitants. For example, in Victorian times, houses were divided into rooms with specific functions (drawing room, dressing room, and so on), providing a series of intimate spatial encounters.

The psychic state of a loft-dweller, argued Zukin, was that of a search for authenticity – an attempt

Bare walls, exposed beams, and unexpected architectural details provide the authenticity sought by buyers of urban loft apartments.

Chelsea Market is a New York food hall created in the 1990s in a derelict factory in the Meatpacking District. Zukin says the area is a far cry from the one-time "no-go zone" of butchery.

benefits specific groups at the expense of others. She claims that regeneration leads to a process whereby poor or marginalized groups are effectively pushed out of the areas in which they have been living, sometimes for generations, to make way for more elite groups. The result can be a uniform urban experience, which Zukin has identified in parts of New York and other cities around the world.

The steps of gentrification

Zukin argues that gentrification is more than, as she puts it, a "change of scene". It is a "radical break with suburbia... toward the social diversity and aesthetic promiscuity of city life." Gentrifiers, according to her, have a distinctive culture and milieu (they are interested, for example, in restoring historical architectural detail), which leads to "a process of social and spatial differentiation". In her study of Lower Manhattan, Zukin argues that gentrification is a process within which a number of steps can be clearly identified.

The first step was a decline in traditional manufacturing industry. Just a couple of generations ago New York had a working waterfront that employed tens of thousands and a hinterland in Manhattan that was packed, in the areas around Greenwich Village, with small-scale workshops and factories making textiles and clothes. The buildings housing the workshops typically had high ceilings and lots of light, and were known as "lofts".

The textile firms began to go out of business from the 1950s onwards, as more and more of the USA's textiles production was "off-shored" by large corporations to countries in Asia where labour costs were lower. US workers were left unemployed, and the affected districts of New York became deindustrialized and run-down. By the 1970s, much of Lower Manhattan had become derelict.

Creative space

The second step took place in the 1970s, after the abandoned workplaces had become home to the poor and marginalized. Because the buildings were intended to be factories, the floors were not subdivided into multiple rooms, as you would find in an apartment block, but were instead open plan with tall windows. A space that accommodated lots of people needing good natural light, while they worked on sewing machines, also proved to be the ideal studio environment for artists. In the early 1970s, when New York was hit by an economic crisis, private rents citywide went down because demand for properties decreased. Stereotypically, artists struggle to make ends meet and often seek out cheap places in which to live and work. Lower Manhattan's old factory lofts therefore had appeal and the area became home to many artists.

This was an organic regeneration of these old neighbourhoods: there was no official city government plan to convert the lofts into live-in studios.

> Much of what made [New York City's] neighborhoods unique lives on only in the buildings, not the people.
> **Sharon Zukin**

As more artists moved to the area, it developed a cultural vibrancy; the presence of the artists meant that secondary businesses – such as coffee shops, restaurants, and art galleries – opened to support their activities. The area became increasingly funky and edgy, and proved attractive to the new class of young urban professionals who wanted to live somewhere new, exciting, and different from the staid, post-war homes in which they had grown up.

The third and decisive step in gentrification was reached when young professionals began to move into the area – in this case, to become part of the urban bohemian environment and lifestyle. There were now people with money interested in living in what had previously been an undesirable area. The fact that this new and more affluent group suddenly wanted to live in the area attracted the attention of profit-driven developers, who began to buy up comparatively cheap property – often, criticizes Zukin, with subsidies from the city authorities – and convert it into apartments that resembled the lofts in which the artists lived. As a result, rents began to steadily increase. Artists and poor people found it hard to afford to live there anymore, and they begin to move out.

The final step in gentrification was reached when the area was colonized by the more affluent middle and upper classes. The galleries and coffee shops remained, but the mix of people, the vibrancy, and the cultural activity that had made the area popular was lost. In effect, the artists became unwitting accomplices of gentrification, and then its victims: their success in breathing new life into Lower

It's just inexorable, this authenticity in the visual language of sameness.
Sharon Zukin

Manhattan resulted ultimately in their exclusion from what they had helped to regenerate.

The search for urban soul

Zukin's work has been influential in clarifying what drives change in modern cities: the cultural and consumerist needs of some social groups wishing to pursue a certain lifestyle, rather than the development of new forms of industry. However, for Zukin this way of life is just another form of consumerism that is ultimately empty, offering a "Disneyfied" experience in which diversity and authenticity are marginalized by the prevalent cultural forms and lifestyles promoted by multinational media companies. The result is that poor and marginalized groups are effectively excluded from urban life.

A naked city

Zukin's more recent work, such as *Naked City*, has focused on how gentrification and consumerism have created bland, homogenous, middle-class areas and robbed cities of the authenticity that most people long for. She also notices that the pace of gentrification has sped up. What used to take decades to unfold now only seems to require a few years: an area is deemed to be "cool" and very rapidly the developers move in and begin a process that fundamentally alters its character, invariably destroying what was special. In fact, the distinctiveness of a neighbourhood has actually become a tool of capitalist developers – one that results in the exclusion of the characters who first gave an area its real "soul". The challenge for planners is to find ways of preserving people as well as buildings and streetscapes. ∎

Sharon Zukin

Sharon Zukin is currently a professor of sociology at Brooklyn College in New York, and at the CUNY Graduate Center. She has received several awards, including the Wright Mills Award and the Robert and Helen Lynd Award for career achievement in urban sociology from the American Sociological Association.

She is the author of books on cities, culture, and consumer culture, and a researcher on urban, cultural, and economic change. Her work has mainly focused on how cities are affected by processes such as gentrification, and investigating the dominant driving processes in urban living. She is also an active critic of the many changes that are occurring within New York and other cities.

Key works

1982 *Loft Living: Culture and Capital in Urban Change*
1995 *The Cultures of Cities*
2010 *Naked City: The Death and Life of Authentic Urban Places*

IN CONTEXT

FOCUS
Liquid modernity

KEY DATES
1848 Karl Marx and Friedrich
Engels publish *The Communist
Manifesto*, which forecasts the
globalization of capitalism.

1929–35 Antonio Gramsci's
concept of hegemony shapes
Zygmunt Bauman's view that
the culture of capitalism is
highly resilient.

1957 The ratification of the
Treaty of Rome allows for the
free flow of workers within
the European Economic
Community.

1976 Bauman is influenced by
Michel Foucault's *Discipline
and Punish*, and in particular
by his ideas on surveillance.

2008 British sociologist Will
Atkinson questions whether
Bauman's notion of liquid
modernity has been subject
to sufficient critical scrutiny.

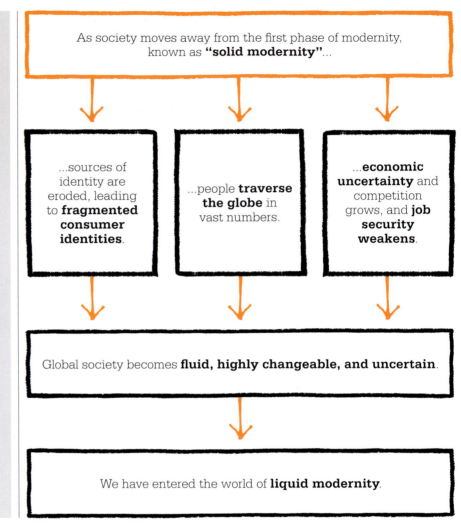

As society moves away from the first phase of modernity,
known as **"solid modernity"**...

...sources of identity are eroded, leading to **fragmented consumer identities**.

...people **traverse the globe** in vast numbers.

...**economic uncertainty** and competition grows, and **job security weakens**.

Global society becomes **fluid, highly changeable, and uncertain.**

We have entered the world of **liquid modernity**.

In the late 19th century, societies began to coalesce around urban centres, and Western Europe entered a phase known as modernity, characterized by industrialization and capitalism. According to Polish sociologist Zygmunt Bauman, societies have moved away from that first phase of modernity – which he termed "solid modernity" – and now occupy a period in human history called "liquid modernity". This new period is, according to Bauman, one marked by unrelenting uncertainty and change that affects society at the global, systemic level, and also at the level of individual experience. Bauman's use of the term "liquid" is a powerful metaphor for present-day life: it is mobile, fast flowing, changeable, amorphous, without a centre of gravity, and difficult to contain and predict. In essence, liquid modernity is a way of life that exists in the continuous, unceasing reshaping of the modern world in ways that are unpredictable, uncertain, and plagued by increasing levels of risk. Liquid modernity, for Bauman, is the current stage in the broader evolution of Western – and now also global – society. Like Karl Marx, Bauman believes that human society progresses in a way that means each "new" stage develops out of the stage before it. Thus it is necessary to define solid modernity before it is possible to understand liquid modernity.

Defining solid modernity
Bauman sees solid modernity as ordered, rational, predictable, and relatively stable. Its defining feature is the organization of human

See also: Karl Marx 28–31 ▪ Michel Foucault 52–55 ▪ Max Weber 38–45 ▪
Anthony Giddens 148–49 ▪ Ulrich Beck 156–61 ▪ Antonio Gramsci 178–79

activity and institutions along bureaucratic lines, where practical reasoning can be employed to solve problems and create technical solutions. Bureaucracy persists because it is the most efficient way of organizing and ordering the actions and interactions of large numbers of people. While bureaucracy has its distinctly negative aspects (for example, that human life can become dehumanized and devoid of spontaneity and creativity), it is highly effective at accomplishing goal-oriented tasks.

Another key characteristic of solid modernity, according to Bauman, is a very high degree of equilibrium in social structures – meaning that people live with a relatively stable set of norms, traditions, and institutions. By this, Bauman is not suggesting that

Auschwitz concentration camp
in Poland was built and run by the Nazis. Bauman cites the Holocaust as a product of the highly rational, planned nature of solid modernity.

social, political, and economic changes do not occur in solid modernity, just that changes occur in ways that are relatively ordered and predictable. The economy provides a good example: in solid modernity, the majority of people – from members of the working class through to middle-class professionals – enjoyed relatively high levels of job security. As a consequence, they tended to remain in the same geographical area, grow up in the same neighbourhood, and attend the same school as their parents and other family members.

Bauman regards solid modernity as one-directional and progressive – a realization of the Enlightenment view that reason leads to the emancipation of humankind. As scientific knowledge advances, so does society's understanding of, and control over, the natural and social worlds. In solid modernism, according to Bauman, this supreme faith in scientific reasoning was embodied in the social and political institutions that »

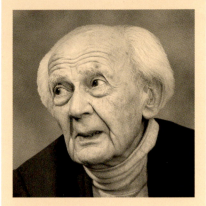

Zygmunt Bauman

Born in 1925, Zygmunt Bauman is a Polish sociologist from a non-practising Polish-Jewish family who were forced to relocate to the Soviet Union in 1939 following the Nazi invasion. After serving in the Polish division of the Red Army, he moved to Israel. In 1971 he settled in England, where he is now professor emeritus of sociology at the University of Leeds.

Bauman is the author of more than 40 books, of which 20 or so have been written since his retirement in 1990. In recognition of his contribution to sociology, he was awarded the Theodor W Adorno Award in 1998 and the Prince of Asturias Award in 2010. The University of Leeds created the acclaimed Bauman Institute in 2010 in his honour, and in 2013 the Polish director Bartek Dziadosz produced a film of his life and views entitled *The Trouble With Being Human These Days*.

Key works

1989 *Modernity and the Holocaust*
2000 *Liquid Modernity*
2011 *Culture in a Liquid Modern World*

addressed primarily national issues and problems. Enlightenment values were institutionally entrenched in the figurehead of the State – the primary point of reference from which emerged the development of social, political, and economic ideals.

At the level of the individual, claims Bauman, solid modernity gave rise to a stable repertoire of personal identities and possible versions of selfhood. Solid modern individuals have a unified, rational, and stable sense of personal identity, because it is informed by a number of stable categories, such as occupation, religious affiliation, nationality, gender, ethnicity, leisure pursuits, lifestyle, and so on. Social life under the conditions of solid modernity – like the individuals it created – was self-

Bauman's idea of solid modernity was embodied by Enlightenment thinkers such as Isaac Newton (depicted here by William Blake), who used reason to transform society.

assured, rational, bureaucratically organized, and relatively predictable and stable.

From solid to liquid

The transition from solid to liquid modernity, according to Bauman, has occurred as a result of a confluence of profound and connected economic, political, and social changes. The result is a global order propelled by what Bauman describes as a "compulsive, obsessive, and addictive reinventing of the world".

Bauman identifies five distinct, but interrelated, developments that have brought about the transition from solid to liquid modernity. First, nation-states are no longer the "key load-bearing structures" of society; national governments today have considerably less power to determine events both at home and abroad. Second, global capitalism has risen and multi- and transnational corporations have proliferated, resulting in a decentering of state authority.

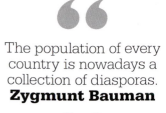

Third, electronic technologies and the Internet now allow for near-instant, supranational flows of communication. Fourth, societies have become ever more preoccupied by risk – dwelling on insecurities and potential hazards. And fifth, there has been huge growth in human migration across the globe.

Defining liquid modernity

As Bauman himself observes, attempting to define liquid modernity is something of a paradox, because the term refers to a global condition that is characterized by unrelenting change, flux, and uncertainty. However, having identified the traits of solid modernity, he claims it is possible to define the most prominent aspects of liquid modernity.

At an ideological level, liquid modernity undermines the Enlightenment ideal that scientific knowledge can ameliorate natural and social problems. In liquid modernity, science, experts, university-based academics, and government officials – once the supreme figures of authority in solid modernity – occupy a highly ambiguous status as guardians of the truth. Scientists are

increasingly perceived as being as much the cause of environmental and socio-political problems as they are the solution. This inevitably leads to increased scepticism and general apathy on the part of the general public.

Liquid modernity has undermined the certainties of individuals regarding employment, education, and welfare. Today, many workers must either retrain or change occupation altogether, sometimes several times – the notion of a "job for life", which was typical in the age of solid modernity, has been rendered unrealistic and unachievable.

The practice of "reengineering", or the downsizing of firms – a term that Bauman borrows from the US sociologist, Richard Sennett – has become increasingly common, as it enables corporations to remain financially competitive in the global market by reducing labour costs significantly. As part of this process, stable, permanent work – which typified solid modernism – is being replaced by temporary employment contracts that are issued to a largely mobile workforce. Closely related to this occupational instability is the shifting role and nature of

> We live in a globalizing world. That means all of us, consciously or not, depend on each other.
> **Zygmunt Bauman**

The key differences between solid and liquid modernity were identified by Bauman as two sets of four characteristics.

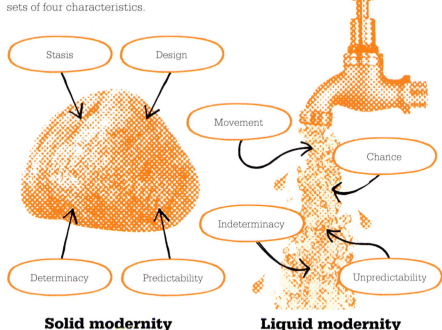

Stasis

Design

Movement

Chance

Indeterminacy

Determinacy

Predictability

Unpredictability

Solid modernity   **Liquid modernity**

education. Individuals are now required to continue their education – often at their own expense – throughout their careers in order to remain up to date with developments in their respective professions, or as a means of ensuring they remain "marketable" in case of redundancy.

Concurrent with these changes to employment patterns is the retreat of the welfare state. What was once regarded historically as a reliable "safety net" guarding against personal misfortune such as ill-health and unemployment, state provision of welfare is rapidly being withdrawn, especially in the areas of social housing, state-funded higher education, and national health care.

Fluid identities

Where solid modernity was based on the industrial production of consumer goods in factories and

industrial plants, liquid modernity is instead based on the rapid and relentless consumption of consumer goods and services.

This transition from production to consumption, says Bauman, is a result of the dissolution of the social structures, such as occupation and nationality, to which identity was anchored in solid modernity. »

Welfare states, as Bauman says, have been under pressure recently. In the UK, for example, the National Health Service is being eroded, despite widespread support for the system.

destabilizing forces are not evenly distributed across global society. Bauman identifies and explains the importance of the variables of mobility, time, and space for understanding why. For Bauman, the capacity to remain mobile is an extremely valuable attribute in liquid modernity, because it facilitates the successful pursuit of wealth and personal fulfilment.

Tourists and vagabonds

Bauman distinguishes between the winners and losers in liquid modernity. The people who benefit most from the fluidity of liquid modernity are the socially privileged individuals who are able to float freely around the world. These people, who Bauman refers to as "tourists", exist in time rather than space. By this he means that through their easy access to Internet-based technologies and transnational flights, tourists are able – virtually and in reality – to span the entire globe and operate in locations where the economic conditions are the most favourable and standards of living the highest. By stark contrast, the "vagabonds",

The self-creation of personal identity is undertaken through consumption as traditional sources of identity, such as employment status and family ties, have withered under liquid modernity.

But in liquid modernity selfhood is not so fixed: it is fragmented, unstable, often internally incoherent, and frequently no more than the sum of consumer choices out of which it is simultaneously constituted and represented. In liquid modernity, the boundary between the authentic self and the representation of the self through consumer choice breaks down: we are – according to Bauman – what we buy and no more. Depth and surface meaning have fused together, and it is impossible to separate them out.

Consumption and identity

The central importance of consumption in the construction of individual self-identity goes beyond the acquisition of consumer goods. Without the unchanging

sources of identity provided by solid modernity, individuals in the modern world seek guidance, stability, and personal direction from an ever-broadening range of alternative sources, such as lifestyle coaches, psychoanalysts, sex therapists, holistic life-experts, health gurus, and so on.

Self-identity has become problematic for the individual in ways that are historically unprecedented, and the consequence is a cycle of endless self-questioning and introspection that serves only to confound the individual even more. Ultimately, the result is that our experience of ourselves and everyday life is increasingly played out against a backdrop of ongoing anxiety, restlessness, and unease about who we are, our place in the world, and the rapidity of the changes taking place around us.

Liquid modernity thus principally refers to a global society that is plagued by uncertainty and instability. However, these

> In a liquid modern life, there are no permanent bonds, and any that we take up... must be tied loosely so that they can be untied... when circumstances change.
> **Zygmunt Bauman**

> If you define your value by the things you acquire... being excluded is humiliating.
> **Zygmunt Bauman**

as Bauman calls them, are people who are immobile, or subject to forced mobility, and excluded from consumer culture. Life for them involves either being mired in places where unemployment is high and the standard of living is very poor, or being forced to leave their country of origin as economic or political refugees in search of employment, or in response to the threat of war or persecution. Anywhere they stay for too long soon becomes inhospitable.

For Bauman, mass migration and transnational flows of people around the globe are among the hallmarks of liquid modernity and are factors contributing to the unpredictable and constantly changing nature of everyday life: Bauman's social categories of tourists and vagabonds occupy two extremes of this phenomenon.

Applying Bauman's theory

Zygmunt Bauman is considered one of the most influential and eminent sociologists of the modern age. He prefers not to align himself with any particular intellectual tradition – his writings are relevant to a vast range of disciplines, from ethics, media, and cultural studies to political theory and philosophy. Within sociology, his work on liquid

modernity is regarded by the vast majority of thinkers as a unique contribution to the field.

The Irish sociologist Donncha Marron has applied Bauman's concept of liquid modernity to a critical rethinking of consumer credit within the USA. Following Bauman's suggestion that consumption of goods and brands is a key feature of how individuals construct personal identity, Marron notes that the credit card is an important tool in this process because it is ideally suited for enabling people to adapt to the kind of fluid ways of living Bauman depicts. The credit card can, for example, be used to fund shopping trips to satisfy consumer desire. It makes paying for things easier, quicker, and considerably more manageable. The credit card of course also serves the function, says Marron, of meeting day-to-day bills and expenses, as people move between jobs or make significant career moves. And the physical card itself

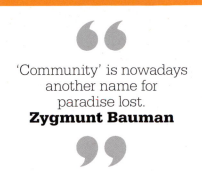

> 'Community' is nowadays another name for paradise lost.
> **Zygmunt Bauman**

can often be co-branded with things the owner is interested in, such as football teams, charities, or stores. These co-branded cards represent a small but revealing means whereby a person is able to select and present a sense of who they are to the outside world. ■

Bauman's global "tourists" are mobile members of the social elite who possess the wealth and occupational status necessary to enjoy the most positive aspects of liquid modernity.

THE MODERN WORLD-SYSTEM
IMMANUEL WALLERSTEIN (1930–)

FOCUS
World-system theory

KEY DATES
16th century The foundations for global capitalism are laid as European powers "discover" and colonize parts of the Americas and Asia.

1750 The Industrial Revolution begins in Great Britain.

1815–1914 New industries and social and economic transformations spread to Europe, North America, Japan, and parts of Australasia – countries in these regions form the "core" of the modern economic system.

1867 Karl Marx publishes the first volume of *Das Kapital*, highlighting the exploitative tendencies of capitalism.

From the 20th century Global trade develops, with new states, including former colonies, integrating into the "system" of global capitalism.

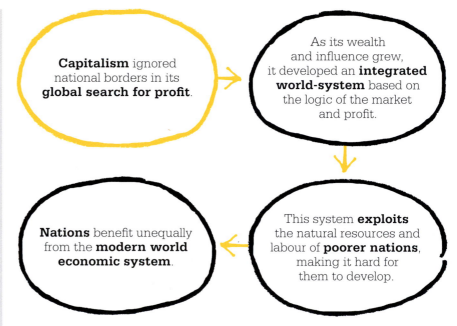

Capitalism ignored national borders in its **global search for profit**.

As its wealth and influence grew, it developed an **integrated world-system** based on the logic of the market and profit.

This system **exploits** the natural resources and labour of **poorer nations**, making it hard for them to develop.

Nations benefit unequally from the **modern world economic system**.

V arious nations of the world are interconnected by a global system of economic relationships that sees more-developed nations exploiting the natural resources and labour of developing nations, according to US sociologist Immanuel Wallerstein in *The Modern World-System* (1974). This "world-system" makes it difficult for poor nations to develop, and ensures that rich nations continue to be the primary beneficiaries of global commodity chains and the products and wealth that are created by industrial capitalism.

The world economic system, says Wallerstein, began to emerge in the 16th century, as European nations such as Britain, Spain, and France exploited the resources of conquered and colonized lands. These unequal trade relationships

See also: Karl Marx 28–31 ▪ Roland Robertson 146–47 ▪ Saskia Sassen 164–65 ▪ Arjun Appadurai 166–69 ▪ David Held 170–71

produced an accumulation of capital that was reinvested in expanding the economic system. By the late 19th century, most of the world had been incorporated into this system of commodity production and exchange.

The global stage

Wallerstein's ideas on the origin of modern capitalism extend the theories of Karl Marx to the global stage. Marx focused on how capitalism produces a struggle over "surplus value", which refers to the fact that a worker produces more value in a day than he or she is paid for, and this extra value translates as profit for the employer. Under capitalism, the working class is exploited by wealthy social elites for the surplus value of their labour.

Wallerstein develops this idea to focus on those who benefit from global commodity chains, arguing that there are class-like groupings of nations in the world-system, which he labels "core", "semi-periphery", and "periphery". Core nations are developed societies,

The modern world-system is based on a class-like grouping of nations, and results in unequal economic and trade relationships between those nations.

- **Periphery nations** are powerless and dispossessed; they have narrow economic bases in agriculture and minerals, and provide the semi-periphery and core nations with commodities, raw materials, and cheap labour.

- **Semi-periphery** nations have intermediate levels of affluence and some autonomy and economic diversity.

- **Core nations** are developed, industrialized, and affluent; they dominate at the heart of the modern world-system.

which produce complex products using technologically advanced methods of production. The core nations rely on periphery nations for raw materials, agricultural products, and cheap labour. Semi-periphery nations have a mix of the social and economic characteristics of the other categories.

The unequal nature of this economic exchange between the core and the periphery means that

core nations sell their developed commodities at higher prices than those from the periphery. Those nations in the semi-periphery also benefit from unequal trade relationships with the periphery, but are often at a disadvantage with regards to their economic exchanges with the core.

This world-system, Wallerstein suggests, is relatively stable and unlikely to change. While nations can move "up" or "down" within the system, the military and economic power of states in the core, along with the aspirations of those in the semi-periphery, make it unlikely that global relationships will be restructured to be more equitable.

Wallerstein's ideas on the modern world-system, originating in the 1970s, predate the literature on globalization, which only emerged as a central concern of sociology from the late 1980s and early 1990s. His work is therefore recognized as an early and important contribution to economic globalization and its socio-political consequences. ∎

Global patterns of wealth and inequality

Social scientists originally discussed global inequalities using the terms "First World" (developed Western nations), "Second World" (industrialized communist nations), and "Third World" (colonized nations). Nations were ranked according to their levels of capitalist enterprise, industrialization, and urbanization, and the argument was that poorer nations simply needed more of the economic features of developed societies to escape poverty.

Wallerstein rejected the idea that the Third World was merely underdeveloped. He focused on the economic process and links underpinning the global economy to show that, although a nation's position in the world-system was initially a product of history and geography, the market forces of global capitalism serve to accentuate the differences between the core and the periphery nations, thereby effectively institutionalizing inequality.

GLOBAL ISSUES, LOCAL PERSPECTIVES
ROLAND ROBERTSON (1938–)

IN CONTEXT

FOCUS
Glocalization

KEY DATES
1582–1922 Beginning with the Catholic countries of Europe and finally the states of East Asia and the Soviet Union, the Gregorian calendar is adopted as the most widely used calendar internationally.

1884 Greenwich Mean Time (GMT) is recognized as the world's time standard, becoming the basis for a global 24-hour time-zone system.

1945 The United Nations (UN) is founded to promote international cooperation.

1980s Japanese businesses develop strategies to adapt global products to local markets, a process they call "glocalization".

1990s Roland Robertson expands the Japanese concept of "glocalization" in his work on globalization.

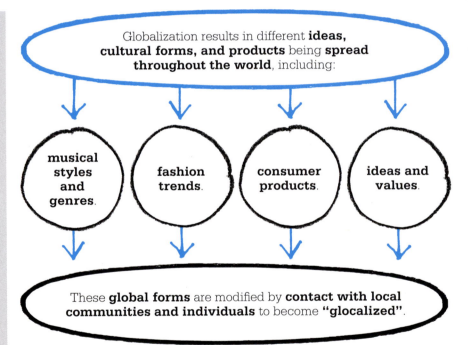

Globalization results in different **ideas, cultural forms, and products** being **spread throughout the world**, including:

musical styles and genres.

fashion trends.

consumer products.

ideas and values.

These **global forms** are modified by **contact with local communities and individuals** to become **"glocalized"**.

Globalization is giving rise to new cultural forms, as global products, values, and tastes fuse with their local equivalents. This intermixing of the global and the local, says British sociologist Roland Robertson, is a key feature of modern societies and is producing new creative possibilities.

In *Globalization: Social Theory and Global Culture* (1992), Robertson argues that the cultural dynamics at the heart of globalization can be understood by focusing on the relationships between four areas: "individual selves", "nation-state", a "world system of societies", and "a notion of a common humanity". This focus allows him to examine

See also: George Ritzer 120–23 ▪ Immanuel Wallerstein 144–45 ▪ Saskia Sassen 164–65 ▪ Arjun Appadurai 166–69 ▪ David Held 170–71

Football is the "glocal game". Communities identify with their team and develop distinctive traditions and football cultures, which they then bring to international competitions.

the interacting aspects of a person's self-identity and their relationship with national and global cultural influences.

One's self-identity, for example, is defined in relation to a nation, to interactions between societies, and to humankind (ideas regarding sexual orientation, ethnicity, and so on). In this context, Robertson explores the tension between global and local influences on a person's experiences and actions.

Robertson emphasizes "global unicity": the ways in which globalization and cultural exchange seem to be giving rise to a global culture. This is a movement towards a world dominated by Western cultural products and beliefs – such as Hollywood movies and US pop music – and is made possible by the increasing connectivity of societies and by people's awareness of the world as a single sociocultural entity.

But Robertson stresses that the emergence of "global unicity" does not mean the world is moving towards a single global culture in which everything is the same, or "homogenized". On the contrary, he argues that the differences between cultural groups and their products can be sharpened as they encounter cultural flows from other communities. This can lead to a dynamic interaction between local and global cultures, as people modify cultural forms to suit their particular sociocultural context.

Mixing "global" and "local"

To reflect how the global and local relate and intermix, Robertson popularized the term "glocalization". The concept was developed from the practices of transnational companies and their strategy of taking a global product and adapting it for a local market. For example, the fast-food corporation McDonald's has created many "glocalized" burger products in an attempt to appeal to customers outside the USA (such as the Chicken Maharaja Mac in India, where Hindus do not eat beef). In sociology, glocalization also refers more broadly to the localization of global cultural products or forms.

Globalization is, then, a twofold process of "universalizing and particularizing tendencies". Some cultural forms, products, and values are transported around the world, where they may be adopted or modified by different societies and individuals. A creative tension then emerges between the local and the global, which can result in cultural innovation and social change; for example, when people tell "local stories" through their adaptation of globally recognized music genres such as Hip Hop, K-Pop, and Indie. ▪

Cultural mélange

The recent rise of global communications has produced what Roland Robertson describes as a "cultural interconnectedness". As global influences mutate and hybridize locally the result is "glocalized" diversity, or a cultural "mélange", according to Dutch sociologist Jan Nederveen Pieterse. A good example of this global-to-local process is film-making.

Hollywood movies inspired the Indian film industry in the early 20th century. But Indian film-makers focused on modifying Hollywood's output: they were keen to make the art form their own, to appeal to local culture and reflect its distinct forms of expression. In so doing, they initiated a creative engagement between the global and local. Indian cinema draws on a rich body of themes – ranging from the country's ancient epics and myths to traditional drama – and retells them in colourful, distinctive ways. The Hindi films known as "Bollywood" attract audiences well beyond the Indian diaspora.

Local cultures adopt and redefine any global cultural product to suit their particular needs, beliefs, and customs.
Roland Robertson

CLIMATE CHANGE IS A BACK-OF-THE-MIND ISSUE
ANTHONY GIDDENS (1938–)

IN CONTEXT

FOCUS
Giddens' paradox

KEY DATES
1900 Modernity continues to spread as nations develop industrial economies and generate economic growth.

1952 The Great Smog, a toxic, smoke-like air-pollution event over London, kills an estimated 4,000 people and leads to the Clean Air Act (1956).

1987 The Montreal Protocol is agreed, protecting the ozone layer by phasing out the production of substances responsible for ozone depletion.

1997 Agreement of The Kyoto Protocol, a United Nations convention intended to reduce greenhouse gas emissions from industrialized countries and prevent climate change.

2009 A renewed commitment to the reduction of greenhouse gas emissions is made in the Copenhagen Accord.

The world is in danger and globalization is at least partially to blame, according to British sociologist Anthony Giddens. He believes that modernity has produced a "runaway world" in which governments and individuals face global risks such as climate change. One of his contributions to this important area of research is to provide a sociological explanation for why governments and individuals are reluctant to take immediate action to address the causes of global warming.

Globalization of modernity
Giddens has been highlighting the effects of globalization and how it has been transforming society's institutions, social roles, and relationships since the publication of his book *The Consequences of Modernity* in 1990. He notes that the world's developed and newly industrialized societies are now characterized by experiences and relationships that are dramatically different from those in pre-industrial societies.

This globalization of modernity and its consequences marks a new stage in human civilization, which

Giddens calls "late modernity". He uses the analogy of "riding onboard a juggernaut" to illustrate how the modern world seems to be "out of control" and difficult to direct. While life in late modernity is at times "rewarding" and "exhilarating", individuals must also confront new uncertainties, place trust in abstract systems, and manage new challenges and risks.

Giddens sees anthropogenic (human-induced) climate change as one of the most important risks, and indeed challenges, confronting humanity. Industrialized societies burn significant amounts of fossil fuels to generate power.

> "
> People find it hard to give the same level of reality to the future as they do to the present.
> **Anthony Giddens**
> "

See also: Zygmunt Bauman 136–43 ▪ Manuel Castells 152–55 ▪ Ulrich Beck 156–61 ▪ David Held 170–71 ▪
Thorstein Veblen 214–19 ▪ Daniel Bell 224–25

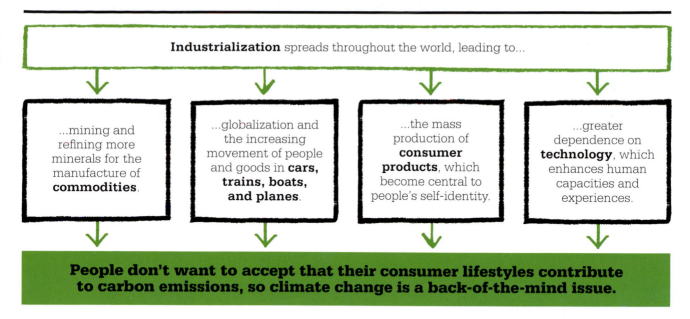

Industrialization spreads throughout the world, leading to...

...mining and refining more minerals for the manufacture of **commodities**.

...globalization and the increasing movement of people and goods in **cars, trains, boats, and planes**.

...the mass production of **consumer products**, which become central to people's self-identity.

...greater dependence on **technology**, which enhances human capacities and experiences.

People don't want to accept that their consumer lifestyles contribute to carbon emissions, so climate change is a back-of-the-mind issue.

A by-product of this energy production is carbon dioxide, which builds up in the upper atmosphere and traps energy from the sun, leading to "global warming" and extreme weather events, such as droughts, floods, and cyclones.

Innovative solutions

In *The Politics of Climate Change* (2009) Giddens argues that because the dangers posed by environmental degradation and climate change are not obvious or immediately visible in everyday life, many people "...do nothing of a concrete nature about them. Yet waiting until such dangers become visible and acute – in the shape of catastrophes that are irrefutably the result of climate change – before being stirred to serious action will be too late."

"Giddens' paradox" is the label that he gives to this disconnect between the rewards of the present and the threat of future dangers and catastrophes.

However, Giddens is optimistic about the future. He believes that the same human ingenuity that gave rise to industrial and high-tech societies can be used to find innovative solutions to reducing carbon emissions. For instance, international cooperation is seeing countries introducing carbon trading schemes and carbon taxes, which use market forces to reward companies that reduce their greenhouse gas emissions. New technologies are also being researched, developed, and shared, which could potentially end the world's reliance on fossil fuels, and provide cheap and clean sources of energy for both developed and developing societies. ▪

Future discounting

According to Giddens, the concept of "future discounting" explains why people take steps to solve present problems but ignore the threats that face them in the future. He notes that people often choose a small reward now, rather than take a course of action that might lead to a greater reward in the future. The same psychological principle applies to risks.

To illustrate his point Giddens uses the example of a smoker. Why does a young person take up smoking, when the health risks are widely known? For the teenage smoker it is almost impossible to imagine being 40, the age at which the dangers start to take hold and have potentially fatal consequences. This analogy applies to climate change. People are addicted to advanced technology and the mobility afforded by fossils fuels. Rather than tackle an uncomfortable reality, it is easier to ignore the warnings of climate scientists.

NO SOCIAL JUSTICE WITHOUT GLOBAL COGNITIVE JUSTICE

BOAVENTURA DE SOUSA SANTOS (1940–)

IN CONTEXT

FOCUS
**Epistemologies
of the South**

KEY DATES
1976 G-7 is formed by the world's seven wealthiest and most influential nation-states to discuss global affairs.

1997 Indian scholar Shiv Visvanathan coins the term "cognitive justice", in his book *A Carnival for Science: Essays on Science, Technology and Development.*

2001 The World Social Forum is founded in Brazil by anti-globalization activists to discuss alternative pathways to sustainable development and economic justice.

2014 British sociologist David Inglis uses de Sousa Santos's ideas about the plurality of knowledge to critically consider the development of cosmopolitan society.

A **Western capitalist world order** has taken root, stratifying nations not only along economic and political lines but also by **forms of knowledge**.

⬇

This has resulted in a **cultural battle** in which the global North, with its **culture rooted in science**, regards the global South as **culturally inferior**.

⬇

Global equality can only be achieved when cultures enter into a **dialogue based on mutual respect** and acknowledgment of **different forms of knowledge**.

⬇

There can be no social justice without global cognitive justice.

The notion that knowledge and culture are inseparable was proposed by French sociologist Émile Durkheim. He claimed that the culture of a group – its collectively produced ideas and ways of thinking about situations and events – shapes the ways in which its members accumulate socially specific knowledge about the world.

Portuguese sociologist Boaventura de Sousa Santos accepts that this link exists and, building upon Immanuel Wallerstein's concept of the world

See also: Zygmunt Bauman 136–43 ▪ Immanuel Wallerstein 144–45 ▪
Roland Robertson 146–47 ▪ Arjun Appadurai 166–69 ▪ Antonio Gramsci 178–79

system, he has extended the idea
to what he says is the cultural
battle created by globalization. He
claims the world is divided into an
uneven conflict between dominant
("hegemonic") groups, states,
and ideologies on one side, and
dominated ("counter-hegemonic")
groups, collectives, and ideas on
the other. The battle takes place
at a number of levels, including the
economy, technology, and politics.

Culture and power
De Sousa Santos says that the
cultures of the world – and the
knowledge embedded within
them – are hierarchically arranged
and unevenly accessible, in line
with wider capitalist power
relations. Referring to the
philosophical term "epistemology"
(from *episteme*, "knowledge"), he
argues that the marginalization
of some nations by others on the
world stage is intimately related to
epistemological exclusion. Because
the dominant models of social
research are those imposed by the

Indigenous tribes, such as Brazil's
Kayapó, understand the properties of
healing plants. Western pharmaceutical
companies exploit this knowledge, but
fail to reward the tribes adequately.

global North, he refers to different
agendas from the peripheral states
as "epistemologies of the South".

In his work, de Sousa Santos
acknowledges that his goal is to
end these hierarchies of exclusion,
because "there is no social justice
without global cognitive justice".
He maintains that the cultural
diversity of the world is matched
by its epistemological diversity;
recognition of this has to be at
the core of any global effort to
eradicate current inequalities.
The biggest obstacle to this,
argues de Sousa Santos, is that the
scientific knowledge of the global
North is "hegemonic" within the
social hierarchy of knowledge.

Technological dominance
The capitalist and imperial order
imposed on the global South by the
global North has an epistemological
foundation. Western powers have
developed the capacity to dominate
many parts of the world, not least
by elevating modern science to
the status of a form of universal
knowledge, superior to all other
types of knowledge. Other, non-
scientific, forms of knowledge, and
the cultural and social practices of
different social groups informed by
these knowledges, are suppressed
in the name of modern science.
Modern science has colonized our
thinking to such an extent that
diverging from it is classified as
irrational thought. An example
of this is the Western media's
portrayal of Middle Eastern culture
as irrational and excessively
emotionally charged, which has
"destructive consequences".

Instead, de Sousa Santos is
keen to develop a transnational
cultural dialogue that will result in

Boaventura de Sousa Santos

Boaventura de Sousa Santos is
a professor at the University of
Coimbra, Portugal. He earned
his doctorate in the USA, at
Yale, and is a visiting professor
at the University of Wisconsin-
Madison. He is a defender
of strong social and civic
movements, which he regards
as essential for the realization
of participative democracy.

In 2001 de Sousa Santos
founded The World Social
Forum as a meeting place
for organizations opposed to
forms of globalization led by
neo-liberal economic policy
and transnational corporate
capitalism. He has published
widely on globalization,
sociology of law and the state,
democracy, and human rights.

Key works

2006 *The Rise of the Global
Left: The World Social Forum
and Beyond*
2007 *Cognitive Justice in
a Global World: Prudent
Knowledges for a Decent Life*
2014 *Epistemologies of the
South*

plurality: an "emancipatory, non-
relativistic cosmopolitan ecology
of knowledges", which will have
at their heart the recognition
of difference, and of the right to
difference and coexistence.
Only by these means, says de
Sousa Santos, can we achieve
a truly global understanding of
how societies work. This vision
informs the efforts of groups
such as The World Social Forum,
which seeks to bring about social
and economic justice using
alternatives to capitalism. ■

THE UNLEASHING OF PRODUCTIVE CAPACITY BY THE POWER OF THE MIND

MANUEL CASTELLS (1942–)

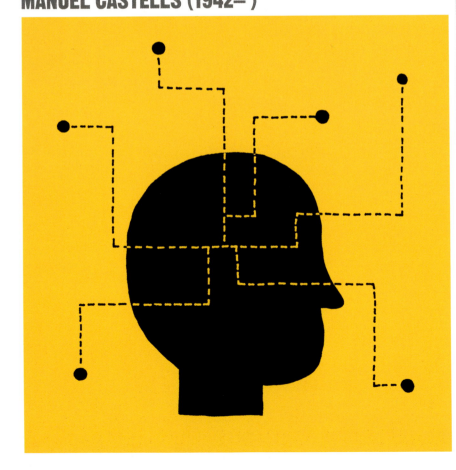

IN CONTEXT

FOCUS
Network society

KEY DATES
1848 Karl Marx and Friedrich Engels' *The Communist Manifesto* forecasts the globalization of capitalism.

1968 Manuel Castells studies under French sociologist Alain Touraine on the subject of social movements and resistance to capitalism.

From 1990 The corporate use of Internet-based technology increases, spreading out to the wider public and domestic life.

1992 US sociologist Harrison White writes "Markets, Networks, and Control", a discussion of network theory.

1999 Dutch sociologist Jan Van Dijk writes *The Network Society*, focusing on social media such as Facebook.

The last 50 years have seen giant leaps in science and developments in Internet-based and digital technologies. According to Spanish sociologist Manuel Castells (whose work straddles communication and information studies and is strongly influenced by Karl Marx), these advances have been shaped by – and played a key role in contributing to – economic, social, and political developments on the world stage. This has led Castells to focus on globalization and its economic and social effects.

For Marx, industrial capitalism was based on the production of consumer goods and commodities.

See also: Karl Marx 28–31 ▪ Niklas Luhmann 110–11 ▪ Zygmunt Bauman 136–43 ▪ Anthony Giddens 148–49 ▪ Ulrich Beck 156–61 ▪ Daniel Bell 224–25 ▪ Harry Braverman 226–31

> The "network society" is an **interconnected global community** of interests...

> ...where access to the network, or the **"space of flows"**, is no longer the preserve of a dominant social group.

> This means almost **anyone, anywhere**, can use telecommunications-based technology for any **creative purpose**.

During the 1970s, US sociologist Daniel Bell invoked the term "post-industrialism" to designate the shift towards a service-led economy. Castells argues that the rise to prominence of Internet-based technologies means capitalism now centres on information and knowledge. Human societies, he claims, have left behind the Industrial Age and entered the Information Age, the social–structural expression of which is the "network society".

A networked world

The Information Age is defined by the creation and dissemination of various specialist knowledges such as fluctuations in world oil prices, the financial markets, and so on. In advanced capitalist societies, networks of financial capital and information are now at the heart of productivity and competitiveness.

The shift from the production of goods and services to information and knowledge has profoundly altered the nature of society and social relations. Castells claims that the dominant mode of organizing interpersonal relations, institutions,

and whole societies is networks. Moreover, the malleable and open-ended nature of these networks means that they span the globe.

When classical sociologists such as Karl Marx, Émile Durkheim, and Max Weber use the term "society" it refers primarily to that of a given nation-state. So, for example, it is possible to talk of US society as something different from, as well as sharing similarities with, say, British society. However, in Castells' work, the nation-state has become the globe and everything in it. The world of relatively autonomous nation-states, with their own internally structured societies, is no longer – it has been re-imagined as multitudes of overlapping and intersecting networks.

The idea of a fully connected world, wired through the Internet, conjures up images of people in all corners of the planet engaging productively in different types of relations with one another in constantly shifting networks – constrained not by geography or nationality, but only by the capacity of human imagination. It is now possible to access information 24 hours a day through search engines such as Google, and to join chat rooms with people thousands of miles away and engage in instantaneous communication.

Castells elaborates on the concept of networks in a variety of ways. Microelectronics-based networks define the network society and have replaced bureaucracy as the main way of »

Bᴍ&ꜰBᴏᴠᴇsᴘᴀ in São Paulo, Brazil, is the largest stock exchange in Latin America. The exclusively electronic trading environment exemplifies the global economy in the Information Age.

The network society is a result of affordable, globally unifying telecommunications technology that has changed how we live, think, and do things. People who may never meet one another can now communicate instantly to trade goods or to exchange information and ideas.

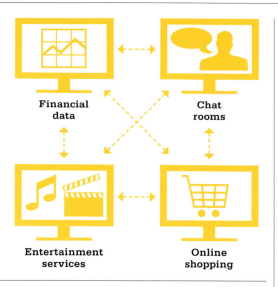

Financial data

Chat rooms

Entertainment services

Online shopping

organizing social relations, because they are far better at managing complexity. As well as the economic networks of financial trade and capital investment, microelectronic networks include political and interpersonal networks. The "network state" includes transnational political bodies such as the European Union, while examples of interpersonal networks are enacted through the Internet, e-mail, and social networking websites such as Facebook and Twitter.

Castells says a network can be defined as follows: it has no "centre"; it is made up of a series of "nodes" of varying importance but nevertheless all are necessary in order for the network to operate; the degree of social power peculiar to a network is relative depending on how much information it is able to process; a network only deals with a certain type of information – namely, the type of information relevant to it; and a network is an open structure, able to expand and compress without limits.

Castells emphasizes the high levels of adaptability characteristic of network society. Key here is that

a social order organized into and around networks can lay claim to being highly dynamic, innovative, and geared to ongoing, fast-moving social changes. Castells describes networked social relations as a "dynamic, self-expanding form of human activity" that tends to transform all spheres of social and economic life.

Social dynamics

The matter of whether individuals and institutions participate in, or are excluded from, certain social networks provides Castells with a window on the power dynamics at work in the network society. He concludes that networked relations have changed the structure of society over time.

Castells' initial argument was that individuals working within large multinational finance houses and institutions, and whose professional work is structured within and through networks of global financial flows, comprised the dominant social group – what he calls the "technocratic-financial-managerial elite". Occupying the key posts of command and control within the worldwide system,

this elite's preferred spatiality is the global city – from here it is able to reproduce its cosmopolitan practices and interests.

Meanwhile, in contrast, the lives of the masses tend to be local rather than global – organized around and clustered in places where people live in close physical proximity and social relations are characterized by shared ways of life. Therefore, said Castells, most people build meaningful identities and lives in actual geographically specific locales, the "space of places", rather than in the ethereal and placeless world of electronic networks, the "space of flows".

With the spread of the Internet and social media, however, this view of a unified, cosmopolitan, global elite using the space of flows to exert power came to be seen as overly simplistic. Economically impoverished social groups may find it harder to incorporate into, and centre their lifestyles on, Internet-based technologies to the same degree as socially dominant groups, but this is less and less the case. Castells now claims that "people of all kinds, wishing to do all kinds of things, can occupy this space of flows and use it for their own purposes".

Networks have become the predominant organizational form of every domain of human activity.
Manuel Castells

Anti-capitalist organizations, such as the Anticapitalist Initiative (which expressly refers to itself as a network on its website), have made use of the Internet in creative ways to connect people through a burgeoning network that occupies the space of flows. Castells uses the example of the Zapatistas in Mexico to acknowledge that social power can be accrued through the space of flows by marginalized groups in order to challenge the state and elite institutions. The Zapatistas have been successful in attracting media attention in cyberspace and have used the Internet to perform virtual sit-ins, with software clogging government servers and websites, as well as to plan and coordinate offline events.

Dystopia or utopia?

Castells' twin concepts of Information Age and network society provide a powerful set of analytical tools for understanding the transformative effects that information technology and globalization are having on human life and social relations.

Marx's concept of alienation resonates throughout Castells' work, which represents an attempt to make sense of the furiously paced changes and processes unfolding in the world around us with a view to reclaiming control over them. However, the idea that humans have created a global society they have lost control of and are alienated by is in part indebted to other theorists of globalization such as Anthony Giddens, Ulrich Beck, and Zygmunt Bauman.

Castells' work has many critics. Sociologists such as Bauman say it is utopian considering the "reality" of the social, economic, political, and environmental problems confronting humanity

today. Others deny that the present social and economic order is historically unprecedented; British sociologist Nicholas Garnham argues that the network society is more accurately a development of industrialism than a novel stage in human society. British sociologist Frank Webster charges Castells with technological determinism – the view that social relations are intimately shaped by technological developments but are not determined by them; rather, the two influence one another.

Whether or not the network society is novel or beneficial, there is no doubt that the world is increasingly interconnected and reliant on digital technologies, which are reshaping social relations. For Castells, the rise of a global society bound by myriad networks is, ultimately, a positive thing. Enabling people from far-flung places to interact offers the potential for humanity to draw upon its collective productive resources to create a new and enlightened world order. He argues that if we "are informed, active, and communicate throughout the world" then we "can depart for exploration of the inner self, having made peace among ourselves". ■

> While organizations are located in places... the organizational logic is placeless.
> **Manuel Castells**

Manuel Castells

Manuel Castells Oliván was born in 1942 in Spain. After being active in the student anti-Franco movement, he left Spain for France to study for a PhD in sociology at the University of Paris during the politically turbulent late 1960s.

In the 1980s Castells moved to California, USA – the home of Silicon Valley. A decade or so later he wrote an influential three-volume study about the network society entitled *The Information Age: Economy, Society, and Culture*.

Castells is an influential social scientific thinker. He is a sociologist at the University of Southern California (USC), Los Angeles, contributed to the establishment of the USC Center on Public Diplomacy, and is also a member of the Annenberg Research Network on International Communication (ARNIC).

Key works

1996 *The Information Age: Volume I: The Rise of the Network Society*
1997 *The Information Age: Volume II: The Power of Identity*
1998 *The Information Age: Volume III: End of Millennium*

WE ARE LIVING IN A WORLD THAT IS BEYOND CONTROLLABILITY

ULRICH BECK (1944–2015)

IN CONTEXT

FOCUS
Risk society

KEY DATES
1968 The Club of Rome think tank is founded and in 1972 publishes a report "The Limits to Growth", which identifies the risk posed by excessive population growth.

1984 US sociologist Charles Perrow publishes *Normal Accidents: Living with High-Risk Technologies*.

1999 US sociologist Barry Glassner draws on Ulrich Beck's concept of risk in *The Culture of Fear: Why Americans Are Afraid of the Wrong Things*.

2001 The 9/11 attacks on the USA lead to worldwide changes in the perception of the risks posed by international terrorist organizations.

We are entering a new period of **"reflexive" modernity**, which is characterized by **uncertainty and insecurity**.

The **scientific and technological revolution** that delivered progress is now viewed as having **introduced problems of development and global risks**.

Nothing appears fixed any more and **contradictions emerge between scientists and policymakers** about the **appropriate risk response**.

Loss of respect for institutions and experts creates uncertainty and doubt as we begin to fear we are living in a world that is beyond controllability.

Human societies have always faced dangers, and historically these have usually been "natural" in origin. In recent years, science, technology, and industry have created prosperity, but have also brought about new dangers (for example, those posed by the production of nuclear power), which have focused the thoughts of individuals and societies on a quest for safety and the idea of calculable risk. In the mid-1980s the German sociologist Ulrich Beck claimed that our relationship to society and its institutions had changed profoundly over the past decades, and that this required a new way of thinking about risk. Beck argues that social life is progressing from a first stage of modernity to an emergent second, or "reflexive", stage. This is shaped by an awareness that control of – and mastery over – nature and society may be impossible. This awareness may itself lead to disenchantment with existing social structures as providers of safety and reassurance.

A key characteristic of this new stage is the emergence of a global "risk society", by which Beck means that individuals, groups, governments, and corporations are increasingly concerned about the production, dissemination, and experience of risk. We now have to confront problems that previous generations could not imagine, and this requires new societal responses.

In his earlier work, Beck points in particular to the risks posed by nuclear energy, the chemical industry, and biotechnology. He says that the application of science and technology to meet human needs has reached a critical

See also: August Comte 22–25 ▪ Karl Marx 28–31 ▪ Max Weber 38–45 ▪ Anthony Giddens 148–49

threshold; that our advances have opened up the possibility of disasters on an unprecedented scale. Should such a catastrophe occur, it would be so grave that it would be almost impossible to contain its impact or to return to the way things were before.

Qualities of risk

Beck identifies three significant qualities of risk. First, global, irreparable damage: accidents cannot be compensated for, so insurance no longer works. Second, exclusion of precautionary aftercare: we cannot return conditions to the way they were before the accident. Third, no limit on space and time: accidents are unpredictable, can be felt across national borders, and impose their effects over long periods of time.

In terms of dealing with the possibility or likelihood of such calamities happening in the future, traditional methods of risk calculation have become obsolete in relation to many of the new kinds of risks that concern us in the 21st century, such as health pandemics, nuclear meltdowns, or genetically modified foodstuffs. As a result, how do scientists, corporations, and governments try to manage such potentially catastrophic risks?

Real and virtual risk

Beck identifies a strange ambiguity in how society understands risks. On the one hand, they are real – they exist as objective, latent threats at the heart of scientific and technological progress. They cannot be ignored, even if authorities try to pretend they do not exist. At the same time, however, risks are also virtual; that is, they represent current anxieties about events that have yet to – or may never – happen. Nonetheless, it is the apparent threat posed by these risks, the anticipation of disaster, which ushers in new challenges to the power of scientists, corporations, and governments.

Beck observes that no one is an expert on questions of risk, not even the experts themselves. The intrinsic complexity of many risks

> “
> Neither science, nor the politics in power... are in a position to define or control risks rationally.
> **Ulrich Beck**
> ”

means that scientists often cannot agree on questions of likelihood, possible severity, or how to set up proper safety procedures. In fact, in the public mind, it is these same experts – in their manipulation of genes or splitting of atomic nuclei – who may have created the risks.

However, while there is public scepticism about scientists, Beck notes that they are nevertheless essential in the risk society. Precisely because we cannot feel, hear, smell, or see the risks that »

Ulrich Beck

Ulrich Beck was born in 1944 in the town of Stolp, Germany, which is now part of Poland. From 1966 onwards he studied sociology, philosophy, psychology, and political science at Munich University. In 1972 he received his doctorate at Munich University and in 1979 he became a full university lecturer. He was subsequently appointed professor at the universities of Münster and Bamberg.

From 1992 Beck was professor of sociology and director of the Institute for Sociology at Munich's Ludwig Maximilian University; he was also Visiting Professor at the London School of Economics. Beck was one of Europe's most high-profile sociologists; in addition to his academic writing and research he commented on contemporary issues in the media and played an active role in German and European political affairs. He died in 2015.

Key works

1986 *Risk Society*
1997 *What is Globalization?*
1999 *World Risk Society*
2004 *The Cosmopolitan Vision*

we face, we need these experts to help measure, calculate, and make sense of them for us.

Making risks meaningful

Beck notes the important role played by so-called "new social movements" in raising public awareness of risk. For instance, Greenpeace, an independent organization committed to environmental protection, runs many high-profile publicity campaigns to draw attention to the environmental risks both caused and downplayed by corporations and governments.

The media feed on public anxieties about risk, claims Beck. To increase sales, news providers latch on to stories of corporate or institutional failures to adequately manage risk, or sensationalize stories of the hidden threats posed by technological developments.

While ultimately self-serving, Beck sees this as a positive thing because it helps develop public consciousness about risks and promote open debate. The media make risks visible and meaningful for people by giving abstract risks

> Reduced to a formula, wealth is hierarchic, smog is democratic.
> **Ulrich Beck**

a powerful symbolic form. For example, the consequences of rising global temperatures over many decades into the future can feel slightly unreal and abstract. However, "then-and-now" imagery of retreating glaciers, or footage of polar bears perched perilously on top of dissolving chunks of ice, delivers a powerful message about the immediacy of the risks the world faces.

Among the wider social consequences of living in a risk society is a change in the nature of inequality. In the past, wealthier individuals could protect themselves from risks, perhaps by paying more to live in a safer community or by having private insurance to provide better medical care. However, people can no longer buy their way out of many modern-day risks. Up to a point, someone could spend their way out of one risk by eating more expensive organic food to avoid the perceived hazards of industrial pesticides. Similarly, wealthier nations might avoid the polluting effects of heavy industry by outsourcing production to rapidly developing nations such as China. Sooner or later, however, these risks "boomerang" back. Here, Beck emphasizes the third quality of risk – that it does not respect boundaries of space and time. Wealth itself provides no certain way to avoid risk – the affluent West cannot ultimately escape the consequences of global warming that will be exacerbated by China's industrialization.

Globalized fears and hopes

In his more recent work on the concepts of "world risk society" and "cosmopolitanism", Beck argues that the process of globalization –

Today's technological societies create risks that may be unknown or almost impossible to quantify. According to Beck, when faced with such unknowable risks, we have three main responses – denial, apathy, or transformation.

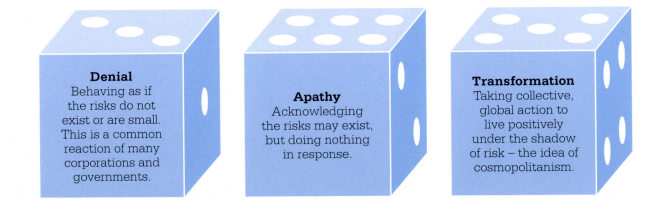

Denial
Behaving as if the risks do not exist or are small. This is a common reaction of many corporations and governments.

Apathy
Acknowledging the risks may exist, but doing nothing in response.

Transformation
Taking collective, global action to live positively under the shadow of risk – the idea of cosmopolitanism.

Surveillance, of both public spaces and private communications, has grown in the Western world in response to the real and perceived dangers posed by terrorist violence.

the growth of interdependency that undermines the influence and power of nation-states – produces its own negative consequences.

These include financial risks and terrorism risks. With the global growth of hedge funds, futures markets, derivatives trading, debt securitization, and credit default swaps, no country can hide behind its borders from the consequences of something going wrong. Acts of terrorist violence, planned and carried out by ideological groups, permeate the boundaries between states by striking at the heart of global cities such as New York and London. Interestingly, Beck observes that global terrorism is one of the few risks that governments are happy to draw attention to for political purposes.

While Beck's overriding focus on risk seems bleak, he also highlights what he sees as the positive possibilities inherent in the growth of risk. He points to the development of what he terms "cosmopolitanism", a concept comprising several components.

First, the existence of global risks calls for a global response: catastrophic risks affect humanity as a whole and must be responded to collectively, beyond the confines of national borders. Second, the level of media attention devoted to risks and catastrophes has the effect of giving more attention to how disasters impact most heavily upon the poor; the media coverage of Hurricane Katrina in the USA in 2005, for example, demonstrated to a global audience how poverty worsens the experience of catastrophe. Third, public experience and awareness of risk today draws groups into dialogue with one another; for example, Beck notes how environmental groups and businesses have joined forces to protest at the US government's lack of responsiveness to the problem of climate change.

Risk and reward

Beck's work has been read widely beyond the world of sociology, because it deals in an all-encompassing way with many of the key changes and concerns of recent decades. First published in German in 1986, at a time of new environmental concerns about acid rain and ozone layer depletion, his original concept of the risk society encapsulated and anticipated a number of high-profile environmental issues and accidents, such as the 1984 Bhopal disaster in India – where a gas leak from a chemical plant caused widespread poisoning – and the 1986 Chernobyl nuclear plant explosion in Ukraine. More recently, Beck's analysis has been applied to issues of global terrorism and the near-collapse of the financial system in 2008; it has been taken on board by others as a way of making sense of a diverse array of issues, including international relations, crime control, human health, food safety, social policy, and social work.

Ultimately, a positive strain runs through Beck's work. He argues that the experience of responding to global risk can lead to innovative solutions and constructive social changes. It is only in new encounters with the possibility of catastrophe that collective welfare and common interests can prevail over narrow, selfish concerns and our modern institutions can be reconfigured accordingly. ■

Fears about acid rain and global warming led to the Intergovernmental Panel on Climate Change. Formed in 1988, it reviewed the state of knowledge of the science of climate change.

IT SOMETIMES SEEMS AS IF THE WHOLE WORLD IS ON THE MOVE

JOHN URRY (1946–)

S ince the 17th century, new technologies have been emerging that have enabled people, objects, and ideas to move around the world more easily than before. British sociologist John Urry advises that the consequences of this increase in global mobility demand that the social sciences develop a "new paradigm" for the study of how goods, people, and ideas circulate. For Urry this movement creates new identities, cultures, and networks, giving rise to cultural diversity, economic opportunities and, at times, new forms of social inequality.

Systems and mobilities

Urry's primary contribution to the study of globalization is his focus on the social systems that facilitate movement. The 20th century, in particular, saw the emergence of cars, telephones, air power, high-speed trains, communications satellites, networked computers, and so on. These interconnecting "mobility systems" are the dynamic heart of globalization, says Urry.

> Being physically mobile has become… a 'way of life' across the globe.
> **John Urry**

He argues that the study of "mobilities" makes apparent the impacts and consequences of globalization. Likewise, the study of the forces preventing mobility – "immobilities" – is essential for comprehending contemporary social exclusion and inequality.

By understanding this global flow, sociology can better explore globalization's social and environmental advantages and costs (such as economic growth or industrial pollutants), as well as the forces driving social change. ∎

See also: Zygmunt Bauman 136–43 ▪ Manuel Castells 152–55 ▪ Saskia Sassen 164–65 ▪ David Held 170–71

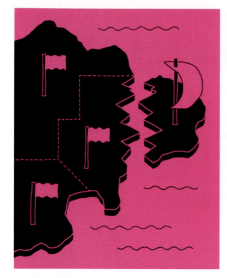

NATIONS CAN BE IMAGINED AND CONSTRUCTED WITH RELATIVELY LITTLE HISTORICAL STRAW
DAVID McCRONE

IN CONTEXT

FOCUS
Neo-nationalism

KEY DATES
1707 The Act of Union is ratified and the United Kingdom is officially formed.

1971 British ethnographer Anthony D Smith publishes his highly influential study, *Theories of Nationalism*.

1983 British sociologist Benedict Anderson publishes *Imagined Communities*, which examines the formation of nationhood.

1998 British sociologist David McCrone argues in *The Sociology of Nationalism* that nationalism operates as a vehicle for a variety of social and economic interests.

2004 Japanese sociologist Atsuko Ichijo explores the apparent contradiction of an "independence in Europe" policy in *Scottish Nationalism and the Idea of Europe*.

The economic, political, and cultural forces that globalization brings to bear have, according to British sociologist David McCrone, coincided with a rise in neo-nationalism, which occurs when a social group within a nation tries to redefine its identity. He argues that all neo-national identities concern smaller entities within larger nation-states: for example, Scotland in the United Kingdom, Catalonia in Spain, the Basque Country that straddles southwestern France and northern Spain, and French-speaking Quebec in Canada.

Both national and neo-national identities are forged from the "raw historical materials" of a common language, cultural myths and narratives, and social ideals. McCrone says that solidarity comes into being whenever enough people invoke these raw materials, or "historical straw", in pursuit of a common cause. Moreover, relatively little historical straw is required to galvanize neo-nationalist sentiment; often only a few symbols are needed to evoke strong feelings in people, such as the Senyara flag of Catalonia, or the fleur-de-lis symbol in Quebec. Although a sense of being distinctively different from the larger state may be the main factor that prompts calls for more autonomy or outright independence, the motivations for neo-nationalist identities or separatism can differ widely. They may, for example, be motivated by perceived unfairness in taxation or resource allocation. ■

The Basque separatist organization ETA engaged in political and armed conflict with the Spanish and French states from 1959 to 2011, in a quest for political independence.

See also: Émile Durkheim 34–37 ■ Paul Gilroy 75 ■ John Urry 162 ■ David Held 170–71 ■ Benedict Anderson 202–03 ■ Michel Maffesoli 291

GLOBAL CITIES ARE STRATEGIC SITES FOR NEW TYPES OF OPERATIONS
SASKIA SASSEN (1949–)

IN CONTEXT

FOCUS
Global cities

KEY DATES
1887 Ferdinand Tönnies says urbanization affects social solidarity by giving rise to a more individualistic society.

1903 Georg Simmel suggests that cities can cause people to adopt an "urban reserve" and blasé attitude.

1920s–40s "Chicago School" sociologists claim that cities have an "urban ecology", in which people compete for employment and services.

From the 1980s British sociologist David Harvey and Spanish sociologist Manuel Castells separately argue that cities are shaped by capitalism, which influences not only their character but also the various interactions of their inhabitants.

Globalization does not take place by itself. According to Saskia Sassen, professor of sociology at Columbia University, New York, USA, certain cities play a key role in generating the economic and cultural flows that connect the world together. These "global cities" exert power and influence well beyond the territory in which they are located.

Sociologists study cities to understand what impact they have on the behaviour, values, and opportunities of occupants. In the 20th century they noted that the large industrial cities of the developed world were forming

Wall Street is the economic engine of the global city of New York. Such cities, Sassen says, are the "terrain where a multiplicity of globalization processes assume concrete, localized forms".

new connections and becoming economically interdependent. These changes were resulting, in part, from trade liberalization and the global expansion of industrial capitalism. Within this new "global economy" central clusters of economic and cultural activity, or "global cities", were forming.

The modern metropolis
Global cities, Sassen advises, produce goods in the form of technological innovations, financial products, and consulting services (legal, accounting, advertising, and so on). These service industries are highly intensive users of telecommunications technologies and are therefore integrated into business networks that stretch across national borders. They are also part of the post-industrial or "service" economies of the developed world, in that their main products are knowledge, innovation, technical expertise, and cultural goods.

Sassen argues in *The Global City* (1991, revised 2001) that the emergence of a global market for financial and specialized services gives global cities a "command and control function" over economic

See also: Ferdinand Tönnies 32–33 ▪ Georg Simmel 104–05 ▪ Henri Lefebvre 106–07 ▪ Zygmunt Bauman 136–43 ▪ Immanuel Wallerstein 144–45 ▪ David Held 170–71

Globalization is **transforming industrial cities** and giving rise to **"global cities"**, which are...

...**command posts** for the direction and policies driving the global economy.

...**key locations for service industries**, including financial and legal firms.

...**sites of knowledge production** and innovation for new industries and sectors.

...**markets** in which the products of new industries and services are bought and sold.

Global cities are strategic sites for new types of operations.

globalization. This is because the headquarters of many major transnational companies are located in global cities. Consultant firms are also "over-represented" in these urban hubs. These companies make the decisions that direct global flows of money and knowledge, and that can cause economic activity to expand or contract in other regions.

The global marketplace

Global cities are also marketplaces where financial goods are bought and sold. New York, London, Tokyo, Amsterdam, Hong Kong, Shanghai, Frankfurt, and Sydney (among others) are major financial centres, home to large banks, businesses, and stock exchanges. In the global city, national and global markets interconnect, which leads to a concentration of financial activity.

Global cities are supported by multi-functional infrastructure. Central business districts provide employment clusters where the employees of local, national, and multinational firms interact. Influential universities and research facilities also contribute to the production of knowledge and innovation, which are central to information-based economies.

Sassen's research shows that global cities are sites where the human activities behind the processes of globalization are performed and their consequences dispersed through the socio-economic networks of the global economy. While global cities are not free from poverty and other forms of social inequality, they are nevertheless cosmopolitan sites of diverse economic and social opportunities. ▪

Multinational urban culture

Sassen's work highlights that global cities are increasingly cosmopolitan. As migrants add new foods, cultural expressions, fashions, and entertainments to the host national culture, this diversity enriches a city.

In a nation-state that encourages multiculturalism and social inclusion, global cities can become even more vibrant sites of cultural innovation as ideas and values are freely shared. This multicultural texturing of a pre-existing national culture also increases economic activity. This is because global cities are more appealing for transitory visitors and migrants, who can maintain aspects of their ethnic and national identities, while embracing the new experiences and values of a cosmopolitan city. The cultural diversity of global cities also means that they are orientated towards supporting the activities of a global economy and a cosmopolitan global culture.

DIFFERENT SOCIETIES APPROPRIATE THE MATERIALS OF MODERNITY DIFFERENTLY

ARJUN APPADURAI (1949–)

IN CONTEXT

FOCUS
Globalization and modernity

KEY DATES
1963 Jacques Derrida introduces the concept of "différance" (difference), which later informs ideas about cultural heterogeneity.

1983 British social thinker Benedict Anderson says that groupings based on the perceptions of their members rather than direct interaction are "imagined communities".

1991 Economic liberalization opens India to globalizing forces as the country tries to integrate into the global order.

2008 Postcolonial studies thinker Richard Brock applies Appadurai's notion of "scapes" to critically consider the cultural construction of the HIV/AIDS pandemic.

The term "globalization" has become associated with the spread of free-market capitalism and the development of borderless economies – the idea of a global trading village. In a sociological context, however, globalization is not just an economic, but a cultural, social, and ideological phenomenon.

Much debate among cultural theorists has addressed the issue of whether globalization necessarily means that the world will become more homogenous – moving towards a "one-world" culture – or whether reactions to the forces of globalization will reinforce diversity in language, culture, and ethnicity.

See also: Zygmunt Bauman 136–43 ▪ Immanuel Wallerstein 144–45 ▪
Roland Robertson 146–47 ▪ Manuel Castells 152–55 ▪ Jeffrey Alexander 204–09

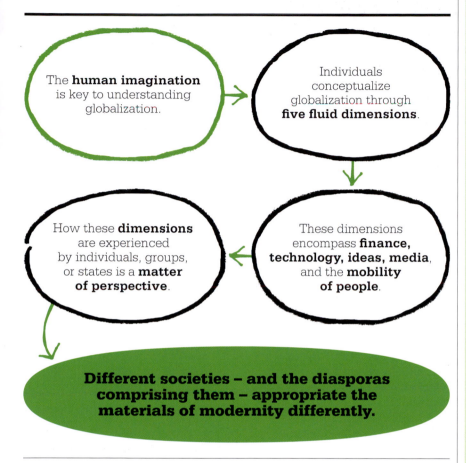

The **human imagination** is key to understanding globalization.

Individuals conceptualize globalization through **five fluid dimensions**.

These dimensions encompass **finance, technology, ideas, media**, and the **mobility of people**.

How these **dimensions** are experienced by individuals, groups, or states is a **matter of perspective**.

Different societies – and the diasporas comprising them – appropriate the materials of modernity differently.

Arjun Appadurai

Born in Mumbai, India, Arjun Appadurai went to the USA to study at Brandeis University, near Boston. He attained his master's degree in 1973 and his doctorate from the University of Chicago in 1976.

Appadurai is currently the Goddard Professor in Media, Culture, and Communication at New York University, where he is also Senior Fellow at the Institute for Public Knowledge. He has served as an advisor to the Smithsonian Institution, the National Endowment for the Humanities, the National Science Foundation, the United Nations, and the World Bank. Appadurai founded and is president of the non-profit group Partners for Urban Knowledge Action and Research, based in Mumbai, and he is one of the founders of *Public Culture*, an interdisciplinary journal focused on transnationalism.

Key works

1990 "Disjuncture and Difference in the Global Cultural Economy"
1996 *Modernity at Large: Cultural Dimensions of Globalization*
2001 *Globalization*

Indian social anthropologist and sociologist Arjun Appadurai has taken this debate in a different direction. He argues that the conventional view of globalization as a form of cultural imperialism fails to reflect the reality of the changes globalization has set in motion. Instead, Appadurai suggests that different societies appropriate the materials of modernity differently.

What this means is that one society, such as China, may take up one aspect of global change (such as economic change) very rapidly, and another aspect (such as ideological change) very slowly, while another society will be different altogether. The result is that globalization does not necessarily denote a uniform and all-encompassing process; rather, nations are more positively disposed towards certain facets of globalization than others, depending on a range of factors, such as the state of the economy, political stability, and strength of cultural identity. For example, China has embraced industrial and information technologies and global economic expansion, while retaining a strong sense of political autonomy.

For Appadurai the process of globalization is one that leads to "disjunctures" where areas such »

> One man's imagined community is another man's political prison.
> **Arjun Appadurai**

as the economy, culture, and politics do not move in the same direction, thereby causing tensions in society. An example of this is the distance between a promise of consumer goods made by global companies and the ability of local people to afford them.

Appadurai's work addresses how globalization diminishes the role of the nation-state in shaping cultural identity and argues that identity is increasingly becoming deterritorialized by mobility, migration, and rapid communications. People no longer hold coherent sets of ideas, views, beliefs, and practices based on their nationality or membership of a state; instead, new cultural identities are emerging in the interstices between different states and localities – what Appadurai calls translocalities.

Globally imagined worlds

The key to understanding globalization, says Appadurai, is the human imagination. He argues that rather than living in face-to-face communities, we live within imagined ones that are global in extent. The building blocks are five interrelated dimensions that shape the global flow of ideas and information. He

calls these dimensions "scapes" – ethnoscapes, mediascapes, technoscapes, finanscapes, and ideoscapes. Unlike landscapes, which are characteristically fixed, Appadurai's "scapes" are constantly changing, and the manner in which they are experienced depends largely on the perspective of the social actors involved.

In this context, social actors may be any one of a number of groupings, such as nation-states, multinational corporations, diasporic communities, families, or individuals. The different ways in which these five scapes can combine means that the imagined world that one person or grouping perceives can be radically different, and no more real, than that seen by another observer.

Shifting scapes

Appadurai first used the term "ethnoscape" in a 1990 essay, "Disjuncture and Difference in the Global Cultural Economy", to describe the flow of people – immigrant communities, political exiles, tourists, guest workers, economic migrants, and other groups – around the globe, as well as the "fantasies of wanting to move" in pursuit of a better life. The increasing mobility of people between nations constitutes an essential feature of the global world, in particular by affecting the politics of nation-states.

Mediascapes refer to the production and distribution of information and images through newspapers, magazines, TV, and film, as well as digital technologies. The multiplying ways in which information is made accessible to private and public interests throughout the world is a major driver of globalization. Mediascapes

provide large and complex repertoires of images and narratives to viewers, and these shape how people make sense of events taking place across the world.

Technoscapes represent the rapid dissemination of technology and knowledge about it – either mechanical or informational – across borders. For example, many service industries in Western Europe base their customer-care call centres in India; and Indian software engineers are often recruited by US companies.

Finanscapes reflect the almost instantaneous transfer of financial and investment capital around the globe in the fast-moving world of currency markets, stock exchanges, and commodity speculations.

Ideoscapes are made up of images that are "often directly political", either state-produced and intended to bolster the dominant ideology, or created by counter-ideological movements "oriented to

France has embraced many economic dimensions of globalization yet seeks to limit the influence of foreign cultures by, for example, charging a ticket levy to help fund the French film industry.

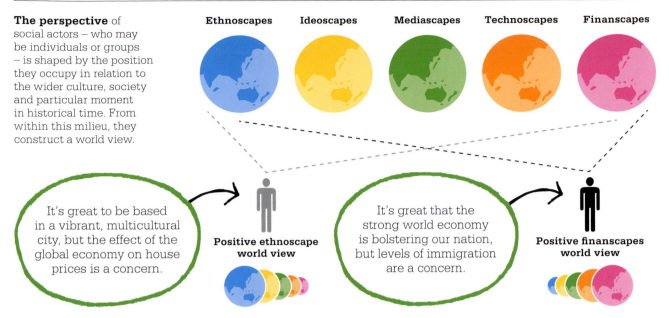

The perspective of social actors – who may be individuals or groups – is shaped by the position they occupy in relation to the wider culture, society and particular moment in historical time. From within this milieu, they construct a world view.

Ethnoscapes   Ideoscapes   Mediascapes   Technoscapes   Finanscapes

It's great to be based in a vibrant, multicultural city, but the effect of the global economy on house prices is a concern.

Positive ethnoscape world view

It's great that the strong world economy is bolstering our nation, but levels of immigration are a concern.

Positive finanscapes world view

capturing state power or a piece of it". Examples include ideas about a state built through concepts such as "national heritage", countered by social and political movements that promote the rights of minority groups and freedom of speech.

Sameness and difference

The different "scapes" identified by Appadurai may be, and often are, incongruous and disjointed. For example, social actors in one place may be positively disposed towards economic developments brought about by globalization (that is, they see a positive finanscape), while simultaneously regarding immigration as a threat to national identity and culture (a negative ethnoscape).

By conceptualizing globalization in terms of the five scapes, Appadurai is able to undermine the view of globalization as a uniform and internally coherent process; instead, globalization is understood as a multi-layered, fluid, and irregular process – and one that is characterized by ongoing change.

The different scapes are capable of moving together or of following different trajectories, in turn serving either to reinforce or destabilize one another.

Appadurai states that the scapes are constructs of perspective because they are determined by the relation of the viewer to the viewed. If this relation changes, so in turn does the view. In sum, the world view constructed by any social actor is exactly that: it is a view dependent upon the social, cultural, and historical positioning of the actor; and for this reason, who and where we are determines what scapes we see and how we interpret them. There are multiple ways of imagining the world.

The impact of Appadurai's contribution to globalization theory is a significant one, primarily because it does not try to provide an integrated theory of globalization in the orthodox manner of social thinkers such as Immanuel Wallerstein from the USA and Spain's Manuel Castells. Quite the opposite; it is Appadurai's

intention to critically deconstruct what he considers the naive view that something as complex and multi-faceted as globalization can be explained through one master theory. That said, Appadurai's work has been criticized by the likes of Dutch social thinker Gijsbert Oonk, who questions whether or not his concept of global landscapes can be meaningfully applied when conducting empirical research. ∎

" The new global order cultural economy has to be understood as a complex, overlapping, disjunctive order.
Arjun Appadurai
"

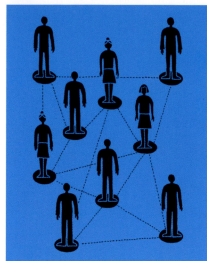

PROCESSES OF CHANGE HAVE ALTERED THE RELATIONS BETWEEN PEOPLES AND COMMUNITIES
DAVID HELD (1951–)

IN CONTEXT

FOCUS
Globalization

KEY DATES
1960s Canadian media theorist Marshall McLuhan claims that the world is contracting into a "global village" through technology.

1974 US sociologist Immanuel Wallerstein publishes *The Modern World-System*, highlighting the social effects of a global economy.

1993 US sociologist George Ritzer claims that systematic methods of production are influencing the operations of institutions and corporations around the world.

2006 German sociologist Ulrich Beck argues that states must embrace multilateral cooperation, transnational institutions, and cosmopolitan identities if they are to prosper in the global age.

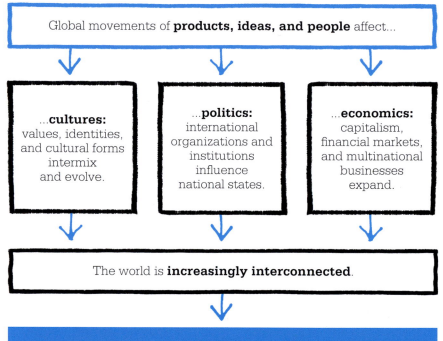

Global movements of **products, ideas, and people** affect...

...**cultures:** values, identities, and cultural forms intermix and evolve.

...**politics:** international organizations and institutions influence national states.

...**economics:** capitalism, financial markets, and multinational businesses expand.

The world is **increasingly interconnected**.

Processes of change have altered the relations between peoples and communities.

The world is becoming smaller due to the mass movement of people and the exchange and flow of products, ideas, and cultural artefacts. These changes, suggests British sociologist David Held, are altering the way communities and individuals are interacting and communicating with one another.

Migration, for example, creates an intermixing of cultures and the development of multicultural societies. People also connect

See also: George Ritzer 120–23 ▪ Immanuel Wallerstein 144–45 ▪
Roland Robertson 146–47 ▪ Ulrich Beck 156–61 ▪ Arjun Appadurai 166–69

Bollywood films in India represent the assymetrical flow of culture around the world. Despite selling more tickets than Hollywood, they make far less revenue from international distribution.

with global cultures, such as music genres or cuisines, blending the global with the local to produce new cultural products.

Held suggests globalization is best understood as a set of processes and changes. Cultural dimensions include the distribution of media products and movement of ideas and people across societies. Political dimensions include the rise of international organizations, institutions, and multinational companies. The economic dimensions include the expansion of capitalism and consumerism.

Change for better or worse?

In *Globalization/Anti-Globalization*, Held examines the views of different sociologists on globalization, organizing them into "hyper-globalists", "sceptics", and "transformationalists".

The hyper-globalists see the forces of globalization as powerful, unprecedented, and as facilitating the development of a global civilization. Some hyper-globalists praise globalization for driving economic development and spreading democracy; others are critical of the spread of capitalism and its social consequences.

The sceptics, by contrast, downplay the extent to which globalization is a new phenomenon and reject the idea that global integration and institutions are undermining the power of the nation-state. They see globalization as marginalizing the developing world, while at the same time benefiting corporations based in developed nations.

The transformationalists, according to Held, best explain the contradictory processes of globalization. They argue that boundaries between the global and local are breaking down, and that the human world is becoming interconnected. They also argue that there is no single cause of globalization, and that the outcomes of these processes are not determined.

Globalization, Held suggests, is giving rise to a new global "architecture" comprised of

David Held

David Held was born in Britain in 1951 and was educated in Britain, France, Germany, and the USA. He holds an MSc and a PhD in political science from Massachusetts Institute of Technology (MIT), USA.

In 1984, Held co-founded Polity Press, the highly influential international publisher of social-science and humanities books, where he continues as Director. He has written and edited more than 60 books on democracy, globalization, global governance, and public policy. In 2011 Held resigned his professorial position in political science at the London School of Economics to become Director of the Institute of Global Policy at Durham University in the UK.

Key works

1995 *Democracy and the Global Order*
2002 *Globalization/Anti-Globalization* (co-author)
2004 *Global Covenant*

multinational companies and institutions, and characterized by asymmetrical cultural and economic flows.

The precise nature of the emerging patterns of inequality and prosperity brought by globalization is not yet clear. Importantly, however, Held sees globalization as a dynamic process that can be influenced: nation-states can embrace policies and relationships that address global problems or risks, be they poverty, pandemics, or environmental damage and change. ∎

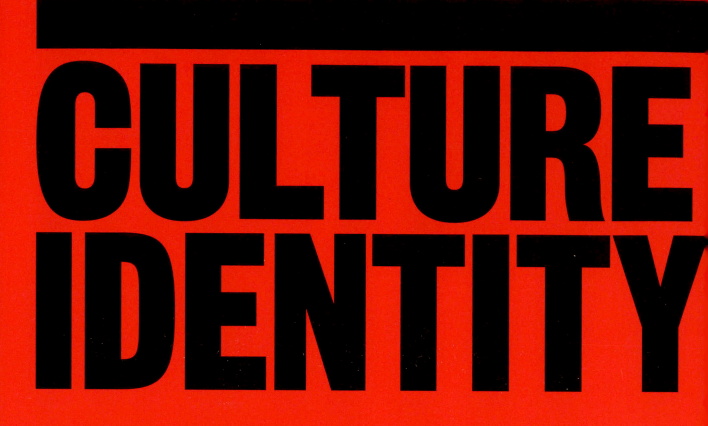

CULTURE
IDENTITY

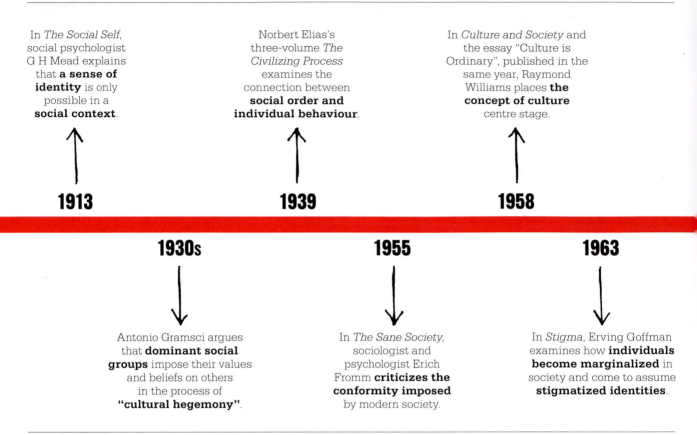

In *The Social Self*, social psychologist G H Mead explains that **a sense of identity** is only possible in a **social context**.

1913

Norbert Elias's three-volume *The Civilizing Process* examines the connection between **social order and individual behaviour**.

1939

In *Culture and Society* and the essay "Culture is Ordinary", published in the same year, Raymond Williams places **the concept of culture** centre stage.

1958

1930s

Antonio Gramsci argues that **dominant social groups** impose their values and beliefs on others in the process of **"cultural hegemony"**.

1955

In *The Sane Society*, sociologist and psychologist Erich Fromm **criticizes the conformity imposed** by modern society.

1963

In *Stigma*, Erving Goffman examines how **individuals become marginalized** in society and come to assume **stigmatized identities**.

From its beginnings in the early 19th century, sociology sought to examine not only the institutions and systems that created social order, but also the factors that maintained social cohesion.

Traditionally, this had come from the shared values, beliefs, and experiences of communities, but with the advent of "modernity" in the form of industrialization and secularization, the structure of society was radically transformed. Although it was recognized that modernity had changed the way people associated with one another, it was not until the 20th century that culture – the ways that people think and behave as a group, and how they identify themselves as members of a society – became an object of study in its own right.

The emergence of sociology – the systematic study of how society shapes human interaction and identity – had coincided with the establishment of anthropology and psychology, and there was a degree of overlap between the three disciplines. It is unsurprising, then, that one of the first cultural sociologists was also a pioneering social psychologist, G H Mead. He set the scene for a sociological study of culture by highlighting the connection between the individual and society, and especially the notion of a social identity. An individual, he argued, can only develop a true sense of identity in the context of a social group, through interaction with others.

The connections with social psychology continued throughout the 20th century, notably in the work of Erich Fromm in the 1950s, who argued that many psychological problems have social origins. In the process of connecting with wider society and identifying with a particular culture, individuals are expected to conform with society, and this stifles our individualism so that we lose a true sense of self. Around the same time, Erving Goffman began discussing the problems of establishing a sense of identity; and in the 1960s, he focused on the stigma attached to those who do not conform or are "different".

Culture and social order
Norbert Elias, in the 1930s, had described the imposition of social norms and conventions as a "civilizing process", directly regulating individual behaviour.

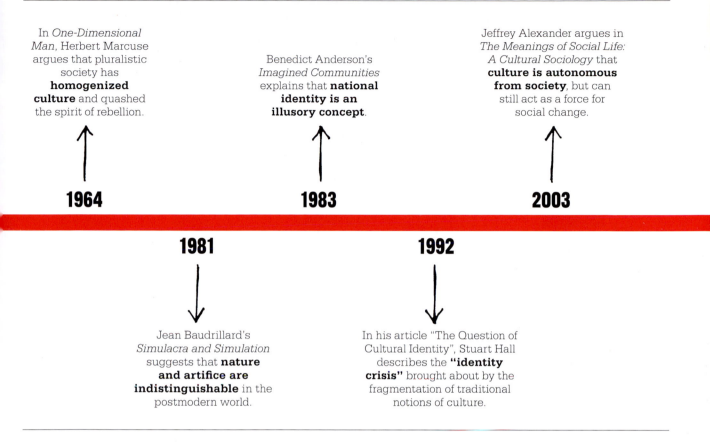

In *One-Dimensional Man*, Herbert Marcuse argues that pluralistic society has **homogenized culture** and quashed the spirit of rebellion.

Benedict Anderson's *Imagined Communities* explains that **national identity is an illusory concept**.

Jeffrey Alexander argues in *The Meanings of Social Life: A Cultural Sociology* that **culture is autonomous from society**, but can still act as a force for social change.

1964

1983

2003

1981

1992

Jean Baudrillard's *Simulacra and Simulation* suggests that **nature and artifice are indistinguishable** in the postmodern world.

In his article "The Question of Cultural Identity", Stuart Hall describes the **"identity crisis"** brought about by the fragmentation of traditional notions of culture.

There is clearly a connection between the regulating power of culture and the maintenance of social order, and some saw it as more than merely a process of socialization. Antonio Gramsci recognized the potential for culture to be used as a means of social control. Through subtle coercion, a dominant culture imposes a "cultural hegemony" in which social norms become so ingrained that anything else is unthinkable.

Michel Foucault developed this idea further in his study of power relations, and others, including Herbert Marcuse, examined the ways in which culture could be used to quell social unrest. Later, another French sociologist, Jean Baudrillard, argued that in the postmodern world, with its explosion of availability of information, culture had become so far removed from the society in which it exists that it bears little relation to reality.

Cultural identity

A distinct branch of culturally oriented sociology emerged in the UK from the latter part of the 20th century: cultural studies. The starting point was Raymond Williams' extensive research into the idea of culture. His work transformed the concept, opening up entirely new areas of study to sociological investigation.

Williams explained that culture is expressed by material production and consumption, and by the creations and leisure pursuits of social groups of a specific time and place – their food, sports, fashion, languages, beliefs, ideas, and customs, as well as their literature, art, and music. Also at the forefront of this British school of cultural studies was Stuart Hall, who suggested that notions of cultural identity are no longer fixed. With significantly improved communications and increased mobility, traditional national, ethnic, class, and even gender identities have all but disappeared – and another British sociologist, Benedict Anderson, goes so far as to suggest that the concept of belonging to any community is illusory.

However, the US sociologist Jeffrey Alexander considered culture to be an independent variable in the structure of society. His cultural sociology examines how culture shapes society through the creation of shared meaning. ∎

THE "I" AND THE "ME"

G H MEAD (1863–1931)

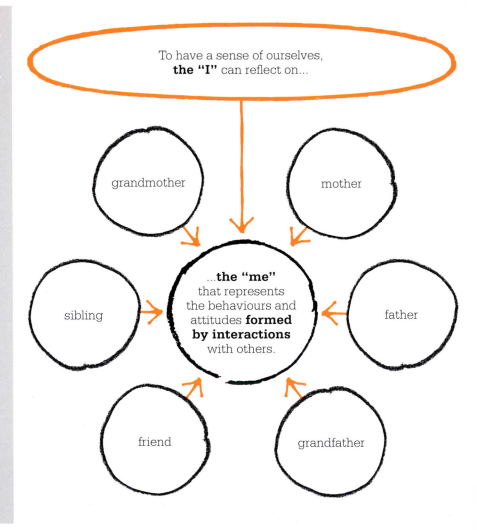

To have a sense of ourselves, **the "I"** can reflect on...

grandmother

mother

sibling

...**the "me"** that represents the behaviours and attitudes **formed by interactions** with others.

father

friend

grandfather

See also: W E B Du Bois 68–73 ▪ Edward Said 80–81 ▪ Norbert Elias 180–81 ▪ Erving Goffman 190–95 ▪ Stuart Hall 200–01 ▪ Benedict Anderson 202–03 ▪ Howard S Becker 280–85 ▪ Adrienne Rich 304–09 ▪ Jeffrey Weeks 324–25

George Herbert Mead was a social psychologist and a philosopher, and he looked to both disciplines in trying to work out what exactly we mean when we talk about the "self". Traditional philosophers and sociologists saw societies as growing from the coming together of individual, autonomous selves, but Mead said the opposite was true – selves emerge from social interactions; they are formed within society.

This concept is prevalent now in psychology and psychotherapy, but when Mead first presented his ideas in 1913 in *The Social Self*, it was a revolutionary point of view. Mead disagreed with the idea that individual, experiencing selves exist in any recognizable way before they are part of the social process. The social process of experience or behaviour is "logically prior to the individuals and their individual experiencing which are involved in it".

By this, Mead is suggesting that an individual's consciousness, with all its intentions, desires, and so on, is formed within the context of social relationships, one or more particular languages, and a set of cultural norms. From birth, babies begin to sense communication through gestures, which function as symbols and build "a universe of discourse". Over time, they learn to mimic and "import" the practices, gestures, and eventually words of those around them, so that they can make their own response and receive further gestures and words from others.

Who we are

The pattern of attitudes that the baby experiences and internalizes (learns) creates the sense of "me". In this way, the "me" represents the behaviours, expectations, and attitudes learned through interactions with others.

But Mead says that we also have another sense of ourselves, which he calls the "I". Both the "I" and the "me" are different functions of the self. The "I", like the "me", keeps evolving, but its function is to reflect on the "me", while also

Our view of ourselves, of who we are, is developed from birth through interaction with those closest to us. Individual selves are not the products of biology but rather of this interaction.

seeing the bigger picture: the "me" acts in habitual ways, while the "I" can reflect on these and make self-conscious choices. It allows us to be different, both from other people and our former selves, through reflection on our actions.

Mead's theory of the development of self was pivotal in turning psychology and sociology away from the idea of "self" as being merely internal introspection, and aligning it firmly within a societal context. ∎

Mind can never find expression, and could never have come into existence at all, except in terms of a social environment.
G H Mead

G H Mead

George Herbert Mead was born in Massachusetts, USA. His father was a minister in the Congregational Church, and he moved the family to Oberlin, Ohio, to teach at the seminary there when Mead was six years old. After graduating from Oberlin College in 1883, Mead worked for a few years as a teacher and then as a railroad surveyor before returning to academia. He began his studies in philosophy and sociology at Harvard University in 1887 and seven years later moved to the University of Chicago, where he worked until his death in 1931. He claimed to have an "activist spirit" and marched in support of women's suffrage and other causes. The philosopher John Dewey acknowledged Mead as having "a seminal mind of the very first order".

Key works

1913 *The Social Self*
1932 *The Philosophy of the Present*
1934 *Mind, Self, and Society*

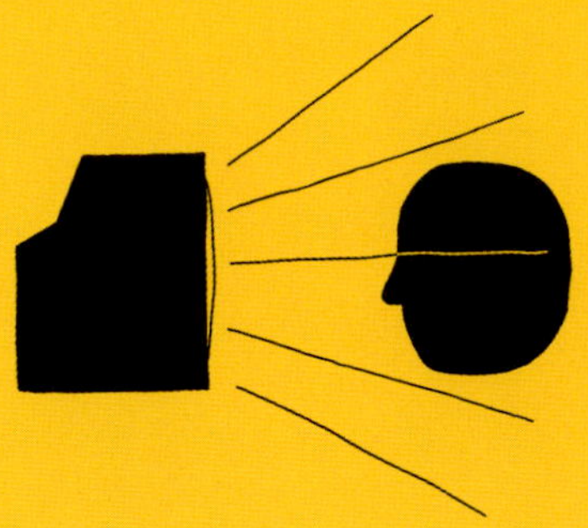

THE CHALLENGE OF MODERNITY IS TO LIVE WITHOUT ILLUSIONS AND WITHOUT BECOMING DISILLUSIONED

ANTONIO GRAMSCI (1891–1937)

IN CONTEXT

FOCUS
Cultural hegemony

KEY DATES

1846 Karl Marx and Friedrich Engels finish *The German Ideology*; not published until 1932, it later strongly influences Gramsci's thinking about ideology.

1921 The Italian Communist Party is founded.

1922 Benito Mussolini becomes dictator of Italy and a leading figure in the development of Fascism.

1964 The Centre for Contemporary Cultural Studies is established at the University of Birmingham, England, and draws heavily on Gramsci's notion of hegemony.

1985 Inspired by Gramsci's concept of hegemony, Ernesto Laclau and Chantal Mouffe develop a post-Marxist manifesto in *Hegemony and Socialist Strategy*.

According to Marx, **the ruling class controls the economic base** and creates the superstructure of institutions and social relations that **dominate the working class**.

↓

Gramsci claims **class domination also occurs culturally**: the working class are subject to the **ideological illusions** perpetrated by the ruling class.

↓

These illusions must be seen through, and **resisted at all costs**.

↓

The challenge of modernity is to live without illusions and without becoming disillusioned.

The Marxist view of society is that life is an ongoing struggle of competing groups; these groups are determined economically, and under modernity the struggle has intensified into a contest for control between a minority ruling elite and the majority, made up of workers. Italian socialist and social thinker Antonio Gramsci tries to explain why revolution is not precipitated

See also: Karl Marx 28–31 ▪ Friedrich Engels 66–67 ▪ Pierre Bourdieu 76–79 ▪ Zygmunt Bauman 136–43 ▪ Herbert Marcuse 182–87 ▪ Jean Baudrillard 196–99

in a crisis, as it should be according to classical Marxist theory. He argues that repression by the ruling class is insufficient to secure a stable social order; there must also be ideological subjugation. This happens in a complex process whereby the ruling elite propagates its views of the world so that they are accepted as common sense and largely beyond contention. Gramsci calls this "hegemony", a concealed mode of class domination that explains why workers can become Fascists rather than revolutionaries.

The hegemonic struggle

Gramsci claims that hegemony is cultural and that it is involved in a struggle between competing class-based world views, by which is meant sets of values, ideas, beliefs, and understandings of what human beings are like, what society is, and – crucially – what it could be.

Hegemony, he says, involves an invisible mechanism whereby positions of influence in society are always filled by members of an already ruling class – largely with the consent of the subordinated. The ruling class's ideas, which are the dominant ones permeating the whole of society, are propounded by intellectual groups working in its service (often only partially knowingly) such as journalists who disseminate these ideas to the wider population. Constant exposure to them means that the lower classes experience them as natural and inevitable, and come to believe them. Hegemonic ideas shape the thinking of all social classes. It is for this reason, says Gramsci, that the challenge of modernity is not to become disillusioned with the ongoing struggle but to see through the "illusions" – the views propounded by elite groups – and resist them.

Because individuals have the capacity to think critically about the view imposed upon them, which Gramsci calls "counter-hegemonic" thinking, the ruling class's ideological dominance is often in the balance. In Western liberal democracies the challenge to hegemony is an everyday reality.

The nature and extent of these struggles between competing world views is contingent upon social, political, and economic circumstances. A series of prolonged economic crises leading to high unemployment, for example, is liable to result in a situation in which various counter-hegemonic forces arise in the form of trade unions or protest movements. Gramsci notes that in most capitalist societies the ruling classes face constant opposition and dissent "from below" and have to devote a vast amount of time and energy to managing this situation, with complete control highly unlikely, even for short periods.

Gramsci's ideas emphasize the role of individuals and ideologies in the struggle for social change, and thereby challenge the economic determinism of traditional Marxism. His concept of "cultural hegemony", which recognizes human autonomy and the importance of culture, has had a lasting impact on a number of academic disciplines. ▪

Antonio Gramsci

Antonio Gramsci was born in Sardinia, Italy, in 1891. He was a co-founder of the Italian Communist Party. While serving as the party's leader, he was sentenced to 20 years imprisonment in 1928 by Benito Mussolini, Italy's prime minister and dictator at the time.

Gramsci wrote prolifically while in prison. Although he had a prodigious memory, without the help of his sister-in-law, Tania, who was a frequent visitor, his ideas would not have come to light. This intellectual work did not emerge until several years after World War II, when it was published posthumously in what are known as the *Prison Notebooks*. By the 1950s, his prison writings had attracted interest not only in Western Europe, but also in the Soviet bloc. Due to the poor diet, illness, and bad health he suffered in prison, Gramsci died of a stroke at the age of only 46.

Key works

1975 *Prison Notebooks* (three volumes)
1994 *Pre-Prison Writings*

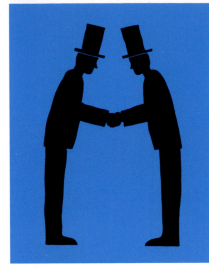

THE CIVILIZING PROCESS IS CONSTANTLY MOVING "FORWARD"
NORBERT ELIAS (1897–1990)

IN CONTEXT

FOCUS
The civilizing process

KEY DATES
c.1500 Feudalism in Western Europe comes to an end and court society emerges.

1690 English philosopher John Locke describes "civil society" as a united body of individuals under the power of an executive.

1850s Auguste Comte asks how the individual can be both a cause and consequence of society.

1958 Max Weber says values and beliefs can cause dramatic change in the social structure.

1962 US anthropologist Robert Redfield says that civilization is a totality of great and little traditions.

1970s Antonio Gramsci says the ruling classes maintain their dominance through the institutions of civil society.

As nations stabilized in the West after the 1500s, **power was centralized** and became the preserve of a small number of people.

These people were no longer revered for their physical strength, but for their **social standing**, reflected in their courtly manners.

To be identified with power, people are encouraged to display the same **"civilized behaviour"** as a nation's governing elite.

People (and nations) lacking the right behaviour are seen as **inferior and need "civilizing"** into following the rules of the powerful.

To shed light on the West's centralization of national power and increasing global domination over the last 500 years, Norbert Elias turned his attention to the "psychical process of civilization" – the changes in behaviour, feeling, and intentions of people in the West since the Middle Ages. He describes these changes, and the effect they have had on individuals, in his famous book *The Civilizing Process*.

Elias draws on history, sociology, and psychoanalysis to conclude that the way in which Western society believes itself to be superior to others is summed up by the concept of "civilization". This is both historical and

See also: W E B Du Bois 68–73 ▪ Paul Gilroy 75 ▪ Pierre Bourdieu 76–79 ▪ Edward Said 80–81 ▪ Elijah Anderson 82–83 ▪ Stuart Hall 200–01

"Good" table manners and "correct" etiquette and deportment were, according to Elias, key components of the cultural template in the spread of the European "civilizing" process.

contemporary, and can refer to all sorts of facts about nations: from general ones such as lifestyles, values, customs, and religions, to personal ones such as levels of bodily hygiene, ways of preparing food, and so on. In every case, Western society stresses that "its" version is the standard against which all others should be judged.

The rise of manners

Elias studied etiquette books and found that a transformation in attitudes towards bodily behaviours was key to this sense of civilization. Westerners had gradually changed their ideas of what was acceptable in terms of facial expressions, control of bodily functions, general deportment, and so on.

Behaviours considered normal in the Middle Ages were thought "barbarous" by the 19th century.

These minor changes resulted in the formation of a courtly class, identifiable by its highly codified manners and disciplined way of living. Warrior knights became quiet courtiers, expressing restraint and maintaining strict control of impulses and emotions. "Civilized" behaviours soon became essential to everyone wishing to trade and socialize with others, from tradesmen to noblemen and women.

Elias says that the process spread ever more widely from the 1500s onwards, because "good manners" help people get along more peaceably, and growing towns and cities require such cooperation. The process, he said, at some point became a question of internalizing the social rules of one's parents, rather than one's "betters". However, the rules about what constitutes "good manners" have always been dictated by the upper classes, so "civilization" continues to work towards furthering the interests of the powerful elite.

Elias saw the transformation of manners as an important part of the centralization of power within Western nations, and a sign of the growing interdependency of people during urbanization. But it was also important in colonization during Elias's lifetime. He was writing during the 1930s, when colonial powers such as Britain and France, secure in their sense of national self-consciousness, justified the morality of colonization by claiming it brought civilization, which would be "good" for colonized peoples. ▪

Norbert Elias

Norbert Elias was born in Breslau (now the Polish city of Wrocław) in 1897, to a wealthy Jewish family. After leaving school he served in the German army during World War I. Elias studied philosophy and medicine at Breslau University, gaining a PhD in philosophy in 1924. He then studied sociology with Max Weber's younger brother, Alfred, at Heidelberg, Germany, before moving to Frankfurt University to work with Karl Mannheim.

In 1933 Elias went into exile in Paris and then London, where he finished *The Civilizing Process*. In 1939 the book was published in Switzerland, but sank into oblivion until its re-publication in West Germany in 1969. A sought-after lecturer, Elias spent his final years travelling in Europe and Africa.

Key works

1939 *The Civilizing Process* (3 volumes)
1939 *The Society of Individuals*
1970 *What is Sociology?*

MASS CULTURE
REINFORCES POLITICAL
REPRESSION

HERBERT MARCUSE (1898–1979)

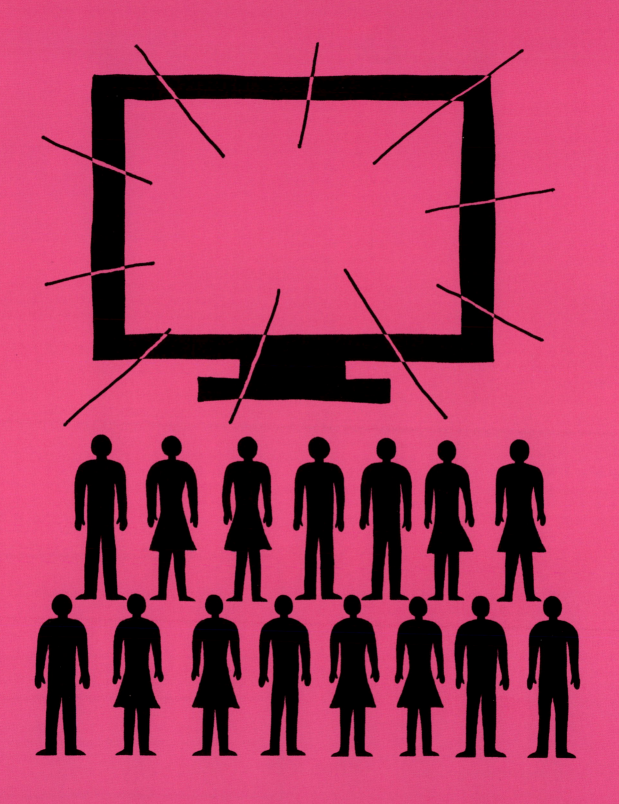

During the 20th century, it became apparent that the transformation of society theorized by Karl Marx had failed to materialize. The sociologist and philosopher Herbert Marcuse tried to determine what had happened by urging Marxists to move beyond theory and take into account the real, lived experience of individuals.

Marcuse said that capitalism had somehow integrated the working class: workers who were supposed to be the agents of change had accepted the ideas and ideals of the establishment. They had lost sight of themselves as a class or group and become "individuals" within a system that prized individuality. This seemed to be the route to success, but in abandoning their group, the workers lost all bargaining power.

Freedom to choose

How had the workers been so easily silenced? There was no obvious moment at which this had taken place, so Marcuse examined how rebellion against the status quo seemed to have been so effectively quashed during the 20th century. He started by looking much further

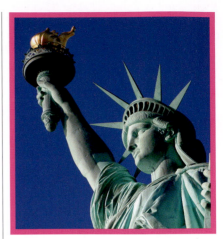

The Statue of Liberty symbolizes the American Dream of a "classless" society with equal opportunity – through hard work, anyone can improve their lives and fulfil their potential.

back, to the end of feudal society in Europe in the late Middle Ages. In this time of transition, people moved from being bound to work for a landowner to being free to find work anywhere, for their own benefit alone. But this "freedom of enterprise was, from the beginning, not altogether a blessing", says Marcuse. Although free to work wherever they wanted, the majority of people had to labour extremely

---

Culture has always played a key role in pointing to possible ways of living that are **outside the social "norm"**.

But from the 1960s, even **art forms once thought subversive** were subsumed into daily life and appropriated by the media.

By absorbing the media's messages **people accepted society's rules and values** as their own; they realized that to step beyond them would seem neurotic.

The possibility of rebellion has effectively been quashed: mass culture reinforces political repression.

See also: Karl Marx 28–31 ▪ Michel Foucault 52–55 ▪ Antonio Gramsci 178–79 ▪ Erving Goffman 190–95 ▪ Jean Baudrillard 196–99 ▪ Thorstein Veblen 214–19 ▪ Daniel Miller 246–47

hard, with no guarantee of work from day to day, and they were frightened about the future.

Centuries later, the machines of the Industrial Revolution promised to lift national economies to such an extent that it was thought a person would no longer need to worry about survival, but might "be free to exert autonomy over a life that would be his own". This was the American Dream, and the hope of most Westerners during the 20th century. If the longed-for freedom was synonymous with choice, individuals were free as never before, because choices in work, housing, food, fashion, and leisure activities continued to widen over the decades.

"False needs"

However, when Marcuse looked closer, he discovered that "a comfortable, smooth, reasonable, democratic un-freedom prevails in advanced industrial civilization" – far from being free, people were being manipulated by "totalitarian" regimes that called themselves democracies, he said. Worse still, people were unaware of the manipulation, because they had internalized the regimes' rules, values, and ideals.

Marcuse goes on to describe government as a state apparatus that imposes its economic and political requirements on its people by influencing their working and leisure time. It does so by creating in people a set of "false needs" and

Desire for "must-have" clothing, gadgets, and inessential goods stems, says Marcuse, from a false sense of "need" that is implanted in us by advertising and the media.

then manipulating people through those needs. Essentially, by convincing people that they have certain needs, and then making it look as though there is a route to satisfying these needs (even though there is not), "vested interests" effectively control the rest of the population.

False needs are not based on real ones such as the necessity for food, drink, clothes, and somewhere to live, but are instead artificially generated and impossible to satisfy in any real sense. Marcuse cites the need "to relax, to have fun… and consume in accordance with the advertisements, to love and hate what others love and hate" – the actual content of these needs (such as the latest "must-have" gadget) is proposed by external forces; it does not naturally arise in someone like the need for water does. Yet these needs feel internally driven because we are bombarded by media messages that promise happiness if you do that or go there. In this way we begin to believe that false needs are real ones.

> The cultural center is becoming a fitting part of the shopping center.
> **Herbert Marcuse**

Marcuse suggests that: "People recognize themselves in their commodities; they find their soul in their automobile, hi-fi set, split-level home, kitchen equipment."

Everything is personal; the individual is paramount, and his or her needs are what matter. This apparent empowerment of the individual is in fact its opposite, according to Marcuse. Social needs – for job security, a decent living standard, and so on – are translated into individual needs, such as your own need for a job to buy »

> "The classics have left the mausoleum and come to life again, but… they come to life as other than themselves; they are deprived of their antagonistic force.
> **Herbert Marcuse**

consumer products. If you think you are badly paid, your employer might invite you in to talk "about you". There is no longer any sense of being part of a group that is treated unfairly – all hopes of Marxist rebellion are lost.

A dimensionless world

According to Marcuse, we are caught in a bubble from which there is no escape, because it has become almost impossible to stand outside the system. There used to be "a gap" between culture and reality that pointed to other possible ways of living and being, but that gap has disappeared. Traditionally, the forms of art considered to represent "culture" – such as the opera, theatre, literature, and classical music – aimed to reflect the difficulties encountered by the transcendent human soul forced to live in social reality. It pointed to a possible world beyond gritty reality.

Tragedy, says Marcuse, used to be about defeated possibilities; about hopes unfulfilled and promises betrayed. He cites Madame Bovary, in Gustave Flaubert's novel of that name (1856), as a perfect example of a soul unable to survive in the rigid society in which she lived.

However, by the 1960s, society had become so pluralistic that it could apparently contain everyone and all their chosen lifestyles. Tragedy is no longer even possible as a cultural motif; its discontent is seen as a problem to be solved.

Art has lost its ability to inspire rebellion because it is now part of a mass media, claims Marcuse. Books and stories about individuals who will not conform are no longer

Flaubert's Madame Bovary chose to die rather than "fit in". But modern society has absorbed all forms of lifestyle; so today, Marcuse suggests, she would be offered therapy.

incendiary calls to revolution but must-read "modern classics" that someone might consume on a self-improvement programme. The "avant garde and the beatniks" now entertain without troubling people's consciences. Culture is not in a position of dangerous "other", but has been stripped of all its power. Even great works of alienation, he

Herbert Marcuse

Born in Berlin in 1898, Herbert Marcuse served with the German army in World War I before completing a PhD in literature in 1922 at the University of Freiburg. After a short spell as a bookseller in Berlin, he studied philosophy under Martin Heidegger.

In 1932 he joined the Institute for Social Research, but he never worked in Frankfurt. In 1934 he fled to the USA, where he was to remain. While he was in New York with Max Horkheimer, the latter received an offer from Columbia University to relocate the Institute there and Marcuse joined him.

In 1958 Marcuse became a professor at Brandeis University, Massachusetts, but in 1965 he was forced to resign because of his outspoken Marxist views. He moved to the University of California, and during the 1960s gained world renown as a social theorist, philosopher, and political activist. He died of a stroke, aged 81.

Key works

1941 *Reason and Revolution*
1964 *One-Dimensional Man*
1969 *An Essay on Liberation*

says, have become commercials that sell, comfort, or excite – culture has become an industry.

This flattening of the two dimensions of high culture and social reality has led to a one-dimensional culture that easily determines and controls our individual and social perspectives. There is no other world, or way to live. Marcuse claims that in saying this he is not overstating the power of the media, because the social messages we receive as adults are merely reinforcing the same ones that we have been hearing since our birth – we were conditioned as children to receive them.

The disappearance of class

The compressing of culture and reality is reflected in an apparent levelling of class structure. If all art forms and mass media are part of a homogenous whole, where nothing stands outside of societal approval, people from all social classes will inevitably start doing some of the same things. Marcuse points to the examples of a typist who is made up as attractively as her boss's daughter, or the worker and his boss enjoying the same

> Intellectual freedom would mean the restoration of individual thought now absorbed by mass communication and indoctrination.
> **Herbert Marcuse**

The power of the media

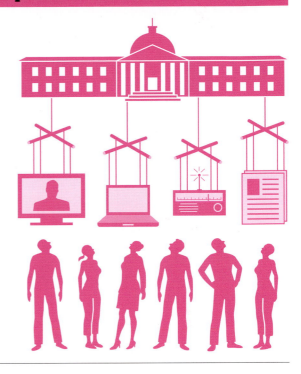

The state and its consumerist forces control the media in the modern world.

The media reflects and disseminates the state's dominant values and ideologies, and manipulates society into buying goods, services, and lifestyles.

Society and individuals are lulled into believing and conforming to the media messages.

TV programme. However, according to Marcuse, this kind of assimilation does not indicate the disappearance of classes – it actually reveals the extent to which the needs that serve the establishment have become shared by the underlying population.

The result of this is that classes are no longer in conflict. The social controls have been internalized, and Marcuse says that we are hypnotized into a state of extreme conformity where no one will rebel. There is no longer a sublimated realm of the soul or spirit of inner man, because everything has been or can be translated into operational terms, problems, and solutions. We have lost a sense of inner truth and real need, and can no longer critique society because we cannot find a way to stand outside of it without appearing to have lost our sanity.

Marcuse's ideas about a society that includes everything – in which pluralism defeats the oppositional power of any idea – is particularly relevant in a global age that is dominated by a proliferation of new media. Marcuse was always aware of the importance of scientific knowledge in shaping and organizing not just society but myriad aspects of everyday life. Crucially, and often from a radical and politicized perspective, he could see the potential for both emancipation and domination, which makes his emphasis on the cultural conversation and the role of new technologies in its service especially pertinent. Do these things really bring about social change and liberation, or are they simply tools for increasing manipulation and social oppression by a powerful ruling class? ■

THE DANGER OF THE FUTURE IS THAT MEN MAY BECOME ROBOTS
ERICH FROMM (1900–1980)

IN CONTEXT

FOCUS
Alienation of self

KEY DATES
1844 Karl Marx says humans become alienated from their own essence as a systemic result of capitalism.

1903 In *The Metropolis and Mental Life*, Georg Simmel suggests urban life breeds alienation and indifference.

1955 Erich Fromm publishes *The Sane Society*.

1956 US sociologist Leo Srole develops an alienation scale.

1959 US sociologist Melvin Seeman says alienation results from powerlessness, normlessness, social isolation, cultural estrangement, and self-estrangement.

1968 Israeli-American sociologist Amitai Etzioni says alienation results from social systems that do not cater to basic human needs.

The German sociologist and psychoanalyst Erich Fromm claimed that during industrialization in the 19th century, God was declared dead, "inhumanity" meant cruelty, and the inherent danger was that people would become slaves.

However, in the 20th century, the problem changed: alienated from a sense of self, people had lost the ability to love and reason for themselves. "Man" effectively died. "Inhumanity" came to mean lacking humanity. People, Fromm advised, were in danger of becoming like robots.

He attributed this sense of alienation to the emergence of Western capitalist societies and believed that a state's social, economic, and political factors intersect to produce a "social character" common to all its citizens. In the industrial age, as capitalism increased its global dominance, states encouraged people to become competitive, exploitative, authoritarian, aggressive, and individualist.

In the 20th century, by contrast, individuals were repositioned by capitalist states to become cooperative consumers, with standardized tastes, who could be manipulated by the anonymous authority of public opinion and the market. Technology ensured that work became more routine and boring. Fromm advised that unless people "get out of the rut" they are in and reclaim their humanity, they will go mad trying to live a meaningless, robotic life. ∎

> Synthetic smiles have replaced genuine laughter... dull despair has taken the place of genuine pain.
> **Erich Fromm**

See also: G H Mead 176–77 ▪ Robert Blauner 232–33 ▪ Arlie Hochschild 236–43 ▪ Robert K Merton 262–63 ▪ Erving Goffman 264–69 ▪ Ann Oakley 318–19

CULTURE IS ORDINARY

RAYMOND WILLIAMS (1921–1988)

While Karl Marx had a keen interest in culture, especially in literature, he regarded the economy as the driver of history: culture and ideas were secondary. Later Marxist thinkers such as Antonio Gramsci and Hungarian theorist Georg Lukács paid more attention to cultural matters; but culture only came to the centre of radical theory in the mid-20th century with Raymond Williams' extensive body of work, which included his hugely influential text *Culture and Society*.

Williams detaches the idea of culture from a politically conservative understanding of "tradition", enabling an analysis of what he calls "the long revolution": that difficult but persistent effort to democratize our whole way of life.

The shape of culture

In his essay "Culture is Ordinary" (1958), Williams offers a personal reflection of a journey from the farming valleys of South Wales to the colleges of Cambridge, England. For Williams, the shape of his culture includes mountains, farms, cathedrals, and furnaces; family relationships, political debates, trade skills, languages, and ideas; as well as literature, art, and music, both popular and serious. He describes the shape as a characteristic "structure of feeling", which might be defined as the lived experience (ordinary life) of a community beyond society's institutions and formal ideologies.

Structure of feeling operates, Williams explains, "in the most delicate and least tangible part of our activities". The concept suggests a combination of something that is visible and organized enough to be the subject of study (structure), yet elusive enough to convey the complexities of lived experience (feeling). Williams' emphasis on lived experience served to open up to sociological study whole swathes of popular culture such as television, film, and advertising, which had earlier been seen as culturally insignificant. ∎

See also: Karl Marx 28–31 ▪ Antonio Gramsci 178–79 ▪ Herbert Marcuse 182–87 ▪ Jean Baudrillard 196–99 ▪ Stuart Hall 200–01

STIGMA

REFERS TO AN ATTRIBUTE THAT IS DEEPLY DISCREDITING

ERVING GOFFMAN (1922–1982)

IN CONTEXT

FOCUS
Stigma

KEY DATES
1895 Émile Durkheim explores
the concept of stigma and its
relation to social order.

1920s The concept of
symbolic interactionism
emerges at the University
of Chicago as the leading
US social theoretical model.

1934 *Mind, Self, and Society*
by US social psychologist
G H Mead is published and
later influences Goffman's
ideas about identity.

2006 In *Body/Embodiment*,
Dennis Waskul and Phillip
Vannini (eds) see Goffman's
work as a "sophisticated
framework" for understanding
the sociology of the body.

2014 US sociologist Mary Jo
Deegan applies Goffman's
theories to the analysis of sex,
gender issues, and feminism.

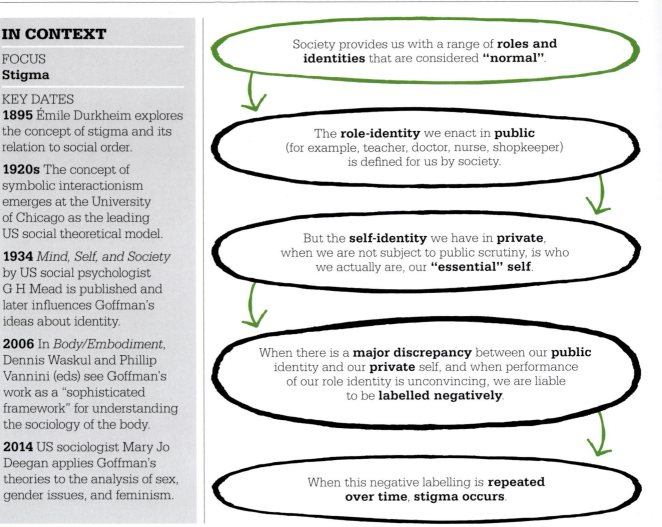

Society provides us with a range of **roles and identities** that are considered **"normal"**.

The **role-identity** we enact in **public** (for example, teacher, doctor, nurse, shopkeeper) is defined for us by society.

But the **self-identity** we have in **private**, when we are not subject to public scrutiny, is who we actually are, our **"essential" self**.

When there is a **major discrepancy** between our **public** identity and our **private** self, and when performance of our role identity is unconvincing, we are liable to be **labelled negatively**.

When this negative labelling is **repeated over time**, **stigma occurs**.

Erving Goffman was a
Canadian sociologist whose
work draws heavily on
the US social theoretical tradition
known as symbolic interactionism.
This tradition focuses on micro-
level interactions and exchanges
between individuals and small
groups of people, rather than on
the far more impersonal, macro-
level relationships between social
structures or institutions and
individuals. Interactionist thinkers
examine issues such as personal
identity, selfhood, group dynamics,
and social interaction.

The basic idea underpinning
symbolic-interactionist thought is
that the individual self is first and
foremost a social entity: even the
most seemingly idiosyncratic
aspects of our individual
selves, according to symbolic
interactionists, are not so much
the product of our own unique
psychology, but are socially
determined and culturally and
historically contingent. Who we
think we are, who we imagine
ourselves to be, and perhaps most
importantly, who it is we are able
to be, is inextricably bound up

with and mediated by the types
of people we interact with and the
institutional contexts we inhabit.

Of specific interest to Goffman
was the subject of deviance and
the socially enacted processes
whereby individuals and groups
come to be stigmatized (from
the Greek word *stigma*, meaning
"mark", "brand", or "puncture"), or
marked with disgrace. Deviance
is implicit in the notion of stigma
because, as Goffman points out,
stigma occurs whenever an
individual or group is perceived
to have deviated from the socially

See also: Pierre Bourdieu 76–79 ▪ Georg Simmel 104–05 ▪ G H Mead 176–77 ▪ Howard S Becker 280–85 ▪ Alfred Schütz 335

School teachers perform one of the most "legitimate", highly respected roles in society – Goffman refers to the public roles people enact as their "virtual social identity".

prescribed norms that govern interpersonal conduct. When an individual deviates from these social norms they are stigmatized and marginalized from the wider group or social community to which they belong.

Virtual and actual identity

In his landmark study *Stigma*, Goffman analyses the behaviour of individuals whose identity is believed to be "soiled" or "defective" in some way. He distinguishes between what he refers to as "virtual" and "actual" social identity.

Virtual social identity is the socially legitimate version of selfhood that individuals are expected to present in public – for example, the socially defined traits and behaviours associated with being a medical doctor. Actual social identity is the self-identity

individuals imagine themselves to possess in private – the traits and behaviours the doctor enacts in his or her private life, for example. For Goffman, stigma arises whenever the disparity between virtual and actual social identity becomes untenable – when, for instance, the respected medic is known to drink and smoke excessively outside of work; feelings of embarrassment or shame then ensue, and social interaction breaks down. Stigma results from the fact that members of society share common expectations and attitudes about what to expect from people in certain social situations, and how those people should behave or look.

The concept of stigma

Goffman identifies three important features of the concept of stigma. First, stigma is not inherent to a given individual, attribute, or way of behaving, although some behaviours, such as paedophilia, are universally condemned. The context in which an attribute or behaviour is displayed strongly determines how others respond. »

Erving Goffman

Erving Goffman was born in Canada in 1922 to a family of immigrant Ukrainian Jews. After graduating from the University of Toronto in 1945 with a BA in anthropology and sociology, he moved to the University of Chicago, USA, where he attained his MA and PhD. For his doctoral dissertation, he undertook fieldwork on a remote island in Scotland. The data he collected there formed the basis for his most celebrated work, *The Presentation of Self in Everyday Life*. He was appointed to the University of Pennsylvania in 1968 and in 1981 was the 73rd President of the American Sociological Association. Goffman died in 1982 of stomach cancer.

Key works

1959 *The Presentation of Self in Everyday Life*
1961 *Asylums: Essays on the Social Situation of Mental Patients and Other Inmates*
1963 *Stigma: Notes on the Management of Spoiled Identity*

Stigma constitutes a special discrepancy between virtual and actual social identity.
Erving Goffman

Second, stigma is a negative classification that emerges out of the interactions and exchanges between individuals or groups, whereby one has the power to classify the other as the possessor of what are considered to be socially undesirable attributes or behaviours. (Goffman refers to non-stigmatized people as "normals".) To this extent, it is a relational concept, because things classified as stigmatized are liable to change, depending on the individuals or groups interacting. Goffman suggests that potentially any attribute or act is stigmatizing, and for this reason some degree of stigmatization is present in virtually all social relationships: we are all capable of being stigmatized at certain times.

The third characteristic of stigma, says Goffman, is that it is "processual": this means that being stigmatized or, more precisely, coming to assume a stigmatized identity, is a socially mediated process that takes place over time. For example, if an individual is made to feel uncomfortable by others because they become excessively inebriated at an office party, then the feelings of embarrassment and shame, while not particularly pleasant and comfortable, are not likely to have any long-term effect on the person's

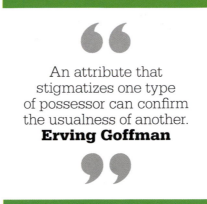

> An attribute that stigmatizes one type of possessor can confirm the usualness of another.
> **Erving Goffman**

actual social identity. However, if the excessive behaviour continues over a period of time, and through interaction with group members the individual is allocated a deviant status, then their self-conception will be altered as they assume a stigmatized identity.

Types of stigma

In addition to explaining the concept of stigma, Goffman identified three types of stigma. The first type of stigma relates to what he refers to as "deformities" of the body, such as physical disability, obesity, uneven skin tone, baldness, and scarring. The second type of stigma refers to blemishes of character, including, says Goffman, "mental disorder, imprisonment, addiction,

alcoholism, homosexuality, unemployment, suicide attempts, and radical political behavior". He identifies the third type of stigma as tribal stigma, which includes social marginalization on the grounds of ethnicity, nationality, religion, and ideological beliefs. The attributes identified in these three categories of stigma are liable, Goffman claims, to impinge negatively on the ordinary and predicted patterning of social interactions involving the possessor of the attribute, and in turn result in exclusion or marginalization.

Impression management

Goffman also focuses on how individuals try to respond to and cope with negative classification. He suggests that people who are stigmatized actively seek to manage or, where possible, resist the negative social identities attributed to them.

His concept of "impression management" is important in this context because it highlights the various ways people try to present a version of selfhood to others that is as favourable as possible: they adopt different strategies to avoid being stigmatized. These include "concealment" through use of "covers", such as prosthetic limbs in the case of people who feel ashamed of having lost a limb. This is in direct contrast to "disclosure", which involves a person openly acknowledging the discrediting feature(s) of their identity. Where these strategies fail or are simply not feasible, the possessor of a stigma is liable to

Wigs are among the "props" or "covers" that are used by some bald people to attempt to "conceal" their baldness and thereby deflect potential sources of stigma.

seek out social types who they believe will act sympathetically towards them.

Goffman identifies three categories of people in particular who are liable to fulfill this role. The first are "the own": people who have a similarly stigmatized attribute – for example, members of a drug-addiction recovery group. The second category is "the wise": people who work in an institution or agency that supports individuals who possess a stigmatizing trait (care workers, disability officers, nurses, mental health therapists, and social workers, for example). The third category identified by Goffman includes individuals that the stigmatized person knows very well and who are likely to be empathetic towards them, such as the partner of someone with a disability or an addiction.

Crossing boundaries

It is generally accepted within sociology that Goffman's detailed observations of human interactions and of the interpersonal dynamics of small-scale groups remain unparalleled. Anthony Giddens, for example, draws heavily on Goffman's ideas about human behaviour and identity formation in his much acclaimed "structuration" theory, which discusses the link between structures and human interaction. Pierre Bourdieu also refers to Goffman's work in his exploration of the extent to which people are able to change who they are and how they feel within certain contexts.

British social thinker Anthony Wootton has argued, however, that Goffman's work universalizes and identifies certain attributes as once and for all liable to be the cause of stigmatizing behaviour. But normative expectations and moral

The causes of stigmatization are numerous, but can include idle gossip and negative attitudes that arise from ignorance and/or class- or race-based tensions. This then leads to negative stereotyping of an individual by the wider group. Over time, the individual internalizes these labels to the extent that they inform the person's self-evaluation and identity. By this point, the individual has acquired a stigmatized identity.

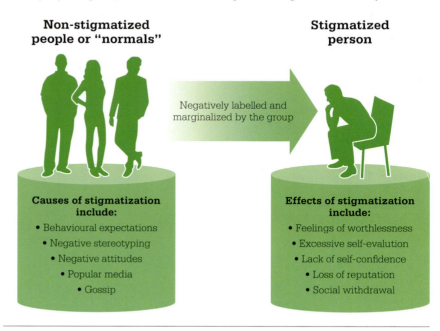

Non-stigmatized people or "normals"

Stigmatized person

Negatively labelled and marginalized by the group

Causes of stigmatization include:
- Behavioural expectations
- Negative stereotyping
- Negative attitudes
- Popular media
- Gossip

Effects of stigmatization include:
- Feelings of worthlessness
- Excessive self-evaluation
- Lack of self-confidence
- Loss of reputation
- Social withdrawal

evaluations of certain attributes and behaviours change as society progresses. So, he says, whether or not mental illness and physical disability could still be said to be the cause of stigma is highly questionable in certain social and national contexts.

Goffman's work straddles the disciplinary boundaries between sociology and social psychology – his theories have therefore been taken up by thinkers from a wide range of academic backgrounds. Within sociology, his ideas about stigma have been applied very effectively by British social thinker Gill Green to consider the experiences of people with long-term illness, including those who have contracted the HIV virus. And social worker John Offer has used Goffman's concepts to consider the reintegration of

stigmatized individuals back into the community. Goffman's work also remains relevant politically – in particular, by offering a means of understanding how to address the problem of the stigmatization of minority groups in modern multicultural societies. ∎

❝

The stigmatized individual may find that he feels unsure how normals will identify and receive him.
Erving Goffman

❞

WE LIVE IN A WORLD WHERE THERE IS MORE AND MORE INFORMATION, AND LESS AND LESS MEANING

JEAN BAUDRILLARD (1929–2007)

IN CONTEXT

FOCUS
Simulacra

KEY DATES

c.360 BCE Greek philosopher Plato says he would banish "the imitator" from his perfect republic.

Early 1800s The Industrial Revolution begins in Europe.

1884 Friedrich Nietzsche says that we can no longer look to God to find meaning in our life, because "God is dead".

1970s Roland Barthes says signs and symbols have ideological functions that they impart to the reader with a "natural" simplicity.

1989 British computer scientist Tim Berners-Lee invents the World Wide Web (www.), an Internet-based hypermedia initiative for global information sharing.

A t the end of the 20th century, the French sociologist Jean Baudrillard announced that "the year 2000, in a certain way, will not take place". He claimed that the apocalypse – the end of the world as we know it – had already occurred, and in the 21st century, we "have already passed beyond the end". He believed this because, he said, there had been a perfect crime – "the murder of the real".

The only way in which we would "know" the year 2000, Baudrillard said, would be the way we now know everything: via the stream of images that are reproduced endlessly for our

See also: Henri Lefebvre 106–07 ▪ Alan Bryman 126–27 ▪ David Held 170–71 ▪ Antonio Gramsci 178–79 ▪ Herbert Marcuse 182–87

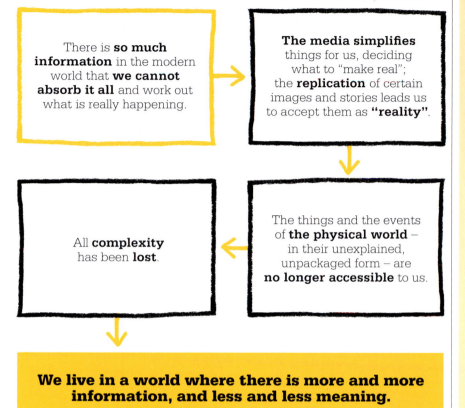

There is **so much information** in the modern world that **we cannot absorb it all** and work out what is really happening.

The media simplifies things for us, deciding what to "make real"; the **replication** of certain images and stories leads us to accept them as **"reality"**.

The things and the events of **the physical world** – in their unexplained, unpackaged form – are **no longer accessible** to us.

All **complexity** has been **lost**.

We live in a world where there is more and more information, and less and less meaning.

Jean Baudrillard

Born in Reims, France, in 1929, Jean Baudrillard was the first member of his family to attend university. His parents were civil servants, but his grandparents were peasant farmers, and he claimed to have upset the status quo when he went to Paris to study, beyond school level, at the Sorbonne.

During the 1950s Baudrillard taught German in secondary schools while writing a PhD thesis under the tuition of the Marxist philosopher Henri Lefebvre. In 1966 Baudrillard took up a post at the University of Paris IX teaching sociology, and later became a professor in the subject. His left-wing, radical attitude made him famous (and controversial) worldwide. He broke with Marxism in the 1970s, but remained politically active all his life. When asked "Who are you?", he replied, "What I am, I don't know. I am the simulacrum of myself."

Key works

1981 *Simulacra and Simulation*
1983 *Fatal Strategies*
1986 *America*
1987 *The Ecstasy of Communication*

consumption by magazines, TV, newspapers, film, advertising, and websites. Reality, according to Baudrillard, is not whatever happens in the physical world (that "reality" is dead), but that which is capable of being simulated, or reproduced. In fact, he says, the real is that "which is already reproduced". During the 20th century, representation started to precede reality, rather than the other way around.

The map comes first
Baudrillard explains his position with reference to a short story by the Argentinian writer and poet Jorge Luis Borges, in which

cartographers draw up a huge map of an empire. The map's scale is 1:1, and so the map is as large as the ground it represents, and covers the physical landscape of empire completely. As the empire declines, the map gradually becomes frayed and finally ruined, leaving only a few shreds remaining.

In this allegory, the real and its copy can be easily identified; the difference between them is clear. Baudrillard maintains that this is how it used to be in the Renaissance world, when the link between a thing and its image was obvious. The image was a reflection of a profound reality, and we recognized both its **»**

similarity to that reality and its difference. With the start of the industrial age, however, the link between the object and its representation became far less clear, as the original object, or a model of one, could be reproduced hundreds or thousands of times.

Remaking reality

Baudrillard was aware of other Marxist thinkers of the 1960s, such as French theorist Guy Debord, who had drawn attention to the shift in cultural thinking that occurred with the onset of mass production. Debord notes that at this point in history, "the whole life of those societies... presents itself as an... accumulation of spectacles". Thus life becomes condensed into a set of recorded pictures: a family wedding, a holiday in France, and so on. People are more interested in capturing the image – becoming spectators – than in *doing* things: the image, not the event, is central (the modern obsession with taking "selfies" emphasizes how pervasive this has become).

Baudrillard points out that through capitalism, commodities also became detached from themselves. Wheat was no longer simply wheat, for instance, but a

good investment, or a breakfast cereal. Presentation, not substance, dictated value. This was the start of the age of advertising, where the message of the brand overtook the reality of the substance in question. Image became everything.

Simplifying the world

Baudrillard followed the trajectory of this bizarre world of images and spectacles still further. As technology progressed, he says, it became obvious that there was no need to refer to a real object or model at all. The image – which was originally abstracted from something real – could now be created from nothing. It did not need to connect to or reflect anything in the physical world at all. This kind of image he calls a "simulacrum".

As long as an image or set of images is reproducible, Baudrillard maintains, it can create reality. The real is "that which can be reproduced". Once images are replicated and widely disseminated (in magazines or websites, for example), they create a shared reality that people can discuss, in a way that they cannot do with the messy, unstructured physical reality that we used to try to

engage with. They simplify the world and make it manageable. In addition, the reality they create is more exciting and perfect in every way than the one around us.

Dangerous utopias

"Simulacra" – images that have no original in reality – can be produced to create a much more satisfying effect than images that reflect reality. An actress can be "digitally enhanced" to look closer to a culture's ideal image of womanhood, but even this refers back to some kind of reality. For this reason, Baudrillard says that "the territory" of the real has not yet disappeared entirely – fragments remain. But people who find pleasure in looking at these enhanced images may find even more pleasure in images that are completely digitally created – that do not refer back to a "real person" at all. For example, we can look at "perfect" digitally created people

> The real is produced from miniaturized units, from matrices, memory banks and command models – and with these it can be reproduced an indefinite number of times.
> **Jean Baudrillard**

and worlds, and even re-create ourselves in any shape or form online, in virtual worlds where we are invited to interact with other real/virtual people.

And herein lies the danger, says Baudrillard. Constructed realities can be built to maximize pleasure, so they are far more appealing than reality. We are constructing utopias, because if you have the freedom to construct a world, why not aim at a utopia? But the utopia we are creating in our virtual worlds is tantamount to death: we no longer want the real experience of something, but the experience of being told about the experience of something – in such a way that it is hyperreal, or more real than real. For instance, we prefer to sit in a cinema and enjoy the hyperreal experience of a family reunion than go to one of our own. On screen it is more colourful, noisy, and complete – it seems "so true". Our own lives pale by comparison, except perhaps our virtual lives, on Facebook or elsewhere. Meanwhile, we sit, not moving, looking at a screen.

Too much information

According to Baudrillard, our reality is now dictated by the incredible amount of information that streams into our lives from so many forms of media. He says that, strangely, although the real is disappearing, "it is not because of a lack of it, but an excess of it". An excess of information pouring into our awareness puts an end to information, he says, because we drown in complexity, and reach for the simple solution that is handed

In Disney World, USA, countries such as "China" are re-created. These virtual models, says Baudrillard, are far more appealing to Disney's customers than the world "outside".

> The age of simulation thus begins with a liquidation of all referentials – worse: by their artificial resurrection in systems of signs.
> **Jean Baudrillard**

to us. Simulacra make sense of the world, even if this is at the cost of complex meaning. The world is becoming ever more superficial.

The simulacra that make up our reality today have been constructed to immediately gratify our desires. Baudrillard says that as virtual reality increases, our ideals and imaginations will recede. We accept what is given, just as we find it far easier to travel from "Germany" to "France" in Disney World than in Europe. There is no longer a requirement for systems or things to be rational, just to work well, or be "operational". We have created a hyperreality that is, he says, "the product of an irradiating synthesis of combinatory models in a hyperspace without atmosphere". We seem not to have noticed the fact that only robots can "live" without an atmosphere.

Some critical theorists, such as US philosopher Douglass Kellner, have criticized Baudrillard for moving away from a Marxist interpretation of culture. Marxist geographer David Harvey takes a similar stance, saying that Baudrillard is wrong to insist that there is no reality behind the image. Many theorists, however, including Canadians Arthur and Marilouise Kroker, praise his celebration of postmodern culture and see his work as a vital guide to the cultural dangers of the 21st century. As media ecologist Kenneth Rufo notes, Baudrillard is "full of interesting things, and even his misses... still pack a wallop." ■

MODERN IDENTITIES ARE BEING DECENTRED
STUART HALL (1932–2014)

IN CONTEXT

FOCUS
Cultural identity

KEY DATES
17th century "The self" becomes a noun for the first time, gaining currency as an idea worthy of investigation.

1900s Max Weber says that individuals act according to their subjective interpretations of the world.

1920s G H Mead's idea of symbolic interactionism examines the symbols that allow people to communicate to each other despite their subjective interpretations.

1983 Anglo-American professor Benedict Anderson says that national identity is an "imagined community".

2010 British sociologist Mike Featherstone examines self-driven identity change through bodily transformations such as cosmetic surgery.

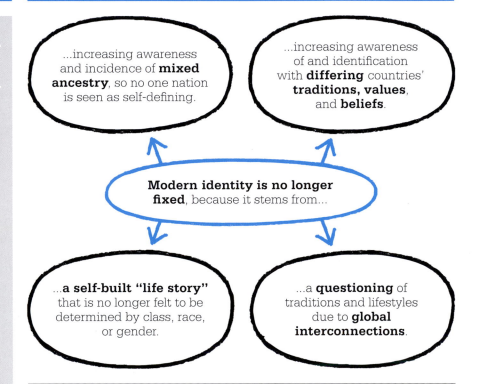

...increasing awareness and incidence of **mixed ancestry**, so no one nation is seen as self-defining.

...increasing awareness of and identification with **differing** countries' **traditions, values**, and **beliefs**.

Modern identity is no longer fixed, because it stems from...

...**a self-built "life story"** that is no longer felt to be determined by class, race, or gender.

...a **questioning** of traditions and lifestyles due to **global interconnections**.

In the late 20th century, sociologists began to speak about a new "crisis of identity", because identity – once seen as a simple idea – was becoming increasingly hard to pin down. Professor Stuart Hall claims that this is due to the way in which structural change has been transforming modern societies, fragmenting the cultural landscapes of class, gender, sexuality, ethnicity, race, and nationality. These are the frameworks that we have traditionally relied upon to tell us who we are, both within society and as individuals.

See also: W E B Du Bois 68–73 ▪ Roland Robertson 146–47 ▪ David Held 170–71 ▪ G H Mead 176–77 ▪
Norbert Elias 180–81 ▪ Erving Goffman 190–95 ▪ Benedict Anderson 202–03 ▪ Howard S Becker 280–85

In modern cities different cultures are thrown together. The more our lives are influenced by these diverse cultural traditions, the less sense we have of a fixed national identity.

Hall names three modern ideas of identity: the Enlightenment "self", the sociological "self", and the postmodern "self". The Enlightenment sense of self prevailed from the 17th to the early 20th centuries, and was held to be a complete, autonomous being: a person was born with a firm inner "core" that unfolded with age, but remained unchanged.

In the 1920s, sociologists such as G H Mead suggested that identity is formed in relationship with the environment and "significant others", who explain and transmit the values, meanings, and symbols of the child's world. The self in this definition was still seen as an inner core, but it could be modified by society, through internalizing cultural values and meanings. This "interactionist" view of the self, which bridges the gap between the personal and public worlds, became the classic sociological view of the self.

The postmodern self, on the other hand, says Hall, has no stable inner core. It is not fixed in any way, but instead is formed and transformed continuously according to the ways that it is addressed or represented in society. This is a self in process, defined historically rather than biologically. It contains contradictory identities that pull in different directions, and only seems continuous or stable because of the narrative that each of us constructs about ourselves (our "life story").

Detached identities

Hall says that the rapid, continuous, and extensive change that began to take place at the end of the 20th century has added to a sense of instability. Traditions and social practices are constantly examined, challenged, and often transformed by new information stemming from increased global interconnection. The global marketing of styles, places, and images means they pop up in every country, disrupting a traditional sense of fixed nationality and cultural identity.

This "mash up" of global culture means that identities have become detached from specific times, places, histories, and traditions, and we are now faced with a range of identities from which we can choose, when they appeal to us. Within the "discourse" (meanings system) of global consumerism, the differences and cultural distinctions that are used to define identity have become a kind of global currency. For example, jeans and trainers – once associated with "being American" – are now just as much a part of being a young person in India or Kenya.

Where to the Afro-French philosopher Franz Fanon, black people were always defined as "other" to whites, Hall says that in the global arena, cultures are thrown together "with each 'Other'", where that other is "no longer simply 'out there' but also within". People increasingly come from a mixture of living spaces, ancestry, and birthplaces, and are aware of internally holding a range of identities that may come to the fore at different times. This inner and outer diversity, Hall says, is the force that is shaping our times. ▪

Stuart Hall

Known as the "godfather of multiculturalism", Stuart Hall was born into a Jamaican family that he says played out the conflict between the local and imperial (colonizing) context. His parents were from different social classes and from mixed ancestry; Hall rebelled against their suggestions to play only with "higher colour" friends.

In 1952, Hall went to Oxford University, England, and became a key figure in the emerging New Left political movement. He was a co-founder of the *Left Review* in 1957, director of the Centre for Contemporary Cultural Studies, Birmingham, UK, and in 1979, a professor of sociology with the Open University. He also worked with film-makers and artists on black subjectivity.

Key works

1979 *The Great Moving Right Show*
1980 *Encoding/Decoding*
1992 "The Question of Cultural Identity"

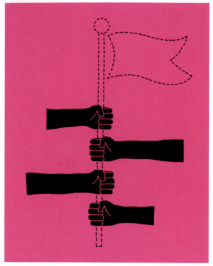

ALL COMMUNITIES ARE IMAGINED
BENEDICT ANDERSON (1936–)

IN CONTEXT

FOCUS
Nationalism

KEY DATES
1800 German philosopher Johann Fichte argues for a centralized state that could isolate itself from the world to develop a *volksgeist* – a nation's distinct sense of self.

1861 Soon after Italian unification, politician Massimo d'Azeglio announces: "We have made Italy. Now we have to make Italians."

1965 British-Czech anthropologist Ernest Gellner suggests that "nationalism is not the awakening of nations to self-consciousness: it invents nations where they do not exist".

1991 French philosopher Étienne Balibar says that "every 'people'… is the project of a national process of ethnicization".

Before the 16th century, the idea of nationalism did not exist. It is a modern concept that we have imagined into being and then convinced ourselves that it has an immemorial past. These are the views of social and political theorist Benedict Anderson, who says that we take the idea of nationalism as a given: if you are born in a certain place, you have a certain nationality, just as you are born a particular gender.

Anderson's book *Imagined Communities* (1983) questions the entire basis of nationalism. He defines "the nation" as "an imagined political community

With the **development of printing**, publishers appealed to the masses with books written in **the most widespread vernacular** languages as well as in Latin.

↓

This gave the **languages more stability**, and helped to **define groups of people** according to the language they spoke.

↓

This **unification via a common language** allowed the growth of shared ideas and values, and the idea of **belonging to a nation** grew.

↓

In a time when belief in **religious rule was in decline**, the concept of **"nationhood"** gave the populace **something to believe in**, and a **cause to die for**.

See also: Paul Gilroy 75 ▪ Edward Said 80–81 ▪ Elijah Anderson 82–83 ▪ Saskia Sassen 164–65 ▪ David Held 170–71 ▪ Stuart Hall 200–01

that is imagined as both limited and sovereign". He explains that it is "imagined" because members of even the smallest nation in the world will never know or even meet most of their fellow-members, but "in the minds of each lives the image of their communion".

National consciousness

The idea of the nation is "limited", Anderson argues, because even the largest of nations has finite boundaries, although these are "elastic" (due, for example, to movement from immigration, emigration, and contested territories). No nation has ever entertained the possibility of making everyone in the world part of "their nation", he says, in the way that a religion, such as Christianity, would like to see everyone joined in one, unified belief system.

Anderson claims that one of the ways in which nationalities revealed their "elastic borders" was via the printing industry. In the 16th century, booksellers catered to the educated, Latin-speaking minorities, but realized they needed to reach larger markets for bigger profits. Unable to cater for

Nationality, or… nation-ness, as well as nationalism, are cultural artefacts.
Benedict Anderson

the many regional dialects, they chose the larger ones, and as these dialects gained stability in print, so they created unified fields of communication and helped define what the nation should "look like".

Giving life purpose

Sovereignty is also part of this idea of the nation, Anderson says, because the concept arose during the Enlightenment and an era of revolution. Religions lost their unquestioned grip on people's minds, and it was no longer accepted that monarchs had been divinely chosen by God to rule. The sovereign state allowed the structure of a nation to exist without calling on its people to believe in religious dogma. But with the death of religious rule, questions about the meaning of life went unanswered, according to Anderson. The rationality of the Enlightenment did not suggest any reason for living, or dying – but with the idea of the nation, a new purpose arose. Here was something worth dying for, and it also provided a sense of continuity of purpose that people had previously gained from an idea of the afterlife (such as heaven).

Some have questioned Anderson's theory, in particular with respect to the Arabic world, which continues to use a classical form of language and is still defined by religious belief. However, at a time in which political unrest is rife within "sub-nations" (such as Scotland or Catalonia) around the world, Anderson's idea of imagined nationhood has proved both controversial and hugely influential. *Imagined Communities* has been published in 29 languages. ▪

Benedict Anderson

Benedict Richard Anderson is professor emeritus of international studies, government, and Asian studies at Cornell University, USA. Born in Kunming, China, in 1936, he was the son of an Irish father and English mother who had been active in Irish nationalist movements. The family emigrated to California in 1941, and thereafter to Ireland. Anderson was educated at Eton College in Berkshire, England. He took a degree in classics at the University of Cambridge in 1957.

A fascination with Asian politics led Anderson to undertake a PhD at Cornell University, USA, which included a period of research in Jakarta, Indonesia. His public response to the 1965 communist coup there resulted in him being deported from the country, after which he travelled in Thailand for several years before returning to Cornell to teach.

Key works

1983 *Imagined Communities*
1998 *The Spectre of Comparisons*
2007 *Under Three Flags*

THROUGHOUT THE WORLD
CULTURE
HAS BEEN DOGGEDLY
PUSHING ITSELF
CENTRE STAGE
JEFFREY ALEXANDER (1947–)

IN CONTEXT

FOCUS
Cultural sociology

KEY DATES
1912 In *The Elementary Forms of the Religious Life*, Émile Durkheim discusses how culture and meaning are interrelated.

1937 US sociologist Talcott Parsons emphasizes the autonomy of culture in *The Structure of Social Action*.

1973 US anthropologist Clifford Geertz stresses the importance of meaning for human social life in *The Interpretation of Cultures*.

1995 In *Fin de Siècle Social Theory*, Alexander criticizes Pierre Bourdieu, the world's leading sociologist of culture.

2014 British sociologist Christopher Thorpe applies Alexander's ideas in his examination of how the British experience Italy.

Sociologists have tended to regard culture as of **secondary importance**.

Material factors – **such as economic wealth and social class** – have been seen as **more influential**.

Alexander **emphasizes the role of culture** for determining social life.

Without culture, **no communication, event, or human interaction** is intelligible.

Within sociology, culture has been doggedly pushing itself centre stage.

M any of us live our lives without examining why we habitually do what we do and think what we think. Why do we spend so much of each day working? Why do we save up our money? Why are we interested in gossip about people we don't know? If pressed to answer such questions, we may respond by saying "because that's what people like us do". But there is nothing natural, necessary, or inevitable about any of these things; instead, we behave like this because the culture we belong to compels us to.

The culture that we inhabit shapes how we think, feel, and act in the most existentially pervasive ways. It is not in spite of our culture that we are who we are, but precisely because of it.

US sociologist Jeffrey Alexander argues that culture – the collectively produced ideas, beliefs, and values of a group – is integral to an understanding of human life. Only through culture can humans prise themselves apart from a primordial state to reflect upon, and intervene in, the world around them. In spite of its central role, Alexander

maintains that sociologists have historically seen culture as being of secondary importance. As one of the most influential social theorists in the world, Alexander has sought to ensure that the subject of culture takes centre stage in the analysis of late-modern society.

Sociology and culture
While early sociological theorists recognized the central importance of culture, they failed – according to Alexander – to take seriously the idea that culture is essential to understanding why people think

See also: Karl Marx 28–31 ▪ Émile Durkheim 34–37 ▪ Max Weber 38–45 ▪
Erving Goffman 190–95 ▪ Talcott Parsons 300–01 ▪ Herbert Blumer 335

> We are not anywhere
> as reasonable or rational
> or sensible as we would
> like to think.
> **Jeffrey Alexander**

and act in the ways they do. Karl Marx, for example, saw mainstream culture as a function of the ideas and values of the ruling class; accordingly, culture served as little more than a veil to blind the majority of people to the profoundly unjust society in which they lived. Max Weber took a different view and argued that Western culture was rational and involved viewing the natural and social worlds in a dispassionate and scientific way; it was devoid of any wider meaning or worth.

For Alexander, both of these views are lacking: Marx's account is overly reductive because it holds that culture is determined by the way society is organized; Weber's account is overly rational because it fails to acknowledge the highly irrational aspects of Western culture – in particular the role of emotions and values in directing the responses of individuals, and even entire nations, to the events taking place around them.

Alexander's theoretical approach was very different, and built upon ideas about religion proposed by French sociologist Émile Durkheim. For Durkheim, religion involved the separation of the sacred – meaning the ideas, icons, and representations of the divine – from the profane, or the functions of everyday life. Alexander saw culture as akin to the sacred – autonomous from, rather than dependent upon, society; enabling rather than solely constraining; and containing both irrational and rational elements. His cultural sociology focuses on understanding how individuals and groups are involved in the creation of meaning by drawing upon collectively produced values, symbols, and discourses – ways of talking about things – and how this in turn shapes their actions.

Three aspects of culture

Alexander defines cultural sociology in terms of three main points, relating to origination, interpretation, and structure. First, culture can be completely autonomous from the material dimensions of social life. Marx's theories about culture became the orthodox way of conceptualizing the relationship between the "social" and the "cultural". In Marx's view, the material base of society (the economy, technologies, and the division of labour) determined the ideal superstructure (the norms, values, and beliefs of culture).

In contrast, Alexander believes that culture cannot be understood as a mere by-product of the "harder", more "real" material dimensions of social life. The notion that material factors determine ideal ones – that economy determines culture – is fundamentally misguided. »

Jeffrey Alexander

Jeffrey Alexander, born in 1947, is the Lillian Chavenson Saden Professor of Sociology at Yale University, USA, and Co-Director for the Center for Cultural Sociology. As part of this role, Alexander established *Cultural Sociology* as a new academic journal to promote cultural sociological ideas and methods.

In the USA, and arguably on the world scene generally, notably through his work on *Remembering the Holocaust: A Debate* (2009), he is one of the most distinguished social thinkers of his time. Originally taught by the influential US sociologists Talcott Parsons and Robert Bellah, Alexander carried forward structural-functionalism to its logical conclusion before abandoning it and founding his cultural sociological paradigm.

Key works

2003 *The Meanings of Social Life: A Cultural Sociology*
2012 *Trauma: A Social Theory*
2013 *The Dark Side of Modernity*

> …the heart of current
> debates lies between…
> 'cultural sociology' and
> the 'sociology of culture'.
> **Jeffrey Alexander**

Instead, culture is, and should be, according to Alexander, considered "an independent variable", detached from the life conditions from which it emerged but able to exert power over the individuals and collectives within that culture.

People's understanding of events is neither natural or inevitable but is determined by the culturally specific language and symbols they use to interpret, code, and make sense of the world. As Alexander says, whether a society is defined as capitalist, socialist, or authoritarian does not bring us any closer to understanding the collective meaning attributed to an event. Instead, this is something that needs to be explored from "inside", in terms of the collectively produced structures, meanings, and symbols that people use to make sense of it.

Second, in order to understand culture, sociologists must adopt an interpretative approach. Alexander compares culture to a text – something that people read and interpret in ways that are socially

> The failure of Bourdieu... is that he doesn't recognize that culture has relative autonomy from social structure.
> **Jeffrey Alexander**

structured, but partially unique to them, and for this reason cannot be understood in terms of simple cause and effect. How people interpret an event cannot ever be fully predicted but instead requires to be understood retrospectively and from the perspective of the people concerned.

Third, Alexander claims that in the same way that there exist social structures – patterned ways of behaving that exist above and beyond individuals – there are also

cultural structures. These are symbolic resources, constellations of signs and symbols that members of a culture draw upon to invest the world with meaning and relevance. People are often only partially aware of these structures – they do not consciously reflect upon the extent to which their conscious and unconscious minds are shaped by them. Nevertheless, those structures are socially produced and patterned. The goal of cultural sociology is to make these structures visible. The ultimate aim is to understand better – and, where desirable, intervene in – the collective actions and reactions to events that take place in the world.

Meaning and the Holocaust

To demonstrate the way social groups are compelled by value-laden meanings and symbols, Alexander draws upon the example of the Nazi Holocaust of World War II. He uses this example because the Holocaust is recognized as one of the most powerful symbols of

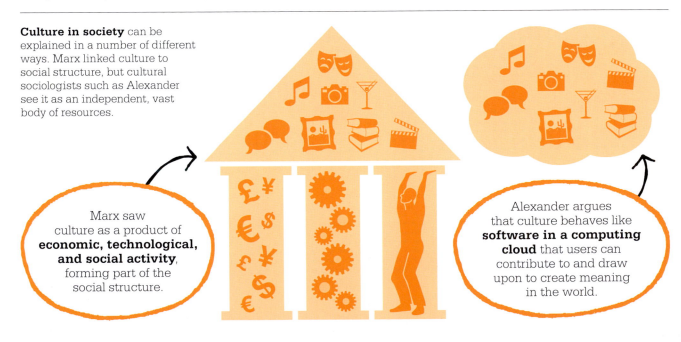

Culture in society can be explained in a number of different ways. Marx linked culture to social structure, but cultural sociologists such as Alexander see it as an independent, vast body of resources.

Marx saw culture as a product of **economic, technological, and social activity**, forming part of the social structure.

Alexander argues that culture behaves like **software in a computing cloud** that users can contribute to and draw upon to create meaning in the world.

human suffering and evil; it is (almost) beyond question that this event could be understood in any other way. Unbelievable as it may seem now, he argues, it is neither natural or inevitable that those events came to be understood as an act of unprecedented evil; rather: "...the category of 'evil' must be seen not as something that naturally exists but as an arbitrary construction, the product of cultural and sociological work."

In his 2001 essay "On the Social Construction of Moral Universalism: The 'Holocaust' from War Crime to Trauma Drama", Alexander demonstrates in rich detail that in the years immediately after World War II the Holocaust was not viewed with anything like the same horror and condemnation as it is now. As a socially distinct ethnic group, European Jews were typically negatively regarded in many societies, which in turn led to a less than empathetic response to their plight. Only as they became more integrated into wider society, and their distinctness as a social

Willy Brandt's kneefall at the memorial to the Warsaw Ghetto Uprising in 1970 was an act that symbolized German repentance, triggering a shift in collective identity.

group lessened, did it become possible for individuals and institutions to identify with them psychologically. By the early 1970s, the necessary cultural structures were in place for the Holocaust to be re-evaluated, re-narrated, and symbolically recoded as an act of evil. Only then was it elevated to the level of a traumatic event for all humankind and not just the Jews. On a state visit in 1970, the West German chancellor's "kneefall" at the Warsaw Ghetto memorial has been described by Valentin Rauer, in Alexander's *Social Performance* (2006), as a "symbol in action".

Alexander's cultural sociology is rapidly establishing itself as one of the most innovative and insightful sociological theoretical frameworks. As part of the wider "cultural turn" within the social sciences, his work has helped retrain the analytical focus of social thinkers onto the topic of "meaning". In particular his adaptation and application of Durkheim's work to understanding

An earthquake in 1997 destroyed Giotto's frescoes of St Francis in the basilica at Assisi, Italy. Mira Debbs reflected on how this loss resulted in socially constructed cultural trauma.

the creation of meaning and its maintenance across a range of areas – including the Holocaust, democracy and civil society, and the 9/11 attacks – have led to more scholars developing and extending his ideas. For example, US sociologist Mira Debbs has analysed the response in Italy to the destruction in 1997 of the artist Giotto's iconic frescoes in the basilica at Assisi. Such was the sacred status allocated to them in the national imagination that their loss has often been given more prominence than that of human life. Debbs draws upon Alexander's ideas to demonstrate how the narration and coding of the artworks in a particular way – as sacred national treasures – led to such a strong, seemingly irrational, collective emotional response by the majority of Italian people. ∎

IN CONTEXT

FOCUS
Conspicuous consumption

KEY DATES
1844 Karl Marx discusses class structure in capitalist society in *Economic and Philosophical Manuscripts of 1844*.

1859 Charles Darwin explains his theory of evolution in *On the Origin of Species by Means of Natural Selection*.

1979 Pierre Bourdieu reworks Veblen's theory of conspicuous consumption in *Distinction*.

1992–2005 Studies by US sociologist Richard A. Peterson suggest that snobbery is no longer a determining factor in the consumption practices of the middle class.

From 2011 Veblen's concept of conspicuous consumption influences economic ideas about irrationality and consumer behaviour.

The work of US economist and sociologist Thorstein Veblen focuses on the relationship between economy and society, and on how different class groups consume specific goods and services. He draws on the ideas of a number of key theorists, including Karl Marx, British sociologist Herbert Spencer, and British naturalist Charles Darwin. Veblen's insights into capitalist society and the types of consumer behaviour it gives rise to are outlined in his most celebrated work, *The Theory of the Leisure Class: An Economic Study of Institutions* (1899).

Capitalism and class

Veblen sees the transition from traditional to modern society as propelled by the development of technical knowledge and industrial production methods. Like Marx, Veblen argues that capitalist society is split into two competing social-class groups: the industrious class made up of workers; and the leisure class, also referred to as the pecuniary or business class (which also includes politicians, managers, lawyers, and so on), which owns the factories and workshops.

> The motive that lies at the root of ownership is emulation.
> **Thorstein Veblen**

The industrious class forms the vast majority of the population and engages in productive labour, such as manual craft and machine work. By contrast, the leisure class is a numerically far smaller, but nevertheless socially and economically privileged, group that is parasitic on the labour of the industrious class. For Veblen, members of this predatory leisure class do not produce anything of any real benefit to the wider good of society. The wealth and privilege they possess derive from driving competition and manipulating workers, with the sole aim of increasing their personal wealth.

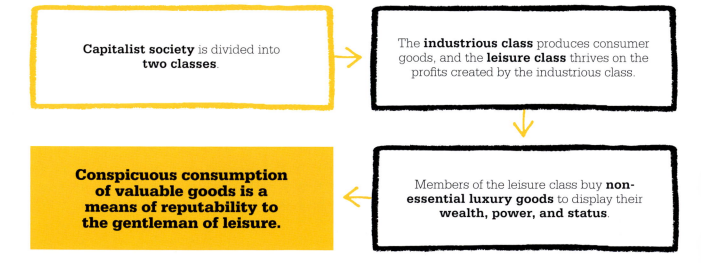

Capitalist society is divided into **two classes**.

The **industrious class** produces consumer goods, and the **leisure class** thrives on the profits created by the industrious class.

Members of the leisure class buy **non-essential luxury goods** to display their **wealth, power, and status**.

Conspicuous consumption of valuable goods is a means of reputability to the gentleman of leisure.

See also: Karl Marx 28–31 ▪ Charles Wright Mills 46–49 ▪ Pierre Bourdieu 76–79 ▪ Anthony Giddens 148–49 ▪ Herbert Marcuse 182–87 ▪ Colin Campbell 234–35 ▪ Herbert Spencer 334

Worse still, the privileged class consistently impedes positive social advancement through its deliberate mismanagement of industry and society generally.

Social recognition

Veblen's concept of "conspicuous consumption" is his most renowned contribution to economic and sociological theory. Framed by the Darwinian notion that all life represents an ongoing struggle for resources in the pursuit of advancement of the species (or in the case of human societies, the groups to which individuals belong), Veblen argues that under capitalism the majority of human behaviour is determined by struggles for social recognition, status, and power. This is most evident in relation to patterns of consumption and leisure.

Conspicuous consumption refers to spending money on, and consumption of, non-essential luxury goods in order to display to other members of society one's own economic and material wealth. An example of this is the modern business tycoon who buys an expensive yacht so that he can entertain friends and clients. It is not the utility value of the yacht (whether or not it is an effective means of transport) that matters to the tycoon; rather, its value is as a highly conspicuous signifier of the wealth at the tycoon's disposal, for which he will receive both admiration and respect.

Leisure and waste

Closely bound to Veblen's concept of conspicuous consumption is the notion of conspicuous leisure: the vast amount of time that members of the leisure class spend in pursuit of activities that are neither economically nor socially productive. Very simply, leisure implies an absence of work. For members of this privileged class who have sufficient distance from economic necessity (the need to work), the non-productive use of time can be used to further their social prestige and class position. Going on exotic foreign holidays and learning about other countries are classic examples of conspicuous leisure, according to Veblen.

The inevitable consequence of conspicuous leisure and consumption is the production of unnecessary waste. Conspicuous waste, argues Veblen, derives from the amalgamation of conspicuous consumption and conspicuous leisure. The net result of these two activities is that socially valuable resources (the raw materials and human labour essential for the production of consumer goods and services) and time are wasted. A glaring example of this culture of waste is the depletion of natural resources such as oil and minerals in the manufacture of luxury »

The concept of "Veblen goods", or luxury goods that signal high status, appeared in economic theory in the 1970s. In a reversal of usual trends, the higher the price of these items, the more they are desired.

Desire for goods increases as price increases.

PRICE OF LUXURY ITEM

DESIRE FOR LUXURY ITEM

Travel to foreign lands, learning languages, and acquiring knowledge about other cultures were powerful status symbols for wealthy Europeans in the 18th and 19th centuries.

goods and commodities, which in turn gives rise to increased carbon emissions and climate change.

Veblen's concepts of conspicuous consumption and conspicuous leisure are "political" ones because they contain within them a strong moral stance towards the actions and lifestyle of what he sees as the predatory and parasitic leisure class.

Pecuniary emulation

Aside from the wastefulness that the lifestyle of the leisure class necessitates, a further negative consequence of their activities is captured in Veblen's notion of pecuniary emulation. This concept refers to the idea that individuals from lower social-class groups try

> "
> Wealth is now itself intrinsically honourable and confers honour on its possessor.
> **Thorstein Veblen**
> "

to emulate, both consciously and unconsciously, the consumption practices of their social "superiors" – members of the leisure class. This is an attempt to signify to others their affiliation to the most socially powerful and dominant groups in society.

Pecuniary emulation is firmly rooted in the idea of ownership: once the immediate material needs of individuals are met, consumer goods are purchased for their utility as signifiers of social-class status and affiliation to the identity and lifestyle of a given social group. In capitalist society, social-class groups are stratified hierarchically. Attached to each class group is a specific amount of social status. Ownership, power, status, and dominance become inextricably bound together, such that the struggle for status is founded primarily in displays of economic wealth and pecuniary respect. Veblen claims that people are constantly comparing themselves – and what they have – to those around them. There are, he says, a number of very real and negative unintended consequences arising from this phenomenon.

Individuals and entire groups are subjected to the pressures of "invidious", or unjust, comparison with one another,

The carbon-copy lifestyle of some middle-class neighbourhoods arises from pressure to emulate the consumption practices of residents in an attempt to gain status and prestige.

according to Veblen. As capitalism becomes increasingly competitive, so the process of invidious comparison proliferates. The dominant mode of evaluating other people is "with a view to rating and grading them in respect to relative worth or value". But in addition to generating even more waste across the population, the process of pecuniary emulation does not guarantee the accumulation of social respect or prestige. Here Veblen uses the term "nouveau riche", or recently acquired wealth, to describe people who engage in conspicuous acts of consumption, such as buying flashy cars or designer-brand clothes. This may result in disapproval from people whose wealth or status – and what may be considered as more understated or subtle taste dispositions – is inherited from previous generations. This could serve to alienate the nouveau riche even further from the dominant social groups they aspire to emulate. Purchasing conspicuous consumer goods can lead to the attainment of social prestige, but not in those cases in which the consumers are perceived to be, and often are, exceeding the financial means available to them.

Veblen's legacy

Veblen's ideas on the conspicuous nature of consumption have been influential in the development of sociological analysis and continue to attract controversy and debate in equal measure.

For example, the work of the French theorist Pierre Bourdieu is indebted to Veblen's notions of pecuniary emulation and conspicuous consumption, even though he modified them to fit his theoretical model. Bourdieu maps out how individuals and social-class groups constantly compete with, and differentiate themselves from, one another through the consumption of certain types of socially distinguishing goods and services.

British-born sociologist Colin Campbell, however, sees Veblen's work as overly reductive. He claims that Veblen fails to acknowledge that the acquisition of consumer goods plays an essential and positive part in the way people

> Individuals... seek to excel in pecuniary standing and... gain the esteem and envy of fellow-men.
> **Thorstein Veblen**

are able to construct a sense of self-identity and worth through the products they buy and the activities they pursue.

More recently, sociologists have questioned whether a socially distinct leisure class can really be said to exist at all. British sociologist Mike Savage, for example, has argued that the shifting dynamics of modern class relations means there is no aristocratic leisure class in the modern world. This also means, according to Savage, that there is no longer a clearly identifiable social group whose taste

dispositions and consumption practices are emulated by all other social groups.

Developing this idea further, US sociologist Richard Peterson devised the concept of "cultural omnivore" to refer to an emergent social group – the educated fraction of the middle class working in the new media industries and advertising – that accrues prestige from consuming an eclectic mix of high- and low-brow consumer goods. Social prestige, according to Peterson, is now no longer derived from conspicuous consumption of luxury goods alone, but from the "knowing" and "ironic" consumption of purposively non-luxury items such as retrograde clothing, baseball caps, Dr Martens boots, and so on.

Despite criticisms and modification of his ideas, Veblen's *The Theory of the Leisure Class*, with its detailed examination of the intended and unintended social consequences of consumer spending and wider consumption patterns in capitalist societies, nevertheless remains an essential reference for economists and sociologists alike. ∎

Thorstein Veblen

Thorsten Veblen was born in Wisconsin, USA, to Norwegian immigrant parents. He obtained his undergraduate degree in economics from Johns Hopkins University in 1880; four years later he received his doctorate from Yale University.

Veblen's relationship with the world of institutional academia was a fractious one. In the late 19th century, many universities were strongly affiliated with churches, and Veblen's scepticism about

religion, combined with his odd manner and allegedly monotonous teaching style, meant that he struggled to gain employment. As a result, from 1884 to 1891 he depended on the largesse of his family.

In 1892, his former mentor, J. Laurence Laughlin, joined the University of Chicago, taking Veblen with him as a teaching assistant. It was here Veblen wrote and published *The Theory of the Leisure Class*. Shortly after, he was fired from the University of Chicago and, later, also from the University of Stanford for

his notoriously promiscuous behaviour. This culminated in divorce from his wife in 1911. He moved to California, where he passed his remaining years in depressed solitude.

Key works

1899 *The Theory of the Leisure Class: An Economic Study of Institutions*
1904 *The Theory of Business Enterprise*
1914 *The Instincts of Workmanship and the State of the Industrial Arts*

THE PURITAN WANTED TO WORK IN A CALLING; WE ARE FORCED TO DO SO

MAX WEBER (1864–1920)

IN CONTEXT

FOCUS
Protestant work ethic

KEY DATES
1517 German theologian Martin Luther posts his "Ninety-Five Theses on the Power and Efficacy of Indulgences", which is a catalyst for the Protestant Reformation.

From the 1840s Karl Marx focuses on economic – rather than religious or cultural – factors for understanding the rise of capitalism.

1882 A world-view hostile to Christianity is articulated by the German philosopher Friedrich Nietzsche, who declares "God is dead".

1920 Max Weber's book *Sociology of Religion* is published and becomes a major influence on sociological theories of religion.

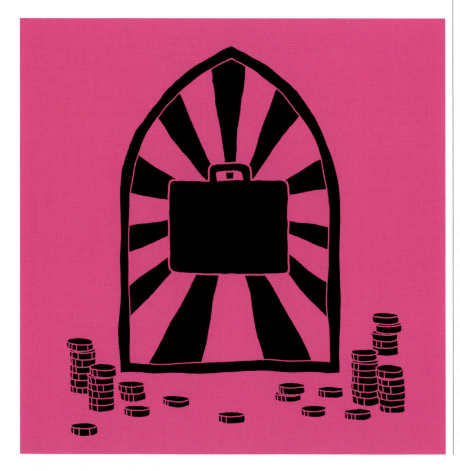

Max Weber, a founding father of sociology, provides a very different account of the rise of capitalism to that outlined in the work of the two other traditional founders of the discipline, Karl Marx and Émile Durkheim. In *The Protestant Ethic and the Spirit of Capitalism* (1904–05), Weber's most acclaimed work, he offers an analysis of the role played by religious ideas, beliefs, and values – particularly Protestantism – in the rise of modern capitalism.

For Weber, the definitive feature of capitalist society is the particular "work ethic" or "spirit of capitalism", as he refers to it, that

See also: Émile Durkheim 34–37 ▪ Zygmunt Bauman 136–43 ▪ Jeffrey Alexander 204–09 ▪ Colin Campbell 234–35 ▪
Karl Marx 254–59 ▪ Bryan Wilson 278–79

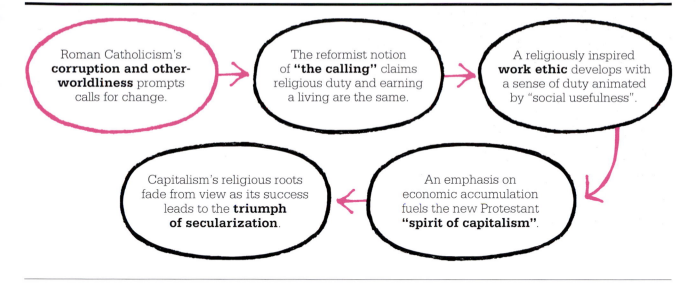

Roman Catholicism's **corruption and other-worldliness** prompts calls for change.

The reformist notion of **"the calling"** claims religious duty and earning a living are the same.

A religiously inspired **work ethic** develops with a sense of duty animated by "social usefulness".

An emphasis on economic accumulation fuels the new Protestant **"spirit of capitalism"**.

Capitalism's religious roots fade from view as its success leads to the **triumph of secularization**.

drives modern economies and the pursuit of wealth and profit. He claims that this "work ethic" is founded on the values of rationality, calculability, individual self-regulation, and gain.

The pursuit of profit

Weber's focus on the part played by cultural factors was partly intended to counter Marx's view that the rise of capitalism was a natural and inevitable process. Weber rejected the notion that human history is driven by underlying, inexorable "laws" that determine the path society will take.

The buying and selling of goods and services for more than they are worth is, Weber says, not unique to capitalism. Throughout history people have always traded with one another with a view to accruing profit. What is historically unique

to capitalism, he argues, is that the pursuit of profit becomes an end in itself. A modern-day example is the transnational banking group HSBC, which made a pre-tax profit of US $22.6 billion in 2013. If this profit was distributed among all of the firm's employees they could stop working and still live materially comfortable lives. Instead, firms such as HSBC use the profit they make to reinvest in the corporation, improve its efficiency, and pursue further profit.

Where, wondered Weber, did this ideal – the unrelenting pursuit of profit, or wealth for wealth's sake – that animates the "work ethic" at the heart of capitalism, actually come from?

Weber believed that to answer this question, we must look not to changes in social solidarity or technology but to one of the oldest features of all human societies – religion. He looks back in time to religious developments that were taking place in 16th-century »

The vast profits of the US retail giant Walmart should, staff say, be redirected into paying better wages. The corporation came under scrutiny in 2014 as a low-paying employer.

Europe, when Protestantism emerged as a reaction to the perceived corruption and failings of the Roman Catholic Church. Nascent Protestantism offered a very different vision of the relations between God and his subjects and the ethics overseeing them.

The Protestant "calling"

Weber identified in particular the importance of "the calling" to the new Protestant system of ethics, by which was meant the position that God has called people to occupy in this world. Whereas the Roman Catholic Church urged monastic retreat from the world of mundane affairs (such as daily life and work), Protestantism demanded that its followers fulfilled their worldly duties and responsibilities.

In drawing attention to this difference in religious ideals, Weber identified the German theologian Martin Luther (1483–1546) as the man whose thinking was essential to the development of Protestant theology. Luther was the first person to suggest that fulfilling the duties of secular life also demonstrated reverence to God. He claimed that at the heart of the concept of "the calling" is the belief that earning a living and religious duty are one and the same thing.

Luther's ideas were taken up within two decades and developed in important ways by arguably the most influential of all the reformers, John Calvin (1509–1564). However, contained within the otherwise coherent ethical system Calvin formulated was a significant inconsistency or contradiction: if God is all-seeing and all-knowing, then our destiny as individuals is predetermined because God made the world and everyone in it.

Calvin's notion is referred to as the concept of the "elect". Because God already knows how we are fated to live our lives, he also knows whose souls he has elected to save and whose souls will be damned. The problem for Protestants, however, is that there is no way of knowing in advance the category – the saved or the damned – to which they belong. According to Weber, this unknown gave rise to "salvation anxiety" and led to psychological terror among the followers of Protestantism. To resolve their unease, Protestants convinced themselves and one

Calvinist church aesthetics stress simplicity: Protestantism focused on austerity and thrift in contrast to the grandeur and ostentation that was often associated with Catholicism.

another that there were certain distinct signs that revealed who was predestined to be saved.

Social usefulness

Protestants felt that the most obvious way in which they could tell whether or not they were saved was by succeeding in the world, especially in economic affairs. Essential to this outcome was, they believed, a specific work ethic – historically novel and uniquely Protestant – that emphasized the absolute need for austerity, self-monitoring, and self-control in the conduct of economic affairs. Weber referred to this as the "spirit of capitalism".

A further aspect of this spirit was the drive towards increasing rationalization, control, and calculability within the sphere of economic action. To prosper economically is to demonstrate to one's self and others adherence to the notion of "the calling": the more

Modernity and the Holocaust

For Weber, the spread of the values of calculability, rationality, and self-restraint that defined the Protestant work ethic were also central to the development of modernity.

German-Polish sociologist Zygmunt Bauman argues that the value-basis of that ethic also explains how the Nazi Holocaust was able to occur. Instead of the traditional view of the Holocaust as the triumph of irrationality and a regression to primitive, pre-modern ways of thinking and acting, Bauman sees it as a highly rationalized event. Not only did modernity's rationality make the Holocaust possible, it was a necessary condition for it because the extermination was run on bureaucratic, organized lines. Bauman argues that the high levels of rationality and self-discipline exhibited by the Holocaust's perpetrators are inextricably bound up with the religious culture and values that were found throughout Protestant Europe.

hard-working, austere, and self-controlled individuals are in their actions, the greater will be the economic rewards they reap; and the more wealth they accumulate, the more this is understood as proof of their religious purity and the promise of salvation.

The inverse of the Protestant ethic is to shy away from work – to commit the sins of idleness and indolence and to fail to prosper financially.

Secularization

With the steady decline of formal religion (secularization) from the Industrial Revolution onwards, the Protestant ethic that underpins the "spirit of capitalism" has been eroded. When Weber claims that early Protestants "wanted to work in a calling" but that today "we are forced to", he is suggesting that although the values of hard work, self-control, and self-discipline upon which capitalism is founded have remained and are valued socially, their religious roots have disappeared from view.

In identifying the strong affinity between the work ethic contained within Reformation Protestantism – particularly the teachings of John Calvin – and the spirit of capitalism, Weber draws attention to a great historical irony. The Protestant Reformation was intended to salvage the message of God from the corrupting influences of the Roman Catholic Church. Nearly 500 years later, formal religion has gone into significant decline. What began as an attempt to salvage the Word has given rise to a work ethic that has been essential to the proliferation of capitalism. And as capitalism has developed, the power of formal religion to influence our actions has greatly diminished.

More than 100 years after its original publication in German, Weber's theory of the Protestant ethic remains hotly debated among contemporary sociologists and historians. The Italian sociologist Luciano Pellicani, for example, has argued that the spirit of capitalism arose much earlier than Weber suggests and that it was already present in medieval society.

In Weber's defence, English historian Guy Oakes points to the fact that medieval capitalism was fuelled by greed rather than by the sober, mundane sense of duty promoted by Calvinism. However, the fact that industrial capitalism first took hold in the Protestant countries of Europe, such as the Netherlands, Britain, and Germany, confirms the link that Weber made between Protestantism and the enterprising impulse that was necessary for the development of capitalism. And

> Fulfilment of worldly duties is... the only way to live acceptably to God.
> **Max Weber**

in *The Romantic Ethic and the Spirit of Modern Consumerism* (1987), Colin Campbell uses Weber's theory to account for the rise of consumer culture in Europe and the USA. This extension of Weber's ideas confirms that his religion-inspired account of the rise of capitalism continues to exert a powerful influence over sociological thought. ∎

The Protestant world view was shaped by the concept that worldly duties show reverence to God and promote his glory. Material success is interpreted as God's approval – a reward for effort, thrift, sobriety, and other "correct" ways of living.

Worldly duties:
Hard work
Self-control
Discipline

Honour your calling and you shall be rewarded

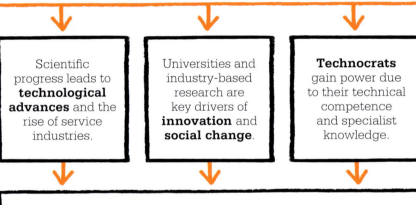

TECHNOLOGY, LIKE ART, IS A SOARING EXERCISE OF THE HUMAN IMAGINATION
DANIEL BELL (1919–2011)

IN CONTEXT

FOCUS
Post-industrialism

KEY DATES
1850s–80s Karl Marx argues that the social power of the bourgeoisie, or capitalist class, derives from ownership of industrial machines.

1904–05 Max Weber's *The Protestant Ethic and the Spirit of Capitalism* points to the increasingly rational nature of modern culture.

1970s Leading US sociologist Talcott Parsons defends the values and advancement of modern industrial society.

1970–72 Daniel Bell forecasts the rise of the Internet and the importance of home computers.

From the 1990s The concept of post-industrialism informs the theories of globalization experts Ulrich Beck and Manuel Castells.

Post-industrial society is characterized by the proliferation of **scientific and theoretical knowledge**.

Scientific progress leads to **technological advances** and the rise of service industries.

Universities and industry-based research are key drivers of **innovation** and **social change**.

Technocrats gain power due to their technical competence and specialist knowledge.

Advances in technology lead society in imaginative and unpredictable **new directions**.

During the 1960s and 1970s profound changes swept through the economic basis of society in Western Europe and the USA. In his influential work *The Coming of Post-Industrial Society* (1973), political journalist and sociologist Daniel Bell developed the concept of "post-industrialism" to refer to these changes. Having lived in New York and Chicago, Bell had first-hand experience of the rapid and extensive urban development that was taking place.

Bell agrees with Karl Marx that the bourgeoisie, or capitalist class, was the most powerful social group in industrial society because they owned the means of production – the factories and machines that produced the goods consumed by the wider population. In Bell's post-industrial society,

See also: Karl Marx 28–31 ▪ Manuel Castells 152–55 ▪ Ulrich Beck 156–61 ▪ Max Weber 220–223

however, the most valuable social "resource" is scientific and theoretical knowledge, and those who control it hold the power.

He also claims that social change occurs at an unprecedented pace as scientific progress and developments in technology interpenetrate and propel human societies into the future. The post-industrial era is therefore, he says, a period in the history of society in which advances in science and technology are as unpredictable and boundless as the human imagination.

Post-industrial society

According to Bell, post-industrial society differs from industrial society in three interrelated ways: first, the production of consumer goods is surpassed by the growth and progress of "theoretical" knowledge; second, developments in science and technology become increasingly intertwined as universities and industry-led

Modern cities are no longer dominated by the factories essential to manufacturing. In the post-industrial world of service industries, futuristic architecture has space to thrive.

initiatives form ever-tighter and interpenetrating relations; and finally, the number of unskilled and semi-skilled workers declines as the majority of the population work in, and draw upon, the expanding service industries. Bell refers to service industries as those spheres of human activity that are devoted to managing and guiding the application of information and knowledge.

Another key aspect of post-industrial society, according to Bell, is the rise in power of "technocrats", or people who exercise authority through their technical knowledge and ability to solve problems logically. The social power of technocrats is determined by their skill in forecasting and guiding new scientific ideas.

Bell believes that technology encourages imagination and experimentation – in so doing, it opens up new ways of thinking about the world. He points to the fact that the Greek word *techne* means "art". For him, art and technology should not be seen as separate realms: technology, he says, is "a form of art that bridges culture and social structure, and in the process reshapes both". ▪

Daniel Bell

The influential social thinker, writer, and sociologist Daniel Bell was born in Manhattan, New York City, USA, in 1919. His parents were Jewish immigrants from Eastern Europe. His father died when Bell was just a few months old; his family's name was changed from Bolotsky to Bell when he was a teenager.

In 1938 Bell received a BSc from City College of New York. He worked as a political journalist for more than 20 years. As managing editor of *The New Leader* magazine and editor of *Fortune*, he wrote widely on social issues. In 1959, in recognition of his contribution to political journalism, he was appointed professor of sociology at Columbia University; he was later awarded a PhD from the same university, even though he did not submit a doctoral thesis. He was a professor of sociology at Harvard University from 1969 to 1990.

Key works

1969 *The End of Ideology*
1973 *The Coming of Post-Industrial Society*
1976 *The Cultural Contradictions of Capitalism*

THE MORE SOPHISTICATED MACHINES BECOME THE LESS SKILL THE WORKER HAS

HARRY BRAVERMAN (1920–1976)

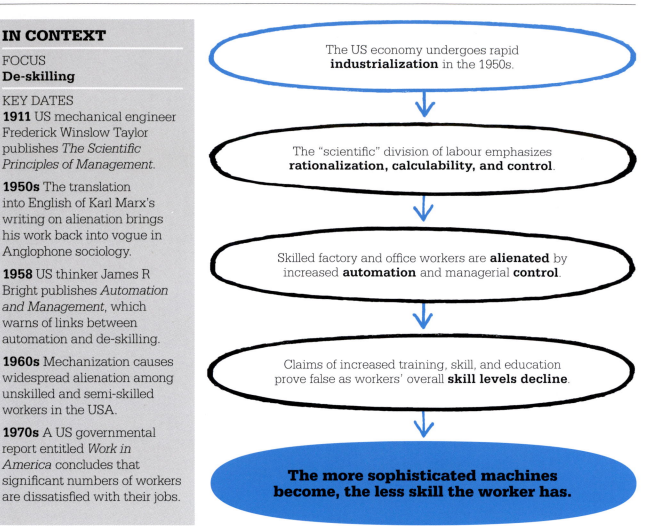

The US economy undergoes rapid **industrialization** in the 1950s.

The "scientific" division of labour emphasizes **rationalization, calculability, and control**.

Skilled factory and office workers are **alienated** by increased **automation** and managerial **control**.

Claims of increased training, skill, and education prove false as workers' overall **skill levels decline**.

The more sophisticated machines become, the less skill the worker has.

Since the 1950s, Karl Marx's concept of alienation has been the leading analytical lens through which sociologists from North America and Europe have sought to understand the modernization of employment and its effects on the workforce.

Both Marx and Max Weber had predicted that the rise of industrial technology would be accompanied by a drive towards ever-greater levels of efficiency, and the rationalization of the workforce into increasingly differentiated and specialized parts. Explicitly acknowledging that he is following in this intellectual tradition, Harry Braverman's classic 1974 study, *Labor and Monopoly Capital: The Degradation of Work in the Twentieth Century*, is a systematic enquiry into the nature of industrial work and the changing composition of the working class under the conditions of monopoly capitalism.

Braverman's analysis pivots on the notion of "de-skilling": that advances in industrial technology and machine production have led to the alienation and "deconstruction" of skilled members of the industrial working class and craftsmen. He believed that the de-skilling of work and the degradation of industrial workers was a process that had been gathering momentum since World War II. Although his focus was on factory workers, he also dealt with, albeit in less detail, office and clerical workers.

Myths of skilled labour
The idea that the industrialization of factory work is empowering for workers is tackled head on by Braverman and found seriously wanting. Drawing on his own

See also: Karl Marx 28–31 ▪ Max Weber 38–45 ▪ George Ritzer 120–23 ▪ Manuel Castells 152–55 ▪ Erich Fromm 188 ▪ Daniel Bell 224–25 ▪ Robert Blauner 232–33

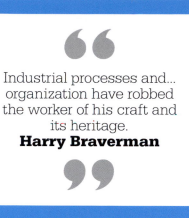

> Industrial processes and... organization have robbed the worker of his craft and its heritage.
> **Harry Braverman**

experience of such factory work, Braverman challenges official statistics and governmental classifications of workers to demonstrate the progressive and ongoing "de-skilling" of the US working class.

So, for example, the notion that increasing technology in the workplace calls forth a more technically proficient and educationally qualified workforce is, he argues, simply not true. Terms like "training", "skill", and "learning" are vague and open to interpretation, and the amount of training required to operate factory and office machinery often takes only a matter of minutes or, at most, a few weeks. Merely pointing to the fact that workers can operate machinery does not necessarily mean their skill levels have increased significantly. Tending to machinery and knowing how to operate it – a good example is learning how to use a photocopier – does not mean that a worker should be reclassified as "skilled".

Moreover, Braverman found that while general levels of educational achievement have increased among the workforce, typically this has a negative and unintended consequence for the individual entering paid employment.

In the course of surveys and interviews undertaken by Braverman, it was often found that the attainment of educational qualifications made the experience of factory and office work even more frustrating, or lacking in fulfilment, because opportunities for individuals to utilize and apply the knowledge obtained from their schooling simply did not exist. Greater educational achievement can lead to a far more acutely perceived sense of alienation.

Progressive skills erosion

Before the Industrial Revolution, notes Braverman, material goods were made by skilled and semi-skilled craftsmen and artisans. Advances in technology had enabled the scale of industrial production to reach unprecedented levels. The capacity for machines to perform so many of the tasks hitherto performed manually by skilled workers meant certain skills and technical knowledge were no longer required, while the need for new competencies and expertise grew in their place.

Understood in this way, argues Braverman, automation removes the need for some skills while creating a need for different, new skills in their place. Technological progress alone does not necessarily lead to a decline in workers' skill levels. Neither does alienation follow as a direct result.

Braverman was not arguing nostalgically for a return to the pre-industrial model of the craft worker; on the contrary, he acknowledges that automation can be a positive development. The effects become wholly negative, he claims, when automation of the workplace is coupled with radical changes to the social relations of production: the way in which the total labour process is organized, managed, and manipulated. He emphasizes the distinction between advances in science and technology and how those are implemented in the workplace on the one hand, and changes to the social relations of production – the drive for ever-more efficient ways to organize and divide up the labour force – on the other.

Just as machines are built to do jobs in the most efficient way, the workforce is structured to increase productivity and profit. Braverman's aim is to show that the embodied knowledge and technical competencies of skilled workers have been eroded and forgotten. »

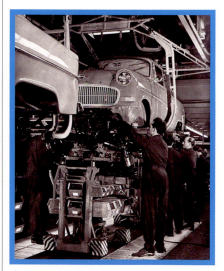

The production line at Opel in 1950s' West Germany. Subdivision of labour improved efficiency but, claimed Braverman, such processes de-skilled and degraded the worker.

What Braverman means by the degradation of work is the decline in the number of jobs that require a worker to conceptualize and execute a task. He argues the workforce has been reorganized into a mass of workers, whose jobs require little conceptualization, and a smaller number of managers.

The rise of management
Influenced by the work of US engineer and industrialist Frederick Taylor, who had developed a theory of scientific management and workflows, Braverman argues that three novel and significant developments have accelerated and accentuated the de-skilling of the labour force.

First, knowledge and information of the entire labour process is known only to, and closely controlled by, management and not the workers. Second, and as a direct result of the first development, the worker performs his set task in the total division of labour on a "need-to-know" basis. Workers are kept completely in the dark about the impact of the tasks they perform and about the role these tasks play in the

> "
> The alienation of the worker presents itself to management as [a] problem in costs and controls.
> **Harry Braverman**
> "

overall labour process. Third, empowered by knowledge of the total labour process, management is able to control in highly exacting ways what it is that each individual worker does. Careful monitoring and regulation of productivity levels means that management is able to intervene whenever productivity is perceived to be dipping, or whenever a worker can be shown to be underperforming.

Braverman argues that the ultimate negative consequence of organizing work in a manner that above all else emphasizes efficiency, calculability, and

productivity is the separating out of what Braverman refers to as "conception" from "execution". Invoking a biological metaphor, Braverman states that the workers are like a hand, whose every move is controlled, supervised, and corrected by the distant brain of management.

The cold logic of capitalism
As the total range of skills possessed by workers diminishes over time, so in turn their value decreases. Workers can be paid less because the tasks they perform are increasingly menial and unskilled. Robbed of their expertise, they are more dispensable and, crucially, interchangeable. For Braverman, the cruel and unforgiving logic of the capitalist system inextricably ties his analysis to the concept of social class. The deconstruction of craftsmanship among the labour force works to ensure that entire sections of the population are prevented from climbing the social hierarchy.

Braverman's study focuses primarily on industrial factory work but his attention also turns to the de-skilling of office workers.

In Braverman's metaphor, managers are the brain and workers the hand of all-seeing management in the workplace. When labour is organized to maximize efficiency, productivity, and profit, there is a negative outcome for the workers. Braverman attributed this to the rise of management, which now observed, monitored, controlled, and regulated every action of the workforce. The effects of technology were first felt in factories; today, even retail outlets are supervised by distant, centralized head offices.

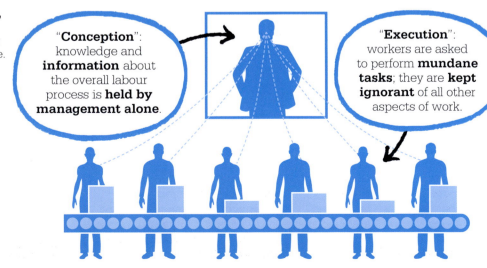

"**Conception**": knowledge and **information** about the overall labour process is **held by management alone**.

"**Execution**": workers are asked to perform **mundane tasks**; they are **kept ignorant** of all other aspects of work.

Women typists at a mail-order firm in 1912. By the early 20th century the profession of clerk had given way to large-scale, efficiently arranged, and scientifically managed offices.

He notes that control over the daily round of activities involved in clerical work – including bookkeeping, scheduling, and the responsibility that ensues from this – have been degraded to endless paper-chasing, photocopying, and other menial tasks. He also observes that because – at the time he was writing – office workers in Britain and the USA were typically female, they could be paid less, which in turn reduces costs and maximizes profit.

Expertise diminished

Labor and Monopoly Capital is considered a classic contribution to the discipline of sociology, but it is the only academic book that Braverman ever wrote. The book's influence on the application of critical Marxist thinking to the empirical study of industrial work has been profound. Like Marx, Braverman never held a university post and it is perhaps for this very reason that he was able, without

fear of censorship, to write such a penetrating and biting critique of the injustices of industrial capitalism and their impact on the majority of the workforce. While Braverman was not the first or only thinker to identify and denounce the relationship between automation and de-skilling, his work was crucial for revitalizing the analysis of work across a broad range of disciplines, including history, economics, and political science. Since the publication of *Labor and Monopoly Capital*, Braverman's ideas have continued to generate debate among sociologists of work. Writing in 1979, US sociologist Michael Burawoy was strongly supportive of Braverman's work, as was US sociologist Michael Cooley in his study of computer-aided design.

While the conviction with which Braverman presented his arguments has led to criticism from some quarters (in the work of Robert Blauner, for example), his central ideas have survived and been carried forward in the work of Manuel Castells, the highly influential Spanish sociologist of globalization and the network society. ∎

Harry Braverman

Harry Braverman was born in 1920 in New York, USA, to Polish-Jewish émigré parents. He attended college for one year before leaving for financial reasons. He later worked as an apprentice coppersmith in Brooklyn, where he developed a powerful insight into the effects of science-based technology on the "de-skilling" of the working class.

Deeply affected by his experience, Braverman joined the Socialist Workers Party (SWP) and absorbed himself in the work of Marx and other socialist thinkers of the period. In 1953 he was expelled from the SWP, and went on to found the Socialist Union and to become editor of *The American Socialist*. In 1963 Braverman finally completed a BA from the New School of Social Research.

Key works

1974 *Labor and Monopoly Capital: The Degradation of Work in the Twentieth Century*

Marxism is not hostile to science and technology... but to how they are used as weapons of domination.
Harry Braverman

AUTOMATION INCREASES THE WORKER'S CONTROL OVER HIS WORK PROCESS
ROBERT BLAUNER (1929–)

Workers in different industries experience **varying levels of alienation** in automated work processes...

...those who **lack knowledge** of and control over technology have **high levels of alienation**.

...those with **expert knowledge** of technology have **low levels of alienation**.

Knowledge of automation increases the worker's control over work processes and reduces alienation.

Alienation occurs when workers are disconnected from and lack control over their work, according to Karl Marx. In his influential book on industrial society, *Alienation and Freedom: The Factory Worker and His Industry* (1964), US sociologist Robert Blauner draws heavily on Marx's concept of alienation to examine the possibility that alienation in the workplace can be significantly reduced by the effective use of technology.

Blauner claims alienation is central to understanding the negative impact of automation on workers during and after the Industrial Revolution. His text critically assesses Marx's claim

See also: Karl Marx 28–31 ▪ Erich Fromm 188 ▪ Daniel Bell 224–25 ▪
Harry Braverman 226–31 ▪ Arlie Hochschild 236–43 ▪ Michael Burawoy 244–45

that all workers are necessarily alienated due to the increased automation of work. Blauner suggests, on the contrary, that automation can actually facilitate, empower, and liberate workers.

Using a wide range of data (including statistics, interviews with workers, and attitudinal surveys), Blauner examines four types of industry: craft printing, car assembly lines, textile machine-tending, and chemical-processing. Alienation levels are tested according to four criteria: job control, social isolation, sense of self-estrangement, and meaningfulness of work.

Technology and alienation

Blauner describes his results as conforming to an "inverted U curve". According to his study, alienation is typically very low among print workers. He suggests that the use of machinery is empowering for these employees because it provides them with greater control and autonomy. The same is true for workers in chemical-processing plants: again, these individuals are empowered,

Automated technology on car assembly lines should be organized and deployed in ways that enable the manufacturing workers to regain a sense of control over their environment.

he proposes, because they possess expert knowledge of the relevant technology, which in turn is meaningful and fulfilling because it furnishes them with a significant degree of control over their work experience and environment.

By contrast, the automated technology used in car production and in textile factories leads to relatively high levels of alienation. These findings seem to contradict Blauner's claim that greater automation diminishes alienation. To explain this, however, he argues that it is not technology itself that alienates workers, but a lack of control over the way it is used, how work is organized, and the nature of the relationships between workers and management.

Blauner concludes that under the right organizational conditions, automation increases the worker's control over his work process and diminishes a sense of alienation in equal measure.

Blauner's study has greatly influenced the sociology of work, as testified by follow-up studies

Alienation exists when workers are unable to control their immediate work processes.
Robert Blauner

Robert Blauner

Robert Blauner is an emeritus professor of sociology at the University of California, Berkeley, USA. He was awarded his undergraduate degree from the University of Chicago in 1948.

Blauner was a staunch communist, and after graduating he worked in factories for five years, aiming to inspire a working-class revolution. Unsuccessful in those efforts, he completed his MA and PhD at Berkeley in 1962. His PhD thesis became the 1964 study that established his reputation. In addition to his contributions to the study of alienation and work, Blauner has made penetrating analyses of race relations in the USA.

Key works

1964 *Alienation and Freedom: The Factory Worker and His Industry*
1972 *Radical Oppression in America*
1989 *Black Lives, White Lives: Three Decades of Race Relations in America*

conducted by sociologists in the USA, as well as in Britain and France during the 1970s and 1980s. Furthermore, the "political" character of Blauner's work means studies of alienating work environments have fed into, and strongly influenced, commercial working directives and policies. The global technology firm Apple, for example, is renowned for investing heavily in training staff to use Apple technology to enhance their working experience as well as their own personal lives. ▪

THE ROMANTIC ETHIC PROMOTES THE SPIRIT OF CONSUMERISM
COLIN CAMPBELL (1940–)

IN CONTEXT

FOCUS
The Romantic ethic

KEY DATES
1780–1850 The Romantic movement in Europe reacts to the overly rationalistic, abstract ideals of the Age of Enlightenment.

1899 In *The Theory of the Leisure Class*, US social and economic thinker Thorstein Veblen suggests that consumption is driven by groups "emulating" one another to gain social status.

1904–05 Max Weber identifies a connection between the "Protestant work ethic" and the rise of capitalism.

Present Scholars such as US sociologist Daniel Bell and Italian sociologist Roberta Sassatelli draw heavily on Colin Campbell's ideas in their studies of consumption.

Why have Western Europe and the USA developed consumer cultures? British sociologist Colin Campbell, emeritus professor at the University of York, discusses this question in his important study, *The Romantic Ethic and the Spirit of Modern Consumerism* (1987), intended as a sequel to Max Weber's similarly named and hugely influential *The Protestant Ethic and the Spirit of Capitalism* (1904–05).

Weber claims that the values of self-discipline and hard work, which lie at the heart of modern

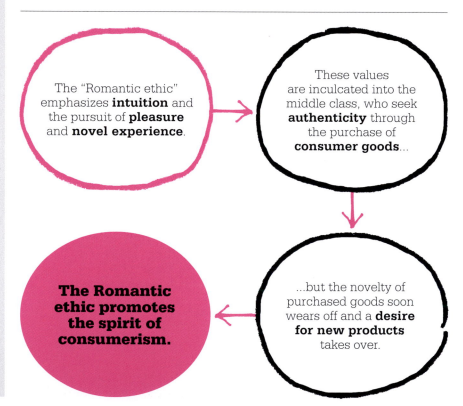

The "Romantic ethic" emphasizes **intuition** and the pursuit of **pleasure** and **novel experience**.

These values are inculcated into the middle class, who seek **authenticity** through the purchase of **consumer goods**...

...but the novelty of purchased goods soon wears off and a **desire for new products** takes over.

The Romantic ethic promotes the spirit of consumerism.

See also: Karl Marx 28–31 ▪ Max Weber 38–45 ▪ Herbert Marcuse 182–87 ▪ Jean Baudrillard 196–99 ▪
Thorstein Veblen 214–19 ▪ Daniel Bell 224–25

Designer goods stimulate the desire for purchase, possession, and for a lifestyle far removed from the mundane realities of existence. But desire, by its very nature, is insatiable.

capitalist societies, have their basis in the Protestant work ethic of the 16th and 17th centuries. Campbell, building on Weber's work, advances the theory that the emotions and hedonistic desires that drive consumer culture are firmly rooted in the ideals of 19th-century Romanticism, which followed on the heels of the Enlightenment and the Industrial Revolution.

Desire, illusion, and reality
The Enlightenment conceived of individuals as rational, hard-working, and self-disciplined. But the Romantics saw this as a denial of the very essence of humanity. They stressed intuition above reason, and believed that the individual should be free to pursue hedonistic pleasures and new and exciting feelings.

The Romantic ethic was inculcated into and carried forward by the burgeoning middle class, and by women in particular, Campbell argues. Within consumer culture this ethic is expressed as a self-perpetuating loop: individuals project their desire for pleasure and novelty onto consumer goods; they then purchase and make use of those goods; but the appeal of the product quickly diminishes as the novelty factor and initial excitement fade; the desire for excitement, fulfilment, and novelty is then projected onto, and re-stimulated by, new consumer items. And so the cycle of consumption, fleeting fulfilment, and ultimate disillusionment, repeats itself.

The engine of capitalism
The cycle described by Campbell is one of highs and lows for the consumer. Consumer desire is the very engine of capitalism because it drives individuals to search for that elusive yet satisfying experience amid the endless tide of new products. The consequences of this process for economies based on consumption are vast because consumers are forever chasing the latest commodities.

Campbell's concept of the Romantic ethic has had immense influence on sociology and anthropology. His work not only dispels the overly simplistic view of humans as necessarily disposed to acquire things, but it also attempts to shed light on the more positive aspects of consumer society.

It is simply wrong, according to Campbell, to suggest that consumerism is an inherently bad thing. Instead, the pursuit and projection of our innermost desires onto consumer goods form a fundamental part of our own self-realization in the modern world.

Campbell's highly original and powerful correctives to more economically reductive and cynical accounts of consumerism have provided contemporary thinkers with fertile soil in which to develop more positive and historically informed appraisals of modern-day consumer society. ∎

Consumerism as mass deception

The uniqueness of Campbell's focus on the Romantic ethic as the key to modern consumerism lies in its engagement with the impact of long-term historical processes. His ideas differ greatly from those of the highly influential French post-structuralist and postmodern thinkers such as Roland Barthes and Jean Baudrillard a decade or so earlier.

For them, unlike Campbell, the triumph of consumer culture is to be resisted at all costs.

They see the failed social and political revolutions of the late 1960s as signifying the "death of Marxism" and therefore also the triumph of capitalism. Barthes' work on semiotics identifies the advertising industry as playing a key role in blinding consumers to their true wants and desires, whereas for Baudrillard the media is responsible for overwhelming the consumer and concealing the vacuous nature of modern capitalist society.

IN PROCESSING PEOPLE THE PRODUCT IS A STATE OF MIND

ARLIE RUSSELL HOCHSCHILD (1940–)

IN CONTEXT

FOCUS
Emotional labour

KEY DATES
1867 Karl Marx completes the first volume of *Das Kapital*, which inspires Hochschild's concept of emotional labour.

1959 Canadian sociologist Erving Goffman publishes *The Presentation of Self in Everyday Life.*

1960s The burgeoning service industries of Europe and North America start to be heavily gendered towards women workers.

1970s Feminist thinkers begin to turn their attention to the negative consequences of capitalism for women.

2011 Sociologists Ann Brooks and Theresa Devasahayam publish *Gender, Emotions and Labour Markets*, which combines Hochschild's ideas with globalization theory.

When Karl Marx, in *Das Kapital*, expressed concern about mother- and-child factory workers and the "human cost" of labour, he said they had become an "instrument" of labour. This observation, and the environment of brutalizing physical work, led to his alienation concept, whereby lack of fulfilment and control leads workers to feel disconnected and estranged.

Alongside Marx's insights, two models of emotion emerged in the late 19th and early 20th century. The "organismic" model, built from the work of Charles Darwin, William James, and Sigmund Freud, identifies emotion as mainly a biological process: external stimuli trigger instinctual responses that people express in similar ways. From the 1920s, John Dewey, Hans Gerth, Charles Wright Mills, and Erving Goffman created an "interactional" model. They accepted emotion had a biological component, but they maintained that it is more interactive and differentiated by a range of social factors: culture is involved in the formulation of emotion and people manage feelings subjectively.

'Sincerity' is detrimental to one's job, until the rules of salesmanship and business become a 'genuine' aspect of oneself.
Charles Wright Mills

Following the translation of Marx's work into English in the 1960s, alienation became a powerful analytical tool for sociologists trying to make sense of the changes then taking place to working conditions in North America and Western Europe.

A state of mind
Inspired by these various ideas, and drawing upon women thinkers such as Simone de Beauvoir, US feminist and sociologist Arlie Hochschild has made the analysis of the emotional dimensions of

New service industries require workers to possess **"emotional resources"**.

Because women are stereotyped as more **emotional** these industries are heavily **gendered towards a female workforce**.

Women workers are asked to act in ways that **create positive emotional states** to help ensure future custom.

Under capitalism, human emotions are commodified: in processing people, the product is a state of mind.

See also: Karl Marx 28–31 ▪ G H Mead 176–77 ▪ Erving Goffman 190–95 ▪ Harry Braverman 226–31 ▪
Christine Delphy 312–17 ▪ Ann Oakley 318–19

Children are exposed to "childhood training of the heart", says Hochschild. Whereas girls learn to be caring and to master aggression and anger, boys mask fear and vulnerability.

human interaction her life's work. More specifically, she concentrates on the ways in which social and cultural factors condition the experience and display of emotions in capitalist society.

Her work charts the rise of the service industries in North America from the 1960s onwards, and the emergence of forms of employment in which the emotions of workers have become marketable commodities sold for a wage: "emotional labour", as she calls it.

Hochschild says that her interest in how people manage emotions probably began when she was growing up in a household where her diplomat parents acted as hosts to foreign embassy staff. Where, she wondered, did the person end and the act begin? Later, as a graduate, she was inspired by the chapter "The Great Salesroom" in Wright Mills' *White Collar*, in which he argued that we sell our personality when selling goods and services.

Hochschild felt that this had the ring of truth, but that it missed the sense of the active emotional labour involved in the selling. Unlike 19th-century factory work, where output could be quantified and it mattered little whether you loved or hated what you made, employment in a service industry is qualitatively different. It means that "the emotional style of offering the service is part of the service itself", which makes it necessary for the worker to sustain a certain outward appearance in order to produce a proper state of mind in others. Whereas for Marx the individual in the factory becomes alienated from the products they create, Hochschild argued that in the service-based economy "the product is a state of mind".

In Hochschild's view, the increasing use of emotionally based rather than manually based labour has a greater impact on women than men, because women are conditioned since childhood to supply feelings. But she believes that this can come at a cost to the individual, who may become estranged from their own emotions, which feel like they belong to their work rather than to them.

Managing interaction

One of the major influences on Hochschild is symbolic interactionist Erving Goffman. The idea underpinning his work is that selfhood is created during social interaction. Only by interacting with others – and managing the way we present ourselves – are individuals able to obtain a personal sense of identity. In essence, our innermost sense of selfhood is inextricably bound up with the social contexts in which we are implicated.

Hochschild extends this idea in a critical way by arguing that emotions, as well as being something external – residing in interactions between individuals and groups – are subject to self-management too. Emotions and feelings are also tied directly to behaviour and are experienced by individuals as they prepare to act and interact with others.

In a similar way to the sensory faculty of hearing, "emotion communicates information", as Hochschild puts it. She likens emotion to what Freud referred » to as a "signal function", whereby messages such as fear or anxiety are relayed to the brain, indicating the presence of danger, and so on. Hochschild says that: "From feeling we discover our own viewpoint on the world." Emotions engender a mental component that reconciles past events with actual situations in which we put or find ourselves.

In addition to putting these emotional dimensions at the heart of social interaction, Hochschild stresses the myriad ways in which emotions are mediated and shaped by wider processes. Society and culture intervene in the emotional economy of the individual through socialization. For example, through primary socialization people learn to make sense of their emotions and, with varying degrees of success, manipulate and manage them. Hochschild is saying that emotions are not simply things that happen to passive human actors. Rather, individuals are actively involved in producing and creating their feelings and emotions.

Emotional work and rules

As individuals, claims Hochschild, we "do" emotions. Feeling emotional and acting in emotional

...the action is in the body language, the put-on sneer, the posed shrug, the controlled sigh. This is surface acting.
Arlie Russell Hochschild

ways is purposively enacted. She calls this process "emotional work", and uses it to describe how people alter and intensify particular feelings, while simultaneously trying to suppress unpleasant emotions. She identifies three main ways that people work to produce emotion: cognitive emotional work, bodily emotional work, and expressive emotional work.

In cognitive emotional work, individuals use images, ideas, and thoughts in order to call forth, or stifle, the various emotions associated with those ideas. Bodily emotional work refers to any attempt to control the physical reaction accompanying a particular emotional state, such as sweating when anxious, or shaking when angry. Expressive emotional work involves attempting to manage the public display of particular emotions with a view to realizing a specific feeling, or set of feelings.

The purpose of Hochschild's typology of emotions is to highlight the extent to which individuals are actively involved in shaping and managing their inner emotional states in order to call forth certain feelings. Earlier work in this area focused on outward appearances: the physical behaviour and verbal cues we use to communicate emotions; what Hochschild refers to as "surface acting". She extends her analysis to focus on "deep acting", referring to "method acting" when trying to explain it: "Here, display is a natural result of working on feeling; the actor does not try to *seem* happy or sad but rather expresses spontaneously, as the Russian theatre director Constantin Stanislavski urged, a real feeling that has been self-induced."

It is not Hochschild's intention to suggest that people consciously manipulate or deceive one another,

Many women work in service-industry jobs, where employers ask them to exude real emotion to satisfy customers. All in the line of, as Hochschild puts it, "being nice".

although this is always possible. She is attempting to demonstrate the ways and extent to which people interact and work together to define a particular social situation and how, in turn, this feeds back into, and intimately shapes, their emotional states.

Hochschild maintains that rationalization and the marginalization of the more emotional aspects of human behaviour have meant that the often tacit rules that underpin interpersonal conduct have begun to develop in new directions. To explain this, she introduces the notion of "feeling rules". These are socially learned and culturally specific norms that individuals draw upon in order to negotiate and guide the display and experience of emotions and feelings. In modern capitalist societies, there are two types: display rules and emotional rules. Display rules are, like "surface acting", the outward verbal and non-verbal cues people communicate to one another. Emotional rules refer to the level of people's emotions, the directions they take, and how long they endure. For example, if a loved one dies, there is a strong social expectation that the grieving process will take time to run its course. In essence, emotional rules exist that influence what constitutes an appropriate response to death, how powerful the response should be, and the length of time it should last.

Delta Airlines

The interconnected notions of emotional labour and emotional work were explored by Hochschild in her most celebrated book, *The Managed Heart: Commercialization of Human Feeling* (1983). The study focuses primarily on US company Delta Airlines. She demonstrates that the airline consistently hired people who it perceived could be

controlled physically – in terms of their personal appearance – and emotionally. Keen to increase passenger numbers, Delta focused on employing young, attractive, single women, although a small number of men were employed too. The appeal of the women was that they were perceived to embody, in the most literal ways, the very specific ideals and image the corporation wanted to project to customers. Especially important was that flight attendants did not use surface acting when displaying emotion. In order to ensure passengers felt the emotional experience they were receiving was authentic, flight attendants were taught to practice "deep acting" by producing within themselves emotional displays that were sincere and genuine. Delta Airlines recognized that authentic displays of emotion and emotional performances are far easier to perform and sustain "when the

> "In the case of the flight attendant, the emotional style... is... the service.
> **Arlie Russell Hochschild**"

feelings are actually present". Training manuals and guidelines were issued so that flight attendants could perform emotional labour and produce authentic performances. The manuals taught an array of sophisticated strategies with which to produce corporately calculated emotional states and feeling repertoires. If these were genuine, passengers would feel »

Surface acting

I'm tired, fed up, and I want to go home.

Champagne, sir?

Deep acting

You're my guest and I'm happy to help you in any way I can.

Emotional labour is, according to Hochschild, the "commercialization of human feeling". Delta Airlines, she says, trained recruits so that they could transcend "surface acting", whereby postures or expressions are deceits and feel faked. The company urged trainees to imagine the cabin as their home, into which they welcomed customers as "personal guests". Once staff had mastered the art of "deep acting", feigning sincerity became unnecessary as real feelings were self-induced.

reassured, happy, and at ease. By evoking in passengers positive emotional states and feelings of comfort and safety, Delta believed it could secure the loyalty and future custom of passengers.

Ingenious and innovative as the corporate philosophy might at first seem, Hochschild argues that the deep acting and emotional labour demanded of flight attendants was ultimately damaging to their psychological wellbeing. Constantly having to control, manage, and subvert their own feelings, while simultaneously working to produce and display a range of positively authentic emotions, proved harmful.

She identified two particularly negative consequences arising from long-term emotional labour. First, the fusing together of the flight attendants' private sense of selfhood with their public self – the roles they played as attendants – was liable to lead to emotional and psychological burnout. Second, a sense of self-estrangement often

occurred: trying to manage the very real disparity between their personal feelings and the emotional states they strived to evoke in passengers, typically led to one of two outcomes among them – either they began to resent themselves emotionally or they developed resentment for the job.

Hochschild claims that even if individuals actively engage in strategies aimed at self-preservation, resenting the work as opposed to themselves, the net result is the same. The emotional and psychological wellbeing of the individual is harmed, with the result they feel increasingly alienated from their innermost self and their emotions too.

Gender inequality

As a feminist sociologist, Hochschild's study of Delta also provides a window onto the ways in which wider gender inequalities are sustained and reproduced within US society. Since the 1960s, increasing numbers of women have

> Women make a resource out of feeling and offer it to men.
> **Arlie Russell Hochschild**

entered into the workforce, with many joining the burgeoning service industries. For Hochschild, this is not necessarily a positive development, because it serves to push the highly uneven division of emotional-labour characteristics of modern capitalist society further in the direction of women. In making this argument, Hochschild claims that women are more inclined to make a resource out of feeling, which they in turn sell back to men. Although the increasing numbers of working women seem to testify to a shift in the occupational status of women in modern society, a closer examination of the statistics shows that women are far more likely than men to work in the service industries – most shopworkers, call-centre operatives, and hotel and bar staff are women.

Within modern capitalist society it falls to women to undertake the vast majority of the total emotional labour. In the long term, this is a negative and unintended

Many nurses claim their emotional labour is invisible to some colleagues. They give loving, daily care to patients, often in an attempt to compensate for the insensitivity of more senior staff.

consequence of capitalism because it makes women more emotionally prone to burnout, and psychologically and socially susceptible to feelings of self-estrangement and alienation.

Insatiable capitalism

Hochschild's notion of emotional work and her analysis of the emotional labour performed by airline flight attendants marks a key moment in the history of sociological thinking. For Marx, capitalism leads to physical and mental degradation for the worker as the nature of work becomes increasingly repetitive, menial, and specialized. Social thinker Harry Braverman argued that automation of the workplace leads to the steady deconstruction of a once highly skilled workforce. Remaining with the Marxist tradition, Hochschild demonstrates that even the most personal aspects of individual selfhood – our emotions, feelings, and affective life – are turned into commodities and exploited by the capitalist market in order to make profit. Her ideas have been developed by many other scholars involved with the sociology of work and emotions, and applied to a

Call-centre operatives experience high levels of emotional burnout and distress, induced by their emotional labour, according to research by Dutch sociologist Danielle van Jaarsveld.

number of occupations, ranging from nurses and caregivers to waitresses, telemarketers, and call-centre operatives.

Hochschild gives particular credit to a cross-cultural study of emotion management, between Japan and the USA, by Aviad Raz in his 2002 book *Emotions at Work*. She relates his story about "smile training" in which the Japanese managers at Tokyo Dome Corporation were not happy with the weak, "spiritless, externally-imposed smiles" that they thought managers in the USA were prepared to settle for. Instead, the Japanese felt it necessary to appeal to the underlying *chi* ("spirit") of the workers. This they enticed from their employees through the culturally powerful force of shame. Cameras were placed at the cash registers of unfriendly sales clerks, whose videotaped behaviour was shown later to their fellow workers.

The smile may now be a global fad but Raz confirms Hochschild's insight that capitalism exploits emotional aspects of culture. ■

...when a worker abandons her work smile, what kind of tie remains between her smile and her self?
Arlie Russell Hochschild

Arlie Russell Hochschild

Arlie Russell Hochschild was born in 1940 and is a US feminist and sociologist of work and emotion. Her parents were both US diplomats. Hochschild claims that growing up in a social milieu defined by the need for people to control and manage their emotions in very subtle and convincing ways instilled within her a fascination with the emotional dimensions of modern social life.

Hochschild obtained her MA and PhD at the University of California, Berkeley. During this time she became a feminist and developed an ongoing interest in the dual roles women play as workers and primary caregivers in capitalist society.

The overtly political pitch of Hochschild's work has strongly influenced feminist thinking in the USA and Western Europe. It has also led to an ongoing dialogue with captains of industry and high-level politicians.

Hochschild's work has informed social policy at a number of levels, including the US state of California's Child Development Policy Board as well as former US vice president Al Gore's working families' policy directives.

Key works

1983 *The Managed Heart: Commercialization of Human Feeling*
2003 *The Commercialization of Intimate Life: Notes from Home and Work*
2012 *The Outsourced Self: Intimate Life in Market Times*

SPONTANEOUS CONSENT COMBINES WITH COERCION
MICHAEL BURAWOY (1947–)

IN CONTEXT

FOCUS
Manufacturing consent

KEY DATES
1979 The effects of the global oil recession impact on US manufacturing industries, causing tension between workers and management.

1981 British sociologist Anthony Giddens refers to Michael Burawoy's book, *Manufacturing Consent: Changes in the Labour Process Under Monopoly Capitalism*, as "one of the most significant contributions to industrial sociology".

1998 In "Manufacturing Dissent? Burawoy in a Franco-Japanese Workshop", French sociologist Jean-Pierre Durand and British sociologist Paul Stewart apply Burawoy's concept of manufacturing consent to a Nissan automobile plant.

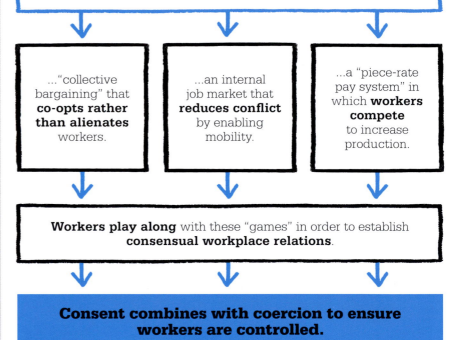

Management pacifies workers with **the illusion of choice** by playing **workplace "games"**, such as...

..."collective bargaining" that **co-opts rather than alienates** workers.

...an internal job market that **reduces conflict** by enabling mobility.

...a "piece-rate pay system" in which **workers compete** to increase production.

Workers play along with these "games" in order to establish **consensual workplace relations**.

Consent combines with coercion to ensure workers are controlled.

Why workers in the capitalist system work as hard as they do and how the interests of workers and management are negotiated are issues that Anglo-American sociologist Michael Burawoy analyses from within a Marxist theoretical framework. From this perspective, the interests of labour and capital are seen as being in fundamental opposition; Burawoy

See also: Karl Marx 28–31 ▪ Michel Foucault 52–55 ▪ Pierre Bourdieu 76–79 ▪ Anthony Giddens 148–49 ▪ Harry Braverman 226–31 ▪ Robert Blauner 232–33

contends that modern management now manufactures and channels workers' consent to work harder.

He rejects Marx's explanation that workers are simply exploited and coerced into working as hard as they do. The rise in the power of labour unions and workers' collectives has done a lot to curb the use of power by managers, which was once exerted through the bullying of workers. Burawoy acknowledges that within any organization there is always coercion and consent but their relative proportions and mode of expression have changed.

Management, he claims, now seeks to control workers by creating restrictive social relations and organizational structures that give them the "illusion of choice", but that ultimately serve to mask and maintain unequal power relations.

Workplace "games"

Burawoy worked in a factory called Allied Corporation, where he researched his ideas about the "games" played within the workplace, such as collective bargaining (negotiation of wages and conditions of work), ensuring internal job mobility for workers, and the piece-rate pay system, in which workers are paid more if they produce above quota. This system, he says, gives the illusion that work is a game; the workers are the players and compete with one another to "make out"– surpass their expected production quotas. Job satisfaction is achieved by mastering the intricate and often devious and informal strategies workers use to "make out" under various production conditions. Burawoy claims that the games

workers play are not attempts to reduce job discontent or oppose management, because often lower-level management participates in the games and the enforcement of their rules. Playing the game creates consent among workers about the rules upon which workplace games are based – and, crucially, the arrangement of social relations (owners–managers–workers) that define the rules.

Moreover, because managers and workers are both involved in playing games, the numerous opposing interests that define the social relations between the two are obscured, ensuring that manager–worker conflict is kept to a minimum. Burawoy claims such methods of manufacturing and eliciting cooperation and consent are more effective than the coercive measures of early capitalism.

Burawoy's work is a seminal contribution to the sociology of industrial relations and has inspired follow-up studies, including those by British social thinkers Paul Blyton and Stephen Ackroyd, focusing on workplace resistance and coercion. ■

> "
> Conflict and consent are not primordial conditions but products of the organization of work.
> **Michael Burawoy**
> "

Michael Burawoy

Michael Burawoy is an Anglo-American Marxist sociologist at the University of California, Berkeley, USA. He obtained his first degree in 1968 in mathematics from the University of Cambridge, England, before going on to complete his doctorate in sociology at the University of Chicago, USA, in 1976.

Burawoy's academic career has changed direction and focus over time. His early work involved a number of ethnographic studies of industrial workplaces in the USA as well as in Hungary and post-Soviet Russia. In the latter part of his career he turned away from the factory floor to focus on raising the public profile of sociology by using sociological theories to address prominent social issues.

In 2010, in recognition of his considerable contribution to the discipline, and in particular to promoting sociology more widely to the general public, Burawoy was elected President of the International Sociological Association (ISA) at the XVII ISA World Congress of Sociology. He is editor of *Global Dialogue,* the magazine of the International Sociological Association.

Key works

1979 *Manufacturing Consent: Changes in the Labour Process Under Monopoly Capitalism*
1985 *The Politics of Production: Factory Regimes Under Capitalism and Socialism*
2010 *Marxism Meets Bourdieu*

THINGS MAKE US JUST AS MUCH AS WE MAKE THINGS
DANIEL MILLER (1954–)

Modern societies are **materialistic and consumerist**.

Consumerism is often perceived negatively – as a signifier of **wastefulness** and **superficiality**, for example.

But **material objects** and possessions can help **shape and strengthen** people's **self-identity** and their interactions and **relationships with others**.

Things make us just as much as we make things.

Sociologists, drawing on the pioneering work of Thorstein Veblen in the late 19th century, have traditionally conceived of consumer goods symbolically, as objects people acquire to communicate specific meanings to one another – for example, the type of lifestyle they lead and the amount of social status they possess.

However, British sociologist Daniel Miller in his book *Stuff*, published in 2010, points out that the myriad ways in which consumer goods inform personal identity, selfhood, and interactions with others have been understood primarily in negative terms. Consumerism is, he says, considered by the majority of commentators to be wasteful and bad; desiring consumer goods is thought to be superficial and morally reprehensible; and consumerism is alienating and socially divisive – it separates the "haves" from the "have-nots" and can lead to serious social problems, including theft.

Miller puts a very different slant on things by emphasizing the various positive ways in which material artefacts contribute to

See also: Karl Marx 28–31 ▪ Pierre Bourdieu 76–79 ▪ Herbert Marcuse 182–87 ▪ Thorstein Veblen 214–19 ▪ Colin Campbell 234–35 ▪ Theodor W Adorno 335

making us who we are and how they mediate in our relationships and interactions with others.

Rethinking the house

Miller gives the example of his own family home. The architectural style and physical design, he says, feed into and shape his identity in relation to the property, but they also affect the interactions with and between family members.

His property retains "many of the original features", including an oak staircase, fireplaces, and window surrounds. These physical and aesthetic features frame his experience of and relationship to the house, he says. For example, his predilection for furniture and design by the popular Swedish furnishing store IKEA creates a tension within him: he feels that his taste for the modern, clinical, and clean lines that are characteristic of this brand means that he has "demeaned" and betrayed the house, that it deserves someone with "better taste". To resolve this tension, he describes

how ongoing discussions with family members enable him to find a compromise with regard to furnishing and decoration.

Miller claims that he and his family imagine and relate to the house as though it were a family member, with a unique identity and its own needs. His argument here is that the materiality of the house is not necessarily oppressive, alienating, or divisive; on the contrary, it not only positively shapes the relationships of the family to it, but also facilitates interaction and increasing solidarity between family members.

A counterbalance

Miller's work is designed to provide an alternative to the accounts of consumerism given by Frankfurt School thinkers such as Herbert Marcuse and Theodor W Adorno, who read mass consumer culture as "symptomatic of a loss of depth in the world". At a time when the global economic and environmental crises have cast serious doubt over the

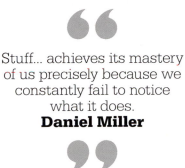

> Stuff... achieves its mastery of us precisely because we constantly fail to notice what it does.
> **Daniel Miller**

sustainability of a materialistic, consumer culture, Miller's work is thought by many, including sociologists Fernando Dominguez Rubio and Elizabeth B. Silva, to provide a provocative riposte to views that denigrate material culture in society. Miller's ideas are permeating sociological analysis and inform part of the increasing interest in the examination of material objects (the "materiality of cultural forms"), spearheaded by French sociologist Bruno Latour. ▪

Tight blue jeans are popular in Brazil because they are thought to enhance the natural curvature of a woman's buttocks.

The denim phenomenon

Since 2007, British sociologist Sophie Woodward, in collaboration with Miller and other sociologists, has been interested in blue denim as a phenomenon of consumerism. She suggests that despite being available everywhere, denim garments are often revered as highly personal items, with which their owners have an intimate relationship – a favourite denim jacket or pair of jeans, for example.

Drawing on ethnographic studies of denim jeans as fashion items throughout the world, Woodward has found that the appeal of denim is inextricably bound up with the cultural mores and frames of meaning specific to particular locales. In London, England, for example, blue jeans are often used by many different types of people to resolve anxieties about what to wear – their anonymity and ubiquity protect the wearer from negative judgement. In Brazil, however, jeans are often worn by women to emphasize their sensuality.

FEMINIZATION HAS HAD ONLY A MODEST IMPACT ON REDUCING GENDER INEQUALITIES

TERI LYNN CARAWAY

IN CONTEXT

FOCUS
The feminization of work

KEY DATES
From the 1960s The rise of globalization and industrialization in the developing world attracts the attention of feminist scholars of work.

1976 Michel Foucault's *The History of Sexuality, Volume I: An Introduction* claims that gender roles and relations are socially constructed discourses.

1986 Sylvia Walby publishes *Patriarchy at Work: Patriarchal and Capitalist Relations in Employment.*

1995 R W Connell's fluid conception of gender categories as things that are flexible and open to change is articulated in *Masculinities.*

More women are entering – and **feminizing** – the workforce.

Although globalization has helped to erode **men's domination of the economy**, the **unequal gender division of labour** persists.

Significant feminization of the industrialized economy can occur only if...

...**labour demand** outstrips the capacity of the male workforce available.

...women are more available for work due to better **access to higher education and childcare**.

...the trade unions either support the access of women or are **unable to exclude them** from "male" occupations.

See also: Karl Marx 28–31 ▪ Michel Foucault 52–55 ▪ R W Connell 88–89 ▪ Roland Robertson 146–49 ▪ Robert Blauner 232–33 ▪ Jeffrey Weeks 324–25

In recent decades, despite a big growth in the participation of women in the workforce in Southeast Asia, the gender division of labour has been redrawn rather than eliminated. US feminist and sociologist Teri Lynn Caraway studied industries in Indonesia in her book *Assembling Women: The Feminization of Global Manufacturing*. Building upon the work of Michel Foucault, she says that gender in the workplace is fluid and constantly renegotiated, and it is even influenced by the ideas of femininity and masculinity held by factory managers, who may determine machine operations that suit male or female workers.

Caraway rejects mainstream economic theory because it views individuals as rational and genderless, reflecting the male, middle-class characteristics of those who developed it. She also dismisses Marxist analyses because they prioritize social class over gender. Whereas the conventional wisdom is that employers pay women lower wages,

Female factory workers in Indonesia, like these garment workers in Sukoharjo, receive equal wages with men. According to Caraway's research, this is not the case in East Asia.

which has led to more women entering the global workforce, Caraway claims that this underestimates the power of gender in labour markets. Instead, ideas and practices about men and women providing distinct forms of labour – what she terms "gendered discourses" – play a key role in the feminization process.

Conditions for feminization

Caraway says three conditions are necessary for the feminization of industrial labour to occur. First, when demand for labour exceeds supply (for example, when there are insufficient male workers), industry turns to women. Second, only when family planning and mass education are available can women enter the workforce. And third, work for women becomes possible when barriers such as trade unions – which protect male-dominated workplaces from being undermined by cheap female labour – are no longer effective. In Indonesia this happened when the state weakened Islamist organizations and trade unions, both of which are potential opponents of female labour.

Caraway notes the general assumption that some employers pay more to men because they perceive their work to be superior, while others consider women to be unreliable in the long-term (due to motherhood or marriage). In fact, Caraway argues, both are examples of complex "gendered cost benefit analysis"; how female workers are perceived and treated, and therefore why women are seen as better for certain types of labour, can be explained by wider cultural ideals, values, and beliefs about gender roles within a society. ▪

Globalization and gender wellbeing

The economic changes created by globalization and the new, flexible requirements of labour markets are thought to benefit women. Although feminization "opens the door of job opportunity to women", as Teri Lynn Caraway puts it, the outcome is mixed. Caraway, Sylvia Walby, and Valentine Moghadam have all shown that female workers are far more likely to suffer ill health. Moreover, women's disproportionate burden of domestic work means that employment outside the home places greater strain on them.

German sociologist Christa Wichterich argues, in *The Globalized Woman* (2007), that rather than liberating women into the workplace, globalization has bred a new underclass. She shows how, from Phnom Penh to New York, women's lives have been devastated by having to respond to the demands of transnational corporations, surviving in low-paid employment, and coping with the erosion of public services.

> " Employers feminize their workforces only if they imagine women are more productive than men.
> **Teri Lynn Caraway**

Karl Marx says religion is **"the sigh of the oppressed creature**... the opium of the people" in his essay "A Contribution to the Critique of Hegel's Philosophy of Right".

Max Weber explains the process of **secularization and rationalization** of modern society in *The Protestant Ethic and the Spirit of Capitalism*.

Antonio Gramsci uses the term **"hegemony"** to explain how the views of the dominant class become seen by the rest of society as **"common sense"** and indisputable.

In *Asylums*, Erving Goffman describes how **"total institutions"** reorder people's **personalities and identities**.

1844　　　　**1904–05**　　　　**1930s**　　　　**1961**

1897　　　　**1911**　　　　**1949**　　　　**1963**

In *Suicide*, Émile Durkheim introduces the idea of **"anomie"** to account for differing suicide rates, revealing this personal act as a social phenomenon.

In *Political Parties*, Robert Michels argues that bureaucracies render **democratic government impossible to achieve**.

In *Social Theory and Social Structure*, Robert K Merton proposes that **"anomie"** is at **the root of deviant behaviour**.

In *Outsiders*, Howard S Becker suggests that **any behaviour can be considered deviant** if society labels it as such.

For centuries, the dominant institutions in Europe were the Church and the ruling class of monarchs and aristocrats. It was not until the Renaissance that the authority of the Church was challenged by humanist ideas and scientific discovery, and republican democracy began to threaten claims of a God-given, inherited right to rule. The age of Enlightenment thought further weakened these institutions, and in the 18th century the old order was overturned with political revolutions in the USA and France, and an Industrial Revolution spreading from Britain.

Secularism and rationalism

A recognizably modern society rapidly emerged, which was shaped by the rational ideas of the Enlightenment and the economic demands of industry. The social cohesion based on community values and shared beliefs gave way to new secular institutions, and government of society was transferred to representatives of the people. Together with this secularization came a rationalization suited to the increasingly material nature of modern society. Industrialization, and the capitalism that grew from it, required a much greater degree of administration, and the idea of bureaucracy spread from the sphere of commerce to government too.

The institutions of modern society evolved from these bureaucracies: financial and business institutions, government departments, hospitals, education, the media, the police, armed forces, and so on. The new institutions formed a prominent part of the social structure of modern society, and sociologists have sought to identify the roles they play in creating and maintaining social order.

Bureaucracies, however, are organized for efficiency and consequently tend to follow a hierarchical structure. As Robert Michels pointed out, this leads to their being ruled by a small elite, an oligarchy, which far from helping to promote democratic government actively prevents it. As a result, people feel as much under the control of the new institutions as they did under religious and monarchical rule. Michel Foucault later examined the nature of the (often unnoticed) power of institutions to shape society and

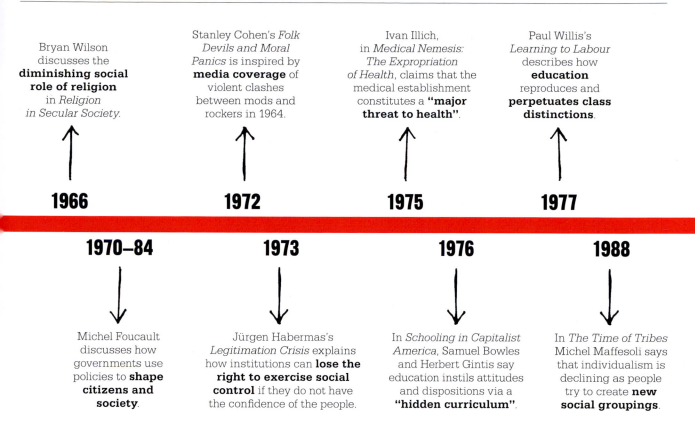

Bryan Wilson discusses the **diminishing social role of religion** in *Religion in Secular Society*.

Stanley Cohen's *Folk Devils and Moral Panics* is inspired by **media coverage** of violent clashes between mods and rockers in 1964.

Ivan Illich, in *Medical Nemesis: The Expropriation of Health*, claims that the medical establishment constitutes a **"major threat to health"**.

Paul Willis's *Learning to Labour* describes how **education** reproduces and **perpetuates class distinctions**.

1966

1972

1975

1977

1970–84

1973

1976

1988

Michel Foucault discusses how governments use policies to **shape citizens and society**.

Jürgen Habermas's *Legitimation Crisis* explains how institutions can **lose the right to exercise social control** if they do not have the confidence of the people.

In *Schooling in Capitalist America*, Samuel Bowles and Herbert Gintis say education instils attitudes and dispositions via a **"hidden curriculum"**.

In *The Time of Tribes* Michel Maffesoli says that individualism is declining as people try to create **new social groupings**.

the behaviour of its individual citizens – imposing social norms, and stifling individuality. Jürgen Habermas was similarly critical of institutional power, but argued that this can only be wielded so long as the institutions are trusted by the people. More recently (and controversially), Michel Maffesoli has suggested that as people become disillusioned with institutions, they form new social groupings along tribal lines, with corresponding new institutions.

The social influence of religious institutions, described famously by Karl Marx as "the opium of the people", declined with the growth of bureaucracies, and during the 20th century most states had (at least nominally) a form of secular government. Nevertheless, today some 75 per cent of the world's population still identify themselves as belonging to a recognized faith community, and in many places religion is increasingly becoming a social force.

Individualism and society

As well as studying the nature and scope of institutions in society, sociologists in the latter part of the 20th century have taken a more interpretive approach, examining the effects of these institutions on the individual members of society. Max Weber had warned of the stultifying effects of bureaucracy, trapping people in the "iron cage" of rationalization, and later Erving Goffman described the effects of institutionalization, when individuals have become so used to living with an institution they can no longer do without it. A particular example of this is our increasing reliance on medicine as a means of curing all ills, as described by Ivan Illich. Education, too, came under scrutiny as an institutional means of fostering social attitudes and maintaining a desired social order.

But it was Émile Durkheim who recognized the conflict between individualism and institutional expectations of conformity. His concept of "anomie", a mismatch between an individual's beliefs and desires and those of society, was taken up by Robert K Merton in his explanation of what was considered deviant behaviour. Howard S Becker developed this further, suggesting that any behaviour could be considered deviant if an institution labels it as such, and, according to Stanley Cohen, the modern media demonizes things in just this way. ■

RELIGION
IS THE SIGH OF THE
OPPRESSED
CREATURE

KARL MARX (1818–1883)

IN CONTEXT

FOCUS
Religion

KEY DATES
1807 German philosopher Georg Hegel's work *The Phenomenology of Spirit* introduces the concept of alienation.

1841 *The Essence of Christianity* by German philosopher Ludwig Feuerbach draws on Hegel's idea of alienation and applies it critically to Christianity.

1966 Religion has lost its authority, according to British sociologist Bryan Wilson in *Religion in Secular Society*.

2010 German sociologist Jürgen Habermas, in *An Awareness of What is Missing: Faith and Reason in a Post-Secular Age*, muses on why religion has failed to disappear.

Economic hardship prevents most people from achieving **comfort** and true **happiness** in this world.

Religion distorts this reality and encourages people to **work hard**, passively **accept their lot**, and **endure suffering**.

Religion provides **false hopes** and says that true happiness can only be attained in the heavenly **afterlife**.

Although it provides solace, religion is the sigh of the oppressed creature, the heart of a heartless world.

According to the German philosopher Georg Hegel, liberty in a full sense consists of participation in certain ethical institutions. More infamously, he also said that only in the state "does man have rational existence". He believed that Christianity was the perfect ("consummate") religion for the emerging age of modernity because it reflected its spirit or *geist* – faith in reason and truth. However, because of the process of contradiction known as "dialectic" (in which, by its own nature, something can contain its

opposite), the social structures and institutions that people create to serve them can instead come to control and even enslave them. The process of rational self-discovery can lead to "alienation" – a concept of estrangement that went on to have a profound influence on the social sciences.

Ludwig Feuerbach, a German philosopher and former student of Hegel's, used the concept of alienation to criticize religion. Feuerbach argues that people endow God with human qualities and then worship him for those

qualities, so they unconsciously worship themselves. This prevents them from fully realizing their own potential; the divine is no more than a projection of alienated human consciousness. Karl Marx's collaborator, Friedrich Engels, acknowledged that Feuerbach's *The Essence of Christianity* had a profoundly liberating effect on them both in the 1840s.

Man makes religion

Karl Marx's father had converted from Judaism to Christianity merely to ensure his job security,

See also: Auguste Comte 22–25 ▪ Karl Marx 28–31 ▪ Friedrich Engels 66–67 ▪ Sylvia Walby 96–99 ▪ Max Weber 220–23 ▪ Bryan Wilson 278–79 ▪ Jürgen Habermas 286–87

> Religion is used by those in temporal charge to invest themselves with authority.
> **Christopher Hitchens**
> British-US writer (1949–2011)

and yet he instilled in his son a belief that religion is necessary for morality. However, from a relatively young age Karl Marx criticized the idea that a spiritual realm was needed to maintain social order. He later became convinced that secularization (decline in the social significance of religion) will liberate people from mystical forms of social oppression. He outlined many of his ideas about religion in "A Contribution to the Critique of Hegel's Philosophy of Right" (1844).

Expanding upon the idea of alienation, Marx argues that "man makes religion, religion does not make man". People, he says, have forgotten that they invented God, who has come to have a life of his own and now controls the people. What people have created, they can destroy. The revolutionary working class, he believes, will realize that the ideologies and institutions of capitalist society, which enslave

The wealth of the Catholic Church
has been criticized by many. For Marx, religion serves capitalist interests and is a tool used by wealthy elites to control and oppress the working class.

them, are not natural or inevitable but can be overthrown. Until then, religion will remain as a symptom of the disease caused by material deprivation and human alienation, which creates such pain for its sufferers that they need the solace provided by religion.

Like the French philosopher Auguste Comte, for whom religious belief is an infantile state of reason, Marx believes in society progressing scientifically towards secularism. However, Marx is more critical of religion as a reflection of society, rather than as a set of beliefs. His goal is to liberate the working class from the oppression of capitalism, and he argues that the ideas of the ruling class are those dominating society – and one of the apparatuses transmitting those ideas is the Church.

The Church and the state
In 18th-century England, an unknown wit described the Church of England as a political party "at prayer". For Marx, any institution

that serves capitalist interests, including religion, has to be contested, and ultimately done away with. The replacement will be a humanist society based on socialism and communism.

According to Marx, religion is "consolation and justification" for the existing state and society. Churches proclaim that the authority of the ruling class is ordained by supernatural authority, thus the lowly position of the workers is inevitable and just. When a society is riven by inequality, injustice is perpetuated rather than eased. Marx declared: "The struggle against religion is, therefore, indirectly the struggle against that world whose spiritual aroma is religion." This sentiment was echoed in the 1960s by British sociologist Bryan Wilson, who claims that the role of the Church is to socialize each new generation into accepting their lot.

Marx aims to expose the illusory nature of religion and reveal it as an ideological tool of the »

Marx argues that religion is a belief system that enables the ruling class to maintain power in the present by promising the working class that things will be better in the hereafter. The poor find solace in moral teachings because, ultimately, they will reap a reward for their suffering; social change is averted because religion stabilizes society and upholds the status quo.

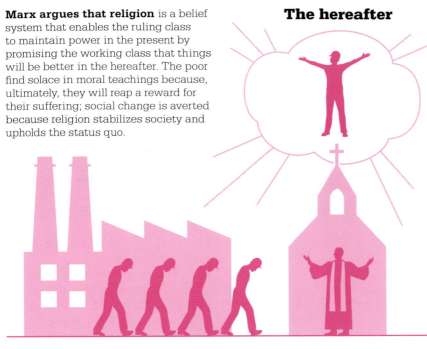

The hereafter

The here and now

ruling class. Because a belief in the hereafter serves as a comfort to the poor and the oppressed, Marx described religion as "the opium of the people". Russian revolutionary Vladimir Ilyich Lenin said it is "spiritual gin": religion deadens the harsh realities of working-class life, and through it people are drugged into accepting their lowly positions in return for a better afterlife. In effect, religion can be understood as a potent form of social control that keeps the poor in their place and obstructs social change.

Religion and radicalism

Marx does not overlook the fact that Christianity is a religion that grew out of oppression, and that it has sustained and comforted those who are miserable and without hope. Religious suffering is both an "expression of real suffering and a protest against real suffering" – it is the "sigh" of oppressed people,

which suggests that religion has a radical or potentially revolutionary aspect. In 17th-century England, for example, Puritanism led to the execution of a king and the establishment of a republic. However, Marx says that religion is the "*illusory* happiness of

the people" when the situation demands their *real* happiness: "To call on them to give up their illusions about their condition is to call on them to give up a condition that requires illusions." The task of history and philosophy, he declares, is "to unmask self-estrangement in its unholy forms once the holy form of human self-estrangement has been unmasked".

Marx agreed with German sociologist Max Weber's premise that Protestantism had played a big role in establishing capitalism because it better satisfied the commercial needs of 16th-century merchants and later industrialists. Hard work accompanied by reward was at the heart of Protestant philosophy, and Calvinists in particular looked upon material success as a sign of God's favour.

Marx describes the Reformation as Germany's revolutionary past – a revolution that began in the brain of a monk, as he puts it. Luther, he says, "overcame bondage out of *devotion* by replacing it with bondage out of *conviction*"; Luther turned priests into laymen because he turned laymen into priests. In Marx's view, Protestantism did

Feminism and religion

Elizabeth Cady Stanton, 19th-century US author of *The Woman's Bible*, said the Word of God was actually that of a man and was used to subjugate women. Feminist theories of religion since then have generally echoed this theme of sexism and gender inequality.

Women tend to participate more than men in religious observation, but they are usually marginalized and discriminated against, with fewer rights and heavier punishments. Egyptian

writer Nawal El Saadawi says religion may be used to oppress women, but the cause is patriarchal forms of society, which has reshaped religion. Many Muslim women use their religion and dress to symbolize their liberation, notes British sociologist Linda Woodhead.

Within some religions, the position of women is changing significantly; since the Church of England permitted female ordination in 1992, women now make up one in five of the clergy.

not offer the true solution to the problem, but it did provide a "true setting" whereby a man's struggle was now no longer against the clergy outside but the "priestly nature" inside himself.

Meanwhile, the social status quo presented a further obstacle to real human emancipation. Whereas the landowners and capitalists became richer in this world, the reward for the working class for toiling long hours for little pay was a place in heaven; suffering is made into a virtue. Marx is concerned by the role of the Church as a landowner and employer in the 19th century and sees this as further evidence that religion is one more ideological tool used by the ruling classes to control the workers.

An irreligious workforce

In Britain, the establishment feared that working people were losing touch with organized religion and turning instead to other Christian religious groups or working-class political movements, such as Chartism. For this reason, a Census of Religious Worship was carried out in 1851. This revealed working-class apathy as well as a divide in society between the conservative, established Church of England and the meeting houses and chapels where followers of newer, popular religions, such as Quakerism and Unitarianism, gathered.

Methodism – a Protestant denomination focused on helping the poor – was extremely popular in many working-class areas in the manufacturing centres of Britain.

Christian groups like the Quakers were perceived as a threat to the religious-political status quo. Opposed to war and slavery, and refusing to swear oaths to others, they rejected the idea of hierarchies in the Church.

> The roots of modern religion are deeply embedded in the social oppression of the working masses.
> **Vladimir Ilyich Lenin**
> **Russian political theorist (1870–1924)**

It also attracted the new factory owners, who were both perturbed by the apparently irreligious nature of their workers and shocked by their vices, such as drunkenness. Offering Marxists further evidence of religion being used as an ideological tool by the ruling classes, some owners coerced workers into attending services, Bible study classes, educational talks, and hobbies in an attempt to "educate" them into a "decent", sober, existence – one that would enable them to work more efficiently. Divesting them of energy

in this way also thwarted their revolutionary potential and ensured they became the compliant workhorses of industry.

Western intellectuals such as A C Grayling, the late Christopher Hitchens, and Richard Dawkins, sometimes branded the "New Atheists", share many of Marx's sentiments about religion. Namely that, as arguably the first attempt at philosophy, religion is interesting but is a form of alienation, both emotional and intellectual, and a poor substitute for social justice and happiness. However, Marx himself – in his observations about the Reformation – acknowledged religion's potential for radical thought and social action. The part that Nonconformist religions played in Britain during more than a century of progressive social reform later demonstrated this. In seeking an answer as to why religion has not faded away by the 21st century, Jürgen Habermas acknowledges the important public role played by religious communities in many parts of the world. Today, in spite of widespread secularization, no one speaks of the extinction of religions or the religious. ∎

THE IRON LAW OF OLIGARCHY
ROBERT MICHELS (1876–1936)

IN CONTEXT

FOCUS
Oligarchy

KEY DATES
1904–05 Max Weber's *The Protestant Ethic and the Spirit of Capitalism* sees the rationalization that results from bureaucracy as an inevitable feature of modernity.

1911 In *Political Parties*, German social and political theorist Robert Michels contends that organizational democracy is an impossibility.

1916 Italian sociologist Vilfredo Pareto argues that democracy is an illusion; the elite will always serve itself.

2009 The launch of the Chilcot Inquiry in the UK into the 2003 invasion of Iraq shows the extent to which officials, such as ex-Prime Minister Tony Blair, are protected from being publicly accountable for their actions. Many argue that Blair should be tried for war crimes.

Bureaucracy is an enemy of individual liberty, according to Robert Michels. In the early 20th century he pointed out the link between bureaucracy and political oligarchy (the rule of the many by the few). In his observations of political parties and unions, he saw that the size and complexity of democracies require hierarchy. A leadership, with a clear chain of command, and separate from the masses, is needed – resulting in a pyramid-like structure that places a few leaders in charge of vast and powerful organizations.

Michels applies Max Weber's idea that a hierarchy of responsibility increases efficiency, but argues that this concentrates power and endangers democracy. The interests of the elites of organizations, rather than the needs of the people, become the key focus, despite professed democratic ideals. Michels stresses that the self-interest of those at the top of organizations always comes to the fore.

Keeping their positions of power becomes an important role of bureaucracies such as political parties; and maintaining an air of mystery and superiority through complex voting systems, use of arcane language, and sub-committees helps to ensure this. Officials tend to be well insulated from the consequences of their decisions – bureaucracy protects them against public accountability. Oligarchy thrives in the hierarchical structure of bureaucracy and frequently undermines people's control over their elected leaders. ∎

> Who says organization, says oligarchy.
> **Robert Michels**

See also: Karl Marx 28–31 ▪ Max Weber 38–45 ▪ Friedrich Engels 66–67 ▪ Michel Foucault 270–77 ▪ Jürgen Habermas 286–87

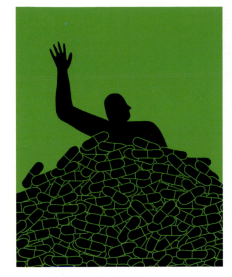

HEALTHY PEOPLE NEED NO BUREAUCRACY TO MATE, GIVE BIRTH, AND DIE
IVAN ILLICH (1926–2002)

Society has become acutely
aware of the dangers posed
by medicine. Over-use of
diagnostic x-rays in pregnancy,
which can lead to childhood
cancers, and harmful prescription-
drug interactions are examples.
The Greek word "iatrogenesis" –
"brought forth by a healer" – is used
to describe such problems. Radical
Austrian thinker Ivan Illich argues
that the medical establishment has
become a serious threat to human
life because, in conjunction with
capitalism, it is an institution
that serves itself and makes more
people sick than it heals.

Illich suggests there are three
main types of iatrogenesis. Clinical
iatrogenesis is when a harm arises
that would not have occured
without medical intervention;
less resistance to bacteria from
the over-prescription of antibiotics,
for example. Social iaotragenesis
is the medicalization of life: more
and more problems are seen as
amenable to medical intervention,
with expensive treatments being
developed for non-diseases. Minor

Hospital births, uncommon before
the 20th century, are cited by some
as an example of social iatrogenesis
– the increasing, and unncecessary,
medicalization of life.

depression is, for example, often
treated with habit-forming drugs.
The agencies involved, such as
drug companies, have a vested
interest in treating people this way.

Even worse, for Illich, is cultural
iatrogenesis – the destruction of
traditional ways of coping with
illness, pain, and death. The over-
medicalization of our lives means
that we have become increasingly
unwilling to face the realities of
death and disease: doctors have
assumed the role of priests. ∎

See also: George Ritzer 120–23 ▪ Robert Putnam 124–25 ▪ Ulrich Beck 156–61 ▪
Erving Goffman 264–69 ▪ Michel Foucault 270–77; 302–03

SOME COMMIT CRIMES BECAUSE THEY ARE RESPONDING TO A SOCIAL SITUATION

ROBERT K MERTON (1910–2003)

IN CONTEXT

FOCUS
Anomie or strain theory

KEY DATES
1897 In *Suicide*, Émile Durkheim uses the concept of anomie to account for differing suicide rates among Protestants and Catholics.

1955 US criminologist Albert Cohen, a former student of Talcott Parsons, says the disadvantages faced by lower-class men cause status frustration, or strain, leading to delinquency, which is seen as a way to command respect.

1983 British criminologist Steven Box says some accounts of delinquency, such as those of Albert Cohen, fail to explain the crimes of the powerful in society.

1992 US sociologist Robert Agnew insists that anomie, or strain theory, can be used to explain crime and deviancy but should not be tied to class.

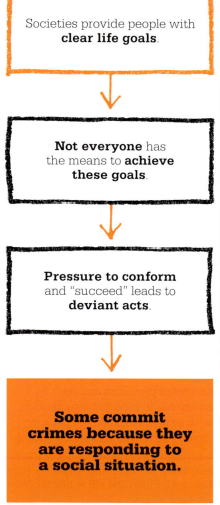

Societies provide people with **clear life goals**.

Not everyone has the means to **achieve these goals**.

Pressure to conform and "succeed" leads to **deviant acts**.

Some commit crimes because they are responding to a social situation.

Deviance is universal, normal, and functional, according to French theorist Émile Durkheim. He argues that when people no longer feel integrated into society and are unsure of its norms and rules – for example, during times of rapid social change – they are more likely to turn to deviant acts or suicide. This condition is known as *anomie*, a Greek word meaning "without law". In his article "Social Structure and Anomie", published in 1938, US sociologist Robert K Merton adapts Durkheim's analysis of deviance, applying it to contemporary US society and arguing that such behaviour occurs as a direct result of strain.

The American Dream

Merton suggests that the ideals and aspirations connected with individual "success" in the USA – the "American Dream" of, for example, material prosperity, and home and car ownership – are socially produced. Not everyone can achieve these goals through legitimate means because certain constraints, such as social class, act as barriers to achieving them. According to Merton, deviance

See also: Richard Sennett 84–87 ■ Robert D Putnam 124–25 ■
Max Weber 220–23 ■ Howard S Becker 280–85 ■ Talcott Parsons 300–01

The American Dream of leading a charmed life, owning a home and a car, and accumulating wealth is a fantasy for many, especially those caught in the clutches of poverty and unemployment.

(which is also socially constructed) is likely to occur when there is an obvious tension or discrepancy between social expectations and the ability or desire to attain them. This "strain theory", for Merton, explains the direct correlation between unemployment and crime: for example, a lack of money means that the legal routes to buying a car, a house, or other items are not accessible, but the pressure to conform to what is expected can lead people to theft.

Rebel or conformist?

Merton extends his theory by dividing people into five categories according to their relationship to culturally accepted goals and the means of achieving them. "Conformists", he suggests, have invested in the American Dream and, through the accepted routes of education and gainful employment, are able to attain it. "Ritualists" do not aspire to society's cultural goals, but nevertheless respect the recognized means of achieving them. They may, for example, go to work every day and perform their duties conscientiously, but they do not attempt to climb the corporate ladder to "success".

"Innovators" (often seen as criminals) are those who believe in the goals of society but choose less legitimate and traditional means to achieve them. "Retreatists" are society's dropouts – they reject not only conventional goals but also the traditional means of attaining them. Finally, "Rebels" are similar to Retreatists, but they create alternative goals and means of achieving them and seek to advance a counterculture. It is this group (which often includes terrorists and revolutionaries) that, according to Merton, can effect social change.

Merton's strain theory has been criticized for focusing on individual deviance at the expense of group or gang behaviour. It is also argued that the theory relies too heavily on official crime statistics, which often obscure middle-class crime. ■

Robert K Merton

Robert K Merton was born as Meyer R Schkolnick in 1910 in Philadelphia, USA. His parents were working-class Russian-Jewish immigrants; the first few years of his life were spent living above their dairy shop (which later burnt down). He adopted the stage name Robert Merlin at the age of 14 as part of his magician act, but changed it to Robert K Merton when he won a scholarship to Temple University.

Merton is credited with coining the phrases "self-fulfilling prophecy" and "role models", and is said to have pioneered the focus-group research method. He was elected president of the American Sociological Association in 1957.

Key works

1938 "Social Structure and Anomie"
1949 *Social Theory and Social Structure*
1985 *On the Shoulder of Giants: A Shandean Postscript*

> Anti-social behaviour is... 'called forth' by... differential access to the approved opportunities for legitimate... pursuit of... cultural goals.
> **Robert K Merton**

TOTAL INSTITUTIONS STRIP PEOPLE OF THEIR SUPPORT SYSTEMS AND THEIR SENSE OF SELF

ERVING GOFFMAN (1922–1982)

situation. In such places, the inmates can create new currencies – for example, bargaining with tobacco or sweets – or develop particular ways of communicating through a creative use of language. Some may try to maintain a defiant feeling of independence by discreetly urinating on a radiator, which will evaporate any signs of misbehaviour, rather than ask for permission to go to the toilet. Institutions will often turn a blind eye to such relatively minor indiscretions in the knowledge that these keep the inmate tractable for the most part.

Not everyone is successfully socialized into the norms of "total institutions". Although Goffman does not focus in detail on this, some inmates may retain a spirit of resistance and rebel by sabotaging the plumbing, organizing mass refusal of particular foods, riots, or even arranging for a member of staff to have "an accident".

Self-serving institutions

Despite writing in a cool, detached tone, Goffman has been accused by some of over-identifying with the patients he observed. Others, such

as the US sociologist and criminologist John Irwin, have suggested Goffman's study was a little narrow in its focus and was limited by only observing inmates while in the institution.

Nevertheless, in seeing "total institutions" as places that, rather than operating in the best interest of inmates, effectively dehumanize them, Goffman's work has been cited as precipitating changes in the treatment of mental health patients. He lays bare the ways in which "total institutions" are self-legitimatizing organizations – through defining their goals they legitimate their activity, which in turn legitimates the measures they take to meet those goals.

His work is also important for the sociology of identity because of his claims that names, possessions, and clothes are symbols imbued with meaning and importance for identity formation. He highlights the clear gap between officially imposed definitions of the self and the self that the individual seeks to present.

Goffman's studies remain of social relevance. Despite the fact that, in Britain, many mental health

One Flew Over the Cuckoo's Nest, a novel by Ken Kesey, is set in an asylum. It deals with patients adopting coping strategies, and how institutions crush challenges to their authority.

facilities have been closed from the 1960s onwards as part of a process of deinstitutionalization in favour of domiciled ("in the community") care, a significant proportion of people will still end their days in an institution. An ageing population means that many citizens may be unable to live independent lives and therefore have to spend time in nursing or care homes, which can exhibit some of the negative hallmarks of "total institutions". ∎

US city jails confine those arrested but not yet charged or convicted. It is argued such institutions expose normal citizens to inmate culture.

A crisis of incarceration

John Keith Irwin had a different kind of first-hand experience of a "total institution" than Goffman: in 1952, he served five years in prison for robbery. He used that time to study and later gained a PhD in Sociology, becoming an expert in the US prison system and the forms of social control demanded by society.

Based on his own insight and interviews with prisoners, Irwin wrote *The Jail: Managing the Underclass in American Society* (1985), which he dedicated to

Erving Goffman. He argued that city jails, which confine those arrested but not yet charged or convicted, degrade and dehumanize people. Rather than controlling the disreputable, they indoctrinate inmates into particular ways of behaving.

He claims that these jails are designed to manage the "underclass", or "rabble", who are seen as threatening middle-class values. The jails are perceived to be holding-tanks for petty thieves, addicts, and sexual nonconformists, which confirms their outsider status.

GOVERNMENT IS THE RIGHT DISPOSITION OF THINGS

MICHEL FOUCAULT (1926–1984)

IN CONTEXT

FOCUS
Governmentality

KEY DATES
1513 In *The Prince*, Florentine political theorist Niccolò Machiavelli offers advice on how to maintain power.

1567 French writer Guillaume de la Perrière argues in *Le Miroir Politique* that the word "governor" can apply to a broad array of people and groups.

1979 Michel Foucault publishes an article entitled "On Governmentality".

1996 British sociologist Nikolas Rose examines how institutions such as prisons and schools shape the behaviour of citizens.

2002 German sociologist Thomas Lemke applies Foucault's concept of governmentality to modern day neo-liberal societies.

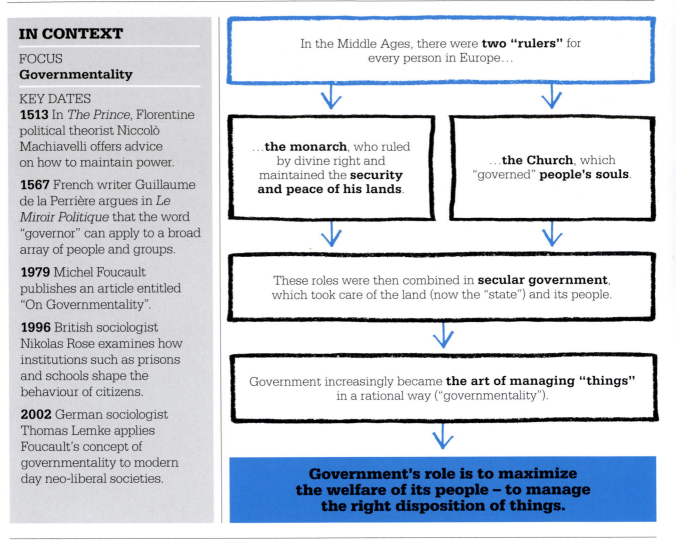

In the Middle Ages, there were **two "rulers"** for every person in Europe…

…**the monarch**, who ruled by divine right and maintained the **security and peace of his lands**.

…**the Church**, which "governed" **people's souls**.

These roles were then combined in **secular government**, which took care of the land (now the "state") and its people.

Government increasingly became **the art of managing "things"** in a rational way ("governmentality").

Government's role is to maximize the welfare of its people – to manage the right disposition of things.

Throughout history, people have been concerned with the nature of government, where and how it is needed, and the question of who has the right to govern other people. French philosopher Michel Foucault focused his study on the workings of power, and became particularly interested in the processes and legitimacy of government in Western Europe from the 16th to 20th centuries.

As a professor at the prestigious Collège de France in Paris between 1970 and 1975, Foucault delivered a series of lectures that became a prominent feature of intellectual life in the city. One of these lectures was later published in the influential journal *Ideology and Consciousness* in 1979, under the title "On Governmentality". In this work, Foucault argues that it is impossible to study the formation of power without also looking at the practices – the techniques and rationality – through which people are governed. This rationality is not an absolute that can be reached by pure reason, as most philosophers have suggested,

but a changing thing that depends on both time and place. What is "rational" in one space and time may be thought irrational in others. To summarize this concept, Foucault joined the French words "governeur" (governor) and "mentalité" (mentality) to create a new term – governmentality – to describe the way that a government thinks about itself and its role (its "rationality").

Foucault's approach to philosophical analysis focuses on the "genealogy of the subject". So rather than relying on the

See also: Michel Foucault 52–55; 302–03 ▪ David McCrone 163 ▪ Norbert Elias 180–81 ▪ Max Weber 220–23 ▪ Robert Michels 260

traditional approach to enquiry, where philosophers look for the universal and invariant foundations of knowledge, Foucault looks at how a subject is constituted across history, and how this leads to its modern appearance.

Foucault's series of lectures on governmentality examined the ways in which the modern idea of an autonomous, individual self developed in concert with the idea of the nation-state. He was particularly interested in seeing how these two concepts co-determined each other's existence, and changed with the political rationality of the time.

Medieval governance

Foucault's investigations trace the shifts in ways of governing that have taken place in different eras and places. Looking back to Europe in the Middle Ages (c.500–1500), he says that the modern nation-state as we know it did not exist; nor did governmentality. People lived in a "state of justice" that imposed blunt laws and customs, such as putting

I wanted to study the art of governing, that is to say, the reasoned way of governing best and, at the same time, reflection on the best possible way of governing.
Michel Foucault

offenders in the stocks, in order to integrate people into their community. This was the age of feudalism, when monarchs, who were seen as God's divine representatives on Earth, relied on various lords to keep the local people under control. The network of lords with allegiance to a king offered a way of maintaining order across large areas of land.

The lords earned their titles, castles, and land rights by providing military service and support to the monarch. Eventually these privileges became hereditary. Peasant farmers, or serfs, were obliged to work the land, making large profits for their rulers. Such a system, in which there was a very clear and obvious exercise of power by individuals, meant that there was little sense of coherent governance: the various nobles often ruled in very different ways. Conflict and internal warfare were also common. Monarchs' subjects did not think of themselves as bound to a national identity but instead were tied to their locality and aligned to their feudal lord.

Peasant farmers worked on the land during the Middle Ages making vast profits for their lords. Feudal systems imposed control on people, rather than coherent government.

A new way to govern

According to Foucault, the question of governing became a far greater problem in the 16th century when medieval feudalism fell into decline. As the ideas of empire and territorial expansion began to take hold, the question of how to govern the individual, the family, and the state became a central issue. Governmentality was born.

The break with the feudal system also led to a rise in conflict between states. As a result, it became increasingly important that a state knew both its own capacity and strength and the strength of its rivals. Foucault claims this is why the phenomenon of the "police" emerged in the 16th century. These forces not only provided the government with security but were also able to measure and assess the strength of the state. The police enabled the easy governance of »

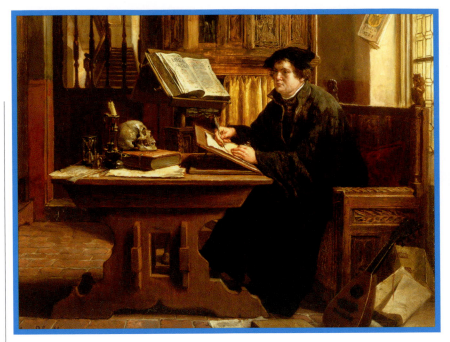

German priest Martin Luther led the Protestant Reformation, which challenged the power of the Catholic Church and, argues Foucault, marked the beginning of a shift in governance.

citizens, ensuring that individuals under surveillance remain productive and compliant.

The 16th century also saw a significant shift in religious practice in Europe. The Protestant Reformation, which began in 1517, was a major challenge to the Catholic Church and its power. According to Foucault, the conflict that took place between the Protestant and Catholic Churches, together with the rise of territorial states, led early modern theorists of government to combine two very differing ways of thinking. Theologians had always approached governance from a spiritual perspective: the pastoral leader's ultimate duty was to save souls by watching over his "flock" as a shepherd would guard his sheep. Secular statesmen had approached the art of government in much more worldly terms – seeing their role as managing conflict, protecting the territory, and securing peace. These two ways of thinking, Foucault argues, came together to form a new hybrid art of governance in the late 16th and 17th centuries.

Death of the prince
For the first time, it seemed possible that the citizens and their rulers could be brought together in a system that was mutually beneficial. The personal interest of the rulers was no longer the sole guiding principle for ruling; with this shift, the idea of "ruling" was transformed into "governing". Foucault traces the shift from a sovereign notion of power to

government as an efficient mode of operation through an examination of the political treatise *The Prince* (1513), by Florentine diplomat Niccolò Machiavelli. In this short work, the prince is seen as being fundamentally concerned with maintaining and expanding his territories; his subjects living on those lands are of little interest or consequence, as long as they are behaving themselves. The prince remains morally detached from his territory – he owes no one any obligation or debt. This is the way of thinking that came to an end as monarchs lost their sovereign rights, the Churches lost power, and new technologies (such as the printing press) allowed for the spread of revolutionary ideas.

From the late Middle Ages to the 17th century, the Renaissance ushered in a return to Classical ideas of freedom and democracy, followed by more revolutionary thinking that threatened the physical safety of monarchs as well as their right to rule. In England, for

example, King Charles I's belief that he had a divine right to rule brought him into armed conflict with parliamentary forces in the English Civil War. Charles was tried, convicted of high treason, and executed in 1649.

Benevolent government?
Foucault highlights French Renaissance writer Guillaume de la Perriere's 1567 definition of government, which was significant because of its lack of reference to "territory". Instead, government was described here as the correct disposition of things, organized to lead to a convenient end. Under an ideology of benevolence, the responsibilities of governments were expanded to include the welfare of their citizens, although in reality, this form of governance was really concerned with managing people's lives – and the material products of their efforts – in order to maximize the nation's strength. Ensuring the growth of wealth was seen as crucial in governing, but it

was also important to have a healthy populace that would multiply if the government wanted to secure long-term prosperity and productivity. Foucault says that from this point onwards, "men and things" (the relation people have to wealth, the environment, famine, fertility, the climate, and so on), rather than territories, needed to be administered in an efficient way. Governance was now an "art".

Citizen or subject?

Foucault contends that early liberal ideas of civil society, as espoused by John Locke and Adam Ferguson in the 18th century, made a social government possible. The liberal art of government has as its organizational principle "the rationale of least government"; in other words, it advocates less state intervention and an increased focus on the role of the population. At this time the concept of a "population" and its centrality to the success of the state became paramount, and led to the idea of "an individual member of the population" as a living, working, and social being. The new idea of an autonomous individual was to lead to many new

political questions, including the rights and responsibilities of the individual and the state. In what ways can an individual be free, if he or she is governed by the state? The link between the "autonomous" individual's self-control and political control became an important issue, as did the possibility of domination and economic exploitation.

In examining this period, Foucault revisited his work on "passive bodies". In *Discipline and Punish*, he had traced how the body was seen as a target (to be used and improved) by those in power during the 17th and 18th centuries. He also examined how techniques of surveillance drawn from monasteries and the army were used to control people's bodies and produce passive subjects who were incapable of revolt.

In this earlier work, Foucault maintained that discipline creates docility, but when focusing on governmentality, he began to think this placed too much emphasis on domination and was too simplistic an argument. Individuals, he now said, have more opportunities to modify and construct themselves than he had thought previously.

Let us not... ask... why certain people want to dominate... Let us ask, instead, how things work at the level of... processes, which subject our bodies, govern our gestures, dictate our behaviours.
Michel Foucault

Governmentality refers to the ways in which societies are decentred and citizens play an active role in their own self-governance; it is the relationship between public power and private freedom that is central.

The art of government

Foucault claims that govermentality is important because it provides a link between what he calls the "technologies of the self" (the creation of the individual subject) and the "technologies of »

Slimmers regulate and discipline themselves according to mass standards and cultural requirements rather than through individual choice.

Governing the body

Weight-loss organizations, such as Weight Watchers and Slimming World, illustrate Foucault's notion of governance of the self that sits in line with "normal" ideas of the time. While these organizations develop a person's sense of self and worth, they also envelop them in a web of power that ultimately benefits huge corporations.

Many feminists, such as US writer Kim Chernin, have argued that the quest for the perfect body through dieting places women within a "tyranny of slenderness".

Slimming companies and diets constitute disciplinary practices that promise an "improved self", but they also subject women to patriarchal (male-dominated) ideas about what a woman "should" look like and how she should behave. This necessity to conform to current standards of "normal" transforms dieting from an eating behaviour into a moral imperative. US feminists Sandra Bartky and Susan Bordo argue that this is indicative of the ways in which women become, simultaneously, both subjects and subjected.

> If one wants to analyze the genealogy of the subject in Western civilization, he has to take into account not only techniques of domination but also techniques of the self.
> **Michel Foucault**

domination" (the formation of the state). This is because, according to Foucault, "government" does not have a purely political meaning. From the 18th century until relatively recently, government was a broad concept that embraced guidance for the family, household management, and guidance for the soul, as well as more conventional politics. Foucault describes this all-embracing form of government as "the conduct of conduct". In the modern world, governing is more than simple top-down power relationships, Foucault says; it rests

on a multi-layered web. Where once governing rested on violence – or the threat of violence – this is now just one element of control. Other systems that hold sway in current forms of governing are coercive strategies, and those that structure and shape the possible forms of action citizens may take. Governing by fear and violence is much less effective than employing more subtle forms of control, such as defining limited choices or using disciplinary institutions like schools to guide the behaviour of individuals. In this way, self-control becomes linked to political rule and economic exploitation. What appears to be individual choice just "happens to be" also to the benefit of the state. In this way, Foucault suggests that the modern nation-state and the modern autonomous individual rely on one another for their existence.

Governmentality in action

Foucault's view of governmentality as the effort to shape and guide choices and lifestyles of groups and individuals has been further developed by many contemporary scholars. For example, US anthropologist Matthew Kohrman

> The dream or nightmare of a society programmed… by the "cold monster" of the state is profoundly limiting as a way of rendering intelligible the way we are governed.
> **Nikolas Rose**
> British sociologist (1947–)

considered governmentality in relation to cigarette smoking among Chinese physicians. His 2008 paper "Smoking Among Doctors: Governmentality, Embodiment and the Diversion of Blame in Contemporary China" looks at the ways smoking among health professionals was suggested to be the cause of high smoking rates among the public. Public health campaigns targeted these doctors, blaming them for tobacco-related diseases in China and calling on them to govern their own bodies and stop smoking.

The individual and the state

The individual became recognized as important in politics, Foucault claims, when the ideas of the divine right of kings and the infallibility of the Catholic Church were challenged. The task for any government then became how to find a way to conspicuously act for the people, while nevertheless continuing to build its own strength.

Domination by the monarchy and the Church (c.6th–16th centuries).

The rise of the individual (late 16th–17th century).

Citizens participate in their own governance (from the 18th century).

Foucault's vision of the modern nation-state as a governmentalized whole is not without its critics. He has, for instance, been charged with being vague and inconsistent in his definition of governmentality. Philosopher Derek Kerr has argued that Foucault's definition "beheads social subjectivity", by seeming to do away with free, subjective choice. Canadian sociologists Danica Dupont and Frank Pearce accuse Foucault of taking a rather simplistic and idealistic reading of Western political history, seeing it as "the growth of a plant from a seed", which overcomes obstacles to realize its true potential (as though this were always implicit, in some way).

Neo-liberalism

Nevertheless, Foucault's idea of governmentality remains a powerful conceptual tool with which to unpick and critique neo-liberalism. This is the post-war, post-welfare politics and economics of the late 20th century, whereby the state, in many respects, rolled back its responsibilities to its citizens. In his lectures, Foucault discussed neo-liberalism in three post-war states: West Germany, France, and the USA. This form of governance has been described as the triumph of capitalism over the state, or as "anti-humanism", owing to its emphasis on the individual and the destruction of community bonds. In neo-liberal thinking, the worker is viewed as a self-owned enterprise and is required to be competitive.

Neo-liberalism relies on the notion of responsible, rational individuals who are capable of taking responsibility for themselves, their lives, and their environment, particularly through "normalizing technologies" – the

agreed-upon goals and procedures of a society that are so "obvious" that they are seen as "normal". In the 21st century these include behaviours such as recycling, losing weight, being involved in Neighbourhood Watch schemes, or stopping smoking.

Foucault claims that the ways we think and talk about health, work, family and so on, encourage us to behave in particular ways. People govern themselves and others according to what they believe to be true. For instance, many societies view monogamous, heterosexual marriage as the "correct" environment for bringing up children, and this "truth" is

> ❝
> Foucault's work permanently changes one's understanding of how people are governed in modern society.
> **Brent Pickett**
> **US political scientist**
> ❞

Barack Obama's 2008 US presidency campaign had supporters chanting "Yes We Can!", implying government by the people. The tactic echoes Foucault's concept of self-government.

established in many ways, from cultural artefacts to government discourse on family values. Political policies may also be used to put weight behind particular ideas, such as the family, through incentives such as tax breaks.

British academic Nikolas Rose, drawing on Foucault's key ideas, has written persuasively on the "death of the social" and the ways in which the individual in the neo-liberal state has to govern his or her access to state services with little or no help. It is through perspectives such as this, Foucault says, that we can see the ways in which power is repressive, even while it appears to be acting in the interests of the individual. Foucault argues that political control – the art of governance – is most effective when it presents everything it offers as an act of free choice. Modern neo-liberalist governments have found perhaps the most dangerous way to govern – by giving the impression that they are not governing at all. ∎

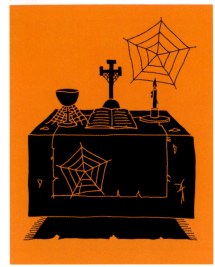

RELIGION HAS LOST ITS PLAUSIBILITY AND SOCIAL SIGNIFICANCE
BRYAN WILSON (1926–2004)

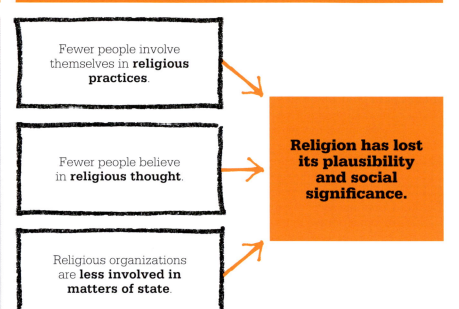

Fewer people involve themselves in **religious practices**.

Fewer people believe in **religious thought**.

Religious organizations are **less involved in matters of state**.

Religion has lost its plausibility and social significance.

Towns and cities across Britain contain churches and chapels that have been converted into pubs, showrooms, and apartments. British sociologist Bryan Wilson, writing between the 1960s and early 1990s, argues that a process of secularization is taking place. By this he means that the importance of the supernatural and the sacred is declining; religion, he suggests, has less influence on social life, institutions, and the individual. Using statistical data on various aspects of religious life, he notes that, according to polls, fewer children are being baptized in the Church of England, fewer people take part in the Easter communion, and more people say that they do not believe in God.

Wilson cites modernity – industrialization, the development of the state, and the advances in

See also: Auguste Comte 22–25 ▪ Karl Marx 28–31; 254–59 ▪ Émile Durkheim 34–37 ▪ Max Weber 38–45; 220–23 ▪
Jürgen Habermas 286–87 ▪ Michel Maffesoli 291 ▪ Michel Foucault 302–03

science and technology that come with it – as contributing to this decline in the importance of religious thought in society.

Initially, he suggests, religion was not defeated outright in the modern world, but had to compete with other claims to truth. But eventually science became too formidable an adversary. There has been a consequent disengagement of state and church into separate domains, in contrast to their closeness in the Middle Ages. And the role of religion in schools is negligible, as it is in the workplace, where the principles of organization have little room for religious myths.

God is dead?

Wilson, like Karl Marx, believes that world religions such as Christianity and Judaism play a role in maintaining the status quo by socializing new generations into accepting social divisions. But with modernity, religion has lost its authority to instruct people in what to believe and how to behave. He states that churches are aware of

their marginalized position and have to adapt to changing moral values. As old orders crumble, people seek new assurances.

Social fragmentation has brought with it cultural pluralism: alternative beliefs compete for popularity, and religions have become more private. In this sense, for Wilson, secularization is linked to a decline in community. Rather than being indicative of the longevity of religion, he sees new religious movements (NRMs), such as Scientology, as "anti-cultural": they symbolize a destructuring of society and do not contribute to the maintenance of social order and control. They are unable to channel their religious expression into a form that might have significant repercussions in modern society.

Many key thinkers of the 19th century, such as Marx, Durkheim, and Comte, believed that religion would lose its significance with the advent of industrialization. But in recent years, despite having several supporters, including British sociologist Steve Bruce, the

The Unification Church is one of several new religious movements that, according to Wilson, point to fragmentation and secularization in the modern world.

idea of secularization has received stark criticism. British journalist Michael Prowse, for example, says the idea is out of date and that there is evidence for the continuing vitality of religion. The popularity of church-going in the USA and the growth of non-Christian religions in Britain, particularly Islam, certainly endorse this view. ▪

[The] content of the message that the churches seek to promote, and the attitudes and values that it tries to encourage, no longer inform much of our national life.
Bryan Wilson

Bryan Wilson

Bryan Ronald Wilson was born in Leeds, England, in 1926. He was awarded his PhD from the London School of Economics and went on to become a lecturer at the University of Leeds, where he taught for seven years. He then moved to the University of Oxford, and remained there for 30 years, until his retirement in 1993. Wilson was president of the International Society for the Sociology of Religion from 1971 to 1975. Although an agnostic, he had a lifelong interest in new religious movements and sects, and was a staunch advocate of freedom of religious thought. In addition to his fascination with religion, he wrote extensively on youth culture and education. Wilson suffered from Parkinson's disease for several years. He died in 2004, aged 78.

Key works

1966 *Religion in Secular Society*
1973 *Magic and the Millennium*
1990 *The Social Dimensions of Sectarianism*

OUR IDENTITY AND BEHAVIOUR ARE DETERMINED BY HOW WE ARE DESCRIBED AND CLASSIFIED

HOWARD S BECKER (1928–)

IN CONTEXT

FOCUS
Labelling theory

KEY DATES
1938 Austrian-US historian Frank Tannenbaum argues that criminal behaviour is the result of conflict between one group and the community at large.

1951 *Social Pathology*, by US sociologist Edwin Lemert, introduces the idea of primary and secondary deviancy.

1969 Authorities create deviant identities, says US sociologist David Matza in *Becoming Deviant*.

1976 US sociologist Aaron Cicourel suggests that the police operate with a stereotype of the deviant as a young, working-class male; these youths are therefore far more likely to be sentenced than middle-class youths who commit crimes.

Powerful people in society define certain acts as **deviant**.

Individuals are found guilty of these acts and labelled as **outsiders**.

All their **future actions** are **tagged** with the label.

So they **internalize the label** and behave accordingly.

Our identity and behaviour are determined by how we are described and classified.

A lthough many people in society break the law – for example, by exceeding the speed limit or stealing stationery from work – only some are regarded as real criminals. Labelling theory, which emerged from a mistrust of government powers in post-war Britain and the USA in the 1960s and 70s, considers why this is so.

Proponents of labelling theory argue that criminologists once tended to conceptualize criminals as types of people, asking why particular individuals, or groups of people, committed crime. In contrast, labelling theory questions why some acts are thought to be deviant and who has the power to label some people's behaviour as deviant; it then examines the impact of such labelling on society and the individual.

Consider this example. If a group of young, middle-class men on a stag night are drunk and disorderly in a town centre, the authorities are likely to attribute their behaviour to youthful exuberance. But if a similar disturbance is caused by young, working-class men, they are far more likely to be labelled as hooligans or criminals.

According to labelling theorists, this is because rule-makers, such as judges and politicians, tend to be middle or upper class and treat the infractions of their own kind more leniently than the deviance of working-class people. Our concept of deviance comes, the theorists argue, not so much from what people do, as how others respond to it – labelling is a political act. This school of thought – which has connections with the work of Émile

See also: Émile Durkheim 34–37 ▪ Ferdinand Tönnies 32–33 ▪ Edward Said 80–8 ▪ Elijah Anderson 82–83 ▪ G H Mead 176–77 ▪ Erving Goffman 190–95 ▪ Samuel Bowles and Herbert Gintis 288–89 ▪ Stanley Cohen 290

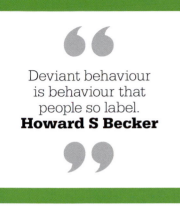

> Deviant behaviour is behaviour that people so label.
> **Howard S Becker**

Durkheim, G H Mead, and the Chicago School in the USA – is particularly associated with the work of US sociologists Howard S Becker and Edwin Lemert.

Types of deviancy

Lemert distinguished between the ideas of "primary" and "secondary" deviancy. According to him, primary deviance is when a crime or other act is committed, but is not officially labelled as deviant, either because it went unnoticed or because the perpetrator was considered to be acting out of character. Either way, it does not attach a label of "deviant" to the individual. Secondary deviance is the effect that society's reaction has on an individual. If someone commits a crime, and is caught and labelled as criminal or deviant, they may change their behaviour in the future to live up to that label.

In *Outsiders* (1963), Becker developed a number of Lemert's ideas and laid the foundations for what became known as labelling theory. He argued that there is no such thing as a deviant act: how we respond to an act depends on whether a particular form of behaviour has become sanctioned within a given society. For example, "terrorists" are accused of murder but the army may legally kill terrorists. And among Western nations, as recently as the 1990s, a husband forcing intercourse on his wife was not guilty of rape, according to the law. Becker claims that it is not the act itself that is deviant; the response of society defines it as such and, crucially, the responses of the powerful determine how society is expected to view such behaviours. Only those who have power can make a label stick; institutions such as the criminal justice system can ensure that a deviant label will follow an individual. Rather than being universal, deviance is relative – it depends on who commits it and how it is responded to.

Moral entrepreneurs

Coining a label that has proved extremely useful in the social sciences, Becker identifies **»**

A group of privileged undergraduates who smash up a restaurant when fuelled by drink may be accused of student high jinks, while a group of working-class boys displaying identical behaviour may be labelled as delinquents.

Privileged students   **Working-class youths**

↓   ↓

Criminal damage or youthful exuberance?

↓   ↓

HIGH JINKS   **DELINQUENT**

The film *Reefer Madness* (1936) was a thinly disguised piece of propaganda that charts the downfall of a respectable high-school couple who are corrupted by marijuana use.

"moral entrepreneurs" as the people in society who have the power to label others. They task themselves with the role of persuading others to see the world in a way that suits their own moral beliefs. They fall into two types: rule creators and rule enforcers. The position and identity of moral entrepreneurs varies between societies, but they

> The process of making a criminal... is a process of tagging, defining, identifying, segregating.
> **Frank Tannenbaum**
> **Austrian-US historian (1893–1969)**

are always people in positions of relative power, who use that power to get their own way by either imposing their will on others, or by negotiating with them.

Becker illustrated the actions of moral entrepreneurs through the case study of a publicity campaign that was run by the Federal Bureau of Investigation (FBI) in the USA in 1937. The goal was to ban the recreational use of marijuana. The moral entrepreneurs' distaste for public displays of enjoyment or ecstasy, coupled with a Protestant concern for respectability and self-control, led to the push for legal change. The FBI, according to Becker, used various means to achieve their goals; these included propaganda such as the film *Reefer Madness*, as well as public debate and political lobbying.

Deviant "careers"
Becker was particularly interested in individuals who internalized the label of deviancy, making it their defining characteristic, and went on to adopt lifestyles with deviancy as a central feature. He studied marijuana users to

investigate how they progressed through the various stages of a deviant "career" and noted that first-time marijuana smokers had to learn how to perceive and subsequently enjoy the effects of the drug. Without this learning process, he said, taking the drug could be unpleasant or apparently have no effect whatsoever. Learning was central to the meaning of the deviant act – people only willingly learned what was meaningful to them – and individuals became fully fledged "dope smokers" only when they learned how to hide the habit from the "straight" or "square" world. If the smoker was caught and charged or arrested, their deviant status was likely to be confirmed. Becker reasoned that following a deviant career has its rewards, though they do not come from wider society; instead, they come from feeling a sense of belonging to a group that is united by its opposition to the world at large.

Labelling critics
Despite its influence and continued popularity, a number of criticisms can be leveled at labelling theory. The British sociologist Jock Young, for example, points to the fact that much labelling theory focuses

> The rule-breaker might feel his judges are outsiders.
> **Howard S Becker**

> Social groups create deviance by making the rules whose infraction constitutes deviance.
> **Howard S Becker**

on marginal deviancy rather than more "serious" crimes, and therefore ignores the fact that some crimes, such as murder, are almost universally condemned, and are not subject to alternative perceptions of deviancy. Alvin Gouldner, a US sociologist, has

In a study of jazz musicians, Becker proposed that their "deviant" lifestyle set them apart from society, which caused them to develop values that reinforced their deviancy.

complained that Becker's deviants passively accept the labels forced upon them, rather than fighting back. Gouldner challenges Becker's theory by saying people frequently fight back in their own defence: free will is far stronger than Becker's work implies.

Academics such as Becker have also been accused of romanticizing the underdog; in response, Becker has stated that "unconventional sentimentality… is the lesser evil". But Becker's work forces us to ask important questions about power relationships and justice in society and has been significant for a number of theorists who focus on deviancy. US sociologist David Matza, for instance, develops many of Becker's ideas by arguing that what becomes a crime is the outcome of decisions and actions taken by governments and agents of the state. According to this process, both the criminal and their act are seen as abnormal and yet from the perspective of the deviant, the deviancy is entirely normal behaviour. ∎

Howard S Becker

Born in Chicago, USA, in 1928, sociologist Howard Saul Becker became involved in the world of music from an early age. By the age of 15 he was working as a semi-professional pianist in bars and clubs and was regularly exposed to the drug culture that he later made the subject of his studies. After reading sociology at the University of Chicago, most of his academic career was spent at Northwestern University. Becker has received many awards during his academic career, including the Award for a Career of Distinguished Scholarship from the American Sociological Association in 1998. Becker is known for his academic generosity – although mainly retired, he continues to help doctoral students with their work and offers advice on how to publish their theses. Music – jazz in particular – remains a subject of personal and research interest for him.

Key works

1963 *Outsiders: Studies in the Sociology of Deviance*
1982 *Art Worlds*
1998 *Tricks of the Trade*

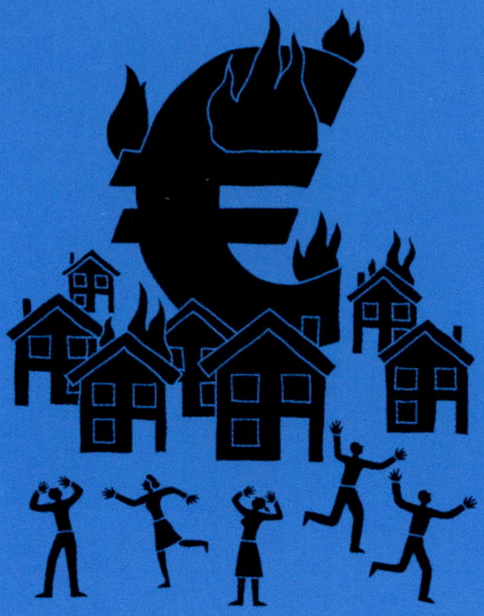

ECONOMIC CRISIS IS IMMEDIATELY TRANSFORMED INTO SOCIAL CRISIS

JÜRGEN HABERMAS (1929–)

IN CONTEXT

FOCUS
Legitimation crisis

KEY DATES
1867 In *Das Kapital*, Karl Marx suggests that capitalism is prone to economic crises.

1929 The stock exchange crash in Wall Street, New York, USA, leads to a ten-year economic depression that affects all Western economies.

1950–60s Talcott Parsons discusses legitimation and soical order, claiming that through socialization people acquire values that lead them to conform to social norms.

2007 Global economic recession results in a swing across Europe to parties of the political right.

2009 Chilean sociologist Rodrigo Cordero Vega argues, contrary to Habermas, that Marx remains relevant to contemporary society.

Late-capitalist societies experience periodic **economic downturns**.

↓

Policies to cope with this may seem **unfair** to the majority of voters.

↓

When this happens, citizens **question the authority** of government.

↓

Demonstrations and protests threaten the legitimacy of the state.

↓

Economic crisis is immediately transformed into social crisis.

Karl Marx argued that capitalist societies are prone to economic crises and that these will worsen over time, culminating in a workers' revolution. But why is it that when a society has such a crisis, a somewhat different change in the political climate often follows?

This was the question posed by the German sociologist Jürgen Habermas in the early 1970s. He was intrigued by the relationship between capitalism and crises, having seen the system survive a series of extraordinary events such as the Wall Street Crash of 1929 in the USA, the subsequent Great Depression, the rise and fall of fascist movements in Europe, World War II, and the Cold War.

Habermas suggests that traditional Marxist theories of crisis tendencies are not applicable to Western late-capitalist societies. This is because these societies have become more democratic and have changed significantly thanks to welfare-state policies, such as free healthcare provision, that make up for economic inequalities. In addition, he says, collective identities have fragmented and

See also: Adam Ferguson 21 ■ Karl Marx 28–31 ■ Herbert Marcuse 182–87 ■
Daniel Bell 224–25 ■ Michel Foucault 270–77 ■ Stanley Cohen 290

there is evidence of increased individualization and fewer class-based conflicts.

Crisis of legitimacy

Although the economic cycles of prosperity and recession continue, policy measures by nation-states have enabled them to avert major crises. Unlike earlier capitalist societies, under state-regulated late-capitalism the primary site of crisis and conflict has shifted to the cultural and political spheres.

The crisis of modern Western society is, according to Habermas, one of legitimation. Legitimacy has become the focal concern because the state, as manager of the "free market" economy, has simultaneously to solve economic problems, ensure democracy, and please the voters. If the public feels government policies are unfair, it withdraws its support for the government. The state therefore

Riot police in Athens, Greece, in 2011 confront demonstrators claiming that government austerity measures to deal with sovereign debt favour the few at the expense of the many.

has the difficult task of balancing the pursuit for capital with maintaining mass support. In other words, state policies must favour business and property owners while appearing to represent the interests of all. This means the conditions exist for government institutions to suffer a large-scale loss of legitimacy.

If citizens sense that the government is just and benevolent, then they will show support. If, however, they feel that policies are not in their interests, people will respond with political apathy or even large-scale discontent and protests. Given a threat to the status quo, a government may try to appease its citizens with short-lived social welfare measures.

Habermas says democratic capitalism is an "unfinished project", implying the social system can be further improved. Western governments' actions since the global financial crisis began in 2007 have exposed many social tensions between narrow capital interests, the public interest, mass democracy, and the need to secure institutional legitimacy. ■

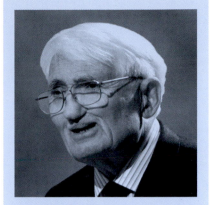

Jürgen Habermas

Born in Düsseldorf, Germany, in 1929, Jürgen Habermas's political awakening came when, as a teenager in the Hitler Youth, he witnessed the aftermath of World War II and the Holocaust – events that inform much of his work.

Habermas is one of the world's foremost contemporary social thinkers. Many of his writings are concerned with knowledge communication and the changing nature of the public and private spheres. He was born with a cleft palate, which affected his speech and, at times, left him socially isolated in his youth. The experience influenced his work on communication.

He studied sociology and philosophy in Frankfurt at the Institute for Social Research, under Max Horkheimer and Theodor Adorno, who both helped originate critical theory, and in the late 1960s he became director of the Institute for Social Research.

Key works

1968 *Knowledge and Human Interests*
1973 *Legitimation Crisis*
1981 *The Theory of Communicative Action*

SCHOOLING HAS BEEN AT ONCE SOMETHING DONE TO THE POOR AND FOR THE POOR

SAMUEL BOWLES (1939–) AND HERBERT GINTIS (1940–)

Schools prepare the poor to **function well and uncomplainingly** within the hierarchical structure of the modern workplace.

Schools for the poor are established as part of the popular programme of **free education** to achieve **social equality**.

Schooling has been at once something done to the poor and for the poor.

IN CONTEXT

FOCUS
The hidden curriculum

KEY DATES
1968 In *Life in Classrooms,* US sociologist Philip W Jackson claims that children are socialized in the classroom via a "hidden curriculum".

1973 According to Pierre Bourdieu, the reproduction of "cultural capital" (the ability to recognize cultural references, to know how to act appropriately in different social situations, and so on) explains middle-class success.

1978 Kathleen Clarricoates' British study indicates that gender inequity, to the detriment of girls, forms part of the implicit curriculum.

1983 Henry Giroux, US cultural critic, suggests that hidden curriculums are plural, operating along lines of gender and ethnicity as well as social class.

Schools exist to prepare children for adulthood and society, but in the 1960s the benign consensus about this fact of modern life began to fragment. At the end of that decade the term "hidden curriculum" was coined by Philip W Jackson, who claimed that elements of socialization take place in school that are not part of the formal educational curriculum. Although Émile Durkheim had observed this imparting of values decades earlier, it was now given a less favourable interpretation and since then several sociological approaches have developed.

The most radical perspective comes from US economists Samuel Bowles and Herbert Gintis, who argue in *Schooling in Capitalist America* (1976) that education is not a neutral sphere but one where the needs of capitalism are reproduced by implicitly creating attitudes among young people that prepare them for work that alienates them in their future lives.

See also: Émile Durkheim 34–37 ▪ Pierre Bourdieu 76–79 ▪ Erving Goffman 264–69 ▪ Paul Willis 292–93 ▪ Talcott Parsons 300–01

According to Bowles and Gintis, schools exist to reproduce social inequalities. Therefore, the best predictor for a child's future is the economic status of parents, rather than academic achievement or intelligence. Although the explicit curriculum is about equality of opportunity, education's prime role is not to teach the skills needed in the world of work, but to instil into children the "hidden curriculum".

Working-class children are taught their place in society and learn that qualities such as working hard, deference, punctuality, and following orders are prized. These traits are rewarded, while creativity and independent thought are not valued. This maintains the economic status quo, which needs industrious, uncritical employees.

Bowles and Gintis claim that early 19th-century schools in the USA were set up to assimilate immigrants into the "American" work ethic. Crucially, there is a "correspondence" between the hierarchical social relations within the school system and those found in the economic system. The nature of work also has similarities: pupils have little control over what they study and neither do they study for the inherent value of knowledge; like workers, they are "alienated". Schools teach children that social inequalities are just and inevitable, and therefore education can be seen as a form of social control.

Class matters
In France, Pierre Bourdieu took a different view and suggested that the hidden curriculum is achieved through the cultural reproduction of knowledge. The dominant class is able to define its culture and values

> The structure of social relations in education… inures the student to the discipline of the workplace.
> **Samuel Bowles & Herbert Gintis**

as superior and this shapes what is taught, thus people learn to respect things perceived as upper class and deride those considered working class. For example, working-class children might be taught that classical music is superior to popular music, and that it is too difficult for them to understand, whereas middle-class children are taught how to appreciate it. In a similar way, middle-class children are taught the qualities that will enable them to become leaders. So, lower-class children face systematic bias against them in the system.

Many sociologists, such as British academic Diane Reay, contend that schools have not become vehicles for economic opportunity. The work of Bowles and Gintis still has much resonance because there has been little progress for the working classes over the last century. The poor are simply better educated than in the past. Throughout Western society, "real" incomes for the poorest have been falling, inequality has been increasing, and it is common to find graduates in low-paid work. ∎

Samuel Bowles and Herbert Gintis

Both Samuel Bowles, born in New Haven, Connecticut, USA, and Herbert Gintis, born in Philadelphia, Pennsylvania, received doctoral degrees from Harvard University and they have since worked extensively with one another. They were invited by the US civil rights leader Martin Luther King Jr to write educational background papers for the Poor People's March of 1968. Much of their work, which has been described as Marxist, argues that many social institutions, such as schools, are characterized by the disciplinary exercise of power.

They were both hired in 1973 to join the economics department at the University of Massachusetts. Gintis still works there, but Bowles left in 2001 to join the Santa Fe Institute as research professor and director of behavioural sciences, and he is also a professor of economics at the University of Siena. Recent collaborations have focused on cultural and genetic evolution, asking why large groups of unrelated individuals gather together cooperatively.

Key works

1976 *Schooling in Capitalist America: Educational Reform and the Contradictions of Economic Life*
1986 *Democracy and Capitalism: Property, Community, and the Contradictions of Modern Social Thought*
2005 *Unequal Chances: Family Background and Economic Success* (eds)

SOCIETIES ARE SUBJECT, EVERY NOW AND THEN, TO PERIODS OF MORAL PANIC
STANLEY COHEN (1942–2013)

IN CONTEXT

FOCUS
Moral panics

KEY DATES
1963 *Outsiders: Studies in the Sociology of Deviance*, Howard Becker's study of labelling, lays the foundations for moral panic theory by discussing how people's behaviour can clash with societal norms.

1964 Media exaggeration of clashes between "mods" and "rockers" youth subcultures in the UK sparks a moral panic.

1971 In *The Drug Takers: The Social Meaning of Drug Use*, Scottish academic Jock Young, a friend of Stanley Cohen, discusses the idea of moral panic in relation to the social meaning of drug-taking.

1994 US sociologist Erich Goode and Israeli academic Nachman Ben-Yehuda develop Cohen's ideas in their book *Moral Panics: The Social Construction of Deviance*.

So important is the sociological concept of "moral panics" that the term is now widely used by journalists and politicians. The idea emerged in the 1970s, partly from South African-born sociologist Stanley Cohen's *Folk Devils and Moral Panics* (1972), which was inspired by media-aggravated conflicts in 1964 in the UK between youth groups known as mods and rockers.

Cohen examines how groups and individuals are identified as a threat to dominant social values, and how the media plays a key role in amplifying this, presenting them in negative or stereotyped ways, thus creating a national panic. The media is an influential institution that often reflects the values of the powerful and represents issues so that the public are enticed to agree with "experts" (politicians and the police, for example) on how best to deal with the problem.

Those seen as blameworthy become scapegoats, or what Cohen terms "folk devils", for problems that often lie with the state; moral panics reflect deep-seated anxieties. Media attention may create a "self-fulfilling prophecy" by encouraging the behaviours it reports. Moral panics can be short-lived and die down when they are seen to be dealt with, or they may form part of a larger, ongoing panic.

The concept of moral panics continues to be used by academics, such as British sociologist Angela McRobbie, to describe the role the media plays in creating deviant acts and justifying increased social control of marginalized groups. ∎

The 9/11 attacks in New York, USA, sparked moral panics about "terrorism", leading to widespread Islamophobia – prejudice against Muslims or those perceived as Muslims.

See also: Harold Garfinkel 50–51 ▪ Edward Said 80–81 ▪ Herbert Marcuse 182–87 ▪ Stuart Hall 200–01 ▪ Howard S Becker 280–85

THE TIME OF THE TRIBES
MICHEL MAFFESOLI (1944–)

IN CONTEXT

FOCUS
Neo-tribalism

KEY DATES
1887 Ferdinand Tönnies identifies an important shift in social ties from *Gemeinschaft* (community) to *Gesellschaft* (society).

1970s and 1980s Building on the work of US sociologist Robert Merton, subcultural theorists argue that youths form ties based on class and gender.

1988 French sociologist Michel Maffesoli's *The Time of Tribes: The Decline of Individualism in Mass Society* is published.

1998 British sociologist Kevin Hetherington expands Maffesoli's concept and argues that neo-tribes, a reaction to the fragmentation of postmodern society, are communities of feeling.

We live in "the time of the tribes", according to French sociologist Michel Maffesoli. In a world of rapid change, characterized by risk and unpredictability, individuals need new ways to find meaning in their lives. New collectives, or tribes, have emerged, says Maffesoli: they are dynamic, fleeting, and "Dionysiac" (after the Greek god Dionysus: sensual, spontaneous). A shared social experience, or collective aesthetic sensibility, is far more important to the tribes than individuality, and the repetition of shared rituals is a way of forging strong group solidarity.

The rave movement of the 1980s and early 1990s, featuring "raves" (parties with rhythmic music and a specific dance style), was characterized less by a common identity than a shared consciousness (love of rave music and dance). Not as fixed as class-based subcultures such as punk, the movement exemplifies the tribal forms of solidarity described by Maffesoli. Unlike traditional

> The metaphor of the tribe... allows us to account for... the *role*... each person... is called upon to play within the tribe.
> **Michel Maffesoli**

institutions and ties, these new forms of belonging and community are actively achieved, rather than being something one is born into.

Maffesoli sees the modern-day tribes as short-lived, flexible, and fluid rather than fixed, so a person can move between different groupings in everyday life and achieve a fulfilling plural existence. Tribal membership, says Maffesoli, must be worked at and requires a shared belief or consciousness to maintain coherence. ■

See also: Ferdinand Tönnies 32–33 ■ Pierre Bourdieu 76–79 ■ Zygmunt Bauman 136–43 ■ Benedict Anderson 202–03

HOW WORKING-CLASS KIDS GET WORKING-CLASS JOBS

PAUL WILLIS (1950–)

IN CONTEXT

FOCUS
Cultural reproduction and education

KEY DATES
1971 Influential research by British sociologist Basil Bernstein suggests that working-class children are disadvantaged in the education system.

1976 US academics Samuel Bowles and Herbert Gintis suggest that schools are institutions that teach people their place in society.

1979 British journalist Paul Corrigan's *Schooling the Smash Street Kids* argues that working-class boys reject middle-class understandings of success through hard work.

1994 A study by British sociologist Máirtín Mac an Ghaill, *The Making of Men*, reflects some of Paul Willis's findings, showing how "macho lads" react against school.

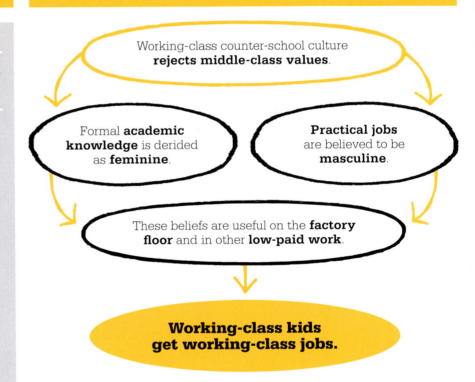

Working-class counter-school culture **rejects middle-class values**.

Formal **academic knowledge** is derided as **feminine**.

Practical jobs are believed to be **masculine**.

These beliefs are useful on the **factory floor** and in other **low-paid work**.

Working-class kids get working-class jobs.

A repeated claim is that society is meritocratic: people can achieve to the level of their ability. But Paul Willis, in his study of working-class youths in an industrial town in England in the 1970s, asks why it is, then, that working-class boys end up in working-class jobs.

Following 12 boys, or "lads" as he refers to them, in their final two years of school and first year of employment, Willis claims it is the culture and values surrounding these young men that inform their life choices. They develop a counterculture that resists the philosophy of school, namely that

See also: Michel Foucault 52–55 ▪ Friedrich Engels 66–67 ▪ Pierre Bourdieu 76–79 ▪ R W Connell 88–89 ▪ Stuart Hall 200–01 ▪ Samuel Bowles and Herbert Gintis 288–89

academic hard work will lead to progress. Through language, dress, and practices such as smoking and drinking, they make clear their rejection of middle-class ideals, and instead emphasize their belief in practical skills and life experience, developing what Willis sees as a chauvinistic or patriarchal attitude.

School's out

The boys see academic knowledge as "feminine", and pupils who aspire to achieve – the "ear'oles" (conformists) – as "sissies" and inferior. Factory work and similar employment is viewed, says Willis, as suitably masculine. Many of the boys work part-time, for example as shelf-stackers or key-cutters, and learn the value of and culture connected to such work.

Their attitudes to girls are exploitative and hypocritical ("sexy" girls are desired but also become figures of contempt), and are based, Willis claims, on a belief in the gendered division of labour. Another challenging aspect of their culture is racism, which serves to distinguish their white, working-class group identity. The factory or shop-floor culture mirrors the boys' experiences in school – with a stress in both places on having a laugh and resisting too much work.

Factory fodder?

Willis argues that, in effect, the boys' "performance" of working-class masculinity supports both patriarchy and – crucially, from a Marxist perspective – capitalism by providing the low-paid (male) workforce. The lads, however, experience their employment as a matter of their own free choice rather than as exploitation.

Willis says that this is not simply an example of Friedrich Engels' "false consciousness", whereby the dominant ideology is imposed from above. Instead, ideas about class, gender, and ethnicity also emerge from within their culture; they are very aware that they would have to sacrifice their class identity to move up the social ladder. Their teachers often have low expectations of the boys, leading them to gradually give up on the idea of teaching them. Schools thus play a crucial role in reproducing cultural values, economic divisions, and working-class trajectories.

New questions

Willis's work has been criticized, for example by British sociologists David Blackledge and Barry Hunt, for being based on insufficient sampling. But in the 1990s British sociologist Inge Bates reframed Willis's question to ask why working-class girls end up with working-class and gender-stereotyped jobs. One of her studies showed that girls who wanted to

The fierce opposition to school exhibited by working-class boys in the UK is evident, according to Willis, in their "struggle to win symbolic and physical space from its rules".

work in childcare ended up on training schemes for care of the elderly. Another study focused on girls who were keen to enter the gender-stereotyped world of fashion. These aspirations confirm, says Bates, that working-class girls have limited horizons. Overall, Bates suggests that a constrained labour market, few qualifications, and socialization into "choosing" gendered jobs means there is little evidence of social mobility. ∎

Paul Willis

A cultural theorist, sociologist, and ethnographer, Paul Willis was born in Wolverhampton, UK. After graduating from the University of Cambridge with a degree in literary criticism, he studied for his PhD at the Centre for Contemporary Cultural Studies at the University of Birmingham.

From 1989 to 1990, Willis was a member of the Youth Policy Working Group for the Labour Party. Much of his recent work has focused on ethnographical studies of culture; in 2000 he co-founded the journal *Ethnography*. Having been a professor of social and cultural ethnography at Keele University, he is now a professor in the sociology department of Princeton University, USA.

Key works

1977 *Learning to Labour: How Working Class Kids Get Working Class Jobs*
1978 *Profane Culture*
2000 *The Ethnographic Imagination*

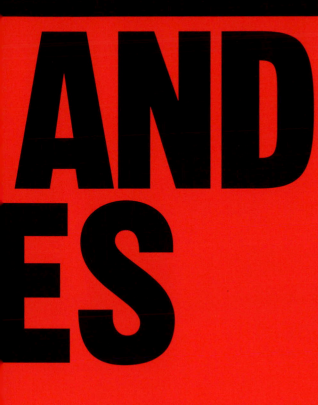

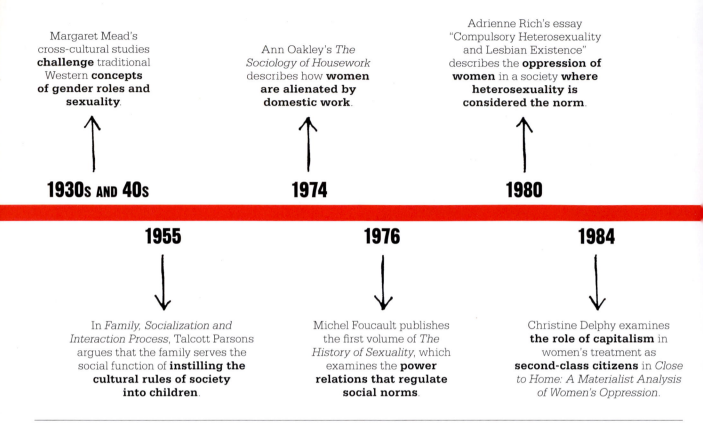

Margaret Mead's cross-cultural studies **challenge** traditional Western **concepts of gender roles and sexuality**.

Ann Oakley's *The Sociology of Housework* describes how **women are alienated by domestic work**.

Adrienne Rich's essay "Compulsory Heterosexuality and Lesbian Existence" describes the **oppression of women** in a society **where heterosexuality is considered the norm**.

1930s AND 40s

1974

1980

1955

1976

1984

In *Family, Socialization and Interaction Process*, Talcott Parsons argues that the family serves the social function of **instilling the cultural rules of society into children**.

Michel Foucault publishes the first volume of *The History of Sexuality*, which examines the **power relations that regulate social norms**.

Christine Delphy examines **the role of capitalism** in women's treatment as **second-class citizens** in *Close to Home: A Materialist Analysis of Women's Oppression*.

For many years, sociologists had used scientific methods to study institutions and the structure of society as a whole. However, the middle of the 20th century saw a shift in emphasis towards understanding the social actions of individuals – a study of reasons and meanings rather than quantities and correlations. This came to be known to sociologists as the interpretative approach.

From the 1950s, the scope of this interpretive method widened slightly to include the study of families, which could perhaps be seen as a social unit somewhere between the individual and institutions. As such, it was possible to identify not only the relationships between individuals and their families, but also the connections between families and wider society. This area of study progressed to examine interpersonal relationships and how they are shaped by society.

Family roles

Among the first sociologists to examine the family in this way was US scholar Talcott Parsons, who combined the interpretive approach of German social theorist Max Weber with the concept of functionalism. For Parsons, the family is one of the "building blocks" of society, and has a specific function in the working of society as a whole. Its primary function, he argued, was to provide an environment in which children can be prepared for roles they will later play in society, by instilling in them its rules and social norms. Adults too benefit from another function of the family unit – to offer a framework in which they can develop stable relationships.

Others were more critical of the conventional notions of family. Traditionally, families reflected the norms of wider society – patriarchal in their structure, with a male breadwinner and a female child-carer and houseworker. But attitudes changed rapidly after World War II. The idea of the stay-at-home mother was increasingly regarded as a form of oppression, and feminist sociologists such as Ann Oakley and Christine Delphy described the alienation that these women experienced.

Gender roles within the family and, by extension, within society as a whole, began to be challenged, as did the idea that there is such a thing as a "typical" or "normal"

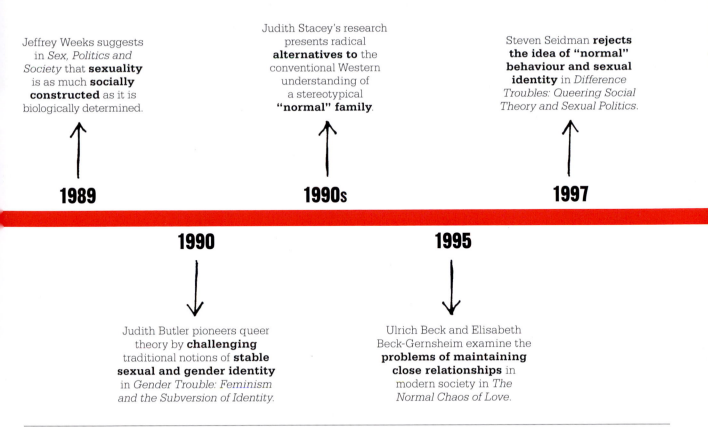

Jeffrey Weeks suggests in *Sex, Politics and Society* that **sexuality is as much socially constructed** as it is biologically determined.

Judith Stacey's research presents radical **alternatives to** the conventional Western understanding of a stereotypical **"normal" family**.

Steven Seidman **rejects the idea of "normal" behaviour and sexual identity** in *Difference Troubles: Queering Social Theory and Sexual Politics*.

1989

1990s

1997

1990

1995

Judith Butler pioneers queer theory by **challenging** traditional notions of **stable sexual and gender identity** in *Gender Trouble: Feminism and the Subversion of Identity*.

Ulrich Beck and Elisabeth Beck-Gernsheim examine the **problems of maintaining close relationships** in modern society in *The Normal Chaos of Love*.

family. As a result of the decline of the traditional patriarchal family model, the conflicting pressures of home and work now affect both partners in many couples, putting a strain on their relationship. The nature of families, according to Judith Stacey, is continually changing to meet the demands of the modern world and also responding to and shaping social norms, so that, for example, single-parent families and same-sex couples are no longer considered unusual in Western societies.

Interpersonal relationships
The more liberal attitude towards sexual relationships and sexuality in the West was, however, slow in coming. In the 1930s and 1940s, the anthropologist Margaret Mead helped to pave the way with her study of gender roles and sexuality in various cultures around the world, showing that ideas of sexual behaviour are more a social construction than a biological fact. In the West, despite increasing secularization, religious morality continued to influence the social norms of heterosexual relationships within marriage.

Attitudes towards relationships changed greatly during the 1960s. An anti-establishment youth culture helped break taboos surrounding sex, advocating hedonistic free love and a relaxed view of homosexuality. This change in culture was echoed by the academic work of French scholar Michel Foucault and others.

Foucault believed that the new openness towards intimate relationships of all kinds was a way of challenging the sexual norms imposed by society, and his ideas paved the way for the sociological study of sexuality itself.

In the 1980s, Jeffrey Weeks applied the idea of sexual norms as a social construct to his study of sexuality, and specifically homosexuality, while Christine Delphy described the experiences of lesbians in a predominantly heterosexual society. Perhaps the most influential sociologist in this field of study, however, is Judith Butler, who advocated challenging not only notions of sexuality, but the entire concept of gender and gender identity too, opening up a new, and radical, field of study now known as queer theory, which calls into question conventional ideas of what constitutes normal sexual behaviour. ∎

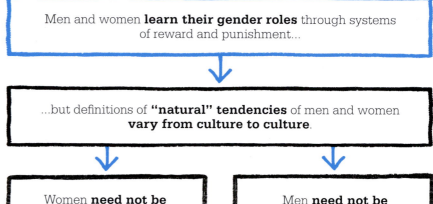

DIFFERENCES BETWEEN THE SEXES ARE CULTURAL CREATIONS
MARGARET MEAD (1901–1978)

IN CONTEXT

FOCUS
Variation in gender roles across different cultures

KEY DATES
1920 Women in the USA are given the right to vote.

1939–45 Women in the UK and subsequently in the USA prove themselves capable of doing "men's work" during World War II; factory worker Rosie the Riveter becomes a US icon of female capability and economic potential.

1972 British sociologist Ann Oakley argues in *Sex, Gender and Society* that gender is a matter of culture.

1975 In her article "The Traffic in Women: Notes on the 'Political Economy' of Sex", US cultural anthropologist Gayle Rubin argues that heterosexual family arrangements give men power and oppress women.

Men and women **learn their gender roles** through systems of reward and punishment...

↓

...but definitions of **"natural" tendencies** of men and women **vary from culture to culture**.

↓   ↓

Women **need not be nurturers** of children.

Men **need not be** the **dominant** sex.

↓   ↓

Differences between the sexes are cultural creations.

In early 20th-century US society, a man's role was to provide for his family, while women were relegated to the private sphere and considered responsible for childcare and housework because they were thought to be naturally more inclined to such roles. Margaret Mead, however, believed that gender is not based on biological differences between the sexes, but rather reflects the cultural conditioning of different societies.

Mead's investigations of the intimate lives of non-Western peoples in the 1930s and 1940s crystallized her criticisms of her own society: she claimed that the ways in which US society

See also: Judith Butler 56–61 ▪ R W Connell 88–89 ▪ Talcott Parsons 300–01 ▪ Ann Oakley 318–19 ▪ Jeffrey Weeks 324–25

expressed gender and sexuality restricted possibilities for both men and women. Mead claims that men and women are punished and rewarded to encourage gender conformity, and what is viewed as masculine is also seen as superior.

Comparing cultures

Mead takes a comparative approach to gender in her studies of three tribes in New Guinea. Her findings challenge conventional Western ideas about how human behaviour is determined. Arapesh men and women were "gentle, responsive and co-operative" and both undertook childcare – traits the West would see as "feminine".

Similarly, it was the norm for Mundugumor women to behave in a "masculine" way by being as violent and aggressive as the men. And in a further reversal of traditional Western roles, women in Tchambuli society were dominant, while men were seen as dependent.

The fact that behaviours coded as masculine in one society may be regarded as feminine in another, leads Mead to argue that temperamental attitudes can no longer be regarded as sex-linked.

Her theory that gender roles are not natural but are created by society established gender as a critical concept; it allows us to see the historical and cross-cultural ways in which masculinity, femininity, and sexuality are ideologically constructed.

Change can happen

Mead's work laid the foundations for the women's liberation movement and informed the so-called "sexual revolution" of the 1960s onwards. Her ideas posed a fundamental challenge to society's rigid understandings of gender roles and sexuality.

Following on from Mead, feminists such as the American cultural anthropologist Gayle Rubin argued that if gender, unlike sex, is a social construction, there is no reason why women should continue to be treated unequally. Viewing gender as culturally determined allows us to see, and therefore

Gender roles are cultural creations, according to Mead. There is no evidence that women are naturally better than men at doing the housework or caring for children.

challenge, the ways in which social structures such as the law, marriage, and the media encourage stereotyped ways of conducting our intimate lives.

In comparison to the early 20th century, gender roles for both men and women in the 21st century have become far less restrictive, with women participating more in the public sphere. ▪

Margaret Mead

Margaret Mead was born in Philadelphia, USA, in 1901. Her father was a professor of finance; her mother was a sociologist; she herself became curator emeritus of the American Museum of Natural History, New York.

Mead received her PhD from Columbia University in 1929, and went on to become a leading cultural anthropologist, best known for her studies of the people of Oceania. Her early work on gender and sexuality was labelled as scandalous and she was denounced as a "dirty old woman". She nevertheless

became a popular figure, lecturing widely on key social issues such as women's rights, sexual behaviour, and the family. Mead was the author of more than 20 books, many of which were part of her mission to make anthropology more accessible to the public. She died in New York in 1978.

Key works

1928 *Coming of Age in Samoa*
1935 *Sex and Temperament in Three Primitive Societies*
1949 *Male and Female*

FAMILIES ARE FACTORIES THAT PRODUCE HUMAN PERSONALITIES
TALCOTT PARSONS (1902–1979)

IN CONTEXT

FOCUS
Socialization of children and stabilization of adults

KEY DATES
1893 In *The Division of Labour in Society*, sociologist Émile Durkheim suggests that divisions in work are essential for maintaining economic, moral, and social order.

1938 US sociologist Louis Wirth claims industrialization is destroying extended families and communities.

1975 British sociologist David Morgan, influenced by feminist theory, argues in *Social Theory and the Family* that privileging the nuclear family is potentially harmful.

1988 In *The Sexual Contract*, British political scientist Carole Pateman reveals that the notion of "separate but equal" hides the power men have in both the private and public spheres.

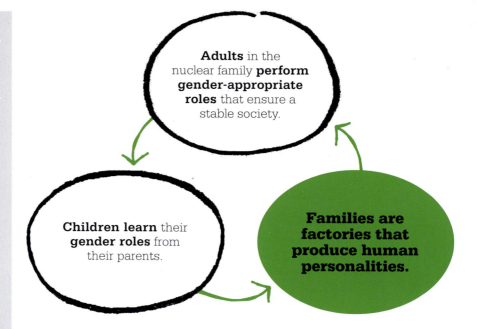

Adults in the nuclear family **perform gender-appropriate roles** that ensure a stable society.

Children learn their **gender roles** from their parents.

Families are factories that produce human personalities.

Many of the writings of the sociologist Talcott Parsons focused on American society in the 1940s and 1950s. Parsons (influenced by the work of Émile Durkheim and Max Weber) claimed that the US economic order required a smaller family unit. The family, Parsons believed, is one of several institutions, such as the education system and the law, that have roles that support one another and enable the stable functioning of society as a whole.

From Parsons' perspective, the modern nuclear family – in which a husband, wife, and their children live relatively isolated from their extended family and community – is the prime agent of socialization. People derive status and roles from their various positions in the family. Although during World War II

See also: Émile Durkheim 34–37 ▪ Max Weber 38–45 ▪ Margaret Mead 298–99 ▪ Judith Stacey 310–11 ▪ Ulrich Beck and Elisabeth Beck-Gernsheim 320–23

women showed that they were perfectly able to do work previously considered "men's work", many non-feminist authors typically assume a natural division of labour between men and women, and Parsons is no exception.

Happy families

The separation of home life and paid employment, with women remaining at home, is logical, according to Parsons, because women are natural carers. Men are then able to take the lead in the role of breadwinning. This division is considered efficient because there is less competition for the family wage. Staying out of paid employment allows women to focus on their caring role: child-rearing and the stabilization of adult personalities.

In addition to cooking and cleaning, this role demands psychological management to ensure a happy household. Parsons is of the opinion that personality is not born but made, and the family is the first place this happens.

He argues that women are able to use their emotional bond with children to steer them into becoming socialized human beings. For example, children learn their sex roles by identification with their same-sex parent. These roles are internalized so that girls become "feminine" women and boys become appropriately "masculine" men, ready to take their place in heterosexual family life. So, in much the same way as a factory produces goods, each stable family unit produces grounded individuals who are groomed to contribute positively to society.

Nuclear power

For Parsons, this neat division avoids tainting the household with the rational, competitive outside world, although the father can provide the link between the outside world and the home when the child is ready. The nuclear family, from a Parsonian perspective, can be seen as the lynchpin of civilization and crucial for the moral health of society.

The nuclear family was once considered the traditional family unit. But the existence of diverse family types is now acknowledged, including same-sex and single-parent families.

This way of understanding families remained dominant in the social sciences until the 1970s and 1980s, when feminists, among others, began to question it. The nuclear family, it is argued, only pertained to privileged white, middle-class Western families and ignored the differing realities of many other groups in society. It also served to justify and perpetuate inequality between the genders. ▪

The importance of the family and its function for society constitutes the primary reason why there is... differentiation of sex roles.
Talcott Parsons

Talcott Parsons

Talcott Parsons was born in Colarado, USA, in 1920 and belonged to one of the oldest families in US history. His father was a liberal academic and a congregational minister.

Parsons graduated from Amherst College with a degree in philosophy and biology and thereafter studied at the London School of Economics, UK, and at the University of Heidelberg, Germany. He was a fierce critic of both fascism and communism, and a staunch advocate of US

society. For most of his academic career, he was based at Harvard University until he retired in 1973, after which he continued to develop theories and give lectures. Parsons died of a stroke in 1979 in Munich, Germany, where he had been lecturing.

Key works

1937 *The Structure of Social Action*
1951 *The Social System*
1955 *Family, Socialization and Interaction Process*

WESTERN MAN HAS BECOME A CONFESSING ANIMAL

MICHEL FOUCAULT (1926–1984)

Why do people talk so much about sex these days? This is one of the key questions posed by the influential French philosopher Michel Foucault in *The History of Sexuality: Volume I* (1976). Foucault claims there is an important relationship between confession, truth, and sex. He suggests that to understand sexuality in the West we must consider how knowledge operates and how particular forms of knowledge, such as the science of sexuality (*scientia sexualis*) and

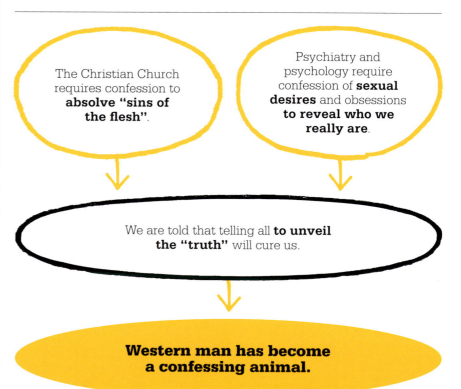

The Christian Church requires confession to **absolve "sins of the flesh"**.

Psychiatry and psychology require confession of **sexual desires** and obsessions **to reveal who we really are**.

We are told that telling all **to unveil the "truth"** will cure us.

Western man has become a confessing animal.

See also: Michel Foucault 52–55; 270–77 ■ Norbert Elias 180–81 ■ Arlie Hochschild 236–43 ■ Karl Marx 254–59 ■ Jeffrey Weeks 324–25

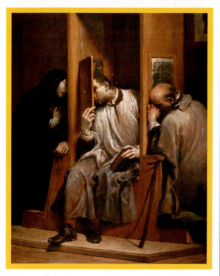

In confessing, we give power to "experts" (priests, therapists, doctors) to judge, punish, and correct us. The confessor suffers an endless cycle of shame, guilt, and more confession.

psychology, have increasingly dominated our ways of thinking about gender and sexuality.

These knowledges are a form of "discourse" – ways of constructing knowledge of the world that create their own "truths". Incitement to discourse, says Foucault, began in the West four centuries ago. The Christian Church's emphasis on "sins of the flesh" in the 17th century led to a greater awareness of sexuality, and to the rise in the 18th century of "scandal" books – fictional accounts of illicit sexual behaviour. The discourse culminated in the 19th-century science of sex that created modern sexuality – from being an act, it was transformed into an identity.

The confession

With the advent of psychiatry and psychology at the end of the 19th century, the Christian ritual of confession – admitting to sins and seeking penance from a priest in order to regain the grace of God – became reconstructed in scientific form. Revealing sexual habits and desires was seen as a way to unearth the "authentic" self.

According to Foucault, the confession has become one of the most valued ways to uncover "truth" in our society. From being a ritual, it has become widespread and is now part of family life, relationships, work, medicine, and policing. As Hungarian sociologist Frank Furedi posits, confession now dominates personal, social, and cultural life, as evident in reality TV programmes and in social media platforms such as Facebook and Twitter.

Healthy relationships, we are continually assured, require truth-telling. Thereafter, an "expert" (a therapist or doctor, for example) is required to reveal our "authentic" self. The compelling promise of the confession is that the more detailed it is, the more we will learn about ourselves, and the more we will be liberated. A person who has experienced trauma is often told that re-telling the experience will have a curative effect. But this "will to truth" is a tactic of power, says Foucault, that can become a form of surveillance and regulation. Confession, he claims, does not reveal the truth, it produces it.

Foucault's work has had an immense impact on feminism and studies of sexuality since the 1980s. In particular, his ideas have influenced British sociologist Jeffrey Weeks, who uses Foucault to unearth the ways in which legislation has served to regulate gender and sexuality in society. ■

Therapy culture

The Hungarian sociologist Frank Furedi, emeritus professor of sociology at the University of Kent, UK, argues that we are obsessed with emotion in the modern age. Experiences and emotions that were once thought normal, such as depression and boredom, are now believed to require treatment and medical intervention.

We read constantly about sports stars' addictions and celebrities' sex lives. And in order to heal, the emotionally injured are encouraged to share their pain with others, to ignore the boundaries separating public and private. To seek help publicly – through a revealing autobiography, for example – is seen as a virtue in a therapeutic culture. Emotions have come to be seen as defining features of identity and we are encouraged to understand them as being indicators of illness. This phenomenon, Furedi argues, is intensely disabling. Ironically, the supposedly "therapeutic" culture leaves society feeling vulnerable.

> Everything had to be told... sex was taken charge of, tracked down.
> **Michel Foucault**

HETEROSEXUALITY MUST BE RECOGNIZED AND STUDIED AS AN INSTITUTION

ADRIENNE RICH (1929–2012)

What if heterosexuality is not innate or the only "normal" sexuality? Heterosexuality is often seen as a "natural" foundation for society, but Adrienne Rich challenges this idea in her important essay "Compulsory Heterosexuality and Lesbian Existence" (1980). Rich was influenced by the French intellectual Simone de Beauvoir, who argues that women have been urged to accept the roles placed upon them in a society that views women as inferior.

Rich suggests that, far from being natural, heterosexuality is imposed on women and must be seen as a system of power that encourages false binary thinking – heterosexual/homosexual, man/woman – in which "heterosexual" and "man" is privileged over "homosexual" and "woman". Compulsory heterosexuality, she says, presents "scripts" to us that are templates for how we conduct relationships and "perform" our gender. We are, for example, encouraged to think of men as being sexually active and women as sexually passive, even though there are no studies to prove this.

> The most pernicious message relayed by pornography is that women are natural sexual prey to men and love it; that sexuality and violence are congruent.
> **Adrienne Rich**

Women are therefore expected, according to Rich, to behave in restrictive ways, as passive and dependent on men; behaviour that does not conform to these expectations is considered deviant and dangerous. Sexually active women, for instance, are labelled as abnormal or called promiscuous. Patriarchy (a power system that assumes male superiority) is a useful conceptual tool for Rich in explaining women's oppression over time; she suggests that it is necessary to think about male

Heterosexuality is constructed as **normal**; men are seen as active and women as passive.

Heterosexuality is **promoted** and maintained by **ideology** and **force**; **lesbianism** is denied and **denigrated**.

Heterosexuality must be recognized as an institution and a system of power that benefits men and subjugates women.

See also: Karl Marx 28–31 ▪ Judith Butler 56–61 ▪ R W Connell 88–89 ▪ bell hooks 90–95 ▪ Sylvia Walby 96–99 ▪ Steven Seidman 326–31

power over women as the key to understanding women's subordinate position.

The power of ideology

Rich discusses many of the ways in which the ideology of compulsory heterosexuality "forces" women into sexual relationships with men. The unequal positions of men and women in the labour market, for instance, can result in women being financially dependent on men. And the pervasive myth that women are at risk of male violence in public spaces, and should restrict their movements and seek male protection, is another example of how women are coerced into heterosexual relationships. Women are encouraged to view themselves as sexual prey, and men as "natural" sexual predators (reinforced by beliefs such as stranger danger), so entering into heterosexual relationships offers women a (false) sense of security.

Despite increasing numbers of people opting to delay marriage, many young women still perceive it as a normal and inevitable part of their lives: this expectation is an important aspect of Rich's argument about the compulsory nature of heterosexuality. Once again, ideology helps shore up heterosexuality through the promotion of romantic narratives in films such as *Titanic* and fairy tales like *Cinderella*.

So prevalent is the idea of heterosexuality in society that people are assumed to be heterosexual unless they declare otherwise. The irony then is that when lesbians or gay men "come out" they are viewed as being more sexual than those who do

not have to. Heterosexuality therefore carries with it an insidious assurance of normality.

Oppressive tactics

Karl Marx argued that capitalism is, in part, maintained through violent actions such as conquest and enslavement. Heterosexuality, Rich contends, can be viewed in a similar way. Under conditions of compulsory heterosexuality, men and women no more choose to be heterosexual or homosexual than a worker chooses wage labour.

Alongside the symbolic violence of ideology, physical violence is often used to control the behaviours of women. Acts such as female genital mutilation and punishment for female adultery or lesbianism **»**

Hollywood films such as *Basic Instinct* that depict lesbians as killers provide an ideological endorsement of lesbianism as threatening and deviant and heterosexuality as normal.

Modes of dress that restrict women's movements are designed, Rich argues, to inhibit women's freedom and prevent them from moving outside and participating in the public sphere, independent of men: they can then, she says, be kept under control by men within compulsory heterosexuality.

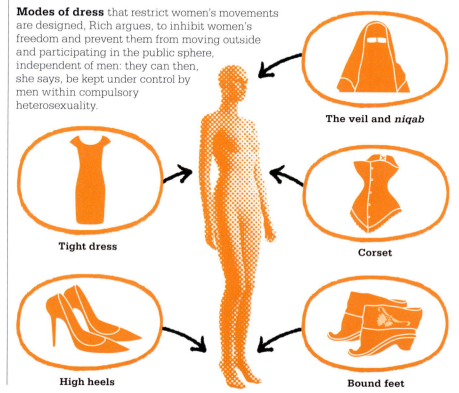

The veil and *niqab*

Tight dress

Corset

High heels

Bound feet

deny women sexuality. Child and arranged marriage, pornographic images that depict women enjoying sexual violence and humiliation, child sexual abuse, and incest – all force male sexuality on women. Rape is another violent tactic; marital rape was not recognized in many Western nations until the 1990s – a reflection of the belief that a woman must be sexually submissive to her husband. And Rich says that "using women as objects in male transactions" is another oppressive tactic of compulsory heterosexuality – as revealed, for instance, in the trafficking of women for sexual exploitation and the use of prostitutes for sexual pleasure.

The view, persistent in some cultures, that it is preferable to send the son to school because sons will stay in the family, whereas girls leave to join the husband's family after marriage, means that across the globe only 30 per cent of girls get a secondary-school education. A poor education will inevitably mean poor employment prospects.

Another method whereby male power is maintained is through the barring of women from exclusive

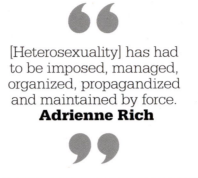

> **66**
> [Heterosexuality] has had to be imposed, managed, organized, propagandized and maintained by force.
> **Adrienne Rich**
> **99**

clubs, and from leisure pursuits such as golf where important business deals might be made.

It is in these many different ways that heterosexuality can be understood as an institution that operates through rigid social constructions of gender and sexuality. Considerable social control, including violence, is used to enforce these ideas of gender. The effect is to keep women inside heterosexuality and to ensure that they remain subordinate within it. A direct consequence of heterosexuality, for Rich, is the oppression of women.

Erasure and denial of lesbianism in history and culture is one of the ways in which heterosexuality is maintained. Rich contends that society is male-identified, meaning it is a place where men and their needs are placed above women's needs. Women feel the need to look beautiful for men, and place more value on romantic relationships with men than on their friendships with women. Rich calls upon women to try and reshape their lives around other women – in other words, to be woman-identified. This does not mean that she urges all women to give up men and sleep with women but, rather, she wants all women to experience that which has arguably only been available to lesbian communities – namely, to love other women.

The lesbian continuum

Rich challenges preconceptions about what a lesbian is – it is not someone who hates men or sleeps with women, but simply a woman who loves women. This idea is known as "political lesbianism": Rich and others saw it as a form of resistance to patriarchy rather than simply a sexual preference.

Adrienne Rich

Feminist, poet, and essayist Adrienne Rich was born in 1929 in Maryland, USA. Her home life was tense, due to religious and cultural divisions between her parents.

Despite later identifying as a lesbian, Rich married, in part to disconnect from her family. During this time she took a teaching post at Columbia University. Her experiences as a mother and a wife impeded her intellectual potential and radicalized her politics. She was committed to anti-war protests, and was also actively engaged in feminist politics and the civil rights movement. In 1997, in protest against the inequalities in the USA, she refused the National Medal of Arts from President Bill Clinton.

Key works

1976 *Of Woman Born: Motherhood as Experience and Institution*
1979 *On Lies, Secrets and Silence: Selected Prose, 1966–1978*
1980 "Compulsory Heterosexuality and Lesbian Existence"

Female witches were often feared and persecuted for their "otherness". In the late 15th century it was believed that they possessed the power to cause impotence and infertility in men.

Lesbianism can, then, be placed on a continuum, which includes those who are sexually attracted to women and those who may be heterosexual but are politically connected to other women. This does not mean there are degrees of lesbian experience, with those who are "less" lesbian being more socially acceptable. Instead, Rich is suggesting that there have always been women who have resisted the compulsory way of life and existed in and out of the continuum for hundreds of years – from the many women in Europe, in the 16th and 17th centuries in particular, who were hanged or burnt as witches, often for living outside of patriarchy, to the late 19th-century "Wigan Pit Brow Lasses", colliery workers who caused scandal in Britain by insisting on wearing trousers.

Rich's idea of a lesbian continuum has caused considerable debate, partly because it can be seen as desexualizing lesbianism and allows feminists to claim to be part of the continuum without examining their heterosexuality.

Sheila Jeffreys, a British radical feminist, argued that it allowed heterosexual women to continue their relationships with men while feeling politically validated. But the strength of Rich's work is that rather than critiquing heterosexual women, it critiques heterosexuality as an institution.

Rich's ideas also challenge the hetero/homo binary and thus anticipate queer theorists such as US scholar Eve Kosofsky Sedgwick, who argues that sexual identity is a construct of Western culture. Sedgwick also opposes the assumption that these constructions of sexuality are only an issue for "minority" groups such as lesbians and gay men.

A conceptual shift
The ideas put forward in Rich's 1980 essay have arguably provided the most important conceptual shift in studies of sexuality by inviting an examination of heterosexuality as an institution. This had never been done before because, as British sociologist

Carol Smart suggests, heterosexual identity, like white colonial identity, has maintained an effortless superiority and an ability to remain invisible because it has constructed itself as the norm. Heterosexual feminists such as British sociologist Stevi Jackson have gone on to unpick heterosexuality as a direct result of Rich's work. French feminist Monique Wittig argued in 1992 that heterosexuality is a political regime that relies on the subordination and appropriation of women.

The recent revelation in the UK of the sexual abuse of girls by celebrities and the abduction of more than 200 schoolgirls in Nigeria, Africa, by the militant Islamist group Boko Haram, are glaring examples of how heterosexuality is still forced on women and girls. The arguments put forward by Rich thus continue to inform important explorations of heterosexuality as a social and political structure. ∎

> **"**
> The patriarchal institution of motherhood is not the "human condition" any more than rape, prostitution, and slavery are.
> **Adrienne Rich**
> **"**

WESTERN FAMILY ARRANGEMENTS ARE DIVERSE, FLUID, AND UNRESOLVED
JUDITH STACEY

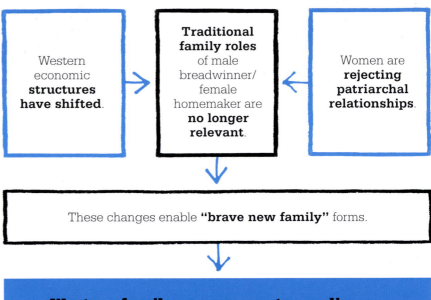

Western economic **structures have shifted**.

Traditional family roles of male breadwinner/ female homemaker are **no longer relevant**.

Women are **rejecting patriarchal relationships**.

These changes enable **"brave new family"** forms.

Western family arrangements are diverse, fluid, and unresolved.

The "modern" US family unit, praised by the likes of Talcott Parsons, is a dated and potentially oppressive institution. This is the view of Judith Stacey, professor emerita of social and cultural analysis at New York University, USA, whose work has focused on the family, queer theory, sexuality, and gender.

Based on her detailed research into families in Silicon Valley, California, Stacey suggests that, in line with demands from a changing economic structure resulting in poverty and unemployment, the family has undergone a radical shift. Marriage is also weaker because women are rejecting patriarchal relationships. Instead,

See also: Sylvia Walby 96–99 ▪ Talcott Parsons 300–01 ▪ Adrienne Rich 304–09 ▪ Ulrich Beck and Elisabeth Beck-Gernsheim 320–23 ▪ Jeffrey Weeks 324–25

there is a move towards blended families, lesbian and gay families, cohabitating couples, and single parents – all of which are part of what she calls the "postmodern" family (although many have argued that these forms have always existed and that Parson's nuclear family was only relevant for a few privileged middle-class families). To reflect this new reality, Stacey insists that the work structure needs to ensure equal pay for men and women, and universal health and child care should be provided.

A pioneering spirit

The economic role of the family has declined, Stacey argues, and as a result, intimacy and love have become more important. Despite the decline of marriage, Stacey does not believe that individuals no longer form meaningful social ties, but rather that complex ties continue to be formed as a result of divorce and remarriage.

Because traditional roles and legal- and blood-ties within the family are less relevant today than they were in the past, family members now have greater choice and are therefore creating more experimental intimacies. She suggests that the heterosexual/homosexual binary is becoming less stable and is being replaced by a "queering" of family relations. These "brave new families" are endeavouring to fully embrace change and diversity and forge more unconventional and egalitarian relationships.

Stacey is in line with other key thinkers, such as Jeffrey Weeks and British sociologist Gillian Dunne, in suggesting that lesbian and gay families are at the forefront of

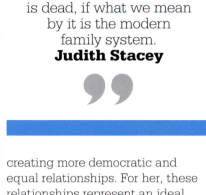

> The family indeed is dead, if what we mean by it is the modern family system.
> **Judith Stacey**

creating more democratic and equal relationships. For her, these relationships represent an ideal of postmodern kinship for which traditional roles are less applicable.

Equal love?

The British sociologist Anthony Giddens is in agreement with Stacey when he suggests that contemporary family forms bring greater equality to relationships and undermine stereotypes and traditional gender roles. In contrast, recent studies in Britain have revealed that in heterosexual couples, women are still largely responsible for housework.

Some have questioned the extent to which same-sex relationships are more equal. Canadian researcher Janice Ristock, for example, has pointed to the prevalence of domestic abuse among same-sex couples. Others, such as sociologists Beck and Beck-Gernsheim, have emphasized the many difficulties associated with living a detraditionalized life. Nevertheless, Stacey contends that social experiments in ties of love are ongoing. ▪

Gay parenthood

Stacey notes that US pressure groups are claiming that the country is facing a crisis due to fatherlessness: heterosexual men are abandoning pregnant partners or opting not to have children at all. New technologies and the availability of contraceptives have separated sex from procreation. And having a child no longer guarantees a future income for parents. Thus Stacey argues that parenting is now more about emotion than finances.

Yet increasing numbers of gay men are opting for parenthood, even though they face many more challenges than lesbian and heterosexual couples, including access to the means of reproduction (eggs and a womb). When straight couples adopt, they are often given healthy babies. Gay men tend to be offered older children or those who are unwell or thought of as "difficult" in some way. Thus it is gay men, says Stacey, who are giving homes to some of society's most needy children.

Gay men who choose to become fathers challenge many of society's stereotypes about masculinity, fatherhood, and gay promiscuity.

THE MARRIAGE CONTRACT IS A WORK CONTRACT

CHRISTINE DELPHY (1941–)

IN CONTEXT

FOCUS
Material feminism

KEY DATES
1974 British sociologist Ann Oakley puts housework under feminist scrutiny in *The Sociology of Housework*.

1980 US writer and feminist Adrienne Rich suggests that heterosexuality is a political institution that continues to give men power and control over women.

1986 According to British sociologist Sylvia Walby, the gender division of labour in the household is one of the key structures that maintain patriarchy in society.

1989 French materialist feminist Monique Wittig publishes *On the Social Contract*, suggesting that the heterosexual contract is a sexual and labour contract.

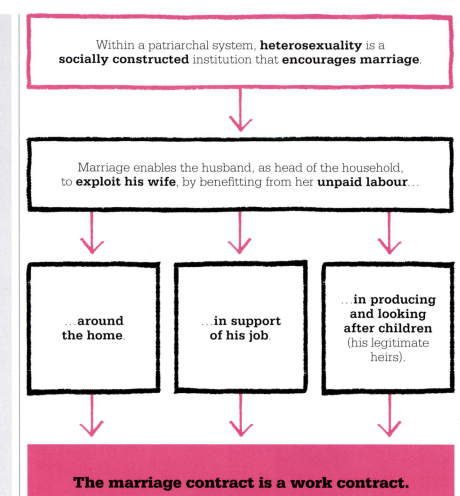

Within a patriarchal system, **heterosexuality** is a **socially constructed** institution that **encourages marriage**.

Marriage enables the husband, as head of the household, to **exploit his wife**, by benefitting from her **unpaid labour**…

…**around the home**.

…**in support of his job**.

…**in producing and looking after children** (his legitimate heirs).

The marriage contract is a work contract.

For hundreds of years in many societies, marriage has been the destiny and often the dream of every young girl. Numerous cultural artefacts – from fairy tales to novels and films – have reinforced this view. However, in the 1980s, feminists such as Ann Oakley and Christine Delphy argued that, in reality, marriage is a highly abusive institution that is fundamental in aiding men's continuing oppression of women.

Christine Delphy is a Marxist theorist, who claims that the only way to investigate oppression of any sort is through a Marxist-style analysis that looks at the material benefits accruing to any party. But where Marx investigated oppression through examining class structure, Delphy investigates women's oppression through the power structure of patriarchy (the power and authority held by men). She says that within a patriarchal system, heterosexuality (and the resulting male–female couple) is not an individual sexual preference but a socially constructed institution, which acts to maintain male domination. This is demonstrated, she argues, in the way that women are channelled into marriage and motherhood, so that their labour can be exploited by men.

Domestic production
Delphy argues that Marx's concepts can be applied to the home environment, which she sees as a site of the patriarchal mode of production. Within this workplace, men systematically take advantage of, and benefit from, women's labour. Under these conditions, women labour for the male head of the household, carrying out

See also: Judith Butler 56–61 ▪ Friedrich Engels 66–67 ▪ Sylvia Walby 96–99 ▪ Arlie Russell Hochschild 236–43 ▪ Teri Lynn Caraway 248–49 ▪ Adrienne Rich 304–09 ▪ Ann Oakley 318–19 ▪ Steven Seidman 326–31

The narrative of films such as *Pride and Prejudice,* adapted from the novel by Jane Austen, reinforce the idea that what every woman wants is to find the "perfect" man and marry him.

potentially limitless work. This role, she says, has no job description, no agreed wage, and no limit in terms of the hours. In any other working position, such conditions would be viewed as exploitative. And in marriages where a woman is engaged in paid employment outside the home, she is also – in most cases – expected to be responsible for household and childcare duties. According to Delphy, when the domestic situation is viewed in these materialist terms, it becomes obvious that married women are working for nothing.

Delphy points out that for Marxists, classes only exist in relation to one another: there can be no bourgeoisie (owners of the means of production) without the proletariat (the workers). Friedrich Engels wrote extensively on how

the development of a class society is the basis for women's oppression. He said that with the rise in private property during the 19th century, there was a corresponding rise in inequality, because men increasingly controlled the public sphere of production, and so became increasingly wealthy and powerful. In addition, men were keen to ensure that their property would be inherited by their legitimate male heirs, and the most effective way of doing this was through the institution of the monogamous patriarchal family. In this way, marriage became a relationship of property.

Unpaid assistants

Demand for labour increased during and following the Industrial Revolution. Women were required to produce more children to supply that demand. But the more children a woman had, the more tightly she was tied to the household and unable to work elsewhere. Delphy also suggests that unmarried women become "wives" too, in

the sense that their labour was often appropriated by brothers, fathers, or employers. This view was partly influenced by the book *Married to the Job*, by British sociologist Janet Finch. This work documents how women are co-opted by employers into a male relative's job, but without pay. This might be through indirect help, such as entertaining (for businessmen or politicians); direct involvement, such as acting as an assistant (for tradesmen or academics); or providing welfare, for example cooking and cleaning (for members of the clergy).

Materialist feminism

Delphy sees capitalism and patriarchy as two distinct social systems, both of which share the appropriation of labour, and which influence and shape each other. Her materialist feminist approach to the family marks a departure from earlier forms of feminist analysis, which did not consider the role of capitalism. Delphy pointed out, however, that a »

Women's exploitation in the home is, says Delphy, a consequence of the combined effects of patriarchy and capitalism, both of which function to perpetuate male dominion and control.

Surveys conducted among OECD countries (Organisation for Economic Co-operation and Development) between 2009 and 2011 have shown a hugely unequal division of labour in the home, with women spending far more time than men caring for family members (preparing food, for example) and doing domestic chores.

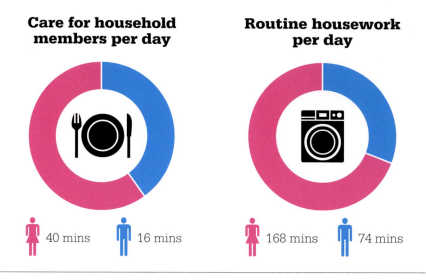

Care for household members per day

♀ 40 mins   ♂ 16 mins

Routine housework per day

♀ 168 mins   ♂ 74 mins

wife's obligation to perform domestic duties is institutionalized on entering marriage, making marriage a labour contract.

This idea has proven to be controversial, but has received support from other academics including the British political theorist Carole Pateman. Drawing on the ideas of British philosopher John Locke, who envisaged a social contract whereby individuals act as good citizens and in return receive protection from the state, Pateman saw heterosexual relations in terms of a sexual contract. Women might be seen to receive protection from men by being married; but husbands had acquired a right to their wives' work and their bodies ("rape in marriage" was not yet a criminal offence in England when Pateman wrote her book *The Sexual Contract* in 1988).

Delphy claims that it is not simply a case of women's work being devalued, as some feminists have argued. The problem will not

go away by paying women more. This is because – as Marxist class analysis has shown – the system only works if there is a group that can be exploited. If there is no exploited group, there is no profit. The creation of an exploitable group in turn depends on the existence of a dominant ideology that runs throughout a society, continually positioning a group of people in a certain way. In a capitalist, patriarchal society, this ideology is sexism (prejudice against women because of their sex).

One critique raised against Delphy's ideas is that they do not take account of the fact that some women benefit from marriage, financially and/or sexually. Delphy does not deny this; she claims, however, that there is an unequal exchange. Wives may enjoy some of the tasks they complete for their own sake and because they love their husbands, but this does not mask the fact that they are expected to do large amounts of

unpaid work. Writing with Diana Leonard, Delphy notes that married men and women may love each other – but "loving women does not prevent men from exploiting them".

A woman is made, not born

Delphy argues that a person's sex is far from self-evident: maleness is not determined solely by the presence of a penis or chest hair, for example, nor is femaleness a function of being able to bear children. Sex is emphasized in society because we live in a world where the simple binary division by gender gives men priority over women, and values heterosexuality over homosexuality. In this way, gender dictates, or "precedes", sex, and the classification of people by sex maintains hierarchies and power structures.

Delphy argues that using sex as a system to classify people is misguided and leads to serious errors in thinking. Why should a person's sex be more prominent than other physical traits that are equally distinguishable? Why is biological sex the only physical trait that splits the world's

> The fact that domestic work is unpaid is not inherent to the particular type of work done, since when the same tasks are done outside the family they are paid for.
> **Christine Delphy & Diana Leonard**
> **British sociologist (1941–2010)**

Signing a marriage contract means entering a legal partnership. This has different implications in different countries, but Delphy suggests it always benefits the man.

population into two groups, which are then loaded with apparently "natural" traits and roles? This idea of sex as a wholly false classification is a crucial concept within Delphy's radical appraisal of patriarchy because it undermines the notion of sex being used to differentiate between those who will dominate (financially, socially, and sexually) and those who will be dominated.

In developing her theories, Delphy was greatly influenced by the writings of the French feminist Simone de Beauvoir, who argued that men had made women "other" in order to support an unequal patriarchal system. By challenging the categories of "men" and "women" as meaningful, Delphy's ideas can be seen as a precursor to queer theory, which questions previously accepted ideas of sex, sexuality, and gender, and their role in establishing identity.

Feminism and Marxism

Delphy's ideas created a furore in feminism when they were first published. This was at a time when feminists were interested in domestic labour and how to understand it, but there was considerable disagreement about the relationship between feminism and Marxism. Some Marxist feminists, such as British scholars Michele Barrett and Mary McIntosh, were extremely hostile to the accusation that men benefit from their wives' labour and therefore directly exploit them. Others argued that it is impossible for two modes of exploitation (patriarchy and capitalism) to exist at the same time in a given society.

Continuing inequality

Delphy and many other feminists since the 1980s have taken on board these criticisms and worked them through in detail, making Delphy's work a continuing influence on feminists around the world. US philosopher Judith Butler, for instance, has used many of Delphy's concepts in her work, in particular her questioning of the sex/gender distinction. In developing Delphy's ideas, French feminist Monique Wittig has argued that the division of society into two sexes is the

product, not the cause, of inequality. In *The End of Equality* (2014), journalist and campaigner Beatrix Campbell charted the ways in which women continue to be exploited in their intimate relationships; for instance, there are few societies in the world where men equally share the work of childcare with women. For Campbell, contemporary global capitalism has served to strengthen and further men's domination over women.

Material oppressions in forms other than economic exploitation, such as the ongoing debate about abortion in some countries, also benefit from Delphy's analysis. If child-bearing and -rearing are understood as labour extorted from women, as Delphy suggests, men may fear that women will escape this form of exploitation by limiting births. In this way the withdrawal of the right to abortion in places such as Northern Ireland, and the fierce debates about abortion in the USA, can be seen as a form of male control over women's choice, keeping them as an exploited class so as to sustain both capitalism and patriarchy. ∎

Christine Delphy

Christine Delphy was born in France in 1941 and educated at the universities of Paris, France, and California, Berkeley, USA. Inspired by the political protests in Paris in 1968, she became an active member of the French women's liberation movement. In 1977 she co-founded the journal *New Feminist Issues* with French philosopher Simone de Beauvoir.

Delphy was a member of Gouines Rouge (Red Dykes), a group that attempted to reclaim the insulting term "dykes" used for lesbians by referring to it as a revolutionary position. More recently, she voted against the law that banned Muslim girls from wearing the *hijab* (veil) in French schools, calling the act a piece of racist legislation.

Key works

1984 *Close to Home: A Materialist Analysis of Women's Oppression*
1992 *Familiar Exploitation* (with Diana Leonard)
1993 *Rethinking Sex and Gender*

HOUSEWORK IS DIRECTLY OPPOSED TO SELF-ACTUALIZATION
ANN OAKLEY (1944–)

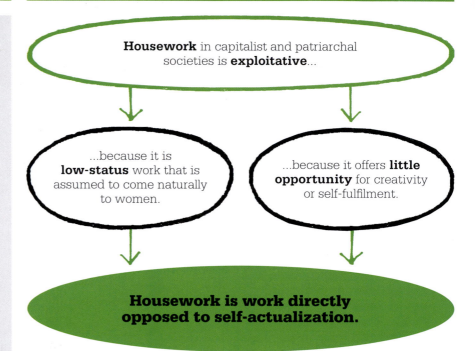

Housework in capitalist and patriarchal societies is **exploitative**...

...because it is **low-status** work that is assumed to come naturally to women.

...because it offers **little opportunity** for creativity or self-fulfilment.

Housework is work directly opposed to self-actualization.

The majority of women's work is still domestic labour that takes place in the home. More than a generation ago, in 1974, sociologist Ann Oakley undertook one of the first feminist sociological studies into domestic labour when she interviewed 40 London housewives between the ages of 20 and 30, all of whom had at least one child under five. The pioneering study looks at housework from the perspective of these women.

Oakley argues that housework should be understood as a job in its own right and not a natural extension of a woman's role as a wife or mother. This was a controversial standpoint at a time

See also: Sylvia Walby 96–99 ▪ Harry Braverman 226–31 ▪ Robert Blauner 232–33 ▪ Arlie Hochschild 236–43 ▪ Talcott Parsons 300–01 ▪ Christine Delphy 312–17

when housework was not seen as "real work". Women are compelled to engage in domestic duties for no wages – an essential form of exploitation that enables capitalism to function and succeed: by providing the needs of the male worker, housewives ensure male workers are able to provide the needs of the economy.

A woman's role?

Domestic duties have often been regarded as natural for women, due to their ability to give birth; although why that capacity means a woman is better able to iron out creases in clothes is unclear. Arguably, it does not occur to most women to demand wages for the work they give "for free".

Karl Marx's argument that male workers are exploited in paid employment is applicable to women's exploitation in the home. Ideology serves to disguise this fact by presenting housework as "natural" for women and also not worthy of a wage. Oakley contends, however, that gender, and gender

roles, should be seen as reflecting cultural and historical processes, rather than as being tied to biology.

Alienation

Marx claims that workers, in a system of private ownership, experience alienation or estrangement from their work because they do not own the fruits of their labour. Similarly, Oakley insists, the majority of housewives are dissatisfied with their lot, finding nothing inherently satisfying about their work, which is lonely, monotonous, and boring. They resent the low status that is associated with being a housewife. Like factory workers, they find their jobs repetitive, fragmented, and time-pressured.

Oakley's studies reveal that women report feelings of alienation from their work more frequently than factory workers. This is due in part to their sense of social isolation as housewives – many of them had careers before marriage, which they subsequently gave up. These women, Oakley says,

> Women's domesticity is a circle of learnt deprivation and induced subjugation.
> **Ann Oakley**

have no autonomy or control; responsibility for the work is theirs alone and if it is not done they risk an angry husband or sick children.

Viewed in this way, housework prevents women from reaching their full potential. Oakley's findings remain significant today: recent research by, among others, British sociologist Caroline Gatrell shows that 40 years later women are still doing most of the housework, despite engaging more in paid employment. ▪

Ads for household products from the 1950s stereotype women as happy housewives who have an emotional attachment to the cleaning agents that form such a key part of their lives.

Ann Oakley

The sociologist and feminist Ann Oakley was born in the UK in 1944. She is professor of sociology and social policy at the University of London. After completing a degree at Oxford, where she was one of the first students to take a sociology option, she wrote two novels but was unable to find a publisher for them. She then enrolled for a PhD and her first academic book, *Sex, Gender and Society*, introduced the term "gender" into everyday use.

Oakley's first novel, *The Men's Room*, was published in 1988 and in 1991 it became a popular BBC series starring Bill Nighy. Oakley remains committed to feminism, and much of her work addresses gender issues. She also has an interest in developing environmentally friendly cleaning products.

Key works

1972 *Sex, Gender and Society*
1974 *The Sociology of Housework*
1974 *Housewife*

WHEN LOVE FINALLY WINS IT HAS TO FACE ALL KINDS OF DEFEAT

ULRICH BECK (1944–2015) AND ELISABETH BECK-GERNSHEIM (1946–)

IN CONTEXT

FOCUS
The chaos of love

KEY DATES
1992 Anthony Giddens' *The Transformation of Intimacy* presents an optimistic view of egalitarian relationships in a reflexive (self-aware) society.

1994 US right-wing thinker Charles Murray asserts that traditional family values need to be emphasized to halt a breakdown in society.

1998 British sociologist Lynn Jamieson suggests that "intimacies" is the most useful term for describing the organization of our personal relationships.

1999 British academics Carol Smart and Bren Neale suggest parental relationships with children are far more enduring than fragile intimate partnerships.

S ustaining a happy, intimate relationship can be a difficult and tiring business, yet at the same time a compelling one. In *The Normal Chaos of Love* (1995), German husband-and-wife team Ulrich Beck and Elisabeth Beck-Gernsheim try to explain why this is so. They trace the development of a new social order that has transformed the ways in which we conduct our personal lives, arguing that one of the main features of this new order is "a collision of interests between love, family, and personal freedom". The traditional nuclear family – "built around gender status" – is disintegrating "on the issues

See also: Ulrich Beck 156–61 ▪ David Held 170–71 ▪ Colin Campbell 234–35 ▪ Talcott Parsons 300–01 ▪ Adrienne Rich 304–09 ▪ Judith Stacey 310–11

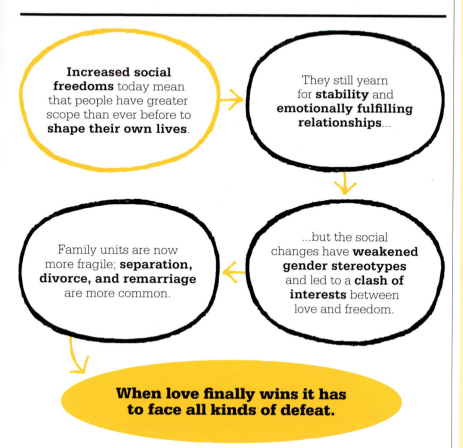

Increased social freedoms today mean that people have greater scope than ever before to **shape their own lives**.

They still yearn for **stability** and **emotionally fulfilling relationships**…

…but the social changes have **weakened gender stereotypes** and led to a **clash of interests** between love and freedom.

Family units are now more fragile; **separation, divorce, and remarriage** are more common.

When love finally wins it has to face all kinds of defeat.

Elisabeth Beck-Gernsheim

Born in Freiburg, Germany, in 1946, Elisabeth Beck-Gernsheim is a sociologist, philosopher, and psychologist. Her partly Jewish heritage meant that many of her family members fled Nazi Germany in the 1930s, with some of her uncles moving to London, UK.

She has produced several key works in collaboration with her husband, Ulrich Beck (who had his own links to London through the LSE), but has also written extensively on issues from social change to biotechnologies. More recently, she has developed an interest in transnational marriage, migration, and ethnic identities. She is currently a senior research fellow at the Institute for Cosmopolitan Studies, University of Munich. (See pp.156–61 for Ulrich Beck.)

Key works

1995 *The Normal Chaos of Love* (with Ulrich Beck)
2002 *Individualization* (with Ulrich Beck)
2002 *Reinventing the Family*

of emancipation and equal rights". The fading away of traditional social identities means that the antagonisms between men and women over gender roles emerge "in the very heart of the private sphere", with the result that more couples are divorcing or separating, and different family forms are taking shape. All this is part of "the quite normal chaos called love".

Individualized living

Following on from Beck's earlier *Risk Society* (1986), which suggests that women are torn between "liberation" and the continuance of traditional gender roles, the couple make the case that a new age of

"reflexive modernity" has produced new risks and opportunities. The particular social and economic conditions of global capitalism have led to a greater sense of individual identity; life is less predictable and personal narratives have more of a sense of "do-it-yourself".

The couple explain that "individualization" is the opposite principle to that used in Germany's Code of Civil Law in the late 19th-century, which established that "marriage is to be viewed [as] a moral and legal order independent of the will of the spouse". Individualization has facilitated new forms of personal and social experimentation. »

People marry for… love and get divorced for… love.
Ulrich Beck & Elisabeth Beck-Gernsheim

The pursuit of love and marriage remains a feature of modern society, despite the fact that the pressures on our lives mean that marriages are more likely to end in divorce than in the past.

The couple's views echo those of Anthony Giddens who, in *The Transformation of Intimacy* (1992), argues that in contemporary society we make our identity rather than inherit it. Such a change has, he says, altered how we experience the family and sexuality.

According to Giddens, in the past, when marriages were economic partnerships rather than love matches, expectations were lower and disappointments fewer. Now that men and women are increasingly compelled to reflexively create their identity through day-to-day decisions, Giddens argues that they are able to choose partnerships on a basis of mutual understanding, leading to what he describes as "pure relationships" – entered for their own sake and only continuing while both parties are happy. Such partnerships, he says, bring greater equality between individuals and challenge traditional gender roles.

Intimate but unequal
Although Beck and Beck-Gernsheim agree with Giddens that there is far more scope in the modern world for men and women to shape their own lives and thus weaken gender stereotypes, they are not wholly optimistic.

Individuals are subject to forces beyond their control; life may be do-it-yourself but it is not do-as-you-like. Women and men, say the couple, are "compulsively on the search for the right way to live" – trying to find a model of the family that will offer a "refuge in... our affluent, impersonal society".

Individualization may have released people from the gender roles prescribed by industrial society, but the material needs of modern life are such that they are forced to build up a life of their own that is adapted to the requirements of the labour market. The family model, Beck and Beck-Gernsheim say, can mesh "one labour market biography with a lifelong housework biography, but not two labour market biographies", because their inner logic demands that "both partners have to put themselves first". Inequality will

> ❝
> For individuals who... invent... their own social setting, love becomes the... pivot giving meaning to their lives.
> **Ulrich Beck & Elisabeth Beck-Gernsheim**
> ❞

persist until men become more accepting of women's participation in the workplace and until men engage in more domestic labour.

Fragile yet resilient
Beck and Beck-Gernsheim contend that, for the most part, intimate relationships cannot be egalitarian; if equality is what is required, then relationships must be abandoned: "Love has become inhospitable."

Men and women face choices and constraints that differ significantly from those faced by their counterparts in previous eras because of the contradiction between the demands of relationships of any kind (family, marriage, motherhood, fatherhood) and the demands of the workplace for mobile, flexible employees. These choices and constraints are responsible for pulling families apart. Rather than being shaped by the rules, traditions, and rituals of previous eras, Beck and Beck-Gernsheim argue that contemporary family units are experiencing a shift from a "community of need", where ties and obligations bound us in our intimate lives, to "elective affinities" that are based on choice and personal inclination. In spite of these difficult changes, the lure of the romantic narrative remains strong. In an uncertain society, "stripped of its traditions and scarred by all kinds of risk", as Beck and Beck-Gernsheim put it, love "will become more important than ever and equally impossible".

Individuals now have a greater desire for emotionally fulfilling relationships, which has fuelled industries such as couples' therapy and self-help publishing. But the ties that bind are fragile and people tend to move on if perfection is not achieved. As the couple say, even when individuals do fall in love ("when love finally wins"), there are often more battles ahead – division, resentment, and divorce, for example.

Beck and Beck-Gernsheim suggest that nurturing personal relationships and attending to the demands of a rapidly changing economic world require a delicate balancing act; as a consequence, there is a rise in divorce. Yet so strong is the hope of happiness that many divorcees marry again.

The importance of children
While Beck and Beck-Gernsheim argue that we have come too far to return to old ways, and neither men nor women would wish to, the pressures of an individualized life mean that it can be tinged with nostalgia and a longing for certainties that perhaps never existed – those "family values" that governments often hark back to. The more fragile our relationships are, the more we hanker after love.

One way in which this yearning for the past exerts itself is through the increased significance placed upon children in contemporary society. While love between adults might be viewed as temporary and vulnerable, love for children becomes more important, with both parents investing emotionally in their children, who are seen as providing unconditional love.

In this respect, Beck and Beck-Gernsheim suggest that men may be challenging women for the role of emotional caretakers in the family. This can be seen in the increased numbers of fathers who seek custody of their children post-divorce and the rise of groups advocating equal parenting rights for fathers, such as Fathers4Justice.

The feminist academic Diana Leonard supports this view, saying that parents are "spoiling" their children with gifts to keep them close to them. Connection with

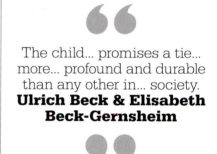

> The child... promises a tie... more... profound and durable than any other in... society.
> **Ulrich Beck & Elisabeth Beck-Gernsheim**

the child in this context becomes ego-driven and intense, providing a feeling of permanence not found in the chaos of adult relationships.

Inevitably, criticisms have been levelled at Beck and Beck-Gernsheim's arguments. Several theorists, including Swedish scholars Diana Mulinari and Kerstin Sandell, have objected to the implication that women are responsible for the increased divorce rates. Nevertheless, *The Normal Chaos of Love* transformed academic work on the family – from being seen as an institution that responds to social change, it was acknowledged as one that actually contributes to change. ∎

Marriage and divorce rates
in the Western world during the past 50 years have altered significantly. Changes in the law and society have seen marriage decline and divorce increase. Although the pattern seems to have stabilized, the family unit is now more fragile.

1960:
- Marriage
- Divorce

2012:
- Marriage
- Divorce

* Divorce not permitted in Spain until 1981. Earliest data is from 1990.

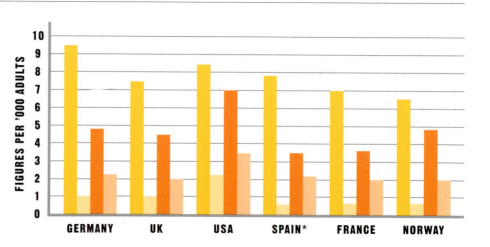

FIGURES PER '000 ADULTS

GERMANY UK USA SPAIN* FRANCE NORWAY

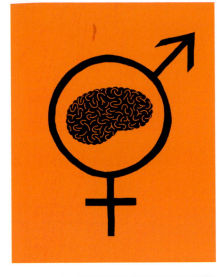

SEXUALITY IS AS MUCH ABOUT BELIEFS AND IDEOLOGIES AS ABOUT THE PHYSICAL BODY
JEFFREY WEEKS (1945–)

Jeffrey Weeks, arguably the most influential British writer on sexuality, offers a detailed historical account of how sexuality has been shaped and regulated by society. He sees sexuality not so much as rooted in the body, but as a social construct that is ideologically determined.

Inspired by the work of British sociologist Mary McIntosh, he argues that industrialization and urbanization consolidated gender divisions and increased the stigma of male same-sex relations.

Weeks examines how Victorian society used the new "sciences" of psychology and sexology (the study

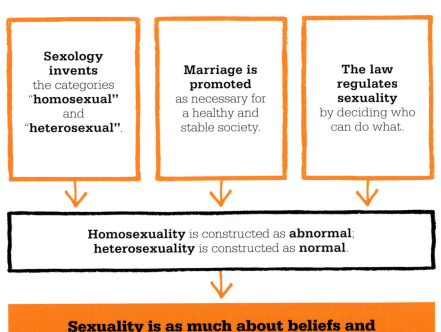

Sexology invents the categories **"homosexual"** and **"heterosexual"**.

Marriage is promoted as necessary for a healthy and stable society.

The law regulates sexuality by deciding who can do what.

Homosexuality is constructed as **abnormal**; **heterosexuality** is constructed as **normal**.

Sexuality is as much about beliefs and ideologies as about the physical body.

See also: Sylvia Walby 96–99 ▪ Margaret Mead 298–99 ▪ Michel Foucault 302–03 ▪ Adrienne Rich 304–09 ▪ Steven Seidman 326–31

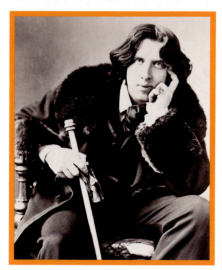

Oscar Wilde was tried and convicted in the late 19th century of "gross indecency" with other men. The trials of the Irish writer helped construct homosexuality as a social problem.

of sexuality that claimed to be a science but was often undertaken by wealthy amateurs) to pass sentence on homosexuals.

The growing interest in classifying sexuality assumed that women were naturally sexually passive and men were naturally active, without having any evidence for such assumptions. Anything contrary to these "essentialist" views (that sexuality reflects biology) was often considered abnormal. The new sciences thus firmly upheld existing patriarchal ideas.

Weeks observes that there was an increasing tendency to view the institution of marriage as essential to the maintenance of a stable, "healthy" society. There was also, therefore, a concern to regulate men's "natural" lustfulness by steering them towards marriage. At the same time as marriage was

heralded as the norm and essential for society, "homosexuality", Weeks says, was invented. Acts that might be homosexual had been criminalized previously, but for the first time in history, sexologists identified a new type of people: "homosexuals" (the category "heterosexuality" was invented soon after). Many of the studies on sexuality were influenced by the teachings of the Christian Church.

Sexuality as social control

Male homosexuality was viewed as a perversion and, increasingly, as a social problem, leading to tighter legal and social control. The 1885 Criminal Law Amendment Act, for example, broadened and redefined the legal definition of homosexual acts. This construction of homosexuality as abnormal, along with essentialist ideas of femininity and masculinity, served to support the belief that heterosexuality was normal and the only legitimate form of sexual behaviour.

It is possible, Weeks suggests, to see this defining of sexuality as both a social construction and a form of social control. The law can decide who is allowed to marry, adopt children, have sex, and at what age. Religion can instruct society that any sex that does not lead to procreation is sinful.

But cultural ideals about who should have sex, and who should not, can have a significant negative impact. There has, for example, been a notable rise in sexually transmitted diseases among the over-50s in the UK because ideas that sex between older people is, among other things, distasteful has led to fewer older people seeking medical advice. ∎

Jeffrey Weeks

The social historian Jeffrey Weeks was born in Rhondda, Wales, UK, in 1945. His work has been influenced by his early participation as a gay rights' activist in the Gay Liberation Front (GLF).

Weeks was a founding member and editor of the journal *Gay Left*, and his work continues to be informed by ideas from lesbian and gay politics, socialism, and feminism. He has published over 20 books and numerous articles on sexuality and intimate life, and is currently a research professor at the eponymous Weeks Centre for Social and Policy Research at South Bank University in London, England. In 2012 he was awarded an OBE for his services to social science.

Key texts

1977 *Coming Out: Homosexual Politics in Britain*
1989 *Sex, Politics and Society*
2001 *Same Sex Intimacies: Families of Choice and Other Life Experiments*

Social processes construct subjectivities not just as categories but at the level of individual desires.
Jeffrey Weeks

QUEER THEORY QUESTIONS THE VERY GROUNDS OF IDENTITY

STEVEN SEIDMAN (1950–)

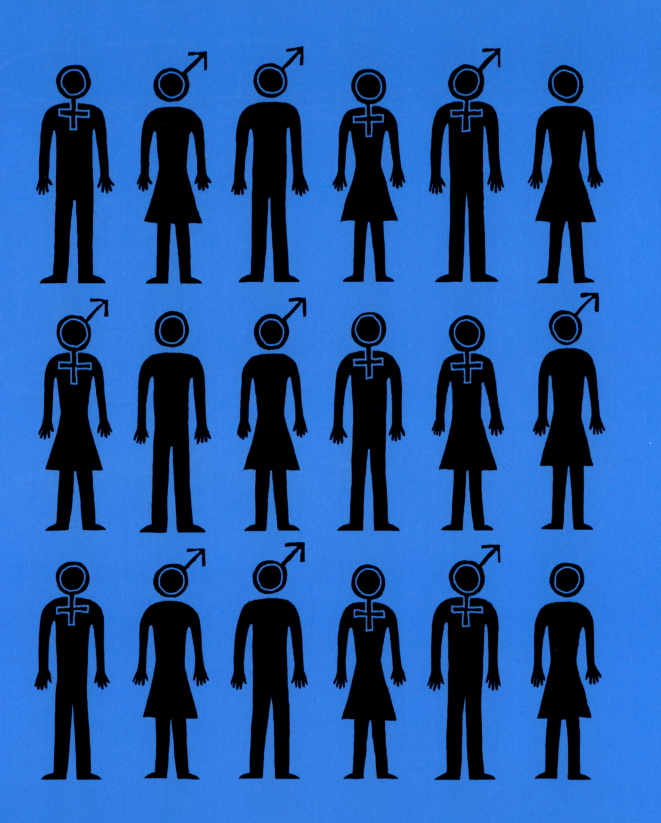

IN CONTEXT

FOCUS
Queer theory

KEY DATES
1976 Michel Foucault's work
*The History of Sexuality.
Volume I: An Introduction*
traces the social construction
of sexuality; he sees sexual
identities emerging through
history and produced by
power, and thus not based
on nature or biology.

1987 ACT UP (AIDS Coalition
to Unleash Power) forms in
New York as a response to
homophobic AIDS campaigns.

1990 In *Gender Trouble*,
Judith Butler argues that
gender is socially constructed
and produced from actions
and behaviours that are
constantly repeated.

1998 US academic Judith
("Jack") Halberstam examines
masculinity without men in
Female Masculinity.

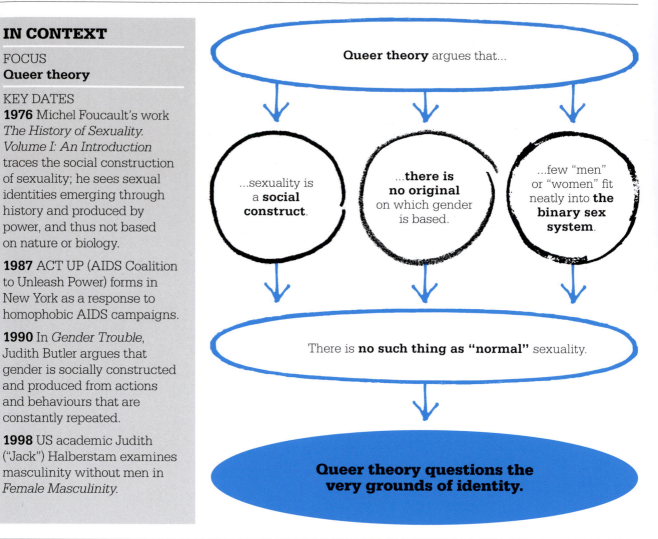

Queer theory argues that...

...sexuality is a **social construct**.

...**there is no original** on which gender is based.

...few "men" or "women" fit neatly into **the binary sex system**.

There is **no such thing as "normal"** sexuality.

Queer theory questions the very grounds of identity.

In the early 1980s the AIDS crisis was wrongly identified in the public mind as an epidemic that mainly affected gay men. The resultant health panic and growth of homophobia made the lesbian and gay community feel isolated and marginalized.

Politically activist gay men and lesbians responded by originating "queer" politics and theory, trying to deprive the term "queer" of its derogatory power. As a reverse affirmation of a pejorative word, "queer" is still a contentious term for some. In its widest sense it includes any category that debunks the heterosexual male–female "natural" model – not just gays and lesbians, but transgendered people, cross-dressers, and others, including heterosexuals who reject the "norm".

Queer theory and its political approach has grown out of feminist and lesbian and gay theory. Influenced by Michel Foucault and Judith Butler, the key queer theorists, such as Eve Kosofsky Sedgwick, Gayle Rubin, and Steven Seidman, have disrupted traditional unitary identity – or social – categories, believing that the differences within categories such as "woman" or "gay" undermine their usefulness. Queer theory, like some feminist theory, was also initially critical of the lesbian and gay communities, which were seen as assimilationist – seeking to enter the mainstream by campaigning for things such as marriage rights.

Constructed sexuality
Steven Seidman is an important figure in the history of queer thinking due to his interpretation

See also: Judith Butler 56–61 ▪ R W Connell 88–89 ▪ Michel Foucault 302–03 ▪ Adrienne Rich 304–09 ▪ Christine Delphy 312–17 ▪ Jeffrey Weeks 324–25

and critique of other queer theorists. Seidman argues, like Foucault and British sociologist Jeffrey Weeks, that sexuality is "constructed". Industrialization and urbanization, which gendered social space by creating the public male world of work and the private female world of the home, produced significant changes in how we understand masculinity and femininity, and the regulation of sexuality. Many of the qualities of gender and sexuality that we now see as natural ("heteronormative" means heterosexuality deemed to be the normal sexual orientation) were established at this time, such as women being seen as nurturing and caring, men being regarded as sexually active, and homosexuality being viewed as a perversion.

Seidman suggests that up until the late 20th century, the study of sexuality can be seen as a history of homosexuality. To the sciences of the 19th century, as well as to sexology and Freudian psychology, heterosexuality was normal and not in need of examination. In effect, this moment in history established

In India, the Supreme Court in 2014 upheld the right of transgender individuals, an ancient group called *hijra*, to self-identify their sex, thereby creating a third gender status in law.

many of the social inequalities that persist, such as the divisions between men and women.

Questions of identity

Because queer theorists such as Seidman regard identity as socially constructed, it is considered unstable and lacking coherence; even something seemingly as stable as biological sex is questioned. Few individuals fit neatly into the categories "man" or "woman" – when tested on chromosomes, hormones, genes, or anatomy most will fit somewhere on a continuum. Some men may look very masculine but have high levels of "female" hormones, or a micropenis, while some women may be very tall or hairy, which are qualities we are encouraged to view as masculine.

When babies are born with ambiguous sex, surgeons have often intervened, removing a boy's small penis and suggesting that he be brought up a girl: a paradoxical response that is at one and the same time essentialist, by assuming that a characteristic of "real" men is that they have large penises, and social constructionist, by implying that identity is really a matter of social conditioning. By challenging the idea of unitary identity, such as straight, and rejecting binary ways of thinking, such as man/woman, Seidman is fundamentally critiquing identity-based theory and politics.

Feminism and the lesbian and gay movements emerged as forms of identity politics to challenge patriarchal and heteronormative society. However, critics argued that these movements were promptly dominated by the white

Let's declare war against the center, against all centers, all authorities in the name of difference.
Steven Seidman

middle class (and men, in the case of lesbian and gay politics). At times, such groups also took essentialist approaches to identity, meaning that they saw identities as rooted in biology and therefore natural or normal. As Butler argues, in this context the marginalized identities themselves, by producing fixed meanings, become complicit in reaffirming the binary regimes. Seidman argues that queer theory provides a necessary challenge to the normative gay and lesbian politics because these sexual identities reproduce the processes of power they seek to challenge.

Challenging the norm

In his influential text *The Trouble with Normal: Sex, Politics, and the Ethics of Queer Life* (1999), Michael Warner argues that the concept of "queer" is not just about resisting the norm but challenging the very idea of normal behaviour. Because "queer" is about attitude rather than identity, anyone who challenges the norm or the expected can be "queer" – for instance, couples who decide not to have children. ❯❯

Seidman, in *Difference Troubles: Queering Social Theory and Sexual Politics* (1997), while acknowledging the important contribution that queer theory has made to modern politics and culture, explores the difficulties that can arise for those who champion the politics of difference. How do social thinkers conceptualize differences, such as sexuality or race, without falling into the trap of reducing them to inferior status?

His pragmatic response is to argue for what he calls a "less repressive view of difference" – a social postmodernism in which "queer" is a verb, describing actions, and no longer a noun.

His aim is to challenge all norms by recognizing difference and having "an affirmative politics of difference" rather than an "illiberal kind of identity politics", such that "difference and democracy might co-exist". Seidman insists that queer theorists must, just as other social thinkers do, take into account other forms of social theory and continue to critique key social institutions and examine how people live their lives.

There are many criticisms of the "queer" concept and its theoretical approach. Although it argues against the concept of identity, it has nevertheless become an umbrella term that particularly

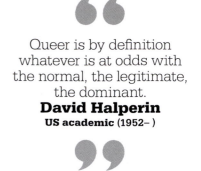

> Queer is by definition whatever is at odds with the normal, the legitimate, the dominant.
> **David Halperin**
> US academic (1952–)

refers to gay men, lesbians, bisexuals, and transgender people. In essence, "queer" can be seen as a new label for an old concept. In this way it has been used to unify many diverse categories of people and has been accused of ignoring important differences and inequalities.

A flawed approach?

Because queer theorists such as the American David Halperin have understood "queer" as a position that can be taken by anyone who feels they have been marginalized due to their sexual preferences, Australian academic Elizabeth Grosz warns that it could be used to validate ethically questionable practices, such as those by "sadists, pederasts... pimps".

Queer theory has been accused of focusing on sexuality to the exclusion of other categories: when Warner argues that pornography is "queer" because – as a result of its uninhibited enactments of sexual fantasies – it is the opposite of "normal", he ignores the ways in which the use of women in much pornography relies on assumptions of "normal" masculinity. In *Queer Race*, South African academic Ian

Groups asserting self-identification sexuality have in recent years challenged the assumption that male–female heterosexuality is the normal sexual orientation. The symbols below are just a few of the many now used to declare to the mainstream that different sexual identities exist.

Self-identification symbols

Symbol	Orientation	Inspiration
♀♀	Female couple	Paired mirror of Venus astrological and alchemical signs, traditionally used to denote an organism of female gender.
♂♂	Male couple	Paired shield and spear of Mars astrological and alchemical signs, traditionally used to denote an organism of male gender.
◯	An intersex or genderless person	The circle element of the Venus and Mars signs, without the gender-defining additions.
⚧	A transgender person	A combination of the male and female gender signs.
☾☽	A bisexual person	The double-moon symbol is widely used in northern Europe, in preference to a "reclaimed" Nazi-era pink triangle used in some countries.

Barnard contends that queer theory has created a whitewashed, Western version of "queer" that ignores race. British historian Jeffrey Weeks has accused it of ignoring the material constraints, such as a lack of money, that mean the decision to be transgressive is not available to all. It could, then, be argued that queer theory has become a white, middle-class, gay male position.

Queer theory also claimed to be the first social theory to challenge the sex/gender distinction. But as British sociologist Diane Richardson points out, this claim is exaggerated: radical feminists such as Christine Delphy, author of *The Main Enemy* (1970), had begun this task as early as the 1970s.

Despite such criticisms, queer theory has influenced a range of academic areas, particularly in studies of masculinity. For example, the work of US academic Judith Halberstam has been lent a "queer" bent by arguing that if we want to understand masculinity it is important to consider marginalized or subordinate forms such as female masculinity. Seidman contends that a queer theory

approach also yields a great deal when applied to novels and films. He argues that the goal of contemporary literary criticism has been to deconstruct the binaries present in much literature – and "queer" makes this possible.

For those whose sexualities are marginalized and who often find that their representations are limited, a "queer" reading that reinterprets the narrative opens up possibilities that the author or creator may not have foreseen – for example: Conan Doyle's *Sherlock Holmes* novels can suggest a

"Queer" interpretations have now been given to many films. In *Alien Resurrection*, Ellen Ripley – part human, part alien – has a potentially erotic liaison with a female android.

romantic friendship between Holmes and Watson; the cross-dressing in Shakespeare's plays can also be given a "queer" interpretation; and films in the *Alien* series are open to a new twist on the "predatory female" trope. "Queer" has also filtered into TV shows such as the US reality series *Queer Eye for the Straight Guy.* ■

US drag king Murray Hill (shown here) is described by Halberstam as "transforming masculinity and exposing its theatricality".

Female masculinity

Judith ("Jack") Halberstam argues that masculinity can exist without men, and challenges the ways in which "masculine" females, such as tomboys, are denigrated. Femaleness does not necessarily produce femininity; maleness does not always lead to masculinity.

This idea poses a fundamental challenge to the gender/sex distinction whereby socially constructed gender (masculinity) is perceived as the natural expression of biological sex (man). Halberstam, whose work is understood as "queer", argues that there has been a tendency to lump all gender-"queer" women under the umbrella term lesbian; but words like "lesbian" and "gay" are not sufficient to explain the broad array of erotic activity that is not conventionally heterosexual. Female maleness becomes a gender rather than an imitation.

"Drag kings" (women who dress as men) highlight the ways in which male masculinity is not based on an authentic essence but is produced through repeated everyday actions.

DIRECTORY

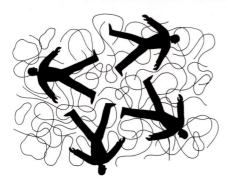

Although sociology was recognized only relatively recently as a social science, its roots go back to the ancient philosophers, such as Plato, who reflected on the "ideal" society. Its main themes have long been of interest to rulers, who had much to gain from understanding the ways in which people form large groups (societies), and how they distribute information, cultural values, wealth, and power. Social reformers realized that such theories could be used to change society, and their voices became ever louder as sociology came of age as a "science". Leaders in the field have been described already in the main part of the book; this section includes other thinkers who have also made key contributions to the discipline and to our understanding of social life.

HERBERT SPENCER
1820–1903

British sociologist and philosopher Herbert Spencer was one of the earliest evolutionary theorists. He coined the phrase "the survival of the fittest", and suggested that societies follow the same evolutionary principles as the human body: they change naturally, evolving from simple states to highly complex forms, and only the stronger societies survive and grow. This view became known as "social Darwinism".
See also: Harriet Martineau 26–27 ▪ Karl Marx 28–31

CHARLES H COOLEY
1864–1929

Charles Horton Cooley, from Michigan, USA, developed the theory of the "looking-glass self", which claims that our sense of identity develops mainly from a sense of how we are perceived by others, and therefore through social interactions. The concept formed the basis for the sociological theory of "socialization".
See also: G H Mead 176–77 ▪ Erving Goffman 190–95

ROBERT E PARK
1864–1944

Robert E Park, a US sociologist, is widely recognized for his work on collective behaviour, race relations, and "human ecology" (the idea that humans function similarly to plants and animals). His approach to urban sociology – treating the city as a "research laboratory" – was a hallmark of what became known as the Chicago School of sociology.
See also: Georg Simmel 104–05 ▪ G H Mead 176–77

SIEGFRIED KRACAUER
1889–1966

Born in Frankfurt, Germany, Siegfried Kracauer is best known for his theories on modern culture and his idea that technology threatens to supersede memory. Kracauer joined Walter Benjamin and Ernst Bloch at the *Frankfurter Zeitung* newspaper as film and literature editor and began analysing society's cultural artefacts, from advertising to films. In 1933 he fled from the Nazi threat, first to Paris and then the USA. Kracauer was a major influence on Theodor W Adorno.
See also: Walter Benjamin 334 ▪ Theodor W Adorno 335

WALTER BENJAMIN
1892–1940

Born in Berlin, Walter Benjamin became a well-known cultural theorist. He was awarded a PhD in literature from the University of Berne, Switzerland, in 1919. He returned to Germany, but fled from the Nazis in 1933. While in exile, he contributed articles on art and culture to the Institute for Social Research in Frankfurt. In 1939 he was interned in a camp in France, and after his release tried to flee to Spain across the Pyrenees. When refused entry, he took his own life.
See also: Jürgen Habermas 286–87 ▪ Siegfried Kracauer 334

KARL MANNHEIM
1893–1947

Karl Mannheim co-founded the sociology of knowledge, which looks at the processes involved in "knowing" the world. He claimed that we "see" the world through the lenses of our culture and ideologies, and as a function of our position in society; "truth" is relative and depends on subject-positions. Hungarian-born, Mannheim studied under Georg Simmel in Berlin, Germany. In 1933 he joined the London School of Economics.
See also: Karl Marx 28–31 ▪ Max Weber 38–45 ▪ Georg Simmel 104–05 ▪ Norbert Elias 180–81

BARBARA ADAM WOOTTON
1897–1988

Sociologist Barbara Adam Wootton is best known for her work *Crime and the Criminal Law* (1963), which reversed commonly accepted views about "the criminal personality". She studied economics at the University of Cambridge, UK, in 1919, and for an MA in 1920, but as women then were not formally recognized as students, she was not awarded the degrees. She later taught sociology at the universities of London and Bedford.
See also: Sylvia Walby 96–99 ▪ Ann Oakley 318–19

ALFRED SCHÜTZ
1899–1959

Alfred Schütz gained a PhD in the philosophy of law at the University of Vienna, Austria, and became interested in the work of Max Weber and the philosopher Edmund Husserl. In 1938 he moved to Paris, and then to New York. Following Husserl's phenomenological approach, which examines how the world is experienced in a person's subjective consciousness, Schütz set out the basis for the new field of phenomenological sociology, which focuses on the nature of social reality.
See also: Max Weber 38–45 ▪ Peter L Berger 336

HERBERT BLUMER
1900–1987

Herbert Blumer gained his PhD in sociology at the University of Chicago, USA, where he taught for 27 years. In 1952 he became the first chair in sociology at the University of California, Berkeley. In *Symbolic Interactionism* (1969), his best-known work, he suggested that individual and collective actions reflect the meaning that people place on things, and these meanings arise from within the context of human group life.
See also: G H Mead 176–77 ▪ Howard S Becker 280–85 ▪ Charles H Cooley 334

THEODOR W ADORNO
1903–1969

Theodor W Adorno was a proponent of neo-Marxist "critical theory". Born in Frankfurt, Germany, he studied under Siegfried Kracauer and received a PhD in philosophy from the University of Frankfurt in 1924. In 1931 he co-founded the Institute for Social Research (also known as the Frankfurt School) with Max Horkheimer, but with the rise of Nazism he moved to the UK, while the institute moved abroad. He was reunited with it in the USA and helped it to become a leading voice against US capitalism's "illusory" pleasures. In 1949, the institute and Adorno returned to (West) Germany. Adorno spent his retirement in Switzerland.
See also: Herbert Marcuse 182–87 ▪ Jürgen Habermas 286–87 ▪ Siegfried Kracauer 334 ▪ Walter Benjamin 334

ANSELM L STRAUSS
1916–1996

US sociologist Anselm L Strauss developed, with Barney Glasser, an innovative method of qualitative analysis known as "grounded theory", which sought to build a theory from research, rather than find research to prove a theory. Strauss studied at the University of Chicago under Herbert Blumer, then later wrote *Social Psychology* (1949) with Alfred R Lindesmith. He became part of the "Second Chicago School", with Howard S Becker and Erving Goffman.
See also: Erving Goffman 264–69 ▪ Howard S Becker 280–85 ▪ Herbert Blumer 335

LOUIS ALTHUSSER
1918–1990

French Marxist philosopher Louis Althusser was a major figure of the structuralist movement of the 1960s, a philosophy that analysed society through the study of signs (semiotics). His reinterpretation of Marx pointed to the role of "ideological state apparatuses" that underlie and perpetuate particular ideologies. Born in Algeria, he moved to France in 1930. He spent most of World War II in a prison

camp in Germany, and began to suffer the psychological problems that would afflict him for the rest of his life. In 1945 he began studying philosophy at the prestigious l'École Normale Supérieure (ENS), Paris. He received great acclaim for his essays and books, despite writing them between hospitalizations. In 1980, he murdered his wife and died, aged 72, in a mental hospital.
See also: Karl Marx 28–31 ▪ Antonio Gramsci 178–79

PABLO GONZÁLEZ CASANOVA
1922–

Pablo González Casanova is a Mexican historian and sociologist who wrote a groundbreaking 1965 article, "Internal Colonialism and National Development". The idea of a "nation within a nation" was first raised by W E B Dubois in the 1930s, but Casanova revealed the structural underpinnings of the idea in practice. His in-depth analysis of the political and social structures of Mexico have provided insights into developing countries in general. In 2003 his work was recognized by UNESCO, when it awarded him the prestigious International José Martí Prize.
See also: W E B Dubois 68–73 ▪ David McCrone 163

DOROTHY E SMITH
1926–

Dorothy E Smith is from Yorkshire, UK. She developed "a sociology for women" that adopted a phenomenological viewpoint, using the subjective, everyday experience of lives, rather than the intellectual theories from the dominant male standpoint. Smith read sociology at the London School of Economics and in 1955 studied at the University of California, Berkeley, USA. She later taught one of the first courses in women's studies, at the University of British Columbia.
See also: Karl Marx 28–31 ▪ Alfred Schütz 335

ROBERT N BELLAH
1927–2013

US sociologist Robert Neelly Bellah is arguably the leading sociologist of religion in the 20th century. He first won acclaim with the essay "Civil Religion in America", which examined the political use of religious symbolism. Born in Oklahoma, USA, Bellah graduated in social anthropology from Harvard University, staying there to gain a PhD under the mentorship of Talcott Parsons. After spending two years reading Islamic studies at McGill University, Montreal, Canada, he returned to Harvard to teach. In 1967 he became professor of sociology at the University of California, Berkeley.
See also: Bryan Wilson 278–79 ▪ Jürgen Habermas 286–87 ▪ Talcott Parsons 300–01

DAVID LOCKWOOD
1929–2014

British sociologist David Lockwood was an influential figure in the theory of class stratification. His father died when he was 10, and his mother struggled financially, which forced him to leave school at an early age to start work. While doing National Service in the armed forces he discovered Marx, and went on to study sociology at the London School of Economics. Lockwood taught at Cambridge and Essex universities. In 1998 he was honoured for his contributions to sociology and made a Commander of the Order of the British Empire (CBE).
See also: Karl Marx 28–31 ▪ Émile Durkheim 34–37

PETER L BERGER
1929–

Born in Austria, Peter Ludwig Berger is best known for his idea that "reality" is constructed through a kind of social consensus, as explained in his book, *The Social Construction of Reality* (1966), written with Thomas Luckmann. Berger emigrated to the USA at the age of 17 and received an MA and PhD in sociology from the New School for Social Research, New York. He became professor of sociology and theology at Boston University, and in 1985 director of Boston's Institute for the Study of Economic Culture, which examines the relationships between economic development and sociocultural change.
See also: Karl Marx 28–31 ▪ Karl Mannheim 335 ▪ Alfred Schütz 335

FERNANDO HENRIQUE CARDOSO
1931–

In 1986, Fernando Cardoso became senator for São Paulo, Brazil, and in 1995 and 1998 he was elected as the country's president. He is acclaimed for bringing economic stability and social reforms to Brazil. Cardoso studied sociology

at the University of São Paulo, becoming a professor there in 1958. His left-wing articles made him popular with the public, but they antagonized the military regime, which forced him into exile in 1964. He taught at universities in Latin America, Europe, and the USA, before returning to Brazil.
See also: Karl Marx 28–31 ▪ Immanuel Wallerstein 144–45

CHRISTOPHER LASCH
1932–1994

The US political theorist and historian Christopher Lasch was an only child of left-wing intellectuals. He graduated from Harvard University in 1954 and took an MA in history at Columbia. While on a sabbatical in the UK, he wrote *The New Radicalism in America* (1965). It portrayed intellectuals as self-indulgent strivers, who professed to offer guidance, but were really interested in status and power. An iconoclast who tried to disrupt consensus thinking, his work included strong critiques of democratic citizenship, elite groups, consumerism, mass culture, US institutions, and the idea that Western societies are making some kind of "progress".
See also: Karl Marx 28–31 ▪ Jürgen Habermas 286–87 ▪ Theodor W Adorno 335

JOHN GOLDTHORPE
1935–

John Goldthorpe was born in Yorkshire, UK, and attended the London School of Economics. An expert in social mobility and class stratification, he invented the Goldthorpe Class Scheme, a seven-

layer structure now used in Europe, Australasia, and North America. He is a critic of the concepts of "cultural capital" and "habitus", especially as formulated by Pierre Bourdieu. He was a fellow of Oxford University from 1969 to 2002 and holds a US visiting professorship at Cornell University, USA.
See also: Max Weber 38–45 ▪ Pierre Bourdieu 76–79

MICHAEL LÖWY
1938–

The French-Brazilian sociologist and professor Michael Löwy grew up in São Paulo, Brazil, in a family of immigrants from Austria. He is best known for developing Georg Lukács' idea of "romantic anti-capitalism", which seeks to disrupt capitalism not through socialism, but by a return to a pre-industrial past and way of thinking. Löwy was politicized by reading the Marxist theorist Rosa Luxemberg, and studied sociology at the University of São Paulo under Fernando Cardoso and Antonio Candido. He gained a PhD from the Sorbonne, France, focusing on Marxist theory.
See also: Karl Marx 28–31 ▪ Pierre Bourdieu 76–79 ▪ Walter Benjamin 334

JON ELSTER
1940–

Norweigan sociologist Jon Elster focuses on rational-choice theory – the idea that people make decisions based on rational considerations of fact (although his later work reveals his disenchantment with the power of reason). Elster's ideas have influenced governments,

economists, sociologists, and psychologists. He has taught in the UK, USA, and France. In 1995 he became the first Robert K Merton Professor of the Social Sciences at Columbia University, USA.
See also: Karl Marx 28–31 ▪ Max Weber 38–45 ▪ Talcott Parsons 300–01

JULIA KRISTEVA
1941–

Julia Kristeva was born in Bulgaria. Her writings on linguistics, semiotics, psychoanalysis, and feminism have received worldwide acclaim. After graduating from university in Sofia, she gained a scholarship to study in Paris. She became part of the left-wing intellectual group associated with St Germain (the Parisian "Left Bank"), and her study of language and linguistics was heavily influenced by the work of contemporaries such as Michel Foucault and Roland Barthes. She became a psychoanalyst, and increasingly interested in the nature of the relationship between language and the body.
See also: Michel Foucault 52–55; 302–03 ▪ Elizabeth Grosz 339

NANCY CHODOROW
1944–

Born in New York, USA, Nancy Chodorow is a leading theorist in feminist thought. She studied anthropology at Radcliffe College, Massachusetts, then trained as a psychoanalyst in San Francisco. In 1975, she received a PhD in sociology from Brandeis University, Boston. Using an interdisciplinary approach, she formulated a

psychoanalytic theory of feminism that opened up the field of feminist psychology. She teaches at the University of California at Berkeley.
See also: Harriet Martineau 26–27 ▪ Judith Butler 56–61 ▪ Erich Fromm 188

DONNA HARAWAY
1944–

"Technoscience" expert Donna Haraway, from Colorado, USA, studied evolutionary philosophy and theology in Paris, before returning to the USA to take a triple major in zoology, philosophy, and literature. Her PhD in biology at Yale examined the use of metaphor in shaping experiments – she sees biology as part of politics, religion, and culture. Professor emerita in the History of Consciousness department at the University of California, Santa Cruz, Haraway is the leading authority on the now-intimate relationship between people and technology. Her essay "A Cyborg Manifesto" suggests that people are already part-human, part-machine, and that this blend allows women to reconstruct themselves anew, in an age of "cyborg feminism".
See also: Karl Marx 28–31 ▪ Michel Foucault 52–55; 302–03 ▪ Bruno Latour 338

SHULAMITH FIRESTONE
1945–2012

Revolutionary feminist Shulamith Firestone was born in Ottawa, Canada. She studied art at Washington University, St Louis, USA, and then at the Art Institute of Chicago, where she became part of the Chicago Women's Liberation Union, the first such group in the USA. She wrote the influential book *The Dialectic of Sex: A Case for Feminist Revolution* (1970), arguing that women are an oppressed class, and gender inequality is ultimately dictated by biology. Echoing Marx, she felt the answer was for women to seize control of the means of human reproduction (made possible by new forms of contraception). She subsequently produced only one book, but her impact on feminism remained undiminished.
See also: Harriet Martineau 26–27 ▪ Karl Marx 28–31

WALDEN BELLO
1945–

Walden Bello was born in Manila, the Philippines, and became a political activist in the 1970s, following the declaration of martial law by Ferdinand Marcos. Bello's official roles have included a professorship in sociology at universities in the Philippines, the USA, and Canada; Chairperson of the board of Greenpeace South Asia; and Member of the Philippine House of Representatives. Bello is a leading critic of globalization.
See also: Robert N Bellah 336 ▪ Michael Löwy 337

BRYAN S TURNER
1945–

Born in Birmingham, UK, Bryan S Turner is a world authority on the sociology of religion. His first book, *Weber and Islam* (1974), is a classic. He became professor of sociology at the University of Cambridge in 1998, and has held professorships in Australia, the Netherlands, and the USA. His interests include globalization and religion, religious authority and electronic information, religious consumerism and youth cultures, and human rights and religion. In *The Body & Society* (1984; 2008), he argues that the body, not abstract ideas such as class, should be the focus of sociological analysis.
See also: Edward Said 80–81 ▪ Max Weber 220–23

BRUNO LATOUR
1947–

Bruno Latour was born in Burgundy, France, and trained as a philosopher, then anthropologist. In the 1980s, along with Michel Callon and John Law, he developed "actor–network theory" (ANT) – the idea that knowledge does not depend on a "truth" waiting to be found, but is gained by analysing the interaction between actors and networks, where the "actors" involved in creating meaning are both physical and symbolic. Latour is professor at Sciences Po, Paris.
See also: Harold Garfinkel 50–51 ▪ Michel Foucault 302–03 ▪ Donna Haraway 338

THEDA SKOCPOL
1947–

US sociologist and political theorist Theda Skocpol is Victor S Thomas Professor of government and sociology at Harvard University, USA. Her research focuses on US social policy, health reform, and civic engagement in US democracy. She began her career studying the French, Russian, and Chinese revolutions, and in the 1970s she became the main advocate of state autonomy theory. As a result, she is

credited with the creation of a new paradigm, in which institutions (including the state) are seen as structuring political life and embodying ideas, and therefore open to causal analysis. Her 1992 book, *Protecting Soldiers and Mothers: The Political Origins of Social Policy in the United States*, won five major awards.
See also: Max Weber 38–45 ▪ David McCrone 163 ▪ Arjun Appadurai 166–69

ANGELA McROBBIE
1951–

Cultural theorist Angela McRobbie is a professor at Goldsmiths College, London, UK. She claims that in the 1990s there was a backlash against feminism, despite a general consensus that gender equality had been achieved. In her 2009 book, *The Aftermath of Feminism*, she draws on the work of Ulrich Beck and Anthony Giddens to argue "female individualization" is a post-feminist masquerade that reinforces masculine hegemony.
See also: Anthony Giddens 148–49 ▪ Stuart Hall 200–01 ▪ Beverley Skeggs 339

ELIZABETH GROSZ
1952–

Cultural and feminist theorist Elizabeth Grosz was born in Sydney, Australia, where she studied philosophy. Influenced by post-structuralist thinkers such as French philosopher Jacques Derrida, her work focuses on gender studies (particularly sexual difference), female sexuality, and the nature of time from a feminist perspective. She is professor of women's studies at Duke University, Durham, North Carolina, USA. Her best-known work is *Becoming Undone* (2011), in which she outlines a feminist theory of postmodern Darwinism.
See also: Michel Foucault 52–55; 302–03 ▪ Julia Kristeva 337

TARIQ MODOOD
1952–

Tariq Modood was born in Karachi, Pakistan, but raised in the UK. After studies at Durham and Swansea universities, in 1997 he became founding director of the Centre for Study of Ethnicity and Citizenship at the University of Bristol, UK. Also a professor of sociology, politics, and public policy at Bristol, he is an expert on racism, multiculturalism, and secularism. He argues that contemporary Muslim assertiveness is inspired by identity politics, rather than theological demands. Modood is the co-founding editor of the international journal *Ethnicities*.
See also: Stuart Hall 200–01 ▪ Bryan S Turner 338

HARTMUT ROSA
1965–

German sociologist Hartmut Rosa is best known for his theory of "social acceleration", the title of his 2013 book. The theory suggests that not only is society accelerating in three ways (technological innovation, societal change, and the pace of life), it also has zones of deceleration, in which large groups of people may be left behind. He also claims that the world is at a point of "frenetic standstill" where nothing remains as it is, while nothing essential actually changes. Rosa is professor of general and theoretical sociology at Friedrich Schiller University, Jena, Germany.
See also: Karl Marx 28–31 ▪ Max Weber 38–45 ▪ Jürgen Habermas 286–87

TOM SHAKESPEARE
1966–

Tom Shakespeare studied at the University of Cambridge before spending five years working for the World Health Organization (WHO) in Geneva, Switzerland. A medical sociologist who is disabled himself, he is an important voice in the sociology of difference. He is interested in the ethical aspects of genetics and disability studies, particularly in the areas of sexual politics and human rights. Now a lecturer in medical sociology at the University of East Anglia, UK, he claims that people "are disabled by society and by their bodies".
See also: G H Mead 176–77 ▪ Erving Goffman 190–95 ▪ Howard S Becker 280–85

BEVERLEY SKEGGS

Beverley Skeggs studied sociology at the universities of York and Keele, before becoming Director of women's studies at Lancaster University (with Celia Lury). In *Formations of Class & Gender* (1997), she argues that class should feature prominently in theories of gender, identity, and power. Skeggs is a professor of sociology at Goldsmiths College, London.
See also: Karl Marx 28–31 ▪ Pierre Bourdieu 76–79 ▪ Ann Oakley 318–19

GLOSSARY

Agency Within sociology, self-determination or free will.

Alienation As identified by Karl Marx, the condition of workers who feel estranged from themselves or society due to a lack of power, control, fulfilment, and satisfaction. Marx attributed this to **capitalist** society, where the **means of production** are privately owned. The concept has been developed since the post-war era by various thinkers, including Robert Blauner.

Anomie A state of confusion or "normlessness" resulting from rapid social change. When the social **norms** and values governing daily conduct change suddenly, people are liable to feel disorientated and purposeless until a social order is re-established. See also **deviant**.

Bourgeoisie In Marxist theory (see **Marxism**), the **social class** of people that owns the industrial **means of production**.

Bureaucracy Defined by Max Weber as a system of organization that is characterized by a hierarchy of rule-bound officials who keep detailed records of every action.

Capital Financial assets (such as machinery) or the value of financial assets (cash) used to produce an income. One of the key ingredients of economic activity, along with land, labour, and enterprise.

Capitalism An economic system based on the private ownership of property and the **means of production**, in which firms compete to sell goods at a profit and workers labour for a wage.

Capitalists The **social class** of people that owns the **means of production** in industrial societies.

Chicago School Not to be confused with a free-market economic way of thinking, this sociological school of thought developed in the 1920s and 30s. Although its interests were eclectic, it is often identified with the origin of urban sociology.

Class conflict The tension that can arise between different **social classes** as a result of competing socio-economic interests.

Colonialism A phenomenon whereby one country exerts control over another, often exploiting it economically. The term commonly refers to the conquest, settlement, and exploitation of parts of the world by European powers.

Communism An economic system based on collective ownership of property and the **means of production**.

Construct, social A concept or perception created in society.

Consumer An individual who buys goods or services for personal use or consumption.

Consumerism The state of an advanced **capitalist** society in which the buying and selling of various goods and services define the era. The term also refers to a perception that individuals desire goods to construct self-identity.

Conspicuous consumption A concept originated by Thorstein Veblen that describes members of a wealthy leisure class using luxury goods to display their status. See also **material culture**.

Culture The languages, customs, knowledge, beliefs, values, and **norms** that combine to make up the way of life of any society. May also refer to the arts (such as music, theatre, literature, and so on).

Delinquency Minor crime committed by a young person; the term can also describe behaviour judged "unacceptable", according to a society's **norms**.

Determinism The belief that a person's behaviour is determined by some form of external force (such as God, genetics, or the environment) so that genuinely free choice is not possible. See also **economic determinism**.

Deviant A behaviour or type of person deemed "rule-breaking" in terms of the **norms** of a particular society or social group.

Discourse In general use, communication in speech or writing; in sociological use, a framework or system of ideas that provides a perspective on life and governs the way in which it can be discussed. Discourse imparts a meaning to events, and varies in different eras, geographical areas, and within social groups.

Domestic labour Unpaid work in the home, such as cooking, cleaning, childcare, and looking after the sick and elderly.

Economic determinism A materialistic view of history which claims that economic forces cause all social phenomena and the evolution of human society.

Elite A small group of people who hold a disproportionate amount of wealth and power in a society.

Emotional labour As defined by Arlie Hochschild, paid work that requires an employee to display certain emotions with the aim of inducing particular responses.

Empirical evidence Evidence that can be observed by the senses and measured in some way.

Enlightenment, the A cultural and intellectual movement in 17th- and 18th-century Europe, which fused ideas about God, rational thought, and nature into a world view that prized logic and reason over emotion and intuition.

Essentialism The belief that entities or people have inherent characteristics, properties, or "essences" that define who or what they are. This idea leads to the view that specific categories of people possess intrinsic traits.

Ethnicity The shared **culture** of a social group (such as language or religious belief) that gives its members a common identity and differentiates it from others.

Ethnography The study of peoples and **cultures**.

Ethnology The comparative study of the differences between peoples and **cultures**.

Feminism A social movement that advocates the social, political, and economic equality of the sexes. Feminism is recognized as having had several "waves", or eras, each with a different agenda of issues.

Feudalism A dominant historical social system in which a warrior nobility was rewarded with land for providing military services to the monarch, and then ruled over those lands, benefiting from labour and produce offered by vassals, or peasants, in return for protection.

Frankfurt School A school of interdisciplinary social theory, originally known as the Institute for Social Research, and affiliated to the University of Frankfurt. The school fostered new **Marxist** thinking in the 20th century.

Functionalism In sociology, the idea that society is structured like a biological organism, with specialized functions. Every aspect of this society is interdependent and contributes to the overall functioning and stability.

Gender The socially constructed, rather than biological, differences between men and women.

Gender identity The way that individuals are seen, by themselves and others, in terms of their **gender roles** and biological sex.

Gender role The social behaviour expected from men and women.

Gentrification A change in the character of a run-down urban community that is observable through rising property prices and an influx of wealthier individuals.

Globalization The increasing interconnectedness and interdependence of societies around the world, as media and **culture**, consumer goods, and economic interests spread globally.

Glocalization The modification of global forms – from fashion trends to musical genres – by contact with local communities and individuals.

Habitus Building on Thomas Aquinas's idea that each of us thinks of ourselves as a certain kind of person, Pierre Bourdieu's concept refers to a set of acquired dispositions whereby people of a **social class** share cultural values.

Hegemonic masculinity A given society's ideal of manliness. In Western nations, this is associated with heterosexuality, "toughness", wealth, and the subordination of women. The idea emphasizes that masculinity is an acquired identity.

Hegemony The winning and holding of power and the formation of social groups during that process. Antonio Gramsci says that hegemony is how the dominant **social class** maintains its position.

Heterosexuality An attraction towards people of the opposite sex.

Homosexuality An attraction towards people of the same sex.

Hyperreality As defined by Baudrillard, the idea that there is no longer a separate "reality" to which images and symbols refer, but instead a simulated version of reality that seems more real than anything that exists in the physical world.

Iatrogenesis The danger that arises from a medical system that harms more people than it heals.

Identity The ways that individuals see and define themselves, and how other people define them.

Ideology A framework of ideas that provides a viewpoint or set of beliefs for a social group.

Industrial Revolution A stage of development, originating in the UK in the 18th century, during which the economy was transformed by new forms of mechanization from a mainly agricultural economy to an urban, industrialized one.

Interpretive The subjective approach to examining society, which contrasts with the objective and scientific **positivist** approach.

Left-wing In the political spectrum, the ideas of those who favour reforming or **socialist** ideas.

Marginalization The process by which a person or group of people is pushed outside a powerful or ruling group, with a consequent loss of power, status, and influence.

Marxism A **structural** theory of society developed by Karl Marx and Friedrich Engels, which claims that history consists of epochs and that social change arises out of conflict between **social classes** – the owners of the **means of production** and the exploited working masses.

Mass culture Products (books, TV shows, and so on) that are created as entertainment for sale to the general public.

Material culture The history and philosophy of objects; relationships between people and things.

Means of production The key resources (such as land, factories, raw materials, and machinery) needed to produce society's goods.

Mode of production A **Marxist** concept about the way a society is organized to produce goods and services; this includes the **means of production** and the relations among the labour force.

Modernity The condition of society from the 17th century onwards, especially the social change created by the **Industrial Revolution** and **urbanization**.

Nation A body of people united by **culture**, history, or language, and usually sharing a particular geographical area.

Nationalism A shared sense of identification that is attached to a **nation** and stems from a commitment to a common **ideology** and **culture**.

Neo-liberalism Political and economic philosophies rooted in a belief that free markets, limited government, and the responses of individuals provide better solutions to problems than action by the **state** can.

Neo-tribalism Short-lived, flexible, and fluid groupings that people, in a world of rapid change, seek out to provide meaning in their lives.

Norms Social rules that define what is expected behaviour ("normal") for an individual in a particular society or situation.

Nuclear family A two-generation household of parents and children – a prime agent of socialization.

Other, the A concept introduced by Simone de Beauvoir to explain how a group (men, in her example) sees itself as the **norm**, and judges anyone outside the group (women) in terms of its own standards and attributes, rather than seeing that group independently, with the attributes it actually has.

Patriarchy A social stratification system in which men dominate, exploit, and oppress women.

Positivism Within sociology, the idea, pioneered by Auguste Comte, that it is possible to observe social life in a measurable, verifiable, scientific way and establish truths about a society. This belief gave rise to the "positivist" opinion that science could build a better world.

Postmodernism A perspective that denies there can be a defining "truth" about anything, instead suggesting that a text, person, or society can be deconstructed according to many different perspectives into many different "truths". By its nature, postmodern social theory rejects being defined and it is difficult to define.

Poverty Seebohm Rowntree defined poverty as a state in which earnings are insufficient to provide a person's bare necessities, which is a subsistence level of poverty. The term absolute poverty refers to a living standard based upon providing basic wants such as food, housing, fuel, and clothing. In wealthier countries today, poverty is usually measured in relation to the generally accepted standard of living of the time, known as relative poverty. Some definitions of poverty now take account of factors, such as skills or health, that might produce social exclusion.

Proletariat In Marxist theory (see **Marxism**), the **social class** of people who labour for a wage.

Queer theory A cultural theory that challenges binary notions of sexuality and instead suggests that sexualities are cultural **constructs** influenced by time and place.

Racism Discriminating against people, typically identified by skin colour, on the basis of alleged biological differences, when in fact such biological differences have been proved by science not to exist.

Right-wing In the political spectrum, the conservative ideas of those who favour traditional social arrangements and values.

Roles The patterns of behaviour that are expected from individuals in society. See also **gender role**.

Secularization The process whereby religion and its institutions lose social significance.

Self-estrangement The sense of **alienation** from oneself, either through a negative view of self or a sense that one's labour belongs to another person or organization.

Sexism Prejudice, discrimination, or stereotyping of people because of their male or female sex.

Sexual orientation An individual's attraction towards people of a particular biological sex.

Simulacra Images that have no basis in reality yet appear to reflect things in the physical world.

Social class A status hierarchy within the social system, reflecting power, wealth, education, and prestige. Although these classes vary by society, Western models generally recognize three broad groups. The upper class is a small social group that has the highest status and owns a disproportionate amount of society's wealth. The term middle class refers to well-educated people who do non-manual work, often in offices. Working class refers to people with manual jobs, such as factory or agricultural work.

Social mobility The movement of people or categories of people, such as families, from one **social class** to another.

Social networks The links between individuals, families, and groups with similar interests.

Social structure The social institutions and relationships that form the framework of a society.

Socialism A political doctrine that aims to establish social and economic equality. Socialists argue that if the economy were under the control of the majority of the population, a more equitable **social structure** would be created.

State An organized authority that has legitimate control over a territory, and a monopoly of the use of force within its territory.

Status The amount of prestige or importance a person has in the eyes of other members of society.

Stereotype A widely held but overly simplified image of a person or social group.

Stigma A mark of disgrace or an undesirable characteristic, physical or social, that disqualifies an individual from being fully accepted by society. The **marginalization** of individuals in society, because they evoke negative responses from others, has been attributed to their having assumed stigmatized identities, which are demeaning in some way.

Structuralism The idea that we must understand things – such as a text, human mind, or society – by examining the elements, or pattern of relationships, in its structure.

Subculture A group that is seen as a distinct and separate one within the larger society because while its members may agree with most of a society's values, beliefs, and customs, they differ in others.

Symbolic interactionism The theory that the self is an entity that arises through social interactions.

Urbanization The process of people moving from rural areas to live in towns and cities, and the social changes accompanying that. The world is increasingly urban.

Values Ideas or beliefs about the worth of a thing, process, or behaviour. A person's values govern the way they behave; a society's values dictate what is important or not important, and what is acceptable or unacceptable.

INDEX

Main page references are in **bold**.

A

Adorno, Theodor W 59, 139, 247, 287, **335**
Agnew, Robert 262
Alexander, Jeffrey 175, **204–09**
alienation 40–45, 87, 122, 123, 155, 186, 213, 228–230, **232–33**, 236, 239, 242, 259, 293, 297
   and Marxism 155, 232, 238, 319
   and religion 256, 257
   of self **188**
Althusser, Louis **335–36**
Anderson, Benedict 175, **202–03**
Anderson, Elijah 65, **82–83**
anomie 29, 30, 31, 34, 37, 188, 252, 253
   and strain theory **262–63**
Appadurai, Arjun 135, **166–69**
asabiyyah (solidarity) **20**
Atkinson, Will 138

B

Barthes, Roland 235
Bates, Inge 293
Baudrillard, Jean 126, 175, 189, **196–99**, 235
Bauman, Zygmunt 105, 134, **136–43**, 155, 222
Beck, Ulrich
   chaos of love 297, **320–23**
   risk society 134, 135, **156–61**
Beck-Gernsheim, Elisabeth 297, **320–23**
Becker, Howard S 252, 253, **280–85**
Bell, Daniel 212, 213, **224–25**, 234

Bellah, Robert N 118, 207, **336**
Bello, Walden **338**
Benjamin, Walter **334**
Berger, Peter L 278, **336**
Bernstein, Basil 292
Blauner, Robert 212, 213, **232–33**
Blumer, Herbert **335**
Bourdieu, Pierre 14, 65, **76–79**, 195, 208, 213, 219, 288, 289
Bowles, Samuel 253, **288–89**
Braverman, Harry 212, 213, **226–31**, 243
Bryman, Alan 103, **126–27**
Burawoy, Michael 213, 231, **244–45**
bureaucracy **40–45**
   and political oligarchy **260**
Butler, Judith 19, 54, **56–61**, 297, 317, 329

C

Calvin, John 222, 223
Campbell, Colin 212, 213, 219, 223, **234–35**
capitalism 174–75
   and alienation of self **188**
   and cognitive justice **150–51**
   commodities and value **198**
   and competition 33
   and consumer desire 235
   cultural hegemony **178–79**
   and dehumanization 42–43
   digital technology **152–55**
   emotional labour **236–43**
   and gentrification **128–31**
   hierarchy 93
   historical materialism 29–31
   and individualism 21, 43–45, 94, 321–22, 337
   industrious and leisure classes 216–17, 219

legitimation crisis **286–87**
marriage as labour contract 316
and Marxism 18, 107, 134, 145, 221, 307
medieval 223
monopoly and de-skilling **226–31**
neo-liberalism 277
and patriarchy 98
and pecuniary emulation 218–19
pre-industrial past, disruption by return to 337
Protestant work ethic 41–42, **220–23**, 258
pursuit of profit 221–22, 231
rational modernity **38–45**
and religion *see* religion
and self-interest 21, 30–31
social class and de-skilling 230–31
workforce oppression 47
world-system theory **144–45**
see also consumerism; work and consumerism
Caraway, Teri Lynn 213, **248–49**
Cardoso, Fernando Henrique **336–37**
Casanova, Pablo González **336**
Castells, Manuel 135, **152–55**
Chicago School 102, 104, 105, 128, 164, 334
Chodorow, Nancy **337–38**
Cicourel, Aaron 282
civic spirit **21**
civilizing process **180–81**
class
   class structure, levelling of 186–87
   conflict **28–31**
   consciousness 30, 64
   and cultural hegemony **178–79**
   cultural reproduction and education **292–93**
   and de-skilling 230–31
   exploitation **66–67**
   and feminism 95, 338
   and gender 339
   habitus **76–79**
   identification 181

inequality **84–87**
  leisure, and capitalism 216–17, 219
  and Marxism **28–31**, 64, 315, 316
  and pecuniary emulation 218–19
  and queer theory 331
  stratification 336
  see also culture and identity
climate change **148–49**
Cobb, Jonathan 64, 84, 87
cognitive justice **150–51**
Cohen, Stanley 253, 266, **290**
colonialism 94, 95
  and Orientalism **80–81**
  and world-system theory **144–45**
communication systems **110–11**,
  152–55
communitarianism **112–19**
community 12, 13, 20, 21, 108–09,
  112–19, **124–25**
  neo-tribalism **291**
  and society **32–33**
competition, and capitalism 33
compulsory heterosexuality 308
Comte, Auguste 18, **22–25**, 29, 35, 36
confession 302–03
Connell, R W 65, **88–89**
conspicuous consumption **214–19**
consumerism
  and advertising industry 235
  conspicuous consumption **214–19**
  consumer credit 143
  and gentrification 131
  globalization and modernity 168
  and liquid modernity 141–42
  and self-identity 142, 143, 201
  see also capitalism; work and
    consumerism
Cooley, Charles H 176, **334**
Cooley, Michael 231
Crenshaw, Kimberlé 92–93
crime **282–85**
  criminal personality 335
  strain theory/anomie **262–63**
culture and identity
  alienation of self **188**
  civilizing process **180–81**
  cultural capital and class habitus 78,
    79
  cultural exchange, and globalization
    170–71

cultural hegemony **178–79**
cultural identity **200–01**
cultural reproduction and education
  292–93
cultural sociology **204–09**
culture, independent nature of
  207–08
culture industry **182–87**
culture and reality, lack of gap
  between 186–87
culture and social order 174–75
development of self **176–77**
emotional labour **236–43**
"false needs", government imposition
  of 185–86
gender performativity **56–61**
gender roles across different cultures
  298–99
globalization and modernity **166–69**
nationalism and imagined
  communities **202–03**
sacred nature of 207
secularization 279
simulacra **196–99**
stigma **190–95**
structure 44–45, 208–09
structure of feeling **189**
symbolic interactionism 192
virtual and actual social identity 193
working-class integration 184–85
see also class

Darwin, Charles 35, 217
de Beauvoir, Simone 58, 59, 306, 317
de Sousa Santos, Boaventura 134,
  150–51
de-skilling **226–31**
Deagan, Mary Jo 192
Declaration of Independence, US
  26–27
Delphy, Christine 296, 297, **312–17**,
  331
democracy, and political oligarchy **260**
Devasahayam, Theresa 238

deviance
  labelling theory 282–83, 284
  stigma **190–95**
  strain theory/anomie **262–63**
Disney 126–27, 199
Disneyization **126–27**
division of labour 13, 19, 33, 35–37, 102,
  212, 238, 243, 248, 293, 300, 301
domestic violence 98–99
Du Bois, W E B 64, 65, **68–73**, 82
Dunne, Gillian 311
Durkheim, Émile 13, 19, 24, 31, 33,
  34–37, 44, 77, 102, 206, 207, 209,
  220, 252, 253, 262

education
  communitarian school 118
  compulsory heterosexuality 308
  and cultural reproduction **292–93**
  de-skilling 229
  hidden curriculum **288–89**
  liquid modernity 141
  and Marxism 293
  "separate but equal" schools, US 70
  standardization of 123
efficiency 31, 40–45, 122–23, 221, 228–31
Elias, Norbert 174, **180–81**
Elster, Jon **337**
emotional labour **236–43**
Engels, Friedrich 18, 64, **66–67**, 134,
  212, 256, 315
Enlightenment, the 12, 21, 23, 24, 54,
  64, 139–40
environment
  climate change and Giddens paradox
    148–49
  and neo-liberalism 277
  risk assessment 160, 161
  waste and conspicuous consumption
    217–18
epistemologies of the South **150–51**
ethnomethodology **50–51**
etiquette, and civilizing process 181
Etzioni, Amitai 21, 103, **112–19**, 188

F

families and intimacies 296–97
  chaos of love **320–23**
  children in contemporary society 323
  communitarianism 117–18, 119
  compulsory heterosexuality **304–09**
  confessions and truth 302–03
  family roles 296–97
  gay parenthood 311
  gender roles across different cultures
    298–99
  housework as alienation **318–19**
  and industrialization 300
  interpersonal relationships 297
  marriage and divorce rates 323
  marriage as "healthy" 325
  material feminism **312–17**
  men as breadwinners, women as
    carers 301
  nuclear family 300, 301, 311, 320–21
  postmodernism **310–11**
  queer theory **326–31**
  same-sex relationships 311, 324
  social construction of sexuality
    324–25
  socialization of children and
    stabilization of adults **300–01**
  therapy culture 303
Featherstone, Mike 200
feminism
  and class 95, 338
  and communitarianism 119
  compulsory heterosexuality **304–09**
  feminist psychology 337–38, 339
  feminization of work **248–49**
  "first-wave" 97–98
  housework as alienation **318–19**
  and intersectionality **90–95**
  and Marxism 92, 97–98, 319
  material feminism **312–17**
  and queer theory 329, 331
  and religion 258
  "second wave" 26, 58, 65, 92, 98
  and slimming and dieting 275
  and social justice **26–27**
  "third wave" 98

women's liberation movement 299
  see also gender; patriarchy; sexuality
Ferguson, Adam 18, **21**
Feuerbach, Ludwig 256
Finch, Janet 315
Firestone, Shulamith **338**
Foucault, Michel
  governmentality 252–53, **270–77**
  power/resistance 15, 19, **52–55**, 267
  sexuality 19, 302–03
  will to truth 58–59, 296, 297, **302–03**
Frankfurt School 31, 44, 232, 247
French Revolution, effects of 24–25
Fromm, Erich 174, **188**
functionalism **34–37**, 267, 296
Furedi, Frank 303

G

G-7 formation 150
Garfinkel, Harold 19, **50–51**
gender
  cultural reproduction and education
    292–93
  inequalities and emotional labour
    242–43
  performativity **56–61**
  queer theory 58, 61, 297, 309, 310,
    311, 317 **326–31**
  roles across different cultures **298–99**
  see also feminism; sexuality
gentrification and urban life **128–31**
Gerth, Hans Heinrich 19, 44
ghetto, iconic **82–83**
Giddens, Anthony 44, 135, **148–49**,
  195, 311, 322
Giddens paradox **148–49**
Gilroy, Paul 65, **75**
Gintis, Herbert 253, **288–89**
Glassner, Barry 158, 335
global warming **148–49**, 160
  see also environment
global world 15, 134–35
  climate change and Giddens paradox
    148–49
  cognitive justice **150–51**

  cosmopolitanism and risk 161
  and culture *see* culture and identity
  digital technology **152–55**
  downsizing of firms 141
  epistemologies of the South **150–51**
  feminization of work **248–49**
  financial risk 161
  gender wellbeing 249
  global cities **164–65**
  globalization **170–71**
  globalization and modernity **166–69**
  glocalization **146–47**
  hyper-globalism 171
  liquid modernity **136–43**
  mobilities **162**
  neo-nationalism **163**
  network society **152–55**
  and patriarchy 317
  post-industrialism 153
  risk society **156–61**
  sceptics 171
  solid modernity, move from 138–40
  terrorism risk 161
  transformationalist 171
  world-system theory **144–45**
  see also modern living
glocalization **146–47**
Goffman, Erving
  institutionalization 252, 253, **264–69**
  stigma 174, **190–95**
Goldthorpe, John **337**
Gouldner, Alvin 285
governmentality **270–77**
Gramsci, Antonio 174, 175, **178–79**,
  252
Green, Gill 195
Grosz, Elizabeth 330, **339**
grounded theory 335

H

Habermas, Jürgen 253, 259, **286–87**
habitus **76–79**
Halberstam, Judith 328, 331
Hall, Stuart 175, **200–01**
Haraway, Donna **338**

health and medicine, iatrogenesis **261**
Hegel, Georg 29, 111, 246, 256
  dialectic view of history 29
hegemonic masculinity **88–89**
Held, David 135, **170–71**
hidden curriculum **288–89**
Hochschild, Arlie Russell 213, **236–43**
hooks, bell 65, 89, **90–95**
housework as alienation **318–19**
hyperreality 199

I

iatrogenesis **261**
Ibn Khaldun 18, **20**
Ichijo, Atsuko 163
Illich, Ivan 253, **261**
imagined communities **202–03**
imperialism see colonialism
individualism
  and capitalism 21, 43–45, 94, 321–22,
    337
  and communitarianism 114, 116,
    118–19
  and institutionalization 268–69
  institutions 253
  and social interaction 239–40
industrial relations, workers' consent,
  managing **244–45**
Industrial Revolution 12, 13, 15, 66, 196
industrialization 102–03
  automation and alienation **232–33**
  class exploitation **66–67**
  and de-skilling **226–31**
  division of labour 33, 36–37, 293,
    300, 301
  and families and intimacies 300
  female unpaid labour 315
  and sexuality 329
inequalities see social inequalities
Inglis, David 150
innovation, technological see
    technological innovation
institutions 14–15, 37, 252–53
  anomie/strain theory **262–63**
  causal analysis 338–39

cultural reproduction and education
    292–93
  education and the hidden curriculum
    288–89
  female domestic duties 316
  governmentality **270–77**
  iatrogenesis **261**
  individualism and society 253
  institutionalization **264–69**
  labelling theory **280–85**
  legitimation crisis **286–87**
  moral panic theory **290**
  neo-tribalism **291**
  oligarchy **260**
  religion **254–59**
  secularization 252–53, **278–79**
  surveillance and control 54
intersectionality **90–95**

JKL

Jackson, Philip W 288
Jacobs, Jane 102, 103, **108–09**
job satisfaction, and workplace "games"
    245
knowledge
  actor–network theory (ANT) 338
  as "law of three stages" 24
  and power 55
  sociology of 335
Kracauer, Siegfried **334**
Kristeva, Julia **337**
labelling theory **280–85**
Lasch, Christopher 310, **337**
Latour, Bruno 247, **338**
Lefebvre, Henri 103, **106–07**
legitimation crisis **286–87**
leisure classes, and capitalism 216–17,
    219
Lemert, Edwin 283
Lemke, Thomas 272
Leonard, Diana 316, 323
liquid modernity **136–43**
Lockwood, David **336**
love, chaos of **320–23**
Löwy, Michael **337**

Luckmann, Thomas 278, 336
Luhmann, Niklas 103, **110–11**
Lutz, Helma 92

M

McCrone, David 135, **162**
McDonaldization **120–23**
McGrew, Anthony 135
McRobbie, Angela 290, **339**
Maffesoli, Michel 253, **291**
management
  empowerment, and worker
    productivity 230
  workers' consent, managing **244–45**
Mannheim, Karl 181, **335**
Marcuse, Herbert 175, **182–87**, 247
Marron, Donncha 143
Martineau, Harriet 18–19, 25, **26–27**,
    64–65
Marx, Karl 13, 14, 22, **28–31**, 40, 41, 45,
    64, 138, 144, 189, 220, 228, **254–59**
    see also Marxism
Marxism
  and alienation 155, 232, 238, 319
  and capitalism 18, 44, 107, 134, 145,
    184, 221, 307
  and class **28–31**, 64, 66–67, 315, 316
  and economics 25, 31, 178, 179, 286
  and feminism 92, 97–98, 319
  and religion 252, 253, **254–59**, 279
    see also Frankfurt School; Marx, Karl
material culture **246–47**
material feminism **312–17**
materialism, historical 29–30
Matza, David 285
Mead, G H 174, **176–77**, 201
Mead, Margaret 13, 58, 296, 297,
    298–99
media
  and class conflict 187
  and consumerism 235
  and globalization 168
  moral panic theory **290**
  public anxieties, feeding on 160
mental life of the metropolis **104–05**

meritocracy, and cultural reproduction 292
Merton, Robert K 252, 253, **262–63**
Michels, Robert 252, **260**
Miller, Daniel 213, **246–47**
mobilities **162**
modern living 134–35
  bureaucracy restrictions 42–43, 45, 139
  civic engagement 125
  communication systems **110–11**
  communitarianism **112–19**
  Disneyization **126–27**
  emotional labour 127
  gentrification and urban life **128–31**
  globalization and modernity **166–69**
  liquid modernity **136–43**
  McDonaldization **120–23**
  rational modernity **38–45**
  right to the city **106–07**
  sidewalks, importance of 109
  social capital **124–25**
  see also global world; urbanization
Modood, Tariq **339**
moral panic theory **290**
morality
  and communitarianism 117, 118, 119
  moral entrepreneurs 283–84
  and religion 256–57
Morgan, David 300
multiculturalism **200–01**
multinational urban culture, and global cities 165

N

nationalism
  and imagined communities **202–03**
  neo-nationalism **163**
Neale, Bren 320
neo-liberalism 277
neo-nationalism **163**
neo-tribalism **291**
network society **152–55**
nuclear family 300, 301, 311, 320–21

Oakley, Ann 296, **318–19**
oligarchy **260**
Orientalism **80–81**
Park, Robert E 102, **334**
Parsons, Talcott 44, 50, 111, 207, 296, **300–01**
Pateman, Carole 316
patriarchy **96–99**
  domestic violence 98–99
  and gender equality 65
  and global world 317
  hegemonic masculinity **88–89**
  and lesbianism, political 308–09
  and material feminism **312–17**
  rules of 94, 95
  and slimming and dieting 275
  see also feminism
pecuniary emulation, and class 218–19
Perrow, Charles 158
Peterson, Richard 219
phenomenological sociology 335, 336
Pickett, Kate 65
positivism **22–25**, 36, 40, 44
post-industrialism **224–25**
postmodern family **310–11**
poverty, relative **74**
power, political and social, sociological imagination **46–49**
power/resistance **52–55**
Protestant work ethic 41–42, **220–23**, 258
Putnam, Robert D 20, 103, 115, **124–25**
queer theory 58, 61, 297, 309, 310, 311, 317, **326–31**

R

race and ethnicity **68–73**
racism 64–65, **75**, 92–93
  iconic ghetto **82–83**
radicalism, and religion 258–59

rational modernity **38–45**
rational-choice theory 337
rationalization 40–45, 228–31
  and McDonaldization **120–23**
  and social control 240–41
  sociological imagination **46–49**
Raz, Aviad 243
reality
  hyperreality 199
  and simulacra **196–99**
  social construction of 336
religion
  and identity politics 339
  and Marxism 252, 253, **254–59**, 279
  political use of religious symbolism 336
  Protestant work ethic 41–42, **220–23**, 258
  and secularization 252–53, **278–79**
  and social inequalities 257–58, 259
  sociology of 338
Rich, Adrienne 296, **304–09**
Richardson, Diane 306, 331
right to the city **106–07**
risk society **156–61**
Ritzer, George 103, **120–23**, 127
Robertson, Roland 134, **146–47**
Romantic ethic **234–35**
Rosa, Hartmut **339**
Rose, Nikolas 277
Rousseau, Jean-Jacques 29, 302
Rubin, Gayle 299
Rubio, Fernando Dominguez 247

S

Said, Edward 65, **80–81**
Saint-Simon, Henri de 13, 18, 23, 24
Sassatelli, Roberta 234
Sassen, Saskia 134, **164–65**
Savage, Mike 219
Schütz, Alfred **335**
Scull, Andrew T 266
secularization 252–53, **278–79**
  and Protestant work ethic 223
Sedgwick, Eve Kosofsky 309

Seeman, Melvin 188
Seidman, Steven 297, **326–31**
self-identity
  alienation of **188**
  and consumerism 142, 143, 201
  cultural identity **200–01**
  development of **176–77**
  and globalization 147
  and institutionalization 267–69
  looking-glass self 334
  self-respect and class inequality 84–86
  sexuality symbols 330
self-interest, and capitalism 21, 30–31
semiotics 235, **335–36**
Sennett, Richard 64, **84–87**, 119, 141
service industries, and post-
    industrialism 225
sexuality
  compulsory heterosexuality **304–09**
  and confession 302–03
  feminism and social justice **26–27**
  gender performativity **56–61**
  gender roles across different cultures
    298–99
  hegemonic masculinity **88–89**
  and industrialization 329
  lesbianism, political 308–09
  masculinity and queer theory 331
  and patriarchy 98–99
  and power 55
  queer theory 58, 61, 297, 309, 310,
    311, 317, **326–31**
  same-sex relationships 311
  self-identification symbols 330
  social construction of **324–25**
  women's liberation movement 299
  see also feminism; gender
Shakespeare, Tom **339**
Siisiäinen, Martti 124
Silva, Elizabeth B. 247
Simmel, Georg 102, **104–05**
simulacra **196–99**
Skeggs, Beverley **339**
Skocpol, Theda **338–39**
slavery 27, 71–72
Smart, Carol 309, 320
Smith, Dorothy E **336**
social acceleration theory 339
social capital **124–25**
  and class habitus 78–79

decline 116
social change, and dehumanized
    society 47–48
social Darwinism 334
social inequalities
  abortion 317
  class consciousness 64
  class exploitation **66–67**
  class habitus **76–79**
  class inequality **84–87**
  double-consciousness of African-
    Americans 71
  education and the hidden curriculum
    288–89
  education of working classes, effects
    of 86–87
  feminism see feminism
  and gentrification 130–31
  global patterns of wealth 145
  hegemonic masculinity **88–89**
  iconic ghetto **82–83**
  immigration and unskilled labour
    85–86
  and liquid modernity 142–43
  Orientalism **80–81**
  patriarchy **96–99**
  patriarchy and gender equality 65
  poverty, relative **74**
  public space in cities, loss of 107
  race and ethnicity **68–73**
  racism see racism
  and religion 257–58, 259
  and risk society 160
  self-respect and class inequality
    84–86
social mobility, and cultural capital 79
social movements 49, 160
social science, sociology as 13–14,
    18–19
social solidarity 20, 26
society
  communitarianism **112–19**
  development as historical process
    29–30
  and modernity 12–13
  risk **156–61**
sociological imagination **46–49**
sociology of difference 339
sociology foundations
  civic spirit **21**

class conflict **28–31**
community and society **32–33**
ethnomethodology **50–51**
feminism and social justice **26–27**
French Revolution, effects of 24–25
functionalism **34–37**, 267
gender performativity **56–61**
industrialization and division of
    labour 33, 36–37, 293, 300, 301
positivism **22–25**
power/resistance **52–55**
rational modernity **38–45**
science of society 24–25, 35–36
social solidarity (asabiyyah) **20**
sociological imagination **46–49**
verifiability of observation 24
solidarity (asabiyyah) **20**
sovereignty, and nationalism 203
Spencer, Herbert 18, 19, 34, 35–36,
    334
Spencer-Brown, George 111
Stacey, Judith 297, **310–11**
stigma **190–95**
strain theory **262–63**
Strauss, Anselm L **335**
structuration theory 195
surveillance techniques 273–74, 275
symbolic interactionism 192, 239, 335

T

Taylor, Laurie 266
technocrats, and post-industrialism 225
technological innovation 15
  and alienation **232–33**
  and alienation of self **188**
  class conflict, disappearance of 187
  and de-skilling **226–31**
  and global cities 164
  and globalization 168
  hierarchies of exclusion 151
  information excess 199
  and memory 334
  mobilities **162**
  online communities 117
  post-industrialism **224–25**

and risk 158–59, 160
technoscience 338
virtual worlds and simulacra 198–99
terrorism
and cultural structures 209
moral panic theory **290**
and risk 158, 161
therapy culture 303
Thorpe, Christopher 206
Tomlinson, John 123
Tönnies, Ferdinand 18, **32–33**, 102, 105, 114, 115–16
tourism, and liquid modernity 142–43
Townsend, Peter 65, **74**
transnational companies, and global cities 165
Turner, Bryan S **338**

UV

UK
Chilcot Inquiry 260
Clean Air Act 148
industrialism 66, 67, 144
Poverty and Social Exclusion survey 74
same-sex marriage 324
UN
Kyoto Protocol 148
Universal Declaration of Human Rights 64
urbanization 102–03, 145, 181, 325
class inequality **84–87**
and gender 329
gentrification and urban life **128–31**
global cities **164–65**
mental life of the metropolis **104–05**
public and private spaces 107
rational modernity **38–45**
right to the city **106–07**
sidewalks, importance of 109
stranger, social role of 104, 105
urban community **108–09**
urban regeneration 129–30
see also modern living
Urry, John 135, **162**

USA
black ghettos 82–83
Civil Rights Act 64, 70
Continental Congress 27
Declaration of Independence **26–27**
double-consciousness of African-Americans 71
female emancipation 26–27, 298
Freedmen's Bureau 71–72
McCarthyism 46
marital rape as crime 306
New Left 49
racial segregation and violence 72–73
"separate but equal" schools 70
slavery history 27, 71–72
Veblen, Thorstein 212, 213, **214–19**, 246
Vega, Rodrigo Cordero 286
voluntarism 124–25

W

Walby, Sylvia 65, **96–99**, 213, 249
Wallerstein, Immanuel 134, **144–45**, 150–51
Warner, Michael 329–30
waste, and conspicuous consumption 217–18
Weber, Max 13, 14
class conflict 31, 64
Protestant work ethic 19, 102, **220–23**, 234–35, 258
rationalization 19, 37, 38–45, 47, 122–23, 252
Webster, Frank 155
Weeks, Jeffrey 297, 303, 311, **324–25**, 329, 331
welfare state, and liquid modernity 141
White, Harrison 152
Wichterich, Christa 249
Wilkinson, Richard 65
Williams, Raymond 174, **189**
Willis, Paul 253, **292–93**
Wilson, Bryan 253, 257, **278–79**
Wittig, Monique 309, 317

Woodhead, Linda 258
Woodward, Sophie 247
Wootton, Anthony 195
Wootton, Barbara Adam **335**
work and consumerism 212–13
alienation 40–45, 87, 122, 123, 213 228–230, **232–33**, 236, 239, 242
American Dream 262–63
capitalism and consumer desire 235
conspicuous consumption **214–19**
consumer society 212–13
consumerism as mass deception 235
de-skilling **226–31**
denim phenomenon 247
emotional labour **236–43**
feminization of work **248–49**
labour unions and workers' collectives 245
material culture **246–47**
pecuniary emulation 218–19
post-industrialism **224–25**
Protestant work ethic 41–42, **220–23**, 258
pursuit of profit 221–22
Romantic ethic and consumer culture **234–35**
social prestige and cultural omnivores 219
taste and material culture 247
workers' consent, managing **244–45**
workplace "games" 245
worldly success and salvation 222–23
see also capitalism; consumerism
worker empowerment, automated work processes 232
workforce mobility 33
World Social Forum 150, 151
world-system theory **144–45**
Wortham, Anne 74
Wright Mills, Charles 14, 19, 44, **46–49**, 131, 238, 239

YZ

Young, Jock 284–85, 290
Zukin, Sharon 103, **128–31**

ACKNOWLEDGMENTS

Dorling Kindersley would like to thank John McKenzie for his contribution to chapter 3, Christopher Westhorp for proofreading the book, and Margaret McKormack for providing the index.

PICTURE CREDITS

247 Corbis: ZenShui (bl). **249 Getty Images:** Bloomberg/Contributor (bl). **257 Corbis:** Godong/Robert Harding World Imagery (br). **259 Getty Images:** Egbert van Heemskerk the Elder (br). **261 Corbis:** Ariel Skelley/Blend Images (cr). **263 Bridgeman Art Library:** Peter Newark American Pictures (tl). **267 Corbis:** Cameron Davidson (tr). **Getty Images:** Stock Montage/Contributor (bl). **269 Alamy Images:** Moviestore collection Ltd (tr). **Dreamstime.com:** Photographerlondon (bl). **273 akg-images:** British Library (tr). **274 Corbis:** Fine Art Photographic Library (tr). **275 Corbis:** 68/Ocean (bl). **277 Dreamstime.com:** Walter Arce (tr). **279 Getty Images:** Chung Sung-Jun/Staff (tr). **283 Dreamstime.com:** Ayse Ezgi Icmeli (bc). Ayse Ezgi Icmeli (br). **284 The Kobal Collection:** G&H PRODUCTIONS (tl). **285 Corbis:** Sophie Bassouls/Sygma (tr). 13/Nick White/Ocean (bl). **287 Dreamstime.com:** Markwaters (tr). **Getty Images:** Milos Bicanski/Stringer (bl). **290 Corbis:** Neville Elder (br). **293 Getty Images:** Evening Standard/Stringer (tr). **299 Corbis:** Mika (tr). Bettmann (bl). **301 Alamy Images:** ClassicStock (tr). **303 Corbis:** Leemage (tl). **307 Alamy Images:** Carolco Pictures (tr). **Dreamstime.com:** Zakaz (br). **308 Corbis:** Christopher Felver (bl). **309 Alamy Images:** SuperStock (tl). **311 Corbis:** Nick Cardillicchio (br). **315 The Kobal Collection:** WORKING TITLE (tl). **Getty Images:** Mel Yates (br). **317 Alamy Images:** Wavebreak Media ltd (tl). **319 Getty Images:** Heritage Images/Contributor (bl). **322 Dreamstime.com:** Rolfgeorg Brenner (tr). **325 Corbis:** Bettmann (tl). **329 Alamy Images:** epa european pressphoto agency b.v. (bl). **331 Alamy Images:** Photos 12 (tr). WENN Ltd (bl).

All other images © Dorling Kindersley. For more information see:

www.dkimages.com